Psyche's Press
Raleigh, North Carolina
©2007 G. G. Bolich

Printed in the United States of America. All rights reserved. No part of this book may be used or reproduced in any manner whatsoever without permission, except in the matter of brief quotations employed in reviews or critical works. For permissions, please contact G. G. Bolich at ggbolich @earthlink.net.

ISBN 978-0-6151-5720-7

Crossdressing in Context.
Dress, Gender, Transgender, and Crossdressing

Vol. 3

Transgender History & Geography

G. G. Bolich, Ph.D.

Psyche's
Press

Ultimately, America's answer to the intolerant man is diversity, the very diversity which our heritage of religious freedom has inspired.

           Robert F. Kennedy

If we cannot end now our differences, at least we can help make the world safe for diversity.

           John F. Kennedy

Our duties originate, not from difference of sex, but from the diversity of our relations in life, the various gifts and talents committed to our care, and the different eras in which we live.

           Angelina Grimké

This volume is respectfully dedicated to all those whose breadth of spirit embraces and celebrates diversity in human experience and expression. We find in both history and other societies in today's world an astonishing variation in ways to be human. May we prove that what unites us and makes us fully human is our common commitment to letting each and every one of us be who we are while not being only for ourselves.

Table of Contents

The Questions

Volume 3: Transgender History & Geography

Preface to the Set	1
Introduction to the Set	5
Q. Set 6: What is the history of crossdressing?	15
Q. 41 What did the ancient world think?	17
Q. 42 Who are some famous crossdressers of mythology?	29
Q. 43 Who are some famous ancient crossdressers?	41
Q. 44 What is the history of crossdressing and the theater?	47
Q. 45 What was the history of gender, transgender and crossdressing in the Middle Ages?	73
Q. 46 What is the history since the Middle Ages?	85
Q. 47 What is the history in the United States?	101
Q. 48 Who are some famous crossdressing women?	149
Q. 49 Who are some famous crossdressing men?	167
Q. 50 What will the present likely be noted for?	177
Q. Set 7: Where in the world are crossdressing and transgender realities found?	193
Q. 51 Is crossdressing only found in the Western world?	195
Q. 52 Where is it found in the East?	201
Q. 53 Where is it found in the Middle East?	227
Q. 54 Where is it found in Africa?	241
Q. 55 Where is it found in Latin America?	261
Q. 56 Where is it found in Europe?	271
Q. 57 Where is it found in the Pacific Ocean nations?	287
Q. 58 Where is it found in North America?	299

	Q. 59	Where is it found in Native American groups?	307
	Q. 60	If it is so common, what roles does it play in culture?	321

Notes 327
Appendix: Overview of Set Contents 401
Author Index 407
Country Index 411
Subject Index 413

Detailed Table of Contents

The Questions

Volume 3: Transgender History & Geography

Preface to the Set   1

Introduction to the Set   5

Q. Set 6: What is the history of crossdressing?   15

    Q. 41 What did the ancient world think?   17
        Was there crossdressing in the ancient East?   20
        Was there crossdressing in the ancient Middle East?   21
        Was there crossdressing in the ancient West?   22

    Q. 42 Who are some famous crossdressers of mythology?   29
        Who is Achilles?   30
        Who are the Amazons?   31
        Who is Amba?   32
        Who is Astygetes?   33
        Who is Bhima?   34
        Who is Herakles?   35
        Who is Hervör?   36
        Who is Leucippus?   37
        Who is Odysseus?   38
        Who is Pentheus?   39
        Who is Theseus?   39
        Who is Tiresias?   40

    Q. 43 Who are some famous ancient crossdressers?   41
        Who is Pharoah Hatshepsut?   41
        Who is Clodius Pulcher?   42
        Who are the crossdressing Roman Emperors?   43

    Q. 44 What is the history of crossdressing and the theater?   47
        What place has crossdressing held in Eastern theater?   48
        What role did crossdressing play in ancient Western theater?   53
        What part did crossdressing occupy in early Modern theater?   59
        Are crossdressing performance acts found in other cultures?   62
        What part did crossdressing play in the history of American theater?   63
        What role does crossdressing occupy in contemporary films and plays?   63

Q. 45	What was the history of gender, transgender and crossdressing in the Middle Ages?	73
	How was gender viewed in the Middle Ages?	74
	What role did changes in fashion play?	76
	Why did people crossdress in the medieval world?	78
	Were there crossdressing men in the medieval world?	81
	Why did crossdressed women get so much attention?	82
	What were the sumptuary regulations?	82
Q. 46	What is the history since the Middle Ages?	85
	What was the relation of gender to dress after the Middle Ages?	86
	Why were women crossdressing?	89
	Why were men crossdressing?	95
	How was crossdressing received?	98
Q. 47	What is the history in the United States?	101
	What role has fashion played in American crossdressing?	102
	What was dress like in early America (16th-18th centuries)?	103
	What was dress like in 19th century America?	105
	What was dress like in 20th century America?	109
	How might we sum up the relation of fashion and crossdressing?	112
	Why did crossdressing occur?	114
	Who were some noted early American crossdressers?	116
	What was crossdressing like in 19th century American stories?	121
	Who were some noted 19th century female crossdressers?	130
	How did crossdressing figure in 19th century entertainment?	136
	Was there crossdressing on the Western frontier?	136
	What role did crossdressing play in the 19th century women's movement?	138
	How were crossdressing men depicted in 19th century America?	140
	What was crossdressing like in the 20th century?	142
	What was crossdressing like in 20th century American stories?	143
	What role does crossdressing have in the United States today?	146
Q. 48	Who are some famous crossdressing women?	149
	Who is Elena de Cespedes?	150
	Who is Mary Frith?	151
	Who is Catalino de Erauso?	152
	Who is 'King' Nzinga of the Mbundu people?	153
	Who is Queen Christina of Sweden?	154
	Who is Christian Davies?	155
	Who is Mademoiselle Maupin?	156
	Who is Mary Anne Talbot?	158
	Who is Kaúxuma Núpika/Qánqon Kámek Klaúla?	159
	Who is George Sand?	160
	Who is Nadezhda Andreevna Durova?	161
	Who is Loreta Janeta Velazquez?	162
	Who is Billy Tipton?	165
Q. 49	Who are some famous crossdressing men?	167
	Who is Ulrich von Lichtenstein?	167
	Who is King Henry III of France?	168

	Who is Francois Timoleon Abbe de Choisy?	169
	Who is the Chevalier de Eon?	169
	Who is Virginia Prince?	171
	Who are some other famous men who crossdressed?	173
Q. 50	What will the present likely be noted for?	177
	Why does male crossdressing receive most of today's attention?	180
	How are male crossdressers responding to the attention?	186
	Why is crossdressing being reappraised now?	190

Q. Set 6: Where in the world is crossdressing found?   193

Q. 51	Is crossdressing only found in the Western world?	195
	How many places are transgender realities like crossdressing found?	196
	But is it 'crossdressing'?	198
Q. 52	Where is it found in the East?	201
	What are transgender realities in China?	203
	What are transgender realities in India?	207
	What are transgender realities in Japan?	210
	What are transgender realities in Korea?	214
	What are transgender realities in Myanmar (Burma)?	216
	What are transgender realities in Nepal?	218
	What are transgender realities in Pakistan?	219
	What are transgender realities in Thailand?	220
	What are transgender realities in Vietnam?	224
	What might we conclude about transgender realities like crossdressing in the modern East?	225
Q. 53	Where is it found in the Middle East?	227
	Were there transgender realities in the premodern Middle East?	228
	What are transgender realities in the modern Middle East?	231
	What are transgender realities in Bahrain?	233
	What are transgender realities in Egypt?	234
	What are transgender realities in Iran?	234
	What are transgender realities in Israel?	235
	What are transgender realities in Oman?	237
	What are transgender realities in Saudi Arabia?	238
	What are transgender realities in Turkey?	239
Q. 54	Where is it found in Africa?	241
	How widespread are transgender realities in Africa?	242
	What role does gender play among traditional African societies?	244
	Are there instances of gender variance among females?	247
	Are there instances of gender variance among males?	250
	What are other examples of gender-variant realities in Africa?	252
	How do transgender realities display in transition rites?	254
	Are there sacred gender crossings?	256
	How are crossdressing and transgendered people viewed in modern Africa?	257

Q. 55	Where is it found in Latin America?	261
	What are transgender realities in the Caribbean Islands?	263
	Cuba (263) Dominican Republic (264) Puerto Rico (264)	
	What are transgender realities in Central America?	265
	Costa Rico (265) Guatemala (266) Mexico (266)	
	What are transgender realities in South America?	267
	Argentina (267) Brazil (268) Chile (269) Columbia (270)	
Q. 56	Where is it found in Europe?	271
	What are transgender realities in Central and Eastern Europe?	273
	Albania (273) Austria (274)	
	Czech Republic (274) Lithuania (275)	
	Poland (275) Russia (276)	
	What are transgender realities in Northern and Western Europe?	277
	Denmark (277) Finland (277)	
	France (278) Germany (278)	
	Luxembourg (280) Netherlands (280)	
	Norway (280) Sweden (281)	
	United Kingdom (281)	
	What are transgender realities in Southern Europe?	283
	Cyprus (283) Greece (283)	
	Italy (284) Portugal (284)	
	Spain (284)	
Q. 57	Where is it found in the Pacific Ocean nations?	287
	What are transgender realities in Australia?	288
	What are transgender realities in the Cook Islands?	288
	What are transgender realities in French Polynesia?	289
	What are transgender realities in Indonesia?	291
	What are transgender realities in Malaysia?	294
	What are transgender realities in New Zealand?	295
	What are transgender realities in Okinawa?	295
	What are transgender realities in Papua New Guinea?	296
	What are transgender realities in the Philippines?	296
Q. 58	Where is it found in North America?	299
	What are transgender realities in Canada?	300
	What are transgender realities in the United States?	303
Q. 59	Where is it found in Native American groups?	307
	What does *berdaches* mean?	309
	Who are the *berdaches*?	310
	What roles are played by the *berdaches* in Indian society?	313
	What is the relation between the *berdaches* and crossdressing?	314
	What are some examples among Indian peoples?	315
Q. 60	If it is so common, what role does it play in culture?	321
	How do gender, transgender, and crossdressing fit into culture?	321
	What place do crossdressers occupy in society?	322
	How does crossdressing serve noncrossdressers?	323

Notes	327
Appendix: Overview of Set Contents	401
Author Index	407
Country Index	411
Subject Index	413

Preface

Can we be honest?

What can you expect?

Let's be candid from the start. The subject matter of this book is controversial. Worse, it is the kind of controversy that often moves beyond mere intellectual disagreement to result in broken relationships and sometimes violence. In preparing this work one particular remark has stayed with me. In a report on violence experienced by transgendered people, the authors wrote, "What is common to most studies of transpeople is their staggering irrelevance to the community at issue."[1]

My intention has been to set forth information that is not irrelevant, either to the transgendered, or to those who find themselves related in some manner to them—which I think is all of us. As the title suggests, this work is about raising questions and offering answers. In the effort to do so, I have drawn both on academic material and on accounts set forth by transgendered people themselves. For example, one question asks how crossdressers describe themselves (Q. 26), while the next offers the results of various formal psychological tests to answer the same question (Q. 27). I have throughout tried to let others speak for themselves. You will find brief quotes from various sources to offer a bit of the flavor of how these other voices sound. In summarizing studies, theories, or personal accounts I have aimed at being concise but fair—and pointed you in directions to follow in order to learn more. Because of the ubiquity of the World Wide Web, whenever possible indication has been made in the endnotes as to where material can be accessed online. At the same time, I have not shied away from offering my own critique of what others have said or my own assessment of the matters about which they speak.

Despite the large number of questions raised, this work barely scratches the surface of transgender realities, including crossdressing. I often refer to 'transgender realities' and I do so quite consciously. I want us to remember that we are examining *realities*—lived experiences that range from very temporary occurrences of minor personal significance to profoundly meaningful matters of personal identity felt and expressed every day. I want us to consider how the *trans* in *trans*gender can mean different things to different people. Nor do I wish us to ever lose sight of how *gender* is basic to trans*gender*. And, because the organizing framework is built around crossdressing, we must also know something about the role clothes play in our lives.

Obviously, I am very ambitious. I hope you are as well. Even something that superficially seems easy enough to describe, like crossdressing, which after all is simply the act of dressing in clothes typically associated with a gender other than the one assigned the wearer, is not really simple when once looked at closely. To understand crossdressing—to begin to truly see transgender realities—takes work. I want to do that work alongside you, serving as a partner in dialog while also offering my modest services as a guide to the vast literature on the subjects considered. Since I am functioning as a guide, you have every right to ask about my qualifications.

Who am I to talk?

One question you may have right away is what my 'position' or 'bias' is on the subject. For example, you might wish to know if I identify myself as a transgendered person. Unfortunately, in my experience, many people screen what they are willing to expose themselves to as they study a controversial topic by using this kind of query. Of course, I know *you* are more fair-minded than that, but the next reader might not be. So, whatever my stance—or identity—may be will have to become a matter of your own judgment (or speculation) as you read the work. I have conscientiously spoken of 'we' and 'us' throughout the book, both when speaking of crossdressers and when referring to noncrossdressers. I wish to convey my conviction that the fundamental humanity that unites us is greater than the differences that we too often let divide, separate, and isolate us. It is a small world we all have to share and a short life we all live.

What I am willing to tell you upfront about myself concerns my qualifications for tackling the subject. I caution you not to infer anything about my being 'for' or 'against' crossdressing from these qualifications.[2] As you know, qualifications do not guarantee people holding reasonable positions or even necessarily knowing what they are talking about! Still, I think you have a right to know relevant portions of my background because they may speak to my level of preparation for talking to you about these things. I don't expect you to take my word on anything from blind trust, but I do hope your confidence in the reliability of my remarks will be strengthened both by my background and by the actual material I set forth.

My background includes more than 30 years working professionally with people, primarily as an educator, but also as a counselor. I hold advanced degrees in the fields of religious studies and psychology, and my teaching and counseling have been in both areas. Because some people view crossdressing as a psychological disorder, my experience in psychology seems relevant. Because some people regard crossdressing as morally or religiously wrong, my experience in religious studies seems relevant, too. In fact, between these two areas, I find most of the questions and concerns about crossdressing that I have encountered from students, clients, and others.

In terms of religious studies, I am seminary trained, holding a M.A. in Theology, and the Master of Divinity—or M.Div.—the degree used to prepare people for professional ministry. My first Ph.D., in Educational Leadership, also focused on religious studies, culminating in a dissertation in the area of New Testament introduction. I am trained in biblical and classical languages (Hebrew, Greek, Latin), and in both traditional and modern methods of translating and interpreting sacred texts. Beginning in 1974, as an instructor at a Bible School, I have taught courses in religious studies at undergraduate and graduate levels in a wide variety of settings, including churches and synagogues, community college, public university, private college, and seminary extension program. These courses have covered matters of ethics, ancient and modern world religions, theology, history, sacred texts, and the relation of religion to psychology. My area of particular interest and specialization has been the religious writings of the period extending from about a century or so before Christ, to the end of the second century after Christ. In addition to scholarly work, I also have been involved in ecumenical work, notably between the Christian and Jewish communities. As a counselor, many people have identified my background in religious studies as an important reason why they chose to come see me.

My second doctorate is in psychology (Ph.D.). I started working with people as a counselor in 1973, while still a college student, on a crisis line. As time passed, my interests began to turn more and more to matters of human development and human sexuality. As a counselor I gradually developed a specialization in Trauma Resolution Therapy, principally working with adult survivors of sexual abuse. Today I teach graduate students in counseling about human sexuality. Both as a teacher and as a therapist I have continually encountered curiosity about crossdressing and transgender people. Because of my additional background in religious studies this curiosity by my students and clients has often extended to specific matters of faith and practice as well as the more specific psychological concerns about whether being a transgender person or engaging in crossdressing is deviant, sick, sinful, or harmful.

Accordingly, this work grows out of many years of interest and experience. I think my background contributes some layers of knowledge that may not be as easily accessible to other professionals whose experience is confined to only one or another of the areas relevant to a full consideration of crossdressing. To these credentials I will add my intention of being fair-minded and honest throughout this work. I intend this work to be educational in nature. At the same time, I am aware that when educating people on controversial subjects it may not be either feasible or even particularly desirable to attempt being completely above the fray and studiously neutral. In truth, I am not neutral on the subject—and I do not know anyone who is. Even scholarly works serve social and political ends, and every work—including mine—must be soberly appraised for fairness. I have every confidence that fair-minded readers who pursue the logic and evidence set down within this work will be able to accurately assess the value of this endeavor.

Introduction

What do you need to know to get started?

Why does any of this matter?

Chances are you aren't looking at this unless you already believe the subject matters. I agree. The fundamental assumption of this work is that transgender realities matter to all of us, whether we are transgendered ourselves or not. They matter because such realities by their very existence pose opportunities for us to explore and expand our sense of sex and gender. In a culture like our own, where sex and gender are so central to the way we define our identities and relationships, such an opportunity must not be missed.

We must also acknowledge from the very beginning that any discussion of these things will generate feeling, and quite often strong feeling. How can it not when the stakes—identities and relationships—are so high? Transgender realities in a culture where sex and gender are rigidly paired at two poles raise a challenge to our sense of what we think and know. But more critically than challenging the narrowness of our perceptions, they prompt questions about our own felt sense of sex and gender. In short, transgender realities matter because they disturb senses of identity and relationship founded and attached to a bipolar duality allowing us only to be masculine men or feminine women.

It seemed to me in framing this work that the most natural and appropriate choice was to mirror what happens in us when we encounter transgender realities like crossdressing. So herein everything is framed by questions. Though 100 questions are used to create what you may think of as 'chapters,' there are literally hundreds of questions raised and considered in this work.

Why this title?

The scope of this work, with all its queries, can be overwhelming—but then sex and gender are precisely that in our culture. You may already feel in over your head just holding this material in your hands. The subject of 'transgender' and 'crossdressing' is perhaps a lot larger than you initially thought—and then 'gender,' 'sex,' and 'dress' are thrown in for good measure! My choice of titles, then, requires a word of explanation.

Crossdressing in Context is meant both to be descriptive and to be implicitly critical of most other works on crossdressing. There are a number of important contexts in which crossdressing must be situated and the separate volume titles indicate these. First and most immediately there is *dress*, especially clothes, without which crossdressing is impossible and by which *gender* is experienced and expressed. Perhaps the greatest failing of studies of crossdressing is the general neglect of the role played by apparel. It is certainly appropriate to focus on gender, but such a focus needs to begin with gender-differentiated clothing. The first volume explores dress and gender, separately and together, in the context of a rich experience and expressive system.

The second volume examines another principal context: *transgender realities*, the actual lived experiences of human individuals. This material opens by introducing basic terminology and provides an overview of crossdressing behavior. The next set of questions considers a variety of possible causes of transgender behavior like crossdressing. Then it moves to a history of transgender realities, revolving around historical depictions of crossdressing, from ancient to modern times. This material also includes special attention to the history of theater, including modern movies and television. The volume then continues with a survey of transgender realities around the world. Collectively, these materials demonstrate that transgender realities like crossdressing have been persistent across times and cultures. The volume concludes by examining contemporary transgender experience from a variety of perspectives, including how transgender people experience it, examined by a variety of psychological tests, understood legally, and regarded by other people.

The third volume highlights the importance of *religion*. Not only is personal spirituality and religious observance as valued by transgender people as by anyone else, the long history of religions around the world show an involvement with transgender realities that make this area of critical value in properly understanding phenomena like crossdressing. Acknowledging the cultural context in which this work is produced, the first religious sphere considered belongs to Western religions. Thus a careful examination of what the Bible says about crossdressing is followed by how biblical material has been commented upon by Christian and Jewish scholars through the centuries. Following this material a survey is made of the principal religions of the world, both East and West. As in volume 2, the evidence documents an awareness and dialog with transgender realities throughout history and around the globe.

The final volume acknowledges the weight of modern *mental health* in discussions about crossdressing and other transgender realities. Since the medicalization of sex has firmly joined crossdressing behavior to sexuality, this volume begins by examining the theories and evidence allegedly connecting crossdressing and sexual behavior. This is followed by a broader examination of the question whether transgender people, especially those who crossdress, are mentally ill. First this matter is explored by providing a broad historical context—the medicalization of sex—and examining how transgender people often come to mental health professionals' attention. Special terminology like 'gender dysphoria' is explained. The possible connection of transgender behavior to various mental disorders is considered. Then follows a review of contributions on the subject by various scholars since the late 19th century. Given the dominant position the American Psychiatric Association's *Diagnostic and Statistical Manual of Mental Disorders* (popularly referred to as DSM) has attained, a careful look at how crossdressing and other transgender realities have been handled by this model throughout its history also is provided. This, in turn, leads to looking at a variety of treatment approaches that have been tried with transgender clients. The issues involved in such treatment lead to a careful consideration about the wisdom of retaining in the DSM model the categories concerning transgender. Finally, the volume—and the work at large—concludes with a last consideration of whether transgender people need to be changed.

Collectively the four volumes represent one sustained approach to placing crossdressing in context. Although this work broadly is about all transgender realities, the focal point has been the behavior most visibly associated with transgender: *crossdressing*. I treat the subject of crossdressing both as a topic of great interest in its own right and as an entrance into transgender realities. As large as the resulting work is, it could be much larger with a more sustained examination of other transgender realities.

What are the goals of this work?

The structure of this work is dialogical in nature. Questions—many, many questions—are raised and considered. The choice of these questions and the way in which they are answered reflects various goals. There are several principal, intentional goals sought by this work, all with the purpose of establishing an understanding in context:

1. to put dress back into crossdressing by situating crossdressing within an experiencing and expressing system built around clothes as the primary vehicle for communicating gender, which is central to our sense of self and relationships;
2. to highlight and explicate the role dress plays both in our affiliations, such as our membership in a gender group, and in our individuality;
3. to explore the basic distinctions between 'sex' and 'gender' in order to better see what transgender is about and how crossdressing is related to each;

4. to use crossdressing—a transgender reality—as entry into other transgender realities, and to see how these realities are similar and dissimilar;
5. to clarify the meaning of terms (e.g., 'transgender,' 'transvestite,' 'transsexual'), while questioning their usefulness;
6. to document transgender realities, especially crossdressing, throughout history and around the world, and to do so with enough depth and breadth to convince even the most skeptical reader of the pervasiveness and significance of these realities;
7. to broaden our understanding of crossdressing by exploring and illustrating the many various motivations behind it and thereby to simultaneously challenge such narrow and erroneous beliefs as that all crossdressing is done because of disturbed gender identity or sexual perversity;
8. to keep in view always that transgender realities are inevitably human experiences, lived by real people, who are worthy of respect and dignity;
9. to set out and place in context the work of others who have written about transgender realities, especially crossdressing, and in doing so engage in dialog with them;
10. to let transgendered people speak for themselves, especially in addressing matters such as what it is like to live as a transgendered person;
11. to examine basic issues of concern to people, such as the morality of crossdressing, the way in which religious traditions have related to transgender realities, the legal issues connected to transgender experience, the relational aspects of being with a transgendered person as a partner, family member, friend, or helper, and the role of sexuality in the life of the transgendered; and,
12. to address the critical matter of the involvement of mental health professionals, including looking closely at the history of study by professionals about transgender (especially crossdressing), detailing the discussion of transgender in today's dominant diagnostic classification system, reviewing the history of treating transgender conditions, considering whether changes need to be made, and examining new models of therapeutic support.

To meet these dozen goals requires some space; hence the size of this work.

Yet, for all this, there are some things underdeveloped. For example, you should know right off that this book is *not* principally about homosexuality. Because that is the transgender reality that receives by far the most attention this work is organized around a different principle: crossdressing. Yes, some homosexuals (but not all) crossdress. And yes, some crossdressers (but not all) are homosexual. Thus, homosexuals are included within this work. But they are not the focus.

What are 'transgender realities'?

The focus, through the lens of crossdressing, is 'transgender realities.' In choosing the term 'transgender realities' I want to emphasize the multiplicity of expressions that do not fit at the gender poles of masculinity and femininity. A prominent transgender reality—a behavior shared among many transgender people—is crossdressing. I treat all crossdressing as a transgender reality even though not all people whom crossdress identify themselves as transgendered. In other words, just as a self-professed vegetarian may occasionally eat meat, so a non-transgendered person may occasionally enact a transgender reality like crossdressing. In this work I use the broad transgender reality of crossdressing as both entry into other transgender realities and to remind us how pervasive transgender expressions are. But to properly comprehend them they must be retained in their natural contexts.

How is the work structured?

A glance at the questions in the Table of Contents shows an almost bewildering breadth of matters. They are organized into 100 specific questions, each of which entails asking further questions. Yet these questions collectively still by no means exhaust the subject. Instead they aim to reflect a logical organization of reflection based on a variety of the more commonly asked questions related to our interests. Those questions cover all kinds of topics, everything from sex and gender to morals and religion. It takes time to cover so much ground and the length of this work reflects my commitment to taking that time and offering at least enough to cover the basics and point the way to more research. However, this structure allows you to enter wherever you like and get answers quickly.

In truth, this study could be shorter. Part of the length is attributable to the structure. By setting everything as answers to questions and encouraging you to dip in wherever you like, an element of repetition is needed to ensure every answer stays embedded in context with enough detail to make full sense to you. So, in reading through the work in a progressive fashion the effect of this repetition will be felt, though hopefully not in too tedious a fashion. I have tried to be varied in restating matters, but if nothing else the repetition serves pedagogically to reinforce basic concepts and themes.

A significant factor adding to the length is my insistence on fleshing out each context with reason and evidence. Too many people disregard arguments because they only see one or two illustrative cases and fail to recognize them as signifying a vast number of others. I wish to create the sense for you of a phenomenon so common and richly varied around the world and throughout history that it cannot be casually dismissed or superficially examined. Comprehension requires a sense of the complexity and fullness of transgender realities like crossdressing. If you are impatient to press on you can do so, but if you are looking for detail, you will find it here.

I recognize that your interest may not be in all forms of crossdressing, but only a particular kind. You may even only want information on a very specific matter related to that particular kind. As I mentioned above, that is why the organization of this material has been set out as answers to questions. I think this is an intuitive and practical approach that will prove useful to you now with the questions you presently have and later with questions still to come. Hopefully, the net effect will be to also prompt other questions and lead you into a larger, ongoing investigation.

While I like to think the optimal way to use this work is to read it completely from start to finish, it may not be the best way for you at this time. Instead, you might wish to browse it, looking for specific information. This can be done through the questions, a complete list of which is found in the Detailed Table of Contents. Once you locate an interesting question, you can explore it through three levels of interaction. The quickest and most superficial level is 'The Short Answer' provided at the beginning of each answer section. In a few lines you will get a summary answer. Next comes 'The Longer Answer.' This offers a detailed discussion to more fully answer the question. Finally, by using the endnotes for each answer you can find important sources and resources as well as pursue the discussion on some finer points. In sum, the work is organized in a user-friendly manner to meet your needs now and later.

On the use and misuse of this work: Who makes the rules?

A final matter about using this work is important to me. Scholarly work is often proof-texted. In other words, readers pick and choose what conveniently supports the position they want to hold. I don't imagine that any of us entirely escape selective recall or purposeful choosing of 'facts' for presentation, but I ask that you play fair with the material included in these pages. A dialog requires two parties, and fruitful dialog mandates both parties be allowed to speak with an effort to hear them. When once the whole matter is on the table, or as much of it as can be had, then is the time for making a respectful decision based on evidence and reason. I covet for us all making careful judgments and always treating others with respect and charity.

I know—and so do you—that the matters discussed in this work often engage strong feelings in people. None of my goals include telling you how to feel. However you feel about the matters we discuss I will hope you subject those feelings to scrutiny, evaluate the evidence honestly, and behave with respect toward all. This really matters to me—too many people continue to be harmed. Let's think about this matter a moment longer.

One of the curious things about freedom is that most of us demand it in very liberal portions for ourselves, but are less charitable toward others. We want to be left alone to do as we see fit, while often insisting that other folk conform to our personal standards as to what is 'right.' Naturally, we generally have at hand one or another rationale for our judgments. Frequently, our logic centers in an opposition to someone else's behavior on religious or moral grounds. After all, it is unseemly to prioritize the fact that the behavior we condemn makes us personally uncomfortable, so we set that truth in second place and justify it by reasoning that we feel uneasy *because* the behavior is inherently—and to us also *obviously*—wrong. Thus we enjoy the best of all solutions: moral and/or religious justification for our felt discomfort. If we can get a law passed against the behavior then the justification for our feeling is further strengthened—as may be the feeling itself.

We may even find ourselves justifying unkind remarks, avoidance, harassment, discrimination, or physical violence. Once we convince ourselves something is wrong, it is easy to think whatever is done in opposition must be right. But two wrongs never make a right. No matter how we excuse ourselves, violation of another person's human rights is evil.

Unfortunately, our real motivations often remain unconscious. We don't see that our reasoning is actually just rationalization—a way of thinking that has as its real aim making us less anxious rather than knowing the truth. All we know is that by thinking and judging in certain ways we shield ourselves from uncomfortable feelings. While this may seem useful, when it leads to disruption in our relationships with others and prompts us to words and deeds hurtful to others, then we have become the very makers of evil that we despise.

We are best served in the long run by opening our eyes and trying to see matters as clearly as we can. So let us agree to start in as neutral a position as possible. Instead of assuming that crossdressing is 'right' or 'wrong,' 'healthy' or 'mentally ill,' let us just let it be—and then examine it as best we can. If the subject elicits certain feelings, simply let them be as well. In the privacy of your own reading there is no need to let these feelings be more than they are—one source of information among others. Feelings do not have to motivate you to do anything right now. Simply accept them or set them aside and move on to a sober consideration of the topic.

You can do this—and you *must* if you are to be fair to yourself and to others. I know that it is very likely you are holding this book either because you crossdress or someone you care about does. Your feelings may be clear, or they may be mixed, but they are not facts that by themselves must determine what you think or do. In fact, by learning more your feelings may change. So be patient with yourself and with others.

Ready? Then let's start asking some questions.

Volume 3: Transgender History & Geography

The Questions

A Special Note: In this volume the writing uses, as much as possible, the present tense. In the discussion of historical figures this is intended to make the reality of their lived experience more immediate and, hopefully, accessible. In the presentation of research results the same effect is intended. Most often reporting of anything in the past is done through past verb tenses. While this reminds us that such events are limited and closed, such writing tends to distance us from the actual experience. Since this volume intends to confront us with transgender *realities*—actual, immediate, and forceful—the decision was made to rely on present tense writing to contribute to a better awareness that at every time such realities exist and merit reckoning. Then, too, the past remains as alive as the effect it has on present experience. The hope is that the writing style in this volume keeps this awareness of the past's relevance always in front of us.

Question Set 6:

What is the history of transgender and crossdressing?

The historical study of gender, transgender, and crossdressing is beset by any number of obstacles. First, the conception of gender has not been static. Even in our own time fierce debates exist over exactly what gender is, and such debates—albeit in different forms—have marked previous eras. Second, the concept of transgender as such is relatively recent and still somewhat unformed. To apply today's incomplete and sometimes controversial labels to people of the past may help make them feel accessible to us but comes at a cost: in their own context such labels were not used and the meaning today attached to them may or may not have existed then. Third, crossdressing also has been subject to changing conceptions and preoccupations. Because it involves clothing—and clothes are central to a rich experiencing and expressive system—crossdressing cannot be considered without some reference to clothes and particularly to fashion. Exactly what constitutes crossdressing is not as straightforward a matter as it may superficially appear. Then, too, through much of history the principal fascination of the general public seems to have been over crossdressing women rather than crossdressing men. This means in one era our knowledge of a particular gender's gender-crossing behavior may be much richer, only to find a much different situation in studying another era. This complicates drawing any general observations applicable across the span of history. So fashion, gender, changing focuses in historical reporting, and a host of other factors all enter into the discussion.

In light of such obstacles—and many more could be produced—what are we to do? For our purposes it seems sufficient to adopt a modest course through our purview of history. As elsewhere in this work we shall focus on crossdressing, seeking to explore and understand it in its own right, while retaining a belief that it offers some entry into a broader, if more tentative consideration of transgendered realities and gender itself. We need a flexibility of mind sufficient to seek relevant links to the past without insisting that past ideas and experiences are identical to our own. If we keep in view the notion that crossdressing offers a window, or perhaps even a door, into a wider world of gendered realities pertinent to helping us better understand our own time, we should be okay.

The quest to bridge time and space in order to shed light on today is obviously complex and difficult. We already have mentioned one problem that merits reiteration: we often share neither language nor culture with those we study and our labels—questionable and controversial in our own day—may be completely inappropriate and meaningless when applied to other times and cultures. We can (and will) seek to bridge the distance between our own culture and other cultures through attention to their own language and cultural logic. Toward that end we will listen as often as we can to native scholars. The past also presents challenges, not the least of which is the relative inaccessibility of the people the further back we go. Many of us find it difficult to relate to people long dead, whose stories are recounted in past tense. One technique sometimes employed to help bring the past into the present and retain its aliveness is to write in the historical present. This simply means writing about people as though they were currently among us. This helps create an immediacy that may make contact with their experiences easier. For those of us unacquainted with such a style it may seem a little jarring at first, but staying in present tense throughout our discussion is meant to provide a consistency and immediacy that promotes accessibility. We must never forget that the people we study were, like ourselves, human beings caught up in culture, confronted by the challenges of living from day to day, and unique in their individuality. We must try to let them live again for us.

Crossdressing is sometimes called a ubiquitous phenomenon. The designation is warranted. In cultures around the world and across history crossdressing by both males and females is well documented. If what we know about today's crossdressers provides any clue to past experience, we may presume that many more people practiced crossdressing than either we (or their contemporaries) could ever know. One matter we do know: crossdressing has been motivated by a variety of reasons in different times and places. In the answers to the following questions, some indication is offered of the rich diversity of crossdressing experiences. We begin with ancient history.

Q. 41

What did the ancient world think?

The Short Answer. Crossdressing likely is as old as the practice of dressing. While we cannot know with certainty either when or where crossdressing began, we do know the practice dates back at least 3500 years. We possess references to crossdressing in ancient plays and novels. The sacred literature of the world's great religions know of it, and religions long dead also knew of it. In sum, an abundance of materials document the reality of crossdressing in the ancient world. Ancient people held no uniform view on crossdressing. At various times and in various places its practice drew a range of responses from sanction for sacred purposes, to indifference, to mild disapproval, to restrictions to limit or discourage the practice (at least among certain portions of the populace). The response to crossdressing always has been culturally variable. The most influential factor appears to be the values held about gender and how rigidly or flexibly gender roles and identity are construed. Indeed, in this respect it would be accurate to say that even the very definition of crossdressing has varied across cultures and eras. Of course, that complicates any study of the matter. We easily, if errantly, apply modern values, labels, and judgments to matters the ancients experienced differently. Though we try to bridge the distance in language, culture, philosophy and religion, any complete connection eludes us. We are left with doing our best to see what was there and speculating on the ways it is both continuous and discontinuous with what we find today. Toward that end, most of what is offered here focuses on apparent or espoused motivations, which vary from entertainment, to religious practice, to a host of other personal reasons. (In this answer we only touch briefly on a substantial subject, and often present only summaries of matters elaborated in other answers. For example, in describing transgender realities in various societies there are often remarks about things from long ago. Similarly, in discussing various religions, or specific things such as theater, an historical perspective offers further materials about the ancient world.)

The Longer Answer. We need first to know what 'ancient' refers to in this answer. I am using the term very broadly, to refer to the world of the West prior to the Middle Ages and the world of the East down to modern times. I realize this is an arbitrary division and not wholly satisfactory. But the purpose in this answer is to draw together a variety of materials meant to display some of the diversity in time and place for crossdressing prior to the modern world.

Our modern notions of sex, gender, crossdressing, and related notions are neither universal nor timeless. Indeed, we can characterize our culture's views as narrow when compared to notions found elsewhere in the world and in other ages. For example, the rigid dichotomy between the sexes—and the limitation of their number—is not a universal view. To cite a single instance, consider the position put forth by Aristophanes in Plato's *Symposium*. Aristophanes argues that original human nature differed from that seen now:

> [T]he original human nature was not like the present, but different. In the first place, the sexes were originally three in number, not two as they are now; there was man, woman, and the union of the two, having a name corresponding to this double nature; this once had a real existence, but is now lost, and the name only is preserved as a term of reproach.[1]

Though now only two sexes seem apparent, Aristophanes elucidates a number of characteristics flowing from this original reality, including matters often placed today under the umbrella of transgenderism. Thus, Aristophanes reasons that there were three sexes, corresponding to the sun, earth, and moon. Man is the child of the sun, woman of the earth, and 'the man-woman' of the moon, because it is made of sun and earth. He then proceeds to elaborate on the nature of human beings and covers ground any modern reader might find at the same time both strange and familiar.[2]

Like gender itself, the conception of the gender crossing behavior called 'crossdressing' has varied across time and space. At least as far back as the early Roman Empire there was recognition of a cultural element in the practice and acceptance of crossdressing. Today we generally think of crossdressing as something men do, and then for a limited set of reasons, such as gay men in drag purposely violating gender conventions to tweak their nose at cultural stereotypes, or transvestites dressing in secret for sexual arousal or gender role relief. If we simply project these notions back into the ancient world, we err.

In order to try to facilitate our entry into past periods, I am going to adopt a style that keeps history in the present. In short, I will write as though we are there, and here—dwelling in both times simultaneously. So, in presenting people's stories from the past, they will be told as contemporaneous. This artifice is simply intended to help us bridge time, thereby also reminding us that human experience, whenever it takes place, is recognizable to all who share humanity.

Dress Fashion in the Ancient World

We regard crossdressing as behavior equally embracing gender boundaries (cross-) and clothing (dressing). Let's start with the latter. Ancient apparel is significantly different from our own. Differences in general clothing styles are minimal compared to later ages. Males and females both wear unbifurcated garments such as cloak, tunic, *kimono*, or *dhoti*. Though bifurcated garb like trousers exist, they are not widely used and many in the 'civilized' world regard them with distaste. Instead, draped clothing like the Roman toga enjoys regard as 'cultured.' For much of human history to this point the clothes worn by both sexes have looked more similar than dissimilar, and this will continue to be largely the case now and for some time yet to come.

Yet gendered distinctions in appearance seem always to have existed. Hair display, for instance, is utilized as a basic gender differentiator, as it remains today. Masculine hairstyles tend to be shorter than feminine ones and beards are common. There are gender differences in dress as well. Women typically wear head coverings or veils when in public—a practice recognizable to Christian students of the New Testament (see 1 Corinthians 11:4-7). In ancient Iran, pins are associated with women's dress, not men's. In the classical world, to show gender differentiation the length of a garment might vary, the colors used might be different, or the way the clothes are draped or cinched on the body might be distinct. In short, there is always the possibility of crossdressing because there is always gendered distinction in appearance.

Attaining a Historical Perspective

When we turn our eyes on the past, we naturally see through the lens of our present understanding. Though this process is inevitable, and not inherently bad, it does complicate things. Judith Ochshorn, who examines ancient societies for data on gender roles, wonders how we can ever be confident we are doing anything more than "imposing our own familiar assumptions and stereotypes about gender on another time and place."[3] If all we do is superimpose our ideas on ancient cultures, all we can see is an imperfect reflection of ourselves. To comprehend past perspectives on their own terms is a daunting task. It requires we do our best to be conscious of what is largely unconscious about our modern view, then suspend our judgment in the interest of listening to the past rather than putting our own words on their lips. Though we can do this only imperfectly, we cannot profit from their experience if we do otherwise.

Where do we begin? Political scientist Sabrina Petra Ramet observes that historically crossdressing has been a much broader concept than typically envisioned today. For a great many people across history the idea has referred to "any breach across the rigid regulations governing attire."[4] But this does not mean such breaches were uniformly negatively evaluated. Indeed, crossdressing has frequently been a calculated and, within defined contexts, approved gender reversal. Ramet notes that gender reversals occur frequently in mythology, in ancient religions and rituals; they are found "in diverse societies in every era."[5] Within ancient societies—as in our own—the response individuals formed to such behavior reflects a number of things, including cultural values, personal ones, and various contextual factors.

In the classical world, as we shall see (cf. answer to Q. 42), even the greatest of heroes, men like Achilles, Odysseus and Heracles (Hercules) crossdressed.

Yet, while that might suggest they themselves view the practice as commendable, often it reflects situations that do not put these heroes in the best light. Still, evaluations of the merit of the practice vary from context to context. The Stoic philosopher Sextus Empiricus, in a casual remark comparing Roman 'habits' with those of other peoples, observes that the earlier Greek philosopher Aristippus "considers the wearing of feminine attire a matter of indifference, though we consider it a disgraceful thing."[6] There was no consensus.

Roman wits like Martial and Juvenal make fun of crossdressers—but, then, they make fun of almost everyone. Juvenal (early 2nd century), the satirist, describes men who lengthen their eyebrows, use makeup, put up their hair and dress in colors (e.g., green or blue) associated with women.[7] Martial (late 1st century) mocks men who dress or act effeminate, as in this excerpt from one of his epigrams:

> Cottilus, you are a pretty man: many say this, Cottilus. I hear them. But tell me, what does it mean to be 'a pretty man'? A pretty man is someone who has neatly arranged his curls; who constantly smells of balsam and cinnamon; who hums songs from the Nile and Gades, while moving his smooth-shaven arms to varied beats; who all day long is settled among the women's chairs, always whispering in someone's ear.[8]

The type of fellow both Juvenal and Martial describe is, presumably, well-known to their readers.

While we can easily find censure, the practices frowned upon or mocked persist. This certainly tells us that not everyone finds them objectionable. The people who engage in crossdressing probably are not seeking disapproval. Moreover, there must surely be enough folk who don't care, aren't bothered, or see it as acceptable for such behavior to exist in public without severe punishment. And if such things are in the public eye we won't be wrong assuming at least as great an incidence in private. That, too, suggests that unless the crossdresser is acting in total secrecy that some noncrossdressers are, at the very least, putting up with it. So we can hardly say a few well-known stabs of criticism represent a strongly shared social sentiment!

But lest we gain an impression that crossdressing is a practice confined to the West, we must turn our eyes to the rest of the globe. Records of crossdressing in ancient times have been found throughout the world. While we cannot hope to exhaust the subject, the following material gives an indication of the breadth of the practice. In giving special attention to crossdressing in the ancient West, no conclusion should be drawn that it is any more significant or more widely practiced there than elsewhere.

Was there crossdressing in the ancient East?

The lands of the East—China, India, Japan, Korea, and others—know crossdressers in a variety of contexts. In Korea the Flower Boys of Silla, skilled equally in the arts of war and feminine fashion, are famous in the 7th century. At least from the time of the Tang Dynasty in early 7th century China, crossdressing persists as an aspect of theatrical performance, and similar things are happening in other lands (cf. the answer to Q. 44). In India, ancient stories recount crossgender behavior by people and gods alike. Indeed, the religions of Hinduism, Confucianism, Shintoism, Buddhism and Islam all reference transgender realities, including crossdressing, and these often figure in important ways of religious experience and devotion (cf. the answers to Q. 79-82). Transgendered shamans, common to many indigenous cultures, also are found among these lands.

Literary accounts of crossdressing practices among people can be gleaned here and there from documents across the centuries in many Eastern lands. They reinforce the impression gained elsewhere, that crossdressing flows from various motivations, including those we noted above—entertainment and religious devotion—as well as many more. Common folks' individual stories seldom survive, but what we have suggests that all the familiar forces are at work in ancient eastern lands. For example, people sometimes crossdress to gain access to lovers, to escape detection, or to express a sense of a differently gendered self.

Was there crossdressing in the ancient Middle East?

If the Middle East can be called 'the cradle of civilization,' it perhaps also is worthy of the title 'the cradle of crossdressing.' The first famous crossdresser is an Egyptian female, Ma'at-ka-Ra Hatshepsut, Pharaoh in Egypt fifteen centuries before Christ (see the answer to Q. 43). Archaeological findings suggest that transgender dress behavior is known in ancient Iran during the Iron II Age (c. 1100-800 B.C.E.; see the answer to Q. 53). The ancient Jewish scriptures (Tanakh) refer to crossdressing (see answer to Q. 61), and Jewish teachers of the ancient world discuss the meaning of the biblical text in commentaries and the Talmud (see the answer to Q. 63). Both modern Jewish and Christian scholars have produced examples of crossdressing during the centuries covered by the Christian Bible (roughly down to the 2nd century C.E.).

Some of the crossdressing by these ancient peoples of the Middle East is associated with religious practices. This connection helps explain the censure of it in the Tanakh. For example, the *kurĝara*, priests of Sumerian deity Inanna (or Inana), identified with the Akkadian Ishtar, or Astarte of the Semitic peoples of the Mideast, dress so as to conspicuously incorporate mixed gender elements in their public processionals.[9] More pertinently for the Hebrew people, the Canaanites—a people occupying land now part of Israel—incorporate female crossdressing as part of the worship of the goddess Astarte (Astoreth, Ashtoreth): women put on the armor of men. The male priests of Baal are described by 19th century scholar Paul Lacroix (writing under the synonym of 'Pierre Dufour'), as unbearded (unusual for the time and place), with depilated bodies and fragrantly perfumed.[10] In their efforts to keep the Hebrew people separate from the people around them, Israel's priests, prophets, and lawmakers actively discourage such practices.

One of the earliest examples of male crossdressing comes from this region. The Greek writer Ctesias (5th century B.C.E.) records that a guest meeting the Assyrian king Sardanapalus encounters this sight:

> the king with his face covered with white lead and bejewelled like a woman, combing purple wool in the company of his concubines and sitting among them with knees uplifted, his eyebrows blackened, wearing a woman's dress and having his beard shaved close and his face rubbed with pumice (he was even whiter than milk, and his eyelids were painted).[11]

This 'Sardanapalus' has been identified as Ashurbanipal (669-627 B.C.E.) a vigorous military campaigner who extended Assyria's empire. Since the 19th century this account has been regarded as fictitious. Nevertheless, that it was for so many centuries regarded as fact corroborates the notion that the ancients are familiar with actual examples like the fictional portrayal.

Was there crossdressing in the ancient West?

Crossdressing is not unusual in the Greek and Roman classical world. Even a deity might appear in the guise and garb of the opposite sex (see the answer to Q. 76). Among mere mortals it occurs among heroes (e.g., Achilles, Hercules), powerful rulers (e.g., Caligula, Nero), and ordinary folk (e. g., the 1st century Roman philosopher Seneca mentions in passing "a man changed into the likeness of a woman"[12]). Among the Greeks crossdressing is found in religious events (ceremonies and festivals), and is depicted in art forms.[13] The Roman world witnesses crossdressing with relatively wide social toleration.[14]

In human affairs, crossdressing might be motivated by any number of things, including:

- ❑ *entertainment*—traditional classical theater has males filling both male and female roles, and some spontaneous crossdressing may occur in after-banquet revelry;
- ❑ *escape*—on occasion crossdressing is used to evade or escape dire circumstances;
- ❑ *gender identity*—some people probably crossdress because they wish to present as the gender they best identify with rather than as the gender they have been assigned;
- ❑ *gender role-playing*—crossdressing sometimes may be part of a more complete presentation of a gender role different from the one the individual might be expected to fill (e.g., women warriors);
- ❑ *marriage rites*—sometimes crossdressing happens as an aspect of wedding ceremonies;

- ❑ *martial strategy*—on a few occasions soldiers disguise themselves as women in order to gain a military advantage through surprise;
- ❑ *petticoat punishment*—just as in later centuries a boy might be forced to wear girl's clothing to curb his rowdiness, in ancient times men might be punished by forced crossdressing;
- ❑ *puberty rites*—the transition from childhood to adulthood is sometimes marked by crossdressing;
- ❑ *sacred rituals*—some religions feature crossdressing as part of religious ceremonies, such as sacred dances;
- ❑ *special gender status*—as in the case of eunuchs; and,
- ❑ *secret sexual access*—where crossdressing might occur to project an identity that gains sexual access the person otherwise won't have.

While some of these are described more fully elsewhere, all merit at least brief comment here.

Entertainment

The Roman writer Lucian notes in *The Dance* that, "men imitate women."[15] And so they do, in a variety of forums, including the theater, dances, religious festivities, and after-dinner revelries. As discussed at greater length elsewhere (see the answer to Q. 44), crossdressing is well-known in the theater. The practice of males filling both male and female roles stays common in ancient Greece, the Roman Republic and Empire, and early Europe. But crossdressing is hardly confined to professional actors.

Festive occasions might be marked by anyone donning cross gender garb to elicit laughter and add to the merry making. Antiquities scholar Margaret Miller notes that in the Greek world there are spontaneous revels after banquet gatherings (*symposia* and *komoi*), where men put on women's clothes.[16] During the Early Hellenistic period this might even have been the norm for some groups.[17] Miller recalls Philostratus' remark that "*komos* permits women to act like men, and men to dress and walk like women."[18]

Escape

Herodotus recounts in his *Histories* how the wives of the Minyae (descendants of the Argonauts) conspire to save their imprisoned husbands from execution by the Lacedaemonians. On the eve of the sentence being carried out, the wives beg to be allowed a farewell visit with their spouses. The request is granted. The women meet their husbands and exchange clothes with them. In this manner the men are able to escape.[19] This ploy is one found elsewhere as well, including American literature (see the answer to Q. 47).

Gender Identity

Enough examples exist of figures whose depiction suggests they are like our modern transsexuals to plausibly submit the proposal that the ancient world knows transsexualism. These individuals do more than temporarily inhabit a different gender role. Their appearance, demeanor, and manner all suggest a complete identity with a gender different than what others expect based on their sexual anatomy. Some persons make clear their desire to alter their bodies, such as the Roman emperor Elegabulus (see the answer to Q. 43).

Gender Role Playing

Gender role-playing, where a person occupies the role of a gender different than the one assigned at birth, need not be paired with gender identity status. In other words, one can occupy for a time a different gender role while retaining the gender identity they had prior to entering that role. In this regard, the ancient world provides a number of examples, perhaps most notably Achilles, who keeps hidden as a maiden among young women, and Heracles, who serves as a woman to a mistress (for both, see the answer to Q. 42).

Some more ordinary people also crossdress as an aspect of gender role-playing. Either male or female might do so. An epigram of Asclepiades, for instance, refers to a crossdressing woman named Dorcion.[20] Or this might occur within narrow limits, as when a boy dresses as a female to take part in a sexual encounter in which he fills the passive, receptive role for a man. One of the earliest extant Western novels, from the mid-1st century, affords us a look at such a situation. Petronius, in his comic novel *The Satyricon*, has the narrator Encolpius, feeling bitterly betrayed by his love, the boy Giton, and former companion Ascyltus, denounce both with these words:

> And who has saddled me with this solitude? A young scamp polluted with every manner of lustful behaviour, who on his own admission deserved the decree of banishment, a youth not merely free but freeborn devoted to debauchery, his years spent in gambling, hired as a girl even by the person who assumed him to be a man! As for the other one, on the day for donning the man's toga he put on a woman's dress instead, his mother coaxed him to reject his manhood, he played the woman's role in the slaves' quarters, and when he ran out of money he switched the direction of his sexual favours.[21]

In such instances, there is typically no deception intended. Others know the crossdresser's sex. The crossdressing is an aspect of performing the other gender.

Marriage Rites

In ancient Greece, crossdressing is occasionally incorporated into wedding ceremonies[22]—not terribly surprising when we remember the connection to Artemis (see the answer to Q. 76). There are several variations: Plutarch, writing in the 2nd century, mentions the groom might wear feminine apparel as he takes his bride (as found at Kos), or the bride might wear a beard to her wedding night (the practice at Argos).[23] Plutarch also records a curious custom of ancient Sparta. After a man has claimed a woman in marriage ("by a sort of force"), the female superintendent of the wedding "comes and clips the hair of the bride close round her head, dresses her up in man's clothes, and leaves her upon a mattress in the dark."²⁴ The husband then enters, has intercourse with her, and returns to his own apartment. These secret encounters may go on for some time; the man even could have children by the woman before seeing her in plain light! About these kind of acts Monica Cyrino remarks, "Such nuptial transvestism would have served to mark the individual's complete separation from a previously indistinct gender identity and his/her successful passage to the fixed masculine and feminine roles of husband or wife."²⁵ Seen thus, such crossdressing is part of a rite of passage, and the practice is reminiscent of what we find in many societies where crossdressing helps mark transition into adulthood.

Martial Strategy

Spies, whether male or female, often use crossdressing to get around. But on occasion so do soldiers. The maneuver can be successful because women are not expected to be physically dangerous and so are accorded little scrutiny. Soldiers thus disguised are able to infiltrate enemy positions, drop their masquerade, and mount a surprise attack. Pausanias relates one version of an incident in which King Telechus of the Lacedaemonians and some of his men are killed. According to those who kill them, the Messenians, the king had intended to assassinate some of their leading men in order to seize land. To this end he had taken beardless youth, dressed them as maidens, and sent them among the Messenians. However, the plot failed and the conspirators all died.²⁶

Still, the deception does work on occasion, as an incident preserved by Herodotus shows us. In it Alexander, son of Amyntas, cleverly revenges his people on some Persian louts. The latter have come as envoys of King Darius and been honorably received by Amyntas of Macedonia. The envoys request he follow a Persian custom and have women come in and sit with the men while they feast. Amyntas reluctantly agrees. The drunken Persians, as soon as they have an opportunity, begin pawing at the women, trying to kiss them and grabbing their breasts. Alexander, after persuading his father to leave the scene, then approaches the Persians. He tells them they are free to do what they like with the women, only they should wait until the women have cleaned themselves up. The envoys defer to this plan. Alexander then finds beardless men to take the women's place, dresses them in women's clothes, and arms them with daggers. The men take their places beside the Persians and when the latter try to resume their loutish behavior they are killed.²⁷

In a more clearly military situation, Frontinus in his *Strategemata* (*Stratagems*) relates a 2ⁿᵈ century B.C. encounter between Roman forces and their enemy, the Voccaei:

> When the Voccaei were hard pressed by Sempronius Gracchus in a pitched battle, they surrounded their entire force with a ring of carts, which they had filled with their bravest warriors dressed in women's clothes. Sempronius rose up with greater daring to assault the enemy, because he imagined

himself proceeding against women, whereupon those in the carts attacked him and put him to flight.[28]

Petticoat Punishment

Soldiers—avowedly the most manly of men—can be punished through humiliation, and few humiliations can match being publicly paraded as cowards in women's clothing. Diodorus Siculus records the practice of the lawgiver Charondas of Catana in Sicily, a man noted for his exacting penalties for various offenses; soldiers who desert their post, or men who refuse to take up arms, are made to sit for three days in the marketplace dressed in feminine apparel. This preserves their lives, if not their honor, and makes some especially eager for a second chance when later needed.[29]

Perhaps the most famous incident of such forced crossdressing involves the Christian saints Serge (or Sergius) and Bacchus. The account of their martyrdom places these two Roman soldiers as friends of the emperor Maximian (late 3rd-early 4th century). Denounced as Christians, they refuse the imperial order to offer sacrifice to other gods. As punishment they are stripped of all military insignia and clothing, then dressed as women and, in chains, paraded publicly to shame them. The punishment, though, proves ineffective and, following reassignment to a remote province the unrepentant pair are put to death.[30]

Puberty Rites

Various societies around the world have employed crossdressing as part of how they mark coming-of-age transitions. The ancient Greeks and Macedonians appear to have been among such people. In this regard, perhaps the most notable example is the crossdressing male rite of transference from youth to adult citizen in the festival of Ekdusia ('Festival of Disrobing') celebrated at Phaistos.[31] In Macedonia, crossdressing seems to be an aspect of the coming-of-age ritual associated with Dionysus Pseudanor.[32] Less certain is the festival of Oschophoria in Athens where young, wealthy noblemen dress as women, complete with feminine *stolai*, hairstyle and ornamentation, and proceed from the Temple of Dionysius to that of Athena.[33] Standing as substitutes for a whole group, these lads help enact an initiation or transition of a somewhat different character than more individualistic instances.

Sacred Rites

Sacred gender crossings often figure into worship (cf. the answer to Q. 76). They might involve either religious officials, or the worshippers. With reference to the former, we have the example of the priest of Herakles at Cos, who puts on female dress to offer sacrifice.[34] At Argos, worshippers at the feast of Hybristika, both men and women, crossdress.[35]

Crossdressing in the context of sacred events may be termed occasional and circumstantial, assuming that those so dressed do so only within a particular context. Such happenings are notably in connection with celebrations and festivals. Miller observes that comparative anthropological studies suggest the practice may have been widespread and offers as instances the Artemis Orthia festival at Sparta, where both men and women perhaps dance crossdressed, and the festivals of Dionysius found around the Greek world, and others.[36] Among the more often remarked is the Greek festival of Cotyttia in Athens, where males dress as females when they dance.[37]

Of course, not only males crossdress. At the festivals honoring Aphrodite at Argos (called the 'Hysteria'), both sexes crossdress.[38] Especially notable are instances of what classics scholar Fitz Graf terms 'ritual transvestism,' in which crossdressing occurs as part of 'rituals of reversal.' These rituals are typified by the temporary abandonment of ordinary boundaries and restrictions. Graf notes, too, that temporary role reversal is associated with social marginality so that those who always live on society's margin might always crossdress, as do the eunuch priests of Cybele.[39]

Special Gender Status

The eunuchs of the ancient world present a special case in various respects. Those of the classical Western world are derivative of Eastern practice. Their value and functions in different societies—East and West—are typically carefully prescribed because their neutered status often provides them some social access to females that other males do not enjoy. Eunuchs are often connected to religious duties, especially the service of female deities. Crossdressing, including the wearing of earrings, and accompanied by face-whitening, helps set eunuchs apart in a highly visible manner.[40]

Archaeologist Jeannine Davis-Kimball connects their religious affiliations to a common belief in the ancient world that a feminine nature is better suited to communing with the divine. If such is the case, what is a male to do? "Even if they didn't go so far as self-castration," Davis-Kimball says, "male devotees in many cultures adopted the custom of cross-dressing, apparently in an attempt to become more intuitive and spiritual."[41] Both eunuchs and others interested in a religious role, or especially devout, might crossdress, yet the ancients seem to have had little difficulty distinguishing them. Davis-Kimball points to reliefs, statuary and petroglyphs that may represent pictorially the distinction, with the male crossdressers who are not eunuchs "extremely virile-looking with rippling muscles and steely expression, yet still decked out in the flowing robes, jewelry, and long hair usually associated with women."[42]

Perhaps the most famous eunuchs of the classical Western world are those called *Galli* (a term derived from the region of Galatia in Asia). These eunuchs are self-made; they castrate themselves in devotion to the goddess Cybele, whom they serve as priests. In becoming eunuchs, they are following the example of Attis, son and lover of Cybele. Thus, they in effect *become* the goddess' sons and lovers. Like Attis, they crossdress and serve the goddess like handmaidens.[43]

An unusual case concerning eunuchs is hinted at by the Greek historian Herodotus (mid-5th century B.C.E.). He mentions with little elaboration a group among the Scythians known as the *Enarees*. These Scythian males had been divinely punished by Aphrodite after robbing her temple at Ascalon in Syria; they were inflicted with some strange complaint associated with women (*Histories*, I.105). These *Enarees* are later said by Herodotus to be effeminate persons, who practice divination in an unusual manner that they claim has been taught to them by the goddess (*Histories*, IV.67).[44] Whether androgynous or feminine, these mysterious folk clearly come to practice sacred rites that make them valued among the Scythians. Archaeologist Davis-Kimball links them to eunuchs and cites a pseudo-Hippocratic text calling them "eunuchs who belonged to the most powerful nobility, wore women's dresses, performed women's jobs, spoke like women, and enjoyed special respect because of the fear they inspired."[45]

Secret Sexual Access

Some use crossdressing to deceive others. Their intent often is to gain sexual access by fooling those who would otherwise prevent them from gaining their desires. The 2nd century satirist Juvenal describes male 'advisers' of women who seem safe enough to entrust to unchaperoned female company because they present as sexually uninterested in women. But, Juvenal warns:

You cannot, however,
always trust him. Although he sets off his eyes with soot,
and dresses in yellow and wears a hair-net, he's still an adulterer.
The more effeminate his voice, and the more he goes in for resting
his hand on his rounded hip, the more you should have him watched.
In bed he will prove most virile; there the ballet is forgotten.
'Thais' puts off her mask to reveal the accomplished Triphallus.[46]

Curious variants on the secrecy motif also exist, such as the Spartan wedding ceremony remarked upon earlier.

Conclusion

Consistent with what we have seen before, and will certainly see again, crossdressing in the ancient world was not a simple, uniform practice easily understood and predictably interpreted. People—males, females, and intersexed—might undertake crossdressing for any of a number of reasons, for any length of time, and in a variety of ways. Similarly, their actions might be revered or ridiculed, draw curious attention or pass indifferently. No universal judgment can be made.

Q. 42

Who are some famous crossdressers of mythology?

The Short Answer. Mythology persists because it speaks to our deepest selves. Core elements of human experience form the kernel around which stories of divine figures and mortal heroes are spun. Because sex and gender are intrinsic to human experience these matters inescapably prove central in mythology. Not surprisingly, then, issues related to what we call transgenderism are familiar parts of mythology. Mortals and immortals alike cross the boundaries of gender—and often enough they do so through crossdressing. Though examples abound in both Eastern and Western cultures, those most familiar to us come from the world of Classical Greek and Rome. They include divine, mortal, and demigod figures (the divine figures being treated elsewhere in this work). Among the mortals some might surprise us because of their fame as 'manly men.' Few would argue that among the most masculine figures of antiquity are Achilles, Heracles and Odysseus—all of whom crossdressed. Other, less widely known stories, also come down to us from the Greeks and Romans. But later Europe provides its share of examples, too, such as Hervör of Viking fame, a female warrior who took on masculine dress and manner, posing as a man and rising to leadership. The West, of course, has no corner on the market with regard to such tales. In the East, as in the West, we hear of both divine and mortal figures who engage in transgender behavior. Perhaps the most famous figure of Indian antiquity is the masculine god Vishnu who appears as the very feminine Mohini (see the answers to Q. 76, 79). There are human heroes, too, both male and female. Among the former is King Nala, reduced to sharing a single *sari* with his beloved wife Damayanti. Among the latter is Amba, scorned in her life as a woman, reincarnated as another woman, who assumes the guise of a man to exact her vengeance. The stories briefly summarized here in the 'historical present' represent a small portion of those found around the world.

The Longer Answer. Myth offers a way of experiencing that sheds light on our humanity. Ancient stories reflect their cultures but do more than that, which explains their appeal across cultures. Both Western and Eastern traditions are rich in tales we might term transgendered. Perhaps the greatest repository for such tales in the ancient East is found in the Hindu epic poem of love and war known as the *Mahabharata*. Within its pages we find stories of gender-crossing deities and mortals alike. Some like Krishna and Arjuna, are well-known even in the West. Others, familiar in India, are largely unfamiliar to Westerners. Two of these figures—Amba and Bhima—are discussed below.

Western mythology includes among its crossdressers such famous figures as Achilles, Heracles (Hercules), and Odysseus. But this tradition, too, has its share of little known gender-crossing figures, such as the mysterious person Sithon, about whom the Roman poet Ovid simply remarks was one who 'hovered' or 'alternated' between male and female.[47] Ovid's *Metamorphoses*, whose very name reflects transformations, has many stories where gender crossing occurs, sometimes as cross-dressing (e.g., Achilles and Heracles), sometimes more radically (e.g., Caeneus[48] and Iphis[49]). But he is not the only writer of antiquity to mention such events in connection to various figures, as we shall see.

In one respect the ancient accounts of gender-crossing mythic figures, at least in the West, mirrors our own age: an especial interest in crossdressing men. Of course, there are female figures, both divine and mortal, who cross gender boundaries, but it is remarkable that the most renowned male warriors of myth—Achilles, Hercules, Odysseus, and Theseus—are all connected with transgender realities. Moreover, there is a lack of censure or hostility about the acts described that we might find hard to imagine if the writers were mid-20th century men depicting the deeds of a George Washington or Ulysses Grant. In the ancient Western world, despite a gender order with masculine men on top, the boundaries of gender were often more negotiable without censure than would be true in the supposedly more liberal and enlightened modern age.

Who is Achilles?

Achilles is the famed warrior hero on the side of the Greeks in their campaign against the fabled city of Troy (c. 1200 B.C.E.). Though regarded as the manliest of men, and remembered as the greatest warrior on either side during the Trojan war, Achilles almost misses the conflict because he is hiding out, crossdressed, among maidens. His mother, Thetis, insists on the ruse for fear of a prophecy that foretells his death. On the island of Scyros, Achilles grows from boyhood into youth while dressed as a girl.

The Roman poet Statius (1st century) recounts the story in his unfinished *Achilleid*. Thetis' determination to impose on her son the masquerade of a daughter is aided by Achilles' own appearance. Statius describes him in a manner we might think more fitting of a maiden: his yellow hair gleams like gold, his face purples easily like a blushing girl, and he is the image of his mother. When she undertakes to dress him in her own apparel, she persuades by appeal to the example of Heracles (see below). His last resistance to the act is undone by his desire for the beautiful lass Deidamia, whom his mother points out will be more easily approached if he is in disguise. Carefully made up by his mother, Achilles is successfully passed off as his own sister. Under the tutelage of Deidamia he even learns how to be more feminine. Achilles' masquerade reaches its climax when he participates as a maenad in a female-only ritual.[50]

The Greek general Odysseus penetrates this masquerade when he brings presents to the court where he suspects Achilles is hiding. Odysseus later brags:

"Achilles' mother Thetis
Knew of his doom, and had disguised her son
In a girl's dress, and fooled them all. Even Ajax!
I was the one who hid, in the women's trinkets,
Arms that would rouse a warrior. As he stood there,
Still in his dresses, and reached out his hand
Toward shield and spear, I told him: 'Son of Thetis,
Troy, doomed, is waiting for you: why delay her?'"[51]

Interestingly, while so disguised Achilles succeeds in his lust. He impregnates Diomedeia, daughter of King Lycomedes, in whose court he has hidden. This romance, however, is but a brief interlude. Achilles' bisexual nature is better remembered through his passionate relationship with his cousin Patroclus, who precedes him in death at Troy. In that fabled war, Achilles also encounters the warrior queen Penthesilea, leader of a transgendered society—the mighty Amazons.

Who are the Amazons?

The most famed female warriors of history are undoubtedly the Amazons (Greek: Αμαζων, 'breastless'), known through Homer's *Iliad*, but gaining greater fame in later stories. The name derives from the notion that they destroyed their right breasts, as in this brief explanation: "they cultivated the manly virtues, and if ever they gave birth to children through intercourse with the other sex, they reared the females; and they pinched off the right breasts that they might not be trammeled by them in throwing the javelin, but they kept the left breasts, that they might suckle."[52]

Early Greek tales locate them along the southern shores of the Euxine Sea (in modern Turkey, the 'Asia' of the classic West), though later accounts place them elsewhere. Archaeologist Jeannine Davis-Kimball, in remarking on depictions of them, observes that early pieces typically show Amazons dressed in the masculine crested helmets and short tunics typical of the ancient Greek soldier.[53] Other depictions in art and literature display them in different garb, whether the skins of animals they hunt or in the styles of other peoples. What the accounts agree on is that their dress does not fit cultural parameters for femininity. By the standards of the world they dwell in, the Amazons are all crossdressers, for their garb is uniformly masculine no matter how depicted.

Whatever we might say of them is complicated by the multitude of conflicting accounts we have received. Some texts, for example, suggest an antipathy toward men, while others reflect a more positive stance of the Amazons to men. It is represented that they limit sexual contact to males from other societies, mating once a year, and then seemingly interested only in procuring new members for their society. They are said to either kill any male offspring, or to give them to nearby villages to be raised by others. Some accounts suggest a limited and subordinate presence of men among the Amazons. Either the Amazons constitute a female-dominant society, or a female-exclusive one.

In the latter event, we might be wrong to think of the Amazons as a society of 'women' (especially remembering that 'woman' means 'man's wife'). They do not live the lives expected of women. Rather, their masculine pursuits and dress, juxtaposed with their female sex, can be said to present a distinctive 'third gender.' This label traditionally is eschewed in the West, but the Amazons clearly present as a collective group—a society—that experience themselves and present to the world as individuals who are neither masculine males nor feminine females. Nor are they androgynous. Rather, they are clearly biological females (making no effort to disguise this) who live like men with no effort to present as men. They manage to defy the conventions of both femininity and masculinity—in other words, to present as an alternative gender.

Despite the many variations in the stories told of them, certain themes emerge: though female the Amazons engage in manly dress and occupations, especially hunting (their patron deity being Artemis—herself a transgendered deity (see the answer to Q. 76)) and warfare. Fiercely independent, they nevertheless regularly engage in interactions with other people. Said to have their own lands, they occasionally invade other nations, or fight off expeditions to their own. Perhaps reflecting the male unease at such females, the wondrously skilled Amazons still manage to come out on the losing end in their many conflicts, siding with the ill-fated Trojans in the *Iliad*, defeated by the most notable foes, including Heracles, Theseus, Achilles, and even Alexander the Great.[54]

Who is Amba?

The epic Indian poem the *Mahabharata* recounts the travails of a woman named Amba, a victim of tragic circumstances. Amba is betrothed to a man when the supreme warrior Bhishma kidnaps her and her two sisters. He intends to give the three women to others. However, because Amba has been promised to someone already, she is permitted to go home—only to find her beloved no longer available; Bhishma's actions have deprived her of her expected future. Her association with the feared Bhishma makes Amba unavailable to other men, so she returns to him. But Bhishma refuses to marry her, because he had long ago taken a vow to remain unmarried. Thus Amba becomes the ultimate scorned woman—and she vows revenge. After six long years of seeking in vain for a champion to oppose Bhishma and address the wrong she has suffered, the god Shiva takes pity on her. He tells her that in her next life she will avenge herself on Bhishma. At once Amba throws herself onto a funeral pyre.

Book 5 of the *Mahabharata* tells how Amba is reborn as the daughter of King Drupada. His wife receives Siva's promise that the child, 'born a daughter, shall become a man.' But in the meantime, the female form appears not at all suited to the justice the woman Amba had sought. Nevertheless, the queen acts in a manner faithful to the promise she has received. The text (5.CXCI) reads:

> And in due time, O monarch, that goddess, the queen of Drupada, gave birth to a daughter of great beauty. Thereupon, the strong-minded wife of that king, the childless Drupada, gave out, O monarch, that the child she had brought forth was a son. And then king Drupada, O ruler of men, caused all the rites prescribed for a male child to be performed in respect of that misrepresented daughter, as if she were really a son. And saying that the child was a son, Drupada's queen kept her counsels very carefully. And no other man in the city, save Prishata, knew the sex of that child. Believing these words of that deity of unfading energy, he too concealed the real sex of his child, saying,—*She is a son*. And, O king, Drupada caused all the rites of infancy, prescribed for a son, to be performed in respect of that child, and he bestowed the name of Sikhandin on her.[55]

The artifice proves a great success—at least until the time comes when Sikhandin is of an age to be married. The queen insists on a bride being found, but when the marriage is commenced, the secret of Sikhandin's sex becomes known. The outraged father of the bride determines to depose King Drupada for the deceit (5.CXCII). Heartsick, Drupada and his queen ponder their options, while Sikhandin, filled with shame, resolves to end her life (5.CXCIII-CXCIV). Entering a dense forest she encounters the *Yaksha* there, who takes pity on her and grants her the boon of his own maleness—for a time. The prophecy has been fulfilled, though the matter of revenge remains. Still, the immediate crisis is now resolved. When Sikhandin returns, the thoroughly bewildered bride is rebuked for having told such a lie about an obviously masculine man (5.CXCV).

Vengeance for Amba is at last attained in a great battle when Bhishma, knowing Sikhandin has been born a woman, refuses to fight him (5.CXCV; 6.CXIX). Sikhandin, however, shows no such reluctance and leads the force that finally slays Amba's nemesis (6.CXXff.).[56] Thus, the greatest warrior then known among men is brought down by a transgendered person.

Who is Astygetes?

Astygetes wins a crown partly by virtue of crossdressing. As told by Antoninus Liberalis (c. mid-late 2nd century), Astygetes and his sister Aspalis have the misfortune of living within the reach of a despot named Tartaros. This tyrant, upon learning of the beauty of Aspalis, resolves to take his pleasure of her. But the virtuous virgin hangs herself before this can happen. Astygetes, taking advantage of the fact that her death is not yet known, disguises himself in his sister's clothes. Presenting himself in her stead, he is admitted into the presence of Tartaros. Then Astygetes brings out a sword he has concealed beneath the clothes and kills the tyrant. The grateful people of Melite throw the old ruler's body into the nearby river and crown Astygetes their new ruler. Thus, in stark contrast to Achilles, who used crossdressing to avoid violence, Astygetes crossdresses to perpetrate it, though fully in the name of justice.[57]

Who is Bhima?

The Hindu epic, *Mahabharata*, recounts any number of crossdressing incidents beyond the story of Amba (recounted above). One involves a man named Bhima (or Bheema), one of the five sons of Pandu (known together as the Pandavas). Bhima is renowned for his might, being both great in stature and strength. In fact, in his time he is reckoned as perhaps the strongest among men, as well as one of the most adept warriors with his weapon of choice—a mace.

The Pandavas, to promote unity among themselves, resolve to share things in common. So, when Bhima's brother Arjuna wins a princess by his skill as an archer, she becomes the wife of all five brothers (though each, in turn, has separate wives, too). This woman, Draupadi of Panchala, proves over and over to be as high-spirited and high-minded as she is lovely. When foolish gambling leads the brothers into slavery, her courage and cunning wins freedom back for them. Later, when their repeated folly loses them their kingdom for a time and sends them into exile in Kamyaka Forest, she faithfully goes with them.

After a dozen years, the period of exile in the forest ends. For a further year, though, they live hidden in the kingdom of Matsya. Each of the Pandavas and Draupadi take on a disguise. In an episode known as the 'Kichaka-badha Parva' ('Slaying of Kichaka'; *Mahabharata* 4.15-22), their disguises both lead to trouble and afford a way out from it. Bhima, whose appetite is perhaps as famous as his might, has undertaken cover as a cook named 'Valala.' Draupadi has become a handmaiden named 'Sairandhri,' who serves the queen. These disguises, while keeping them from being recognized, also complicate their lives.

The queen's younger brother is a strong fellow named Kichaka. Intent on seducing Draupadi, Kichaka vexes her at every turn, even going so far as to literally chase her into the presence of the royal court, which stands idly by while he insults and pushes her before striding angrily away. Hearing of this, Bhima becomes as outraged by this situation as Draupadi, and when she uses her sexuality that night to persuade him to avenge her, Bhima is more than willing.

A plan is formed. Not long after, according to the plan, Draupadi easily persuades Kichaka to meet her at night at the hall of dancing girls, long after those girls have all gone home. Bhima, disguising himself as a woman, meets Kichaka instead. (Given his reputed size, this must have made for a remarkable sight! But the text says the darkness aids his ruse.) While Draupadi watches, Bhima attacks the prince. In the ensuing great struggle, Bhima beats and chokes Kichaka to death. The royal family, fortunately, believe Kichaka has been killed by a *Gandharva* (a male spirit that appears as part human, part animal—in short, in a shape Bhima easily might have been mistaken for given the darkness and his disguise). So Bhima and Draupadi escape retribution—with the aid of a little crossdressing.[58]

Who is Heracles?

Heracles, more familiar to the modern West under his Latin name of Hercules, is a mythic figure who enjoys immense popularity in the ancient world, especially among the Romans. The son of Zeus and a mortal woman, Heracles grows to renown through feats of immense strength and bravery. The most celebrated of these are his twelve labors. But our interest lies with his relationship with women's clothes, a surprisingly rich and significant relationship for a demigod.

Diodorus Siculus (1st century B.C.E.) tells us that Athena, the goddess who looked out for Heracles, presents him with the gift of a *peplos*, a full-length woman's garment especially associated with her. This is not the garb of war (he has the lion skin Athena helped him with for that), but of leisure. In the view of Nicole Loraux, the *peplos* dramatizes the complex interaction of masculine and feminine, weakness and strength in the hero.[59] Nowhere is the *peplos* more dramatic in Heracles' life than when the woman who loves him, Deianira, also gives him one as a wedding gift, unwittingly sealing his doom because of the poison an enemy has smeared upon it.[60]

Heracles most famous encounter with feminine dress comes from his time with Omphale, Queen of Lydia. In one familiar version of the tale Heracles, in a fit of madness, kills Iphitus and for punishment is afflicted with a disease. The only cure, he learns through an oracle, is to serve as a slave for three years, as well as to pay compensation. So he is sold to Omphale.[61]

What happens next is told by the Roman poet Ovid (43 B.C.E.-17 C.E.) in his *Heroides* (*Heroines*). In the following excerpt the speaker is Deianira, wife of Heracles, to whom she is writing a letter:

Were you not shamed when your arms were bound with gold
    and gems were set on your bulging strength?
Indeed, these arms crushed life out of the Nemean
    nuisance, a horrid beast whose pelt drapes
the left side of your body, but you do not
    hesitate to wrap your long unkempt
hair in ribbons cut for a woman. The white
    poplar is more proper to your curls;
you have shamed yourself by tying up your waist
    with Lydian belts like some reckless girl.[62]

Heracles himself recounts his experience when appealing to devotees of Bona Dea, 'the Woman's Goddess,' for a drink from their sacred spring. In the Roman poet Propertius' *Elegies* the hero says:

"I, too, clad in Sidonian robe, have done a servant's
Chores and a daily stint with Lydian distaff.
A soft breast-band confined my hairy chest;
I was a proper girl, though heavy-handed."[63]

Herakles, in woman's finery, spins wool while his master Omphale dons his lion's skin. Perhaps the dual crossdressing contributes an erotic element. The two become lovers. In his three years of servitude, Heracles has four children by her. He also finds the time and energy to impregnate Barge, another of Omphale's slaves. Apparently, crossdressing does not compromise his sexual vitality despite his wife Deianira's complaint about his effeminacy.

Because Romans regard Hercules as especially their own, and as the most manly of men to be emulated, his time with Omphale seemingly demands explanation. Yet by our standards they offer little. Not surprisingly, modern scholars have interpreted Heracles' crossdressing in a variety of ways. In commenting on the text in Propertius, Tara Welch notes that Heracles' act has been seen as confounding traditional gender categories, or as reaffirming them.[64] Importantly, as Monica Cyrino observes, Heracles' crossdressing does nothing to emasculate him: he accomplishes every task to which he is set and retains his sexual vigor, impregnating Omphale with a son.[65] What ancient and modern commentators generally agree upon is that the act matters enough to be preserved in the telling of his exploits. Heracles may be a different figure for having crossed genders than if he had not. But how he may be different is unclear, subject to individual perspective both in ancient times and in our own.

Who is Hervör?

Hervör is the heroine of the Hervarar Saga, a medieval composition about a female warrior of the 4th century. The daughter of a powerful lord, it is advised at birth that if she resembles her father's kinsman she should be exposed because she will not possess a woman's disposition. Though her life is spared, the prediction proves true. A beautiful maiden, she makes herself skilled with bow, shield, and sword—and leaves home to cause trouble. But she is apprehended and returned to her father's household.

The text then recounts that she again leaves home, this time "dressed and armed like a man," joining some Vikings and staying with them for a time, calling herself Hervarth.[66] She is accepted as a man and rises to the position of chief of the band, proving braver than any of her men. In her greatest deed, she obtains the mighty sword Tyrfing, which once drawn cannot be put up again until a man has died by it. Yet, perhaps inevitably, some recognize her female sex: after slaying a man who has drawn her sword, an observer cautions those eager for vengeance with the words, "Don't stir—you will not be avenged on the man so easily as you think, for you don't know who he is. This woman-man will cost you dear before you take his life."⁶⁷

Hervör/Hervath multiplies adventures, including a long period of success as a pirate. Then she returns home, where she behaves "like other girls, working at her embroidery and fine needlework."⁶⁸ She is courted and marries, bearing two sons. One of them, Heithrek, becomes king by wielding his mother's sword. Interestingly, as a kind of footnote to her story, the saga recounts that Heithrek has a daughter who not only bears her mother's name, but also her beauty and skill with the weapons of war.⁶⁹

Who is Leucippus (Leukippos)?

Leucippus is a name associated with more than one transgender tale. These various stories involve both crossdressing and, in one case, a sex change.

Perhaps the most famous tale is that of a daughter given a son's name. This myth echoes a situation not uncommon in the ancient world. The story happens at Phaestus on the island of Crete. A woman named Galatea, daughter of Eurytius, is married to one Lampros, son of Pandion, a poor man. On finding his wife pregnant he does what many have done in such circumstances: he prays for a son and prepares for a daughter! But the latter, in his mind, means requiring his wife to expose their child should it be a girl.⁷⁰ Galatea, as luck would have it, delivers while her husband is absent. So she takes advantage of the circumstances and disguises the infant as a boy, giving the child the name of Leucippus. Thus, in the manner and dress of a male the daughter is raised. But the danger of discovery is always present, especially as the child matures. So Galatea seeks divine aid at the Temple of the goddess Leto. Her persistent and heartfelt prayers are answered when Leucippus is miraculously changed to become a male in anatomical fact as well as appearance.⁷¹

In honor of Leucippus, recounts German scholar Hans Licht, a festival called Apodysia ('Festival of Undressing') was held at Phaestus on the island of Crete. At Phaestus, sacrifice was made to Leto Phytia, the 'creator' or 'generator' (phytia) of male genitals. Brides before their wedding night slept next to a wooden image of Leucippus, female in form and garb save for possessing male genitals.⁷²

Another Leucippus is a young man who desires a woman he cannot have. This maiden, Daphne, surrounds herself with female companions, who like herself have chosen to remain virgins. Leucippus, a prince, is determined to be near her. So he adopts the manner and appearance of a virgin girl in order to join Daphne's band of huntresses. He is successful in passing as a girl, claiming he is the king's daughter, and gaining the confidence and affection of Daphne. But when she and the other maidens decide to bathe, hapless Leucippus cannot join in without his secret being discovered. But the band of maidens force the issue when they seize and strip him. With his maleness thus exposed, they feel their friendship betrayed. Furious, they kill him with their spears and daggers.⁷³

A related name, 'Leucippe,' attaches to the story of a young woman who crossdresses for a heroic purpose. Her sister, Theonoe, has been captured by pirates and sold to the King of Caria. Leucippe's father goes off to search for his daughter, only to be shipwrecked and made a slave of the same king. Leucippe resolves to find both her father and sister. At the advice of the oracle at Delphi, she cuts her hair and disguises herself as a male priest of Apollo. She first finds her sister, who has been made a concubine. Theonoe is attracted to this new young priest and tries to seduce 'him.' When that fails, Theonoe orders 'his' arrest, oblivious to the fact that this is her sister. Theonoe then orders a slave—none other than her own unrecognized father—to kill the uncooperative priest. But rather than carry out such sacrilege, her father makes to kill himself, only to be prevented by Leucippe, who recognizes him. The reunited father and daughter proceed to hunt down the wicked woman who has set them against one another. But when she is confronted by the sword she had meant for Leucippe, Theonoe makes herself known as the missing daughter. Thus she, too, is reunited with Leucippe and father, and all are sent home with presents.[74]

Who is Odysseus?

Odysseus (Ulysses), the protagonist of Homer's *Odyssey* and a Greek hero in the *Iliad*, is King of Ithica and a man renowned equally for courage and cunning. Though Homer presents him as an epic hero, other writers tend to be less kind. His reliance on deception, including the use of disguises, often is seen as less than manly. Moreover, some regard his choice of bow with poison-arrow as a weapon also less manly.[75] Odysseus thus presents as a complicated and controversial figure, one inviting close scrutiny.

In his long journey home, Odysseus encounters many dangerous challenges. He must outwit enemies he cannot forthrightly overcome by force, and rely on allies where he can find them, be they male or female. Thus, after being sent on a raft from Calypso's island, when Neptune wrathfully raises against him a turbulent sea, Odysseus is in no position to refuse the aid offered by the sea goddess Ino (Leukothea). She instructs him to strip off his clothes and put her enchanted veil about his chest. Dressed thus he is able to swim safely to land.[76]

Though this crossdressing takes place far from the eyes of mortals, Dianna Rhyan Kardulias regards it as a pivotal event. She sees the loan of the feminine veil (κρηδεμνον), which in the story literally saves Odysseus' life, as symbolically transitioning him from a world of war and fantastic adventure to the more mundane domain of human society. Kardulias comments:

> When the hero of the *Odyssey*, already especially sensitive to female experience (as his handling of Kalypso demonstrated), undergoes a rite of passage in *Odyssey* 5 that features crossdressing, his assumption of feminine garb helps reorient him as a human being. Paradoxically, at this crucial transition, his re-

sumption of mature masculine identity depends upon transvestism, a ritual behavior that magically readies him for interactions and negotiations with the mortal women who will facilitate his return.[77]

Perhaps it is especially fitting, as Kardulias notes, that this incident involves the favorite of a goddess (Athena/Minerva) known for her own transgender experiences (in the guise of Mentor and Mentes).[78]

Who is Pentheus?

Pentheus is a king of Thebes who makes the error of refusing the worship of Dionysus. He then compounds his error into a fatal one by imprisoning the disguised Dionysus, who upon his escape brings about Pentheus' downfall. Angered by reports of the maenads (female devotees of Dionysus) brought out from among the women of Thebes, Pentheus is persuaded by Dionysus, now disguised as a priest, to covertly spy upon the maenads before going out in force against them. Going up on Mount Cithaeron in women's dress to accomplish his mad purpose, Pentheus is discovered and meets a gruesome end, being torn to pieces by the frenzied women, led by his own mother, Agave.[79]

Who is Theseus?

Theseus is among the most renowned of all Greek heroes. King of Athens, alleged son of Poseidon (Neptune), Theseus' life is filled with adventure. Among his most famous exploits are the taming of the bull at Marathon and the slaying of the Minotaur at Crete. As king he succeeds in unifying the region under the leadership of Athens. A contemporary and sometimes compatriot of Heracles (Hercules), Theseus' connection with crossdressing is somewhat more complex than for many of the others included in this answer.

Though Theseus does not ostentatiously crossdress, one tradition remarks that upon his entrance to Athens he is mistaken by some workmen for a woman because of his neatly plaited hair and style of tunic, whose length reaches his feet.[80] He is also associated with crossdressing in one variation of the story of his adventure in Crete. Theseus goes to Crete as part of a contingent of seven young men and seven young women to be offered as a sacrifice to the Minotaur. However, as the 2nd century Greek biographer Plutarch tells it:

> [Theseus] . . . selected two youths of his acquaintance, of fair and womanish faces, but of manly and forward spirit, and having, by frequent baths, and avoiding the heat and scorching of the sun, with a constant use of all the ointments and washes and dresses that serve to the adorning of the head or smoothing the skin or improving the complexion, in a manner changed them from what they were before, and having taught them farther to counterfeit the very voice and carriage and gait

of virgins so there could not be the least difference perceived, he, undiscovered by any, put them into the number of the Athenian maids designed for Crete. 81

Theseus' renowned journey to Crete becomes associated with various cults and their rituals, most notably the Oschophoria. One aspect of the Oschophoria is explained as recalling the cunning deception practiced by the Athenians: two male youth of noble standing lead a procession while dressed as maidens.82 Another connection to gender crossing behavior is also connected to a ritual established to honor Ariadne, the Cretan maiden whose aid helps Theseus escape the Labyrinth of the Minotaur, and whom he marries, only to leave her, late in pregnancy, behind on the island of Cyprus. According to Plutarch, on the second day of Gorpiaeus, "which is sacred to Ariadne, they have this ceremony among their sacrifices, to have a youth lie down and with his voice and gesture represent the pains of a woman in travail . . . ."83

Who is Tiresias?

Tiresias (or Teiresias) of Thebes is arguably the most famous 'seer' (soothsayer) of Western mythology. He may also be the most celebrated 'transgender' person of Greek mythology. Tiresias is the son of the mortal shepherd Everes and the nymph Chariclo. Stories concerning Tiresias do not all agree on how he comes to be blind. The version of interest to us relates to his experience as having lived both as a male and as a female. In this version, the male Tiresias chances upon two snakes copulating. He strikes at them with his staff, hitting the female, and then being himself transformed into a woman as a consequence. In this condition he lives seven years. As fortune would have it, he again encounters the same two snakes, again in the act of mating, and this time Tiresias strikes the male. He is then reverted to male form.84

The pertinence of this experience becomes apparent after Zeus and his spouse Hera debate whether men or women derive more pleasure from the act of love. Zeus argues that women do; Hera takes the opposing side. Because Tiresias has known such pleasure both as a man and as a woman, the deities put the matter to him. Tiresias sides with Zeus.85 Of course, this incurs Hera's displeasure, who strikes him blind. Zeus compensates for his wife's act by granting Tiresias the gift of 'second sight'—the ability to see the future. Among his most famous encounters thereafter are those with Amphytrion, to whom Tiresias discloses that Zeus has impregnated Amphytrion's wife Alcmena (mother of Hercules), and with Oedipus, to whom he reveals the awful truth of Oedipus' patricide.86 Even after death Tiresias is consulted, being visited in Hades by the Greek hero Odysseus.87

Q. 43

Who are some famous ancient crossdressers?

The Short Answer. Transgender realities such as crossdressing apparently have been a part of human experience for as long as human beings have been around. Crossdressing may be something that has been done ever since people adopted clothes that could be distinguished along gender lines. The recorded history of crossdressing spans millennia and our first famous crossdresser dates back at least 3,500 years. The most famous ancient crossdressers—and they are folk who give us one kind of glimpse into transgender realities—are not remembered because of this behavior. Rather, they are famed in their own time for their social standing. History, in preserving the stories of notable rulers, for instance, sometimes includes tales of cross gender behavior. These famous figures likely represent the visible tip of a larger mass of transgendered people, most of whom are not remembered individually, though they may be parts of groups (e.g., shamans or priests) who are recalled in connection with gender crossings of one kind or another.

The Longer Answer. Most of the ancient crossdressers we know are figures whose place in history has the boost provided by social rank. These include a good number of rulers, numbering females as well as males.

Who is Pharaoh Hatshepsut?

Perhaps the earliest recorded crossdresser is Hatshepsut in ancient Egypt, who lived 15 centuries before Christ. Ma'at-ka-Ra Hatshepsut enters the world unambiguously female, the daughter of Pharaoh Tuthmose I. After his death she is married to her half-brother, the new Pharaoh, Tuthmose II. But he dies not long into his reign, leaving an heir—Tuthmose III—by another wife. Hatshepsut is appointed regent to this child. As Queen, she is allowed to rule, though officially it is alongside the boy Pharaoh. However, Hatshepsut takes the unprecedented step of declaring herself Pharaoh, a role previously reserved exclusively for males.

Hatshepsut's solution to this problem embraces several elements. With the backing of the priesthood, she proclaims that the god Amun has made her his wife. She also argues that her late husband had made her his heir, intending for her to rule as Pharaoh. Moving cautiously over time, she abandons feminine titles and adopts masculine titles and roles reserved to Pharaoh. Hatshepsut masculinizes her name by dropping the final 't' and becoming 'Hatshepsu.' She also begins to dress in the masculine garb of Pharaoh, complete to the donning of a fake beard. Even her commissioned royal statuary depict her thus garbed.

Apparently, political expediency rather than gender identity issues motivates Hatshepsut's crossdressing. Indications are that she likely has at least one male lover during her reign. Interestingly, she seems intent on also rearing her daughter Neferura as a prince, rather than princess. A statue shows Neferura also bearing the royal false beard. Hatshepsut rules perhaps two decades, until her death.[88]

Who is Clodius Pulcher?

P. Clodius Pulcher (d. 52 B.C.E.) is a Roman aristocrat of the Late Republic. Although he has a colorful, sometimes violent career, and is influential in steering the course of the Republic toward its eventual demise, he is most remembered for one event. That event involves crossdressing.

In December, 62 B.C.E., during the festival for Bona Dea (the Good Goddess), Pulcher profanes the sacred mysteries. The festivities for Bona Dea, a fertility goddess, are reserved for women only. Conducted by the Vestal Virgins, the ceremonies are held at the house of the Pontifex Maximus (High Priest), who at the time is Julius Caesar. The house is cleared of all males, whether animal or human. The exclusivity and secrecy of the feminine divine mysteries are zealously guarded.

But Clodius disguises himself as a female musician and infiltrates the ceremonies. One apparent motive is that his mistress happens to be Pompeia, the wife of Caesar and thus lady of the house. But Clodius is found out. Brought to trial for his misdeed, his attempted alibi is refuted by the renowned orator Cicero, an act that brings lasting enmity between the two men. Clodius, however, is a man of influence and means. He successfully bribes the judges and is acquitted. But the infamy of his deed is never forgotten.

In the 2nd century C.E., the Roman satirist Juvenal recounts the tale and its far-flung fame:

But every Moor and Hindu
Knows the identity of that 'lady'-harpist
Who brought a tool as long as both anti-Catonian
Pamphlets by Caesar into the sanctuary where
All images of the other sex must be veiled, where even
A buckmouse, ball-conscious, beats an embarrassed retreat.[89]

And so his name persists to our own day with an attachment of wonder and shame for his audacious act.

Who are the crossdressing Roman emperors?

'Rank has its privileges'—so offers a saying that certainly fits the public appearance of some ancient crossdressers. Their elevated social status meant greater freedom of expression in many regards and their power provided substantial protection when they deviated from social norms. Their lofty station also meant they would more likely be remembered to history. Thus, some of the best-remembered crossdressers of the ancient world have been rulers, especially those of the most famous empire of all: the Roman Empire.

Gaius 'Caligula'

The Roman emperor Gaius (rules 37-41 C.E.), better known to history as 'Caligula' ('Little Boot'), is one of history's most infamous rulers.[90] He might be the most certifiably psychologically disturbed of Rome's many emperors. His brief reign is characterized by a host of unusual and often extreme behaviors. It might be truly said that crossdressing is hardly among the most remarkable of Caligula's actions—but it is all we will examine here.

The 2nd century biographer Suetonius, in his *Lives of the Caesars*, writes:

> Gaius paid no attention to traditional or current fashion in his dress, ignoring male conventions and even the human decencies. Often he made public appearances in a cloak covered with embroidery and encrusted with precious stones, a long-sleeved tunic and bracelets; or in silk (which men were forbidden by law to wear) or even in a woman's robe; and came shod sometimes with slippers, sometimes with military boots, sometimes with women's shoes. Often he affected a golden beard and carried a thunderbolt, trident, or serpent-twined staff in his hand. He even dressed up as Venus . . . .[91]

The golden beard, thunderbolt, trident, and serpent-twined staff are all part of Caligula's self-presentation as one or another male Roman deity.

As mentioned above, Gaius also presents as various female deities, not only Venus, but Juno or Diana. Mortal or immortal, Caligula excels at masquerades, as the later historian Cassius Dio (c. 150-235) makes clear in a telling observation:

> Now he would be seen as a woman, holding a wine-bowl and thyrsus, and again he would appear as a man equipped with a club and lion's skin or perhaps a helmet and shield. He would be seen at one time with a smooth chin and later with a full beard. Sometimes he wielded a trident and again he brandished a thunderbolt. Now he would impersonate a maiden equipped for hunting or for war, and a little later would play the married woman. Thus by varying the style of his dress, and by the use of accessories and wigs, he achieved accuracy in

many diverse parts; and he was eager to be anything rather than a human being and an emperor.[92]

If Dio is right in his conclusion, perhaps Caligula's crossdressing is a reflection of deep-seated and abiding identity confusion. Unfortunately, while his position provides him the liberty to act out any efforts to find out who he is, that same position means his instability poses serious problems for others. Eventually, the excesses of Gaius threaten the State to such an extent that there are few tears shed when conspirators succeed in bringing his reign to a bloody end through his assassination.

Nero

Nero (rules 54-68 C.E.) is the last emperor of the Julio-Claudian dynasty that guides the Roman Empire for the first century of its existence. A complex character, who rivals Caligula for infamy, Nero crossdresses for a variety of reasons. He fancies himself an artist in many forms, including singing and acting. The later historian Dio records how Nero, the singer, sports long hair and a smooth-shaven chin; as an actor he portrays a pregnant woman in labor. For women's roles he wears masks patterned after his dead lover, Sabina Poppaea.[93]

Nero also expresses a passionate and bisexual sexuality. In this latter regard, he not only crossdresses himself, but makes his lover crossdress. With reference to his male partner, Sporus (who was said to resemble the dead Poppaea), the biographer Suetonius records: "Having tried to turn the boy Sporus into a girl by castration, he went through a wedding ceremony with him—dowry, bridal veil and all—took him to his palace with a great crowd in attendance, and treated him as a wife."[94]

Later, Nero himself plays the role of wife to another man. The great Roman historian Tacitus—himself a child during Nero's reign—remarks in his *Annals* that just when it seems Nero can degrade himself no further, he does so by marrying a man named Pythagoras. As Tacitus records: "The emperor, in the presence of witnesses, put on the bridal veil. Dowry, marriage bed, wedding torches, all were there. Indeed everything was public which even in a natural union is veiled by night."[95] The later historian Dio adds, "After that, Nero had two bedfellows at once, Pythagoras to play the role of husband to him, and Sporus that of wife."[96]

Nero adores the Greeks and at least some of what many Romans perceive as his effeminacy stems from adopting Greek styles. Nevertheless, that he sometimes dresses—by the standards of his own society—like a woman is clear. Suetonius calls him 'shameless' in his appearance and dress, noting how he often gives audiences while adorned in an unbelted silk dressing-gown.[97] Dio echoes the judgment, offering a description of Nero in a short flowered tunic with a muslin neck-cloth.[98]

As Nero gives less attention to governing and more to performing, unrest grows. Despite the disastrous failure of a major plot in 65 C.E., Nero's enemies prove implacable. Revolt breaks out in 68. Nero pays it scant attention, until it becomes too late to save himself. Even as he prepares his suicide, Nero's thoughts are on himself as a performer; he laments, "What an artist dies with me!"[99]

Commodus

Commodus (rules 180-192 C.E.) is the son of Rome's great philosopher-emperor, Marcus Aurelius. But the son is quite unlike the father. Commodus is fascinated with spectacle. He himself repeatedly engages in presenting a spectacle, sometimes by appearing crossdressed. Commodus passionately identifies himself with Hercules, whom he regards as the manliest of men. As he imagines his hero, Commodus "struck with his club, while clad in a woman's garment or a lion's skin, not lions only, but many men as well."[100] He also desires to appear in Rome's arena dressed as an Amazon.[101] Like many emperors before and after him, Commodus' excesses and disregard for the proper affairs of state lead to his downfall. He is assassinated in a plot masterminded by his concubine and the Prefect of the Praetorian Guard.

Elagabulus

The Roman emperor Elagabulus (rules 218-222 C.E.) exhibits many of the signs that today would be associated with transsexualism. The famed historian Edward Gibbon, in his storied *The History of the Decline and Fall of the Roman Empire*, remarks of Elagabulus, "The master of the Roman world affected to copy the dress and manners of the female sex."[102] The Roman historian Cassius Dio, a contemporary of Elegabulus, characterizes him instead as someone who presentz both as a man and as a woman.[103] Dio's portrait shows the lengths to which Elegabulus will go:

> He married many women, and had intercourse with even more without any legal sanction; yet it was not that he had any need of them himself, but simply that he wanted to imitate their actions when he should lie with his lovers .... He would go to the taverns by night, wearing a wig, and there ply the trade of a female huckster. He frequented the notorious brothels, drove out the prostitutes, and played the prostitute himself. Finally, he set aside a room in the palace and there committed his indecencies, always standing nude at the door of the room, as the harlots do, and shaking the curtain which hung from gold rings, while in a soft and melting voice he solicited the passers-by. ...
>
> And finally,—to go back now to the story which I began,—he was bestowed in marriage and was termed wife, mistress, and queen. He worked with wool, sometimes wore a hair-net, and painted his eyes, daubing them with white lead and alkamet. Once, indeed, he shaved his chin and held a festival to mark the event; but after that he had the hairs plucked out, so as to look more like a woman.[104]

Dio offers at some length tales of Elegabulus' behavior. The emperor's identification with the feminine proves so complete that he enjoins others to "Call me not Lord, for I am a Lady."[105] He also desires to castrate himself and have the court physicians construct for him an artificial vagina.[106] But while today we might view Elegabulus as a male-to-female transsexual, his contemporaries view him as someone whose eccentricities threaten the stability of Roman rule. His actions lead to alienation with the very soldiers he depends upon to maintain power. In the end, they slay him.

Conclusion

As we find time and again when examining crossdressing, no one motive can be found to explain every incidence. In the examples given above and in the previous answer, we find great variety. There is crossdressing for assumption of a different gender role, but not a change in gender identity (Hatshepsut), crossdressing to hide (Achilles), crossdressing as forced submission, possibly tinged with an erotic quality (Heracles), crossdressing for theatrical performance (Nero), and crossdressing as an expression of what we today would likely diagnose as transsexualism (Elegabulus). And these do not exhaust the variety of motivations even among the few examples produced here.

Q. 44

What is the history of crossdressing and the theater?

The Short Answer. For virtually as long as theater has existed, there has been crossdressing onstage. While a large part of the reason for this is a history excluding female performers—thus rendering it necessary that males crossdress to play female parts—this is not the sole reason for theatrical crossdressing. Both on stage and through the movies crossdressing has been a vehicle for examining matters of sex and gender. In one form or another, whether through all-male theater troupes or all-female ones, in societies around the world and in different historical eras, plays exploring gender identities and roles, where crossdressing is often employed as a dramatic or comedic device, have enjoyed great popularity and engendered much discussion. Yet just as these plays generate interest they also occasion controversy, even as crossdressing in the world offstage has occasioned public curiosity and debate. In fact, since ancient times a criticism of theater has been its immorality and one exhibit set forward for this claim has been the incidence of crossdressing—a behavior some would like to stay hidden. On the other hand, an argument has been made that theater affords an important way for society to examine such matters and explore their meaning. Through artifice truth might be disclosed. As in literary legends, where the manliest men dress as women, so also theater and film have drawn actors noted for their masculinity who for a time take on feminine appearance and manner. In the media of film and television crossdressing has often been used as a comedic device—a practice found in theater, too. However, in recent years an increasing proportion of presentations on film and television have been serious, often sensitive and moving portrayals of transgender realities. Transsexualism, in particular, has been a subject of fascination.

The Longer Answer. Cross-gender behavior, including crossdressing, seems to have occupied a continuing presence in the history of theater. While the nature and extent of these things has changed, their vital presence has persisted. Indeed, in modern stage and movie productions crossdressing remains common, as even a casual search in magazines like *Entertainment Weekly* reveals.

Where once cross-gender behavior and crossdressing mainly occurred because males played both male and female roles (or, less commonly, females played the roles of men and women), now it happens largely in order to make comments about modern sex and gender issues, usually in the context of comedy. But make no mistake about it—even in places and times where crossdressing ostensibly exists because only one gender is allowed to perform, commentary on both genders, and gender in general, is being made.

Perhaps the best introduction to the subject is found in the volume *Crossing the Stage: Controversies on Cross-Dressing*, edited by Lesley Ferris. This book examines not only theater, but other staged performances in opera, cabaret, and dance. Its historical range is from ancient Greece to modern times.[107] Our attention here is much briefer, but aims both to survey history around the globe and examine the principal issues. We will begin in the ancient East.

What place has crossdressing held in Eastern theater?

Theater in the lands of the East has a rich and varied history. One notable feature of that history has been cross-gender acting, including crossdressing. This behavior has been an aspect of all male performing troupes playing both male and female parts, or all female troupes enacting male and female roles.

Indian Theater [108]

To India we owe the existence of the world's oldest surviving text on theater. Attributed to Bharata Muni, the *Natyashastra* ('theater science,' also called *Natya Shastra*) is of uncertain date—it is generally placed in the period between 200 B.C.E.-200 C.E. Acting (*abhiniya*) is broken into its constituent parts and the relationship between player and role is set out. In this latter respect, the *Natyashastra* permits actors to undertake cross-gender roles—males playing females or females playing males. Since India's theater traditions know both all male and all female troupes, this allowance facilitated acceptance of theatrical crossdressing.

An example can be found in one of the oldest dramatic forms in the world—India's *Kathakali* theater. Originating in southwestern India, it draws its source inspiration from India's mythology, especially its great epic tales, the *Ramayana* and the *Mahabharata*. The characters represent types; color-coding, elaborate facial make-up, headdresses, and formalized gestures all signal the audience concerning the character's nature. Traditionally, *Kathakali* theater includes only male actors. Female roles are embodied by males done up in highly stylized fashion. In addition to the features already described, they use breast and hip padding, and sometimes skirts, to complete the masquerade.

Yakshagana (or *Bayalata*) theater, a folk art form found in southern India provides another instance of crossdressing performers. Dating back to perhaps the early 12th century, it is similar to *Kathakali* in recreating the legendary stories of India's epics, the *Ramayana* and the *Mahabharata*, as well as others from Indian mythology. Unlike *Kathakali*, modern *Yakshagana* is a popular traveling entertainment performed by troupes who set up tents in villages, offering their performances either indoors or outdoors depending upon the season. *Yakshagana* once featured women as solo performers. Today, troupe players are typically all male, performing both masculine and feminine roles. There remain some female performers—who also occasionally enact masculine roles.[109]

British observer John Campbell Oman, near the end of the 19th century, described his experience of the *Ram Lila*, a drama enacted during the Dasarah festival in northern India. In it the story of Rama, hero of the grand and sacred story the *Ramayana*, is told. Actors in makeup and costumes play both human and nonhuman characters, such as Rakshasas, the demons that plague Rama and his wife Sita. Oman writes about observing this sacred play and witnessing males in female garb: "Two tall men, got up as women, went springing about, brandishing naked swords. They represented female Rakshasas."[110] There was no one upset at crossdressed men involved in this sacred drama, and indeed Oman also saw other participants, sporting painted faces, and impersonating Europeans of both sexes.[111]

Chinese Theater [112]

Theater has been a popular aspect of Chinese culture for centuries and crossdressing an integral part of theater. Chinese playwrights, like the women writers Wang Yun (*Quanfu ji* [*A Tale of Complete Happiness*]) and He Peizhu (*Lihua ming* [*The Dream of a Beauty*]) sometimes crafted crossdressing, or at least androgynous characters.[113] In dramas like *Nan Wanghou* (*The Male Queen*), which portrays an effeminate boy who is kept by the emperor in his harem, dressed as a young woman, the audience could find knowing nods at entirely plausible circumstances.[114] But the best-known aspect of crossdressing in Chinese theater remained its employment by actors.

Male crossdressing actors (e.g., *qiandan* in Beijing Opera) have been known since at least early in the Tang Dynasty (617-908), and female crossdressing actresses (*kunsheng*) since at least the 13th century—with crossdressed men and women both appearing on the stage simultaneously sometimes.[115] Likely influenced by Indian theater, it gained support and flourished especially from the time of the Mongol conquest (13th century). Diverse in its forms, Chinese theater has been a nearly omnipresent aspect of life in the villages, towns, and cities of China. While Peking (or Beijing) Opera is the most famous example, it has roots in older forms. One of these is *Yuan Zaju*, a style of theater arising in the Yuan Dynasty (1279-1368), and commonly regarded as the apex of Chinese traditional theater.

Zaju ('variety shows') combines music and movement around a dramatic plot line that unfolds in a prelude followed by four acts. Its variety is displayed through instrumental music, song, dance, and pantomime, among other things. Both males and females (often prostitutes) act. Characterization in *Zaju* is highly stylized. There were originally three basic roles, which later (especially in Peking Opera) become expanded into four main types: 'male' (*mo*), 'female' (*dan*), 'painted face male' (*jing*), and 'clown male' (*chou*)—each subdivided with distinguishing features signaled to the audience by costuming and other means. Male or female actors can portray characters of either gender (and in productions by prostitutes the male roles were often played by the women).

It was in the 18th century that earlier forms of Chinese 'opera' (which bears little resemblance to what the West knows under that name), gave birth to Peking (or Beijing) Opera. By the mid-19th century it had triumphed as China's most popular form of theater. Like *Zaju* before it, Peking Opera is varied in its elements, mixing singing and dance with dramatic dialogs and other forms of action like acrobatics. Drawing on anything from old legends to popular novels, the number of plays is large. So, too, is the number of facial painting patterns used to convey aspects of character—over 1,000. Costumes, ornaments, and other things are all added to express a role.

Traditionally, all roles are performed by male actors—a circumstance reinforced by a ban originating in the late 18th century on women appearing onstage. To perform female (*dan*) roles their costuming is complete down to the props worn on their feet (*qiao*) to represent the Chinese woman's traditionally bound feet. Among great *dan* performers—the 'four famous actors of female characters'—who gave rise to 'schools' of *dan* acting were Shang Xiaoyun, Cheng Yanqui, Xun Huisheng, and Mei Lanfang. Their influence remains felt in contemporary Peking Opera.

Yufu Huang argues that Peking Opera affords a look at changes in Chinese culture. Huang, examining the period from 1790-1937, identifies three aspects of the Opera displaying social changes in the wider culture. First, female roles gradually grow in importance. This, Huang notes, is largely due to the success and influence of the great *dan* actor Wang Yaoqing. Second, the representation of the female characters grows increasingly positive. Finally, more roles for women with unbound feet occur, led by male actors who as early as the beginning of the 20th century seek to abandon use of the *qiao*.[116]

Foot binding ended with a ban in 1911. Recent decades have seen the decline of Peking Opera's popularity and the large scale replacement of males in female roles by women. Nevertheless, some male actors still choose to perform *dan* roles. On the other hand, an increasing number of females have undertaken male roles.[117] In the face of more modern alternatives like film, the future of Peking Opera is uncertain.

The same might be said about the all-female Xiaobiahua troupe of the *Yueju* Opera. Like other forms of Chinese opera, *Yueju* Opera has lost much of its following and now draws principally an older crowd. In an interview with *China Economic Net*, famed opera star Mao Weitao defends the use of an all-female cast as essential to realizing the opera's spiritual world. She also explains how a woman can successfully play a male role—as she has for more than a quarter century—by remarking that her aim is to "interpret the man through the eyes of a woman," while simultaneously embodying male mannerisms in body language and adjusting her voice to sound masculine. She seeks the male character's most vulnerable aspect, which she believes is the key to touching the audience as a "mysterious, attractive and unique" person comes to life. In her view, male roles in *Yueju* Opera are special because they focus on poetic temperament; gender differences are inconsequential.[118]

Japanese Theater [119]

Japanese performers, both male and female, have practiced crossdressing. Much of Japanese entertainment centers around dance. In the *Shirabyōshi* dancing of the 12-13th centuries, women put on a man's hat and robe while performing.[120] This art form probably influenced the development of *Nõ* theater, and some characters in later *Nõ* drama were *Shirabyōshi* dancers (e.g., Sizuka in the play *Funa Benkei*).

In traditional Eastern theater as in Western, males played female roles. The world's oldest continuously extant professional theater is Japanese *Nõ* (or *Noh*) drama, which took on its present form with the actor/playwright Zeami in the mid- to late 14th century. Males perform all the roles, and employ highly stylized masks. However, as Royall Tyler notes, "Actors playing feminine roles do not 'impersonate' women in any obvious way, for acting in *nõ* is on an entirely different plane from ordinary acting as the term is now understood. Gestures are restrained and miming highly abstract."[121]

Within *Nõ* plays crossdressing by a character sometimes occurs. For instance, I already have mentioned the character of Sizuka in the play *Funa Benkei* (*Benkei Aboard Ship*). A similar event occurs in *Izutsu* (*The Well-Cradle*) when the lady of the title puts on her husband's clothes (hat and robe) and dances under the moon as she pines for him. Again, in *Matsukaze* (*Pining Wind*), the title character dances wearing her beloved's hat and robe. Like the dance they perform, these characters' crossdressing is ritual.

In the early 17th century in Japan arose another form of theater. *Kabuki* theater has its roots in the erotic appeal of a female temple attendant and dancer named Okuni. Her success led to forming a dance troupe whose performers also offered themselves as prostitutes. The government banned women's *Kabuki*, but permitted *wakashu kabuki*, performed by boys. They performed both male and female parts and, like the women before them, aroused such a stir that they also were banned. But *Kabuki* theater did not disappear. The government permitted adult men to continue the performances, though mandating that there be more than merely erotic dancing. So plots were devised, though the theater's appeal remained its erotic qualities.[122]

What makes *Kabuki* theater especially pertinent to our study, though, is the degree to which performers carried their masquerades offstage. Those destined for female stage roles occupied a feminine role offstage from early childhood. In the words of Yoshiro Hatano and Tsuguo Shimazaki, they were "compelled to experience first-hand the everyday life, customs and etiquette of the women they played."[123] English professor and historian Louis Crompton observes of the *omnagata* or *oyama*—the males playing female roles—that they carried "the gender ambiguities" between stage and real life, and he draws upon the comments of one such actor:

> Writing on his art, one successful female impersonator held that "one cannot become an excellent *oyama* without living as a woman in ordinary life. In fact his masculinity betrays itself easily in him who makes an effort of will to become a woman on stage." These popular stars often dressed as women at home and on the street and attracted lovers of both sexes, like their counterparts in the Peking Opera.[124]

Like *Nō* theater, *Kabuki* plays remain a popular form of Japanese entertainment, though the intense cross-gender training and identification of males playing female parts is no longer expected.

The all-male *Kabuki* theater is mirrored by an all-female counterpart. Since 1914, an all-female acting venue has been provided through the traveling *Takarazuka Kagekidan* (or Takarazuka Young Girls Opera, or Takaruzaka Revue Company). The performers are known as *Takarasiennes*. Girls between 15-18 years old compete for entrance into the company. Successful candidates are trained for two years at the *Takarazuka Ongaku Gakkou* ('Takarazuka Music School'), where they learn acting, singing, and dancing. Some are selected to play principally female roles (*otokoyaku*), others especially for the male roles (*musumeyaku*). The *musumeyaku* are trained to enact masculine gender traits in body posture, gestures, movement, and speech. All players must remain unmarried.

The largest all-female theatrical company, *Takarazuka* presently features five troupes with some 400 members total. *Takarazuka's* wide-ranging entertainment offers musical takes on original material as well as adaptations of Japanese literature. Western stories like *Gone with the Wind* and *West Side Story* also offer source material, as do classical opera pieces such as *Figaro* or *Tristan und Isolde*. The troupe's principal star enacts the lead male role in most productions. The audience is mostly female, with *Takarazuka* being especially popular with adolescent females.[125]

In fact, this audience makeup was influential in the decision to adapt a phenomenally popular Japanese manga story, *The Rose of Versailles* (cf. the answer to Q. 52). The story features a crossdressed character, a girl raised as a French general's son, who in adulthood still occupies a male role as captain of the palace guard at Versailles. *Takarazuka* adapted the story into musical theater under the title *Beru-Bara*. In its initial run from 1974-1980 the play proved so popular all five troupes began performing it. Over 700 performances reached more than a million-and-a-half fans. Revivals since the original run also have proven successful; by the end of the century more than three million people had seen the play in one form or another.[126]

Thailand (Siam)

In Thai theater, prior to the modern period, there were all-male and all-female theater troupes. Crossdressing, in the sense of males playing female roles or females playing male roles, was common. Australian scholar Peter A. Jackson, who has made a thorough study of transgenderism in Thailand, notes that traditionally an all-female cast performed both male and female roles for productions within the palace. This was the *lakhorn nai*—'theater of the inner [court].' Elsewhere it was the *lakhorn nork*—'theater outside [the court].' In these productions all-male troupes performed all parts. In modern times, the style is now *lakhorn chai jing ying thae*—'the theater of real men and genuine women.' As Jackson has documented in his work on this society, it is a prime example of how the pressure exerted by Western culture has affected gender-related practices.[127]

Other Non-Western Crossdressing Performances

Gender crossing performances are found in other Eastern lands besides those mentioned above. If we include activities like dance as a form of theater, then the reach of crossdressing in public performance grows even wider. For example, Korea had the all-male *Namsadang* theater troupes (see the answer to Q. 52). Indonesia has a long history of crossdressing in both theater and dance through manifestations such as the Arja on Bali, or the Waria performances on Java (see the answer to Q. 59). In the Pacific, the entertainments of Kia Orana day in the Cook Islands feature young men in feminine dance costumes, complete with coconut bras.[128] In short, the presence of transgender realities like crossdressing are widespread in the Eastern hemisphere, finding a place in secular entertainment as well as sacred dance and drama.

What role did crossdressing play in ancient Western theater?

Crossdressing probably was a part of Western theater from the very beginning. This was inevitable simply because there were both male and female roles, but only male actors were often sanctioned as performers. Western theater is considered in this section down to the time of Ben Jonson and William Shakespeare.

Greek Theater

Certainly crossdressing is well attested in ancient Western theater. In both Greek and Roman plays males played virtually all the parts,[129] a practice that persisted in Western societies for many centuries. Greek actors played female parts with the help of various aids. In addition to a feminine garment, they used *prosternida* (chest padding), perhaps a *progastridion* (a false paunch), special footwear and, of course, a mask. Even where the female character was depicted as nude, as in Aristophanes' *Lysistrata*, males could play the part by wearing a special costume.[130]

The appearance thus achieved could be remarkable. In speaking of Greek actors in his own time (mid-1st century), the Roman satirist Juvenal wrote:

On the stage they remain supreme
In female parts, courtesan, matron or slave-girl,
With no concealing cloak: you'd swear it was a genuine
Woman you saw, and not a masked performer.
Look there, beneath that belly: no bulge, all smooth, a neat
Nothingness—even a hint of the Great Divide.[131]

The use of male actors in female parts has been variously interpreted. Philip Ambrose, following the lead of Jack Winkler, thinks, "there is considerable merit to the notion that by playing and observing female roles, that is, by institutionalized cross-dressing, Athenian youths learned how to be Athenian men."[132] Of course, that meant to be a member of the dominant gender in a hierarchical order. In this light, Sue-Ellen Chase puts the matter rather more harshly. She regards the convention and the plays in which it occurred as "allies in the project of suppressing actual women and replacing them with the masks of patriarchal production."[133]

Perhaps a more nuanced position is articulated by Froma Zeitlin, who argues that Greek drama features male authors depicting the feminine in such a manner that a "continual play with gender categories" results.[134] For her, Greek tragedy represents females so as to raise questions about gender roles. Comedy, too, plays with gender.[135] In Zeitlin's view, Greek theater affords a way for male writers with their male audiences to look at socially constructed ideas about gender, question them, and then reaffirm them to the comfort of the audience.

Nancy Rabinowiyz proposes a variant of this notion by seeing the convention as both upholding patriarchy and simultaneously offering a site of resistance to it. She contends that the crossdressed male in Greek tragedy was for the audience "a third gender, so to speak, that was strictly speaking neither male or female, a figure removed from real life although referring to it, as the actor was removed from the character."[136] The unique place held by such an actor she sees as significant. In fact, she locates the central effect of tragedy in this divorce of gender construction from biology. Theatrical crossdressing, operating at multiple levels, is a powerful force.

Greek plays not only used crossdressed actors, they employed crossdressed characters. Thus an audience could see on stage at the same time men playing women and men playing men pretending to be women. A notable instance of this is found in Aristophanes' comedy *Thesmophoriazusae* (*Women at the Thesmophoria*), produced in 411 B.C.E. The plot involves women gathering at the female-only festival Thesmophoria[137] where they would indict the playwright Euripides for constantly showing them in a bad light. Euripides, aware of this, seeks a way to escape their judgment. At the play's opening he tells his father-in-law Mnesilochus his plan:

EURIPIDES I am going to beg Agathon, the tragic poet, to go to the Thesmophoria.
MNESILOCHUS And what is he to do there?
EURIPIDES He would mingle with the women, and stand up for me, if needful.
MNESILOCHUS Would be present or secretly?
EURIPIDES Secretly, dressed in woman's clothes.[138]

Agathon, an actual historical figure, is then depicted approaching on a litter, upon which he reclines, clad in a feminine saffron tunic, with various feminine toiletries at hand. Mnesilochus is confused, thinking Agathon is a woman. Set straight, Mnesilochus, borrowing from Aeschylus' *Lycurgeia*, refers to Agathon as an 'androgyne.' Agathon is described by Euripides as "good-looking, charming, and . . . close-shaven; you are fair, delicate, and have a woman's voice."[139] Agathon himself justifies his appearance by declaring, "My dress is in harmony with my thoughts. A poet must adopt the nature of his characters. Thus, if he is placing women on the stage, he must contract all their habits in his own person."[140] Despite his own self-contentment in feminine appearance, Agathon declines to infiltrate the Thesmophoria.

Euripides then turns to Mnesilochus, who is persuaded to undertake the masquerade. His appearance suitably altered, Euripides enjoins him to remember to speak like a woman, which Mnesilochus promises to do in a falsetto voice. At the Thesmorphia he speaks on Euripides' behalf by claiming the playwright's criticisms of women are not only well-deserved, but barely scratch the surface of the matter. Predictably, this arouses the women's wrath. Then Clisthenes, a eunuch dressed as a woman, appears onstage to inform the women they have been infiltrated by a man in disguise. Suspicion at once falls upon Mnesilochus, who is bound over to face the Magistrate. Only the cleverness of Euripides, who uses a dancing girl to seduce the guard, saves the day as Mnesilochus is freed and scurries away. Euripides himself promises the women he will henceforth depict them in a more favorable light.[141]

Thesmophoriazusae plays with the notion of presentation at multiple levels. Agathon justifies his feminine presentation as a way of comprehending women. The women at the festival are concerned over the presentation of their gender by the male Euripides. Euripides aims to defend his presentations by convincing Mnesilochus to alter his gender presentation and imitate a woman. That imitation itself offers a dual presentation—Mnesilochus is ostensibly a woman presenting all women in a most unfavorable manner. This imitation is undone by yet another imitation, that of the eunuch Clisthenes. Masking and unmasking abound. In the end, Mnesilochus is saved from the consequences of his imitation by Euripides' agreement to alter his presentation of women even though he at once manipulates another man—the guard—by using a seductive presentation by a dancing girl—a presentation of woman as seductress. The importance, artificiality, and fluidity of gender are all considered in these multiple and multifaceted presentations. Gender is inseparable from presentation, and the gendered presentation may or may not conform to the sexed body of the presenter.

As we might expect, evaluations of Aristophanes' *Thesmophoriazusae* have varied with interpretations tracing the lines of general criticism described earlier. Thus, for example, Lauren Taafe highlights how the women of the play are used to get at male concerns. After all, the 'women' are all actually men. In her view femininity is for Aristophanes the ultimate locus of humor and the playwright relies on stereotypes. Thus we may learn about men's attitudes, but not about real women.[142] On the other hand, Angeliki Tzanetou believes that both structurally and theatrically the play celebrates women's power and affirms women's centrality to the "fertility of Athenian drama."[143] She calls attention to the fact that by play's end every character onstage, save one, is wearing women's dress. In her view, the play moves from male to female, from Dionysus to Demeter. "By the end of the play, male crossdressing does not show how easy it is to become female, but how essential women are to comedy—not only creating laughter but also to the basic function of comedy: affirming and celebrating the continuity of human life."[144]

The presentation of gender on the Greek stage, in both tragedy and comedy, has drawn much attention, especially in recent decades. Exactly how crossdressed actors and crossdressed characters contribute to such presentations remains a matter of speculation and debate. One thing generally agreed upon is that these gender crossing activities mean *something*. More than mere convention is at work in males playing the parts of girls and women. Something worth deciphering is being said about gender when crossdressed characters appear on stage. These matters continued to occupy playwrights and audiences who inherited a theatrical legacy from Greece.

Roman Theater

Roman plays are modeled on Greek ones, and often are Latin translations or adaptations of them. By the 1st century B.C.E., the waning Roman Republic witnessed a diversification from such staged comedies and dramas into rival entertainments like mime and pantomime. While the traditional theater permitted only males, the latter forms—popular but regarded as lower-class entertainment—allowed female participation.

Beyond the use of males to play female parts, Roman plays venture into gender-bending ground. Plautus (c. 254-184 B.C.E.), whose plays are among the earliest examples of Latin literature, and who adapted Greek New Comedy (4th century B.C.E.) for his Roman audiences, provides a case in point. In his play *Amphitryo* he uses the male actor playing the female character Alcmena to engage in gender issues. Classics scholar Pamela Bleisch remarks:

> The character of Alcmena, a female performed by a male actor, is, I argue, emblematic of Plautus' tragicomedy. The transvestism of Alcmena in performance serves as a vehicle for travesties of both gender and genre. Throughout the play Plau-

tus deliberately draws our attention to the fact of cross-gender performance, self-consciously disrupts the dramatic illusion of the feminine, and in so doing highlights the genre-crossing of his play. Plautus' *Amphitryo* is an entertaining romp. It is also a highly sophisticated exploration of reality, mimesis, and the nature of identity—not least, sexual identity.[145]

Bleisch calls attention to the fact that the male actor is costumed as a woman in late pregnancy, with twins in her womb, who offers a song that culminates with praise for manly excellence. The audience knows the character is played by a man, and as Bleisch observes, the spectacle of a crossdressed man singing about manhood while also portraying a pregnant woman singing about life's travails creates comic irony. In addition, Bleisch views Alcmena as not merely the expectant mother of twins, but as herself twinned: adulterous and chaste, tragic and comic, male and female. In various ways and places throughout the play, she argues, Alcmena is used to play with gender identity and to remind the audience of the gender performing going on.[146]

The playwright Terrence (c. 186-159 B.C.E.), who professes to adapt Greek New Comedy for Roman audiences, also plays with gender crossing and masquerade. In his most acclaimed play, the comedy *Eunuchos* (*The Eunuch*), Terrence uses the familiar figure of a eunuch, in this case one described as "an old woman of a man."[147] The character Chaerea, a young man smitten by desire for a servant girl in a certain household, reflects on the eunuch's situation with Parmeno, a household attendant. The eunuch, recently made a gift to the household, has not yet arrived when the following conversation takes place:

CHAEREA: Oh, lucky eunuch, to be a present for that house!

PARMENO: What do you mean?

CHAEREA: Can't you see? He'll always see his fellow slave in all her beauty, he'll speak to her and be under the same roof, he may sometimes take his meals with her . . . and perhaps sleep by her side.

PARMENO [teasing him]: Suppose you were the lucky one—

CHAEREA: How could I be?

PARMENO: You could wear his clothes—

CHAEREA: His clothes? And then?

PARMENO: I could take you in instead of him—

CHAEREA: Yes—

PARMENO: And say you were him—

CHAEREA: I see!

PARMENO: You could enjoy all those advantages you just said would be his; be near her, eat with her, touch her, play with her—and sleep by her side. None of the women there can recognize you or knows who you are. [Bursts out laughing] Besides, you're just the right age and figure to be taken for a eunuch![148]

Chaerea, much to the astonishment of Parmeno, resolves on the disguise. Donning the colored clothes and other adornment of a eunuch[149] he is admitted into the household. Taking advantage of the privilege accorded him as a eunuch to be alone with the object of his affections, he has sex with her. This is one of the oldest motivations behind crossdressing—and perhaps the most common reason it was condemned among the ancients.

Obviously, crossdressing in Greek and Roman theater is more than merely a matter of male actors donning feminine garb to play roles on stage. It also affords opportunities for playwrights to play with social ideas about gender. In some instances, the act of crossdressing—or rather the act of masquerade—itself is a critical component of the play. In their manipulation of gender presentation the Greeks and Romans set a model both followed and extended by later Western theater.

Early European and Medieval Theater

In the Medieval period, the Church utilized theater to convey religious messages. Priests and acolytes might act portions of the mass or present religious themes through drama. Males played all the characters in most such productions. Thus, a boy might be assigned, for example, the role of the Virgin Mary. This practice followed ancient theater and continued a tradition other forms of public spectacle would take. However, as Medievalists Robert Clark and Claire Sponsler point out, women occasionally had roles in religious theater and thus crossdressing males on stage cannot be entirely explained by mere custom or traditional practice.[150]

Clark and Sponsler point to plays wherein males play female characters who are themselves crossdressing to masquerade as males. One example is the 13th century French drama *Miracle de la fille d'un roy*, in which the maiden Ysabel, to avoid pressure from her father to assume the role of her dead mother, disguises herself as a knight.[151] The 14th century French play *Miracle de Théodore* presents another such story, that of a crossdressing saint (see the material on Theodora in the answer to Q. 68). Such plays show women entering a realm of experience made possible only by their crossdressing. In the appraisal of Clark and Sponsler, a drama like *Miracle de la fille d'un roy* manipulates gender in such a way it shows the audience the artificiality and arbitrariness of gender categories.[152]

However, what the theater looses it also binds. As Clark and Sponsler point out, these plays also hem in the danger of crossdressing, both by sanctioning its occurrence in the limited sphere of the stage and, within the play itself, by resolving dramatic tensions in such a manner that gender conventions are upheld. Crossdressing, then, is only a temporary and expedient gesture. In the end the gender status quo still reigns.[153]

This situation is not confined to medieval France. Steven Wright makes similar observations about German theater. He argues that some of the medieval plays could only have worked if their audiences were able to recognize that characters could re-invent themselves by manipulating gendered behavior. Wright comments, "For the plays to have worked at all, spectators must have been able to conceive of a gender role (be it masculine or feminine) as something provisional, that is to say, as a kind of performance in its own right."[154] Thus medieval church drama showed "destabilizing alternatives," even as the plays themselves sought to reinforce prevailing gender conventions.

English theater also followed the convention of males playing all parts irrespective of the character's gender. But here we might also note another phenomenon. The ancient practice of using masks probably lies at the root of Mummers' theater; the term 'mummer' may be related to the Danish word *momme* ('mask'). Mummers' plays are an important aspect of early English folk theater. This form of theater, which has persisted into the present, may be the altered survivor of earlier pagan rituals. It is continuous with earlier theater tradition in that males play all the roles. While some interpret this practice as reflecting old, imitative magic, others see it as an example of presenting a third distinct gender.[155]

What part did crossdressing occupy in early Modern theater?

The early modern period continued the practice of males playing female parts. This phenomenon has been well considered in numerous scholarly works.[156] The practice regularly brought criticism, just as it had since the time of the Church Fathers (cf. the answer to Q. 72). English literature scholar Shasta Turner quotes an anti-theatrical tract from 1580 that warns the reader that an actor's clothing may misrepresent the body beneath it.[157] This fact, though well-known, continued to bother some folk so much it elicited warnings of the most dire kind. Men who crossdress on stage are said to become effeminized and might even 'degenerate' into a woman.[158]

The condemnation of theater by various clerics, though it might give voice to ideas like those described above, typically centered in opposition to masquerades and deceit. For these critics crossdressing at the very least upset social order. The permissiveness of theater, they thought, only encourages a more general breakdown in morality. In support of their criticism they called upon Biblical law to substantiate their charging actors with immorality.

Such criticism did not go unanswered. Ben Jonson, in his comedic play *Bartholomew Fair* (1614), meets the charges of the moral critics head-on. Near the end of Act 5, Scene 5, the character Leatherhead (a hobby-horse seller) uses a puppet show to answer Zeal-of-the-Land-Busy, a Puritan critic anxious to publicly address the 'profanations' he finds at the fair. Busy and the puppet Dionysius engage in the following exchange:

>Busy. "Yes, and my main argument against you, is, that 'you are an abomination: for the male among you puts on the apparel of the female, and the female of the male.'"
>
>Puppet. "You lie, you lie, you lie abominably!"
>
>Bartholomew Cokes (an Esquire). "Well, I believe he has given him the lie three times."
>
>Puppet. "It is your old, stale argument against the Players, but it will not hold against the Puppets, for we have neither male nor female among us. And that you may see, if you will, like the malicious purblind zealot you are . . . ."
>
>[The Puppet takes up his garment.]
>
>Ezekiel Edgeworth (a pick-pocket). "By my faith, there he has answered you, Friend, by plain demonstration."
>
>Busy. "I am confuted. The cause has failed me!"[159]

When the puppet Dionysius takes up his garments to prove he is neither male nor female—and thus guiltless of any charge of crossdressing—his critic is undone.

Jonson, like other playwrights of his time, not only employed male actors in female roles, he made crossdressing itself an important dramatic vehicle. For example, in *Epicoene, or the Silent Woman* Jonson offers a farcical comedy in which a crossdressing masquerade lies at the plot's heart. In the story, a man ('Morose') who cannot abide noise decides to take a wife. His nephew ('Sir Dauphine Eugenie'), threatened with disinheritance should his uncle marry, resolves on a course of action: he arranges for his uncle to meet, court, and marry Epicoene, a silent woman. But once married, Epicoene's 'friends' invade Morose's home and create so much noise that the desperate uncle pledges to his nephew a secure future if only he will get rid of all the noise. This Dauphine does at the play's end by proving that Epicoene, already found to not be silent, is also not a woman.[160]

Shakespeare—the most famous playwright of all—also utilized crossdressing. Michael Shapiro, focusing on the role of the 'female page' in five Shakespearean plays, sees how the varied use of this role by the playwright is able to engage, even exploit, society's struggles over gender. The 'female page' role creates opportunities for gender layering, where a boy actor plays a female character in disguise as a male. The ensuing situations can become complex. For example, in *As You Like It*, the male actor plays the character of Rosalind, who pretends to be the boy Ganymede, who instructs another character to treat 'him' (Ganymede) as a girl! The stage becomes a venue to explore wider cultural debates.[161]

The motivation behind crossdressing by the characters varies in Shakespeare's plays. Some crossdressing serves comedic purpose, as in *As You Like It*.

At other times it is dramatic, as in *The Merchant of Venice* (1600). There the female characters Portia and Nerissa disguise themselves as men in order to come to the rescue of a man, Antonio, threatened by another man, Shylock. The motivation can have political overtones—or prove profoundly psychological (e.g., Viola in *Twelfth Night*). Whether crossdressing is also enlisted in the service of presenting homoerotic desire, as in the relationship of Viola/Cesario and Olivia in *Twelfth Night*, remains vigorously argued.[162] But one thing is clear: Shakespeare capitalizes on his audience's interest in gender and its ambiguities. In one fashion or another, crossdressing figures in several of the Bard's plays: *Cymbeline*, *The Merry Wives of Windsor*, *Twelfth Night*, and *Two Gentleman of Verona* in addition to *As You Like It* and *The Merchant of Venice*.

In the first half of the 17th century, the plays of Francis Beaumont and John Fletcher—such as *Love's Cure* (c. 1606-1610), *Philaster* (1609), *The Maid's Tragedy* (1610), or *The Loyal Subject* (1618)—echo Shakespeare in their interest in cross-gender behavior, but with a different sensibility. English professor Peter Berek argues that, "the echoes of Shakespeare in Beaumont and Fletcher change the subject from gender to power."[163] I don't know that those two matters can ever be separated,[164] but Berek's point is that changing times—and anxieties—are reflected in how crossdressing is used in the theater.

In simple point of fact, regardless of moralizing, people flocked to the theaters. Some plays not merely utilized males in female roles, but made the act of crossdressing a part of the play's content. We have seen that already in Shakespeare, but there are many instances. Consistent with the times, the theater reflected the fascination with crossdressing women. French tragic-comedies in the first half of the 17th century had many examples, mostly disguised as men-at-arms. But as Derval Conroy shows, such plays consistently raised gender questions only to answer by reinforcing the cultural standards: the crossdressed woman is motivated by love and sooner or later fits her proper place as wife.[165] Arguably the most famous of plays featuring a crossdressing woman—and one running counter to the tendency just described—is *The Roaring Girl* (c. 1610), whose central character 'Moll' is based on the real life exploits of Mary Frith.[166]

The Roaring Girl, by Thomas Dekker and Thomas Middleton, is ostensibly a comedy. But unlike most comedies featuring crossdressing, where the humor resides in mistaken identity, Moll's identity as a woman is never at stake. She makes no effort to disguise her sex. Literary critic Mary Beth Rose contends that Moll's mere presence—with its outspoken presentation of a woman dressed as a man—elicits both sexual and social anxieties in the world of the play. Rose finds that the playwrights' constructions of the other characters reveals the kind of social and moral beings they are as they respond to Moll. In this manner, she argues, the central issue of the play becomes how society seeks to comprehend this crossdressed woman. Linking the play's discourse to the wider one in society that a few years later would culminate in publications such as *Hic Mulier* and *Haec-Vir* (cf. the answer to Q. 46), Rose argues that Jacobean

English society's social and moral anxiety was aroused by women in men's clothing because of a deep ambivalence over sexual equality and female independence.[167]

Anxiety over theatrical crossdressing persisted alongside its practice. In the late 18th-early 19th century, British society was divided over the work of an Irish actress, Dorothy Jordan (1762-1816). Jordan, connected to the elite of British society as the mistress of the Duke of Clarence, later King William IV (ruled 1830-1837), gained notoriety for her portrayal not only of boys, but even of men. Many saw her as a dangerous model for other women.[168] Yet despite such controversies crossdressing actors and characters remained an aspect of Western theatrical entertainment into the 20th century.

Even the most ostensibly masculine men, those in armed service, enjoy crossdressing entertainers. For example, David Boxwell points out that the British employed "a corps of drag artists performing in camp and shipboard theatricals that were officially sponsored by the military during the Great War."[169] These female impersonators sometimes engaged in burlesque imitations of women in the 'Dame tradition' that offered little discomfort to prevailing gender notions. But at other times the female impersonation, says Boxwell, was mimesis, where sex appeal was very much a apart of the presentation. Instead of gross parody this latter form of impersonation aimed at as close a representation of an erotically arousing woman as possible.[170] Similarly, in POW camps of the First World War captive German officers employed female impersonation both on-stage and off.[171] But the English and Germans were not the only peoples, and World War I not the only conflict, where participants were offered some relief from the stresses of war by such spectacles.[172]

Are crossdressing performance acts found in other cultures?

Interestingly, this aspect of European theater carried over into colonialism. This is hardly surprising, since the colonizers took their culture with them. For example, when the British established colonies on the African continent they made efforts to recreate English society on foreign soil. Thus the African theater showcased all-male cast performances of Shakespeare.[173]

But that should not suggest that indigenous African entertainments know nothing of crossing gender lines. The Zaouli and Flali mask dances of Africa's Ivory Coast feature male performers donning these female masks. Both mask dances are often done as entertainment and the Flali mask dance parodies feminine movements through exaggerated postures and movements.[174]

What part did crossdressing play in the history of American theater?

European settlers to the United States brought their culture with them. One reflection of that was theatrical crossdressing. Such crossdressing by male actors proceeded along the lines and in the tradition of the English theater, as described above. But there were American innovations as well. In the 1840s, for example, White men in minstrel shows crossdressed and crossed-races to masquerade as Black men and women.[175] In so-called 'primadonna' acts, such female-impersonators enthralled audiences whom, writes Pamela Bown Levitt, "were fascinated by doomed portrayals of interracial love featuring crossdressed men playing mulatto women—the object of both white and black male desire."[176]

Women were crossdressing for entertainment too. In the 18th-19th centuries, women in American theater, like the actress Charlotte Cushman,[177] sometimes played male characters—and did so in breeches. There were also women who impersonated men in venues such as the popular 'British Blondes' burlesque troop of the late 1860s. The appearance of these actresses, says Elizabeth Mullenix, was variously appraised, with some seeing them as androgynous figures and others interpreting them as infantilized women, or more dangerously, as 'proto feminists.' In fact, Mullenix finds connection between what was happening on the stage and early 19th century activism by women (cf. the answer to Q. 47).[178]

In 20th century America 'drag' became more prominent than ever. Associated with homosexuals (cf. the answers to Q. 16-17), drag has acquired a variety of meanings, but they converge in an act of public crossdressing. Here we are interested only in drag as a theatrical staged entertainment. Even as such, this is not theater in the same manner as other forms we have been considering, but it merits some mention. Crossdressed men as drag 'Queens' or as female illusionists offer entertainment, albeit in different ways.[179] But not only males do drag. Crossdressed women as drag 'Kings' also have their own shows; Elvis impersonators, in particular, abound.[180] Such entertainments have proven popular with both homosexual and heterosexual audiences.

What role does crossdressing occupy in contemporary films and plays?

Crossdressing remains a frequent occurrence in the world of film and on the stage. Whether it is Broadway or community theater, crossdressing is part of the dramatic repertoire. For example, a production of Shakespeare's *Comedy of Errors* for the Upstate Shakespeare Festival in South Carolina in 2004 chose to cast all males for the female roles and all women for the men's roles. A member of the production wrote:

The actors seem to be enjoying their roles so much that they won't break character.

Backstage, Alyx Clements has acquired a habit of hocking loogies and grabbing her crotch. . . . Brock Koonce, who portrays Adriana, keeps asking if his dress makes him look fat.

Perhaps worst of all, Lynn Junker, who plays Antipholous of Syracuse and my romantic pursuer in the show, follows me around backstage. She periodically pinches my butt and regularly ogles my low-cut dress. Every time I climb the ladder to the balcony, she insists I go first so she can look up my skirt . . . .[181]

Crossdressing in modern plays adds to the rich tradition of this practice in the theater. The following table offers a glimpse of some productions:

Table 44.1 Examples of Modern Plays Featuring Crossdressing

Play	Author (First Run)	Notes
Charley's Aunt	Brandon Thomas (1892)	Made into films in 1915, 1925, 1941
The Drag & Pleasure Man[182]	Mae West (1920s)	Drag Queens; revenge fantasy.
The Singular Life of Albert Nobbs[183]	Simone Benmussa (1970s)	Female crossdressing for economic reasons.
Beru-Bara[184]	Takaruzaka adaptation of manga classic by Riyoko Ikeda (1970s)	Romantic musical featuring crossdressed woman.
Cloud Nine[185]	Caryl Churchill (1978/9)	Various actors cross gender lines in multiple roles.
Man to Man[186]	Manfred Karge (1980s)	A woman masquerades as her dead husband for economic reasons.
Hedwig and the Angry Inch[187]	John Cameron Mitchell & Stephen Trask (1990s)	Musical about a transsexual rocker.
Kiss of the Spider Woman[188]	John Kander & Fred Ebb (1990s)	Musical about imprisoned drag queen.
Hairspray[189]	Based on John Waters' film by same name (2000s)	Musical; Michael McKean plays Edna Turnblad.
All Shook Up[190]	Based on the book by	Musical; Jenn Gam-

	Joe DePietro (2000s)	batese plays Natalie, and Natalie disguised as Ed.
Diary of a Mad Black Woman[191]	Tyler Perry (2000s)	Comedy; Tyler plays Madea, a grandmother
I Am My Own Wife[192]	Doug Wright (2000s)	Documentary play about German transvestite

Crossdressing in the Movies

Crossdressing also has been a staple in film, both on television and at the movies.[193] Many notable stars—both male and female, Black and White—have done a turn in a crossdressed role (or briefly crossdressed), as the following table of films since World War II shows:

Table 44.2 Examples of Actors & Crossdressing Roles in Movies

Actor(s)	Show	Type	Year(s)
Charlie Chaplin	*The Masquerader*, *A Busy Day*, *A Woman*	Comedy Comedy Comedy	1914-1915
Marlene Dietrich	*Morocco*	Romance	1930
Marlene Dietrich	*Queen Christina*	Drama	1933
Katherine Hepburn	*Sylvia Scarlett*	Dramedy	1935
Jack Benny	*Charley's Aunt*	Comedy	1941
Tim Moore	*Boy! What a Girl!*	Comedy	1947
Cary Grant	*I Was a Male War Bride*	Comedy	1949
Peter Sellers	*The Mouse That Roared*	Comedy	1954
Tony Curtis & Jack Lemmon	*Some Like It Hot*	Comedy	1959
Anthony Perkins	*Psycho*	Horror	1960
Rod Steiger	*No Way to Treat a Lady*	Dramedy	1968
Tim Curry	*Rocky Horror Picture Show*	Mixed	1975
Marlon Brando[194]	*The Missouri Breaks*	Western	1976
Sylvester Stallone	*Nighthawks*	Action	1981
Julie Andrews	*Victor, Victoria*	Comedy	1982
Dustin Hoffman	*Tootsie*	Comedy	1982
Linda Hunt	*Year of Living Dangerously*	Drama	1982
Matthew Modine, Jonathan Prince, Michael	*Private School*	Comedy	1983

Zorek			
Barbra Streisand	*Yentl*	Drama	1983
William Hurt	*Kiss of the Spider Woman*	Drama	1985
Vanessa Redgrave	*Second Serve*	Biographical	1986
Jim Varney	*Ernest Saves Christmas*	Comedy	1988
Kurt Russell	*Tango & Cash*	Action	1989
Jaye Davidson	*The Crying Game*	Drama	1992
Robin Williams	*Mrs. Doubtfire*	Comedy	1993
Terence Stamp, Hugo Weaving, & Guy Pearce	*The Adventures of Priscilla, Queen of the Desert*	Comedy	1994
John Leguziamo, Wesley Snipes, & Patrick Swayze	*To Wong Foo, Thanks for Everything Julie Newmar*	Comedy	1995
Whoopi Goldberg	*The Associate*	Comedy	1996
Nathan Lane	*The Birdcage*	Comedy	1996
Mulan (character)	*Mulan*	Animated	1998
Nick Nolte	*Breakfast of Champions*	Comedy	1999
Martin Lawrence	*Big Momma's House*	Comedy	2000
Keira Knightley	*Princess of Thieves*	Adventure	2001
Miguel Núñez, Jr.	*Juwanna Mann*	Comedy	2002
Rob Schneider	*The Hot Chick*	Comedy	2002
Charles Busch	*Die Mommie Die!*	Comedy	2003
Nia Vardalos & Toni Collette	*Connie and Carla*	Comedy	2004
Marlon & Shawn Wayans	*White Chicks*	Comedy	2004
Billy Crudup	*Stage Beauty*	Romance	2004
Gael Garcia Bernal	*Bad Education*	Drama	2004
Marina Golbahari	*Osama*	Drama	2004
Tyler Perry	*Diary of a Mad Black Woman*	Comedy	2005
Cillian Murphy	*Breakfast on Pluto*	Drama	2005
Felicity Huffman	*Transamerica*	Drama	2005
Amanda Bynes	*She's the Man!*	Comedy	2006
Eddie Murphy	*Norbitt*	Comedy	2007

| John Travolta | *Hairspray* | Comedy | 2007 |
| Robert De Niro | *Stardust* | Romance | 2007 |

This table is by no means comprehensive. If anything, crossdressers are far more publicly visible on film than they are in society.

Typically, crossdressing occurs in comedies. In most instances the crossdressing is subservient to other themes, but the reasons for undertaking it are generally consistent with actual causes. For example, in *Some Like It Hot* the male characters disguise themselves as females to avoid harm—a classic rationale for crossdressing, though historically more often employed by females. In *Mrs. Doubtfire* the crossdressing is to gain employment in a stereotypically female job while simultaneously being close to loved ones. On the other hand, some films employ drag to offer—more or less—social satire. In *Women in Revolt* (1971), three real life drag queens fill the three female leads in a dramedy about feminism. In *To Wong Foo* the characters are Latino, Black, and Caucasian drag queens.

Of concern to some has been the incidence of Black males crossdressing for roles. Eddie Murphy, Martin Lawrence, Miguel Núñez, Jr., Marlon and Shawn Wayans, and, especially, Tyler Perry are all recent examples in movies (see Table above), while Flip Wilson, Jamie Foxx, and Cedric the Entertainer are examples in television (see Table below). Some see racist overtones in the readiness of the industry to put Black men on view as women. Black comedian Dave Chappelle is one noted figure who has expressed dismay over Black actors in crossdressing roles. In an appearance on the *Oprah Winfrey Show* in 2006, Chappelle said, "[W]hen I see they put every black man in the movies in a dress at some point in their career.... I am connecting the dots and I'm like, 'Why these brothers got to wear a dress?'" He also relayed he had been pressured to crossdress for a role as a female prostitute—a move he successfully resisted.[195] The interpretation of what putting a Black man in women's clothes means is likely to remain debated, but it seems plausible to think that at least some part of it may be a White culture's way of reducing its anxiety over Black maleness by feminizing it and putting it on comedic display.

While most movie crossdressing has featured males, some notable films have focused on female characters masquerading as males. In *Victor, Victoria*—one of the relatively few instances revolving around a woman—the character is a woman playing a man playing a woman as an entertainer. The title character in *Yentl* offers the historical example of a girl dressing as a boy in order to have entrance into a portion of the world reserved for males—in this case, education. But this reason is not reserved for stories set in the past. In *Just One of the Guys* (1985), a modern young woman disguises herself as a man to break into the world of journalism. Ten years later, Whoopi Goldberg masquerades as a man to make it on Wall Street in *The Associate* (1996), and a decade after that Amanda Bynes masquerades as her twin brother to take his place at school in *She's the*

Man! (2006). Interestingly, in 2004, both a comedy (*Connie and Carla*, where women pretend to be men pretending to be women) and a drama (*Osama*, where a girl in Afghanistan pretends to be a boy as a survival strategy) featured females masquerading as males.

Crossdressing as a truly central dramatic matter involved with serious issues of sexuality and gender is much rarer in theater and cinema. Probably the best known instances are *The Crying Game* (1992) and *Boys Don't Cry* (1999). The former, a movie filled with twists, features at its heart a poignant relationship between a man a woman—but she is both more and less than she appears to be. 'She,' in fact, is a 'he'—a transvestite man passing as a woman. The latter, based on a true story, follows the tragic course of a female-to-male preoperative transsexual. Both films treat the crossdressing characters with honesty and empathy. So, too, does the lesser-known film *Just Like a Woman* (U. K., 1992; U.S., 1994), a 'dramedy' that offers a look into the world of a transvestite man and his relationships with women. Another critically acclaimed film is *Different for Girls* (1996), about the renewal of relationship between two old friends, after one of them has become a woman. The new millennium also saw transgender reality taken seriously in *Transamerica* (2005), where Felicity Huffman portrays Sabrina 'Bree' Osbourne, a male-to-female transgendered woman.

Not all films featuring crossdressing are fictional accounts. The aforementioned *Boys Don't Cry* is based on a true story. So in its own way is the schlock film by 'the world's worst director,' Ed Wood, entitled *Glen or Glenda (I Changed My Sex)* (1953), which ostensibly looks at transsexualism but basically serves as Wood's own self-presentation as a crossdresser and his plea for tolerance. *The Queen* (1968) is a documentary film, in *cinema verite* style, about the 1967 'Miss All-America Camp Beauty Pageant.' Similarly, *Queen of the Whole Wide World* (2001) is another documentary looking at a drag queen contest spoofing the Miss USA contest. *All Dressed Up and No Place to Go* (1996) is a documentary about four heterosexual crossdressers.

Nor are Hollywood films the only ones depicting crossdressing. The following list offers some sense of the rich variety:

- Brazil: Além Da Paixão, *Happily Ever After* (1985), a drama involving a married woman and a male prostitute.
- Canada: Lip Gloss (1993), a documentary on transvestism; *A Boy Named Sue* (2000), a documentary story of a female-to-male (FtM) transsexual.
- China: Peter Chan's *He's a Woman, She's a Man* (1996), and its companion piece, *Who's the Woman, Who's the Man?* (1996).[196]
- Egypt: *Lil-Rigal Faqat (For Men Only,* 1964), a comedy about a gender-segregated workplace.[197]
- France: *Ma Vie en Rose (My Life in Pink,* 1997), story of a 7 year-old transsexual boy; *Juste Une Femme (Just a Woman,* 2001), a documen-

tary about a male-to-female (MtF) transsexual from Iran. *Chouchou* (2003), a comedy about a crossdressing Moroccan immigrant.

❑ Germany: *Enthüllung einer Ehe* (2000), a drama about a married man disclosing coming out as a transsexual.

❑ Greece: Giorgios Katakouzinos's *Angel* (1982), featuring a look at crossdressing prostitutes, was both acclaimed and popular film in Greece;[198] *Havai*, (*Hawaii*, 1995), a drama about crossdressing male prostitutes.

❑ India: *Bombay Eunuch* (2001), a documentary about the *Hijras*, India's 'third sex.'

❑ Italy/Germany: *Delitto al Blue Gay*, (*Cop in Drag*, 1984), a comedic farce.

❑ New Zealand: *Fa'afafine: Queens of Samoa* (1995), a documentary.

❑ Samoa: *Paradise Bent: Boys Will Be Girls* (1999), another documentary on the transgendered Fa'afafine (see the answer to Q. 57).

❑ Singapore: *China Doll* (1991), a documentary about a Malaysian crossdresser; *Bugis Street* (1997), a look at crossdressing prostitutes of Singapore in the 1960s.[199]

❑ South Korea: *Being Normal* (2003) is a documentary of a hermaphrodite who changes presentation from female to male.

❑ Spain: *Chicas por Sentimiento* (2001) is a documentary concerning five Barcelona transsexuals; *Invasión travesti* (2000) is an action comedy.

❑ Thailand: *The Last Song* (1985), a boy's adventure into Bangok's transgender community.

The list above by no means exhausts the available materials on films from around the world. Some others are mentioned in other answers.

To the above list we might also add various anime, specifically *hentai* anime (sexually explicit). Anime, a Japanese art form, has resulted in both animated films and television episodes, though overwhelmingly anime is produced for the small screen, typically in episodes later collected and released in several volumes. Among anime films are different genres and types, including very adult fare like the *hentai* soft porn comedy titled *Rei Rei: Missionary of Love* (1993), which features a compassionate goddess who turns a young man into a woman to help him win the object of his affections. Another kind of anime story is found in the miniseries *El Hazard: The Magnificent World* (1995), sold in a four volume set. The story revolves around Makoto Mizuhara, a high school boy magically transported to another world in a different universe where he must impersonate a missing princess he bears a striking resemblance to.

Crossdressing on Television

Crossdressing has been featured comparatively less on television. Few regular or recurring characters have crossdressed. The following table offers some of the most notable examples:

Table 44.3 Examples of Actors Portraying Crossdressing Characters on TV

Actor(s)	Show	Type	Year(s)
Milton Berle	The Milton Berle Show	Comedy/Variety	1954-59
Harvey Korman	The Carole Burnett Show	Comedy/Variety	1967-78
Benny Hill	The Benny Hill Show	Comedy	1969-89
Flip Wilson	The Flip Wilson Show	Comedy	1970-74
Jamie Farr	M.A.S.H.	Comedy	1972-83
Timothy Bottoms	Escape	Movie Drama	1980
Tom Hanks	Bosom Buddies	Comedy	1980-84
Robyn Douglas	Her Life as a Man	Movie Dramedy	1984
Dana Carvey	Saturday Night Live	Comedy	1986-1992
Bronson Pinchot	Jury Duty: The Comedy	Movie Comedy	1990
Jamie Foxx	In Living Color	Comedy	1990-1994
Corey Haim	Just One of the Girls	Movie Comedy	1992
Kathleen Turner	Friends	Comedy	1994-2004
Cedric the Entertainer	Cedric the Entertainer Presents	Comedy	2002-2003
Tom Wilkinson	Normal	Movie Drama	2003

Even more so than in movies, crossdressing on television largely has been played for laughs, as in Kathleen Turner's recurring role as Chandler's father on the sitcom *Friends*. Though it can be traced back to the earliest days of television, as in the comedy of Milton Berle, it perhaps received a particular boost in the late 1960s-early 1970s with the sketch comedy of the troupe Monty Python, first in Great Britain and then in the United States. American comedian Tommy Chong remarked in 2005 that, "They were the first to really show the world how funny men dressed as women could look."[200] On British television comedian Eddie Izard has continued, and perhaps perfected, this tradition.

By the 1990s, television sitcoms could still milk crossdressing for laughs, and yet convey a more nuanced awareness of transgender. For example, a 1993 episode of *Designing Women* presented a crossdressing man and woman. The man, Eric, was introduced as a successful lawyer dating Carlene, one of the main cast characters. Eric was warmly received and seen as warm, sensitive, and likable—until his unavailability three days a week raised suspicions he was married. Confronted, he revealed himself as a crossdresser. Carlene's response—after recovering from the shock—was to explore his world by masquerading as a man. That act was used to reveal masculine gender privilege and power as her disguise proves instrumental in securing an important business deal.[201]

Situational crossdressing in the context of comedy continues to show up on television, and occasionally to do more than evoke laughter, such as when Jim Belushi, in *According to Jim*, faces his 4-year old television son's (Owen Pearce) desire to dress as Cinderella for Halloween (season 5, episode 1, 2004); though initially worried his son might be a 'sissy,' dad comes through and dresses in kind. As the new millennium's movies increasingly showcased transgender people in serious dramas, television began to follow suit, as in the 2006 made-for-television movie, *A Girl Like Me*, based on the true story of Gwen Araujo, a male-to-female pre-operative transsexual.[202]

In addition to sitcoms there have also been documentaries such as *Drag Kings on Tour* (2004), and various more limited instances of crossdressing. In 2004, a reality series titled *He's a Lady* premiered on cable television. In it men took on the appearance, dress, and roles of women. Even popular cartoon series depict crossdressing: in episodes of *The Flintstones* (1962, 1966), for example, Fred poses in a dress as 'Fredericka' (episode 70), while some years later Barney dresses to pass as a girl (episode 163). There are also occasions where characters change both sex and gender.[203] In general, television has been more conservative than movies in what it depicts. Female crossdressing, in particular, is relatively unknown—at least in the West.

As mentioned above, Japanese anime has brought transgender realities like crossdressing to television. For example, the immensely successful manga story *The Rose of Versailles* (cf. the answer to Q. 52), was rendered into 40 episodes of 25 minutes each for Japanese television in the 1970s. Another very popular anime television series, with transgender integral to the story, is *Ranma ½*. In this series the protagonist, a boy named Ranma Saotome, falls into a spring with a curse that causes him, whenever splashed with cold water, to change into the shape of whatever had last drowned in the pool (a change reversed by being splashed with warm water). In this instance the last drowning victim had been a girl, a situation producing a change leading to numerous plotlines played out over the nine-year run of the series.

Crossdressing has a long—and frequently controversial—history in theater and film. While more often than not played for laughs, even comedies may have serious subtext. They permit a way of examining various facets of gender without overtly threatening social norms. Dramas also provide avenues for exploring gender issues but have tended to reach a more limited audience. Since most of us principally visit the theater or view a film or television for relaxation, serious examinations of gender-related matters are often less favorably received. Nevertheless, some critically acclaimed productions have won audiences and generated fruitful discussion.

Q. 45

What was the history of crossdressing in the Middle Ages?

The Short Answer. The Middle Ages is notable for its fascination with crossdressing. It appears in various ways: interest in theater presentations (see Q. 44), fascination with powerful people violating gender lines (see Q. 48-49), religious amazement at crossdressing saints (see Q. 68), the spectacle of gender reversals at public festivals (see Q. 71), and many more. Crossdressing was perhaps as widely practiced as in our own times, as fiercely debated, and as often the subject of speculation, rumor, and sensationalism. But one important difference immediately emerges: unlike our own time, the Middle Ages seem more interested in female crossdressing than that done by males. Another, less obvious difference is the apparently greater openness in that era to viewing gender as less fixed. Learned discussions of both sex and gender in this period before the medicalization of sex avoid the rigid categorizations that occur so often in more modern times. Philosophers, theologians, and lawyers joined doctors in speculating about sex and gender. Their proposals may seem startling to our contemporary mind, but they should not be dismissed simply because they derive from the past. Indeed, their thinking can inform our own, broadening it and reminding us not to fall into the error of believing our own views are static and unchanged descendants of prior generations.

The Longer Answer. The medieval period in Europe hardly proves to be the monolithic testament to social stagnation that many contemporary folk imagine. This expanse of history (from the late 5th century to the Renaissance) witnesses many changes, social and technological, intellectual and artistic. Both sex and gender are matters of lively interest, and examined through a variety of approaches and in manifold connections.[204] The expectations placed on boys and girls, men and women, are not invariably the same across all periods and places of the Middle Ages. Yet as a general rule it can certainly be claimed that throughout the medieval period there are individuals who find that their socially prescribed gender identities and role expectations are personally inadequate. These folk—'transgendered' in our use of the term—find various ways in which to experience and express their own sense of gender or to challenge existing conventions.

How was gender viewed in the Middle Ages?

The nature of those gender conventions has been reexamined in our time. Medievalists Robert Clark and Claire Sponsler, reflecting on what the theatre of the Middle Ages says about the times, write that "the supposed massive deployment of a stable two-gender system is something of a modern fiction."[205] Rather, matters of gender are as complex then as they are to prove later. Similarly, historian Joan Cadden argues that while Medieval Europe may maintain a binary system of the human sexes, the gender continuum is anything but static. Instead, both a range of body physiognomies and gender behaviors are acknowledged. Medieval writers try to explain what they observe, drawing variously on Christian scripture, philosophy (especially Plato and Aristotle), historical accounts, and medical speculation.

Certainly these efforts are guided by a desire to justify and maintain a gender order that preserves pride of place for masculine males. Women are often described in unflattering terms: as descendents of Eve, who caused Adam to sin, they are weak-willed, lusty deceivers ever prone to get men in trouble. As Kathleen Bishop puts it, "From the masculine point of view, women's 'true nature' covertly confirms the male agenda of its own innate superiority and consequent license, supported by religious, philosophical, and literary authority."[206] Bishop quotes the medieval author Albertus Magnus, who in his *Quaestiones de animalibus* (*Inquiry Concerning Living Things*), remarks, "there is no woman who would not naturally want to shed the definition of femininity and put on masculinity."[207] The question naturally rises: could she? Is gender inevitably pinned to sexual anatomy, and is the latter immutable?

One of the more prominent Catholic philosophers of the 12th century, the Scholastic theologian William of Conches (c. 1080-c. 1154), is illustrative of how reasoning out of these matters proceeds. Attracted to Platonic rationalism, William seems to be interested particularly in psychological matters, an interest filtered through his creative interpretation of Plato's *Timaeus*. In William's gloss of *Timaeus* 42, he reworks the Platonic notion of reincarnation to make his own statement about gendered souls:

> For it is not to be believed that the same soul is first in a man and then afterwards crosses over into a woman and later into brute animals down to the level of worms, as they maintain a certain Pythagoras once assumed. Neither should it be thought that the soul itself contains anything pertaining to either sex within it, but rather this transformation is held to be according to behaviors. Therefore, so long as the soul acts manfully, it is considered to be a man. But when it becomes

soft through various pleasures, while still remaining something of reason about it, then it is understood to be a woman. . . .

And this is the penalty for wretched souls in this life: "and they shall be relegated," that is to say reduced, "to the weakness of a woman's nature." He did not say "to the nature of women," but rather "to the weakness of a woman's nature" to show that this transformation was being accomplished not in essence but rather in resemblance of manners.[208]

Because William locates such a transformation after fifteen years of age, it becomes a 'second birth' that modern scholar James Cain believes William associates with the age of puberty. In Cain's understanding, William of Conches has placed gender assignment at puberty and likened it to transubstantiation—there is no physical change but the invisible, underlying gender essence has been significantly altered. Any difference between pre- and post-puberty gender is manifest in gender-associated behavior, such as mannerisms, gestures, or general comportment. In Cain's view, this Neo-Platonic model allows for gender change from what was assigned at birth through sheer persistence of habit; a person can become the gender they imitate.[209]

This openness to gender fluidity seems rather widespread and corresponds to a similar, if more limited openness about the sexed body. Historian James Blythe remarks, "Medieval medical and scientific views of sex and gender were complex and not fully determinate, resisting binary categorization and making possible various combinations of masculine and feminine traits."[210] With regard to gender, for example, Blythe refers to the mid-14th century medical professor Jacopo da Flori at the University of Sienna, who formulates three indices of gender: complexion, disposition, and physique. Any individual can be gender-mixed along these indices; for example, feminine on one, masculine on another, and even indeterminate with regard to the third.[211]

The Sexed Body—The Case of the Hermaphrodite

The sexual body likewise can be conceived outside a binary system. As Cary Nederman and Jacqui True document, in 12th century Europe the intersexed ('hermaphrodites'), though subject to opinions ranging from condemnation as unnatural grotesqueries to acceptance as a natural variation, can at least be viewed medically as a distinct 'third sex.'[212]

This judgment is echoed in Church circles. For example, in the midst of his remarks on homosexuality, Peter Cantor (late 12th century) pauses to note that:

The church allows a hermaphrodite—that is, someone with the organs of both sexes, capable of either active or passive functions—to use the organ by which (s)he is most aroused or the one to which (s)he is most susceptible. If (s)he is more active, (s)he may wed as a man, but if (s)he is more passive, (s)he may marry as a woman.[213]

This ecclesiastical stance is echoed by Portius Azo (late 12th-early 13th century), Italian canon jurist, who in his *Summa Codices et Institutionum* distinguishes the hermaphrodite as a third sex alongside male and female.[214]

In sum, people of the Middle Ages explore in a variety of ways not only the potential for gender change, but also the gender possibilities lying between masculine men and feminine women. These other possibilities cover phenomena we today label as intersexed (hermaphroditic) people, transvestism, and homosexuality.[215] Rather like our own age, medieval folk struggle with the construction of gender, often finding a disjunction between tolerated but imagined possibilities and resistance to actual transgender expressions. But they do not ignore these realities in their midst.

As in our own time, dress plays a critical role. Clothing stands at the center of a rich, complex, and evolving system of experience and expression. Males and females alike utilize apparel, adornments, and hairstyles as ways to meet their needs. As fashion itself changes and further elaborates gendered differences between the sexes, crossdressing becomes an ever more potent way to use dress. Therefore, if we are to understand gender, transgender, and crossdressing in the Middle Ages we must have at least a rudimentary sense of how fashion changed across these centuries.

What role did changes in fashion play?

Gender-differentiation in dress had been part of the Western world of antiquity but advances in technology make the possibilities for showing such differentiation greater during the medieval period—the era in which fashion truly makes its debut. Additionally, there are particular social influences in different places so that while it can be said that fashion in one place exercises a pull on fashion in another place, each retains peculiar features. We cannot investigate comprehensively the changes in fashion across the Middle Ages.[216] What we can do is indicate a few widespread and important changes that illustrate the broad tendencies in fashion during this long period of history. Further, we can speculate on the connection of these changes to crossdressing.

Religion plays a decisive role in Europe's transition from the classical world to that of the Middle Ages. The influence of Christianity both religiously unifies Europe's culture and lends it a more conservative bent in dress fashion. Both sleeves and hemlines lengthen as the Christian emphasis on modesty (cf. the answers to Q. 66-67) makes itself felt. But though both sexes are admonished to be modest in dress, the emphasis is particularly placed on modesty in females. Accordingly, their dress becomes more restrictive in showing less of the body, both flesh and form. Women's tunics are longer and bifurcated garments are reserved for men. But with the sober realization in 1000 C.E. that the world will likely continue,[217] a turn to more worldly matters like personal appearance proves inevitable.

The evolution of fashion in the Middle Ages can be traced through three distinct periods. The earliest of these (5th-10th centuries) is often called the Dark Ages. The tunic, an unbifurcated garment, still provides the basic covering for both males and females. Both sexes often wear a short tunic over a longer one. Yet there remain gendered differences in presentation, even with tunics. Men's clothing commonly combines a short tunic with trousers. Sandals are the ordinary footwear, only gradually giving way to shoes.

The 11th-12th centuries witness greater diversification. Trade with the East brings new fabrics and fashion influences. Both the spinning wheel and horizontal loom make production easier. A new interest in clothing—and in differentiation in styles—accompany these greater resources and tools. Europeans learn from the East how to make velvet and the sensuousness of silk makes it a coveted fabric. Sleeves and hems widen, and the wider sleeve begins to mark feminine dress. Fashion fitted to the human figure also begins to appear.

In the closing period of the Middle Ages the tunic persists as a basic garment, especially among the common folk. Though both men and women wear long tunics, a short tunic alone still marks a masculine style of dress. Men often fasten it on the right shoulder with a brooch. Head cloths for women are a distinctive aspect of feminine dress. Yet important changes are transpiring that lead to significant clothing modifications.

Textile production both increases and improves, resulting in better and more accessible goods. A growing wealthy upper class also invests heavily in fashion as a display of status. Along with attention to differentiation of social class comes renewed attention to gender distinctions in dress. Philosopher-historian Ivan Illich observes that high social status makes the gender divide even more obvious because the wealthy have both the time and resources to show off their gender.[218] This leads to competition for ostentatious presentations. The competition for displays in dress in turn encourages fashion innovation, giving rise to new forms and making possible fashion fads.

With advances in the art of tailoring, beginning in the 14th century, bifurcated garments become easier to make and more practical. Trousers are regarded as masculine garb. In the 15th century, even as men's tunics shorten and fit more closely, outer leg-wear begins to appear, particularly among the upper class. Historian and gender scholar Lois Banner depicts medieval European history as a time when both young male bodies and young female bodies are eroticised, but it is male clothing that sets the standard for what reflects gender and sexuality—including erotic sexuality.[219]

Buttons in dress seem to appear first among the wealthy in the 14th century, where they are exclusively an item of male apparel. Once adopted for use in women's clothing buttons become a basic differentiator for gendered dress, with the button always appearing on the right hand side in masculine clothing. However, this practice does not seen to become relatively stable and fixed before the 19th century.

As the above brief account indicates, some of today's most basic and distinctive features of gender-differentiation in dress can be traced to fashion changes in the Middle Ages. These include the reservation for the masculine gender of bifurcated garments, the wider sleeve as a mark of feminine dress, and the gendered distinction of side in the placement of buttons.

Why did people crossdress in the medieval world?

Crossdressing, though it may not always be motivated by a need to express a gender identity at variance with the one assigned at birth, is always and inevitably a matter of gender in some respect. There is no reason to doubt that some of those who crossdress in the Middle Ages are people who today would be called transsexuals. Likewise, we need not doubt that some are sexually aroused by what they wear and employ crossdressing for one or another sexual reason. But as in our own world, crossdressing proves to be motivated by a myriad of reasons.

Among these reasons several stand out from examples culled from various historical sources:

- ❑ *access to privileges or activities typically reserved for another gender*—most often this means women disguising themselves as men to gain entry into professions labeled masculine, such as the religious vocations, the military or sailing;
- ❑ *approval of otherwise forbidden relationships*—by masquerading as another gender, crossdressers can publicly enter into domestic relationships with members of the same sex;
- ❑ *gender identity expression*—some individuals appear to crossdress for experience and expression of a gender different than that assigned to them at birth.

Each of these merits some elaboration.

Access to Another Gender's Sphere of Activity or Privilege

Masculine privilege in a gender hierarchy where men hold power motivates many women to find ways to equalize the power between the genders. One obvious strategy—a kind of 'if you can't beat 'em, join 'em'—is to join the desired gender, often through calculated masquerade. Examples of women crossing gender lines abound in the Middle Ages. These lines are sometimes crossed in ways that retain the person's expression of personal gender identity, as when women undertake masculine activities without disguising themselves, or join masculine dress to masculine activity, but do so in a manner that makes it plain they are female. At other times the gender lines are crossed covertly, with the woman changing herself into a man through dress, manner, and activity. Thus, in seeking access to the sphere of activities society reserved for masculine males, a woman has more than one path.

Involvement in military activities provides a ready illustration of these different paths. Historian James Blythe has produced an introduction to this topic replete with examples. He notes instances in which women undertake martial activities without anyone doubting they are female. In some cases the gender-altered presentation is modest but unmistakable, as in the explanation offered by Bishop Otto of Freising (12th century) in explaining how the Lombards (*Longobardi*, 'long beards') derived their name from the practice of having their female warriors twist their hair around to their chin to imitate a beard.[220] A completely masculine presentation can still be done such that it remains apparent the warriors are female, as Byzantine historian Niketas Choniates (c. 1150-1213) describes during the Crusades: "Females were numbered among them, riding horseback in the manner of men, not on coverlets sidesaddle but unashamedly astride, and bearing lances and weapons as men do; dressed in masculine garb, they conveyed a wholly martial appearance, more mannish than the Amazons."[221] Of course, history's most famous crossdresser, Joan of Arc (see the answer to Q. 68), is an example of this kind of female warrior.

Some females disguise themselves as male and are accepted as male. This is the apparent path of another female warrior mentioned by Blythe: Hervör, the heroine of the Hervarar Saga (see the answer to Q. 42). But such an image is counterpoint to contemporary reality; though unknown by name, Blythe remarks, "there are several reports of brave fighters only being exposed as women after death in battle."[222] They have their counterparts in the religious ranks, where any number of accounts tell of women who 'make themselves into men' for the sake of the kingdom of heaven (cf. the answer to Q. 68).

Of course, as this last example shows, there are motivations other than military ones. The 13th century poetic novel *Le Roman de Silence* (*Romance of Silence*), by Heldris de Cornuälle (whose own gendered identity is in doubt), depicts a father raising his daughter—aptly named 'Silence' ('*Silentius/Silentia*')—as a boy in order that an inheritance may be preserved for her. In her guise as a male, Silence is able to occupy a uniquely masculine occupation as a knight at the royal court. As so often happens in such tales, a woman (Queen Eufeme) makes romantic advances toward Silence, who is then accused of rape after righteously resisting the invitation to adultery. The King offers a way out of a sentence of death: to bring to the royal court the person of Merlin. The catch is that this task can only be accomplished by a woman. Silence succeeds, of course, and when Merlin appears before the king he reveals not only Silence's sex but also her innocence and the queen's wickedness. The queen is thus the one executed and Silence marries the king.[223]

Le Roman de Silence retains interest for its provocative manner of raising intriguing and important questions about identity and gender, among other things. As the brief summary shows, crossdressing is a vehicle sufficient to raise these questions. It also shows aspects of experiences almost certainly encountered by various individuals—including perhaps the author, who may be a woman masquerading as a man in penning the poem. If so, we have an instance of what has come to be called 'narrative crossdressing'—the gender crossing of an author in name or narrative voice.

We know from other accounts of children being raised in a gender not deemed congruent by their culture with their biological sex. We know of women masquerading as men who travel more freely about the country because of their guise, as Silence does. We know of women who embrace male occupations, especially martial ones. And we know of women who face relational complications brought on by their masquerade. It is to this last matter we must direct more attention, for on occasion women crossdress in order to pursue same-sex relationships.

Forbidden Relationships

In any environment where same-sex erotic relationships are repressed a creative response is for one partner to pose as a member of the opposite sex. This is a strategy open to both males and females. A female might crossdress and adopt the mannerisms and occupation of a man in order to enjoy a publicly sanctioned relationship with another female. Of course, a homosexual man can do something similar, adopting the dress and manner of a woman—but evidence is far less for this happening in marriage-like relationships than among women. The presentation of one of the partners as a man does more than facilitate living openly as a married couple. It also removes both partners from the ranks of the eligible for marriage, thus protecting them from unwanted unions with men. In some cases, this motivation may be connected to the next as well: the expression of a gender identity different than the one assigned at birth.

Gender Identity Expression

Although no one uses the term 'transsexual' in the Middle Ages, it seems certain the reality exists. For example, the trial of Katherina Hetzeldorfer in 1477 indicates a likely instance of a female-to-male transsexual. Historian Helmut Puff, who specializes in gender and sexuality issues pertinent to the medieval and early modern periods, examines this case as one of what he terms 'female sodomy'—a clear instance of lesbian homoeroticism.

Katherina, a native of Nuremberg, comes to the city of Speyer with a female partner who is identified publicly as 'a sister.' There they engage in a sexual relationship over a period of time. However, according to testimony at her trial, Katherina also approached other women for sexual liaisons. For some unnamed reason, Katherina is arrested. At her trial, two women allegedly approached sexually by the accused describe Katherina as being like a man in both physique and behavior. That behavior includes visiting women at their homes and acting in a sexually aggressive fashion—like a man.[224]

Indeed, Puff labels Katherina as a 'transvestite,' though perhaps 'transsexual' may be a more accurate label by our current ideas. For example, what evidence there is suggests Katherina attempts a complete presentation as a man, including embodying the sexual stereotypes in place for masculine sexuality, taking the active role in aggressive fashion. Witnesses say of her that she grabs, hugs, and kisses "just like a man." Her sexual behavior apparently develops from manual penetration of her partners using fingers to the use of a dildo she fashions, which she holds between her legs.[225]

Puff places this situation in its social context by noting that, "In late medieval Speyer, there was a growing anxiety about cross-dressing. The magistrate prohibited women from wearing men's clothes and, later, men from wearing women's clothes."[226] Such ordinances indicate that Katherina Hetzeldorfer is hardly an isolated case, though she may represent a more extreme case than others. Whatever the exact nature of her unnamed crime, after being found guilty she is drowned on a Friday in 1477.

Why did crossdressed women get so much attention?

Medieval Europe seems especially fascinated by the phenomenon of the crossdressed woman.[227] The most famous form of this phenomenon is the crossdressed saint (see the answer to Q. 68). But these women undoubtedly represent only the tip of the iceberg; most female crossdressing will pass unrecognized, if not in its own time certainly in the gathering dust of time's passage. Fortunately, we do have preserved instances of women other than saints who crossdress, as the just discussed case illustrates.

Another dark aspect of this era merits some attention. The prevailing Christian ideology views women as especially prone to the wiles of the Devil and crossdressing suggests to some folk that something evil is transpiring that leads a woman to seek what is not hers by nature. In the infamous 15th century *Malleus Maleficarum (The Witch Hammer)*, the matter is put bluntly:

> [B]ecause in these times this perfidy is more often found in women than in men, as we learn by actual experience, if anyone is curious as to the reason, we may add to what has already been said the following: that since they are feebler both in mind and body, it is not surprising that they should come more under the spell of witchcraft.[228]

The *Malleus Maleficarum* believes a male can be a witch, but also that female witches far outnumber them.

The nefarious craft is thought to enable gender transformations, either illusionary or real. In the *Malleus Maleficarum* witches are attributed with the ability to work glamour spells—illusions that can make a man believe he has no penis, or otherwise change someone's appearance. By the work of the devil, a girl is alleged to have been transformed into a boy. No wonder, then, crossdressing at times might be connected with witchcraft.

Richard Carroll believes that in *Malleus Maleficarum* transgender behavior, whether mere crossdressing or full adoption of another gendered identity, is viewed as evidence of witchcraft.[229] This seems somewhat an exaggerated claim for that particular document, but perhaps not for the literature on witches as a whole, or for the (il)logic about witches revealed in it. Witches, after all, are said to possess a drug capable of changing the sex of the person who takes it. More credibly, it is almost certain that some crossdressing women are accused of being witches, and perhaps some crossdressed men as well.

Were there crossdressing men in the medieval world?

Historian of sexuality Vern Bullough argues that crossdressing in the Middle Ages is best understood in cultural terms different than the modern tendency to assign psychopathology to the crossdresser. He believes that the concept of social gain and loss explains how crossdressing is perceived during these times. Crossdressing female saints gain social status in donning masculine attire. On the other hand, because males hold higher social status, a crossdressing man loses status. To explain why any male would take such a step, society assigned an erotic quality to men wearing feminine dress; if they did it for sexual reasons it became understandable while remaining sinful. This interpretation also makes crossdressing a dangerous act, one threatening to social order. By providing sanctioned outlets in festivals like Carnival (see the answer to Q. 71), society attempts to keep such behavior in check.[230]

Why might a man want to present as a woman if the latter represents a loss of status? Of course, in temporary gender-crossings the reasons might range from a disguise to cover illegal activity to theatrical performance to the role relief of Carnival. But what of more enduring presentations? What of males who persist in presenting a feminine persona?

Just as we have seen with regard to female-to-male transsexualism, there is at least limited evidence for what would today be termed male-to-female transsexualism.[231] That such terms are not used in the Middle Ages does not mean such transgender realities are unknown. On the other hand, our contemporary notions of the sexed body and of gender are different enough that we must be careful in applying our labels to supposed instances in former times. When the Medieval sources reference crossdressing men there is typically much too little evidence to form firm conclusions as to whether that individual can fairly be classed in one or another of today's categories. Still, on balance, it seems more reasonable to conclude individuals comparable to today's transsexuals exist in the Middle Ages than that they do not.

What were the sumptuary regulations?

Another aspect of crossdressing in premodern times concerns the crossing not of gender lines but of social ones. In our own time the only kind of crossdressing that excites much comment is that perceived as violating gender boundaries. But there was a time when the larger social concern was the perceived transgression of social lines. As we saw above, the growth of fashion makes possible the use of clothing to display wealth and its attendant status. But rich apparel loses its luster if common folk are able to find cheap imitations or otherwise appear in clothes like their 'betters.' So, just as ordinances and laws are sometimes crafted to punish and discourage gender crossdressing, so also some are made to prevent crossing lines of social status. The most famous of these enactments are a series of laws known as *sumptuary regulations*, enacted in England in the 14th-15th centuries. By specifying who could wear what, these laws intend to keep clear what clothing communicated about social status.

However, English society is hardly alone in trying to preserve for the upper class a distinct and ostentatious presence. For example, historian Daniel Roche notes of France that, "before the sixteenth century, the link between social distinction and sartorial difference was constantly affirmed."[232] Similarly, historian Betül Ipsirli Argit remarks of the Near Eastern Ottoman Empire that the style of dress worn within its boundaries is "based on hundreds of years of traditions," and remains "an institution of great importance, bound by very rigid rules." Laws for dress behavior enforce gender, religious, and social distinctions.[233] Laws regulating dress are found in many societies, from America to Japan.[234]

With explicit respect to gender, in discussing European sumptuary laws, sociologist and legal scholar Alan Hunt points out that they play an important part in the time's 'gender wars.' But the sumptuary regulations defy easy categorization in how they try to regulate gender. Hunt remarks:

> Sumptuary law exhibited considerable variability in its presentation of gender; sometimes it was gender-neutral (e.g. 'no person, man or woman, may wear...'), at other times it was explicit in directing its restrictions against a particular sex (e.g. 'no woman may wear...'), while on occasions women were specifically exempted from the sumptuary rules.[235]

One truism persists, however. They are disproportionately enforced against women.[236]

Examples abound of how specific types of clothing might be singled out for attention, or specific groups—and often the two interests intersect. Thus the wearing of fur, for instance, becomes subject to gender differentiation in this regulatory climate. Prostitutes are forbidden to wear it, in addition to being required to wear their outer garments inside-out and hoods distinctive in color so that all might know their profession.[237]

Today we might find the notion of sumptuary regulations to be ridiculous exercises in attempted social control. But though less formal than laws, our own times are marked by efforts to identify and safeguard boundaries between various social groups. Hunt argues that sumptuary regulations have been important elements of a society's response to pressures on their established hierarchical social order. In the attempted construction of social order and the identities of groups within society—whether organized according to gender, class, or nationality—such laws seek to clarify and preserve existing group identities despite the changes being brought by new means to wealth and other changes associated with the rise of the modern world. These laws, in effect, *imagine* a social order they attempt to visibly construct in the appearance of its members. While such laws ultimately fail, they are instrumental in helping shape both civil law and a certain view about self-regulation.[238]

In sum, then, the premodern period offers much of instructive value for us. Study of these times reveals some continuity with our own in broad strokes—like ourselves, people of these times regard dress and gender as important—but also reveal some important discontinuities. The more relaxed perspective on gender in terms of perceiving it as more fluid, diverse, and changeable, could be of help to ourselves who dwell in a more restrictive, uptight age. Whether we will profit from the past remains to be seen.

Q. 46

What is the history since the Middle Ages?

The Short Answer. While the East has long fascinated Westerners, history has remained relatively Eurocentric. Hence, more is known about crossdressers in Europe since the Middle Ages than in most other parts of the world. This answer focuses on Europe, where transgender realities were known in men and women, rich and poor. Matters of sex and gender were of widespread interest and occasioned lively controversy at times. While the stage was one venue for exploring such matters, and garnered discussion, there were other cultural outlets such as festivals (discussed elsewhere) and popular expressions, such as ballads. Social practices also received comment. The varied voices from this period show a wide range in tolerance for transgender realities, from strong opposition through indifference to enthusiastic embrace.

The Longer Answer. In part because the idea of gender and transgender as they exist today are relatively new notions, the study of what we are calling transgender realities as they have appeared in history is somewhat new and very incomplete. Still, a number of works both shorter and longer have appeared in recent years concerning transgender realities, and especially crossdressing, in Europe after the Middle Ages. Much more of the discussion has been provided by literary scholars, then by historians, and much of it has focused on theatrical practice (see the answer to Q. 44).

As we might expect, we can find evidence of both continuity and discontinuity with the Medieval period. Relevant evidence includes ideas both about sex and about gender. For example, with respect to sex, the intersexed (hermaphrodites) continue for a long period to be accorded recognition as a distinct sex with gender options more liberal than generally seen in modern times.[239] Gender expression in dress, involving more than just crossdressing, remains important and might even be argued to have grown in importance as fashion develops. There are both continuities and discontinuities in the way people dress as the Middle Ages give way to this period. To orient ourselves to the centuries after the Middle Ages we need to at least briefly consider some of these matters.

What was the relation of gender to dress after the Middle Ages?

Because we treat of historical matters for other cultures in answering questions related to different regions of the world, here we will do as we did in the last answer: focus on the history of Europe. Once more we will use crossdressing as an entry into broader considerations of gender and transgender. Once more in order to do so we must attend especially to the relation of dress to gender to provide an important broad context.

We should first note that dress, though gender differentiated, is perhaps more importantly utilized in the period from the 16th century to the Victorian age to indicate group identity, both culturally and in terms of social class. Volumes like Cesare Vecellio's 1589 publication *Habiti antichi e moderni di tutto il mondo* (*Ancient and Modern Dress Throughout the World*) present costumes identifying members of other countries and the hierarchy of social classes within these other societies. This use of dress begins to wane in the 18th century as a "globalization of dress" occurs, a process still evolving to the present.[240]

Ideas about gender continue to be debated between the end of the Middle Ages and the triumph of the medicalization of sex in the 19th –20th centuries. Culture historian Thomas Laqueur marks a decisive turning point in the late 18th century when, he says, Europeans moved from a 'one-sex' model (i.e., male and female are variations on a common type) to our modern 'two-sex' model where the sexes are set opposite one another on a horizontal axis.[241] No matter where one dates the shift, a study of literature across this time supports the thesis that a significant conceptual shift—or narrowing—does indeed occur.

The notions about gender that circulate across this era are often more fluid than our own, which under the impress of modern medicine's way of categorizing and thinking has yielded a static dualistic system with a presumed inflexible pairing of sex and gender. Observations about transgender realities like crossdressing abound during this period, appearing in academic discourses, religious musings, popular literature, journalistic accounts, legal treatises, theater, and even ballads. As the world continues to shrink through increased ease of travel, people around the world become more aware of each other and Westerners continue their fascination with cultural differences, though generally interpreting 'different' as 'inferior.'

Cultural openness to the fluidity of sex and gender can also generate anxiety over how each is shaped. For example, a common belief in early modern Europe is that a pregnant woman's experiences, and even her imagination, can shape the features of her unborn child. Kate Chedgzoy refers to a 1560 broadsheet entitled *The True Description of a Child with Ruffles*, in which a child is born with ruffs because the mother has worn them in violation of her proper place. The description of this child, says Chedgzoy, "constitutes a dire warning to women whose dress is inappropriate either to their gender or their position in the socio-economic hierarchy."[242] If gender violations in dress have such power, then it behooves us to seek out some understanding of the connection between dress and gender as conceived by early modern Europeans.

In this regard, historian David Cressy correctly reminds us:

> We need to know what messages were sent by dress, what signals received, and how costume could be used to entice, to shock, to entertain, to convince, or to confuse. What, for example, was the cultural charge of a codpiece or doublet, a petticoat or bodice, points and ruffs, and how did their resonance change when items were appropriated by the opposite sex?[243]

In early modern England items such as those Cressy names are gendered apparel. The doublet, for example, is masculine. Yet some women are so dressed—a fact that draws the ire of social critics like the Puritan Philip Stubbes. He complains:

> The women also have their doublets and jerkins, as men have theirs, buttoned up the breast, and made with wings, welts, and pinions on the shoulder points, as men's apparel is for all the world; and though this be a kind of attire appropriate only to man, yet they blush not to wear it; and if they could as well change their sex, and put on the kind of man, as they can wear apparel assigned only to man, I think they would verily become men indeed, as now they degenerate from godly, sober women, in wearing this wanton lewd kind of attire, properly only to man.[244]

Instead of becoming men, though, Stubbes holds the view they become *Hermaphroditi*, a grotesquerie such as might only be imagined as the product of sorcery. This result, Stubbes is sure, follows from the curse of violating Deuteronomy's prohibition of crossdressing.[245]

If all we know about gender crossing activities like crossdressing came from Stubbes we would be forced to conclude both that such behaviors occur and that they are regarded as disturbing manifestations of sin. Certainly there are other critics like Stubbes, men like Thomas Beard, Stephen Gosson, Adam Hill, and John Rainolds,[246] who raise a cry against crossdressing. Yet, claims Cressy, we would err in concluding that such voices signify that crossdressing shows a sex-gender system in crisis, or even that most people see it as particularly transgressive.[247]

Against such a view Cressy offers several lines of evidence. First, he puts forth a case in which a young man, Thomas Salmon, with the help of one Elizabeth Fletcher, disguises himself in women's dress in order to visit and partake of the cheer being offered in the quarters of a woman who has just given birth. Cressy points out that the more serious violation here is transgressing a place reserved for women, rather than merely crossdressing, which Salmon does for about two hours. Fletcher and Salmon both receive mild sanctions for their prankish behavior.[248]

Second, Cressy urges a recognition of the various contexts, durations, and purposes attached to crossdressing. With reference to crossdressing on stage, he points out that in the more than two dozen plays of early modern English theater that feature a man masquerading as a woman, the character is not denigrated or seen as a failure. To the contrary, Cressy maintains, such characters are portrayed as "proactive, virile, and effective." They instigate practical jokes rather than fall prey to them, outwit opponents, and achieve sexual success. Cressy wonders in light of this, plus the use of crossdressing for comedic effect, how one might find a gender system in trouble.[249]

Clearly, both in England and elsewhere, there are gendered distinctions in dress. Just as clearly, some members of society are scandalized by the appropriation of gendered elements of dress by anyone whose gender is not typically matched to that fashion style. Yet Cressy is correct in reminding us of lines of evidence that indicate relative tolerance of infractions and even positive appraisals. Crossdressing happens for all kinds of reasons, is done by both men and women, and might be either more enduring in character or very short-lived and specific to context.

Most public crossdressing remains transient and context-dependent. Elsewhere we shall investigate festivals where travesty and gender-reversals are commonplace (see the answer to Q. 71). But in European and American circles gender crossings are also common enough in other social settings. Masquerades are a favored activity, perhaps particularly so in the 18th century, sometimes dubbed the 'Age of Disguise.' Terry Castle, a leading scholar on 18th century English life and literature, writes of this time that, "Transvestite costume was perhaps the most common offense against decorum. Women strutted in jackboots and breeches, while men primped in furbelows and flounces."[250] In their masquerades, men appear as old women, witches, bawdy women, nurserymaids, and shepherdesses, while women disguise themselves as soldiers, sailors, and clergymen. In addition to outright crossdressing, androgynous costumes enjoy great favor. Often enough such dress behavior occasions risqué remarks—and provides fodder for opponents who see in such activity open invitation to sexual sin.[251]

Obviously, the long expanse of time between the Middle Ages and our own defies simple characterization in these matters. While some critics in these times decry any and every instance of gender crossing, many folk practice such crossings with approval or endure the most minor of reproves. Most engage in crossdressing temporarily and generally for social frivolity. Some, however, undertake crossdressing for more serious and long-term reasons. As with our own time, reasons for crossdressing—and degrees of success in attaining and maintaining appearance in a different gender—vary markedly. It is time to investigate some of these motivations, differentiated by assigned gender.

Why were women crossdressing?

In the late 15th century, and for some time thereafter, there is great fascination with crossdressing. The interest can even be found at royal courts. Mary Queen of Scots, who reins in the 1560s, is fond of spectacles, including stories involving crossdressing. She herself participates in the masquerades held at court.[252]

As in previous periods the focus of this fascination remains female crossdressing. The persistence of the practice is such that by the early 17th century King James I, in England, commands London's pastors to speak against the practice of women dressing in mannish attire.[253] However, as Cressy observes, few actual incidences of such behavior have been preserved.[254] Since many—and perhaps most—of those who crossdress have no desire to be found out, we will never know their true numbers, but what records we do have suggest that the public fascination is warranted. Not surprisingly, then, the idea of crossdressing women becomes a common feature of popular English literature in the 17th century, with the masquerading female often portrayed as a heroine.[255]

Why is there such concern over female crossdressers in general life? Shasta Turner observes the coincidence of this fascination in England with the heyday of sumptuary laws in the 16th century—regulations concerning dress appropriate to the various social classes (see the answer to Q. 45). Both, Turner maintains, reflect wider preoccupations with the relation of dress to social identity and both are generally accompanied by other transgressions of the social order in terms of political, legal, or economic norms. In short, crossdressing cannot be understood as an isolated phenomenon divorced from other social concerns.[256]

Historical Examples

This confluence of concerns can be glimpsed in the historical record. Arrest records in England show some female prostitutes who dress in masculine attire.[257] Such women are violating more than one boundary. So, too, are women who masquerade as men to be with a lover, whether another woman in lesbian relationships or, for example, to accompany a male lover at sea or war.[258] In each instance crossdressing is not the only social boundary being violated. In fact, it might be argued that as the crossdressing is adjunctive and instrumental to other goals, these other goals should be seen more as principal concerns.

Perhaps the best source of information about crossdressing women in Europe for the period between the Reformation (16th century) and the modern world (19th century) is the work of Rudolph Dekker and Lotte van de Pol. They document dozens of cases of crossdressing women in the 17th-18th century from Denmark, England and the Netherlands in northern Europe, to Spain and Italy in southern Europe.[259] Despite the impressive number of cases unearthed, they point out the incomplete nature of the historical record and conclude that their cases represent "only the tip of the iceberg."[260] They nicely summarize the attractiveness of crossdressing to many women, and the rise and fall of the practice, in two short sentences:

> In the early modern era passing oneself off as a man was a real and viable option for women who had fallen into bad times and were struggling to overcome their difficult circumstances....
>
> The tradition of female cross-dressing may have had its roots in medieval times, but it became visible in the sixteenth century; it was lost in the nineteenth century.[261]

The examples set forth by Dekker and Van de Pol show that women might be motivated by a variety of circumstances and needs. Of 119 women documented as living as men in Denmark between 1550-1839, most become sailors or soldiers, but some find niches in civilian life.[262] In some cases, women disguise themselves as men in order to remain with their husbands and thus avoid long separations, as when their partners take to the sea. Others are motivated by economic desperation, seeking work in occupations reserved for males. Some use crossdressing to express patriotic fervor by joining the military. Others resort to male disguise to escape unfavorable or threatening circumstances. In sum, no one reason accounts for the choices these women make—and Dekker and Van de Pol believe "the decision to start dressing as a man was never for one reason alone."[263] Regardless of the precipitating reason, the courage and creativity required frequently testify to the extraordinary character of both the women and their circumstances.

Crossdressing also shows that virtually any occupation that might attract a man can also attract a woman. Even extreme occupations such as piracy have their share of crossdressing women. Two of the most famous are the early 18th century pirates Anne Bonny and Mary Read (see the answer to Q. 47). They are members of Calico Jack Rackam's crew, which operates in the Caribbean Sea. Brought to trial in the early 1720s their lives and exploits are publicized in *A General History of the Robberies and Murders of the Most Notorious Pirates* (1724).[264]

Crossdressing, however widely it might be practiced, generally remains against the law. Often the only notice we have of crossdressing women comes from brief notations about their arrest with this as part of, or the sole charge. By the 19th century it is possible in some circumstances to gain a permit for dressing in masculine clothes. Such a permit protects the woman from arrest and relieves her of any special pressure to try to pass as a man. In short, the permit allows a woman to dress as a man without any pretence of being a man. The French artist and early feminist Rosa Bonheur is one such woman; her crossdressing makes no effort to disguise her sex, though it remains a subversive gesture in its cultural context.[265]

Crossdressing in Literature

Not unexpectedly, literature examines the practice, too. Theophile Gautier's novel *Mademoiselle de Maupin* (1835) features as its protagonist a woman who crossdresses in an effort to pass as a man. Calling herself 'Theodore,' Mademoiselle de Maupin uses dress as a vehicle to move freely in a society ruled by men. But her physical features combine with her dress to create an androgynous appearance that proves erotically appealing to both men and women.[266] Interestingly, many of Gautier's readers are able to make the connection between the fictional character and the real life La Maupin, who lives in the 17th century (see the answer to Q. 48).

Gautier uses his protagonist to explore blurred gender lines in terms of sexual attraction and interests. Honoré de Balzac's *Séraphita* (1835) likewise may be inspired by an actual person, but in this case a contemporaneous one—the famed author George Sand, a crossdressing woman who publishes under a masculine name (see the answer to Q. 48). In *Séraphita*, the protagonist is so androgynous that he/she passes under two names: Séraphita and, when in masculine dress, Séraphitus. Like Mademoiselle de Maupin, Séraphitus/Séraphita is loved and desired by members of both sexes. Voluntarily exiting life, the protagonist is revealed—as the name suggests—to be an angel. Certainly the character is presented as an idealized figure, and androgyny is at the heart of the portrait.[267]

Crossdressing Ballads

Crossdressing women also catch the popular imagination, as dozens of ballads attest.[268] Sometimes referred to as 'transvestite ballads,' or 'warrior women ballads,' they feature women entering a masculine world—generally at its most dangerous and violent, as in seafaring or military service. Dianne Dugaw argues that between 1650-1850, the peak of such balladry, these songs reflect lived experience for many women. She also notes the influence of the 17th-18th centuries' interest in the transforming powers of dress, an age where fascination with crossdressing corresponded with this wider interest. Changes in the Victorian world, both in values and in organizational structures, redefine what is permissible for women in dress and occupation, and the age of the woman warrior is surpassed by a different sensibility about women.[269]

But as the following table shows, different motivations of crossdressing women can be found in these songs, though they are generally united by a grand theme.

Table 46.1 Crossdressing Ballads

Ballad	Date	Motivation for Crossdressing/ Summary
"Flower of Serving-Men" ("The Lady Turn'd Serving-Man")	1656	Escape. After her mother orchestrates the death of her husband and baby, the daughter disguises herself as a serving-man at the royal court, where the King falls in love with her.

"Mary Ambree"	1760s	Love & Loyalty. Having joined military service disguised as a man to be near her husband, a woman continues to serve after his death, distinguishing herself with bravery.
"The Rose of Britain's Isle"	1880s	Love & Loyalty. After a father sends his apprentice away to sea his daughter Jane disguises herself and follows the lad, Edmond. Off the coast of Spain she is wounded by a cannonball, her secret is revealed, and the couple are returned home.
"Pretty Polly"	Early 19th cent.	Love & Escape. Polly loves a sea captain disapproved by her parents. Disguised as a man she meets him at an inn. He desires sex with her, but she refuses. Appearing the next day in feminine dress the two are wed.
"Handsome Cabin Boy" ("Female Cabin Boy")	19th cent.	Adventure. A young woman wants to see the world so she disguises herself as a lad and signs on as a Captain's cabin boy.
"Devilish Mary"	Late 19th cent.	Love & Domination. Mary wins a husband, then dominates him, becoming the 'man' of the house even in wearing his pants.
"Martinmas Time"	Early 20th cent.	Escape. Soldiers attempt to coerce a woman to come to their quarters that night. She disguises herself as a man and visits as promised, asking quarters for herself and other troops. She is refused and sent away. As she departs she leaves feminine articles (her garters and ribbons) to prove she had come.

If any theme emerges from the collection of ballads as a whole, it is love—even love gone wrong, or lust masquerading as affection. More specifically, it concerns erotic love. In fact, traditionally interpreters of these ballads have assumed they merely reflect a heterosexual male's reading of the world. But

Pauline Greenhill's analysis of ten such ballads contests this assumption. She agrees that a feminist reading broadens comprehension of these songs as about women's experience as well as about men's. However, she also thinks some of them go beyond heterosexual attraction and suggest the possibility of same-sex attraction.[270] Certainly ballads such as "Flower of Serving Men," "Pretty Polly," and "Handsome Cabin Boy" at least hint at same-sex attraction.

This last named ballad, one Greenhill considers, provides an example of the ambiguity and humor that both surface in some of these songs. In "Handsome Cabin Boy," a popular broadside ballad of sailors, the heroine is a young maiden wanting to see far-off lands.[271] She masquerades as a young man and contracts to be a captain's cabin boy for a year. Her fetching good looks soon draw attention from both sexes:

  And the captain's wife, she being on board,
   She seemed in great joy
  To think her husband had engaged
   Such a handsome cabin boy.
  And now and then she'd slip him a kiss
   And she would have liked to toy,
  But it was the captain found out the secret
   Of this handsome cabin boy.

As things are wont to happen, the lass becomes pregnant. The ship's doctor is amused that "a sailor lad should have a daughter or a son." The crew, of course, all swear they are not responsible, leading to the captain's wife declaring:

   "My dear I wish you joy,
  For it's either you or me has betrayed
   This handsome cabin boy."

The ballad concludes in roaring good humor:

  And then each man took his tote of rum
   And they drunk success to trade
   And likewise to the cabin boy
   Who was neither man nor maid.
  "Here's hoping wars don't rise again,
   Our sailors to destroy,
  And here's hoping for a jolly lot more
   Like the handsome cabin boy!"

Though humorous, the ballad reflects an ordinary sailor's yearning on a long voyage bereft of accessible female companionship. Yet there is also the hidden reality of persistent sexual desire that might make a 'pretty boy' attractive to a man. Also, putting the captain's wife aboard adds another layer; both she and her husband are attracted to the cabin 'boy.' The lass herself, though central to the song's action is incidental to the song's interest in terms of her own motivation. All that motivation does is get her aboard; after that all the focus is on what transpires around a pretty girl masquerading as a boy. Lust, rather than love, seems triumphant.

More pointed is the story of "The Soldier Maid" (or, "When I Was a Fair Maid"). In this ballad the singer is a young woman who at age 16 runs away from home to be a soldier. Her comely form—"gentle waist so slender and my fingers long and small"—soon wins her suitors:

> Oh many is the prank I played upon the field
> And many was the young man his love to me revealed.
> Many a prank have I seen among the French
> And so boldly I fought, though only a wench.

The officer in charge keeps her back from the battle front to protect her. Instead, she is sent home to serve as a recruiter. As a sentry at the Tower of London she again becomes the object of another's affections, but this time with a twist:

> A lady fell in love with me,
> I told her I was a maid.
> She went to my officer,
> And the secret she betrayed.

However, the story has a happy ending. The sympathetic officer is sorry to lose her and promises her a bounty for her service at the siege of Valciennes. She ends by resolving that should war come and the King have need, she will once more "put on my regimentals and I'll fight for him again."

What makes this ballad especially intriguing is the eroticism played at in so many ways. As a woman disguised as a man she fetches the desire of both men and a woman. But how complete is her disguise? Are her fellow soldiers attracted to her as a woman, or as a man? Surely the latter makes most sense, since the singer attests:

> Many a night in the guardroom I have lain;
> I never was afraid to lie down with the men.
> At the pulling off of my breeches I oftimes gave a smile
> To think I lay with a regiment, and a maiden all the while.

In fact, her disguise is only undone after a disgruntled female suitor tells on her. Her act of crossdressing is a complete success in accomplishing her gender transformation as far as others are concerned. Yet we cannot call her transsexual; her sense of herself remains that of a woman, albeit one with a masculine interest. And her 'pranks' on the field indicate a masculine casualness about love as well. In that respect the ballad is atypical.

Most of these ballads position the woman's love as the pretext for crossdressing. The circumstances in which love blooms in these ballads typically are odious: a parent or parents disapprove; social rank is a gulf between the lovers; war or other obstacle separates them. In any event, the solution requires the woman to disguise herself as a man. However, this disguise is purposeful and transient; love won, the masquerade ends. Perhaps amazingly, the loved one rarely objects to the artifice. In fact, the man may actually be knowingly complicit in the subterfuge, as is the case in the early 20th century ballad "William and Nancy" (or, "Men's Clothing I'll Put On"), where William is persuaded by Nancy that she can meet the challenges of war disguised as a man.

An array of twists enrich the possibilities for these ballads. In "The Young Shepherd," for example, the woman is a rich merchant's daughter sought after by a man below her social station. Her father shoots and kills the shepherd, putting an end to the suitor. But the daughter, finding the dying man, takes his simple garb as her own and assumes his place with the flock. In this ballad the transgression that counts the most may be the crossing of the social class line rather than the gender line.

Many variations occur on the 'woman disguises herself as a man to follow her lover to sea/war' storyline. For instance, in "Young Sailor Bold" (or, "The Rich Merchant's Daughter") the disapproving father of the woman has homicidal intentions, but his daughter disguises herself as a sailor to warn the intended victim. Unfortunately, the father mistakenly kills her. Distraught, he then kills himself. The lover dies of grief. On the other hand, in "Mary Ambree" the protagonist succeeds in joining her lover, but he is then killed. Faced with the question of what to do next, she remains in military service. In the ballad "Jack Monroe" (or, "Jackie Frazer") the woman's lover does not die, but is wounded. She tends to him, her secret is revealed, and they marry. On the other hand, in "The Rose of Britain's Isle," it is the woman who is wounded, leading to her discovery as female, but with the happy ending that she and her lover are sent home to live in blissful marital peace. Given what we know of the times, it is not difficult to see in every variation an event that plausibly happened to one or another woman.

Why were men crossdressing?

While crossdressed men receive comparatively less attention than crossdressed women for this time period, they certainly exist. As with women, motives can be many and varied. Those discussed here do not exhaust the matter; they merely illustrate its complexity. For example, what are we to make of the 1633 case of Christopher Willan in England, who participates crossdressed in a traditional ceremonial garlanding of the local church? To assess the act's meaning requires knowledge of the practice of 'bearing rushes,' its connection to religious and secular traditions, the presence of the church as the place where the act occurred, and a variety of other factors beyond merely the fact of a man dressed as a woman.

Any generalization suggesting that all men crossdress for the same reason is patently untrue. But discerning the reason, or reasons, involved must almost always be discerned from context, since rather seldom do the participants leave us an explanation for their behavior. (And even then we must take into account other motivations, such as possibly inventing plausible reasons that might be more easily accepted by their contemporaries.) In the following material, then, we must proceed with caution and careful regard to context.

Gender Identity Expression

Some men in their gender crossing behavior apparently are expressing what today we would recognize as one or another transgender condition. Some of history's most famous male crossdressers (see the answer to Q. 49) would today likely receive a diagnosis as transsexual or transvestite or as a gay man in drag. Yet other men's motivation seems not to be the expression of a felt gender-variant sense of identity. Instead, like some women, they utilize gender disguise for other reasons.

Romantic Motivations

Indeed, if we return for a moment to the so-called 'cross-dressing ballads,' these occasionally tell of men disguised as women for hopelessly romantic reasons. For example, the early 19th century ballad "The Holy Nunnery" tells of a young man named Willie who is in love with the maiden Anna. When she hears of his parent's opposition to their union she resolves to take herself to a nunnery. There she will never kiss a man again. Willie endures seven years before he can bear her absence no more. Disguising himself as a woman he goes to the nunnery. But Anna remains resolute in her vows. This ballad reminds us that a man—like a woman—may be motivated by romantic love to crossdress.[272]

Protest and Rebellion

A motivation for many men is protest against unpopular edicts. Sometimes these are relatively minor matters, which prompt mild responses. For instance, Christian officials often sought to discourage participation in secular festivities, such as Maytide games, where men might dress as 'May Marions.'[273] In Yorkshire, the summer of 1596, such an edict aimed at preserving the sanctity of Sundays and church grounds, is met with protest by a group whose number include men dressed as women—and who dress themselves as such at a church before parading through the town of Cawthorne.[274]

Of course the cause can be weightier, too. For some their behavior flows from a refusal to further endure injustice. For example, in 19th century Wales a band of crossdressed men who style themselves 'Rebecca and Her Daughters' roam rural South and West Wales. Between 1839-1844 these men don the guise of women and attack tollgates around the region. Their motivation appears to be rooted in the desperation of deprivation. The tenant farmers of the time are weighed down by burdensome tolls on use of the roads levied by the Turnpike Trusts. Perhaps drawing their inspiration from a biblical text (Genesis 24:60, which reads in part, "And they blessed Rebekah and said to her, '. . . may your offspring gain possession of the gates of their foes.'" (NIV)), a band of men attack a tollgate in South Wales. The attacks soon spread into West Wales. The men dress in a woman's bonnet and petticoats worn over work clothing. By 1844 the leaders are captured and the attacks end. But an ensuing investigation leads to legal reforms that alleviate the burden felt by the poor. These crossdressing men have helped effect positive social reform.[275]

At about the same time, in Ireland, another group of men are also engaged in agrarian revolt. They are the 'Molly Maguires,' who allegedly take their name from a widow whose house provides the first meeting place for the new secret society. Formed during the potato famine of the mid- to late 1840s, these men fight against overbearing landlords. Consistent with their name, they disguise themselves in women's clothing, as well as masks or blackened faces. The memory of the original Molly Maguires persists and the name is appropriated by a violent band of noncrossdressing men in late 19th century Pennsylvania in the United States.[276]

Historian Natalie Zemon Davis notes a number of other, earlier political acts in which men don female guise: English weavers, including crossdressed men mixed with women, are led by a woman called 'Captain' Alice Clark in a grain riot in Essex in 1629; in 1631 men of Wiltshire, England, led by 'Lady Skimmington'—a crossdressed man—protest the king's enclosure of the forests by rioting and destroying his fences; French peasants in the Beaujolais of the 1770s accost land surveyors measuring the peasants' lands for a new master; in 1812, 'General Ludd's wives'—two crossdressed male weavers—lead a large crowd in Stockport to destroy steam looms and a factory.[277] Davis sees the use of such disguises by men as rooted in the long-established practices of Carnival (see the answer to Q. 71). She comments:

> On the one hand, the disguise freed men from the full responsibility for their deeds and perhaps, too, from fear of outrageous revenge upon their manhood. After all, it was 'merely women' who were acting in this disorderly way. On the other hand, the males drew upon the sexual power and energy of the unruly woman and on her license (which they had long assumed at carnival and games)—to promote fertility, to defend the community's interests and standards, and to tell the truth about unjust rule.[278]

The Medicalization of Sex

Other forces are at work as well. While some crossdressing by men is motivated by sexual desires, as the 20th century progresses this connection becomes ever more the focus of attention and concern over male crossdressing. The medicalization of sex (see the answer to Q. 91) that commences in the late 19th century changes many dynamics, not the least of which is a clearer, formal demarcation between homosexuality and what Western culture considers normative, 'natural' sexuality. One important aspect of that is to change perception of behaviors like crossdressing from acts of sin and criminality to ones of mental disorder.

But that transition proves a gradual one. Through much of the 19th-20th centuries crossdressing and other behaviors associated with transgender realities, remain illegal. Britain, for example, in 1885 reforms its criminal code and adds the so-called Labouchère Amendment—officially Section II of the Criminal Law Amendment Act. The text reads:

> Any male person who, in public or private, commits, or is a party to the commission of, or procures, or attempts to procure the commission by any male person of, any act of gross indecency shall be guilty of misdemeanour, and being convicted shall be liable at the discretion of the Court to be imprisoned for any term not exceeding two years, with or without hard labour.[279]

The Amendment permits linking public crossdressing with the establishment's real concern: homosexual behavior among males. Crossdressing is known to be one aspect of homosexual activity; crossdressed men—especially male prostitutes—are seen in public places rendezvousing with other men.[280] Thus the law can punish crossdressing by virtue of its presumed connection to 'gross indecency.'

How was crossdressing received?

The modern gender hierarchy that promotes and protects masculine privilege so zealously increasingly comes to focus its attention—and wrath—on male crossdressing. It proves able to do this more easily once a connection seems established with taboo male sexual behavior (homosexuality mostly, but also for illicit access to women). The temptation to see all crossdressing as suggestive of sexual impropriety, most especially homosexual activity, grows until the presumed link between crossdressing and homosexuality appears unassailable to many minds—a good number of them in the medical ranks. Other links include fetishism and sadomasochism. In short, a crossdressed man is presumed to be motivated by one or another sexual perversity. David Boswell remarks that in British society, by 1916 there is "no question" that crossdressing means sexual outlawry.[281] Similar conclusions are common throughout Western societies—though from the start there are those who challenge such generalizations.

Lessening concern over female crossdressing accompanies this growing concern over male crossdressing. Increasingly often women, even if grudgingly, are acknowledged as having cause for their crossdressing. Yet appreciation of the circumstances that motivate female crossdressing does not mean universal approval. In fact, women throughout much of this time period can be arrested for such behavior, as any number of court records reveal. One found by Jean Howard provides a convenient example. In 1575 a woman named Dorothy Clayton is charged that, "contrary to all honesty and womanhood [she] commonly goes about the City appareled in man's attire. She has abused her body with sundry persons and lived an incontinent life. On Friday she is to stand on the pillory for two hours in men's apparell and then to be sent to Bridewell until further order."[282]

However, generally speaking, even as concern over male crossdressing grows, with respect to female crossdressing mild disapproval may be the norm. Dekker and van de Pol observe both that "rejection was the most common reaction," and that it tended to be more pronounced among the very social groups where it was most likely to occur.[283] Still, this reaction must be kept in a context of wide social anxiety about appearance and class. The way women are dressing and eliciting criticism extends beyond crossdressing.

A common assumption that may be made about crossdressing women is that they, like men, are doing so to engage in illicit sexual practices. For women this especially means prostitution. The sanctions levied against such behavior sometimes includes standing in the pillory—where the offender's head and hands are secured to a wooden framework and the person is subjected to public ridicule, whipping, and imprisonment.[284]

In the post-Reformation era in England the way some women appear in public occasions a lively 'debate about women' (*querelle des femmes*).[285] In the 17th century, an interesting pamphlet entitled *Hic Mulier (This Woman)* appears. It says:

> Come, then, you Masculine women, for you are my Subject, you that have made Admiration an Ass and fooled him with a deformity never before dreamed of; that have made yourselves stranger things than ever Noah's Ark unloaded or Nile engendered. . . . From the other you have taken the monstrousness of your deformity in apparel, exchanging the modest attire of the comely Hood, Cowl, Coif, handsome Dress or Kerchief, to the cloudy Ruffianly broad-brimmed Hat and wanton Feather; the modest upper parts of a concealing straight gown, to the loose, lascivious civil embracement of a French doublet, being all unbuttoned to entice, all of one shape to hide deformity, and extreme short waisted to give a most easy way to every luxurious action; the glory of a fair large hair, to the shame of most ruffianly short locks; the side, thick gathered, and close guarding Safeguards [petticoats] to the short, weak, thin, loose, and every hand-entertaining short bases [skirts]; for Needles, Swords; for Prayerbooks, bawdy legs; for modest gestures, giantlike behaviors; and for women's modesty, all Mimic and apish incivility. . . .[286]

(This tract is answered the same year by *Haec-Vir (This Man)*, a pamphlet defending crossdressing.)

Nevertheless, despite the bluster and public censure, it is worth repeating that the actual consequences of being caught crossdressing are generally mild, for the offense itself is increasingly regarded as minor.[287] However, though social tolerance might be becoming more widespread with time, and legal consequences generally mild, there are important transitions across this period. Especially the medicalization of sex means that gender crossings like crossdressing are increasingly likely to be seen as connected to sexual motivations, be labeled sexual deviancy, become attached to new ideas about 'sexual orientation,' and be considered symptomatic of mental disorder. All these forces can be traced in the history of the United States, to which we now turn.

Q. 47

What is the history in the United States?

The Short Answer. Transgender realities have been a part of life in America since long before Europeans reached its shores, as students of Native American history are well aware (cf. the answer to Q. 59). Much like Europe, the United States has a rich history of crossdressing men and women among those settlers and their descendants. From pre-colonial days forward transgender realities—intersex conditions, homosexuality, crossdressing—have been part of American life. Since gender is expressed through dress, the fashions of various periods in American life have relatively facilitated or frustrated crossdressing, some of which has intentionally aimed at reforming fashion and, through it, the wider society. Interest about crossdressing has paralleled greater interest, and concern, over dress in general. Particularly since the mid-19th century, dress and crossdressing have caught attention in news accounts, scientific studies, and popular presentations through literature, song, and drama. For much of U.S. history more attention was given to crossdressing women. Their motives were diverse, their stories often told. Although such stories generated attention, most of it was not sympathetic. Only in light of the successful challenge made by women to social dress codes, resulting in greater freedom of dress (and other matters), have such stories been appraised in a generally more favorable light. In recent decades the focus has switched to crossdressing males. Increasingly, it is now their stories being told. Much as happened with women, these stories have been disapproved. On the whole, the U.S. has been somewhat less tolerant of crossdressing than Europe. However, contemporary America shows signs of increasing tolerance for—and more public visibility by—transgender people than in previous generations.

The Longer Answer. Transgender realities past and present typically draw attention from one of three phenomena: intersex conditions (in the past termed 'hermaphroditism'), same-sex sexual relationships, or crossdressing (for whatever reason). Consistent with the approach of this work our attention will be devoted primarily to the last named, cognizant that some crossdressing has been associated with intersex[288] and some has aimed at facilitating same-sex relationships. We will use crossdressing as an entry into transgender realities in the history of our own society, something more easily discerned as we enter into our own time, but glimpsed in previous periods, too. However, to understand crossdressing requires continuing at least a rudimentary reckoning of clothes fashion. After all, crossdressing cannot occur without gendered distinction in dress and every generation has its own fashions organized with respect to such distinctions. Accordingly, we begin with a brief overview of fashion and fashion changes throughout the history of the United States.

What role has fashion played in American crossdressing?

Crossdressing cannot occur without dressing (cf. Question Set 1)—and the apparel put on must be gendered sufficiently to be recognized as 'belonging' to one gender or another. Throughout U.S. history clothing has been gender differentiated. Reflecting the culture's binary sex and gender order, clothing has been styled for masculine men or feminine females with the materials, styles, colors and other features designed to communicate perceived traits about each matching set of sex and gender.

In many Americans' eyes throughout much of our history, to put on the clothes designated for a sex-gender pairing other than the one assigned at birth has meant putting on that different pairing.[289] A woman who dresses as a man puts on masculinity, and may be seen as pretending to the male sex; a man dressing as a woman becomes feminized, and may be seen as trying to be a member of the female sex. Thus gender crossings are serious matters, seen as carrying social consequences, and both fascinatingly attractive and dangerous. While our contemporary perceptions of gender and transgender are not exactly the same as in earlier periods, there is some continuity. For example, at present our society has proven as reluctant to recognize a 'third gender' as ever was the case before. Yet today we are more likely to view a crossdressing individual as *performing* gender than actually *swapping* it, and we are more adept at separating gender from sex. We also increasingly are more likely to be bemused by crossdressing than to feel threatened by it—though the all too frequent accounts of crossdressers violently assaulted reminds us how many in our midst remain far less enlightened.

In part these changes are evident and to some extent may be traced in the dress practices of the periods in question. In the following remarks we briefly sketch some general trends and special distinctions in the fashion of each century. We do so for both men and women, with special attention to gendered distinctions. For each century we also consider the practical issues posed by fashion for crossdressing. After thus looking at each century we can offer a few broad remarks on the whole matter before turning to other topics.

What was dress like in early America (16th-18th Centuries)?

From the beginning of its colonial period to the present Americans prove fascinated by clothing, debate what constitutes its use or misuse, and incorporate it into the construction of social identities. This seems no less true for Native Americans and non-English settlers than for British subjects in the thirteen colonies. For example, ethnologist Diana DiPaolo Loren, studying the interaction between Indians and French subjects in the lower Mississippi Valley of the late 17th-early 18th centuries, describes how clothing plays a key role in creating and protecting social identities challenged by cultural contact.[290] Because dress functions in a complex boundary system (see the answers to Q. 2-3), it has tremendous instrumental utility for expressing social values and protecting social order. At the same time, dress—through the agency of fashion—interacts reciprocally with culture, being influenced by, but also influencing, society.

While Americans today may find it difficult to believe that fashion plays much of a role in the construction of early America, we should be wary of too quickly dismissing it as a creative force. Dress, through fashion, expresses and shapes culture. Indeed, historian Kate Haulman, writing of the culture wars that swirl about Philadelphia in the 1780s, remarks, "At the center of these battles for the character and look of the new nation's capital, contests that pitted calls for republican simplicity against the 'timeless logic of signs of power, brilliant symbols of domination and social difference,' lay fashion."[291] She observes that fashion acts in this place and time as a social screen upon which competing ideas can be expressed. But what are the fashion styles of the time that people draw upon to present conflicting ideas about social status and other values?

Men's fashion in the early 17th century shares more in common with the Middle Ages than it will with the end of the century. The main garment is the close-fitting doublet worn with breeches and accompanied by cape (or cassock); by the end of the century the coat has replaced the doublet.[292] Over the course of the century the waist of the doublet rises and falls while breeches lengthen, as does hair. Even shorter hairstyles frequently fall to the shoulders. Late in the century men begin increasingly to wear wigs. The overall effect in masculine fashion is of a longer-legged figure, an effect also heightened by the gradual trend toward boots rather than shoes.

Women's fashion in the 17th century experiences a trend toward more diversity, particularly with regard to wider choices in informal wear. Dresses, always with some type of neckwear, and gowns are long. The underskirt becomes known as the 'petticoat.' Waistlines rise early in the century, then move back toward a more natural place. Ladies' jackets—called 'waistcoats'—are common garb across social classes.[293] As the century progresses women's sleeves shorten, leaving the lower arms bare, and necklines plunge. When compared to changes in masculine fashion, women's wear similarly accents vertical lines, and ever more so through the period. Later in the century the influence of French fashion makes for more sensuous styles among those who can afford them.

The fashion styles for both men and women in the 17th century facilitate crossdressing. For men, women's wear generally conceals more than it reveals, making feminine appearance through dress feasible. If anything, women have it easier adopting and adapting masculine fashions to pass as male. Hairstyles are long and wigs common; long coats and boots conceal much, and even bustier ladies can bind their breasts and rely on capes and coats to cover any ill-fitting doublet.

The 18th century, says John Crowley, finds the dress of both sexes becoming more highly gendered through developments in apparel structure and fabric. Yet, Crowley maintains, the goal for both genders stays the same: to attain a level of gentility marked by both civility and refinement. The bodily constraints imposed by items like whalebone stays in women's garments encourage a posture associated with a social ideal.[294] Yet, over the course of the century social values gradually change, and with them change styles in fashion.

Among men's hairstyles wigs prevail. The three-piece suit introduced in the latter part of the previous century proves a popular and practical fashion for men. By and large, American men follow the fashions of Englishmen, just then coming to dominate men's fashion in Europe, sporting custom-made clothes fashioned largely from wool or linen. In large measure the century is one in which the trend is toward less formality in dress wear. Alongside this a weakening of class distinctions in dress occurs as folk increasingly dress not according to their existing social rank, but in line with the social rank they aspire to.[295] The tendency to accent vertical lines continues. Coats grow more full-skirted in the first half of the century, then less so in the latter half. Also in the latter part of the century waistcoats grow shorter, though in the last decade a brief fascination with long, high-waisted coats emerges. In general, by century's end the informal (or 'undress') wear of a man typically consists of "a plain broadcloth coat with a square front, worn over a vest that becomes shorter through the years, along with breeches occasionally of suede, shoes with ribbon ties or soft, fawn-colored top boots."[296]

Women's fashion in the early 18th century evolves from simpler, more practical clothing characterized by long, loose dress wear with wide sleeves (the 'sack dress'), toward imposing dresses accented by panniers (or 'paniers'—a hoop framework that extended the skirt), a style reaching its excessive zenith about 1730. At the same time that women's fashion is expanding her space horizontally, fashions in hats and hairstyles are expanding her space vertically. By midway through the century a matron can cut an impressive—and space filling—figure. But as the century wanes, fashion in the 1770s tends back toward a more 'natural' look, though this also means more accentuation of sexual features, with both busts and bottoms filling out. In the 1780s, dress is more revealing with plunging necklines, bare forearms, and full skirt open in front to show the underlying petticoat.[297] However, by century's end the desire for dress *au naturel* has led away from artificial excess to the point where even undergarments are sometimes dispensed with.

Fashion styles through the 18th century perhaps pose more challenges to crossdressers designing to pass as members of another sex. Women's fashions increasingly accentuate the sexual aspects of female anatomy, perhaps encouraging a fetishistic approach to crossdressing for men but certainly complicating any efforts to pass as a woman. Women face the challenges presented by the masculine business suit, but growing informality in male dress and the many practical clothes styles available for men make it relatively easier to appropriate masculine garb than men have using feminine dress. As well, as Valerie Steele notes, "some women wore a more masculine dress that resembled a man's riding coat."[298] As proves true in other eras, in general it is easier for a woman to pass as a man than vice versa.

What was dress like in 19th century America?

Ruth Rubenstein contends that talk about clothing takes on a new dimension in the 19th century, one consistent with the scientific spirit of the age. Serious consideration is given to the origin and meaning of clothing. Various theories about clothing's origin compete in the century, each centered in a particular notion: adornment, modesty, or protection.[299] All three theories can claim counterparts in styles. As the supposed 'scientific' medicalization of sex (see the answer to Q. 91) progresses, gender differentiation, reaching new heights of elaboration, also exercises influence on dress. Sara Melissa Pullum-Piñon observes that this gendered division in elaborateness of dress coincides with American commitment in the century to keeping separate spheres of influence for men and women.[300]

The scientific spirit of the age parallels a more general interest in such matters—one that also helps ensure new analysis of a phenomenon like crossdressing. In fact, Etsuko Taketani remarks, "there is arguably no other epoch in American history so tenaciously haunted, vexed, and titillated by the practice of cross-dressing than the 1840s and 1850s."[301] Coupled with the rise of the medicalization of sex in the latter half of the century this means new meanings will be attached to crossdressing. But since crossdressing cannot be properly understood apart from the fashions of the time, we need to review the more prominent trends.

In men's fashion a transformation is underway that will lead to the 20th century's narrow constriction of what is acceptable masculine dress. Consistent with previous historical trends, the 19th century begins with a display of greater attention and change attending masculine fashion than feminine. Historian Vern Bullough contends that during the latter 18th century and early 19th century men's dress changes much more than women's. But he also observes, "since that time variations in men's costumes have become negligible."[302]

The general drift in masculine fashion as the century proceeds is toward a bland sameness in style. Pullum-Piñon succinctly captures this dominant trend by commenting, "Men's outfits became increasing similar, reaching the almost total uniformity of the modern suit in the mid-nineteenth century."[303] The French fashion historian Farid Chenoue traces this evolution as follows: "Nineteenth-century Anglomania shaped the sartorial fate first of the upper classes, then of the lower classes, and it was England that heralded the advent of a key item in a modern man's wardrobe—the business suit."[304] Alongside 'Anglomania,' the French Revolution (1789-1799) exercises significant influence on fashion both in France and abroad.[305] So, too, does the widespread growth of clothing manufactured by machines rather than by hand. These various forces help make the 19th century one in which trousers triumph over breeches. In men's fashion, another significant change is the abandonment of the formal coat style that prevailed in the previous century in favor of more utilitarian overcoats. Ordinary outerwear in the Victorian era (1830s-1890s) for a gentleman consists of six basic components: hat, coat, vest over shirt, pants, and shoes or boots. Vests prove to be the centerpiece, often colorful, and made from wool, cotton, or silk. They are generally waist long and might be either single or double-breasted. The shirts they cover tend toward more utilitarian styles, sometimes with removable bibs and typically with band collars. Pants have a high waistline, sometimes sport stripes, and are worn long, without a crease. The high collars at the start of the century gradually shorten. Of course, workman's wear remains less formal and westward expansion eventually produces its own styles.

Women's fashion presents different challenges from those faced by men. Perhaps most prominent among these is the need for a sharp differentiation between public and private wear. A proper woman in public must present her gender in unmistakable ways that do not lend themselves either to ease of movement or practicality, to say nothing of comfort. This situation calls for an elaboration of the wardrobe. For the 19th century woman, particularly of the upper class, a satisfactory wardrobe has to be able to meet an array of demands in both the public and private spheres. Since many of the clothes she possesses are suited only for brief periods, changes of clothes are frequent.[306]

Feminine fashion witnesses turns once more toward simplicity in the new century with such garb as high-waisted muslin dresses. Full skirts and corsets to present a narrow waist are fashionable, but the corset increasingly draws fire from women. At mid-century, the 'Bloomer's Costume' debuts, its most notable and controversial feature being trousers. Though it is early championed by leaders in the Women's Movement (see discussion below), it soon recedes behind more conventional women's fashion with voluminous dresses and their prevalence of crinoline (stiff material in petticoats or hoop skirts used to widen the dress and lend it a bell-like form).[307] But the influence of masculine style continues, reflecting itself, for example, in the tailored jacket with collar and lapels that women begin wearing after the Civil War. From the 1870s onward, bustles replace crinoline. Dress sleeves cover the upper arm and are wide. Corsets provide a tight gathering to lend accent to the female form. In the 1890s, the waspish silhouette is perfected by a corset to narrow the waist, complemented by padding at hips, buttocks, and bosom.

The corset—the quintessential feminine garment in the 19th century wardrobe because it so greatly exaggerates anatomical differences between men and women[308]—becomes a focal point of debate in the push for dress reform. Fashion historian Valerie Steele's opening line in her history of the garment is telling: "The corset is probably the most controversial garment in the entire history of fashion."[309] In the 19th century, historian Jill Fields observes, "virtually all freeborn women in the United States wore corsets."[310] The debate over them grows more pronounced throughout the century; tightly-laced corsets are blamed for various women's health issues[311]—a rallying point for dress reformers. Still, the corset will persist as a significant force in women's dress well into the next century.

Although the corset proves the most controversial garment of the century, it also represents most visibly a significant change in women's dress in which undergarments become more prominent than ever. They are, in fact, an aspect of dress reform, one that gains momentum when the Women's Movement shifts away from changes in outerwear back toward more conventional dress so as to not obscure their central message.[312] Breast supporters—precursors to the brassiere—make their way into the marketplace in the 1870s.[313] Somewhat earlier, women begin to don bifurcated 'drawers'[314]—undergarments deriving their name from being 'drawn up' over the legs. Fields remarks, "For women to engage in this masculine act and appropriate their new garment's name from the lexicon of menswear blurred what had been a clearly marked gender boundary."[315] But she also points out that uneasiness attending this move was mediated by adaptations to feminize the garment and appeals to the greater modesty they offered.[316] These shifts in dress practice, and the growing attention they gather, will reach greater significance in the next century.

If feminine fashion seems as the century progresses to be more overtly sexualized in its depiction of the female form and attention to such items as corsets and underwear, it is not without parallel in masculine fashion. Of special note in men's fashion in the 19th century is a trend in its latter stages toward more overt display of the body. Form-fitting, body-revealing styles become increasingly popular in the 1880s-1890s. In Britain, *The Tailor's Review* in June, 1890, opines: "Women are beginning to object to and discuss the garments of men.... If men are shocked by the sight of a lady in tights, or *au naturel*, is it not to be conjectured that women regard with loathing the current habit of mankind clothing the legs in an envelope that reveals only too acutely outlines that might be left to the imagination?"[317]

Paralleling the increased public attention to all matters sexual by the medical and academic establishments' increased devotion to articulating a 'scientific' taxonomy of human sexual behavior—and accompanying system of 'normal' and 'abnormal' sexuality—popular entertainment, literature, and fashion all show an increased boldness. However, any such boldness remains contrasted to the very public Victorian sensibility, creating a creative tension in which issues of sex and gender thrive as lively matters of fascination, titillation, and debate. The rigid—and thanks to medical science authoritative—pairing of sex and gender inevitably mean a greater sexualization of gendered activities like crossdressing.

Given the attention to the sexual body found in the latter part of the century, crossdressing becomes more challenging for both men and women—but perhaps especially for men. For a man desiring to pass as female crossdressing requires taking advantage of styles that cover the body most completely, including using hat, wig, and veil to disguise the face. We know that some men use corsets,[318] and this item benefits a male crossdresser, especially for embracing a feminine gender identity since the corset "legitimated and constructed particular notions about femininity, propriety, and the female body."[319] Some additions are needed to alter the body appearance to look more female, with wider hips, larger bottom, and, of course, a bust. Though such challenges have often presented themselves to male crossdressers desiring to pass as female, any time feminine styles accentuate body differences from men the task grows harder.

The growing use of undergarments in the latter part of the century also offers more opportunity for the development of fetishes attached to these garments worn next to the erogenous zones of the female body. Feminine drawers, early in the century sometimes extending below the hemline to display the lace trim, draw fire on moral grounds and their boundary retreats above the hemline.[320] Glimpses of garments known to cover sexual parts of the body can easily be eroticized. As Fields accurately observes, items like a woman's open-crotch drawers can and are simultaneously erotic and yet argued to advance modesty![321]

During this time the meaning attached to male crossdressing is undergoing revision. The medicalization of sex (see the answer to Q. 91) draws attention to male use of female items of clothing as sexual substitutes for arousal and relief, whether as simple fetishes or in crossdressing activity (cf. the answer to Q. 88). Increasingly male crossdressing, perceived as extremely rare, is also viewed as signifying mental disorder, better suited to medical treatment than incarceration. However, when press accounts present male crossdressing it is generally in connection to criminal activity rather than sexual behavior.

On the other hand, crossdressing for women proves more complicated for other reasons. More and more women object to the impracticality of fashions in a society where their daily lives dictate more comfortable—and safer—wear. They increasingly appropriate and adapt articles of clothing designated masculine, acquiring more frequent charges of crossdressing. For these women, the criminality is explicitly in the act of crossdressing—masquerading as men with the usurpation of privilege that implies—rather than using male guise to cover other criminal deeds. While some women continue to crossdress to pass as men, many are openly crossdressing while still presenting as women and calling for dress reform. The resulting chaos fascinates Americans, generates plenty of comment and controversy, and lays a foundation for the changes of the 20th century.

What was dress like in 20th century America?

Already beginning in the 19th century, but peaking in the early 20th century is a pronounced drive for the democratization of dress. Apparel becomes a great equalizer in a modern democracy; anyone can advantage himself or herself of manufacturing's ability to produce relatively inexpensively a wide array of clothing—including styles imitative of the upper class. Ready-to-wear clothing from the neighborhood department store makes "'equal' dress accessible to everybody."[322] During this same period, it becomes a social ideal to use fashion to express democratic values—a public obligation to show civic virtue.[323]

Men's fashion in the United States at the turn of the century differs from the trends toward greater formality found in Europe. Instead, American men in the Edwardian era (1901-1911) rely less on vests and begin favoring shirts with more color and pinstripes. Sack suit jackets and pants complete the ensemble. The landscape-altering First World War, the 'war to end all wars,' ushers in a distinctively modern world of fashion. Menswear grows simpler and more utilitarian. Already in the period between 1909-1918 men's undergarments, with sartorial symbols of social rank declining, become, as the Cunningtons put it, "more rational and therefore ceased to be interesting."[324] The 'College Man' look of the 1920s parallels the flapper fashion among women in accenting athletic youthfulness. The hard times of the Great Depression blunt much of the rebellious enthusiasm and fashion takes a more conservative turn. Perhaps in response to the androgynous look of the late 1920s, men's styles begin to reemphasize masculinity, for example, padding the shoulders on suits. The Second World War not only puts many men in uniform, it increases the desirability for leisure or casual wear when not in uniform. Even business suits become more relaxed, most notably through the disappearance of the vest, producing the increasingly common three piece suit: shirt, jacket, and pants. Outside work, denim blue jeans are steadily becoming more popular.

The second half of the century for men's fashion holds both continuity and change. The three-piece suit remains a staple of business wear. At the same time, leisurewear diversifies and proliferates. In the 1950s, when a discernible teenager culture emerges, young men are drawn to the sultry look of actor James Dean, though 'cool' can also drift toward the style of the beatniks. T-shirts and blue jeans are favored by youth. Beginning in the 1960s, men's fashion styles introduce more color. Still, clothing scholar Mary Lou Rosencranz, writing in the mid-1960s, remarks, "Although men's clothes have improved in the last two decades, they are neither as comfortable nor as aesthetically appealing as women's clothes."[325] Blue jeans—those great clothing equalizers of social class—become nearly ubiquitous. In the 1970s the innovation of bell-bottoms and designer jeans help younger men and women separate their style of jeans from older adults. Also in the 1970s blue denim work shirts emerge to complement jeans. The last decades of the century are replete with fashion experimentation, including designs that put men into skirts and dresses.

Women's fashion in 20th century America increasingly reflects the strength of the women's movement. The omnipresent corset reaches perhaps its most constrictive zenith at the century's start, then in the face of unrelenting protests is modified, ostensibly to address health concerns, in order to provide more support to the abdomen and spine. The 'New Woman' of the new century often aspires to the look of the 'Gibson girl.' Greater involvement in sporting activities, especially gymnastics and bicycling, further prompt fashion modifications as sportswear for ladies grows in popularity. As the century advances, vertical lines becomes more prominent and the corset begins to give way to the brassiere and other so-called 'light foundation' undergarments like latex girdles. In the period 1909-1918 women's underwear, in the words of the Cunningtons, obliterates an accent on the sexual female body; the new ideal is not Venus but Ganymede.[326]

World War I also paves the road for important ladies' fashion changes, such as the rise of woman's work clothes, which feminizes masculine apparel to create, for example, blouse counterparts to men's shirts. Already by 1923 author Helen Goodrich Buttrick remarks on the growing number of working-women as an important pressure on changes in clothing fashion.[327] The greater tacit acceptance of women in garb typically dubbed masculine can be glimpsed in the media, such as in the World War I recruitment posters for the Navy drawn by Howard Chandler Christy. These show a young woman in sailor's dress with the words, 'Gee! I wish I were a man. I'd join the Navy," or "I want you . . . for the Navy."[328]

The appropriation of masculinity in dress reaches a new peak in the flapper fashion of the last years of America's Roaring '20s. This thoroughly modern style achieves femininity through boyishness: short hair, broader (and bare) shoulders, a flat chest, and narrow hips. Indeed, as Diane Crane points out, the French term the flapper '*la garçonne*' (a feminized form of *garçon*, 'boy' or 'young man'), implying a female boy, though what she embodies are qualities drawn from two alternative visions of femininity expressed in the 19th century—docile helplessness and assertive athleticism.[329] The flapper dress style is short and shapeless, while most other styles continue to feature long hemlines, though these generally shorten as the century progresses, reaching their shortest length in the miniskirt of the 1960s.

Hard reality reasserts itself in fashion after the Stock Market collapse of 1929. Women's hemlines drop again and styles become more conservative, favoring fuller busts and more normal waistlines—a boon for corsetry.[330] The coming of World War II adjusts women's fashion to reflect the reality of more women in the workplace. Because of supply shortages one innovation continues an earlier logic—women's fashion appropriates men's fashion, this time literally as women's work suits are crafted out of existing men's suits, shoulder pads and all.[331] Women are also not merely permitted to wear pants but actively encouraged to do so. A commentator writing in 1940 remarks that a college woman not looking like an Ivy league male risks censure from her peers.[332]

The latter half of the century finds women now entrenched as an important part of the American work force. Wear for that purpose continues to feminize what has been viewed as essentially masculine garb. Outside of work women's wear relaxes into styles featuring a return to fuller, longer skirts. Young women of the 1950s are attracted to the playful style of the 'Bobby Soxers'—ponytail bound by a scarf, a collared blouse with poodle skirt, short socks and saddle shoes. The 1960s witnesses two seemingly contradictory trends in outwear, though both converge in the theme of freedom. On the one hand, women in pants (and jeans) finally gain near universal acceptance and use, while on the other hemlines rise to new heights with the miniskirt. From the 1970s until the end of the century there will be diversity in hemlines, with micro and miniskirts at one extreme, midi in the middle, and maxi skirts at the other extreme. Women's sportswear likewise diversifies, as does swimwear; the latter shows more skin than had been acceptable in the first half of the century. Punk fashion, with roots in the 1970s, attains near mainstream acceptance by the end of the 1990s.

As mentioned earlier (in answering Q. 9), perhaps along its simplest lines we can represent the gendered distinction in dress as the 20th century establishes itself in simple and stark terms: men wear bifurcated garments as outerwear and women do not. Women wear dresses and men do not. We might even say, with only modest exaggeration, that women wear color and men do not.[333] But a dramatic shift occurs over the course of the century, one that requires a re-sorting of gendered distinctions in clothing and essentially ends for most people the notion of female crossdressing. By century's end the battle, for the most part, has shifted from outerwear to underwear.

In some sense, as the 19th century might be fairly termed the century of pants, the 20th century could be called the century of *under*pants. And in that respect, women's fashions lead the way. Long-legged pants as undergarments had debuted under dresses in the early 19th century, but it wasn't uncommon for women in the 19th century to wear nothing at all beyond the chemise (a long shirt). Shorter pantaloons worn by women as an undergarment began to appear in the mid-1860s, and the advent of colored underwear in the latter half of the century was regarded as scandalous by many folk.[334] The modern panty, a much briefer garment, does not become part of everyday use until well into the 20th century (Sears began selling them in the mid-1930s). Nylon stockings premiere at the 1939 World's Fair, but modern pantyhose—undergarment and stockings in one garment—do not appear until 1959.[335] The modern brassiere is somewhat older, having been patented in 1913,[336] though innovations such as adjustable straps and cup sizes are not fully established until the 1930s.[337] With women more active in spheres of work and leisure the bra, as it came to be called, supplants the corset.

The accent on underwear rather than outerwear redefines crossdressing. Since by century's end women may wear any kind of outerwear with little risk of censure, and gendered distinctions in clothing have come to emphasize underwear, male crossdressing using feminine undergarments eventually surfaces as the center of attention. Since these undergarments are closest to the parts of the female anatomy associated with sexuality it is inescapable that male crossdressing using feminine underwear becomes viewed as sexually charged. Hence the idea of fetishistic crossdressing, at least superficially logical, catches on and is typically generalized to cover all male crossdressing (despite what many male crossdressers themselves say).[338]

Other complicating factors include the emergence of androgynous outerwear as a feasible dress alternative for both men and women, and the appropriation of feminine styles for men. In the latter regard, fashion designers persistently try to put men in skirts and dresses specifically designed for the male body,[339] though with limited success despite the apparent openness of many young women to the idea.[340] The whole notion of gendered clothing seems open to debate and the 'borrowings' of style back and forth across the gender divide make the whole question of what crossdressing is, and who is doing it, livelier than ever.

How might we sum up the relation of fashion and crossdressing?

Of course, all of these brief remarks must be couched in qualifiers—they indicate general trends not followed by all, they neglect important social class distinctions in wear at different times, overlook regional differences, and do not at all consider matters of personal taste, religious influence, and so forth. In a certain respect they do not even shed light on gender crossing, since in any period those so inclined find ways to appropriate dress to crossdress regardless of fashion styles. Yet when we examine fashion, even broadly, certain matters do stand forth more clearly.

First, every period of fashion passes into history and later observers offer their judgments about it through an historical lens. For example, at the beginning of the 20th century, fashion historian Elisabeth McClellan characterizes men's costume in 1830s America as "rather effeminate."[341] This, of course, is not a judgment that would be welcomed by the men of the early 19th century, who would certainly take strong exception. Again, from a late 20th century perch much of the male dress of the 17th-19th centuries looks womanish, featuring at different times long, flowing lines, long hair, wigs, and so forth. From the standpoint of an observer of an earlier era modern women would doubtless seem hard to differentiate from men in much of their daily wear—and bring anguished cries about female crossdressing. Simply put, judgments about gender crossing through crossdressing can only fully make sense in terms of contemporaneous appraisals. Comparing crossdressing across centuries can only be done by recognizing that each time period defines its own standards and measures.

Second, in every period the points of fashion most correlated with gendered distinction indicate the most likely points for crossdressing practice and controversy. For example, in an age like the 18th century where it is common for men to wear wigs, the mere wearing of a longhaired wig by a man offers no indication of crossdressing, whereas in the early 20th century the same practice likely occasions suspicion. Men in longhaired wigs in the early 20th century will be seen as emulating a woman's hairstyle. In broad terms, as seen above, the most salient gendered distinction in dress moves from outerwear (prior to the 20th century) to underwear.

However, third, by and large the focal point for gendered distinction in dress centers at bifurcated apparel, whether outerwear or underwear. Men wear bifurcated garments; women do not. But this simple, stark standard comes under constant challenge—and erosion. Shifting perceptions, accompanied by material alterations to keep items designed for a similar purpose looking different, preserve the gendered distinction in dress. For example, Fields in discussing feminine drawers notes the material ways in which they vary from men's drawers (e.g., lace trim; open crotch), but also draws attention to the perceptual accommodation that takes place: "women could be allowed to wear a divided garment if feminized and sexualized, and that feminization of the garment reassured that 'real' trousers were worn by 'real' men."[342]

Fourth, fashion changes—and so crossdressing practices must shift if they are to be reckoned as such. Women in pants at the end of the 20th century raise few if any eyebrows; at the start of the century the practice still arouses criticism as crossdressing. Once pants become gender neutral, crossdressing cannot occur. Yet because gendered distinctions in pants styles evolve, crossdressing can still happen by adopting the style of pants associated with a gender different than that assigned the wearer at birth. Hence crossdressing depends on fashion for its very existence.

Finally, noting fashion trends helps clarify the ease with which a person might or might not successfully pass as a member of another gender. For instance, in the 17th century, when both men and women wear their hair long and vertical lines are accented, women have an easier time passing than would have been the case if radically different fashions existed. Consider, for example, the dilemma of the modern male crossdresser, living in an age when feminine fashions tend toward revealing the female body; to pass the male crossdresser must emulate anatomical differences the styles are designed to highlight. In a period where modesty dictates the sexed body be indistinct a man can with greater ease pose as a woman.

Of course, that last remark points out a problem: we must avoid assuming all crossdressing is to present as a member of a different gender. Our contemporary understanding, alongside the many different examples afforded by history, suggests the necessity of a more nuanced view. Not all crossdressing intends masquerade. Not all crossdressing represents a compelling personal experience and expression of a different gender. Once more we are compelled to consider motivations, in all their variety.

Why did crossdressing occur?

Fashion provides avenues to explore in dress, but *gendered* fashion means any crossing of the gender line will produce gendered interpretations. In other words, regardless of motivation, one cannot crossdress and realistically expect to avoid interpretations by others that a gender crossing has happened and that this crossing *means* something. Obviously, one cannot crossdress without clothes and, as we have seen elsewhere (question set 1), clothes are situated at the center of a complex experiencing and expressive system. One fundamental feature of this system is its appropriation of gender both as part of experience and an aspect of expression. Whenever crossdressing occurs this system, including its use of gender, is engaged. No matter the conscious motivation of the crossdresser, both that individual and those around the person, utilize this system. For a number of reasons this system is fundamental to transgender realities.

Such realities, including crossdressing, prove to be a feature of the American landscape long before the first European explorers reach the shores of this country. The experience in this regard of Native Americans is discussed elsewhere in this work (see the answer to Q. 59), but we may mention at least that it also is seen with reference to something meaningful vis-à-vis gender. But here our focus remains on the immigrants who come to form 'the United States.' Among them crossdressing is a behavior practiced by some since the establishment of the colonies. As in Europe, from which the early colonizers come, the expression of what today we call transgender realities takes various forms, some temporary and situational, others more enduring and across situations. Both biological males and females are involved. And their reasons, though never divorced entirely from gender, are not uniform and can make gender experience and expression intentionally secondary in importance.

As proves true in other cultures, the reasons for crossdressing are many. Among the more prominent reasons are the following:

❑ *Access to otherwise excluded opportunities*—it is often suggested that most crossdressing women in U.S. history are motivated by the desire to improve their lot in society. Since many doors are closed to them, especially in terms of work, some disguise themselves as men to undertake jobs they want (or need). But the same motivation might apply at times to men who seek a feminine vocation.

- *Crime (and counter-crime)*—some crossdressers, both male and female, use masquerading as a different gender in order to conduct criminal activities—and some law enforcement officers crossdress to catch criminals.
- *Festive celebrations*—public male crossdressing in some parts of the country is an accepted aspect of parades and merrymaking at holidays such as Thanksgiving for more than a century (see the answer to Q. 71).
- *Gender experience and expression*—the 20th century makes clear that a substantial percentage of crossdressing is directly related to the experiencing and expressing of an individual sense of gender. There is little reason to doubt some such crossdressing exists in previous centuries.
- *Patriotic fervor*—in America's wars women serve and distinguish themselves. While most of us readily conjure images of women nursing the wounded, a good number of women undertake military service in the guise of men. On the other hand, some men crossdress to avoid military service, or to pursue military work as a spy, or to evade capture, or to escape harm.
- *Pursuit of love*—some women and men crossdress in order to openly conduct relationships with members of the same sex. Since there has never been a stigma against heterosexual unions, posing as a heterosexual couple with one partner masquerading as 'the opposite sex' affords a way to have a public relationship without censure—though not without risk of exposure, with consequential censure and scandal.
- *Social commentary and reform*—some crossdressing is very public and does not intend to disguise the conflict between the presented gender of the dress and the assigned gender of the wearer. Whether women publicly pushing for dress reform and other liberating social changes, or gay men using drag as social commentary, this manner of crossdressing plays a role in educating and effecting cultural movement on gender issues.
- *Survival*—some men and women crossdress because they are in desperate circumstances and the maneuver offers them a chance for escape, whether from prison or some other unhappy circumstance.

As we browse the history of crossdressing in the United States we encounter illustrative cases for each of these reasons. The stories selected below represent both unique experiences of individuals and one or another of the reasons listed above. But before we come to individual stories we would do well to have a wider view.

Many scholars who study American history in relation to issues of gender and gender crossing follow the lead of Marjorie Garber in viewing crossdressing as a sign of crisis in the culture.[343] In this perspective, rather than precipitating crisis in a society, transgender realities such as crossdressing are a reflection and response to cultural anxieties. Or, as Kathleen DeGrave puts it, "The crossing of category boundaries was not a conscious effort to create change in the society; rather, it indicates that change was already occurring."[344] That gender anxiety has been strong in mainstream American culture DeGrave finds reflected in the success of literature like the novels and autobiographies that feature crossdressing protagonists. Women have been at the heart of this phenomena.

In United States history, up until the latter half of the 20th century, there are many more examples of crossdressing women than of crossdressing men. One possible explanation for this is that there actually have been more crossdressing women. The hierarchical nature of the gender order is rigid and women often have been excluded from many spheres of activity. There may have been more incentive for women to crossdress, and many of the motives would have entailed this activity in public. Another possible explanation is that society for a long time was more interested in female than male crossdressing and because there may have been a greater likelihood of its public conductance there were far more occasions of exposure. Crossdressing by men may have been as common, or even more common, but less public. If so, less notice would be generated and fewer notable cases preserved. In addition, it is highly plausible to imagine in a male-dominated social world an aversion to any feminine behavior by males, leading to an aversion to seeing it and a suppression of publicizing it—forces not engaged with reference to women.

In sum, it is impossible to ignore the forces of social anxiety and cultural values around gender and dress. But we would be remiss if we neglected the contributions brought by individuals. It seems too narrow a context to place all crossdressing as a response to social anxieties, especially over gender. Without denying this force we must remain alert to the personal creativity and expression that takes places in any age regardless of what its crises are. Transgender is more than a response to culture; it is also an abiding force in itself, able both to form the individual's adaptation to her or his environment and reciprocally shape that environment. The creative impulse in gender crossing can effect change with or without the impetus of social pressure—the internal pressure in an individual ought not to be underestimated.

Who were some noted early American crossdressers?

Transgender realities are known through crossdressing since colonial days. Both men and women crossdress. Though they do not use our modern vocabulary to speak about homosexuality, transsexualism, or transgender something like those modern descriptions almost certainly existed in earlier times and may be glimpsed in preserved accounts. However, we must be cautious in any inferences because of a lack of evidence, the recognition of different perceptions at play, and the real possibility that the nature of cross-gender realities actually changes across historical periods.

The 18th century sometimes has been characterized as the 'Age of Disguise,' a period marked by fascination with masks and masquerades of various kinds, including crossdressing. Dianne Dugaw claims that, "for people in the eighteenth century, masquerade served not simply as a means of reversing roles or suspending authority for a day, but rather as an end in itself, as an experiment with identity."[345] Ute Kauer, concurring, argues that "cross-dressing, be it literal or in the form of narrative cross-dressing, is not a means to become the other but rather an exploration of the possibilities of gendered identity."[346]

Jemima Wilkinson (1752-1819)

On the other hand, the case of Jemima Wilkinson reflects a distinctive identity in which crossdressing engages the explicit end of serving her self-representation of having *no* gender. Raised as a Quaker in Rhode Island, Jemima moves to Connecticut after the death of her mother. At age 24, in October, 1776, an event happens that shapes the remaining course of her life; she falls ill, lapsing into a comatose state and seeming dead. Indeed, in her own eyes she has died and been returned to life, now living as a Second Redeemer. Asking her followers to refer to her simply as 'the Friend,' she disavows gender and chooses a life of celibacy.[347]

Whatever her intent in how she dresses, she is widely perceived as garbed in masculine clothes. A witness in 1787 describes her as wearing in public a light cloth cloak with a cape like a man's, a man's shirt with a handkerchief or cloth tied round her neck in masculine fashion, her hair short and worn like a man's with a man's hat on top. At the same time, observes Catherine Brekus, "she ridiculed men by implying that their power lay in the trappings of dress rather than in their natural superiority."[348] Her appearance, manner and message all make her controversial—and exciting. She is invited to speak in many churches, often attracts considerable crowds, and by 1790 has made more than 250 converts with whom she establishes the colony of Jerusalem in northwestern New York State.

Jemima Wilkinson may have crossdressed to refute notions of gender, but most who crossdress are espousing gender, though one at variance at variance from what they were assigned at birth. Such seems the case in what is arguably the most renowned case of crossdressing in early America.

Deborah Samson (1760-1827)[349]

On May 20, 1782, a young woman named Deborah Samson (often spelled 'Sampson') disguises herself as a man and enrolls in the Fourth Massachusetts Regiment of the Continental Army under the name 'Robert Shurtleff.' Her life journey leading her to take such an action in her 21st year is instructive. Born of distinguished lineage, a descendant of Captain Miles Standish and Plymouth colony governor William Bradford, her own immediate family is large and poor. Bereft of a father by age 5, when he goes off to sea, her mother is forced to desperate measures, placing the children with various relatives and neighbors. Deborah herself at age 8 is placed in indentured servitude, one small step from abject slavery, in which she remains a decade.

Deborah grows up hearing tales of her family's history, including experiences of war. When only 4, the young girl enquires of a relative, a ship's Captain, if she might be his cabin boy—an idea met with laughter because of her gender. (Interestingly, this same relative had himself crossdressed in connection with war; as a captive in the French and Indian Wars he had disguised himself as a woman to make his escape.) Her hard childhood profits Deborah with enough knowledge and skills to become employed as a teacher, despite her lack of formal education, after she gains release from her servitude in 1779. Among those skills is facility with a musket, something learned from hunting alongside the ten boys of the family she has served. In the winter of 1780 she learns that two of these boys, whom she has grown up alongside, have died fighting for the colonials.

Deborah at the time is residing with a couple whose son, Samuel, already has enlisted for the war. At 5 feet 7 inches, she is tall for a woman and able to take some of Samuel's clothes to wear as her own. Binding her breasts tightly, she tests her disguise with a trip to a local tavern. That proving successful she proceeds to enlist, though her left-handed and peculiar manner of holding the quill as she signs the Articles of Enlistment almost give her away as a bystander remarks on the similarity to the manner of one Deborah Samson! The name 'Robert' that she chooses is that of her deceased brother.

Her masquerade does not go completely unsuspected. The Baptist church she has joined excommunicates her on the rumor and suspicion of her activities. Her comrades-in-arms remark on her clean-shaven face—but if any suspect her sex, none pursue the matter. She participates in several battles, being wounded both by sword and bullet. Despite these wounds, her secret is kept until she falls ill with a fever that requires her hospitalization. Remarkably, the doctor who finds her out keeps her secret; he removes her to his home and cares for her there. Only after she is well is the matter conveyed to her commanding officer.

Deborah is then sent with a letter to General Washington, who acts upon its disclosure of the facts about her with a letter of discharge, funds, and some friendly advice. In October of 1783 she is honorably discharged from the army. In 1785 she marries and eventually bears three children. In 1792, by court order, she is awarded a pension for her military service, a decision applauded by the Massachusetts' legislature, which notes her heroism alongside her chaste virtue. In 1797 her exploits are told in a sensationalist account by Herman Mann entitled *The Female Review; or, Memoirs of an American Lady*. In 1804, following an appeal on her behalf from Paul Revere, she also begins receiving a pension from the federal government. Upon her death in 1827, her children are given aid by a special act of Congress.

Although Deborah had disguised herself as a man to serve her country, her crossdressing does not entirely cease after her military career ends. She reportedly is in male dress when she leaves her mother (who disapproves of what she has done), and goes to the farm of a relative, who mistakes her for one of Deborah's brothers. It is after meeting her future husband that she abandons her guise. In 1802, she undertakes a tour during which she dons her uniform while delivering talks about her military experience. More than a century after her death, in 1983 a grateful State proclaims her an "Official Heroine of the State of Massachusetts." In 1985, a commemorative medal is issued to honor her.[350]

Anne Bonny (c. 1700-??) [351]

Another famous—or rather, infamous—example of female crossdressing associated with 18th century America is Anne Bonny. Born Anne Cormac, perhaps about 1697 in Ireland, or perhaps in 1710 in the South Carolina port of Charleston, she is the illegitimate daughter of a wealthy plantation owner and lawyer, William Cormac. Not surprisingly, perhaps, various accounts say that to avoid scandal from his affair Anne is dressed and passed off by her father as a son of a friend apprenticed to himself. Whether born in Ireland or America, it is in Charleston she is raised and at some point all pretence of her being a son is dropped. Even as a child the red-haired Anne is known for a fiery temper and boyish boisterousness. Reputedly before she has reached adulthood she already has killed a person, her English maid.

She takes up the mannish art of fencing and becomes skilled at it. Her temper continues to rage unabated. She beats a suitor with a chair and when her father disowns her for eloping with James Bonny, she responds by setting his plantation on fire. Settling in the port town of New Providence, in the Bahamas, she draws attention when she pulls a pistol and shoots off the ear of a drunken sailor who gets in her way.

Anne leaves her husband and attaches herself to a pirate captain named Jennings and his mistress Meg. This arrangement gives way to her dalliance as mistress of the island's richest man, Chidley Bayard. Eventually, though, she attaches herself to the pirate Captain John Rackham, popularly known as 'Calico Jack' for the style of trousers he favors. This relationship produces a child who soon mysteriously disappears from the scene. Both with Rackham and with others Anne is involved in various acts of piracy in the Caribbean.

A blockade of the New Providence harbor by the British Navy is met with typical defiance. Calico Jack and Anne break through the blockade, Anne bearing a sword, attired as an Amazon, wearing black velvet trousers and naked from the waist up. As they pass the British she brazenly waves a long silk scarf. Once free, the pirates continue operations, Anne establishing herself as second-in-command.

After a special pardon is obtained on her behalf, Anne returns to New Providence. Now she meets the figure with whom history has forever linked her: Mary Read, an English woman raised as a boy, the replacement of her dead brother Mark. Previously having served in the British army, where she met a man she married and for a time assumed life as a woman, by the time she reaches New Providence Mary is once again 'Mark' Read. She has been a sailor on a Dutch ship, but quickly switches to a pirate's life when English pirates capture the ship.

Anne and Mary/Mark strike up a friendship. Spurning her pardon after a sordid adventure in which her husband James had shown up to reclaim her, Anne returns to piracy, her new companion with her. Their relationship is an intimate one and sparks the jealousy of Calico Jack, who has been unaware of 'Mark' Read's sex. Once this truth becomes known, all pretence is dropped and Mary uses her birth name. Both Anne and Mary freely cross gender lines in dress and behavior alike.

Eventually preying on other ships rather indiscriminately, they draw the concerted ire of the British Navy. This makes their fate inevitable. Captured, they are tried in Jamaica and duly condemned in 1720 to hang. Upon this verdict, both women plead to be spared on the grounds they are pregnant; successful, their death sentences are commuted. (Whether either is, in fact, pregnant, is never established and remains a mystery.) Calico Jack and the other male pirates are not so fortunate. Though spared hanging, Mary Read shortly succumbs to a fever contracted while imprisoned. As for Anne, her final fate remains unknown.

Crossdressing Men in Early America

Less attention attracts itself to crossdressing men in early America. That there are such men is indisputable, but much less is known about male crossdressing in this period. Ironically, the most famous man of the period reputed to crossdress—Edward Hyde, Viscount Cornbury—most likely does not.[352] The scant evidence that he does consists of five letters written by his political opponents[353] and a single portrait of a crossdressed man, alleged to be Cornbury. The latter is probably not him at all[354]—but may offer indirect evidence of the practice. In fact, the very reason the charge of crossdressing brought by his enemies against Lord Cornbury, Royal Governor of New York and New Jersey (1702-1708), and first cousin to the Queen, could possess any force is that the practice, though regarded with disfavor, exists.[355] The censure it elicits is incentive to keep it private.

Interestingly, the rumors that circulate about Lord Cornbury add a rather novel twist on an ancient explanation for crossdressing. Patricia Bonomi recounts a story told in 1796, some 63 years after Cornbury's death:

> He was a clever man. His great insanity was dressing himself as a woman. Lord Orford [Walpole] says that when Governor in America he opened the Assembly dressed in that fash-

ion. When some of those about him remonstrated, his reply was, 'You are very stupid not to see the propriety in it. In this place and particularly on this occasion I represent a woman (Queen Anne) and ought in all respects to represent her as faithfully as I can.'[356]

The symbolic representation of a higher figure of a different sex and gender is a common aspect of ancient religious crossdressing (see the answer to Q. 76), and not unknown in connection with politics (cf. the Confucian practice discussed in the answer to Q. 82). But it is unexpected in 18th century America as an explanation, regardless of whether Lord Cornbury crossdressed or not.[357]

Bonomi's discussion of the political climate is relevant for it highlights the role gender and sexuality play. She notes that satire, gossip and scandal provide ready fuel for political attacks. Few prominent men or controversial groups (e.g., the Quakers) escape sensationalistic charges, and these often present alleged gender violations or sexual irregularities.[358] The social climate does not suffer lightly the juxtaposition of male privilege with female apparel. Yet Bonomi also presents evidence of cases where men in 17th century New York, and early 18th century Philadelphia, are arrested for appearing in public in women's clothes.[359] And a high official in early America is caught crossdressing, though his motive is escape from imprisonment rather than any public expression of being a woman.[360] In sum, the accusation of crossdressing can have teeth because real cases are known.

What was crossdressing like in early American stories?

Crossdressing Ballads

Reflecting the interest of the age, crossdressing is an aspect of story, both in song and in prose. Scores of ballads feature it. Since these are explored more fully elsewhere (see the answer to Q. 46), only a couple broad remarks and short examples need be made here. Most of these ballads involve romance, and center around women, like the 1780s ballad, "Rose the Red and White Lilly." But the stories can move beyond mere heart-stricken lasses desperate to stand by their man. For example, "Mary Ambree" (1765) tells the story of a woman who masquerades as a man in order to join the regiment her lover is in. But when he is killed, she remains in service, becomes an officer, and distinguishes herself by her bravery and leadership. There also are some ballads that feature men, and some ballads explore areas outside strictly conventional heterosexual love. Ballads prove extremely popular, both in the United States and in Europe.[361]

Crossdressing in Early American Literature

The exploration of gender is a lively interest in literature as well. In the 18th century, fiction employs what Ute Kauer terms 'narrative cross-dressing,' where the author adopts a narrator's voice in a different gender (e.g., author Samuel Richardson using the character Pamela as narrator in the novel *Pamela*). Kauer finds in this literary technique a manner to deconstruct society's rigid gender bipolarity and show gendered identity as something constructed rather than essential. Because narrative gender crossing occurs in the context of a gender order within society, the goals and effects are different for men and women writers. For the former, the narrative voice of a woman can "give voice to a suppressed discourse"; for a woman author the narrative voice of a man can be a way to "share the dominant discourse to authorize the text."[362]

The female crossdresser in particular is a subject of interest in works of fiction—and, ostensibly, nonfiction. In regard to the latter kind of work, Deborah Sampson, who fought in the Revolutionary War (and whose story is recounted earlier in this answer) inspires the 'biography' of Herman Mann entitled *The Female Review: Life of Deborah Sampson* (1797), which in the telling of the story becomes much more fiction than historical narrative.[363] But the most remarkable crossdressing character of the period belongs to fiction.

Martinette de Beauvais, in Charles Brockden Brown's Gothic novel *Ormond* (1799), is receiving new attention in our own day as we seek to understand how our forebears wrestled with sex and gender. This bold woman revels in masculine dress and action, proclaiming, "I delighted to assume the male dress, to acquire skill at the sword, and dexterity in every boisterous exercise. The timidity that commonly attends women, gradually vanished. I felt as if embued by a soul that was a stranger to the sexual distinction."[364] She recounts with relish her participation in the French Revolution, including her fighting among the men, assuring her astounded American listener that many other women have done likewise:

> Hundreds of my sex have done the same. Some were impelled by the enthusiasm of love, and some by a mere passion for war; some by the contagion of example; and some, with whom I myself must be ranked, by a generous devotion to liberty. Brunswick and Saxe Coburg, had to contend with whole regiments of women: Regiments they would have formed, if they had been collected into separate bodies.[365]

Here, in a nutshell, are encompassed many of the motivations for masquerade enumerated above. The singularly distinctive Martinette de Beauvais, associated with the most important revolution of the times, is herself a revolutionary figure in the ongoing consideration of sex and gender in post-revolutionary America.

What was crossdressing like in 19th century American stories?

The history of the 19th century for the United States is divided by the singularly important Civil War (1861-1865). The Antebellum period, though ostensibly a time of peace, is subjected to enormous social pressures as the still young nation both expands westward and struggles with its identity and values. After the War attention turns to rebuilding the nation even as wide interest in the Western frontier grows. Although the immediate causes of social tension and pressure change, the underlying quest for an American identity continues. An important aspect of that quest is an ongoing cultural musing over gender. In this context, transgendered realities like crossdressing flourish despite official censure.

Ballads

Ballads remain popular in the 19th century—and continue to feature crossdressing. Many of these weave well-known themes continuous of earlier types. For example, "Pretty Polly" (early 19th century) follows the familiar themes of love and travel as Polly disguises herself as a lad to follow her beloved captain to sea. Others reflect historical trends and events. In terms of the former, the ballad "Devilish Mary" (late 19th century) reveals the anxieties being felt over a perceived encroachment by women on masculine privilege. In the song a hapless young man meets a pretty girl, marries her, and she begins to take over his life, even to the point of wearing his pants. He leaves her vowing henceforth to only court girls whose height makes it impossible for them to don his breeches! With regard to specific historical events there is the ballad "Jeff in Petticoats" (1865), which depicts the Confederate President's desperate attempt to evade capture by putting on women's clothes. The Union soldiers who capture him taunt him, saying, "Oh! Jeffy D. You 'flow'r of chivalree. . . . Your empire's but a tinclad skirt. . . ."

Literature

Literature, too, remains rich with stories where things like crossdressing are important aspects. The transgender realities of lived experience are the fodder both for autobiographical accounts and imaginative ones. The former are drawn upon later in this answer in looking at the lives of some crossdressers well-known in their own time. The latter, which we consider here, find life of their own in novels throughout the century. A few notable examples across this span reveal the versatile—as well as dramatic—uses to which crossdressing can be put in a narrative framework.

The Female Marine (1815-1818)

Early in the century the War of 1812 reveals both the bitter political divisions in the United States and the very open question of what role the country will play in the world. Many ordinary Americans are asking similar questions about their own lives as they decide where they stand on social issues and look anxiously at the world around them. The climate is favorable for literature that explores the anxieties of the age. One very successful venture is the trilogy *The Female Marine*, which appears in installments between 1815-1818 and within these four years undergoes some 19 editions.

The tales center in the figure of narrator Lucy Brewer, a young woman originally from rural Massachusetts outside of Boston. In the first book, the *Narrative of Lucy Brewer*, 16-year-old Lucy falls for a faithless young man who leaves her pregnant and alone. Going to Boston to await her child's birth, the luckless Lucy fails to find employment in the better part of the city and unwittingly wanders into the seamier side of town. There she finds shelter in a brothel. After her baby daughter dies shortly following birth, Lucy is coerced into the 'sisterhood' of prostitutes.

For three years Lucy labors to satisfy her debt to the brothel's madam. In 1812, after hearing other women talk about the freedoms possible through masquerading as a man, Lucy resolves to do just that. Donning a sailor's uniform she makes her escape. Discovering her disguise is completely effective Lucy decides to become a marine. She serves three years aboard a frigate, fighting in the War of 1812, before concluding she is ready to resume her life as a woman.

The second tale, *Continuation of the Narrative of Lucy Brewer*, reprises her earlier adventures then adds new ones. Bored with the narrow life of a domestic woman, Lucy decides to reenter a man's world. This time, though, the stakes are higher: she puts on the garb of an officer. In this dress she revisits Boston, going to the very brothel in which she had served three years. The madam does not recognize her. Having, in a sense, come full circle Lucy returns home.

The final story, *An Awful Beacon*, follows Lucy in her life as a woman alongside her mother, devoted to proper feminine domestic duties. She has given up masculine dress and the world that goes with it. Indeed, her hard-won womanly virtue is now rewarded. She is offered two proposals of marriage, accepting one, and becoming Mrs. Lucy West, a respectable but conventional woman.

Historian Daniel Cohen, who collects and represents these tales alongside two related pieces, views their account of crossdressing in the light of the times. Lucy's story reveals some of the anxieties felt in the period, including the specter of unmarried women at the edge of a man's world, and the natural anxieties of a society recovering from war and still finding itself. Though the novels are ostensibly moralizing tales, Cohen observes that unlike contemporaneous novels whose heroines experience a penitential death, Lucy Brewster enjoys her freedom and subverts her own moralizing by her account. In so doing, her story keeps open possibilities to be explored with regard to gender.[366]

She Would Be a Heroine (1916)

As has been the case in the 17th-18th centuries, both male and female authors use crossdressing characters in 19th century literature. Besides Lucy Brewer, another crossdressing woman in a novel early in the century is Lady Georgina Portmore of Sophia Griffith's *She Would Be a Heroine*, a satire on Gothic fiction.[367] But later characters will offer more dramatic insight.

Hope Leslie (1827)

One of the most memorable is the tragic figure of Rosa in the novel *Hope Leslie* (1827), by Catharine Sedgewick. Rosa masquerades as Roslin, male page to Sir Philip Gardiner, her former lover. Rosa has followed Gardiner to America in the vain hope of regaining his love and with a passionate jealousy that leads to disaster. Inevitably, her disguise is penetrated. Perhaps just as inevitably her desperate passion results in the double murder of Hope Leslie and Sir Philip, and her own suicide as she flings a lamp into an open barrel of gunpowder aboard a small boat.[368] Crossdressing in this instance does not provide the woman new liberty but constitutes a prison broken free from by violence. It provides a startling contrast to a different narrative strand in the novel in which the Indian woman Magawisca successfully crossdresses to literally gain freedom from imprisonment.[369]

Clotel (1853)

Crossdressing characters might be male or female—or both in the same novel. Such was the case in William Wells Brown's *Clotel; or, The President's Daughter* (1853). Brown's novel—the first credited to a Black American—features two crossdressing females (Clotel, Mary) and a crossdressing man (George). Clotel, a fair-skinned Black slave, masquerades as a White man and accompanied by a Black male slave escapes to freedom. This narrative strand echoes the historical events recounted by Ellen Craft (see below). Clotel's daughter, Mary, also crossdresses—simultaneously with George, a Black man in jail awaiting hanging. After the two exchange clothes George, holding a handkerchief to his face, is able to escape.[370] This episode echoes the earlier narrative in Hope Leslie involving Magawisca.

Mark Twain's Writings

Mark Twain, that quintessential American writer, plays with gender conventions and challenges through a number of characters, especially female ones.[371] Some crossdress.[372] For example, in his incomplete short story "A Medieval Romance," a duke's daughter is raised as a son named Conrad as part of the duke's cunning plot to usurp the royal lineage from his brother. This idea of subterfuge for inheritance rights is hardly new to Twain—such a motivation is found in numerous historical incidents and tales. And like such earlier stories this one has the unfortunate crossdresser named as the man who has impregnated another woman, in this case Constance, Conrad's cousin.[373]

Twain's character Nancy Jackson in "How Nancy Jackson Married Kate Wilson" masquerades as a man named Robert Finlay. Her resort to life as a man is not, however, purely voluntary. She has got herself in a mess connected with a murder that makes the masquerade advisable. But Nancy's deception is so successful she finds herself caught in another bind. Kate Wilson, daughter to the man who has hired 'Robert Finlay,' has become pregnant by a man now long gone. Failing to woo 'Robert,' Kate accuses him to her father and a 'shotgun wedding' commences.

But Twain's employment of crossdressing female characters does not mean male characters are not also utilized to explore and comment upon gender matters. In the story "Wapping Alice," for example, the title character is a crossdressed male. Far more famous, though, is the protagonist of his most celebrated novel. In *Huckleberry Finn* (1885), arguably the greatest American novel, crossdressing occurs in a variety of contexts. First, Huck deduces from a recovered drowned body that the victim was not a man, but a crossdressed female. Perhaps inspired by the notion of such deception, Huck later presents himself as a girl named Sarah Williams—a subterfuge he carries forth so clumsily he is soon caught out.[374]

Twain uses crossdressing again in *Pudd'nhead Wilson* (1894), where he draws upon his day's common association of crossdressing with criminal activity. There Tom, the son of a Black slave woman named Roxana (Roxy) crossdresses to cover the thieving he pursues to cover his gambling debts and, later, after committing murder. What makes this case especially intriguing is that Tom has transgressed not only gender lines but those of race and class as well, since his mother has taken advantage of his light color skin to successfully switch him as an infant with her master's White son, who is subsequently raised as a slave.[375]

Of course, transgender manifestations don't require public crossdressing. Twain's "1,002nd Arabian Night" (1883) story posits two infants, one male and one female, whose gender status is reversed. The pair is thus raised and the results are comedic. Darker is Twain's tale, "The $30,000 Bequest" (1904). This time, a married couple exhibits cross-gender traits, a situation underscored by their names: Saladin 'Sally' Foster and his wife Electra 'Aleck' Foster. The husband exhibits qualities more stereotypically assumed for a wife, while the wife demonstrates an interest in and acumen for finance equal to any man.

In an unfinished piece, "Hellfire Hotchkiss" (1897), Twain's characters Rachel 'Hellfire' Hotchkiss and Oscar 'Thug' Carpenter challenge gender stereotypes, too, and to an even stronger degree. Without masquerading as the opposite sex, each presents a mismatch of sex and gender pronounced enough that the summary judgment can be made of them, "Hellfire Hotchkiss is the only genuwyne male man in this town and Thug Carpenter's the only genuwyne female girl, if you leave out sex and just consider the business facts."[376] Hotchkiss, a biological female, distinguishes herself in masculine traits; Thug, a biological male, exhibits so many feminine traits his father disgustedly remarks he ought to put on petticoats. The two cross paths most dramatically when Hotchkiss saves Thug from drowning. But their society defeats them with its unyielding, stereotyped expectations. The adult Hotchkiss comes to the realization, "Thug Carpenter is out of his sphere, I am out of mine. Neither of us can arrive at any success in life, we shall always be hampered and fretted and kept back by our misplaced sexes, and in the end defeated by them, whereas if we could change we should stand as good a chance as any of the young people in the town."[377]

Themes

One thing most of these examples from 19th century literature have in common is their association of crossdressing with figures already in some manner at the margins of their social world. Lucy, in *The Female Marine* trilogy, has been victimized by a lover; crossdressing constitutes a kind of salvation. Deliverance comes in a different, but just as powerful form for characters like Clotel (*Clotel*), who escapes slavery, and George (*Clotel*) and Magawisca (*Hope Leslie*), who escape sentences of death. All three of these characters are marginalized by virtue of race; Clotel and George are Black, Magawisca an Indian. Though Huck Finn's masquerade is of a different nature, he himself is also a figure on the margins of the social world he lives in. Finally, Tom (*Pudd'nhead Wilson*) and Rosa (*Hope Leslie*) are figures marginalized by their own actions—gambling for money by Tom and gambling for love by Rosa. Their desperate acts include crossdressing and marginalize them both.

Pantaletta: A Romance of Sheheland (1872)

A unique specimen of fiction—unique for its extended reliance on what crossdressing allegedly signifies—is the 1872 novel *Pantaletta: A Romance of Sheheland*.[378] Written by an author known only as Mrs. J. Wood (possibly a pseudonym), the tale chronicles the adventures of the narrator, General Icarus Byron Gullible. A wealthy American, he has piloted his flying machine 'The American Eagle' in a quest to explore the Arctic, only to land in the nation of Petticotia. To Gullible's dismay, the gender roles his culture embraces are reversed in Petticotia. Here women (shehes), dressed in masculine garb and sporting false beards, are in charge and regard themselves as the superior sex. The men (heshes), clean-shaven, are described as follows:

> Boys under sixteen years of age were quite at ease in dresses, having during their short lives known no other kind of garment. The adults wore hip and breast pads to a man, in obedience to the nefarious dress laws. Their hair was worn in knots or curls all natural deficiencies being supplied by the hair-dressers. Continual shaving, and hair eradicators, kept all beards at bay. Rings adorned the fingers of the new fair sex, and chains, charms, beads and other ornaments, glistened about their throats. Fans and dainty handkerchiefs fluttered in the breeze. Every gentleman—if I may apply so foreign a word—was unhappy unless his dress was made in the height of fashion.[379]

Toward these heshes Gullible feels a mixture of amusement and disgust. But he is no less unhappy with the shehes. He expresses his sentiment to one of the heshes:

> "I regard as fallen all those who, although born to represent a sturdy manhood in male attire, are found in women's dress, imitating every conceivable folly of the weaker sex and

> losing every grace peculiar to their own. As a man I deplore the misfortune which has befallen you, and I cannot but hope for the speedy emancipation of both man and woman from the degradation into which they have fallen."[380]

Gullible, with an indelible masculine appearance, is promptly arrested, tried, and condemned by the austere shehes of the Dress Reform Court. The charges leveled by Gullible's nemesis, the radical Captain Pantaletta, are explicit:

> "We have received from our most zealous Captain Pantaletta the following formal charges against you: 'Firstly, the prisoner is a Heshe, unlawfully clothed in Shehe apparel; secondly, he has not only usurped the Shehe character, but upheld the obsolete distinctions of man and woman; thirdly, being a Heshe, he wears a beard in defiance of the law; fourthly, he has addressed the Shehes of company D as 'gentlemen;' fifty, he has blasphemed all the Shehes of Petticotia by alluding contemptuously to the sex; sixthly and lastly, he has loaded his speeches with so many clumsy terms, that there rests upon him the suspicion of being a sorcerer from the demon-world, or a spy from some war-bent nation.' These are capital offenses, punishable with death."[381]

Gullible is contemptuous of the court's authority and so swiftly condemned. Nevertheless, he is spared execution, and becomes the romantic object of Petticotia's President, who visits him in disguise—dressed as a proper, beautifully attired lady! While begging him to make some concession to the dress law, she apologizes to Gullible for the rigidity of the judges, explaining:

> "The hateful old heads of the Dress Reform Court are worrying me, day after day, for news of your compliance with the law. They are all confirmed heshehaters. Few of their class have ever been married, and those who were so fortunate have been, with few exceptions, childless or unhappy in their family relations. Thus their milk of human kindness is somewhat soured and they are relentless where heshes and the law are concerned."[382]

Eventually, in order to win a limited degree of freedom, Gullible consents to wear feminine apparel, except he is granted the exemption of retaining his moustache.

Wood's novel is not the only one in which crossdressing is pressed into service for social commentary. Other novelists of the 19th century use crossdressing characters to provide observations about gender and dress. Wood's work, though, stands against most use of crossdressing in other literature, which employ it to oppose prevailing social conventions. In *Pantaletta*, General Gullible—Wood's voice—is an indefatigable champion of American values with regard to gender and costume. Darby Lewes, who has made this novel available to a new generation and has studied it closely, remarks that Wood "has little compassion for any gender that persists in behaving in a perverse, unnatural fashion. Instead, she exploits the comic possibilities of transvestism: her men are grotesque parodies of women, and her women hideous travesties of men . . . ."[383] Lewes sums up Wood's presentation succinctly: "Skirts are a synecdoche for femaleness; trousers represent everything masculine."[384]

Ironically, Wood employs literary crossdressing to mount her attack on crossdressing. Speaking through the masculine male General Gullible—a figure whose wealth, status, and power all exemplify the apex of manliness—Wood's offers a spirited antifeminist battle cry. The last half of the 19th century proves to be one in which the Women's Movement sometimes arms itself with masculine dress to advance feminist causes; Wood represents both men and women who oppose the proposed changes. For Wood, the gender role expectations of her time, including those about dress, are proper, comfortable, and natural.

Crossdressing in Literature for Youth

Finally, an interesting aspect of the literature of the 19th century regarding crossdressing is its appearance in material aimed at youth. In the first half of the century, Eliza Leslie, a popular children's author, brings the subject of crossdressing into a pair of stories, one aimed at girls, the other at boys. In "Lucy Nelson," the protagonist is a tomboy disciplined by her parents through enforced wearing of boy's clothes in order to shame her into gender-conforming behavior. Rather differently, in "Billy Bedlow" the title character is presented as a willing crossdresser. Billy has let his hair grow long so that it lays in ringlets upon his shoulders, and sleeps each night with it in curlers. For attending a party he selects for himself a bonnet, two corsets taken from a sister's bureau (because he covets a waspish waist), blue frock coat and parasol. Yet despite how others might regard them, for Billy they express himself as an attractive boy; he is not attempting to pass as a girl. At the party, when his wearing of the corsets is discovered (because he has laced them too tightly to easily breathe), Billy becomes the object of amusement for the girls and some menace by the boy who is his host. Only after Billy changes from his feminine garb into masculine clothing does he fit back into the group.[385]

Autobiographical and Biographical Accounts

While fictional crossdressers were common enough in 19th century literature, we should note as well the rise in biographical and autobiographical accounts of crossdressing. A good number of these are autobiographies of women who fought in the Civil War.[386] Menie Muriel Dowie offers biographies of a variety of 'women adventurers' who aren't afraid to be unconventional in dress.[387] And fiction could closely echo historical movements as in Lillie Devereux Blake's *Fettered for Life* (1874), a novel whose crossdressing woman in her guise as 'Frank Heywood' gives voice to women and proclaims the cause of suffrage.[388]

Who were some noted 19th century female crossdressers?

Crossdressing Masks and Masquerades

Fiction mirrors life—but usually more dramatically. Especially in the first half or more of the 19th century women often do not crossdress in a manner that makes their assigned gender obvious. Rather than making a statement designed to influence public policy like the women's movement seeks, most of these crossdressing women pursue the more modest goal of improving their individual lot in life. They might do that by completely subsuming themselves in the masculine gender, like Josephine Monaghan, of Bostonian origin, who moves west and lives as a man known as 'Little Joe' until dying in Idaho in 1903. Others only 'borrow' masculinity for a calculated use and time, like Anna Starcy, a middle-aged woman in Michigan. Dressed as a man, not giving her name, she purchases 14 acres of land in the late 1860s, which over the next year and a half she converts into a farm, complete with house, fence, and fields ready for plowing. Her house built, she puts off her old clothes, resumes feminine apparel, and reveals her name to one and all.[389]

Ellen Croft

Some of those who borrow another gender also find it advantageous to borrow another race. Gender crossing is sometimes accompanied by race crossing, in entertainment (see below; cf. the answer to Q. 44), and in the desperate circumstances of life, such as escaping slavery. Perhaps the most celebrated of such instances is the case of Ellen Croft, a Black slave woman who takes advantage of the light color of her skin to pose as a White man. Her motive is to secure freedom for herself and her husband, a fellow slave. Both are born slaves in Georgia, though in different towns. Ellen is the child of a slave mother and her White owner. Her Whiteness proves unbearable to her master's wife, especially as others frequently see the child as a member of the family. So, at age 11, she is given to a daughter as a wedding present.

When she meets and is courted by William Croft, Ellen expresses misgivings both about marriage and becoming a mother, given her own experience and the reality that slave families can so easily and capriciously be separated. William does not press the issue of marriage, but instead joins with her in planning an escape. When escape at last seems impossible to them, they marry. But in December of 1848, a plan presents itself to William's mind. "Knowing that slaveholders have the privilege of taking their slaves to any part of the country they think proper, it occurred to me that, as my wife was nearly white, I might get her to disguise herself as an invalid gentleman, and assume to be my master, while I could attend as his slave, and that in this manner we might effect our escape."[390]

Though initially reluctant, Ellen finally agrees. William begins buying the articles of clothing she will need, save trousers, which Ellen herself makes. They each manage to secure passes from their respective masters for a brief release from their duties as a holiday after Christmas. They are ready to go. With Ellen posing as a young White plantation owner accompanied by a slave, the two travel openly. But because neither can read nor write, some artifice has to be made to explain her not signing her name wherever they might lodge. So Ellen makes a poultice and binds her right hand in a sling, demonstrating she cannot sign for herself. Anyone asking is given a name and graciously signs for her. She similarly disguises her face partially, to hide the absence of a beard. Just prior to leaving at morning's light, William cuts her hair short and she dresses as a man, though not eagerly, as her husband later recounts:

> My wife had no ambition whatever to assume this disguise, and would not have done so had it been possible to have obtained our liberty by more simple means; but we knew it was not customary in the South for ladies to travel with male servants; and therefore, notwithstanding my wife's fair complexion, it would have been a very difficult task for her to have come off as a free white lady, with me as her slave; in fact, her not being able to write would have made this quite impossible. We knew that no public conveyance would take us, or any other slave, as a passenger, without our master's consent. This consent could never be obtained to pass into a free State. My wife's being muffled in the poultices, &c., furnished a plausible excuse for avoiding general conversation, of which most Yankee travellers are passionately fond.[391]

They journey first by train, he in a slave car, she traveling alone among the White passengers, one of whom has known her for years. Feigning a degree of deafness she is mostly left to herself. So they proceed, moving to Savannah, then Charleston in South Carolina. From this port they take a steamer to Wilmington, North Carolina. Once more they board a train, passing to Richmond, Virginia and on northwards until they reach Philadelphia, then onward to Boston. Throughout the journey there are moments when they might be discovered, but Ellen succeeds in passing as a young White gentleman.

Once in Philadelphia, Ellen resumes her normal dress. They settle in Boston, but not for long. Fearing application of the Fugitive Slave Law of 1850, they flee to England. There they receive an education. Later they return to the States, now free, and establish a school for black children in Georgia. Their story is recounted in a book penned by William and published in England in 1860.[392] As in other instances, this crossdressing is notable for crossing lines of both gender *and* race.

Women as Soldiers

Best known and most celebrated of crossdressing women, however, are the masquerades by some as soldiers during the great conflict that tore the country apart early in its second half. Women disguised as men fight on both sides.[393] Nor are such women always White. An account from 1898 notes the passage of a special bill granting a pension to 'Aunt Lucy' Nickols, an escaped slave who fights with the 23rd Indiana Volunteers during the Civil War. Her husband had joined the regiment and been killed in battle; she takes up his rifle and marches in his stead. Even near the age of 70, she continues to march in uniform in local parades.[394]

Sarah Rosetta Wakeman (1843-1864)

Another such woman who dons the uniform of her nation, and is later celebrated for it, is Sarah Rosetta Wakeman. She takes the course set by others of her assigned sex and gender by crossing over from woman to man, at least in guise, and not merely to fight in the war. Though her journey into war seems more accidental than the determined course set by Deborah Samson in the Revolutionary War, Sarah's service is no less honorable and the price she pays is her life. Her letters, preserved and eventually published, afford us a look into her mind and life.

Sarah is born in New York State on January 16, 1843, the oldest of nine children. She grows up with the realization that her opportunities as a woman are limited. Most marry; those who work have fewer possibilities than men and for less pay. In August, 1862, after weighing her options, she disguises herself as a man and goes looking for work in the nearby city of Binghamton. While working on a river coal barge, Sarah encounters some soldiers from the 153rd Regiment of New York Volunteers, who encourage her to join the service. The sizable bonus promised enlistees persuades her to take the soldiers' advice.

On August 30th, 1862, lying about both her age (claiming she was 21 when she was actually 19) and sex, she enrolls as 'Lyons Wakeman.' Her description at enlistment indicates her height as five feet tall, with blue eyes and brown hair. In October the regiment is placed in Alexandria, Virginia as part of the defensive perimeter for Washington, D.C. They are stationed there for nine months before being moved to participate in actions under Major General Nathaniel Banks. This move leads to Sarah's initial taste of battle on April 9th, 1864, in Louisiana.

Unfortunately, during this brief campaign Sarah contracts chronic diarrhea. This condition severely dehydrates her. Sarah is placed in the regimental hospital on May 3rd, later being transferred to a hospital in New Orleans. But she does not recover. She dies on June 19th, 1864.

Sarah Wakeman's initial motivation in crossdressing seems principally economic in nature, and this may have been her chief reason for joining the Union Army. Yet her letters indicate that she adapts to military life, takes pride in many aspects of her accomplishment, and though she may feel ambivalence over many things in her life, her choices consistently express such deep felt American values as the desire to better one's lot in life, loyalty, patriotism and courage. [395]

Mary Edwards Walker (1832-1919)

Perhaps the most celebrated of the crossdressing women in the Civil War is one who does not masquerade as a man to fight on the front lines. In fact, she does not masquerade as a man at all; crossdressing is a calculated mask worn to convey a message without that message disguising her sex or gender. Mary Edwards Walker wins enduring fame as the only woman to win the Congressional Medal of Honor.

She is favored by birth with a place in the socially progressive family of a physician in Oswego, New York. Her father supports the abolitionists and other reform movements, including dress reform for women. He makes sure his five daughters receive an education the equal of that made available to boys. Mary follows in his steps, both in becoming a doctor and in espousing social causes, notably women's rights and dress reform.

She graduates from Syracuse Medical College in 1855 and the following year marries a fellow physician, Albert Miller. In addition to retaining her maiden name, Mary also dresses in a masculine fashion, preferring trousers and a man's coat to blouse and skirt. The masculine mask proves of little avail in securing perceptions of her medical competence; the joint practice she and her husband establish proves unsuccessful. With the outbreak of Civil War in 1861, Mary leaves New York and travels to the capital seeking enlistment as a medical officer in the Union Army. When this is denied her, she successfully gains entry as a volunteer assistant surgeon.

For nearly two years she serves near the front lines, being present at such major battles as Fredericksburg on the Eastern Front and in Chattanooga, after Chickamauga, on the Western Front. Her activities, which may also include spying, bring her back and forth across enemy lines. In 1864 she is captured by the Confederates and imprisoned at Richmond, Virginia. After some four months she is made part of a prisoner exchange. Following this, she spends the remainder of the war engaged in other services in Kentucky and Tennessee.

On November 11, 1865 she is awarded the Medal of Honor. By then her marriage is nearly at its end; after 13 years they divorce. Her post-war life is occupied with writing and lecturing. She tours both in the United States and abroad, promoting women's rights. Elected President of the National Dress Reform Association in 1866, she persistently dresses in masculine fashion, contending that feminine apparel is not only inconvenient, but immodest too. Her conspicuous crossdressing—appearing openly in attire that includes not only pants, but bow tie and top hat—garners her several arrests. Her persistence in using crossdressing as a mask rather than a masquerade confronts society with the capricious judgments made along gender lines and invites a rethinking of gender itself.

In 1917, near the end of her long life, Congress amends the standards for awarding the Medal of Honor and strips her of the medal. But Mary refuses to return it, instead wearing it publicly and proudly—and risking arrest since doing so is a crime—until her death in 1919 at age 87. Congress posthumously reinstates the award nearly 60 years later, in 1977. [396]

Mary Anderson/Murray Hall

Although evidence suggests the majority of women who masquerade as men do so only for a short time and a particular purpose, there are some who choose to remain in this gender identity for substantial periods of time. Among the more notable instances of this sort is the case of Mary Anderson, better known as Murray H. Hall. A prominent local politician, member of the General Committee of Tammany Hall, that infamous political machine in New York City, Mary successfully passes as a man for more than a quarter century. In her guise as 'Murray,' she is a highly visible figure about town, drinking whiskey and playing poker with the boys, recruiting voters, and regularly voting in an age when women are denied that right. Sporting a "peppery" temperament and boldness that once leads to being arrested after assaulting a policeman, Mary manages despite all to keep her biological sex hidden. This is true even though she is twice married, to women who guard her secret zealously. She has an adopted daughter who remains unaware of the secret until after Mary's death in 1901 when the truth of her sex is finally disclosed. A colleague describes 'Murray' as "somewhat effeminate in appearance" and with a feminine-pitched voice, but masculine in action. Another remarks that 'he' dresses and talks like a man, though with an eccentric taste for oversized coats—a choice whose strategy was clear in retrospect. Yet another comments, "If he was a woman he ought to have been born a man, for he lived and looked like one."[397]

Today, of course, such a person would be described as transgender or transsexual. In every respect Mary lives completely as the man Murray. That Mary's situation is not unique is easily believed and, indeed, we find similar cases even well into the 20th century (see the story of Billy Tipton in the answer to Q. 48). Though Mary's motive might be guessed as desiring to live openly with another woman in a lesbian relationship, the facts suggest differently. Rather than living quietly so as not to draw attention, Mary as 'Murray' is well-known and undertakes the characteristic masculine activities of her environment, including politics and poker, drinking and smoking, flirting and fighting. The reaction of friends and colleagues to the revelation of Mary's sex is not one of disgust nor revulsion; 'Murray' earned a man's respect and they continued even after exposure to think of this 'woman' as a 'man.'

Women as Criminals

Not all women earn such respect. Though less common than for men (see below), but certainly not unheard of, there are crossdressed female criminals. Even here, though, a noble cause might be served. It is worth remembering that some slave women crossdress (and even cross races) in their bids for freedom—a combination of acts considered illegal by many. Of course, as previously noted, simply being crossdressed is a violation of ordinances and many women are so charged. Penalties are generally mild, but not always. For example, a newspaper account in 1882 offers up the instance of Jennie Westbrook, arrested for impersonating a man because she wore men's clothing. She is committed for six months to the penitentiary, though her case is appealed and reviewed by a Supreme Court justice who is skeptical that any woman would be committed merely for wearing men's clothes.[398]

In another incident, from 1856, a woman is charged with crossdressing, having married another woman, and other offenses. The woman, about age 40, is said to be "perfect" in her imposture. Under the name of 'Alfred Guelph,' she meets a young woman and becomes married a few weeks later. The bride's father, suspecting something amiss, confronts 'Alfred' and wrests a confession. After a "partial examination," he arrests her. Interestingly enough, the first appearance to the bride's family had been as a woman! With the family's knowledge this dress had been changed to that of a man, the family perhaps supposing the former clothing having been a disguise (though from what is not disclosed). Despite all this, and having lived for some three weeks as husband and wife, the bride "still clings to her woman husband," and argues that the arrest is merely a conspiracy to keep them apart.[399]

Cases like these reveal how complex crossdressing 'crimes' can be. The crossdressing in the first instance is said by the woman's attorney to have been the result of gaining better employment than she could as a woman. In the latter case the motive of the crossdressing appears to have been genuine love—and love reciprocated at that. There is no need to multiply instances; more such cases exist than ever brought to trial.

But at least in some instances the female crossdressing is accompanied by criminal activity such as thieving. For example, a report in *The New York Times* tells the case of one Lizzie Leonard (aka. Lizzie Miller), who under the name of 'Albert Leonhardt,' dressed in fashionable men's clothes including trousers and overcoat, has been charged with theft from a jewelry store. When asked by the jail superintendent why she has so dressed, the young woman bursts into tears and recounts how her lover has deserted her. Soon destitute, she has resorted to such dress in the hope of earning a living. Yet her stories contradict each other and the *Times* reporter observes her manner displays long practice in appearing as a man.[400]

Occasionally a case emerges that baffles everyone. In 1874 *The New York Times* carries a story borrowed from *The Chicago Times* of an individual who can only be called an imposter—but so accomplished at it that no one can be sure if the person is a man or a woman. Appearing in public in masculine dress at times, feminine at other times, the person uses the names 'Christian Lund' of Denmark, 'Alexander Lunti,' 'Don J. D. Le L'Until' of Spain, 'Mrs. Isabella Rothe,' 'Mrs. Isabella Ruper,' and 'Countess Knuth' of Denmark. This person tries on a number of occupations—including newspaper reporter—but evidently possesses only one real skill: lying.[401]

Examples of the various kinds of masquerades described above are abundant and hardly exhaust the motives for crossdressing. In the following material we shall examine specific contexts such as entertainment, the Western frontier, politics, and crime where crossdressing also draws notice. While the 19th century seems most fascinated—perhaps troubled—by crossdressing women, we should not suppose crossdressing men are unknown. They deserve special attention because, as we shall see, the situation of male crossdressing receives a different regard than that done by women.

How did crossdressing figure in 19th century entertainment?

Fiction is not the only form of entertainment where crossdressing is featured. Crossdressing on the American stage continues a long tradition in Western culture (see the answer to Q. 44). Both men and women engage in theatrical crossdressing. Interestingly, crossdressing on stage is also sometimes joined with race-crossing. Prior to the Civil War minstrel shows might feature White men masquerading as Black men or women.[402] After the Civil War, as attention returns to the Western frontier, some Whites present themselves in shows as Indian men or women. Some crossdressing also transpires in carnival settings and parades. Photographs from the 1890s show male crossdressing in just such a connection.[403]

Was there crossdressing on the Western frontier?

Westward expansion opens up new possibilities for Americans beyond expanded opportunities for entertaining. Among these are new ways to explore, experience and express gender. Sometimes, though, as in the mock weddings of the northern plains (Dakotas), the crossdressing serves to temporarily relax and reverse rigid gender roles.[404] Crossdressing on the western frontier sometimes involves more than crossing gender lines. Photographic records show both men and women posing as Indians, and some show White men in the guise of Native American women.[405] But it isn't just men who are crossdressing.

Elsa Jane Guerin/ 'Mountain Charley' (1837-??)

Women in the West also can find crossdressing advantageous.[406] Many use it to manage a single life where passing as a man means better pay and more personal security. For most of these women the posing proves temporary; for some, though, it becomes a permanent way of life. Few of these women ever draw attention, for that is not their aim. But some capitalize on their adventures by publishing accounts of their exploits as members of a different gender. One such enterprising person is Elsa Jane Guerin, a woman who explores many aspects of a man's world. Born in 1837, Elsa Jane marries a river pilot when only 12. By age 16 she is a widow. She metamorphoses into 'Mountain Charley,' and in this guise holds a number of masculine jobs, working on steamboats and trains, prospecting for gold, and perhaps even serving in the military. She chronicles her travels and adventures of 13 years in male guise in an autobiography published in 1861.[407]

Ray/Rae Leonard (1849-1921)

Others who draw attention almost invariably have it happen because their secret is found out despite their efforts to keep it hidden. An example perhaps representative of this situation is the case of Rae Leonard, better known as Ray Leonard. Rae, born in Maine in 1849, goes west with her father. They finally settle in Lebanon, Oregon in 1889. Already she is practiced as passing as a man and accounts agree that her appearance and manner are quite masculine. Her father needs Rae's help in his shoemaker trade and encourages the deception, knowing the opportunities for a man far exceed those for a woman. For decades this masquerade proves successful, with 'Ray' a respected member of the community. But the secret of Ray's birth sex is discovered when, at age 70, illness lands her in the hospital. The discovery leads to her commitment to a mental hospital, with discharge contingent on dressing as a woman and henceforth being known as 'Miss Rae.' The people of Lebanon, stunned and upset, marginalize her upon her return, though with time Rae again wins a measure of acceptance. In time she proves something of a local celebrity and at her death in 1921 she is much mourned.[408]

Jeanne Bonnet

Some crossdressing women are less noble. Jeanne Bonnet, sometimes called 'the Little Frog-Catcher' in reference to her short career catching them in the marshes of San Mateo County, is one of San Francisco's most colorful characters of the 1870s. Known for her crossdressing, Jeanne in 1876 organizes a dozen prostitutes from several brothels into a gang that specializes in shoplifting and other forms of theft. But her career in crime is cut short. Just age 25, she is shot dead, allegedly by pimps of some of the girls she has recruited.[409] Her case perhaps offers evidence of a female-to-male transsexual identity as Jeanne is said to have frequented the brothels as a male customer and to have a female companion, Blanche Buneau, who had been devoted to her.[410]

Josephine Ward

Unfortunately, sometimes the advantage in crossdressing is born of desperation. An 1874 account, for example, recounts the trials and tribulations of 17-year-old Josephine Ward of San Jose, California. Much to her father's dismay, in June of the previous year she eloped with a man, who proved to be a convicted criminal on the lam. Her anxious father at once begins a search that leads him to Chicago and back again. After some months, quite by chance, he hears of a young woman discovered near Salinas City dressed in men's clothes. Following this lead, father and daughter are soon reunited. She tells of her travels and travails, detailing how her husband would drink and then mistreat her. She had become pregnant, but lost the baby just three days after birth. Finally, being spooked by some approaching strangers, her husband deserted her. Josephine cut her hair, donned some of his clothes, and hired out as a shepherd. This job proved beyond her, but still masquerading as a man she had worked what jobs she could, making her way at last to the area where her secret was found out and she was reunited with her father.[411]

Crossdressing in Western Fiction

Popular literature of the West—the famous 'dime novels'—also feature crossdressing women. Literature and gender scholar Tania Modleski believes these characters can be seen as continuing the tradition of women crossdressers established in the ballads of the previous two centuries (see the answer to Q. 46). Like the ballad, the dime novel "spoke to the experience of westering American women whose rugged lives necessitated their violation of feminine norms."[412] Modleski follows Henry Nash Smith in seeing these figures as the extension of gradual transformation of female characters, one in which crossdressing allows women to be more active—like men. In the dime novels the most famous and enduring woman crossdresser is Calamity Jane of the Deadwood Dick series by Edward L. Wheeler.[413]

What role did crossdressing play in the 19th century women's movement?

In the latter half of the 19th century dress reform is on the minds of many, with proposals vigorously debated in the context of the competing theories about the origin and purpose of dress. Some women urge dress reform on men.[414] Some men join women in advocating changes in women's dress. But it is women taking upon themselves new styles of dress and attaching it to a larger platform that garners the most attention. The nascent women's movement utilizes open crossdressing as both social commentary and a practical plea for cultural dress reform. Caroline Field Levander writes of these early activists:

> Arguing that their traditional dress codes amplified the physical differences that supposedly made women "naturally" unsuitable for political responsibility, suffrage proponents suggested that women adopt male attire in order to free themselves from their social and political "fetters." Drawing on the numerous autobiographical accounts of women who crossdressed in order to serve as soldiers in the Civil War and the increasingly common accounts in newspapers after 1850 of "the deaths of men who turned out to be women," equal-rights proponents claimed that female transvestism, because it disguised the physical differences that made women subservient to unscrupulous men, ensured not only women's political equality but their sexual purity as well.[415]

Similarly, literary scholar Susan Gubar argues that in modernist literature and painting done by women, the figure of the female crossdresser is a "heroine of misrule." Unlike crossdressing men—widely viewed in the age as clowns at best, psychopathic criminals at worst—the crossdressing woman is someone engaged in a noble effort to prove herself the equal of the men around her. In this manner crossdressing for women can, and sometimes does, reflect a costume of freedom.[416] In her actions she is proving the rule Flugel set out in his interpretation of dress reform in which it becomes "a welcome symbolic expression of revolt."[417] Crossdressing, then, is a rebellious declaration of independence.

Interest in dress reform becomes attached to early feminism at the century's midpoint. In 1850-1851, a 'new costume' comprised of a Turkish tunic and trousers generates considerable comment, as well as enthusiastic support from women like Elizabeth Cady Stanton and Amelia Bloomer.[418] The latter's name soon becomes associated with the garb.[419] 'Bloomers,' writes Nancy Isenberg, "challenged the symbolic language of dress that identified men with active, aggressive, independent behavior, and it thwarted the desire to see women as soft, weak, frivolous, and stationary."[420] In turn, notes Isenberg, accusations of crossdressing and homosexuality become in the 1850s common rhetorical devices to criticize public women.[421] It matters little that most of the women themselves dispute charges of crossdressing.[422]

The 'Bloomer Costume' proves highly controversial, generating what Fields characterizes as an enormous amount of debate, ridicule and fear. Women wearing them are not just crossdressing, claim opponents, they are taking a stance against masculinity and femininity, throwing gendered distinctions out the window, and presenting themselves shamelessly immodest and erotic.[423] The increased use of the bicycle by women makes some form of bifurcated garment desirable and the resulting garment adopted is commonly referred to as 'bloomers.'[424] *The New York Times* recounts in an 1897 column two instances of the kind of hysteria men can conjure up in the face of such dress: a dentist in California is sued after refusing to pull a woman's tooth because she is dressed in bloomers, and even more dramatically, an Alabama man tries to hang himself because his wife has taken to wearing bloomers.[425]

As the above notices indicate, women across the country are involved. In California, Eliza Ann Hurd DeWolf appears in the streets of San Francisco in 1866 dressed in masculine garb. She is making a public statement with regard to the city's anti-crossdressing ordinance—a law aimed mostly at women though it forbids the practice by either men or women. DeWolf's activism is a reflection of her commitment to women's rights and her protest contributes to the ordinance being struck down by a state superior court judge.[426]

Bemused men grudgingly yield to the new trends, though not without reluctance. At times this resistance takes the form of satire as in a *New York Times* column in 1885 entitled "A Secret Revealed." The author begins by musing on how odd it is dress reformers, "who for the last few centuries" have pursued bifurcated garments for women's lower garments, have not succeeded in their quest. Yet, ignoring the upper raiment, it has steadily become like men's. Beginning with the collar, and working steadily downward, women's clothes are now like men's above the waist. So why have not women adopted bifurcated garments below the waist? Ah, the secret stands revealed: she has not done so because men have been "persistently demanding it." As proof, says the author, look no further than the corset, which men battle against and so women cling to tenaciously. Likewise her footwear; men's resistance to high heels only made them more desirable to women; once he gave up, she changed to the comfortable shoes she desired. "The lesson is easy," concluded the essayist. Once dress reformers fall silent on the subject of bifurcation, then shall such apparel become commonplace.[427]

How were crossdressing men depicted in 19th century America?

Although the focus of public attention remains on women who crossdress, there are men who do so as well. While this is generally brought to the eye of the public individual case by individual case, even groups of men might be so engaged for one or another reason. We already mentioned the mock weddings found in some northern states. In 1871 *The New York Times*, in a bemused manner, relates the case of men living in Mount Pleasant, Ohio. The brief article begins by noting the "humorous prophecies" that envision men and women "changing places, doing each other's work and wearing each other's clothes." The latter circumstance, the article observes, has for some time been partly realized by women wearing bloomers. But now the men of Mount Pleasant—"that progressive place"—have taken to wearing skirts to work in the fields, citing their comfort, and appealing to scripture and health reasons alike to justify their action. After some musings on whether Mount Pleasant might replace Paris as the "throne of fashion," the piece concludes by declaring that the "new theory of masculine dress" really is only a return to the "first principles of civilized humanity, which universally begins life in skirts, without regard to sex."[428]

Crossdressing and Crime

In the 19th century it is a crime to be crossdressed. But it is also common to associate crossdressing with criminal acts, especially where a man is involved. Probably the most famous such incident is reported at the end of the Civil War when Confederate President Jefferson Davis is captured. At the time, *Harper's Weekly* observes, "The captors report that he hastily put on one of his wife's dresses and started for the woods, closely followed by our men, who at first thought him a woman, but seeing his boots while he was running, they suspected his sex at once."[429] That this proves an enduring source of irritation and shame for Davis is seen in a newspaper story from 1880 that recounts how he has a crayon portrait done of himself, purportedly representing how he was dressed when captured and aiming to disprove any idea of crossdressing disguise. Yet the newspaper account editorializes that Davis' sensitiveness on the matter is "abnormal" inasmuch as many heroes of history did likewise with no dishonor attaching to their action.[430]

Newspapers often carry lurid accounts of dastardly deeds done by a crossdressed perpetrator. For example, *The New York Times* reports in its June 21, 1878 edition that two men, one dressed as a woman, have injured a dentist one night. The one dressed as a woman lured the dentist outside to the criminals' buggy. When the dentist peered inside he was splashed in the face with a 'bottle of vitrol,' which resulted in loss of sight in one eye.[431] In another account, from 1873, convicted and imprisoned murderer William J. Sharkey escapes with the aid of two female accomplices, Maggie Jourdan and Sarah Allen. Sharkey shaves his moustache and, as recalled later by witnesses, departs disguised in a full suit of black silk, a panier (used to swell out an outfit at the hips), with shawl, bonnet and silk veil.[432] Of course, not all such stories are as lurid; one account is of John Dermody, who in a drunken stupor agrees to crossdress and secretly enter a woman's race. Women's clothes are accordingly purchased and altered to approximate a woman's 'gaiter,' the apparel of female 'pedestriennes.' He is found out soon after the start of the race and to the jeers of the crowd is arrested.[433]

Accounts like those above are kin in spirit to many found in Richard von Krafft-Ebing's *Psychopathia Sexualis*, a pioneering work in sexology in Europe that persistently links crossdressing with insanity and criminal behavior.[434] Though Krafft-Ebing's work does not appear until 1886, it does not spring from nothing. His conclusions reflect the thinking of the time. His numerous examples are drawn from criminal records. What is circulating in Europe is also being felt in America and the ordinary American reading the newspaper can have reason for anxiety when the only accounts of male crossdressers are associated with crime.

Ironically, on at least one occasion crossdressing is used by law enforcement officers and proves instrumental in catching a crook who himself uses a masquerade for his crimes. At the turn of the century, *The New York Times* carries a piece on the apprehension of one Albert, alias 'Barry' Geldheizer. This man has been opportunistically accosting young couples while posing as a policeman. He confronts his victims, flashes a badge, tells them they are violating a curfew ordinance being out so late, and extorts money or jewelry as a bribe to let them go. When the police get wind of this, four officers proceed to the neighborhood where Geldheizer is plying his con. Two detectives are dressed as women. Posing as two couples, each officer and his companion go for a stroll. When Geldheizer tries his ploy on one of them he is promptly arrested.[435]

What distinguished crossdressing in the 20th century?

The early 20th century continues to be characterized by more attention to female crossdressing than to male. Most of the relatively few clinical cases in psychiatric annals for female crossdressers date from the opening decades.

However, in increasing numbers women are challenging dress norms left over from the previous century. Anti-crossdressing ordinances generate arrests here and there, but many women prove ingenious in finding ways around them. Julie Wheelwright comments that by the 1950s crossdressing women avoid prosecution by wearing the minimum number of feminine items required by law.[436] Anti-crossdressing ordinances are increasingly often struck down by the courts and by the end of the century virtually disappear.

Easily the most remarkable feature of public attention to crossdressing in the 20th century is the shift away from preoccupation with female crossdressing to virtually exclusive attention to male crossdressing. A number of factors contribute to this development. Most prominent among them is the success of the women's movement. Women both encourage dress reform and profit from it. By appropriating styles of dress typically gender-specified for men (e.g., pants and underpants), then modifying them slightly so as to retain some measure of gender distinction, and adopting them widely, women achieve the triumph of dismissing charges of crossdressing. First, crossdressing hardly seems a pertinent charge with so many women doing it, and second, the modest modifications to clothes to make them feminine placates all but the most diehard critics.

As this is occurring other forces are also at work. The psychoanalytic community, and psychiatry at large, moves public perception of male crossdressers away from the notion of masquerading criminals to one of homosexuals and a few mentally disturbed heterosexuals with a sexual fetish. As gay drag becomes more visible through expanding media, and transsexualism begins to garner attention, the spectacle of biological males appearing as women becomes popular fodder for comedy, criticism, and controversy. Most of the general public assumes male crossdressers are gay. Those that protest to the contrary are often dismissed as denying their 'latent' homosexuality or shifted to the category of heterosexual sexual perverts. In either event, the safety of 'normal' heterosexual men is thereby preserved.

When mental health professionals finally remove homosexuality from the list of mental disorders in the 1970s, an inevitable shift happens with regard to crossdressing. Since women are no longer seen as crossdressing, and homosexuals doing so are okay, the only 'crossdressers' left to judge are either transsexuals—pronounced as suffering from 'gender dysphoria'—or the aforementioned heterosexual sexual perverts who are typically described as narcissistic, sexually immature, and fetishistic. Mental health professionals might begrudgingly have to acknowledge they are heterosexual—but certainly *not* like 'normal' healthy Americans![437]

Despite what is going on in mental health circles, transgendered people in the United States are steadily becoming more visible. Activists like Virginia Prince help organize support groups where crossdressers can gather together. Sex reassignment surgery, despite its expense, becomes an increasingly popular treatment. Transgendered people, and their supporters, appeal publicly for more and better understanding, plus changes in the laws to end discrimination in health, employment and health care, among other things. More and more evidence from research studies challenges conventional views and raises doubt about crossdressing's association with mental disorder. Alongside the perennial comedic treatments of crossdressing in the media appears serious dramatic and documentary treatments. Even in educational and religious circles more serious consideration begins to occur, with a slow increase in tolerance accompanying increased understanding.[438]

What was crossdressing like in 20th century stories?

Crossdressing characters remain a feature of the literary landscape in the 20th century. As in previous centuries both male and female authors use such characters. At the century's start, crossdressing continues to be found in popular fiction. As the century progresses it shows up in a variety of works both short and long. With the expansion of pornographic works, a whole subgenre featuring crossdressing develops, further fueling notions of its connection to sexual perversion, especially bondage (cf. the answer to Q. 89). Crossdressed characters both mirror and challenge society's perceptions of sex and gender—just as their real life counterparts are doing. The shifting presentation of crossdressers in the literature of the century mirrors contemporary views of what we would term transgendered people, but also offers insight into views of gender and society at large.

Crossdressing Stories in Popular College Fiction

The generally liberalizing force of education, and especially higher education, has long been recognized. One aspect of this has been a greater egalitarianism between men and women. Another has been a championing of diversity and tolerance of differences. But some among us want those who are different kept separate and believe especially that gender differences should not be minimized but rather accented. These conflicting notions find expressions in various ways, including on college campuses and through fiction aimed at a collegiate audience.

Gender scholar Sherrie Inness observes that at the turn of the last century there are voices raised on this same matter, with particular concern expressed that schools are blurring the gender lines. Indeed, one aspect of this phenomenon is crossdressing by both college men and women. Perhaps it is the spirit of the times. The last years of the 19th century and early ones of the 20th are marked by changes caught in the label, 'the Progressive Era.' The period is also styled by some as the age of the 'New Woman,' whose appearance and manner are seen by many as worryingly masculine. Inness remarks that college women often dress in masculine-styles for reasons either of comfort or fashion.[439]

Inness points out that already in the 1890s, there is a crossdressing tradition among the women's colleges of the Northeast. In this respect, they are following a lead established by male students. Inness reports male crossdressing in the Ivy league schools dates back to the early 18th century, when in 1712 a Harvard undergraduate is reprimanded for the practice—and rules are deemed necessary by 1734 to curtail the practice. As is true into the early decades of the 20th century, latitude is offered to young women (and young men) because they are in college; after graduation they are expected to conform more to society's prevailing gender conventions. Even while in school, dress rules govern when, how, and for what purpose crossdressing is sanctioned. Such rules are conveyed and reinforced in various ways, including through the popular college fiction of the day.[440]

Among the examples Inness produces are stories aimed at college women, like "In the Matter of Room-mates," in which a young woman named Molly, described as a 'girl like a boy,' proves the epithet through behavior like only wearing ties made for men. Other accounts extol female crossdressing for the theater, like the story "At Commencement," or the novels *Betty Wales, Freshman*; *Betty Wales, Sophomore*; *Jean Cabot at Ashton*; and *Brenda's Cousin at Radcliffe*. Stories aimed at college men preserve a sense of masculine privilege: men excel women even at crossdressing! Their success is trumpeted in the short stories "The Hazing of Valliant," and "A Violent Remedy," as well as in novels like *College Days*, or *Harry's Career at Yale*. In Inness' view, such stories for young men seek to reassure them of their masculine identity, strengthen their bonds with one another, and otherwise reinforce the gender hierarchy.[441]

The troubled century that ensues, marked by two world wars and turmoil at home over both gender and race relations, can scarcely escape the employment of such a potent mechanism as crossdressing in serious literary fiction. A few select examples from across the span of the century indicates ways in which crossdressing is used to reflect and comment upon what is happening in society.

The Well of Loneliness (1928)

A semiautobiographical novel by Radclyffe Hall in the first third of the century, *The Well of Loneliness* continues the tradition of female crossdressers in fiction. But the figure of Stephen Gordon—a crossdressing lesbian—reflects the temper of the times, specifically the notions advanced through the medicalization of sex. Stephen, so named because her father had never considered his wife might give birth to a daughter, is christened Stephen Mary Olivia Gertrude. She grows up an individual markedly different, never quite fitting in, whose androgynous body lends itself to masculine dress. Stephen falls in love with a woman named Mary, but their relationship is met with opposition and rejection by others. To save Mary's 'respectability,' Stephen gives her up.[442]

The novel meets a fierce resistance, being banned for obscenity, thus seeming to endanger Hall's career, though the furor helps make it a best-seller. What makes it still notable today is its author's presentation of Stephen as someone who is like she is from birth on. Stephen's is a 'congenital' condition and her 'inversion' is comprehended along the lines of the prevailing science of the day.

While reinforcing such ideas, *The Well of Loneliness* also succeeds in challenging homophobia. As well, it shows the consequences of homophobia in the lives of those at whom it is directed. Stephen's life experience is ultimately well captured by the novel's title.

Nightwood (1936)

One of the more remarkable crossdressers of modern fiction is Dr. Matthew O'Connor, the unlicensed gynecologist of Djuna Barnes' *Nightwood*. In one scene, set at night in his bedroom, he is described as in bed dressed in a ladies nightgown, wearing a blonde wig and with rouged cheeks. He engages in discussions with a lesbian, Nora Flood, with whom he weighs in on matters concerning sexuality and gender.[443] Laura Veltman calls him "perhaps literature's first cross-dressing Catholic" and remarks, "Whereas in anti-Catholic propaganda the priest threatens patriarchal order by desiring sexual relations with his female confessant, Matthew O'Connor wants, not to be with a woman, but to be a woman."[444] He is, in many respects, the embodiment of all the most dramatic elements associated with 20th century anxiety over crossdressing, including religion, sexual orientation, transsexualism, and the nature of gender.

Last Exit to Brooklyn (1964)

Hubert Selby's character of George/Georgette in *Last Exit to Brooklyn* stands as a representative of a common 20th century perception: the crossdresser as a homosexual drag queen—a "hip queer" in the novel's parlance. Georgette glories in being gay and in crossdressing, complete with wig and padded bra. 'She' has an aesthetic longing for culture, while having legitimate fears for safety at home where a non-understanding mother and homophobic brother reside. Georgette is enamored of Vinnie, a local hood, who treats Georgette cruelly. In this unhappy world, her principal interest often seems to be scoring a drink or drug fix. However, the provenance of the novel (a collection of shorter narratives) is the underside of life in the Eisenhower era (1950s), replete with desperate people of the working class in the underbelly of a major American city. In this world there is only occasional tenderness—and very little hope. Georgette is manhandled, knifed, and ultimately killed when struck by a car. [445]

Georgette reflects the life of some, but by no means all, crossdressers at the century's midpoint. Unfortunately, to be visible in public means to be relegated to the margins of society. Since individuals like Georgette are already there, crossdressing adds relatively little further insult. But such images impress more firmly on the American popular consciousness the figure of crossdresser as a troubled homosexual loser in a society that prizes masculine power and success.

Stone Butch Blues (1993)

More recent works like Leslie Feinberg's *Stone Butch Blues* (1993) serve to remind us of 'crossdressing' women in the current society. The narrator, Jess Goldberg, is a thoroughly transgendered person in the modern sense: born female, assigned a feminine gender identity, but carrying an androgynous name and body accompanied with a tenuous 'he-she' identity. In struggling to understand gender as it relates to the self, Jess responds to the questions and taunts of others by exploring gendered identity through things like crossdressing. Jess also experiences what too many transgendered people do—violence at home and school, marginalization and isolation. Identifying as a 'butch' lesbian, but searching for a firmer identity, Jess tries hormones and breast reduction surgery to modify his-her body. These steps further complicate life and Jess' journey to a firmer identity continues, with major self-affirming steps occurring when he-she discovers others like him-herself, struggling with similar matters. The decisive move in Jess' life comes when he-she enters into relationship with Ruth, another 'he-she.'[446]

Whether Jess is labeled a 'masculine-identified woman,' a 'butch lesbian,' a 'transsexual' or 'transgendered' female, or simply a 'crossdresser,' the struggle is one readily identifiable to many of us whose gender identity does not neatly and comfortably fit into a dichotomous scheme of polar opposite genders. More than many novels coming before it, *Stone Butch Blues* captures the ambiguities, tensions, and struggles implicit in not fitting in gender-wise in society. It succeeds in challenging many stereotypes, though Jess' quest, replete with discovering a personal sexuality, may well enforce to some readers a connection between atypical gender and atypical sexuality. At any rate, this novel is perhaps the most celebrated of a wave of such stories appearing in the second half of the 20th century.[447]

What role does crossdressing have in the United States today?

The perception of crossdressing as linked to criminal activity persists well into the 20th century. Anti-crossdressing ordinances are slow to give way and some are still being enforced into the 1960s and 1970s (see the answer to Q. 36). Though perceptions slowly shift, in reality crossdressers can still be arrested for appearing in public.[448] Also, crossdressing remains an alternative for pursuing criminal acts. Just as in previous centuries, in the 21st century cross gender masquerading provides a disguise complicating identification of the suspect. Crimes such as bank robbery committed by thieves in crossdressed disguise continue to be reported on occasion. Still, for the most part, the link between crossdressing and criminality has been broken.

Another misperception slow to yield to the facts is the alleged intrinsic connection between crossdressing and homosexuality. Bolstered by the writings of psychoanalysts, it is not until well past mid-century that this popular view begins to be challenged seriously even within the ranks of psychiatry. It is not until the 1970s that the American Psychiatric Association removes homosexuality from its list of mental disorders and even thereafter crossdressing remains a stigmatized behavior associated with psychological illness (see the answers to Q.

96, 99). However, by the dawn of the 21st century it is more widely recognized than ever before that while some homosexuals crossdress, most crossdressers are not homosexual.

Fashion changes at the start of the 21st century continue a trend toward blurring of gendered distinctions in dress. As has been true for centuries, women's fashions borrow from men's fashions.[449] However, a reawakening of interest in fashion by men, begun in the late 20th century, shows no signs of abating in the early 21st century. Moreover, another trend evident as the 20th century closed also continues: the appropriation of feminine elements in dress designed for men. Perhaps for the first time, men's fashion looks to the leadership in women's fashion to borrow elements to make masculine. These include innovations in both outerwear and underwear.[450]

Where fashion and crossdressing will go in the 21st century is uncertain. Susan Freeman opens a review of several volumes on fashion with the following observation:

> I have taken note of the sexy "boyshorts" in women's lingerie aisles. Will these masculine-cut panties, often detailed with lace, become the underwear of choice for women? Will teenage girls continue to roll down waistbands on their shorts and skirts and sport sweatpants with names of athletic teams emblazoned across the buttocks? Will "metrosexuals"—image-conscious, heterosexual men—persist in their pursuit of beauty practices traditionally associated with women? And what do all these trends reveal about the societies in which they appear?[451]

These questions remain quite open as this work is written.

Q. 48

Who are some famous crossdressing women?

The Short Answer. There are too many crossdressing women known to history to tell all their stories here. While various women are named throughout this book, in this answer a select few are discussed in a bit more detail. These women are those who gained some notoriety in their own time and who have been remembered. As is the case with men, most often the crossdressing is remembered because the person was notable for another reason, such as high social status or having attained fame for some endeavor. These women, however, represent only the most visible tip of a very large iceberg. Many more crossdressing women will forever remain hidden to history, just as they were in their own lifetimes. Of special note are religiously motivated crossdressing women. However, their stories merit special inclusion elsewhere in this work. Those women noted in connection to religion are discussed in the answers to questions in question sets 9 and 10 of volume 4 (particularly in the answers to Q. 68-69). Many of these female crossdressers continued to see themselves as women, though masquerading as men. In other instances the crossdressing appears to have accompanied an internalized masculine gender identity.

The Longer Answer. Crossdressing women once engaged the interest and imagination of the general public the way crossdressing men seem to today. In addition to numerous real life examples—some well known through memoirs—there are representations in fictionalized biographies, novels, the theater, and even opera.[452] Some crossdressing women completely adopted the life of a man. Today we would likely label at least some of these individuals 'transsexual' (see Q. 19), or diagnose some of them as experiencing 'Gender Identity Disorder' (see Q. 96). There were no such designations then, and in truth the motivations for crossdressing prove as varied as the women who crossdressed.

The answer provided here is by no means comprehensive; that would require a sizeable volume in its own right. Rather, the examples selected represent women of note for different reasons. Here is a Queen and a crook, an opera star and a jazz musician, soldiers and sailors, women past and present. Most, but not all, undertake crossdressing willingly. Their stories illustrate a sampling of lives; many more stories can be found in the various volumes referenced in the notes. The examples here also all date from the 16th century forward. Stories of women from earlier times certainly exist, and some are recounted in the answers to other questions (cf. answers to Q. 13, 42, 68-69, etc.).

There are two important matters to note in introducing this material. First, as we have in previous answers, in telling their stories we will employ the 'historical present'—an effort to bridge the distance imposed by time in order to see these women as living figures. Second, in a grudging concession to the way most folk in our culture persist in privileging sex over gender, the pronouns used in this answer and the next refer to the individual by birth sex, not by gender—or by marking the gender the person presented in with simple marks ('he'). A more enlightened and appropriate manner—one we ought to follow in our daily lives—is to refer to any person according to the gender that person intends to present. A biological female who intends to present as a man should be referred to as 'he.' A biological male presenting intentionally as a woman should be called 'she.' However, since this answer sets forth biological females assigned at birth to become women, and their dressing as men is typically regarded in their own times and later as crossdressing masquerade, the pronouns used here (and in the next answer) are consistent with sex, not gender presentation. This convention is only followed to provide consistency (since most of the people discussed varied their gender presentation) and to avoid confusion for the reader.

Who is Elena de Cespedes?[453]

Elena de Cespedes (1545-1588) is a Spanish woman of African descent. Her story fascinates modern scholars, who use it to understand and illustrate various aspects of transgender experience. Legal scholar William Eskridge, Jr., for example, utilizes her story as a case-in-point of the many women who pass as men in order to marry another woman.[454] On the other hand, Spanish scholar Israel Burshatin finds in her story an important example of how minorities are treated by the Inquisition and the lengths to which someone might go to make a better life.[455] What especially excites attention, though, is a particular mystery in Elena's story and its tragic conclusion.

Elena's life seems conventional enough early on. She is raised as a girl, marries, and bears a child. Only after being deserted by her spouse does Elena's life begin the strange course that eventually proves her undoing. She gives up her child and moves to Grenada. There she puts on male clothing and adopts a new identity as a man named 'Eleno.' She will occupy her new role with gusto.

In her male guise Elena/Eleno carries on an affair with the wife of her landlord. Once the affair is uncovered, Elena flees, joining the Spanish army. This leads to involvement in various military actions, including being wounded in battle. Leaving the military, Elena settles in Madrid and plies the craft of a tailor.

In this new life, Elena proposes marriage to a local peasant girl. But Elena's sexual identity is questioned. Submitting to the examination of surgeons, Elena succeeds in passing as male. However, this verdict is challenged by Elena's former lover. At the order of the authorities, a second examination is held; again Elena passes as male. Thus satisfied, a priest marries Elena and the girl.

Yet the questions about Elena's sexual identity will not die. A *third* examination is ordered. This time the verdict proves different: Elena now is declared a woman. This decision brings a charge of fraud. Elena must face the infamous system of Catholic Spain's Inquisition. Of course, her marriage is annulled. Elena also is publicly whipped. But much worse, she is convicted of devilry and sentenced to death by burning.

The great mystery, of course, is how Elena succeeds in passing scrutiny by physicians. On her own behalf, she claims she never lied; previously, she says, she actually had grown a penis! Is she a hermaphrodite? Is her genitalia ambiguous enough to lead examiners to conflicting opinions at different times? Or is Elena skilled enough at presenting as male that she somehow deceives her examiners not once, but twice? We will never know.

Who is Mary Frith?[456]

Mary Frith (1584?-1659) is, arguably, the most famous female crossdresser of the 17th century. Popularly known as 'Moll Cutpurse,' Frith gains notoriety as a member of England's underworld. The name 'Cutpurse' comes from her early occupation as a pickpocket. Scrapes with the law motivate her to take a different course, moving up to highway robbery. This venture almost ends disastrously after her misfortune in picking the wrong victim and finding herself in Newgate prison under sentence of death. However, she bribes herself to freedom. So she becomes, instead, a fence for stolen goods. In this capacity she rises to prominence in criminal circles. Though relatively removed from legal difficulties, Frith becomes accused for her crossdressing, as recounted in this excerpt from *The Newgate Calendar*:

> While she thus reigned free from the danger of the common law, an apparitor, set on by an adversary of hers, cited her to appear in the Court of Arches, where was an accusation exhibited against her for wearing indecent and manly apparel. She was advised by her proctor to demur the jurisdiction of the Court, as for a crime, if such, not cognisable there. But he did it to spin out the cause and get her money; for, in the end, she was there sentenced to stand and do penance in a white sheet at St Paul's Cross during morning sermon on a Sunday.[457]

Unlike most female crossdressers of the time, who use the behavior to disguise themselves and pass as males, Frith makes no such pretence. She is masculine in dress and behavior—but apparently not in gender identity. Her contemporaries are fully aware that she is a woman, though at one point in time she may also claim to be a hermaphrodite. At any rate, her dress varies from more androgynous in nature to more masculine. Her manner, however, earns her the moniker, 'the roaring girl.'

Frith is mentioned in writings by her contemporaries and even becomes the subject of a theater production in her own lifetime aptly titled 'The Roaring Girl' (1611).[458] After Frith's death, there appears an anonymously authored 'autobiography,' *The Life and Death of Moll Cutpurse* (1662). Her story continues to exercise the modern imagination, as Ellen Galford's novel *Moll Cutpurse* attests.[459]

Who is Catalina de Erauso?[460]

Catalina de Erauso (1585-1630) is another remarkable 17th century figure. Born in 1585 in San Sebastian, Spain, her parents place her at the age of four in a Dominican convent. In March, 1600, not long before she is to take her final vows as a nun, the unhappy girl decides to escape. Taking with her a little money, some scissors, needle and thread, she makes her way into the night. Hiding in a chestnut grove on the outskirts of the convent, Catalina spends three days refashioning her outfit into makeshift male clothing and cuts her hair.

She retains this disguise as a practical means of protection and for the freedom of travel it facilitates. After some months, under the name of Francisco Loyola, she gains employment as a page to the imperial secretary. When, after seven months, her father shows up unexpectedly, explaining his plight to the secretary, Catalina decides to move on. She travels to the city of Bilbao, fends off the unwelcome attention of some of the town's youth, injuring one of them in the process, gets herself arrested, and spends a month in jail.

Quitting Balboa, she proceeds to the town of Estella, where she resides two years as a page to a local don. Then she returns to her hometown, where she lives as a bachelor. In 1603 she boards a ship to Punta de Araya as a ship's boy on a galleon and thus makes her way to Cartagena of the Indies. There she becomes cabin boy to her uncle, a ship's captain (who does not recognize her). When the fleet is ready to return to Spain, she steals some of her uncle's money and deserts the ship.

Through various adventures, she eventually reaches South America, seeing both Peru and Chile. Catalina participates as a soldier in the conquest of Chile and altogether spends more than two decades in the Americas. An accomplished swordsman, she gambles, duels (even inadvertently killing one of her brothers), and fights her way to renown, mostly in the mining towns of the Andes Mountains.

Then Catalina confesses her true identity to a bishop. She reveals she is not only a woman, but a virgin still. A celebrity, she returns to her native land. There the king gives her a pension. Pope Urban VIII, in 1624, grants her a special dispensation to continue dressing in men's clothes. She writes out the story of her life, which she finishes in the Americas, laboring as a mule driver and tradesman, before dying in 1630.

Who is 'King' Nzinga of the Mbundu people?[461]

In the late 16th century into the early 17th century, a remarkable woman in Africa catches the attention of Europeans. She is Nzinga a Mbande (c. 1580-1663), who rules as 'king' among the Mbundu people in what today is known as Angola. Her extraordinary achievements keep her kingdom free during her lifetime and secures for herself a lasting reputation. In 2004, Nzinga (or Njinga) is ranked 44th among the 100 'Greatest Africans of All Time' listed in the *New African* magazine.[462]

Nzinga is born into the ruling family of the Kingdom of Ndongo. Her early life appears to have been rather ordinary, with Nzinga pursuing a course normal for a princess in her culture. Her father, Ngola Kilajua, zealously holds onto power, eliminating all he sees as rivals, real or imagined, including a son of Nzinga. When he dies in 1617 a half-brother, Mbande, succeeds him as *ngola* (king). In his reign she enters onto the large stage of world politics.

In 1621, Nzinga is appointed to deal with the Portuguese, a European power which has been exercising increasing pressure in the region since before Nzinga's birth. The Portuguese desire economic and military control of the area and towards that end have established a colony at Luanda, an island off the coast of Ndongo. Seeking slaves and gold, the Portuguese have been encroaching steadily upward from the southern border of the kingdom. In 1619, they had seized Ndongo's capital, forcing a relocation of the ruling family. So Nzinga is sent to Luanda as emissary to the colony's governor.

Nzinga, an intelligent woman, understands how to operate in patriarchal societies. Within her own culture she faces the belief that women are unsuited to rule—a belief she intends to challenge. The Portuguese also underestimate her, at least at first. They intend to use her and her people, and so support a treaty that makes Ndongo an ally of the Portuguese in the region, and which will at least temporarily end Portuguese exploitation of her people in the slave trade. Nzinga has plans of her own. To cement her relationship with the Europeans, she undergoes Christian baptism in 1622, adopting for herself the surname of the Portuguese governor, and becoming 'Ana de Sousa.'

In 1624 her brother, the *ngola*, dies under suspicious circumstances—either murdered, or perhaps by suicide. He leaves as his successor a small son. Nzinga assumes the role of Regent. She is now ruler in all but name. However, by 1626 the Portuguese have made it plain they favor a male rival, Hari a Ngola, as successor. Nzinga responds boldly, renouncing both Christianity and her ties with the Portuguese, gathering those loyal to her, and declaring herself their rightful ruler. The resulting force retreats out of reach of the Portuguese, establishing themselves at Matamba, where they continue a kind of civil war that persists until 1656.

At Matamba, Nzinga performs as masculine a gender role as any *ngola* can. Through shrewd moves she keeps her people free and serves as a check on European power until her death in 1663. She accomplishes this using a variety of means: she negotiates with the Portuguese, she welcomes refugees to add to her numbers, she forges advantageous alliances, she wages guerrilla warfare, and she foments civil unrest and resistance in Ndongo, which is now a mere vassal to the Portuguese.

Ever conscious of the gender rules of two patriarchal societies, Nzinga uses those same gender rules to support her own rule. She insists on recognition as *ngola*—'king'—not 'queen.' She dresses in masculine clothes, often favoring European fashions, and often participates in battle. Nzinga likewise bends gender role rules among her entourage to suit her purposes. She has women who serves her court as 'ladies-in-waiting' trained in the arts of war. She also keeps a harem of male youths, all dressed as women. Not least among her accomplishments is the decisive overthrow of the tradition that only males may attain to the highest rule; after her there will be a number of female rulers—though none will compare with Nzinga's success.

Who is Queen Christina of Sweden?[463]

Queen Christina of Sweden (1626-1689) might be remembered for a number of reasons, as she is one of the more remarkable women of history. First, she is a participant in the Peace of Westphalia, which concludes the Thirty Years War. Second, she is a patron of the arts and scholarship, a woman keenly interested in intellectual matters, especially those of theology. Third, she is a monarch who, at the height of her power, abdicates the throne. Fourth, she converts to Roman Catholicism during a time when that action is illegal in Sweden. But we remember her here for crossdressing.

Christina's birth defies the astrologers to King Gustav II Adolf, who have predicted a son. Actually, at birth there is momentary joy that a son has been born, as the child is hairy and the genitalia not immediately determined, but the truth is quickly discovered and the disappointed mother reacts by rejecting her child. The King, though, intervenes and determines that Christina, as his only heir, shall be raised as a prince. Named her father's successor while not yet five, when her father dies at war when she is five, Christina becomes Queen. At age 13, well-educated and with a good mind, she begins to actively rule her nation. By age 15 she has mastered five languages and remains dedicated to her studies. She falls in love with Charles Gustav while still a teenager, and at her coming-of-age coronation at age 18 expects to marry him after his return from an appointment in Germany.

But then Christina falls in love with another man—Magnus de la Gardie. Unfortunately, her affection is not reciprocated. Charles' eventual return is not enough to rekindle her passion for him and they never marry. Indeed, by this time it seems likely she has reached a determination to never marry. Instead, Christina explores Catholicism and exchanges letters with the great philosopher Rene Descartes. For the next few years she actively studies the religions of the world. In her mid-20s she forms a new love interest, Spain's Don Antonio Pimentel de Pradol. Though they never marry, and appear not to have a sexual relationship, he remains her confidant and proves important in her secret steps to convert to Catholicism.

In 1654, about a decade after her coronation, Christina finally takes the step she has been preparing for—abdication. Cutting her hair and putting on male clothes, she travels through Europe, accompanied by men who remain loyal to her. Christina now converts to Catholicism and, when she reaches Rome in 1655, Pope Alexander VII himself receives her. Christina adds 'Alexandra' as a middle name. Now Catholic, in 1656 she travels to France, where she falls in love with Cardinal Azzolino, with whom she will maintain a close, but apparently nonsexual relationship for the rest of her life.

Returning to Rome, Christina becomes the object of gossip and scandal because of her unconventional behavior. She resolves to seize power in Naples, and seeks aid in France, but her plans come apart and—after one of her party is killed for betraying her—she discovers her reputation seriously damaged. The Pope distances himself from her and Christina finds her fortunes falling further. In 1665, her pension is reduced by half. All of her efforts to recapture power and wealth prove futile and so she settles in Rome, where she writes and dedicates herself to patronage of the arts and the promotion of religious tolerance. With increasing age, she devotes herself more and more to spiritual pursuits. When she dies, Christina is accorded the honor of burial in St. Peter's Church in Rome.

Although the period of Christina's crossdressing occupies but a small portion of her life it is important to us anyway. Like many other women throughout history, Christina adopts male disguise for protection. She has just abdicated and her future course is uncertain despite her hopes and plans. Traveling with men, masquerading as one of them, preserves for her the autonomy she had known as monarch. Her crossdressing is utilitarian and when she reaches safety, she no longer requires it, nor practices it.

Who is Christian Davies?[464]

A woman who travels somewhat a different path is Christian Davies (1667-1739/75). Born in Dublin, Ireland she apparently conforms to social conventions in her early years. Inheriting an inn at age 21, she falls in love with and marries Robert Welch, one of the waiters. She has two sons by him. Then her spouse suddenly disappears. Christian learns a year later, in a letter from him, that he has been pressed into military service.

She forms a bold plan of action. Perhaps drawing on the model of one 'Captain Bodeaux,' a French friend of her father's who had been found to be female after suffering a mortal wound in battle, Christian becomes 'Christopher Welch.' Leaving her children with her mother, and donning some of her husband's clothing, she heads out in pursuit of him. Eventually she joins the British army, is wounded, captured by the French, and even engages in a duel, which results both in wounding her opponent and putting Christian in jail. Through all this she avoids discovery, though a leg wound suffered in 1703 jeopardizes that success.

It requires more than a dozen years for Christian, as Christopher, to catch up to her husband. When she does, though, Christian persuades him to keep her secret and pass her off to others as his brother. This Robert does until a wound in battle results in Christian suffering a skull fracture; while unconscious she is discovered as female. But there happens a happy outcome: dressed again as a woman, Christian and Robert are able to resume life as husband and wife, with she accompanying him in his army service. After his death three years later, in 1709, she marries another soldier, Hugh Jones, who also dies in battle (1710).

Queen Anne of England receives Christian in honor, awarding her a pension of a shilling a day for life. At last she returns home to Dublin, where she marries yet another soldier, a man by the name of Davies. A 1740 volume entitled *The Life and Adventures of Mrs Christian Davies*, purporting to be her autobiography, appears; its genuineness is disputed. Christian survives to a great age; she may have lived to be 108, ending her days at Chelsea Pensioners' Hospital for soldiers.

Who is Mademoiselle Maupin?[465]

Mademoiselle Maupin (1670/73-1707) is a noted French opera star of the late 17th-early 18th century. Born Julia d'Aubigny, to an official in the court of the Grand Squire of France, she receives an excellent education, including instruction in swordplay by her father. By age 16 she has become an accomplished duelist. Tall, athletic, and attractive, Julia engages in an affair with her father's employer, the Count, when only a youth (age 14/15). Perhaps to keep the affair hidden, the following year (c. 1686) a marriage is arranged to a Monsieur Maupin of St. Germain-en-Laye. Not long after, the affair comes to its end and her husband receives appointment to an administrative position that takes him away from Paris. Julia remains behind.

In her husband's absence she indulges herself in various activities, some of which result in physical conflict—and which include at least one love affair. Her lover is accused of having been illegally engaged in a duel, which had left a man dead, and so he is forced to flee the city. Julia, still just 18 years old, follows him to Marseilles (c. 1688), under the name of Mademoiselle d'Aubigny. There the two of them put on dueling exhibitions. She is often found in male dress, though apparently makes little if any effort to disguise the fact that she is female. In fact, when her prowess with the rapier causes an observer to doubt her sex, it is said she throws down her foil and opens her bodice to silence any skeptics.

During this time Julia also pursues singing. Accepted into a musical academy, she makes her debut in Marseilles. As this career develops, she tires of her lover and becomes enamored of another. This time, though, the object of her affection is a young woman, whose disapproving parents place her in a convent. Julia follows (c. 1689). Not long after, under cover of a suspicious fire, she and the girl flee. They are gone three months before Julia abandons the girl and returns to Marseilles. But the scandal brings charges against her; she is tried in absentia (as a man!), and sentenced to death by burning.

Julia flees. She proceeds slowly to Paris, supporting herself along the way by singing in taverns. As remains her custom, she crossdresses. On one occasion—according to a particular account of the tale—in Villeperdue, a young man calls out after a performance that, having heard her 'chirping,' he now wants her to show off her 'plumage.' Angry words ensue and a challenge to a duel soon is proffered. The young man and two of his friends face off against Julia. The duel ends when she wounds her offender, who turns out to be the son of a Duke. Anxious for his health, she visits him dressed as a woman, he apologizes for having been a drunken boor, and they initiate a torrid affair. Though on-and-off again as lovers, this relationship will persist throughout Julia's life.

Dogged by the condemnation on her head, Julia seeks out the Count who had been her first lover. By his intervention the King of France voids the sentence. Now free, she enters Paris (c. 1690/91). Using the name Mademoiselle Maupin, she overcomes some initial resistance and enjoys a debut in the Paris Opera in the role of the goddess Pallas Athena, in a production of *Cadmus and Hermione*. Gifted with an excellent memory, a pleasing contralto voice, skill at dancing, and beauty, over the next few years Julia establishes herself as a star of the Paris Opera.

Julia's tempestuous nature continues to involve her in both affairs of the heart and duels. Indeed, she nearly has a second career as a professional duelist. She continues to dress in male garb, and is often mistaken for a man. Julia plays her crossdressing to advantage whenever she can. In one notable incident (c. 1694), she appears at a Court ball in the dress of a cavalier, though without apparent effort to hide her true sex. When Julia draws the attention of a young woman, and then kisses her openly, three young men rise to defend what they see as the young lady's impugned honor and challenge Julia. In the ensuing duel, Julia again emerges victorious. This nearly results in more legal trouble, for dueling remains illegal.

Once more Julia flees, this time to Brussels. There she becomes mistress to a German prince. When that affair ends, she returns to Paris (c. 1698). There she reconciles to her husband and they spend his remaining years in apparent domestic peace. She also resumes her place in the Paris Opera. In 1702, composer Andre Campra writes an opera, *Tancrede*, expressly for her. In 1705, after the death of her dearest female friend, Julia retires from the opera and enters religious life in the shelter of a convent. She dies two years later, after a brief illness. Despite a highly eventful life, she is only 37 years old.

Who is Mary Anne Talbot?[466]

Not all girls or women voluntarily choose crossdressing and masquerading as male. Born in late 18th century London, Mary Anne Talbot (1778-1808), perhaps the illegitimate daughter of Lord William Talbot, is orphaned when her mother dies in childbirth. Passed from one guardian to another during childhood, she finally comes under the control of Captain Essex Bowen. In 1792, when he is recalled to military service, he insists the teenaged Mary Anne come along, disguised as a lad. She is enrolled in his regiment under the name of John Taylor and functions as Bowen's footboy, later serving during battle as a drummer boy.

Her engagement in military actions leads to various harrowing adventures. In the siege of Valenciennes, France, Captain Bowen is killed. Mary Anne herself receives wounds in chest and back. Fearing discovery, she treats her own wounds. From her late guardian's correspondence she discovers she has no inheritance, but despite this disappointment she has no desire to continue as a soldier. Securing for herself a sailor's uniform she deserts and finds a post as cabin boy aboard a French ship in 1793.

The British capture this ship. Mary Anne tells her story to the commanding officer, who transfers her to the HMS Brunswick, where she serves as a 'powder monkey.' In an ensuing battle in 1794 she is wounded again, this time in hip and thigh, from cannon grapeshot. Though the blast nearly severs her leg, she both survives the wound and eventually regains most of her leg's use. Despite medical examination and four months rehabilitation, Mary Anne escapes discovery.

Upon her recovery she ships out as a British midshipman. Her troubled luck continues as French pirates seize the ship. For some 18 months Mary Anne is imprisoned at Dunkirk. After release in 1796, she returns to London. There it seems her fortunes are at last turning for the better. She finds passage on an American merchant ship as steward and so crosses the Atlantic to New York. But on her return to England the luckless lass is taken by a press-gang. Without her official papers, her only recourse to escape them is to reveal her birth sex. Successful at doing so, but needing money, Mary manages to convince a British magistrate of monies owed her by the British navy. Unfortunately, this does not suffice for long.

Mary Anne's hard luck continues. Bothered by her leg, constantly fighting poverty, she retains masculine clothing and masquerade, finding a variety of menial jobs. She even tries the stage, but without much success. Eventually she finds herself in debtor's prison at Newgate. Finally winning release she comes into the household of publisher Robert Kirby as a servant. Fascinated by her stories he eventually publishes the story of her life in two separate books including the title *Life and Surprising Adventures of Mary Anne Talbot.*

Who is Kaúxuma Núpika/Qánqon Kámek Klaúla?

Kaúxuma Núpika (late 18th-early 19th centuries) is a member of the Kootenai (or Kutenai) people, an American Indian tribe in an area today embracing parts of Idaho and Montana in the U.S. and British Columbia in Canada. Named Qúqunok Patke ('One Standing (Lodge) Pole Woman') at her birth, she apparently has an ordinary childhood, though by the time she reaches adulthood she allegedly is large and muscular for a woman (though at least one source instead refers to her as having 'a delicate frame'). Around 1808, unable to find a suitor among her own people, she marries a Canadian fur trader named Boisverd. After little more than a year she returns to her people.[467]

She tells her people a remarkable story. Alleging her husband has transformed her, she declares she is now a man, who is to be called Kaúxuma Núpika ('Gone to the Spirits'). 'He' now uses a dance to show the sex transformation and begins to claim great spiritual power. These things are met with some skepticism among the Kootenai; some consider her/him crazy. But Kaúxuma Núpika is undeterred. 'He' begins wearing masculine clothing, carries a gun along with bow and arrows, and even approaches various young women with offers of marriage. Being snubbed at every turn, Kaúxuma Núpika's manner now inspires rumors of desired revenge upon those who have rejected 'him.' As a consequence, Kaúxuma Núpika is increasingly feared and avoided. 'He' takes refuge among those who have been divorced or widowed.[468]

Among these folk Kaúxuma Núpika finally finds a partner, a woman abandoned by her husband, who agrees to them living together. Rumors circulate about the couple, along with speculation about their sexual relationship. A claim is made that Kaúxuma Núpika uses an artificial phallus made of leather. Another rumor claims Kaúxuma Núpika has jealously accused the partner of infidelity. At some point, Kaúxuma Núpika loses both bow and arrows, and a bark canoe, gambling with some men. This is the final straw in a troubled relationship and the partner leaves. Thereafter, Kaúxuma Núpika will engage in a series of liaisons with various women.[469]

Increasingly, interests turn to the masculine pursuits of raiding and warfare. To lead a raid a warrior would beat upon a hide while going about the camp, in hopes of attracting volunteers. Apparently, Kaúxuma Núpika's initial raid is to steal horses. In the travel accompanying this raid a brother who has come along, suspicious of how Kaúxuma Núpika holds back when it comes to crossing streams, uses a ruse to spy on such a crossing. He sees that his birth sister remains female despite her claim of changed sex. This incident causes some conflict between them when near the conclusion of the unsuccessful raid the party's leader invites anyone who wishes to adopt a new name. Kaúxuma Núpika claims the name Qánqon Kámek Klaúla ('Sitting-in-the-Water Grizzly'), an allusion to having tried to hide her body sex from her brother by squatting in the water while claiming an injury to her ankle. Her brother derisively refers to her only as Qánqon and threatens to expose her secret to the others.[470]

Such exposure actually happens when Qánqon Kámek Klaúla, as has happened before, in a jealous rage beats a female companion. Her brother interrupts the beating and, in a loud voice, explains to all who can hear why he only uses the part-name Qánqon—that she had sat in the water to try to hide that she is still female. After this, everyone calls her Qánqon. Under this name she serves as a courier and guide in Eastern Washington along the Spokane and Columbia rivers. During these activities she also prophesies the destruction of the Indian peoples of the region by a plague of smallpox and by two enormous men bent on destruction. Such words endear Qánqon neither to White men nor Indians. On the other hand, sometimes Qánqon told other Indians that the Whites would bring them gifts at the behest of the Great White Chief.[471]

Whatever may be the actual facts of the case, Qánqon becomes associated with prophetic utterances and, perhaps, the spread of the Prophet Dance doctrine—a precursor to the famous Ghost Dance of the late 19th century. In any event, over the course of the next 14 years, Qánqon manages to establish a reputation as a shaman. Among those who claim to be healed by her is a Chief David (who by some accounts is really the one who gave her the name Qánqon Kámek Klaúla). In this role Qánqon, called by some 'Bowdash,' also engages in mediation between parties. In fact, in this manner Qánqon finally meets her end. In 1837, a party of Flathead Indians are virtually surrounded by hostile Blackfoot Indians. Qánqon serves as mediator to the Blackfoot and intentionally deceives them to facilitate escape by the Flathead party. In retribution she is killed.[472]

Who is George Sand?[473]

The name of Amandine-Aurore-Lucile Dupin (1804-1876) is virtually unknown today. But the name under which she writes—George Sand—is well-remembered. Born in Paris, she is raised in the country home of her grandmother. As a child she invents an androgynous character named Corambe, who can at will become either man or woman—a precursor to Sand's own adult life. Already in her youth she occasionally crossdresses at home.

But, bowing to pressure, in 1822 at age 18 she marries Baron Casimir Dudevant, with whom she has a son and daughter. The match is not a favorable one. She leaves him in 1831, taking their children, and moving to Paris. Subsequently she has a number of affairs, some with prominent figures, like the composer Chopin. She also writes a substantial body of literature; among her works is an autobiography, *Historie de Ma Vie (Story of My Life)*, published in 1854-55.

Sand's unconventional life excites as much comment as her literary works, which themselves are critical of social conventions like marriage. A devotee of socialism, Sand tirelessly decries gender inequalities. She also occasions comment for her penchant for dressing in male garb. She is not bashful about donning a man's suit, complete to top hat. The whole startling effect is topped off by cigar in hand and a brash personality. In this guise she enjoys a measure of anonymity and freedom of movement.

Though Sand has been married and had affairs with men, she proclaims her one great love in life is another woman. Subsequently, in the 20th century she will be embraced both by feminists and many lesbians. In some lesbian circles it will become fashionable to emulate Sand in her manner of dress. In many ways Sand will become an iconic figure of modern life.

Who is Nadezhda Andreevna Durova?[474]

Nadezhda Andreevna Durova (1783-1866) is a Russian woman who, dissatisfied with living the conventional woman's life assigned her, puts matters into her own hands. She has been born into a life of some privilege as the daughter of a town mayor and member of the lesser nobility in Russia. She spends much of her childhood on horseback—a skill she will later put to great advantage. In her own account of her life, Nadezhda writes of being a child who prefers to play war to the quieter tasks expected of her gender. She has no illusions; her mother had explained to her the 'sad fortune' of being a woman—a life of slavery to others. Although from youth she yearns for freedom from her gender role, outwardly she seems to live a normal life. Then, despite her objections, at 18 she is married and becomes mother to a son.

But in 1806, in her early 20s, she abandons her family. Cutting her hair, she puts on an army uniform, mounts her horse Alcides, and calling herself 'Alexandr Vasilevich,' seeks the adventure she craves by joining the Russian cavalry. This is the Napoleonic era, and Nadezhda soon enough finds herself in battle during the 1806-07 campaign against Napoleon. She distinguishes herself with her bravery, even saving an officer's life. But rumors of an Amazon warrior in the cavalry reach all the way to the Tsar.

Summoned before Emperor Alexander I, who presents her the Cross of St. George, she is granted by him a special dispensation to remain in military service and is promoted to officer's rank. Few know her real identity. Under the name of 'Alexander Sokolov,' Nadezhda participates in the 1812 Battle of Borodino, where she is wounded. This leads to her leaving the army, in 1815, after about a decade of service.

Nadezhda retires to a private life. There she proves an able writer. The diary she kept while in the military she publishes in 1839 as *Povesti i rasskazy* (*Notes of a Cavalry Maiden*). When she dies at age 83, she is buried with full military honors—and in male dress. A century after her notes are published, Nadezhda's life will be celebrated in a 1940 play written by Alexander Gladkov, and a movie made in Russia under the title *Hussar Ballad*.

Who is Loretta Janeta Velazquez?[475]

Loretta Janeta Velazquez (1842-1897?) is one of about 400 women known to have masqueraded as men to fight in the Civil War that tore apart the United States in the mid-19th century. She is also among the smaller number of that company to willingly capitalize on her notoriety as a crossdressing woman. Her autobiography, *The Woman in Battle: A Narrative of the Exploits, Adventures, and Travels of Madam Loreta Janeta Velazquez, Otherwise Known as Lieutenant Harry T. Buford, Confederate States Army* (1876) is generally regarded today as untrustworthy as an historical document, but in her own life it serves to secure Velazquez a measure of fame. Whatever the accuracy of the details, her narrative offers a richly detailed story of a crossdressing woman and its various elements may truly reflect experiences some women had during the Civil War.

Born in Cuba, the sixth and last child of a Spanish official from a distinguished family, Loreta moves with her family to Mexico, in 1844. In 1849, after urging by her mother, her father consents to send Loreta to the United States for schooling. Thus she settles with an aunt in New Orleans for that purpose in the 1850s. During these years her imagination is fired by the example of Joan of Arc. She writes, "I was especially haunted with the idea of being a man; and the more I thought upon the subject, the more I was disposed to murmur at Providence for having created me a woman."[476] It is during this time she first begins crossdressing, appropriating the clothes of a male cousin and trying to perfect the manner of a man.

In New Orleans she falls in love with an American army officer named William, secretly marrying him in 1856. This earns her father's wrath; he promptly declares her disinherited. But after the birth of her first child relations with her family improve. Though Loreta bears William three children, none survive childhood. After the outbreak of the War Between the States, in 1861, Loreta persuades her husband to resign his commission and enter the service of the Confederacy. He does so, but will not consent to her desire to enter into armed service as well.

Loreta, though, has determined to be actively involved in the War. As she explains early in her autobiography:

> I do not know what the good people who will read this book will think of me. My career has differed materially from that of most women; and some things that I have done have shocked persons for whom I have every respect, however much my ideas of propriety may differ from theirs. I can only say, however, that in my opinion there was nothing essentially improper in my putting on the uniform of a Confederate officer for the purpose of taking an active part in the war; and, as when on the field of battle, in camp, and during long and toilsome marches, I endeavored, not without success, to display a courage and fortitude not inferior to the most courageous of

the men around me, and as I never did aught to disgrace the uniform I wore, but, on the contrary, won the hearty commendation of my comrades, I feel that I have nothing to be ashamed of.[477]

Right up until he leaves for his new posting the couple argue over the matter. William, hoping to dissuade her, thinks he might cure Loreta of her desire if she actually tastes masculine life. The night before his departure he has her don one of his suits, put on a fake moustache and a wig to hide her long hair, and brings her to a bar. This experience only confirms her desire to persist in such a masquerade, but to appease her husband she pretends to defer to his wishes.

Fortified by her experience, and still inspired by the examples of female warriors of the past who had dressed as men and fought alongside them, Loreta waits until her husband departs, then disguises herself as a man, complete with fake moustache and goatee. Having ordered two uniforms, she attempts unsuccessfully to alter them herself, then finds a tailor who will do as she wishes without asking too many questions. He makes for her a dozen fine wire net shields. She explains:

> These I wore next to my skin, and they proved very satisfactory in concealing my true form, and in giving me something of the shape of a man, while they were by no means uncomfortable. Over the shields I wore all undershirt of silk or lisle thread, which fitted close, and which was held in place by straps across the chest and shoulders, similar to the shoulder-braces sometimes worn by men. A great many officers in the Confederate army have seen the impressions of these straps through my shirt when I have had my coat off, and have supposed them to be shoulder-braces. These undershirts could be rolled up into the small compass of a collar-box. Around the waist of each of the undershirts was a band, with eyelet-holes arranged for the purpose of making the waistbands of my pantaloons stand out to the proper number of inches. A woman's waist, as a general thing, is tapering, and her hips very large in comparison with those of a man, so that if I had undertaken to wear pantaloons without some such contrivance, they would have drawn in at the waist and revealed my true form. With such underwear as I used, any woman who can disguise her features can readily pass for a man, and deceive the closest observers. So many men have weak and feminine voices that, provided the clothing is properly constructed and put on right, and the disguise in other respects is well arranged, a woman with even a very high-pitched voice need have very little to fear on that score.[478]

Taking the name 'Harry T. Buford,' Loreta assigns herself an officer's rank as Lieutenant and raises a regiment of volunteers for the Confederate Army. During this endeavor Loreta discovers she cuts a masculine figure appealing to young ladies and takes advantage of that knowledge to explore romance from the position of a man. "I flatter myself," she writes, "that during the time I passed for a man I was tolerably successful with the women; and I had not a few curious and most amusing adventures, which gave me an insight into some of the peculiarities of feminine human nature which had not impressed themselves on my mind before, perhaps because I was a woman."[479]

Loreta, as Lt. Buford, leads her troop to Pensacola, Florida, where her husband, who does not recognize her, receives them. She discloses her identity to him and gains his reluctant compliance with her masquerade. Not long after, he is killed by an accidental discharge of a carbine while training soldiers.

Eventually, Loreta makes her way to the front of the Eastern theater of the war. As a Confederate soldier she participates in some of the Civil War's most famous battles, in both theaters of the conflict, including those at Bull Run, Ball's Bluff, Fort Donelson, and Shiloh. At the last named battle she even claims to have had General Grant in her sights while on reconnaissance, but she refrains from shooting him. Though she fares generally well, when in one skirmish she receives wounds in the foot, it alarms her to realize such an event could lead to the discovery of her true sex. She is wounded on other occasions, too, and a dislocated shoulder following Shiloh does lead to her discovery as a woman. Yet despite the horrors of war, Loreta finds the life of a soldier suits her, though she also faces a sobering realization. "To be a second Joan of Arc," she confesses, "was a mere girlish fancy, which my very first experiences as a soldier dissipated forever; and it did not take me long to discover that I needed no model, but that, to win success in the career I had chosen, I must be simply myself, and not a copy . . . ."[480]

After battle experiences in Virginia, Loreta decides she might better serve the Confederate cause as a spy than as a soldier. Persuading a slave woman to procure clothes for her—and thus becoming a woman pretending to be a man pretending to be a woman—she enters the North. Among her adventures there she manages even to have a brief meeting with President Lincoln, who leaves her with a better impression of him than she entertained before. Ironically, back in the South, she is arrested while in New Orleans as possibly a Union spy, and briefly imprisoned.

Following her experiences in the Western theater, she renews her spying activities, this time in New Orleans. From there she again makes her way to Virginia. It is now 1863 as she enters the Confederate secret service, but her activities are now complicated by the growing rumors of a woman masquerading as a soldier. In Lynchburg, Virginia, she is arrested on the charge of being a woman in disguise. After securing her release she forms plans to penetrate the Federal lines, which she does, as a woman. Thenceforth, in both theaters, she operates as a Confederate spy. Among her various adventures she gains recruitment by the North's own spy agency and becomes a double agent. One assignment discussed with her involves assisting the North to apprehend a certain figure traveling as a Confederate agent—namely herself!

Her masquerade leads, by her own account, to many ironies. For example, after the death of her husband she remarries after a long engagement to Captain Thomas de Caulp, who knows her as both a man and as a woman without suspecting the two are the same person. When she finally reveals the truth to him, he handles it with more enthusiasm than William had. Soon after, they are married.

Following the War's conclusion, Loreta undertakes further adventures. She travels abroad to Europe and to various Latin American countries, including Venezuela and Cuba. In Havanna she once more puts on masculine attire for a time, appearing in a Spanish military suit she has been given. Her Latin America journey is done in the company of her third husband, a Major Wasson. Later, she marries a fourth time, to an older widower, whom she meets as she travels through the American West. In her travels there she encounters Indians and meets Mormons, including Brigham Young. While staying in Salt Lake City she gives birth to another child, a son.

Loreta's autobiography appears in 1876. She apparently lives until near the end of the 19th century.

Who is Dorothy/'Billy' Tipton?[481]

Billy Lee Tipton is an entertainer in 20th century America, mostly known as a jazz musician. Born Dorothy Lucille Tipton in Oklahoma City in 1914, she is raised in a family where music is important and she receives a respectable musical education, playing the piano. In Kansas City she is exposed to jazz and teaches herself to be a jazz saxophonist. But when she tries to gain professional work in Oklahoma City playing piano, she discovers how limited are the opportunities for female musicians. Ironically, Dorothy chooses a brother's name as her own for the new identity she crafts.

Dorothy's transition into a full-time male identity and role as 'Billy' occurs in the 1930s. The apparent motive for Dorothy's transformation is a familiar one to women through the ages—a better chance at doing what she loves. Billy plays jazz piano, alto and soprano saxophones, while touring through the Midwest and West. Her first known experience crossdressing, in 1933, is linked to her desire to secure an audition for a job. She cuts her hair, tapes her chest, and puts on a suit. But Tipton also is sexually attracted to females. Thus adopting a masculine gender identity and role helps solve two major life problems. It facilitates entry into the world Dorothy wishes to inhabit, and permits socially acceptable access to relationships with other women.

Early on, some people know Dorothy as a crossdressing woman. But in time Tipton becomes more secretive and increasingly surrounded by people who have no idea that this apparent man is really a woman. In this guise Tipton has a number of successful sexual relationships with women who never suspect their lover's real sex. Using the excuse that a car accident has caused rib damage, Tipton keeps her chest bound and, apparently, no one ever questions this habit.

After years on the circuit as a performer, Tipton more-or-less 'retires' and settles in the Spokane valley, in Washington State, in 1958. Taking a job as a theatrical booking agent, Tipton marries a former stripper named Kitty in 1962 and the couple adopt three boys: John, Scott, and William. They are an apparently ordinary family, with Tipton actively involved in the community. But, like many ordinary families, this one has its secrets. Though married 18 years, the Tiptons maintain separate bedrooms and after Billy's death, Kitty claims they never engaged in sexual relations. The union dissolves in 1982, when the couple separate over a common battleground—how to raise the children. They eventually divorce. When Billy dies in 1989, 'he' stands revealed to be 'she' to a surprised community—and family. It is a secret Tipton has been able to keep from 'his' former lovers, at least three wives, and three children.

Q. 49

Who are some famous crossdressing men?

The Short Answer. Throughout history those most likely to be remembered have been the socially prominent, especially those in power. Thus many of history's most famous crossdressers have been rulers, like Pharaoh Hatshepshut (Q. 42), Queen Christina of Sweden (Q. 48), or those found here, including Roman Emperors (Caligula, Nero, Elegabulus), and European Kings (Henry III of France). But the ruling class, permitted greater freedom but also more gossiped about, only represent the tip of the iceberg; many more men than named here crossdressed, whether known to history or not (cf. the answer to Q. 46). The same theme applies in modern times—the socially prominent enjoy a liberty to publicly crossdress (for whatever reason) that transcends any criticism. Only today these people are likely to be entertainers and sports figures rather than rulers.

The Longer Answer. There have been crossdressing men throughout history, most of whom are unremembered. But some have remained more-or-less familiar names either because of their crossdressing, or because of fame for other reasons. For the most part, a common trait links both cases: the socially prominent are more likely to be remarked upon by their contemporaries and to be remembered to history. Whether principally recalled for other reasons or for their crossdressing, society's elite (and sometimes infamous) dominate the list of remembered crossdressing men. A few samples should suffice to illustrate.

Who is Ulrich von Lichtenstein?

Ulrich von Lichtenstein is an Austrian medieval knight and author. In the 13th century he poses as the Roman goddess Venus, complete with dress and a golden wig. In all, he journeys through more than fifty towns of northern Italy and Bohemia, from Venice to Austria. Along the way, von Lichtenstein jousts with rival knights. He sets down an account of his 'Venus Journey' in his *Frauendienst (Service of Ladies)*, a narrative poem appearing in 1257 C.E. In it he offers as the motivation for his journey his earnest desire to win the love of a lady who has spurned him. At the same time, he maintains, he intends his journey to honor all women. The tale inspires both later literary work, film, and the tourist-oriented Škofja Loka's *Medieval Days*.[482]

Who is King Henry III of France?

King Henry III (1551-1589), born Henry de Valois, the son of King Henry II and Catherine de' Medici, rules France from 1574 until his death in 1789. His mother, who many see as "inclined to feminize her royal sons,"[483] is a strong influence. Only 23 when he comes to the throne, he faces daunting obstacles, not the least of which are concerns and criticisms regarding his sexuality and failure to provide an heir. From the beginning of his reign Henry is forced to address such matters, which he begins doing by combining his coronation with marriage the day after—a move aimed to answer criticism over the effeminacy his society believes he has displayed in his previous casual heterosexual excesses.[484]

Henry's life proves full of intrigue, contradiction, and strife. A devout Catholic, he is a leader in the French War against the Protestants. But he copes poorly with divisions within his own family and with rivals from outside it. In a tremendously ill-chosen maneuver, he arranges the assassination of the Duke and Cardinal of Guise. Already unpopular, this seals his fate. Forced to an alliance with his rival, Henry of Navarre (the future King Henry IV), Henry III becomes himself the victim of treacherous trickery. Informed that a young Dominican monk bears a secret message for him, Henry permits the man to come close. But the monk delivers instead a fatal knife blow. So passes Henry III.

Slender of form and effeminate in manner, Henry allegedly has a long history of crossdressing. He is said to have appeared at a royal ball dressed as a girl when 14 years old. As a man, he prefers furs and luxurious, delicate garments, sports earrings in both ears, and on at least one occasion dresses in the costume of an Amazon, complete with a belt of ivory skulls. He is said to favor being addressed as "Her Majesty," and even to appear in formal session among his court deputies dressed entirely as a woman. Henry also places in his company a group of courtiers known as the Minions (*mignons*), who grow their hair long, apply makeup, and dress in a fashion favored by English women of the day.[485]

Of course, as is often the case, those who oppose the King probably exaggerate descriptions of his behavior. The times are turbulent, the king has many enemies, and fashions can be variously interpreted. Pierre de L'Éstoile (1546-1611), most famous chronicler of the times, writes, "The king made jousts, tournaments, ballets, and a great many masquerades, where he was dressed as a woman, working his doublet and exposing his throat, there wearing a collar of pearls and three collars of linen, two ruffled and one turned upside down, in the same way as was then worn by the ladies of the court."[486] However, modern scholar Catherine Crawford—who reproduces the passage from L'Éstoile—is of the view that outside one Carnival season, "he never again appeared to be cross-dressing."[487] Like so many judgments, the suitability of this one may depend on how 'crossdressing' is perceived or interpreted.

Who is Francois Timoleon Abbe de Choisy?

Although his story is repeated elsewhere (see the answer to Q. 70), de Choisy merits mention here. A noted French writer—and priest—Francois Timoleon, Abbe de Choisy (1644-1724) is dressed as a girl throughout childhood. This ends briefly when he leaves home at 18 for studies at the Sorbonne. However, only a year later—freshly granted an abbacy—he secretly appears on stage as an actress. Continuing to crossdress as an adult, he refers to himself as 'Comtesse des Barres.' When he marries, de Choisy selects Mademoiselle de Charlotte, who also loves to crossdress in the identity of 'Monsieur de Maulny.'

Apparently, none of this prevents his pursuing activities with the blessing of the Church. In 1676, he accompanies Cardinal de Bouillon to witness the coronation of Pope Innocent XI; he appears at the subsequent ball dressed as a woman. In 1685, he is part of a mission to Siam, where he appears in woman's garb and apparently makes quite an impression on the locals. Admitted to the French Academy in 1687, de Choisy enjoys a long and distinguished career, contributing to literature numerous works, mostly religious, including a well-regarded, multi-volume history of the Church (written between 1703-1723). He continues his crossdressing until the end of his life.

Who is the Chevalier d'Eon?

Arguably the most famous crossdressing man of history is Chevalier d'Eon (1728-1810). This is due in no small measure to the influence of the pioneering British sexologist, Havelock Ellis, who chooses to term crossdressing behavior as 'Eonism.'[488] The Beaumont Society, a United Kingdom support group for transgendered people, will also be named after him.[489]

Charles-Geneviève-Louis-Auguste-André-Thimothée d'Eon de Beaumont[5] is born into 18th century France's upper class. His father, Louis d'Eon de Beaumont, is an advocate in the High Court of Justice, and his mother is Lady Françoise de Chavanson, of a wealthy aristocratic family. This grants d'Eon social privileges and advantages, but also helps ensure his later life as a very public figure.

Chevalier d'Eon's childhood is marked by excellence in school. Later, it will also be the subject of speculation. His 1779 book of memoirs, *La Vie Militaire, politique, et privée de Mademoiselle d'Eon* (*The Military, Political and Private Life of Mademoiselle d'Eon*),[490] makes the extraordinary claim that d'Eon has actually been born female, but reared as a boy, only later reverting to 'her' true identity as a woman. In fact, he is biologically male.

In 1749, having completed his studies, d'Eon becomes a secretary in the Paris office of finance, where he writes his first book—on government finance. It marks the beginning of a long literary career. Perhaps his most famous book is his 1764 volume *Lettres, mémoires, et négociations particuliéres* (*Letters, Memoirs, and Private Negotiations*). A 13 volume work, *Les Loisirs du chevalier d'Eon de Beaumont* (*The Leisure Activities of the Chevalier d'Eon de Beaumont*), appears in 1774. His last intended book is a never published autobiography entitled *La Pucelle de Tonnerre* (*The Maiden of Tonnerre*).

Chevalier d'Eon, however, lives more than a life of quiet contemplation. Though comfortably surrounded by books as a royal censor, in 1756 he enters the King's Secret, a network of royal spies for Louis XV. That same year, the king sends him on a secret mission to Russia's Empress Elizabeth I. Though ostensibly a secretary attached to the French secretary Chevalier Douglas, d'Eon meets with the empress while in disguise as a woman. The negotiations are successful; in 1757 France and Russia renew formal diplomatic relations.

Back in France, in 1762 d'Eon is appointed a captain of the renowned Dragoons, and sees action in the Seven Years War. He distinguishes himself in combat, receiving wounds in both thigh and head. At the war's end he is part of the negotiations that lead to the treaty adopted. By age 35, he has earned the Cross of Saint-Louis and is raised to noble rank with the title 'Chevalier.'

In 1763 he is appointed Plenipotentiary Minister to England. It begins a long association with the British. Alongside his official duties, d'Eon continues to operate as a spy for the King, who is planning an invasion of England. But d'Eon's lofty status proves short-lived. In October of the same year he is ordered back to France. Fearing the outcome, he refuses and spends the next fourteen years in voluntary exile. He publishes the aforementioned *Lettres, mémoires, et négociations particuliéres* (1764) and begins amassing a large personal library. Despite whatever concerns d'Eon has about going home, in 1766 the king grants him an annual pension for his previous services.

Interestingly, during his years in England, d'Eon becomes the subject of rumors and betting concerning his true gender. Though he regularly dresses as a man—and a military one at that—speculation swirls that he is actually a woman masquerading as a man. The betting on his gender becomes widespread, even reaching the London Stock Exchange. The wagering reaches hundreds of thousands of British pounds—a truly staggering volume for the time. The Court of the King's Bench finally has to resolve who are the winners and who the losers—all without recourse to proof one way or the other. The matter will not be finally resolved until an autopsy after his death in 1810.

After the death of France's Louis XV in 1774, d'Eon begins negotiations for his return to his homeland. The new king, Louis XVI, is eager to reclaim documents in d'Eon's possession. In their settlement, a startling announcement is made: the Chevalier d'Eon is really a woman! Having lived a very public life as a man, d'Eon in middle age now fully takes on the life of a woman—in which he remains the rest of his days. The king orders d'Eon be publicly recognized as a woman and dress as one—and even grants funds for purchasing a wardrobe. So, in 1777, the now 'Mademoiselle' d'Eon returns to France. There he dresses regularly as a woman, though proudly wearing the Cross of Saint-Louis prominently on his left breast. In such garb he even participates in fencing matches. Through it all, the public accepts the declaration that d'Eon is, in fact, a woman whose earlier life as a man had been the fiction.

But Chevalier d'Eon does not long enjoy the king's favor. In 1778 he is briefly imprisoned, then spends the next six years mostly at the family home in Tonnerre. During this period Christian faith becomes more important to d'Eon. But France is no longer proving a satisfactory home. In 1785 he leaves again for England. There he lives the rest of his life. However, when the French Revolution occurs in 1789 he loses his annual pension, introducing him to financial difficulties that will persist from then on. He is forced to sell his books and to participate in fencing tournaments to earn money. After a serious fencing wound in 1796, he retires from such contests and his last years are marked by poverty. He dies in 1810.[491]

Why does d'Eon give up the life of a man for that of a woman? Biographer Gary Kates finds more than a single reason at work. In part the 'transformation' seems to be a response to his own life events—a public career in decline. But Kates also finds motivation in d'Eon's convictions about the genders. Utilizing the unpublished autobiographical materials d'Eon penned, Kates suggests that the Chevalier gradually came to the conviction that man is as inevitably tied to sin as woman is to virtue. Thus, personal salvation lay in being as like a woman as possible.[492] In this respect, d'Eon pursues a radical but sensible course. Yet having embarked on this life, d'Eon seems guided by a particular vision of the ideal woman. As Kates remarks, "d'Eon did not simply want to be known by his public as a woman; he wanted to be known as a certain kind of woman: Amazonian, pious, virtuous, patriotic; a woman in the mode of the Maid of Orléans, Joan of Arc."[493]

Who is Virginia Prince?

Arguably the most important transgender individual of the 20th century is the person who coined the term 'transgender'—Virginia Prince. Indeed, Riki Anne Wilchens gets it exactly right when quoting a friend: "Virginia Prince made it possible for two crossdressers to look one another in the eye."[494] Unfortunately, for a figure of such significance relatively little is known of Prince's early life. A biological male, born in Los Angeles on November 23, 1912, Prince became the recipient of the first award for lifetime achievement granted by the International Foundation for Gender Education (IFGE; see the answer to Q. 34).

Prince's gender crossings begin in childhood, about age 12, using what is readily available—mother's clothing. As a youth, Prince learns how to pass as a girl, but only does so occasionally. Much of the time now and through early adulthood, Prince occupies a masculine gender role and seems to do so with great success. In public life as a man, Prince earns a Ph.D. in pharmacology, marries a woman by whom a son is born, and works in higher education as an instructor and researcher. The marriage, however, founders—as will a second one some years later, despite the greater tolerance of this second wife to the ongoing crossdressing.[495]

In 1957, Prince publishes an article in the *American Journal of Psychotherapy* titled, "Homosexuality, Transvestism and Transsexuality: Reflections on Their Etiology and Differentiation." This article has attached to it a 'preamble' by the noted expert on transsexualism, Harry Benjamin, who knows the author in both masculine and feminine presentations, and who characterizes 'him' as "highly educated with a fine cultural background." The article itself defends the earlier conclusions of sexologists Magnus Hirschfeld and Havelock Ellis that distinguishes crossdressing homosexuals from what Prince calls 'true' transvestites, who are heterosexual. Prince likewise differentiates transvestites from transsexuals, calling the former people well content with their sexual bodies and not desiring to remove their sex organs.[496]

As Prince moves progressively more into cross gender activities, other important changes occur. To disguise his/her birth name (which Prince prefers not be disclosed), the name 'Charles Prince' is adopted. By the mid-1950s, Prince begins the mission of educating others about crossdressers. During this period 'Virginia' emerges as an identity, the identity Prince eventually will come to live fully within by the end of the 1960s. At the beginning of that decade Prince begins publishing *Transvestia*, a magazine aimed at a male crossdressing audience. Some of the subscribers to this publication form the core in 1961 for the 'Hose and Heels Club' in Los Angeles. About 1962 this club evolves into a national phenomenon, and within a few years, an international one, eventually under the name by which it is known today—Tri-Ess (see the answer to Q. 34). In connection with this expansion, in 1967 Virginia Prince visits 37 cities in 8 European countries.[497]

Prince's Chevalier Publications, publisher of *Transvestia*, also puts out other materials, including crossdressing erotica, some of which Prince writes. These activities bring legal woes. Arrested in the mid-1960s for sending obscene materials through the mail, jail is avoided with the sentencing of 5 years probation. However, public crossdressing could be construed as a violation of parole, so Prince's lawyer argues to specifically permit it as part of Prince's ongoing efforts to educate the public about crossdressing.[498] Not content to leave it at that, Prince successfully lobbies the United States Postal Service to change its regulations so that material on crossdressing will no longer be considered pornography and materials concerning it can be mailed legally.[499]

Prince displays vigor in a range of activities that includes more work spreading support groups for crossdressers, writing, participating in scholarship to further research and education on crossdressers, and even marketing various things of help to transgender people such as artificial breasts.[500] Of special note is her collaboration with Peter Bentler. He is a psychologist at UCLA, an expert in psychometrics and measurement, and a scholar with a long history of involvement in personality research. Together, in the late 1960s, they enlist the aid of male crossdressers in what are then unprecedented large-scale research studies. These include 180 male crossdressers administered a standard personality test, and 504 male crossdressers surveyed on a number of basic matters (research covered in the answers to Q. 26-27). In 1967, Prince publishes her first book, *The Transvestite and His Wife*.[501] Ironically, it comes even as Prince's marriage nears its end.

The year 1968 proves a pivotal one. Prince's second marriage ends—though not because of crossdressing—and a gender Rubicon is crossed: henceforth Prince will live entirely as Virginia. She appears for the first time on television and fully embraces her career working on transgender issues as a full-time transgender person. Of course, at that time the terminology for male heterosexual crossdressers is 'transvestite.'

Prince eventually coins new words to more adequately describe people like herself. In the late 1980s (1987 or 1988),[502] she proposes the term 'transgender' to refer to those who choose to live full-time in a gender different from the one assigned them at birth, but who do so without the sense of being trapped in the wrong sex and without seeking sex reassignment surgery. As a 'transgenderist'—another term originated by Prince—this biological male lives as a woman. She carries out a wide range of activities connected to educating and supporting other crossdressers, as well as informing the general public what this behavior is about.

Virginia Prince continues her work until well-advanced in age. At age 82, she still is thinking about important issues, and offers up a new term: 'transposeur' to describe someone "who sets over or rearranges the order of things or takes a position across from or opposite to his original position"—a description she sees as adequately fitting what a transgenderist does. And she regards the male crossdressers of today as the vanguard of men's liberation in a manner similar to the female crossdressers of an earlier generation.[503] Also in these later years, she is increasingly recognized by an ever wider public as a significant figure in the advancement of awareness of transgender people and issues in the United States and abroad.

Who are some other famous men who crossdressed?

Famous men get remembered. Sometimes their fame is directly related to a transgender reality, as in the case of some of the males discussed above. Others attain renown by virtue of something else, yet are well-known for their gender crossing behavior. Still others gain fame for reasons other than crossdressing, and in many instances their crossdressing is either little known or is acknowledged as a small aspect of their life experience and not worth special mention. In short, though these men participate in a transgender reality the evidence may not strongly suggest they experience a transgender identity. In the cases next briefly considered, we find a range of identification with transgender experience and expression.

Samuel Clemens (Mark Twain)

Samuel Langhorne Clemens (1835-1910), arguably the greatest writer produced by the United States, is better known by his pen name, Mark Twain. As a writer, Twain is never bashful about exploring gender and gender-crossing. At least nine of his works feature crossdressing characters, both male and female (see the answer to Q. 47). Among them is his most famous character, Huckleberry Finn. While Twain often treats gender crossing in ways that reproduce and reinforce conventional notions of his time, he also shows a willingness and ability to think outside the confines of his culture's stereotypes.[504]

Twain's flexibility of mind apparently extends to his personal behavior. Twain scholar Laura Skandera-Trombley asks, in light of his writings, if Twain himself ever engages in crossdressing and concludes it seems he does so quite often. She remarks he is quick to meet whatever seems the demands of family charades and drama productions. She points to a photo taken of Twain near the end of the 19th century. It shows him, alongside his oldest daughter, posing on a cabin porch. His daughter is dressed like a princess. Twain has on a bonnet and a woman's dress worn over rolled-up long underwear, with a hot water bottle hanging from his neck. There is no expression of shame on his face; indeed, Skandera-Trombley comments he looks like he has just been caught dancing a merry jig.[505]

Still, there has never been much biographical attention drawn to this behavior and it seems more plausible to think Twain uses crossdressing as play than as any expression of transgendered identity. That he is fascinated by transgendered realities seems certain, and that he is secure enough in his own identity to publicly employ crossdressing fits what we know about him. But those two facts together suggest that if his identity is transgendered he will have made it plain. Rather, the evidence available only supports his own engagement in crossdressing in the service of social play—not unlike those who masquerade for Halloween or Carnival.

Dennis Rodman

Dennis Rodman (1961-) exemplifies the modern man whose attainment of high social status derives from success in entertaining others. In his case, this comes through his proficiency at basketball. As a star member of world championship basketball teams in Detroit and Chicago in the 1980s-1990s, Rodman gains an audience. He extends that attention and keeps it burning brightly by a number of very public unconventional behaviors—including crossdressing.

In his 1996 autobiography, *Bad As I Wanna Be*, Rodman says, "I grew up around women, and as a kid I would sometimes dress up as a girl."[506] He adds that his play included dressing femininely, wearing makeup, and acting like a woman. In contrast with his childhood crossdressing, Rodman claims as an adult that, "When I cross-dress now, it's just another way I can show all the sides of Dennis Rodman. I'm giving you the whole package. I'm becoming the all-purpose person."[507]

Rodman further claims that crossdressing is not something he gives much forethought or planning to, but rather does as the mood fits and in whatever setting he feels like. He also recounts a progression of the behavior: "I don't remember the first time I decided to do it as an adult; there isn't one time that really sticks out. It was more of a gradual thing, where it progressed from earrings and fingernails to halter tops and tight leather shorts."[508] One item his crossdressing does not include, he says, is lingerie. But what he does wear he buys for himself—and he claims women love a man secure enough in himself to be comfortable in feminine makeup and clothing.[509]

In 1996, Rodman says he has not yet worn a dress, though he has purchased one for an interview with Howard Stern. However, to publicize the release of his autobiography he does show up to a press event clad in full bridal regalia, and signs photos shot of him in that dress as 'Mrs. Dennis Rodman.' Whatever else it may have done for him, it gains him the desired publicity and remains one of the most indelible images many people have of him.

Rodman's own words leave the question of a transgendered identity open. His description of its origin and progress resembles that heard from many transgendered individuals. But the motivation for his public crossdressing seems other than expression of such an identity. There is no question his dress behavior draws notice—but that is exactly the point. Any statement intended by Rodman about himself through his crossdressing, beyond his declaration in his autobiography's title, remains unclear.

Q. 50

What will the present likely be noted for with reference to gender, transgender, and crossdressing?

The Short Answer. Though it is speculative to imagine how the future will look back upon our time, it seems plausible to think certain items will stand out. First, sex and gender are undergoing intense scrutiny and reappraisal. In the realm of sex the reality and frequency of intersex conditions has proved especially influential in eliciting new thinking about sexed bodies and how gender relates to sex. Second, the notion that gender is socially constructed has permitted recognition of gender fluidity and reopened serious consideration of 'third gender' possibilities. Third, transgender has come out of the closet in new ways. Instead of gaining public attention only through entertainment, prostitution, or sensational news stories, transgendered people and their supporters have made strides in 'normalizing' what many saw as 'unnatural' by living transgendered lives openly, through research and publications, and via activism to change laws and policies.

With regard to crossdressing we may also note three matters likely to be remarked upon by future commentators on our time: first, men are the focus of attention. Second, crossdressing men are resisting the stereotyped images often placed on them, and doing so in a variety of ways, some of which are very public. Third, in part because it is men who are garnering attention and in part because some of them are activists for change, and in part because of social changes, crossdressing is receiving more and better attention, with greater understanding and wider tolerance. Thus, this time may someday be regarded as one of meaningful changes for crossdressers.

The Longer Answer. We are too close to our own experience to be able to see ourselves as future folk will through the wider, longer lens of history. The best we can offer is speculation, but perhaps not uninformed speculation. The most prominent change in Western society with respect to our topic may be the changing conversation on gender—an often controversial argument proceeding at multiple levels, and not merely in academic halls. As traced in another work, *Conversing on Gender. A Primer for Entering Dialog*, over the last half-century tremendous changes have transpired in how we think about gender.[510]

Even today, many in our society hold assumptions about sex and gender that more accurately reflect the convictions of an earlier understanding than what we have learned more recently. Although, as we have seen (in answering Q. 47) ideas about gender have been debated and modified throughout our history, for some time in our near past the virtually unchallenged perception of sex and gender was that both are fixed, immutable, essential natural realities that yield a hierarchical order with masculine men on top. Of course, this view complicates life for those of us who aren't masculine men—or more particularly, not masculine men of a certain sort, namely White and at least middle class in socioeconomic status. Women and others are disadvantaged in persistent and systemic fashion. An *essentialist* position on sex and gender posits that Nature intends only two sexes—XX and XY—suited naturally for reproduction, which stands center as the norm for human sexuality. Assuming this nature for sex, gender is thought to be a social reflection—a psychological reality on the individual level—that follows naturally and inevitably from the sex-differentiated body. In short, males (sex) must become men (gender); females (sex) must become women (gender).

This view still enjoys support, especially among those who have never thought it through, nor personally recognized the adverse consequences associated with its reign. However, women in our society's past increasingly experienced frustration with a position that both seemed unassailable and that served to keep them 'in their place,' a secondary status justified by appeal to Nature. Second wave feminists in the 1970s successfully challenged essentialism through the most compelling of means—appeals to both reason and evidence. Scholars in many disciplines, ranging from anthropology to biology to economics to psychology to sociology, and many more, brought forth facts that demonstrated essentialism does not adequately reflect reality. Simultaneously, these scholars advanced ideas about how better gender might be conceived.

Foremost among these was a collection of proposals that have been grouped under the umbrella of *social constructionism*. The title is self-explanatory: gender (and to some extent sex, too) is made by people. There are numerous ideas about how gender comes to be constructed, but the basic point remains that far from being an inevitable outgrowth of sex it is socially framed and more variable than the narrow perspective of essentialism recognizes. A little later, a smaller group of scholars under the name of *queer theory* departed from this framework without returning to an essentialist view. Their ideas include some startling proposals, such as Judith Butler's notions of the 'preformativity' of gender. Inasmuch as these various ideas have been discussed in volume 1 of this work and in many other books, we shall leave this matter as is, since our point here is that this upheaval in how we regard gender will likely prove the most notable event of our times—and it has important consequences for the study of transgender realities, including crossdressing.

Transgender has come out of the closet. The more flexible way of understanding gender—one better able to account for actual reality—helps people more accurately comprehend variances from the gender scheme promoted by essentialism and still widely held. Instead of being consigned to seeing transgender experiences and expressions as 'unnatural,' the new ways of looking at gender permit not merely tolerating gender diversity, but actually accepting— even celebrating—it. Some have suspected this is just political opportunism by sexual minorities, but while social and political activism have been important, the success of the new ways of seeing gender resides mostly in their power to better account for the facts of the world we live in.

The more nuanced views of gender have had other practical consequences. Instead of gaining public attention only through entertainment, prostitution, or sensational news stories, transgendered people are gaining wider access into the world everyone else lives in, with its manifold possibilities for employment and housing. It is science that has promoted and supported the changes in policy and law providing transgendered people equal rights and civil protections. Both the transgendered and their supporters have made strides in 'normalizing' what many saw as 'unnatural' by living transgendered lives openly, through research and publications, and via activism to change laws and policies. It remains a truism that the most effective way to combat bias, prejudice, and discrimination is through education—and the best education is actually knowing a transgendered person and thereby discovering that the negative stereotypes are untrue.

We may also consider that even as the changes in how we talk about gender has positively affected transgendered people, those changes have also facilitated alterations in the experience of gender. In other words, though variously gendered people have always been around, and the newer ways of talking about gender in part exist to reflect their presence more accurately, the new language of gender also offers new avenues for self-perception and self-experience. Today's transgender people are in important respects different from their predecessors in their self-perception, self-experience, and even self-presentation because of the changes in talking about gender.

Comprehending this situation prompts anxiety in some folk. They worry that promoting gender as socially constructed or individually formed opens the way to such wide diversity that gender will descend into chaos—with devastating social consequences. On the other hand, if gender is truly this flexible, then we might be better served with such an overwhelming range of diversity that we finally succeed in dethroning gender as a basis for social status and power. In such a brave new world maybe allowing everyone whatever gender identity and role they desire will truly democratize us. Such a scenario seems very utopian at present.

These kind of musings have their place—but there is inadequate space here to pursue them. We must redirect our attention more completely to crossdressing. In that respect, we may note three matters that appear most likely to be remembered in the future about our own times. These are:

- First, crossdressing males have become the focus of attention.
- Second, crossdressing men are resisting the stereotyped images often placed on them, and doing so in a variety of ways, some of which are very public.
- Third, in part because it is men who are garnering attention and in part because some of them are activists for change, and in part because of social changes, crossdressing is receiving more and better attention, with greater understanding and wider tolerance.

This time we are dwelling within may someday be regarded as one of meaningful, important changes for crossdressers.

Why does male crossdressing receive most of today's attention?

To a student of the history of crossdressing (and there are more interested in the topic than many like to acknowledge), the most remarkable difference between the 20th century and prior centuries is the emergence of male crossdressing as the focus of attention. In answering previous questions we have discussed the forces at play in producing this change. Nevertheless, it is appropriate to review them here in answering our present query.

The forces in view are all embedded in the changes in gender conversation summarized above. That larger conversation must be kept in mind. However, in this section our attention will be narrowed to a few instrumental forces directly involved in moving society's attention away from women and toward men. Although it may be plausible to point to a variety of forces instrumental in moving male crossdressing to the center of attention, three appear especially significant:

- the medicalization of sex;
- increasing pressure on the masculine gender role; and
- the women's movement.

These are interrelated and each is an aspect of the broader gender conversation.

The Medicalization of Sex

As we discussed earlier (answer to Q. 46), the medicalization of sex has had a profound impact on the social perception of sex, sexuality, and gender. The phrase refers to the invention of a new way of understanding and talking about human sexuality that begins in the latter half of the 19th century and is fully developed by the middle of the 20th century. Previous to this new way of looking at things, social focus has been on sexual *behaviors* rather than about the inherent dispositions and psychological states said to produce them.[511] In fact, for most of human history, sexual acts have been judged mostly by practical measures: do they produce offspring? Pleasure? Social accord or discord?[512]

Why did things change? As we have seen, the 19th century in Europe and the United States is marked by lively conversation about gender. Appeals to science are common. Medical science, in particular, emerges as the most prominent voice in talking about sex and sexuality; linked to gender this makes medicine an authority on it as well. Medical researchers then, as they do now, possess an understandable desire to scientifically classify and categorize human behavior related to health—including sexual health and mental health. Today these are largely the domain of professions like psychiatry—spawned by and remaining within medicine—and psychology. But in the latter half of the 19th century, both of these are still nascent; medicine is the branch of science looked to for guidance in matters these other disciplines will soon claim as their own. As medical professionals consolidate their hold in the 19th century as the authoritative voices on human sexuality, they recast its discussion consistent with a new vocabulary. Words like 'homosexual' and 'heterosexual' begin to emerge. The variants of human sexual behavior are being labeled—and sometimes linked to gender (e.g., 'hysteria' as a woman's mental disorder), or gender variance.

The authority of medical science in these matters is both invited and sanctioned by a perceived social need. Historian Angus McLaren says that sexology's emergence coincides with European magistrates increasingly relying on medical experts to inform them about sexual behaviors related to crimes before the court.[513] The rule of law obviously requires clear boundaries for judicial decisions—and such boundaries are not always apparent. Medical science's task, eagerly undertaken, becomes to provide those boundaries. This they accomplish by coining labels to accompany categories into which they can place 'deviant' behaviors. Behaviors like crossdressing—already publicly discouraged by various laws—are now 'officially' linked to mental disorders. 'Normal' and 'healthy' people do not engage in crossdressing; laws sanctioning penalties for the behavior are understandable, though medical professionals prefer the disturbed individuals be treated as ill rather than as criminals. One outgrowth of this way of doing things will be modern psychiatry's diagnostic model set out in the successive volumes of the *Diagnostic and Statistical Manual of Mental Disorders* (DSM model), appearing after the Second World War (considered at length in volume 4 of my work). In this model crossdressing has persistently been included as a mental disorder—for males.

Ostensibly this new medical language of sexuality is scientific and rooted in an objective discernment of natural reality. But as McLaren points out, medical professionals solidly ensconced in the middle class prove oblivious to the efforts of their own social class to impose their values about sexuality and gender on everyone else. Like others of their class, these medical professionals accept certain social conventions about behavior and, especially, about masculine sexuality.[514] Masculine men obviously don't go out in feminine apparel! Masculine men are heterosexual. The temptation to merge 'deviancies' is irresistible: if men aren't dressing like men, they must be emasculating themselves, which isn't normal. Since dress is widely theorized to exist to attract potential sexual partners, crossdressed males must be looking for men; therefore, male crossdressers are homosexual. This 'logic' is driven not by empiricism but by deductively working out unexamined presuppositions about what is 'natural' and 'normal'—presuppositions derived from culture, not Nature.

The medical professionals who construct the new model accept without much scrutiny the aforementioned essentialist perspective. So in practice the quest to accomplish an objective science, blind to the subjective bias of its architects, proceeds as Robert Nye puts it, "to conflate sex, gender, and sexuality and to treat the sexual identity of individuals as biologically or 'naturally' determined."[515] The supposed triumph of science denies—and effectively hides—the cultural values that guide the all-too-human architects of the new science of sexology. But medical professionals are themselves soon to yield at least partial control to emerging disciplines with an even greater claim on the subject matter.

The establishment of psychiatric and psychological disciplines further shifts the emerging discourse on human sexuality and gender. These professions gain a measure of scientific legitimacy by committing to the medical model. But they also uncritically accept the accompanying essentialist perspective. Moreover, their focus is often on people brought to them—willingly or unwillingly—who are socially deemed to suffer from disordered sexuality—people like crossdressers. The medical model and its embedded essentialism thus lead mental health professionals to pathologize much of the behavior they are confronted by—and then to seek for it a causal path, much as a doctor looks for the cause of a physical illness. Similarly, psychiatrists and psychologists often spend considerable energy looking for a physical basis for psychological disturbances, thinking, for example, that sexual abnormalities might be explained by some body deficiency.[516] The essentialist sense of biological determinism sorts everyone into categories, starting with sex. Born either male or female—save for the unfortunate few whose hermaphroditism shows Nature makes mistakes—resulting identities and behaviors are expected to reflect the 'natural' consequences of biological origin. Crossdressers confound expectations by not staying to the expected and prescribed path. This in itself is enough to 'prove' their disorder. Since gender, in this model, is presumed to depend on sex, with both converging in sexual attitudes and behaviors, a crossdresser must have a failed gender sense that correlates to a disturbed sexuality.

When things 'go astray' according to this scheme, whether through intersex birth or influences that prompt socially ascribed deviant behavior, the medicalization of sex points to an authoritative path to follow in response. First, the condition must be properly labeled—sorted to where it belongs. Then it has to be investigated in terms of the biological forces at work. If these cannot be found, the medical model need not be abandoned. Instead, it merely requires shifting its logic to searching out environmental factors as though these can be summed up through either a single causal pathway (a disease), or multiple causes resulting in a coherent symptom pattern (a syndrome).[517] Crossdressing was early on subjected to this process with the initial result linking it firmly with homosexual orientation. Over time that simplistic identification proved inadequate and the model has grudgingly modified itself.

The medicalization of sex conjoins systematic classification through labeling behaviors and 'orientations' into seemingly discrete categories with an implicit essentialist perspective that privileges a narrow view of the world—one in which White heterosexual procreational sexuality and gender conforming to normative masculinity or femininity are what is 'natural' and expected. This places the medicalization of sex as a lynchpin to the continuing success of a gender culture in which both sexuality and gender are rigidly constricted, making inevitable much stress in lived experience with regard to both. It also goes far to explain why male crossdressing receives exclusive attention in the model. What males do matters in a way inconceivable for females. Males serve as the template for normative humanity. It is the same instinct that has kept medical science largely focused on research principally involving males, as in recent years has been so well documented with regard to heart health. Male crossdressing is deeply disturbing to the implicit vision of humanity at the center of the medicalization of sex.

The logical limitations of the medical model in attempting to explain the complexities of human experience and behavior inevitably show up. People will be who they are regardless of what a set of cultural values proclaim they ought to be, and natural variations persist in the face of attempts to define them out of existence or label them dysfunctional. Male crossdressers have not disappeared because physicians, psychiatrists, and psychologists proclaim crossdressing symptomatic of mental disorder. In fact, for the most part male crossdressers have stuck to an instinct that says their behavior is not indicative of mental illness and have stayed far away from mental health treatment (which has proven bankrupt in changing or extinguishing the behavior). Instead, increasingly crossdressers have hearkened to voices they believe speak more accurately to their situation—the voices emerging from the challenge of essentialism. We would be fair in claiming that the new emergence of an invigorated gender concept serves in itself as an indictment of the paucity of language and logic in the medical model when applied to phenomena studiously linked to sex, sexuality and gender.

The inadequacy of the medical model is being seen by more folk today than ever before. However, Western mental health as a system remains largely committed to it with unstinting efforts to rescue it through doing the same things over and over—as though merely trying harder will prove to be the answer. With reference to the DSM model, for example, each succeeding edition has been larger than the one before it as diagnostic categories multiply seemingly without end. The poverty of the fruits of the medicalization of sex also points to problems arising from an uncritical acceptance of essentialism, at least an essentialism rooted in 19th century European values. As doctors, psychiatrists, psychologists, and sexologists try to sort out the different displays of sex and sexuality they are confronted by the need to draw on the concept of gender. In the mid-20th century this need inadvertently contributes to the feminist awakening that reinvigorates the gender conversation.[518] But while that awakening helps further discourage disparagement of girls and women, it does not keep male crossdressers from remaining the subjects of social scorn—and medical judgment.

Increasing Pressure on the Masculine Gender Role

The medicalization of sex has had an unintended influence in helping constrict masculinity. By positing what is 'natural' and 'normal,' and tying both to a set of cultural values conditioned by a bygone age and place, over time pressure has mounted as individuals respond to demands that were always more idealistic than realistic, and that increasingly display their outdated quality. The medicalization of sex lent the weight of an authoritative judgment as to what is 'healthy' to culture's construction of gender identity, gender roles, sexual scripts, and stereotypes about masculinity, femininity, homosexuality, and so forth. As filtered through the mechanisms of the broader culture such as media, politics, school and family, these notions become part of the air we breathe while living in our Western society.

From birth forward these ideas about sex, sexuality and gender exert force on us. Both boys and girls experience pressures to conform to their assigned gender identity. However, these pressures appear to be more pronounced on boys because of the rigid and restrictive patterns of socialization they experience—and a consequence is various kinds of psychological distress.[519] Yet the basic logic boys master growing up is fairly straightforward: don't be feminine. Anything associated with femininity—including homosexuality or crossdressing—is lent a negative appraisal and discouraged, sometimes forcefully. Thus it may be difficult to understand why boys suffer when the demand is so narrow and seemingly straightforward. To better comprehend the situation we must look at the construction of modern Western masculinity more closely. It displays at least these three tendencies:

- ❑ It tends to be prohibitive in its prescriptions.
- ❑ It tends to make demands more than offer opportunities.
- ❑ It tends to rely on negation of others for self-definition.

Developmental psychologist Ruth Hartley long ago noted that prescriptions of desired behavior for boys more often comes in the form of what he ought *not* to do than in encouragement of what he should do.[520] Research has consistently found that boys are more liable than girls to draw attention for negative behavior and are more likely to be punished. This certainly pertains to gender variant behaviors. Crossdressing is typically regarded as far more worrisome in a boy than a girl. In fact, a study examining referrals of children to a clinic treating 'Gender Identity Disorder' over a span from 1978-1995 found boys nearly seven times more likely than comparable girls to be referred to mental health professionals. What is especially telling is that this is despite the fact that, if anything, the girls referred actually showed more extreme cross-gender behavior! The authors are surely right in viewing this as evidence of cultural factors weighing in.[521]

Of course, both boys and girls experience pressures to conform to their assigned gender identity. But the *quality* of these pressures may vary. It appears gender expectations are more rigid and restrictive for boys because of their higher status in the gender hierarchy.[522] More than three decades ago Hartley wrote, "Demands that boys conform to social notions of what is manly come much earlier and are enforced with much more vigor than similar attitudes with respect to girls."[523] If anything, these pressures have intensified. The advances by girls and women, ironically, may increase masculine stress. Girls have been granted latitude to explore wider gender roles; as theirs increase, boys' decrease in order to safeguard masculine privilege. Rather than be offered freedom to explore a variety of ways to be a gendered person, boys are strongly censored for feminine behaviors. In short, they are offered a narrow path along a steep incline to achieve a satisfactory gender.

The necessity of protecting privilege means that the building of modern Western masculinity in boys relies on negation of others for self-definition. There are few worse epithets a boy can hear than to be called a 'sissy'—like his sister, a girl! The label not only threatens his gender, but also his sexuality, for it is associated both with girls (in being a feminine boy), and with nonnormative boys (in being homosexual). A boy must not merely be masculine, but heterosexually so.[524] In this respect, we need to recall the research presented earlier (answer to Q. 47), where a research study not only found 'sissies' more negatively regarded than 'tomboys,' but also more frequently predicted to continue their gender nonconformity into adulthood, to be less 'well-adjusted,' and to be more likely to be homosexual.[525] Such beliefs, irrespective of the facts, reflect the cultural pressure on boys to conform to their assigned gender. To guard his own masculine identity means to denigrate other gender identities, including certain forms of masculinity, to at least some extent. Where a girl has some latitude in desiring and displaying masculinity, a boy has almost none in the opposite direction.

What this means for male crossdressing is that attention by others to such behavior begins very early. Infants are color coded, and while some tolerance is shown to very young boys who 'dress up' like mommy or an older sister, this tolerance is sharply limited. Keeping the attention on males whenever crossdressing is discussed, and then linking it to deviancy and mental disorder, helps emphasize the undesirability of the behavior to boys. Of course, the evidence suggests that a typical response is not to give up the behavior but to hide it. Yet the pressure remains and the boy is likely to incorporate for some time a sense of shame or guilt over crossdressing. Given the connections to femininity ascribed by the culture, social censure also increases the likelihood that crossdressing will be accepted by the crossdresser as meaning what the culture says it means—that he is effeminate, perhaps even really a 'she.' In effect, cultural pressure to protect masculinity may in some cases be driving boys to femininity and a feminine persona in a curious variant of the old saying, 'If you can't lick 'em, join 'em.'

The Women's Movement

Drawing inspiration from cracks in the medicalization of sex, second wave feminists opened wide the conversation on gender—with consequences for crossdressers. In broader strokes, the women's movement put what previously would have been construed as crossdressing into such widespread practice that the label became meaningless. *If* crossdressing is something only a deviant minority does, *then* such dress behavior by the majority of girls and women *can't* be crossdressing! So women wearing pants—the scandal of the mid-19th century—becomes the unremarkable commonplace of the end of the 20th century.

If women can wear whatever they want, as long as they leave some tiny space in dress fashion for men to occupy, then talk of crossdressing is absurd. In part this development follows the logic of the gender hierarchy: what those who are in lesser status rungs does is of far less consequence than what those at the top do. But in part this development also obeys the implicit logic of the view about sexuality reigning in the culture. Males are seen as more highly (and 'naturally') sexualized than females, aggressive and active in sexual behavior, and more prone to sexualize objects and acts. The idea that a girl or woman might be sexually aroused by clothing seems, at best, awkward and easily rejected. Men, on the other hand, sexualize *everything*—why not clothes?

Besides, in view of the culture's values, it is better to regard a crossdresser as doing the behavior for sexual excitement than for reasons more intimately connected to gender identity and role. The former is far less weighty. So all the forces we have been examining collude to push male crossdressing to the forefront, discourage it, pathologize it, and render it in terms the prevailing social system can comprehend. If the result doesn't fit the facts, too bad for the facts.

How are male crossdressers responding to the attention?

Those thrust center stage with the spotlight upon them and grim attendants on every side blocking escape have little choice but to play some part. Among the options are:

- ❏ play the role ascribed;
- ❏ repudiate the role; or
- ❏ hide in the audience.

Each choice carries its own risks and rewards.

Playing the Role: Feminine Males

Some play the role socially imputed to them. They internalize the negative messages sent about their masculinity and flee fully into femininity. In fact, as mentioned earlier (answer to Q. 22), one explanation for male crossdressing is the 'escape from gender role' model. In this model, males who cannot face the demands of the masculine gender as set forth in their society seek relief or escape from such demands by affiliating with femininity. But does this explanation fit all crossdressing males? As we have seen, a large number of reasons are offered for crossdressing and the same pertains to explaining a self-experienced femininity.

For whatever reason, those males who adopt femininity do so in a wide variety of ways—which is what this work is largely about. Some accept the social label of transvestite (though not necessarily the added label of fetishist). They may crossdress partially or fully, seldom or often, mostly in private or commonly in public. The reasons they offer may range from the simple pleasure of the clothes to the sexual pleasure of the behavior to the expression of a distinct feminine persona. Others experiencing and expressing femininity may do so in an abandonment of masculinity, while simultaneously retaining their physical maleness. They are transgendered in the narrow sense. These males live openly as women, often successfully passing as female despite their male anatomy. Still others find a measure of identity in the designation 'transsexual,' rejecting both the maleness of the body and the masculinity to which they were assigned because of that body. These individuals typically seek body modifications, including sexual reassignment surgery, to bring about a conformity of the body to the reality of the mind.

These variations have been covered before (see the answers to Q. 18-20). What we must add here is that today, more so than in the past, such individuals are able to find solace and affiliation in the company of others with similar gender identities. Beginning especially in the latter half of the 20th century, groups began to emerge in England, the United States, and elsewhere to provide contact and support for crossdressing males. The explosive growth of the internet made such connections even easier. In short, crossdressers who in an earlier time would have experienced much more isolation now find resources to draw upon according to their own needs and desires.

In numbers lie strength, and with strength comes voice. Male crossdressers, both individually and as groups, are giving more public expression to their undeniable existence, to its legitimacy as a human expression, and to the necessity that the wider society acknowledge in law and policy their same right to civil protections and opportunities enjoyed by everyone else. An important aspect of finding their voices has been efforts to spread more accurate knowledge about transgender realities. In so doing they challenge stereotypes with the myriad individual truths they embody in the world.

Repudiating the Role, A: Crossdressers in Distress

Some crossdressers repudiate the role assigned them and seek to change parts by conforming to the role originally expected of them as a noncrossdresser. There should be no surprise that not all crossdressers manage the negative social pressures in a way that leaves them able to continue the behavior without grave distress. These individuals may try repeatedly to end the behavior. In fact, as we shall see later, it is very common in the experience of male crossdressers to attempt at least once to stop crossdressing. Many 'purge' by getting rid of all the feminine apparel they have acquired. Some seek out therapy, whether on their own initiative or at the urging of significant others. Few, however, find they are able to permanently stop crossdressing.

The conflict between the need to crossdress and the experience of pressure not to do so can create significant distress. The psychological results are predictable: anxiety and depression, among other things. We must note—in anticipation of material yet to be covered—that research suggests the general population of male crossdressers do not experience any more incidence or severity of mental disorder than noncrossdressing males. Yet there are some males for whom the experience of crossdressing becomes a mix of pleasure and pain, a source of ongoing conflict, and a well of distress.

As we shall document in the fifth volume of this work, attempts to 'cure' crossdressing have proven almost entirely unsuccessful. Increasingly, mental health professionals are considering that such efforts are misguided. More counselors are adopting a supportive approach. In sum, where previous efforts sided with the client's pain and sought to end crossdressing, more and more are siding with the client's pleasure and seeking to alleviate the suffering. In doing so, mental health professionals are inevitably discovering the necessity of addressing the culture and seeking through education and advocacy to change society for the better for all of us.

Repudiating the Role, B: Men Reclaiming Fashion

Some crossdressing males reject the script society writes about them in another way. They contest the label 'crossdresser' and contend they fully embrace masculinity. Some even claim they may be more masculine than other men because they aren't afraid to dress however they please. In effect, these men deny the authority of the Golden Rule of Dress—a male must in no manner appear feminine—and thus seek to undermine its social power. By adopting dress associated with women and doing so openly as men they hope to reclaim an initiative and scope in fashion largely lost by men over the last century.

It probably comes as little surprise that leading the way in this regard are certain male fashion designers. As discussed in volume 1 of this work, fashion designers have for decades been putting male bodies into unbifurcated garb—skirts and dresses made for men. In addition, they have been adding features now associated with women's lingerie (e.g., lace) that once belonged openly and proudly to masculine fashion.

Italian sociologist Francesco Alberoni, in trying to explain these fashion events, offers some plausible hypotheses. First, he notes the economic slump of the early 1990s provided strong incentive to fashion designers to be creative—and adding elements of dress associated with femininity to masculine fashion certainly was creative and got attention. Second, he speculates that the introduction of such elements reflects either a narrowing of the gap between models of masculinity and femininity, or even a cultural dominance by women. In the case of the former, if there isn't that much distance between the genders then there need not be much difference in their dress. In the case of the latter, if femininity has attained dominance then men are doing what women did for centuries—borrowing elements of dress from the dominant gender. Alberoni wonders if perhaps designers are perceiving this "urge for feminization" and responding to it. Of course, other possible explanations exist. Alberoni notes that ours is an increasingly multicultural world with many parts of it less gender divided than Western European and American societies. As Westerners tune in to other cultures they may be relaxing more into wearing styles already acceptable elsewhere. Finally, as rigid gender lines break down, so also do rigid sexual boundaries. Feminists, homosexuals and bisexuals all have helped weaken "the force of heterosexual eroticism." Perhaps male clothing with feminine elements represents a response to a wider anti-hetero trend—a provocation. Alberoni believes all four of these hypotheses are compatible with one another. Hearkening back to Freud's notion that artistic products express different impulses, it is entirely plausible to see in recent men's fashion impulses reflecting the age—and contributing to its change.[526]

What is particularly notable about this response—which remains the road less traveled—is that it presents the sharpest challenge to the prevailing gender hierarchy. Whatever else it is, men dressing more like women parallels earlier historic moves by women in the interest of equality. It is a democratization of dress. Whether such efforts ever succeed in gaining wider adoption remains to be seen.

Hiding in the Audience: Invisible Crossdressers

The prior two responses share in common staying in the spotlight—in other words, not shrinking from public gaze. However, many crossdressing males—in fact, probably the majority—duck the spotlight by taking a place in the audience. In effect, they hide in plain sight. They crossdress, but only in secrecy. Most, perhaps all of the time, the crossdressing occurs in private. If it happens in public great lengths are gone to in order to assure successfully 'passing' so that the crossdressing goes undiscovered. Most of the time, to most who know them, they pass as conforming masculine men. In their public personas they are, to quote the DSM model, "unremarkably masculine."[527]

These individuals remain largely invisible, save perhaps to a few close to them, and so escape in large measure the censure of society. Obviously, this alleviates the concerns many openly crossdressing males experience. But the denial of self carries a price and the fiction typically becomes harder to sustain with age. We all desire to be known—and accepted—for who we are. So it is not uncommon that in middle age the male crossdresser dares more, expanding the scope of those who know and exploring the path of exposure.

In sum, many crossdressing men are resisting the stereotyped images often placed on them, and doing so in a variety of ways, some of which are very public. Through equal measures of courage and creativity many crossdressers are carving out not merely a place for themselves as individuals, but laboring to gentle the world for all who appear gender variant. Of course, there are many in society at large who shrink back from such efforts, others who actively oppose them, and a great number who are simply befuddled by it all. In our present state, too many questions about gender remain unanswered for any of us to feel as comfortable as we might have in the cocoon of a rigid and narrowly described gender hierarchy. But there is no going back: the genie is out of the bottle.

Why is crossdressing being reappraised now?

Perhaps we should ask, '*Is* crossdressing being reappraised now?' In one respect, virtually the entire history of crossdressing has been one of continuous reappraisal. There has never been a complete consensus on the matter, not even in the long period when a narrow psychoanalytic perspective held sway. As documented in the fifth volume of this work (see the answer to Q. 95), there has been a steady stream of scholarly work on male crossdressing. At the same time that review suggests that the scope of this reappraisal, and the number of voices chiming in, have increased in recent years. Though it may be arguable, there do seem reasonable grounds for arguing that our contemporary scene is seriously engaging the reality of crossdressing and transgender realities with special vigor.

The question then becomes, 'Why?'

In part the answer resides in the unsatisfactory answers offered by the medicalization of sex. Scholars outside that tradition, even though bearing the weight of its cultural influence (which affects us all) have created enough space for themselves to frame other perspectives. In so doing they seek to redress the flaws of the dominant model and craft hypotheses that better fit the empirical data. That data, of course, principally comes from crossdressers themselves. So another part of explaining why new attention is being given now rests in the greater voice found issuing from male crossdressers. But we cannot forget that a large part of the reason for the attention today is because the dominant gender scheme articulated from an essentialist perspective has broken down, and as a result the gender hierarchy is experiencing great and creative stress. Precisely because *males* who are supposed to be presenting as *masculine men* are so visible in the dress and often the manner of feminine women, the prevailing gender scheme must pay attention. Such males are not merely hard to comprehend, but pose a perceived threat to masculine hegemony, just as homosexual men did previously (and to some extent still do).

The wonder—perhaps the glory—of it all is the extent to which all of this attention is mostly occurring outside a context of repression and violence. Because of social changes, crossdressing is receiving more and better attention, with greater understanding and wider tolerance. This is not to minimize the very real and unacceptable levels of violence that still transpire (and are covered earlier in this work). But it does seem the reappraisal of transgender realities and crossdressing occurring today is more characterized by openness than before, both by scholars and the general populace. At the very time we are all wrestling with gender in a broader sense, the very uncertainties by which we find ourselves confronted seem for most of us to be producing a greater sense of tolerance. Perhaps in the face of uncertainty we are capable of adopting a wait-and-see attitude, a willingness to live-and-let-live, rather than merely retreating to the security of a gender system that secured order at the price of equality. If so, there is hope for us all.

Question Set 7:

Where in the world are crossdressing and transgender realities found?

In this question set our attention moves from history to geography. Those who argue that transgender realities are rooted in Nature, rather than purely culturally-derived, point to their existence both across time (history) and around the world (geography). Having covered some of the relevant historical materials we need next to investigate transgender realities as they appear in various cultures.

A legitimate question—one that arose in connection to the study of history—remains whether what we find in other cultures is being filtered by our own cultural consciousness in such a manner that we distort what we see to fit our own pre-existing notions. Just as we did with history, we must attempt to let others be as they are, to see them as much as is possible for us as they see themselves. Of course, this is an endeavor in which we cannot hope to entirely succeed. But we do harm by refusing to try, by asserting our own cultural superiority in insisting that other realities fit within the labels and categories we devise for our own society.

By now we ought to be chastened by the realization that our own people ill fit the classification system our 'experts' have devised. Mindful of this truth we should exert all the more effort to let indigenous people describe themselves. At the same time, in the quest to render realities sensible to our own cultural mind, we shall recognize the Western labels and interpretations that have been applied. Thus, our impossible task is twofold: both to let others speak for themselves and to set alongside that the 'translations' of Western scholars. Fortunately, contemporary Western scholars of other cultures today are more aware than ever before of the necessity to understand other peoples as they understand themselves. In so doing we can enter into a legitimate conversation—and that is our goal in our quest to comprehend transgender realities.

Q. 51

Are transgender realities like crossdressing only found in the Western World?

The Short Answer. Crossdressing behavior occurs around the world and across cultures. That fact remains the case in whatever manner 'crossdressing' is defined. The best use of the term is to stand for dress behavior that crosses gender lines in the view of the culture being considered. Probably every society in the world utilizes some form of gendered dress distinctions, whether modest or extensive. However gender is regarded, however it is viewed in relation to sex, the possibility exists that dress behavior by an individual can result in crossing a gender line. Because some societies recognize more than two genders, and because some societies do not tie gender to sex as rigorously as our on does, the occurrence of gender violations may be difficult for a Westerner to recognize and appraise in a culturally-sensitive manner. Even more problematic is another possibility. If we operate out of our own cultural framework, interpreting apparel by Western uses, then we may attribute crossdressing to dress behavior that in its own cultural context may or may not be regarded as gender crossing. For example, our own society strongly associates unbifurcated apparel (like dresses and skirts) to femininity. Other societies do not uniformly connect unbifurcated garb to femininity. If we apply our own cultural predisposition in this regard we are likely in some instances to see male bodies as feminizing themselves because they are clad in unbifurcated garments. In fact, as we shall see, this very tendency in the past has had a profound impact on relations between Western societies and certain others. Naturally, those of us who live in the West are most familiar with crossdressing in our own culture and perhaps give little thought to whether it happens elsewhere. In fact, we may give little attention to whether it even occurs in other Western societies other than the specific one we live in. Yet a little investigation shows that crossdressing is known in a variety of Western societies and in other cultures and societies as well. Before we begin investigating specific examples in geographic regions around the globe, we will do well to attain a broad view. Toward that end we will in this answer both attempt to ascertain how common crossdressing is and to indicate by naming specific countries in diverse regions just how widely distributed the behavior is.

The Longer Answer. Crossdressing is not found only in the United States, or only in the U.S. and Europe. Crossdressing occurs in North and South America, in Europe and Asia, in the islands of the Pacific, in Africa and the Middle East. Indeed, around the globe gender-crossing behavior is a relatively common facet of human experience and crossdressing remains the most visible reminder of that. While answers to subsequent questions will provide more specific information about various places, here we will briefly provide an overview of crossdressing in the world.

How many places are transgender realities like crossdressing found?

Quantifying the incidence of crossdressing in cultures has not been a strong interest of researchers. Robert and Ruth Munroe provide some evidence of extent in their report of a study of 73 societies that found transvestite males could be documented for one-third (24 societies).[528] Earlier research involving 20 societies had discovered that institutionalized male transvestism correlated better with environments that do not emphasize male-female differences than among those that do[529]—a finding confirmed by the Munroes, and one surprising to a people like our own whose culture so closely ties crossdressing to sexuality and the sexed body. Of course, such research accounts for only a particular kind of crossdressing, and a limited number of societies. More commonly, researchers speak in general terms, saying that crossdressing (and usually with male crossdressing in mind) is 'ubiquitous,' or 'universal,' occurring around the world in cultures both 'primitive' and 'modern.'

When the famed anthropologist Margaret Mead mentions crossdressing in her work *Sex and Temperament in Three Primitive Societies*, she carefully notes that it is not only a variation occurring where differing, sex-based personalities are decreed for men and women, but also as a social invention in less restrictive cultures.[530] Similarly, Vern and Bonnie Bullough, who carefully document crossdressing across time and cultures in their many works, note in one of them the summary judgment that, "a number of variations from traditional Western practice of recognizing only two sexes and two forms of gender behavior exist in a number of societies."[531] Freed from the artificial constraints of only two genders, other cultures find it easier than our own for expressions such as crossdressing.

The 11th edition of *Way Out of the Closet. The Tranny Guide* offers in its reports a brief indication of the widespread nature of the transgender community. There are reports concerning Australia, Austria, Belgium, Denmark, France, Germany, Holland, Italy, Spain, Thailand, the United Kingdom, and the United States.[532] Yet these barely scratch the surface. The following table provides a cursory overview of countries where transgendered people reside and crossdressing occurs with enough frequency to have received attention in the research literature and/or media.

Table 51.1 Examples of Countries Where Crossdressing is Documented

Africa & Middle East	Americas	Far East	Europe	Pacific Ocean Nations & Other Lands
Algeria	Argentina	Bangladesh	Czech Republic	Australia
Bahrain	Brazil	Cambodia	Denmark	Dutch Antilles
Egypt	Canada	China	England	Greenland
Iran	Chile	Hong Kong	Finland	Indonesia
Israel	Colombia	India	France	Malaysia
Kenya	Costa Rica	Japan	Germany	New Zealand
Kuwait	Cuba	Korea	Greece	Okinawa
Liberia	El Salvador	Myanmar	Ireland	Philippines
Nigeria	Guatemala	Nepal	Italy	Polynesia
Oman	Honduras	Pakistan	Macedonia	Russia
Saudi Arabia	Mexico	Taiwan	Netherlands	Samoa
South Africa	Nicaragua	Thailand	Poland	Singapore
Tunisia	Puerto Rico	Vietnam	Serbia	Tonga
Turkey	United States		Spain	
Yemen			Sweden	
			Switzerland	
			Ukraine	

This table is not exhaustive, but it is indicative of the wide range of cultures and societies in which crossdressing occurs. Many of these countries are discussed in the answers to other questions.

Today a number of facts seem established beyond reasonable doubt. First, clothing to mark gender appears to be a universal cultural characteristic. Second, wherever gender distinctions in clothing exist, there is a distinct possibility for crossdressing; in most such situations some crossdressing has been documented. Third, crossdressing is not confined to one sex. Females as well as males may crossdress. Fourth, crossdressing is not limited to one particular purpose, nor motivated by a singular desire or need. Indeed, the uses served by crossdressing are manifold. Finally, while there are some commonalities across many cultures with regard to crossdressing, many cultures know of distinct and unique crossdressing groups. In short, crossdressing reflects in microcosm the diversity of human experience and expression as shaped within cultural contexts.

But is it 'crossdressing'?

Thus far, what we have said fits comfortably within our Western cultural framework. However, we must note that 'crossdressing' can—and is—variously construed. Dress behavior in societies differentiates genders—no matter how many genders might be perceived. If we start with the notion that most folk fit themselves within femininity or masculinity, experiencing and expressing themselves as women or men, then we can assume most apparel is made with these two dominant genders in view. Simply put, there is no profit in constructing clothing for genders that have so fewer numbers. This leaves these other genders to creatively borrow and adapt the gendered clothing at hand. In so doing they often shape dress expressions that to Westerners—stuck in a two-and-only-two gender system—seem to be crossdressing.

Let us examine this a little closer, operating within our social framework where sex and gender are paired in predictable fashion and only two such pairings (masculine male or feminine female) are granted legitimacy. From this perspective, starting at the gender poles mixed elements of dress or mixing body sex with clothing associated with a different sex/gender pairing both result in 'crossdressing.' So-called 'third gender' people almost inevitably end up crossdressing in this way of looking at things. They need some manner of expressing the fact they do *not* reside within either of the dominant genders, but in doing so they can scarcely escape the judgment they are crossdressing. In fact, they *are* from this limited Western perspective.

On the other hand, let us grant that a distinct 'third gender' group may adopt for themselves a distinctive manner of dress, albeit one incorporating elements recognizable from their use by the dominant genders. The consistent use of such dress keeps them *within* their gender no less than dressing femininely keeps girls and women within their gender group. In this respect, such people *are not* crossdressing since they have not crossed any line from their gender to another. By this logic, a male body in feminine dress is *not* crossdressing *if* the behavior reflects a distinct gender sense that fits the person in a recognizable gender group that is neither men nor women. Of course, this logic does not prevail—in fact, it hardly registers in any discussion of crossdressing because we continue to operate out of a system recognizing only two genders.

To grasp cultural diversity requires a willingness to move outside our own cultural myopia with all its attendant biases. We are accustomed to think our ways and values are better rather than merely different. We are also prone to interpret what we find in other cultures through the prism of our own. In that regard, another significant obstacle is our predisposition to interpret matters of sexual behavior in terms of sexual orientation. We fixate on object choice—*who* is with whom—rather than the far more common way such matters are interpreted—*what* is being done, actively or passively. In most of the world, sexual acts derive their value from whether they fit into a perceived active role (masculine), or passive one (feminine).

Accordingly, in many places transgender realities facilitate same-sex (non-homosexual) sexual activities by permitting, for example, males who identify as men to have sex with other males, who identify as women (or at least as 'not men'). Thus members of the same sex can engage sexually in culturally sanctioned ways because the acts performed are construed to remain within the identified sex roles: active, penetrative sex by masculine participants and passive, receptive sex by feminine (or third gender) ones. Gender trumps sex.

In sum, studying transgender realities (itself a Western-derived label) across cultures is a task fraught with complications. In what follows we shall attempt to be faithful both to an effort to see others as they seem themselves, and try to understand matters from our own limited cultural perspective. This effort will entail drawing on numerous disciplines, especially anthropology. Pride of place is given as often as possible to the voices of those who reside within the societies under review, but this is not always possible. The study of transgender realities in other cultures and societies remains a work in progress.

Q. 52

Where is it found in the East?

The Short Answer. Culture diversity, including different ways of understanding gender, means we err if we unthinkingly interpret behaviors in other societies through the lens of our own cultural perspective. Perhaps nowhere is such a warning more appropriate than when Westerners observe and describe Eastern practices. Crossdressing certainly is found throughout the East, including countries as diverse as China, India, Indonesia, Japan, Thailand and others. In this answer, 'East' is used broadly, embracing both the lands of Asia and what Westerners commonly call the 'Far East.' Crossdressing in these regions is not a recent phenomenon; historical and literary records show the practice—by both males and females—has long occurred. Moreover, the reasons for crossdressing prove as varied in the East as those discovered in the West. But while there may be many similarities between East and West, there are also important differences. The cultural context frames crossdressing in the East differently than it is situated in Western culture. Perhaps it proves inevitable that we fall back upon the vocabulary and cultural lens we know best, but we cannot excuse ourselves from attempting to see transgender phenomena in the East along the lines those societies embrace. At the same time, we must acknowledge that the West has influenced the East, often inducing many people in Eastern lands to adopt Western values and perspectives. Thus the lands of the East today offer a variety of viewpoints about realities their people have known for centuries. In some cases that has meant traditional tolerance giving way to Western prejudices.

The Longer Answer. Crossdressing practices in the East have been long noted by Western observers. Pioneering sexologist Magnus Hirschfeld, who gave the world the term 'transvestite' (see answer to Q. 95), traces Western accounts of Eastern practices dating back across many centuries. Hirschfeld himself notes several examples of crossdressing in the Far East of the late 19th century. He points to the female impersonators of Japan and to the transvestites of

Java, who live together and go out together at night.[533] He also remarks on a striking practice found in many places, East and West:

> Among the strangest phenomena of intersexuality is *male childbed*, or the couvade. It is amazing that this almost grotesque custom, according to which the man completely assumes, for as long as forty days, the role of the confined woman and even puts on her clothes, should be found in the most widely separated portions of the earth. The traveler Marco Polo described it in the thirteenth century as existing in Chinese Turkistan. In antiquity, Diodorus of Sicily, Apollonius of Rhodes, and Strabo, gave accounts of it, and it has subsequently been discovered among some Indian tribes of California, Central and South America, as well as on the shores of the Black Sea, in Asia Minor and in Corsica.[534]

This excerpt exemplifies both Hirschfeld's attention to such realities in diverse historical and cultural contexts, as well as the way in which such things typically strike Westerners—as 'amazing,' and 'almost grotesque.' But Hirschfeld merely hints at the rich diversity of transgender realities, including crossdressing, found in societies of the East. Both male and female crossdressing occur in the East, for reasons as varied as those offered by crossdressers in the West. Some folks crossdress for entertainment, others for religious purposes (e.g., in shamanism[535])—and some sometimes do both simultaneously. Both in the past and today, some women masquerade as men to gain access to experiences otherwise closed to them and some men disguise themselves as women for similar reasons. In our contemporary world crossdressing has even been used in the fight against terrorism in Asia.[536]

Despite the parallels we might draw between transgender practices of the East and those found in the West, we must be careful to remember that important cultural differences exist. Anthropologist Erick Laurent, a specialist in Japanese culture, in speaking about Asian perspectives, asks us to remember two important matters:

> First, most Asian countries and regions had, and often still have, a tradition of tolerance towards traditional same-sex feelings and practices, culturally determined and accepted by society. There is little overt anti-gay hostility, like one might find in "the West." Secondly, the traditional place of transgender people in society is much more important than in western countries, being recognized by society and bearing a precisely defined place in the culture. Transgender persons appear relatively freely and often on TV shows, at festivals, as guest lecturers, and so on.[537]

As these comments remind us, we shall commonly be dealing both with sexual orientation and transgender matters together because, rightly or wrongly, they are closely linked in Western consciousness.

The following table offers a brief glimpse at some of the countries of the East where transgender realities are documented:

Table 52.1 Examples of Eastern Countries Where Transgender Realities Are Documented

Bangladesh	Korea	Philippines
Cambodia	Malaysia	Polynesia
China	Mongolia	Samoa
Hong Kong	Myanmar (Burma)	Singapore
India	Nepal	Thailand
Indonesia	Okinawa	Tonga
Japan	Pakistan	Vietnam

Limited remarks on various of these countries follow. However, additional material can also be found in other answers (cf. answer to Q. 57 for some of the lands listed above), especially those dealing with the religions associated with these nations (see the answers to Q. 78-82).

Acknowledgment and acceptance of transgender realities varies not only among societies discussed here, but within them as well. Many transgender people find their life opportunities constricted, and occupation in the risky sex trade is a common route to securing some economic foothold in a society. Violence is all too common; in Bangladesh, for instance, a study found that 87% of male respondents had been subjected to sexual assault or rape because they were perceived as effeminate.[538] As we shall see, often the intolerance modern transgender people experience is at least to some extent the result of Western influence. The high status and power enjoyed by Western culture has exerted pressure on many societies—pressure felt in gender and sexuality because these are so important to Westerners in their self-definition.

What are transgender realities in China?

Chinese conceptions of human sexuality and gender have their own distinct form. As we might expect from such a long-lived culture, there have been changes, some significant, now obscured by the mists of time. Mot especially, there has been a debate over the extent to which China once was a matriarchal culture that gave way to the patriarchal orientation now evident. But by any measure, ancient religious and philosophical traditions indigenous to the region have contributed significantly to cultural values. Among these influences the ideas of Yin and Yang, and of *chi*, have been central.[539] But the weight of the

Confucian tradition has been considerable too, especially in its emphasis on hierarchical and ordered social relations (cf. the answer to Q. 82).[540] In today's China, Confucianism is enjoying somewhat of a revival.

Chinese literature makes clear that crossdressing has been a feature of life known throughout various periods of China's long history. The crossdressing was occasioned by various motivations familiar to Western crossdressers, such as women masquerading to gain access to an aspect of a male-privileged world, or a man impersonating a woman for entertainment purposes. A few examples from literature will illustrate the situation in pre-modern China.

Pre-Modern China

As in many other societies, crossdressed actors were a feature of Chinese theater (see the answer to Q. 44). Men were performing such roles by at least about the 7th century and women by the 13th century. In the late 18th century an official ban was placed on women appearing onstage, but this was defied in regions where imperial influence was weak. By the dawn of the 20th century the ban was moot in practice if not in law. Cho Hui-ling observes that the practice on stage by women also carried to offstage as actresses appeared in public wearing masculine apparel both of Chinese and Western styling.[541]

Pre-modern Chinese fiction presents various instances of crossdressing. As in other times and cultures, some stories of crossdressers embrace universal themes of love, lust, and loss. For example, the 17th century novel *Lien-siang-pan* (*Love for the Perfumed Companion*) features a woman who crossdresses in order to marry another woman; when separated, one marries a man so her companion can become his mistress and the lovers once more may be together.[542] Same-sex yearnings—though this time male—are also found in the same century's drama *Nan Wanghou* (*The Male Queen*), which portrays an effeminate boy kept by the emperor in his harem, dressed as a young woman.[543]

Women writers could use gender crossing characters as ways to work out their own culturally denied ambitions. In the novel *Zaisheng Yuan* (*Destiny of the Next Life*), the protagonist, a woman named Meng Lijun, disguises herself as a man and has a spectacularly successful career, culminating in becoming Prime Minister. In *Bi Shenghua* (*Flowers of Literature*), another aspect of life typically closed to women is explored in the heroic tale of a woman masquerading as a man who not only saves the land from her position as a military leader, but who personally saves the emperor's life after sneaking into the imperial palace.[544]

We may also find characters depicting other aspects of transgender identity and behavior. In the famed 18th century novel *Hong Lou Meng* (*The Story of the Stone*, aka *The Dream of the Red Chamber*) the character Jiang Yu-Han is a female impersonator, while the character Jia Bao-Yu displays the characteristics of a transsexual, whose grandmother speculates perhaps he should have been born a girl.[545]

Crossdressing is found in nonfiction literature as well. In the late 18th-early 19th century, Shen Fu's *Fu Sheng Liu Ji* (*Six Records of a Floating Life*), a record of life and love during the Ch'ing Dynasty, recounts a classic instance of a woman disguising herself in male clothing in order to gain entrance into a social world she would otherwise never experience. As the following excerpt makes clear, this crossdressing happens when Shen Fu urges his wife Yün to crossdress in order to attend a festival at the Tungting Temple:

'What a shame that I cannot go just because I am not a man,' said Yün.

'If you wore one of my hats and some of my clothes, you could look like a man.'

Yün thereupon braided her hair into a plait and made up her eyebrows. She put on my hat, and though her hair showed a little around her ears it was easy to conceal. When she put on my robe we found it was an inch and a half too long, but she took it up around the waist and put on a riding jacket over it.

'What about my feet?' Yün asked.

'In the street they sell "butterfly shoes",' I said, 'in all sizes. They're easy to buy, and afterwards you can wear them around the house. Wouldn't they do?'

Yün was delighted, and when she had put on my clothes after dinner she practiced for a long time, putting her hands into her sleeves and taking large steps like a man.

But suddenly she changed her mind. 'I am not going! It would be awful if someone found out. If your parents knew, they would never allow us to go.'

I still encouraged her to go, however. 'Everyone at the temple knows me. Even if they find out, they will only take it as a joke. Mother is at ninth sister's house, so if we come and go secretly no one will ever know.' [546]

The plan proves a spectacular success. Yün, having amused herself with her appearance in the mirror, allows herself to accompany Shen Fu about the Temple—with no one the wiser. To those who enquire who she is, Shen Fu replies that she is his cousin. Only at the last place they visit does the ruse almost fall apart. They come upon some young women and girls chatting. Yün begins to talk to them in her normal manner. At one point she bends over and casually places a hand on the shoulder of a young lady. This excites an indignant outburst from one of the women, who demands to know what kind of rogue would act in such a manner. Before Shen Fu can intervene, Yün takes off her hat and shoes and declares she is also a woman. The women's anger dissolves into laughter and both Yün and Shen Fu stay for tea.[547]

This account nicely illustrates several things. First, as mentioned above, it is motivated by a common reason used by female crossdressers: access to a man's world. Second, it depicts both the crossdressing and the practice accompanying it that are needed to masquerade as a member of the opposite sex. Third, it recounts the anxiety of appearing in public. Fourth, it shows something contemporary crossdressers know—having a supportive partner when going out in public helps. Fifth, the successful passing leads to an embarrassing encounter when Yün forgets her role as a man and acts as a woman. Finally, the whole event is presented as occurring with her husband's active support and with no censure when the truth comes out.

Of course, women are not the only ones who crossdressed. Males, both boys and men, might don female garments for one or another reason. During the reign of Ai-Di, for example, some male royal favorites presented themselves in makeup and ornate silk finery in the guise of women.[548] Much of the material suggests a relatively positive—or at least not outrightly negative—perspective toward the transgendered. However, educator Sam Winter, at the University of Hong Kong, points out that the term *yen-yiu* ("person changed against nature") used to describe transgendered people, carries a negative connotation.[549]

Modern China

A negative judgment certainly reflects the official stance of modern communist China, where the State denies, minimizes or tries to explain away transgender realities. While Chinese history makes plain that crossdressing has long happened in the land, mainland Chinese officialdom apparently prefers to regard most instances of Chinese transgenderism as evidence of Western decadence. This, for example, is the judgment about transsexualism presented by the nation's media.[550] Nevertheless, Chinese transsexuals are perhaps not uncommon—a 1988 estimate of prevalence for Taiwan was 1-in-1,031 for ages 18 and older[551]—and the first documented case of sexual reassignment surgery (SRS) occurred in 1981 in Hong Kong,[552] though the first case in mainland China was not documented until the late 1980s.[553] Despite Chinese efforts to suppress and censor information about transgender conditions, physician and sexual historian Fang-Fu Ruan successfully gathers together material written in letters by seven male-to-female transsexuals, chronicling aspects of their experience.[554]

More recent information comes from John Sik-Nin Ko. He presents data collected between 1991-2001 at the University of Hong Kong. Of 376 identified cases, 28 meet DSM-IV criteria for Gender Identity Disorder. These cases are roughly evenly divided between male-to-female (MtF) and female-to-male (FtM) transsexuals. Ko finds heterosexual, homosexual, and bisexual orientations reported among the 13 FtM clients, but only homosexual orientation among the 15 MtF clients. Most (80%) have pre-pubertal onset of gender dysphoria and almost all (92.9%) have a history of crossdressing at least once a month.[555]

Today, a comprehensive treatment approach to transsexual clients exists in Hong Kong. Ng and Ma report that by the end of 1998 a total of 48 persons had undergone SRS. Though the law at the end of the 20th century still only recognized legal identity based on chromosomal sex, transsexuals could obtain name and identity card changes to create congruence with their gender presentation. Nevertheless, legal barriers (e.g., no right to marry) and discrimination often bring suffering to transsexuals. Despite this state of affairs, Ng and Ma note that no post-operative transsexuals express regret over their surgery.[556]

Ruan, in his brief history of sex in China, documents instances of transvestism as well as transsexualism. Crossdressing, he finds, meets differing degrees of tolerance in Chinese society.[557] It is not illegal in Hong Kong, though public reactions tend to be negative.[558] Transgender people remain generally invisible except when subject to violence or presenting for treatment, which may be less for ending the behavior than for changing the body to better match gender presentation. In Ko's analysis of cases occurring at a Hong Kong sex clinic he finds five male transvestites who presented for sex reassignment surgery but who did not meet criteria for transsexualism.[559] Finally, it should be noted that despite any controversy over crossdressing in general, it remains an accepted theatrical practice (see the answer to Q. 44).

What are transgender realities in India?

India presents an interesting situation in more than one way. Perhaps even more than holds for other societies, dress is instrumental to identity and social relations in traditional Indian culture.[560] India also provides an important situation because of the way in which East meets West. India possessed a long and rightfully proud history before coming under the dominion of Islamic rulers and, later, Great Britain. Prior to the dominance of the British, both male and female crossdressers could be found in Indian society; after colonialism was established much of the overt crossdressing ended.[561] The period of colonization left a collection of laws as well as new customs that continue to mark India. Yet the ideas and ways of the pre-colonial era also persist, albeit often in altered forms. So, for example, the long history of tolerance for transgender behavior has survived colonialism's laws against 'unnatural' or 'obscene' offenses as seen through Western eyes. What once was more widespread in public simply has gone underground or, because it is connected with religion (cf. the answer to Q. 79), is generally overlooked by those who enforce the law.[562]

Indian languages recognize the possibility of gender beyond the dichotomy of 'man' and 'woman.' *Kama Sutra* speaks of *tritiya praktriti* (a 'third nature'; see volume 4). The Sanskrit *napunsaka* and the Urdu *namard* are terms used to cover members of various groups that our term 'transgender' is often applied to: homosexuals, transvestites, transsexuals—all kinds of crossdressers.[563] There are gender variant females as well as males, such as the *sadhin* of northern India, who renunciate sexual relations, or the *basivis* of Madras, who crossdress.[564] Other females engage in same-sex relationships. Today, colloquial terms are used for female same-sex relationships (*sakhi*) and for those among boys (*masti*).[565] Effeminate (uncastrated) males with a homosexual orientation, who crossdress and take the passive, receptive role in sexual interactions are known locally as *Jankhas* (or *Jhankhas*), or *Zenanas*,[566] or *Kothis*.

Kothis

The term *Kothis* is used locally as a self-identifier in India, Bangladesh, and parts of Pakistan; regional equivalents include the *Metis* of Nepal and *Zenanas* of Pakistan. *Kothis* are 'feminized males' who do not regard themselves as members of a masculine gender, but rather as 'not males.'[567] They demonstrate culturally feminine characteristics, often in a highly performed manner in public in order to attract sexual partners. They accept the feminine (passive) role when engaging in sex with men. However, *Kothis* are sometimes married, and occasionally have sex with other *Kothis* (though this is kept secret and denied).[568]

The *Kothis'* reality stands as an exemplar of the construction of gender consonant with cultural rules for sexual interaction. The male-dominated societies of South Asia facilitate environments where males are free to congregate, show public displays of affection, and engage in sex. But what we in the West style homosexuality—same-sex sexual interactions between like-gendered people—is frowned upon. Same-sex sexual behavior between so-called 'real men' (*Giryas* or *Pathi*) and 'not-men' (*Kothis*) is acceptable because they occur between differently-gendered people. The 'real men' occupy the active, penetrating role; the 'not men' a passive, receptive role like that also expected of women.[569]

However, we should be wary of concluding that *Kothis* as a gender status is merely contrived to fit sexual desire. These males, in terms of our Western gender dualism, are noticeably effeminate in behavior before and apart from sexual activity. Those who go into the sex trade are often pressed into it by economic necessity or thrust into it as unwilling victims of sexual abuse. To reduce the gendered nature of the *Kothis* to a cultural convenience for sex simply would be wrong.

Crossdressing Connected to Religion

Not uncommonly, the crossdressing found throughout India is associated with one or another religious tradition.[570] The male Sakhibhava devotees of Krishna venerate Radha and, in imitation of her Gopi attendants, imitate women in dress, marking menstrual periods and even occasionally undertaking a female's passive role in sexual interactions. In central India, among the Gond, both male and female crossdressing is permitted.[571] But two forms of such realities most often receive attention: the *Jogappa/Jogamma* of southern India, and, especially, the *Hijras*.

Jogappa/Jogamma

In southern India, either males or females may become sacred servants to the goddess Yellamma. Males (*Jogappas* or *Jogta*), who may be dedicated to this service while children, must crossdress and enact a feminine gender role (including adoption of a feminine name) as they become Yellamma's preistesses.[572] Similarly, females (*Jogamma*) crossdress, draping themselves in a masculine *dhoti*, or even turban and jacket to wait upon Yellamma as masculine attendants. The *Jogamma* role may come late in a woman's life, and varies in significant ways from the more constricted and particular role of the *Jogappas*.[573]

Hijras/Hijrins

Throughout the nation, but especially in northern India (and Pakistan) the most famous of the country's transgendered people are found—the *Hijras* ('eunuchs').[574] The *Hijras* are regarded as neither 'male' nor 'female'—but a 'third' sex and gender. Nevertheless, a linguistic distinction can be made between those whose bodies are male (*Hijras*) and those whose bodies are female (*Hijrin*).[575] Transgendered *Hijra*, living together in communities (*hijra gharanas*) include ritual categories for those preparing for castration (*akwa*) and those castrated (*nirwaan*).[576] The nirwaan ceremony confers status as irrevocably a 'real' *Hijra*.[577] But while some voluntarily become eunuchs (as an act of religious devotion), and some may be sexually ambiguous by nature (true or pseudo-hermaphrodites), many *Hijras* are neither. They do not easily fit any Western categories, though Western scholars have likened them, variously, to homosexual or heterosexual crossdressers, or to transsexuals. The Indian National AIDS Control Organization (NACO), influenced by Western categorization, specifies four distinct subgroups: transvestites, transsexuals, hermaphrodites, and drag queens/*Satia Kothi*.[578] We do best, though, to leave them as themselves—a distinct and unique group. They are included among crossdressers only because from a Western standpoint (cf. the answer to Q. 51) they are biological males who appear in the dress and gender role of biological females.

Found principally in India's larger cities, like Bombay and Delhi, the number of *Hijras* have not been kept by official census data and estimates range widely; anthropologist Laurent reports unofficial estimates from a half million to 5 million.[579] They belong to a distinct community, with its own order, rules, and customs. Adolescents leave their birth families to join a new household—one of seven lineages preserved by the *Hijras*—organized in communes where at least five *chelas* ('disciples') are led by a *guru* ('spiritual master'). In this new family they take a feminine name, refer to one another by feminine pronouns, put on feminine clothing, and adopt feminine mannerisms. They receive training in *Hijra* traditions and activities such as the ritual performances by which they will earn income. They may have sex with males, typically assuming a passive-receptive role in anal intercourse. Their sexual activity may be motivated by personal desire or as an act of prostitution.

Their place, historically, has been within Hinduism where they are especially associated with the female deity Bahuchara Mata,[580] who has a temple in Gujarat. The *Hijras* served as eunuchs in the royal courts of Muslim rulers and thus gained influence with many adherents of Islam too. Indeed, the influence may have been reciprocal, as *Hijras* follow certain practices more in keeping with Islamic tradition than Hindu, such as burying their dead rather than cremating them—and some *Hijras* have become Muslim.[581] Even today many Muslims, like many Hindus, believe that the *Hijras* mediate a divine ability to bless or curse; refusing them money or gifts is thought by some to bring bad luck. However, British colonialism marked a severe downturn in Hijra fortunes. They increasingly became an ostracized group.[582]

While within their community they have both place and identity, in the larger society *Hijras* remain marginalized. Siddharth Narrain remarks, "*Hijras* in India have virtually no safe spaces, not even in their families, where they are protected from prejudice and abuse." Narrain observes that some *Hijras* have become politically active to redress their lot in society. In Bangalore, they joined with local *Kothis* and other sexual minorities to form an organization named Vividha, with a charter calling for legal reforms (e.g., equal housing and employment rights), repeal of laws such as Section 377 of the Indian Penal Code (which makes even voluntary same-sex sexual behavior illegal), and recognition of *Hijras* as women.[583] This latter move again reflects the practical reality of trying to carve out a gendered place in a system where only two genders are 'official.' Since *Hijras* know they are not men, their only other gendered option in the gender system is to seek recognition as women.

Far more in the past than presently, they fulfilled a social function within society by serving as mediums for the feminine divine. Today they retain a place in society but largely without the social status once enjoyed. They still are sometimes employed at wedding or birth ceremonies to provide entertainment through ritual song and dance. Their sexually suggestive routines constitute a bawdy fertility ritual meant to bless the couple yet often today viewed as rude and offensive. Still, because many common folk worry that not paying the *Hijras* will bring ill-fortune, they are commonly given gifts of food, clothing, or money.

Similarly, *Hijras* often show up at religious festivals. However, they have occasioned controversy and censure in some circles for sometimes involving themselves in public activities whether invited or not, and insisting on remuneration, with rude displays (e.g., not wearing underwear and lifting their skirts to expose themselves) if payment is refused. Accordingly, some characterize them in unflattering terms as 'bitchy," 'bad-tempered,' and 'demanding.'[584] Today they may be thought of as much for their begging and prostitution as for the historical role they have occupied in India's folk spirituality. Still they persist, India's most noted and durable transgender population.[585]

What are transgender realities in Japan?

The island nation of Japan has had an impact on the world disproportionate to its size. Japanese culture remains distinctive while both influencing and being influenced by other cultures. Transgendered realities have been a part of Japan's history and culture for centuries. Crossdressing behavior has deep roots in Japan, but some changes are evident. To better understand such matters we will begin with a brief look at Japan's most famous kind of clothing—the *kimono*.

The Kimono

Few articles of dress are more associated with a particular culture than the Japanese *kimono* ('clothing'). Bernard Rudofsky suggests it as an entry metaphor ('*kimono* mind') into Japanese culture.[586] With Rudofsky in mind, Richard Martin declares, "the kimono mind is the compelling faculty of contemporary fashion; we in the West have seen our world transformed by Japanese dress in my lifetime."[587] The impact of this garment on the thinking of Japanese clothes designers stands as background to Japanese contributions to world fashion.

Yet within Japan itself dressing styles since the end of World War II have been influenced increasingly by Western fashion. As a result, traditional garments like the *kimono* are becoming a rarer sight. They are expensive and difficult to put on properly. Today they are more likely to be reserved for special or ceremonial occasions. In fact, there are different kinds of *kimono* for various situations and seasons.

The Japanese use of the *kimono* can be instructive for us in better comprehending the complex relationship of dress and gender presentation. Although in the Western mind the *kimono* typically is pictured as feminine garb worn by delicate young maidens, men and children may also don a *kimono*. Traditionally, the kind of *kimono* worn can signal the wearer's age, gender and social status as well as the formality of the occasion and the occasion itself. Clearly, the *kimono* occupies in traditional Japanese dress a central role in a rich expressive system.

There are stylistic differences between *kimono* made for men and women. A man's *kimono* is shorter. The sleeve on a man's *kimono* is closed under the arm. The woman's sleeve has an open underarm. Young, marriage-eligible women wear *kimono* with longer, 'butterfly' sleeves. Color also differentiates the genders. A man's *kimono* is simpler, darker, and features more subdued colors than a woman's. At a traditional wedding, both bride and groom wear a *kimono*; hers is white, his is black. Yet we must resist any temptation to conclude that color invariably differentiates gender. At a funeral both men and women may wear a black *kimono*. Context determines appropriateness of color and style. Thus, color differentiation also exists among the *kimono* worn by women; a young, unmarried woman wears a more brightly colored *kimono* than does an older married woman.

More factors enter in. Other garb may be worn with the *kimono*. An outer garment called the *hakama*, which may be either bifurcated (pant-like) or unbifurcated (skirt-like), may be worn over the *kimono*. Today, both men and women wear *hakama*, though once more color (men wear darker, more subdued colors), or other features (e.g., men wear striped *hakama*) serve for gender differentiation.

Traditionally, *kimono* served as daily wear for men. Today Western suits and casual wear have largely displaced them, except for special occasions. In fact, Western values may be seen in the gender portrayals found in contemporary Japanese advertisements. A study reported in 2003 (of data collected in 1996) of gender stereotypes in Japanese television ads notes how often the *kimono* is the dress depicted. The study finds that the *kimono* is most associated with a cluster of characters the research labels as 'beautiful and wise housewives.' Over half (52.9%) of the characters in this cluster are depicted in a *kimono* in contrast to the clusters identified as 'middle- and old-aged people enjoying private time' (23.5%, with both men and women represented); 'young celebrities' (17.6%, with more than three-quarters (78%) female); 'young females attracting people's attention' (2.9%); or 'middle-aged worker bees' (2.9%, mostly male). If we sum the message sent in these advertisements we might well conclude that the *kimono* is the dress of domestically settled females and some older gentlemen. It is not the preferred dress of either young women or, especially, working men.[588]

In light of the above, it should come as no surprise that the *kimono* is used in crossdressing. When this occurs the crossdresser is engaging a powerful expressive system. Even where this system is imperfectly understood, as among most Westerners, it may be utilized for one or another expressive purpose. For example, some Western males use a woman's *kimono* to express what they regard as an exotic feminine persona. Males—both Western and Asian—are known to appear in a woman's *kimono* to serve as hostesses in certain nightclubs. Japanese crossdressers also wear the *kimono*. One of Japan's best-known crossdressers, Maruyama Akihiro, has often been featured in advertisements selling, among many other things, *kimono*. The use to which this kind of clothing is put is hardly uniform. Although a gender presentation accompanies the *kimono* a crossdresser may also be expressing other matters. Yet as the *kimono* becomes a less visible and more gender-stereotyped article within an increasingly Western-influenced society, it seems likely its popularity among crossdressers will increase as a vehicle to express both a distinctive gender performance and a strong cultural identity.

Japanese Crossdressing Expressions

Crossdressing has a rich history in Japan. Much of it has been associated with Kabuki theater (see the answer to Q. 44) or other entertainment (e.g., Mana, the former leader of the band Malice Micer and an inspiration for the Gothic Lolita fashion movement in Japan), but there have been other expressions as well.[589] There were crossdressing male prostitutes who formed their own guild, complete with patron deity.[590] Sometimes, in fact, crossdressing was explicitly connected to religious matters (cf. the answer to Q. 81). Crossdressing prostitutes remain a facet of the Japanese sex trade. Interestingly, so-called 'lesbian play' (*rezupurei*) refers to crossdressed men interacting with female prostitutes rather than two females performing for a male audience.[591] However, it would be erroneous to conclude that crossdressing is an exclusively male phenomenon and one limited to entertainment or the sex trade.

Crossdressers in modern Japan fit many Western categories, including transvestites and transsexuals. Some refer to themselves as *nyuuhaafu* ('new-half'), a 'third sex' or, perhaps better, an 'intermediate sex.'[592] Despite indigenous labels, Western categorization predominates. So, too, does a general perception of transgendered realities as forms of mental illness. Estimates of the number of transsexuals in Japan vary widely, though a 2003 newspaper account cites 'experts' at placing the number somewhere between 7,000-70,000.[593] Authorization of SRS was later in coming than in many other modern nations, but has been happening since the late 1990s. Both FtM and MtF surgeries have since taken place.

The lives of transsexuals prior to 2003 were complicated by the lack of legal recognition after their change in gender identity and role, even when sexual reassignment surgery (SRS) had occurred. Japanese law historically has designated the gender of individuals by their anatomical sex. But this legal tradition is being challenged by people like Masae Torai, a FtM post-operative transsexual, and among the best known members of Japan's transgendered people. In 1987, at age 23, Torai journeyed to the United States for the first of the operations needed to complete a transformation from female to male; a subsequent operation was performed two years later. Torai has written extensively about transsexualism and has been active in his homeland to effect legal and social changes.[594] In 2001, he was part of a group of six post-operative transsexuals to file civil suits seeking recognition and registration of their new status under the Family Registration Law; as of 2003 none of these suits had prevailed.[595] However, that same year the Japanese government approved a law permitting transgendered people to list their changed sex and new names on official documents.

As in other cultures, transgender realities also are found in public art and entertainment. As in the West, Japanese theater displays males in female garb (*onnagata* in Kabuki theater)—and sometimes women in male clothing (*otokoyaku* in Takarazuka). Modern Japanese films continue a theatrical representation of crossdressing (on crossdressing in both theater and film, see the answer to Q. 44). Japanese boy bands commonly feature crossdressing.

Mark McLelland, an Australian interdisciplinary researcher, explores an especially interesting facet of the Japanese interest in transgendered people found in another distinctive Japanese art form. He points to the popularity among heterosexual Japanese females of representations of gay and transgendered men in manga, a form of artistic entertainment that comprises more than a third of all Japanese published materials. The manga McLelland especially references is called *shoojo* manga, and are comics published for girls. They frequently feature *shoonen'ai* ('boy love') between *bishoonen* ('beautiful boys'). McLelland traces this kind of story to the early 1970s, though he points to deeper roots in a literature aimed at a male audience that extends back a long time. Successful *shooju* manga like *June* (pronounced 'ju-neh') can reach high circulation levels; *June* was between 80,000–100,000 in the mid-1990s. And, McLelland, observes, these magazines are increasingly reaching Western women.[596]

This kind of manga received its first substantial boost with the unexpected success of a story entitled *Berusaiyu no Baru* (*The Rose of Versailles*), by Riyoko

Ikeda, a woman in her early twenties. She set out to tell a story about Marie Antoinette in the days prior to the French Revolution. A principal character—who became the fans' favorite—is Oscar Francois de Jarjeyes, a girl raised as a son by her father, a French general. As an adult woman, Oscar rises to the position of captain of the palace guard. Although perceived as a male, Oscar is courted by both males and females. Over 1972-1973, this romantic story appeared in *Margaret* magazine. Collected together into 10 volumes, *The Rose of Versailles* sold more than 12 million copies by the end of the 20th century.[597] *The Rose of Versailles* soon achieved status as a 'classic,' and was rendered into anime in 40 television episodes (25 minutes each), as well as adapted for musical theater by the Takarazuka company (see the answer to Q. 44). Its popularity also helped spawn a multitude of stories in which crossdressed characters play a minor or major role. Some of the more often noted titles include: *Basara*; *Eerie Queerie*; *Girl Got Game*; *Hana-Kimi*; *Kill Me, Kiss Me*; *Lingerie Publicity*; *Pretty Face*; *Princess Prince*; *Ranma ½*; *Tokyo Crazy Paradise*; and *W Juliet*.

At present, Japan appears to be like many other modern nations—at a crossroads with respect to how to understand and respond to transgendered realities. Though Yoshiro Hatano and Tsuguo Shimazaki remark that those who cross gender are not yet widely accepted in Japanese society, with most Japanese maintaining a "dualistic gender bias," this conclusion should be tempered by such other factors as those described above. Hatano and Shimazaki themselves note that attention has been given in recent years to transgendered reality as a human issue.[598] The future remains open.

What are transgender realities in Korea?

Korea occupies an Asian peninsula between two great powers: China and Japan. Steeped in Confucianism, but influenced also by great religions of the East (Buddhism, Taoism) and West (Christianity), Korean culture is androcentric, communitarian, and conservative. Transgendered groups have not found the nation particularly accepting or tolerant, though there have been signs of change. Efforts to secure guarantees of basic human rights through legal reform are ongoing. Sex reassignment surgery is legal, though the matter of gender change registration remains unsettled. In sum, despite centuries of transgender realities lived in the society's midst, Korea remains deeply conflicted over the proper place of such realities. As much as any other society on earth, contemporary Korea experiences the tensions of a people divided in many ways, including powerful and contrary cultural impulses from within and without.

That transgender realities have been known throughout Korean history is illustrated by stories preserved from the past. For example, in the mid-15th century, one Sa Bang-ji, a domestic servant assigned masculine gender status, had a notorious affair with a widow of the upper-class. Bang-ji was beardless and dressed in feminine costume. The affair caused a scandal; after being arrested a second time for pursuing it, Bang-ji was formally examined by physicians and found to be intersexed, manifesting both male and female sexual characteristics. The unfortunate Bang-ji was exiled to a remote place and demoted to the status of a slave.[599] This story became the subject of a 1988 South Korean film titled *Sabangji*.

Historically, Pauline Park and John Manzon-Santos distinguish three traditions with respect to transgender, each found in a different aspect of society:

- ❑ *entertainment*—crossdressing actors like the all-male Namsadang theatrical troupes;
- ❑ *military*—crossdressing elite warriors like the famed Flower Boys of Silla; and,
- ❑ *religion*—crossdressing male and female shamans.[600]

All three of these expressions, however, belong either exclusively to the past or have been largely suppressed in modern Korea. The touring Namsadang troupes, where male actors played both male and female roles, were largely gone by the beginning of the 20th century. The Flower Boys of Silla belong to the 7th century dynasty that united the land. These remarkable youth were skilled both with women's fashion and makeup as well as with the arts of war.

The Mudang and Paksu

The shamanistic tradition (cf. the answer to Q. 76) is well-represented in Korea by the *mudang* (female shaman) and *paksu* (male shaman). Most are women and these female shamans wear masculine clothing. However, as Laurel Kendall points out, "the rare male shaman in Korea (*paksu mudong*) performs *kut* wearing women's clothing, down to the pantaloons that hide beneath his billowing skirt and slip."[601] The mudang culture was suppressed in Communist North Korea, where historically it had been particularly strong, but it persists there, as well as in the South. In modern Korea much of the popularity of the shamans is attached to their proficiency with rites of healing, though they are also sometimes asked to perform other rites, such as for the success of business.[602]

Contemporary Transgendered Koreans

Of course, not all transgendered Koreans are part of a shamanic tradition. Most, in fact, can be fit in modern Western categories such as transsexualism or homosexuality—labels employed that signal Western influence. Homosexuality is widely acknowledged, but often misunderstood. Prior to 2004, the South Korean Commission on Youth Protection listed homosexuality on its list of sexual practices harmful to teenagers. Bowing to pressures both within the country and from human rights groups abroad, including the United Nations, homosexuality was finally dropped from the list. In the effort to expand awareness and pursue legal reform to be granted basic human rights, gays, lesbians, and other transgendered people participate in various events such as the Queer Culture Festival held in Seoul, the capital city. In a deeply patriarchal society, lesbians especially have difficulty.[603]

Transsexuals, too, have been in the public eye in recent years.[604] In this case, the attention may be traced to a single, startling event: a 2001 television commercial for DoDo, a cosmetic company. In the ad, an attractive woman with long dark hair, reaches up and pulls it back to expose a neck with a definite Adam's apple. Though her throat had been digitally enhanced, the model was a transgendered person. Harisu (or Ha Ri-su, 'hot issue'), a now famous model, singer, dancer and actress, is commonly credited with having done much to help inform the public about transsexualism.[605] Born in the mid-1970s as Lee Kyung Yup, the only son in a wealthy family, sex reassignment surgery occurred at age 19 in Japan. Harisu gained more attention when her debut album, *Temptation*, was accompanied by her going public about having undergone a sex change. In 2002, at age 27, Harisu succeeded in winning court approval to change gender status and legally assumed the name of Lee Kyung-eun.[606] In May, 2007, the 31-year-old Harisu married her 27-year-old rapper boyfriend in a ceremony attended by the surgeon who did her sex change surgery and by many of the countries most noted celebrities.[607]

South Korea's number of transsexuals is unknown, but commonly estimated at between 4,000-10,000 (with the Korean Medical Association's estimate at the lower end). Although transsexuals can legally obtain sex reassignment surgery, their assigned gender status remains by law a matter of genetic sex. Efforts to formally grant a legal right to change gender status in the early years of the 21st century followed the decision of a District Court in Pusan to register a gender change.

This prompted some lawmakers in 2002 to introduce legislation authorizing such changes nationally.[608] Such a change appears to be supported by most Koreans; a 2001 Gallup poll found a majority favored the right to change registration card gender status (58.6%), and believed changing gender, as a personal matter, should be left to individual discretion (51.3%).[609] However, the proposed legislation stalled in session for years, leaving the legal muddle still unresolved entering 2006, and still in the discretion of local judges. The results have been predictably uneven. Though Harisu obtained her legal change of gender status in 2002, others have not been so fortunate. The *Korea Times* reports that between 2000-2004, some 81 transsexuals petitioned for changes in gender recognition, with 41 of them having their petitions granted. The land's Supreme Court was set to hear a case in 2006 from some whose petitions had been denied.[610] That case resulted in the Court's decision on June 22, 2006, that transsexuals may change their sex in their family register. In its written remarks the Court said: "[I]t is reasonable to recognize their changed sex if they have the appearance of the gender opposite to the one they were born with and it is clear that their new sex is reflected in their personal and social circumstances and does not militate against public welfare and the social order."[611]

Although Harisu has been instrumental in winning a new hearing for Korea's transgendered population, support resources have remained scant. The first internet support group, Anima, began operation in 1996. The site targets crossdressers, especially transsexuals and transvestites, but welcomes all.[612]

What are transgender realities in Myanmar (Burma)?

Myanmar—formerly known as Burma (a name still preferred by many in light of how the current name came about)—is a land sandwiched largely between India on the west and China, Laos, and Thailand on the east. Incorporated into the British Empire in the 19th century, it was administered as a province of India until 1937, then became a self-governing colony until it gained full independence in 1948. The ruling military government changed the name to Myanmar in 1989.

Culturally, Buddhism (Therevada) remains a major influence, though other world religions (notably Christianity and Islam) have some adherents, and indigenous spiritual traditions exert force too. The latter, in fact, are key to understanding Burma's most noted transgender population, the *Acault* ('spirit-possessed one'), or *Nat kadaw* ('spirit wife').[613] An important indigenous religious influence is belief in 37 spirit deities (*Nat*), whose powers can enact good or ill among the people. Transgender folk play an important role in relation to these spirits. Some are male shamans (*kadaw*) who crossdress as they enact the role of a female *Nat*—and who may experience temporary spirit possession.[614]

A female *Nat* named Manguedon sometimes takes possession of a biological male and changes the individual into someone regarded by others as no longer a masculine male, but as an *Acault*—neither male nor female (but more like a female than a male). This typically occurs at an early age, though such spirit possession can happen at other times. Ceremonially wedded to Manguedon, who bestows femininity upon them, the *acault* stand between the sexes and genders. Their crossdressing reflects this change in status. Given their origin, it is no surprise the *Acault* are connected to spiritual roles, serving as shamans, seers, or in other roles. [615]

Manguedon is a spirit connected to success and good fortune, making her welcome among people. An *Acault* thereby may be petitioned by others, with accompanying gifts, to intercede on their behalf. Should the outcome be favorable, the occasion might lead to celebrations honoring Manguedon. At such events, held in pavilions dedicated to the *Nat*, the *Acault* engage in ceremonial dance while dressed in feminine clothing and cosmetics. During the dance they enter into a special state of communion with Manguedon, serving as a conduit for requests from those present.[616]

Another consequence of their change in status is the *Acault*'s sexual availability to men. Because the *acault* have become a kind of variant of female sex and feminine gender, those who have sex with *Acault* are viewed as engaged in heterosexual behavior—an important factor in a society that finds homosexual activity objectionable. As for the *Acault* themselves, a team of Western researchers who present three case studies in a report in the early 1990s, find both masculine and feminine gender identities. They conclude individual *Acault* might be categorized by one or another Western labels, including transvestite and transsexual; Westerners would be prone to also see them as homosexual.[617]

This discrepancy between Western and native perceptions occurs often around the world, and the situation of the *Acault* when separated from cultural, especially religious, considerations leads to misunderstanding. Sociologist Stephen Murray notes that because Manguedon is thought to be jealous of any contact by the *Acault* with females, the *Acault*s' exclusively same-sex sexual behavior should be regarded as a consequence of the religious proscription against contact with women[618]—an eminently sensible conclusion.

The regard of the *Acault* by others is mixed. On the one hand, their connection to powerful forces must be respected. Manguedon's association with success and good fortune ensures that an *Acault* shaman holds an important position. Their occupation of religious roles fills a recognizably vital communal need. On the other hand, the *Acault* seem not to be envied. Being a masculine male in general means to hold a privileged position in society; the *Acault* do not possess this status. Further, local Buddhist beliefs about reincarnation are unfavorable toward the *Acault*. Prevailing beliefs privilege being male; the *Acault* cannot look forward to attaining nirvana from this life. Also, some believe that a son's spirit possession and becoming an *Acault* is a reflection on past life karma—moral failings having led to the present condition. These ideas help explain why families may not be favorable toward a child exhibiting the characteristics of an *Acault* and may resist such development.[619] However, the ruling Burmese junta appears to more than merely tolerate veneration of the *Nats* and *Acault* activities; they may even tacitly encourage these things.[620]

What are transgender realities in Nepal?

Nepal is a mountainous land sandwiched between India and China. It is distinguished by being the only officially Hindu state in the world. The most often noted transgender realities involve biological males, including masculine homosexual men (*Dohoris*)[621] and feminine males (*Metis*). The latter has received more attention.

The local equivalent of the self-identified *Kothis* of Bangladesh and India (see above), and the *Zenanas* of Pakistan (see below), the *Metis* demonstrate culturally feminine characteristics, including crossdressing. Many are engaged in the sex trade, where they accept the culturally feminine (passive) role when engaging in sex with men. This business exposes them to many risks, including sexually transmitted diseases and aggression from customers.

Unfortunately, violence from lawbreakers is not their only worry. In what locally has been termed 'sexual cleansing,' *Metis* have received beatings from law enforcement officials. In at least one instance the beating was accompanied by the specific declaration that transgender people 'pollute' society and must be 'cleaned out.'[622]

What are transgender realities in Pakistan?

Pakistan is an Islamic nation best known to Americans because of its relations with two bordering countries: India and Afghanistan. A relatively poor nation with a majority of the population relatively uneducated by Western standards, the teachings of Islamic clerics often constitute the primary source of information and forms the basis for many beliefs. Even among the wealthier and better educated, misperceptions and ignorance on sex and gender matters has been remarked upon. One study reported in 2000, involving 188 young (18-30) Pakistani men generally of the middle class, finds a high prevalence of misconceptions about female sexuality, including some 40% who endorse the notion that women find sex less enjoyable than men, and 42% who are ignorant of the ability of females to achieve orgasm.[623] Moreover, women when raped are more likely than not to be accused of adultery and be accordingly punished.

As the above might suggest, sex education (in Western terms) is not widespread.[624] Particularly problematic are matters outside normative heterosexual sexuality. Transgender realities are seldom discussed and remain largely unstudied. That does not mean they are unknown, or even uncommon. One gay Pakistani calls homosexuality "condemned but not opposed."[625] Formally, homosexual sexual practices are illegal, with social ostracism and severe punishment (e.g., public lashing; life imprisonment for sodomy) among the consequences possible for those who are discovered or choose to 'come out'—and they do occasionally occur. Nevertheless, some accept the risk, as indicated by the BBC report in the spring of 2005 of an Afghan refugee with a Pakistani man.[626] Young homosexual males participating in the sex trade are known as *Chawas*.[627]

In late May, 2007, a married couple made news when state authorities arrested them for lying to a Pakistani court in a case brought by the husband, 31-year-old Shumail Raj, against his wife's family for harassment. The arrest was based on the couple's failure to disclose that Raj was born a biological female. Though he had completed sex reassignment surgery some 16 years previously, the father of wife Shahzina Tariq, age 26, wants the marriage annulled as illegal because formed between two women. Raj testified he had married Tariq to save her from being sold into marriage to satisfy an uncle's gambling debts. At the time of this writing the couple were being held pending appearance in court.[628]

Perhaps the most remarkable instance of crossdressing in Pakistan is Ali Saleem, better known as the popular television host Begum ('Lady') Nawazish Ali. Saleem, a male in his late 20s, appears in the role of a middle-aged woman, ostensibly the widow of an army colonel. Saleem dons a silk *sari* for the show. While no effort is made to keep Saleem's real sex a secret, some viewers remain unaware that the Begum is an imposter. However, those who are aware of the fact seem largely unbothered by it. Saleem's "Late Night Show" has been extremely lucrative and the Begum much admired. Even the conservative Islamic clergy of the nation have refused to speak against Saleem. Begum Nawazish Ali is not the first woman Saleem has impersonated. Some years previously he made an impression by appearing on stage and television as former Pakistani Prime Minister Benazir Bhutto, Noor Jehan (an actress), Margaret Thatcher, and Princess Diana. Saleem declares these roles do justice to the 'bisexuality' within himself. His remarkable success has even inspired in him thoughts of entering politics—in the character of Begum Nawazish Ali—in a bid for a parliamentary seat.[629]

However, not all who are privy to Saleem's identity are approving. In his instance, his popularity has provided a layer of protection many others in his society lack. As all-too-common around the world, many transgender people in Pakistan find their opportunities in life narrowed and many turn to the sex trade, with all its attendant risks. A World Bank report on HIV/AIDS in Pakistan notes that while the nation is still considered a low-risk one, the incidence of infection is on the rise. Among the groups most at risk are men engaging in same-sex interactions (4% HIV infection rate) and those having sex with *Hijras* (2% infection rate), who are also noted to have an alarmingly high rate of syphilis (60% in Karachi!).[630]

Zenanas

The most famous population of males who dress as women in Pakistan are called *Zenanas* (a word originally referring to secluded women's quarters), whose presence has been documented for centuries. The *Zenanas* represent a group that might in Western terms be variously construed as transvestite, transsexual, or transgendered in the narrow sense (see the answer to Q. 20). However, such labels are misleading for people who belong to a distinct community found in an area that encompasses Pakistan, India, and Bangladesh. The *Zenana* community is structured into four 'families,' embracing a hierarchical structure headed by a *guru* (teacher). Those who are accepted into a family become *chelas* (disciples). Though biologically male, the *Zenanas* identify as women (including referring to themselves with feminine language forms) and commonly crossdress, wearing feminine clothes and make-up. Some become castrated as a way to further their feminization.[631]

The sex trade is a principal source of income. Not all *Zenanas* engage in prostitution; the more junior *chelas* are most likely to do so, where they take the woman's passive role and are penetrated by other males. Many are pressured into such acts, especially by peers in response to their display of feminine characteristics. Once within the Zenana community their acts are directed by their *guru*. Exploitation and harassment by law enforcement are common experiences.[632]

What are transgender realities in Thailand?

Perhaps no other country in the world is more famous for its crossdressers than Thailand, in Southeast Asia. Some have reckoned them among the country's most famous sights. Formerly known as Siam (before 1939), rule of the land—at least nominally—has rested in the Chakkri Dynasty since 1782, and the kingdom can trace itself to roots in the late 11th century. Unusual for the region, despite the influence and power of colonial powers, the land has remained independent for most of its history. However, both the impact of European colonialism in the region, as well as imperial Japan's occupation of the country during World War II, have impacted Thailand's culture.

Before examining the changes that have made modern Thailand what it is today, we need to step back to attempt a brief and broad perspective on traditional Siam/Thailand. It is a culture characterized by anthropologist Rosalind Morris as astounding in its plasticity and heterogeneity of gender and sexual identity.[633] Historically, three distinct gendered groups have been recognized: masculine (*chai*), feminine (*ying*), and transgendered (*thang ying thang chai*—'both feminine and masculine'; or, *ying pra-phayt song*—'women of the second kind'; or *Kathoey*—variously understood, depending on context, as 'hermaphrodite,' 'transvestite,' 'transsexual,' or 'transgender').[634] Peter Jackson notes that European accounts prior to the last century describe both crossdressing men and women—both called *pu-mia* ('male-female') in the local dialect.[635] Crossdressing women and men called the *Maa Khii* also persist in parts of northern Thailand. Contemporary discussion of transgendered Thai people focuses on the *Kathoey* (discussed below), as well as the *Maa Khii*. With these thoughts in mind we are ready for a short historical review to provide some context for the modern society.

Peter Jackson's 'Bio-History' of Thai Transgender

Both East and West influences from other societies have shaped gender expression in modern Thailand. Peter Jackson, a Research Fellow in Asian and Pacific History at the Australian National University, is perhaps the best-known contemporary student of Thailand's transgender community. He remarks that the nation experienced in the latter decades of the 20th century a proliferation of new gender and sexual identities and cultures. Following the lead of Foucault's *History of Sexuality* and Judith Butler's idea of 'performative gender,' Jackson advances a case that the emergence of these new expressions flows from the Thai state's efforts to 'civilize' gender display as a response to the imperial powers of the last two centuries. Historically in Siam, transgender behaviors like crossdressing occasioned little remark. Yet by the 1960s Thai medical and mental health professionals had come to follow the West's lead in pathologizing transgender realities. The long transition to this state of affairs, Jackson proposes, was inspired by the kingdom's desire to escape Western characterizations as a barbarous land by initiating changes to earn the West's recognition as a 'civilized' nation.[636]

Jackson remarks that Western observers numbered among their criticisms a complaint about the perceived similarity of appearance between Siamese men and women. There was no differentiation in clothing fashions (all wearing the unisex *jong-kraben*) and hairstyles. To 19th century foreign visitors, with their hair cut short like men's Siamese women looked too masculine, especially when wearing *pha chongkaben*, a traditional garment somewhat resembling baggy trousers. Worse, in Western eyes, were those who crossed Western gender lines in dress and action, like the female royal guards of the king's harem outfitted in what seemed like masculine garb, or male actors portraying women onstage. The similarity in gendered appearance of Thai men and women continued to occasion comment through the 20th century until at least the post-World War II period.[637]

The Siamese government did not ignore Western criticism. Jackson says they responded with selective strategic efforts to use legal and institutional forms of power to make the populace 'civilized' in Western eyes. But, he argues, their aim was not the reforming of private sexuality but "refashioning the public gendering of their bodies."[638] Laws were passed, and enforced, to ensure that all Thai people were covered properly and that male and female could be easily distinguished.[639] This meant men wore shirts and trousers, while women wore blouses and skirts; traditional unbifurcated unisex garb was officially set aside.[640] By the mid-1960s an effective Westernization of dress fashion was entrenched.[641]

Today's Thai people experience the effects of a prolonged period of conscientious effort to change traditional sexual and gender identities and cultures. Jackson states frankly that, "Patterns of personal identity have been altered as a result of the Thai gender revolution."[642] He demonstrates the pervasiveness and significance of these changes, reflected not only in dress, but in linguistic changes, social roles, and a variety of other ways. Only in this context can the modern *Kathoey* be understood. Jackson observes that, "the modern *Kathoey* has emerged *together with* gay identities as one aspect of the broader gender revolution."[643]

Kathoey

As noted earlier, the *Kathoey* (or *katoey*, or *kathooi*) represent a third gendered group, in distinction to masculine and feminine. The best English translation of the term has been debated. Rosalind Morris views *Kathoey* as "feminized maleness."[644] But that understanding better fits the modern Thai transgendered expression as strongly influenced by the West. Kittiwut Jod Taywaditep and colleagues trace a progressive change in meaning for the term. Originally referring to someone of indeterminate sex (a hermaphrodite), it came to refer to homosexual men, until the Western term 'gay' supplanted it. Now, they say, it refers to males demonstrating feminine social behaviors and as such is widely viewed by Thai gay men as a derogatory term.[645]

Contemporary Thai *Kathoey* males may be placed in one or more of several Western categories, including effeminate homosexuals, transvestites, transsexuals, or transgendered in the narrow sense (see the answer to Q. 20), meaning men who live as women, perhaps with some body alterations, but without sexual reassignment surgery (which is widely available in Thailand). They are publicly accepted in Thai society, though often with a lower social standing. In rural villages they may participate in local festivities in a feminine role, such as food preparation. In more urban areas they may hold any number of professional positions but are often associated with certain occupations such as prostitute, beautician, hair-dresser, florist, or fashion designer—positions identified with women. Entertainment and media also offer opportunities, though media presentations often reinforce stereotypes of the *Kathoey* as histrionic and emotionally unstable—again, like women. Much of the stereotyping applied to the *Kathoey* may be linked to many Thai people seeing all *Kathoey* as being like gay drag queens.[646]

The public tolerance of the *Kathoey* tells only part of the story. Researcher Andrew Matzner, after a year long study of Thai attitudes toward homosexuals, concludes that while the *Kathoey* may not experience public harassment in Thai society, their private experience is often difficult. Many find parents and extended family are ashamed of them. Also, *Kathoey* run a special risk of sexual violence by males (chai).[647] Matzner's findings resemble those of Walter Irvine, who finds that village *Kathoey* express their awareness of the stigma and subordinate status attached to themselves, including by family.[648] These observations support Jackson's idea that a long modern history about sex and gender presentation in Thailand has created a public reality that may not accurately reflect private realities. Rosalind Morris' explanation is that the public decency accorded the *Kathoey* may merely reflect Thai interests in public shows of respect (*kreng jai*) or propriety (*naa*).[649]

Even public realities may not live up to what the casual tourist encounters. The continued impress of Western ideas and values continues to be felt in Thailand. For example, in 2003 the military determined to make transgendered people exempt from the draft. The reason cited by an army general was "not because we are prejudiced but because we fear that the military will collapse." This, he said, was because they may have "physical attributes" deemed "inappropriate."[650]

The Maa Khii

In northern Thailand another transgendered reality is known. Principally women, but also sometimes men, these folk are called the *Maa Khii* ('possessed ones'). The *Maa Khii* are associated with a spiritual tradition (the *phi* cults) in which they occupy the role of spirit mediums. In this role ancestral guardian spirits 'possess' them during an annual festival. A trance-like state, dancing and cross-gender behavior, including crossdressing, mark this possession. Outside this special spiritual role these persons enact gender-typical behavior.

Most *Maa Khii* are female. This situation is buttressed by the tradition that the ancestral guardian spirits are passed matrilineally from one generation to the next. However, male *Maa Khii* are not unknown. Some are also *Kathoey*. Like the female *Maa Khii*, these males also exhibit cross-gender behavior; in the case of the *Kathoey* this means stereotypically masculine behavior unlike what they normally exhibit.[651]

Walter Irvine's study of the *Maa Khii* concludes that about 15% are not female. Of these, most are *Kathoey*. Irvine's explanation for why some non-females may be able to function as spirit mediums is that the *Kathoey*, like females, are viewed as 'weak-souled,' meaning they are unable to resist spirit possession like males can. He also thinks that the *Kathoey* who became *Maa Khii* do so in response to an earlier illness afflicted by a spirit (*chao*). By yielding to the *chao* and becoming possessed they can regain their health—and become spirit mediums. This choice also improves their social status since the *Maa Khii* enjoy a prestige the ordinary *Kathoey* does not.[652]

Rosalind Morris points to a special relationship that seems to exist between one particular *chao*, the spirit of Queen Chamathewi, and *Kathoey*. The Queen is famous for the legendary manner by which she vanquished an unwanted suitor. Taking cloth from one of her undergarments she had worn during her menstrual flow, she fashioned a hat and gave it to him. As a result his male strength was vitiated and a spear he had cast was blown back and killed him. Now *Kathoey* mediums seem especially likely to be possessed by her.[653]

What are transgender realities in Vietnam?

The history of transgender realities in Vietnam, both past and present, includes both male and female shamans, who embody spirits both male and female, accompanied by appropriately gendered dress. In contemporary times transgendered males have received the most attention—a fact in line with Western culture's preoccupation with this part of the transgendered population. The language terms for crossdressing males vary between the northern and southern parts of the country. In the north *Dong co* ('woman goes into a trance'), with roots in the tradition of indigenous shamans, is used. In the south *Bong cai* ('female shadow') is common.[654]

Transgender individuals have been described in the scientific literature at least since the mid-1970s. At that time, psychiatrists Elliott Heiman and Cao Van Le describe a continuum of social response. At one end, what some term the 'hermaphroditic witch' displays transgender behavior within a culturally prescribed and sanctioned role. Other crossdressers, who do not fit within a shamanic role may nevertheless find ways to fit within cultural parameters for cross-gender behavior, such as young crossdressers. But at the opposite end of this spectrum, where the modern transsexual resides, no cultural sanction exists. Such people—one of whom is described by the authors—remain at best marginalized and are largely invisible.[655]

This sometimes drives individuals to desperate acts. Nguyen Trong Tien, a male-to-female transsexual was repeatedly turned down by hospitals. He finally resorted to attempting to remove his penis by his own hand. The hospital at which he found himself refused to complete removing it and instead reattached it.[656] Apart from self-inflicted injuries, transgender people widely suffer from social exclusion and political persecution, according to a 2003 Amnesty International report.[657]

As is happening around the world, contemporary Vietnam is wrestling with gender issues and laws about transgender people. Vietnamese endocrinologist Nguyen Thu Nhan began studying gender variant children in the 1980s and estimates as many as 1-in-10,000 to 12,000 babies are intersex. Among this population some sex reassignment surgeries occur. In May, 2005, the National Assembly, debated Article 36 of a revised Civil Code, which would for the first time authorize legal sex reassignment through surgery (in cases of 'congenital defects').[658] In July, 2006, the Assembly authorized a gender transition law under which a transgender person who has undergone medical and psychological tests may change their sex and gender statuses.[659]

Not surprisingly, public awareness of many transgendered males starts with those areas drawing attention in many societies: entertainment and the sex trade. In terms of the former, social tolerance may be growing. In the fall of 2006, the Ministry of Culture permitted release of the music CD by the country's best known transsexual singer, Cindy Thai Tai (born Nguyen Thai Tai).[660] With respect to the latter, male transgendered sex workers, research indicates they tend to be young (20s), relatively uneducated, and involved in risky sexual practices, especially as the passive partner in unprotected anal sex with other men.[661] They constitute a small but distinctive minority of sex workers, but are found in various places in the country, including Saigon. There "transvestite sex workers on motorbikes are common in the main tourist area."[662]

What might we conclude about transgender realities like crossdressing in the modern East?

Overall, the East historically has displayed more tolerance toward crossdressing than the West. In modern times the Western world's power has influenced the East such that Western values and views about gender and sexuality have had a restricting effect on transgendered people in many Eastern lands. Some of this has been due to the effects of occupation or colonization by Western powers, like the British. In other cases, though, it has been a self-generated change within Eastern societies desirous of better relations with the West or self-consciously imitating the West because of perceptions of Western economic success. In any event, the influence of the West on the East appears to have been more pronounced than any leavening influence flowing from East to West. As a result, transgendered people in the East have both experienced greater cultural disapproval while simultaneously gaining (in some places) modest legal protections modeled on Western practices.

Q. 53

Where is it found in the Middle East?

The Short Answer. Transgender realities are no stranger to the Middle East, having existed both in ancient times and down to the present. Thus the countries of the Middle East have witnessed crossdressing through their long history. It occurred in biblical days in the area in and around Israel. It happened during the ascension to prominence of Islam. And it continues to be known in modern times. Historically, more tolerance was shown toward transgendered individuals—especially the intersexed—prior to the influence of the Christian West. Today transgendered people are largely marginalized, and homosexuality is a criminal offense in Islamic lands. Transvestites and transsexuals fare somewhat better in some nations, but for the most part remain with other sexual minorities on the fringe of Islamic society. Israel, a modern democracy, provides more legal protection and transgendered people enjoy more civil liberties, but as in the Islamic world those who are most religiously conservative in Israel are generally the least tolerant, and often openly hostile.

The Longer Answer. Crossdressing by both males and females has occurred and still occurs in the lands known today as the Middle East. As seen in answering an earlier question (Q. 51), likely all the countries of the Middle East experience crossdressers and transgender realities, though some deny it officially. In this material we will examine some of the history of crossdressing in this region and provide some modern instances of the practice. Since many of the lands of the Middle East are aligned with Islam, the answer to Q. 78 also provides pertinent material. With reference to Israel, Judaism's interaction with transgender realities is discussed in the answers to Q. 61-63, 77. Some of the countries where transgender realities such as crossdressing are documented are listed in Table 53.1.

Table 53.1 Middle Eastern Countries with Documented Transgender Realities

Bahrain	Iran	Lebanon	Syria
Egypt	Israel	Oman	Turkey
Iraq	Jordan	Saudi Arabia	Yemen

Were there transgender realities like crossdressing in the premodern Middle East?

The value placed on the Middle East by Western culture makes it reasonable to begin this investigation with the past. Elsewhere, this history is looked at both in a more general historical context (the answer to Q. 41), with regard to specific historical figures (the answer to Q. 43), and in terms of religion (the answers to Q. 63, 76-78). Here a general orientation to the region is established by looking at three regions of the Middle East, each important in its own way in the ancient world, and each knowing transgender realities. In turn, these three regions are: Mesopotamia, Egypt, and Israel/Canaan. In addition, because the Middle East today is religiously dominated by Islam, a very brief presentation is offered on early and modern Islam, though the more complete treatment in answering Q. 78 should be reviewed as well.

Mesopotamia

Ancient Mesopotamia, often called the 'Cradle of Civilization,' presents us records of transgender realities. Perhaps the best known—or at least most often remarked—is the lusty hero king Gilgamesh, laid low by his love for the wild man Enkidu, created especially for him. As Enkidu is tamed by a priestess who entices him to sexual intercourse, making him weak but wise, so in turn Enkidu draws Gilgamesh to himself 'as to a woman' (or 'wife'). Indeed, Enkidu's female companion prepares him for his encounter with Gilgamesh by dividing her own garments and clothing him. Enkidu, resembling Gilgamesh though smaller, at last meets the king. They struggle and though Gilgamesh prevails in the contest, his lusts for women are defeated and he makes Enkidu his steadfast companion.

While the *Gilgamesh Epic* is well-known, other less celebrated texts recount gender crossings, like crossdressing, that happened more than two millennia ago in the lands of the Middle East. Indeed, Mesopotamia offers us the earliest written depictions of gender-altering deities and sacred gender crossings by priests. The transgendered appear in an ancient creation account: the god Enki named and decided the fates of the human beings the goddess Ninmah fashioned out of clay. The sixth of these "she fashioned one with neither penis nor vagina on its body. Enki looked at the one with neither penis nor vagina on its body and gave it the name 'Nibru eunuch (?)', and decreed as its fate to stand before the king."[663]

Also in ancient Sumeria, the 'mother of literature' Enheduanna (En-hedu-Ana, 'The High Priestess called Ornament of Heaven') penned praises to the goddess Inana (cf. the answer to Q. 76). Inana (or Inanna), identified with the Akkadian Ishtar, or Astarte of the Semitic peoples of the Mideast, is the daughter of Enki. She is associated with liminal realities and reversals; when she asks Enki what her functions are, he answers, "I covered ...... with a garment. I made you exchange its right side and its left side. . . . I made you tangle straight threads; maiden Inana, I made you straighten out tangled threads."[664] She, then, is a patron goddess of transgendered realities—those states between the sex and gender poles.

In a hymn to Inana her unique qualities in relation to people are put forth as follows:

> Inana was entrusted by Enlil and Ninlil with the capacity to gladden the heart of those who revere her in their established residences, but not to soothe the mood of those who do not revere her in their well-built houses; to turn a man into a woman and a woman into a man, to change one into the other, to make young women dress as men on their right side, to make young men dress as women on their left side, to put spindles into the hands of men . . . , and to give weapons to the women. . . . .[665]

As well as transform mortal men and women, Inana can embrace both genders in her own presentation: "When I sit in the alehouse, I am a woman, and I am an exuberant young man."[666] And just as Inana is made to exchange her garment's 'right side and its left,' so also her devotees: "Dressed with men's clothing on the right side, they parade before her, holy Inana. I shall greet the great lady of heaven, Inana! Adorned (?) with women's clothing on the left side, they parade before her, holy Inana."[667] Apparently, this is not exclusively the right of her priests, the *kurĝara*; the mighty hero Ama-ušumgal-ana is said to cloak his body "as if in your royal robe of office."[668]

Finally, some ambiguous evidence comes from Babylonian Wisdom literature. An Assyrian proverb, incompletely preserved, supposes an Amorite man saying to his wife, "You be the man, [I] will be the woman. [Since . .] . I became a man [. . . . .] female [. . . . .] male."[669] What precisely is entailed in this gender reversal is unknown. But it is not farfetched to imagine it involved crossdressing.

Nor are we confined to literary evidence. Michelle Marcus, in her study of the role played by pins in the dress of ancient Iranian women at Hasanlu (c. 1100-800 B.C.E.), observes that on rare occasions these important feminine items were found on men. Marcus suggests three plausible hypotheses for this happening: cross-dressing, recognition of a third gender, or a potential transition with respect to gender such that when men reached a certain age, "they had the privilege of abandoning the rules of gender difference by adopting elements of dress that were gendered female."[670] While Marcus favors the third alternative, she acknowledges transvestism seems to have been common and that the possibility of a third gender status cannot be ruled out.

Ancient Egypt

Ancient Egypt, that remarkably long-lived and stable world, knew full well transgendered realities on heaven and earth. Despite a fondness for gender-paired gods and goddesses, the Egyptian pantheon has its notably gender ambiguous deities: the principal creator deity Atum originated as an androgynous god with procreative power;[671] Amun-Re is a father deity who gives birth to human-kind; Hapi, god of the Nile, is represented as a masculine deity with feminine breasts.

Human worship can incorporate gender crossings too. In recognition of the complex sexual relationship depicted between the male deities Set and Horus, worshippers might have incorporated homoerotic elements.[672] "Hieroglyphic texts indicate that wine drinking followed by homosexual penetration may have been included in religious rituals honoring Seth and Horus."[673]

Gender crossings could happen for other reasons as well. For example, Ma'at-ka-Ra Hatshepsut—arguably the world's first known crossdresser (see the answer to Q. 48)—was the daughter of Pharaoh Tuthmose I. After his death she reigned first as Queen Regent before assuming the power and role of Pharaoh. In this role she dressed in masculine garb and donned a royal beard. She also apparently attempted to raise her daughter Neferura as a prince.[674]

In the mundane world of everyday human affairs Egyptians recognized sexual differentiation into categories resembling our modern division of male, female, and intersexed. There are hieroglyphs for male (*tie*), female (*hemet*), and 'eunuch' (*sekhet*), one like a male without a male's procreative capacity. But as the 1997 Kelsey Museum exhibition on Women and Gender in Ancient Egypt demonstrates, artifacts from prehistory through late antiquity show representations of an even wider gender spectrum with recognition (often vague) of a variety of 'third genders.' The influence of outside cultures, most notably Greco-Roman and Christian, led to more formal—and to us familiar—gender categories.[675]

Ancient Canaan and Israel

The sacred gender crossings of the Sumerians extended to other societies in the region down through the centuries. In ancient Canaan crossdressing could have noble intentions, as when the woman Pughat put on the martial dress of a man, armed herself with a sword, and gained revenge for her dead brother Aqhat.[676] The ancient Israelites responded to the practice by waging a vigorous and centuries long battle over its appropriateness. In popular Israelite religion the practices of the devotees of Ishtar/Astarte and the Canaanite Asherah were well-known and often incorporated. Late in the debate the Hebrew book *Devorim* (or *Debarim*; known in the English Bible as *Deuteronomy*) weighed in by including a provision in the Torah concerning crossdressing (see the answer to Q. 61-65).

Still later, in the period when the Christian New Testament was being formed, the Jewish military commander and historian Josephus described transgender behavior as one feature of certain Galilean thugs in the days of revolt against the Romans:

> They also devoured what spoils they had taken, together with their blood, and indulged themselves in feminine wantonness, without any disturbance, till they were satiated therewith: while they decked their hair, and put on women's garments, and were besmeared over with ointments; and that they might appear very comely, they had paints under their eyes, and imitated, not only the ornaments, but also the lusts of women, and were guilty of such intolerable uncleanness, that they invented unlawful pleasures of that sort.[677]

The *Talmud*, gradually shaped over the following centuries, also has pertinent materials to our discussion, but these are covered in volume 4.

Early and Premodern Islam

The early history of Islam, centered in the lands of the Middle East, also references crossdressers. These might be male (*mukhannathun*, 'effeminate men') or female (*mutarajjulat*, women 'who assume the manner of men'). The former played an active and varied role in early Islamic society. They experienced both tolerance and intolerance at different times, though their influence and their prominence were effectively ended by the Caliph Sulayman.[678]

Everett Rowson, a noted scholar of Arabic and Islam, observes that in medieval Baghdad, at the court of the Caliph, crossdressing was a feature of entertainment. His investigation of the sources reveals that some crossdressers were so successful in their imitation of another gender that even in sex they could persuade their partner to imagine them as the sex they were pretending. Thus the poet Abu Nuwas remarks of a young female slave masquerading as a boy that she was so skilled he had no trouble imagining her as a boy.[679]

Though more should be said on these matters, the material in the next volume (see answer to Q. 78) provides the proper context of this history in conjunction with Islam.

What are transgender realities in the modern Middle East?

As elsewhere in the world, there has been no uniform social response to transgendered realities. Crossdressing remains a fixture of modern life in the Middle East, and one aspect of transgender realities found in the region. Most prominent by the concern it generates and the attention given to it has been homosexuality,[680] widely reported but most often making the news when individuals are arrested and punished, sometimes by capital punishment, in Islamic societies. Best tolerated have been intersexed conditions; hermaphrodites are known and discussed in Islamic religious/legal traditions. The existence of transsexualism, including individuals seeking sex reassignment surgery (SRS) also has prompted Islamic response, which has varied from place to place. In a region where transgendered people are marginalized and must often fear the State, most remain hidden and those who emerge in public do so largely in barely tolerated niches such as the sex trade. However, as in other places, the most visible road to tolerance has been through public entertainment. Together, the sex trade and entertainment continue to represent the most visible means for supporting themselves open to many transgendered people.

Crossdressing and Entertainment

In the Middle East some crossdressing is associated with entertainment, whether in singing, dancing, theater, or film. With reference to Egypt, Garay Menicucci terms crossdressing "the most ubiquitous coding for gay and lesbian cinematic imaging," and notes that public transvestite performers (*khawalat*) became more prominent in the 19th century after female dancers were banned.[681] Crossdressing is also an aspect of the burlesque theater in Iran, were female roles in the *Tazieh* (morality plays) are performed by males.[682] In Israel, prominent entertainers include the drag queen Bnot Pesia and the MtF transsexual singer Dana International.

Various Transgendered People

But the Middle East transgendered community is far more diverse—and hidden—than a few very public figures might suggest. It embraces Muslims, Jews, and Christians. Repressive laws in some nations keep many transgendered people largely invisible, while others in public view often lead precarious lives, minimally tolerated because they provide a desired but unsanctioned outlet such as through the sex trade, but harshly treated when that role draws unwelcome attention. Many more transgendered people lead lives wearing the mask of social conformity in public to avoid negative social consequences.

However, many hidden transgendered people are by no means entirely silent. The anonymity of the internet, for example, affords an outlet for making connections, expressing concerns, and advocating acceptance. For instance, the Transsexual Alliance of the Kingdom of Jordan maintains Café Trans Arabia, a website for the Middle Eastern Transsexual Community.[683] Moreover, some services have emerged, albeit limited, in various nations. In Egypt and Iran, for example, some doctors perform sex reassignment surgery (SRS), in accordance with strictures set out by the religious authorities.

Violence Faced by Crossdressers

Nevertheless, life is often problematic for the transgendered people of the region. Islamic nations in the Middle East generally uphold a strongly dichotomous gender division. Sexual interactions are typically morally evaluated by whether the person involved is actively penetrating (the 'male' role), or passively receiving penetration (the 'female' role). Homosexual and other transgender people are generally disavowed, afforded few if any legal protections (even in the face of a lack of specific legal prohibitions), and commonly harassed—or worse.

Homosexuality remains a crime punishable by death in many Islamic lands, whether Sunni or Shiite (e.g., Iran (Shiite), Saudi Arabia (Sunni)). Little if any distinction is made among those who crossdress, and crossdressing is a punishable offense in most Middle East countries. Amnesty International, in a 1996 report, cites various reports of violence against crossdressers in Turkey, including beating, hair being torn out, and genitals injured.[684] In Saudi Arabia, males caught crossdressing may be subjected to flogging, and perhaps even execution by beheading.[685] In Yemen, the same penalties may be applied.[686] These examples hardly exhaust the dangers transgender people face.

Changes in the Middle East

Yet, despite the hostility frequently faced by transgendered people in these lands, there have been signs of change. For example, in 2004 a Kuwaiti court ruled that a 25 year old who had undergone male-to-female sex reassignment surgery could henceforth be officially recognized as a woman. The judges justified their ruling on the Islamic permission for gender change when medically supported. This followed presentation by the individual's lawyer of an edict (*fatwa*) issued by Egypt's Al-Azhar the preeminent Sunni legal institution.[687] However, a higher court later overturned this decision.[688] On the other hand, nations as different as Egypt, Saudi Arabia and Iran have all permitted sex changes with religious authorization under certain conditions. In general, the situation for transgendered people remains troubled, and especially so for homosexual males.

The brief remarks that follow examine select nations. The information here is relatively sparse. This is a reflection of the difficulty obtaining reliable reports, not the scarcity of a transgendered population. Most of these nations do not have free presses and information published about transgendered people is rare and typically shrouded in generalities or misleading terms.

Few comments have been made about the homosexual communities in these lands. However, as indicated above, the situation gays and lesbians face is repressive in Islamic lands of the Middle East. Rather than reiterate the matter in each nation only select incidents have been reported. These may be regarded as indicative of the larger social picture. As throughout this work the emphasis here is on crossdressing.

What are transgender realities in Bahrain?

Anthropologist Julanne McCarthy observes in Bahrain a diversity of crossdressing behavior. Crossdressers include the *kaneeth* (*Xanith*, or *khanith*), regarded as specially gendered, and the *benaty*, who are apparently generally tolerated, being mostly ignored, and who are occasionally seen in public. McCarthy notes various motivations for crossdressing by males in different contexts. These include entertainment, gaining access to females, and seeking to evade police detection. In addition to male crossdressers, McCarthy also notes the presence of female crossdressers—lesbian Filipinas, who intentionally flatten their breasts and adopt clothing that permits passing as male.[689]

What are transgender realities in Egypt?

Egypt, long a leader among the Islamic nations of the region, is among the most progressive in some respects with reference to the treatment of transgendered people. SRS has happened for a small number of people since at least the late 1980s. In 1988, Grand Mufti Mohamed Sayed Tantawi, citing *hadith*, issued a religious edict (*fatwa*) in a letter to the Doctors' General Syndicate authorizing SRS in the case of a patient deemed a hermaphrodite.[690] In the mid-1990s, Sheikh Tantawi became the Grand Imam of the Sunni legal body Al-Azhar. The *fatwa* authorizing SRS when medically necessary "to bring out signs of femininity or masculinity which are present but hidden" remains in force but is limited to individuals designated as hermaphrodites. SRS by other individuals remains unsanctioned.

What are transgender realities in Iran?

Like other Islamic lands, Shiite-dominated Iran has long been aware of gender variant individuals. Iranian scholar Afsaneh Najmabadi points out that the modern Western idea of a gender binary does not fit well on the Iranian past. In 19th century Iranian culture the designation of an adult male as *mukhannas* (someone desiring to be the object of other men's desire) did not carry with it an identification of effeminacy. But in the interest of attaining recognition by Europeans as a 'modern' state, Iran's acceptance of realities like homoeroticism was revoked in the interest of what Najmabadi calls the "heteronormalization of eros and sex."[691] The Shiite nation's understanding of Islam reckons homosexuality a crime. Gay men are subject to execution and lesbians to the lash.

While homosexuals have fared the worst, other transgendered people often have faced difficulties too. Prior to the Islamic revolution in 1979 the state generally turned a blind eye to transgender. Since then transgendered people, whether transvestites, transsexuals, or homosexuals, are often grouped together and regarded negatively. That was particularly so in the immediate aftermath of the revolution. Since then the status of transsexuals has improved in comparison to that of homosexuals. Even so, there have persisted incongruities, with some individuals faring better than others and even the same person experiencing tolerance or opposition at different times. In recent years there have been more general signs of tolerance toward many transgendered, particularly by religious scholars and officials, but not toward homosexuals. In fact, with reference to transsexuals and the intersexed there are anecdotal reports of individuals receiving the blessing and support of local clerics in their efforts to transition from one gender to another.[692]

There are varying factors that have influenced this shift. An important one has been that as clerics have become better informed about transgendered realities a creeping tolerance has advanced. Some religious scholars, like cleric Hojatolislam Muhammed Medhi Kariminia, have even undertaken academic examination of the topic. But such things are possible especially because the late Ayatollah Ruhollah Khomeini was persuaded by a transsexual compatriot to issue a *fatwa* supporting a sex change. Maryam Molkara, the person who braved a beating to reach the Ayatollah in person, had previously corresponded with him while the spiritual leader was in exile. In 1975, correspondence Molkara sent explained her own transgender experience and received the Ayatollah's advice to follow Islamic law for women. However, the revolution of 1979 greatly worsened Molkara's situation, including losing employment, being confined in a mental institution, and forcibly given male hormones and made to dress as a man. Upon release, Molkara sought a personal meeting with the Ayatollah, which only happened after Khomeini's kin intervened to stop the beating being done by the guards. The Ayatollah called in experts to learn about transsexualism and then issued a *fatwa* permitting Molkara to receive SRS.[693]

The authorization granted one individual has become by extension a grant to other similar individuals. SRS can proceed with the permission of the government. While it is still common for individuals seeking SRS to obtain it outside the country, many cases are known to have occurred within Iran. One physician, Dr. Mir-djalali, conducted more than 300 over a decade span.[694] However, as *New York Times* correspondent Nazila Fathi observes in a 2004 article, growing tolerance among clerics and doctors does not equal acceptance among the general populace, where prejudice remains strong.[695]

In that respect, Paula Drew remarks that not only crossdressing but "any kind of individualism in unconventional dress or hairstyle is almost impossible" in Iran. She explains that Iranian social structure, which puts great control of offspring into parental hands throughout life serves to reinforce cultural norms.[696] The prevailing Shiite conservatism further enforces rigid gender distinctions in dress and manner. Accordingly, transgendered people remain mostly hidden. When they surface in public view it is along the social margins in venues such as low-brow entertainments that the upper classes of Iranian society look down upon.

What are transgender realities in Israel?

Israel, a state created in 1948 by resolution of the United Nations, exists as a Western-style democracy in a region surrounded by Islamic states. Within Israel's borders Jews and Muslims make up most of the population and Islam is a vital force alongside Judaism. Although Orthodox Judaism exerts the most authority among Israeli Jews, there are also Conservative, Reform, and secular Jews. A visible transgendered population exists and enjoys freedom from the criminal penalties transgender people face in many of the surrounding nations.

Social acceptance of crossdressing and transgendered people varies. Many Jews, whether religious or secular, see nothing objectionable to celebratory crossdressing conducted as part of the festival of Purim, which commemorates a divine reversal of fortune in the days of Queen Esther. The Torah text of Deuteronomy 22:5, which prohibits crossdressing, is variously interpreted with few Jewish scholars seeing the modern practice as that meant by the biblical injunction (see the answers to Q.61-63, 77). Some individuals have been very visible publicly, notably in entertainment. Those most likely to accept transgender realities tend to be secular or religiously moderate. Orthodox Jews are more likely to reject the legitimacy of such realities, appealing to religious grounds (see the answer to Q. 77).

Crossdressers in Israel include individuals who identify as homosexual or heterosexual, transvestite or transsexual. As in many other lands, some find a public outlet through entertaining. Drag queen Bnot Pesia is one well-known entertainer. However, perhaps the best known such figure is an MtF transsexual named Sharon Cohen, better known by her stage name, Dana International. The singer has enjoyed success not only within the transgender community, but throughout Israel (and in Arab lands as well).[697] Other crossdressers often visible publicly, both male transvestites and MtF transsexuals, work in the sex trade. Some research indicates the risk of HIV infection among them is significantly higher than among other prostitutes.[698]

Homosexuals have witnessed advances in public tolerance over the short history of the nation. In 1993, during parliamentary work on gender equality legislation, some 100 gay and lesbian people were invited to appear before a Knesset subcommittee—an event that helped spark various reforms.[699] One participant in that event, Uzi Even, in 2002 became the first openly gay member of the Knesset (Israel's parliamentary body).[700] In 2003, the first openly gay member of Tel-Aviv's city council was elected.[701] Presently, Israel has the most prominent national Gay-Lesbian-Bisexual-Transgender (GLBT) organization in the region, the Agudah ('union,' or 'gathering'), headquartered in Tel Aviv.[702] Gay pride parades take place in a climate of civic tolerance in the capital.[703]

Despite some tension between Israel's homosexual community and other segments of the transgender population, efforts have occurred to show unity for mutual benefit. There are public events to display solidarity and heighten general awareness such as the gathering of transgendered people to observe a 'Transgender Day of Remembrance' in Tel Aviv.[704] Among other resources is the Israel transgender magazine, *Banot* (*Girls*), which at the beginning of the new millennium appeared monthly in Hebrew; an accompanying website provided transgender resources.[705]

Utilizing a schema in which transgendered people are viewed as gender dysphoric, scholars Ronny Shtarkshall and Minah Zemach contend that "gender conflicted persons find it difficult to be evaluated and cared for in an organized and controlled way."[706] There is some truth to this in that supportive therapy and access to sexual reassignment procedures remain limited. Still, Israeli transsexuals generally have more options than those in other lands of the Middle East. Sex change is not illegal, but it is limited. In the late 1990s, only one hospital—Tel Hashomer's Sheba Hospital—was authorized to conduct sex reassignment surgery. In a roughly decade span (1987-1998) only 15 individuals were reported to have undergone such procedures. Recognition of the change stops short of providing full acknowledgment but can include issuance of a new identity card if the applicant provides either a court order or sufficient documentation from medical authorities.[707]

What are transgender realities in Oman?

Oman sits at the edge of Arabia, across the Gulf of Oman from Iran. It is bordered by the United Arab Emirates to the north, Saudi Arabia to the west, and Yemen to the southwest. A mostly Muslim nation with a small Hindu minority, Oman's most noted transgender reality is found in the *Xanith*.

The *Xanith* are transgendered males. Norwegian social anthropologist Unni Wikan, whose fieldwork was among the Arabs of Oman's city of Sohar on the northeastern coast, concluded in the mid-1970s that these distinctive folk constitute perhaps 2% of the adult males of Sohar.[708] Although considered by law as male, *Xanith* speak of themselves as women. However, they are not permitted to dress as women; such behavior is a crime. Instead, *Xanith* speak in a falsetto voice and present in distinctive dress that lies intermediate to the appearance of men and women. For example, while men and *Xanith* both wear ankle-length tunics, those of the *Xanith* are cinched at the waist like a woman's dress. Where a man wears white and a woman wears bright colors in patterned cloth, the *Xanith* wear unpatterned colors. Men keep their hair short, women wear theirs long, and the *Xanith* have hair whose length is in-between men and women styles.

The *Xanith* occupy a distinctive role in Sohar. Unlike other males, they are free to move among women, who may show their face to them. However, if they marry a woman they then lose this privilege and are treated like other males. *Xanith* sing at weddings, and perform other social tasks, but are perhaps best known for their involvement as prostitutes.[709] Both the Euro-American terms of 'transvestite' and 'transsexual' have been applied to the *Xanith*, though they may also be considered an example of a third gender.

What are transgender realities in Saudi Arabia?

Homosexuals in Saudi Arabia, as in other Islamic nations, face arrest and severe punishment. Gay men may even be sentenced to death. In late March of 2005, for example, Saudi security police raided a private party in Jeddah and arrested more than 100 men. The newspaper *Al-Wifaq* reported the men's conduct as 'behaving like women,' and in closed court sessions, without defense representation, 4 men were sentenced to flogging by 2,000 lashes and two years imprisonment; 31 other men were sentenced to prison terms ranging from six months to a year, accompanied by flogging by 200 lashes. Another 70 received one year prison terms.[710]

Other transgendered people also often suffer abuse, ridicule, and legal sanctions. For instance, in 1998, in a raid on a private home, 5 crossdressing Pakistanis were arrested. In addition to deportation they also faced possible flogging. However, interpreting that situation is complicated by the fact the raid was in search of illegal immigrants.[711]

Other stories have surfaced with regard to transgendered individuals. In 2004 the *Sydney Morning Herald* reported a story from *Okaz* newspaper in Saudi Arabia that five siblings of one family all were transitioning from female to male through SRS. The justification for the SRS was that medical examination had determined all of them had more male than female hormones.[712] As the presiding physician, Dr. Yasser Jamal, explained, the sisters were designated intersex rather than transsexual—a condition associated with homosexuality in the society.[713] In accordance with the Al-Azhar *fatwa* on such matters, the operations were approved under Islamic law as medically needed (to resolve hermaphroditic ambiguity) and not granted for purely personal desire.

In another matter, a Saudi court generated controversy when a judge ruled in favor of a woman who had previously been a man concerning an inheritance dispute. The Saudi woman's magazine *Sayidaty* (*My Lady*) reported the story of 'Ahmad,' who told the magazine of growing up a male but identifying with females. Sent abroad to the U.S. for college, Ahmad began crossdressing and developing feminine bodily features. His request for SRS funding from his father met with a threat of disinheritance. However, his father, a wealthy man, died and Ahmad inherited as a son. Ahmad then had SRS and lived as a woman. However, after 9/11, Ahmad returned to Saudi Arabia presenting as a man. When his family learned the truth, his sister and her husband sought in court to have the inheritance reapportioned, which would have cut Ahmad's share in half since daughters do not have the same inheritance rights as sons. However, the judge indicated at a preliminary hearing that the suit would not prevail and it was dropped.[714]

What are transgender realities is Turkey?

Modern Turkey is notable as a land where East meets West, and Islamic traditions coexist with many Western values. Turkish culture traditionally has been androcentric. Indeed, even in contemporary times parents there—by a 86% to 14% margin—strongly prefer male to female children. Division of labor falls along gender lines; a man who does 'woman's work' (e.g., domestic or child-rearing activities) is seen as shameful. Stereotypes about personality differences between men and women are widely embraced. Women are commonly viewed as more childlike, emotional and dependent, while men are regarded as stronger and more active. Nevertheless, over time such stereotypes may be weakening, at least among the young adults attending universities. A study reported in 2005 finds evidence for more endorsement of traits like 'independent,' 'assertive,' and 'self-sufficient' for both men and women.[715] Much like in Europe and the United States, where greater gender equality has meant women becoming more like men, a similar process may be occurring in Turkey.

Nevertheless, the influence of Western cultural values remains tempered by Islamic sensibilities. For example, the critically praised movie *Brokeback Mountain*, about two homosexual men's complicated relationship, was restricted by the Culture Ministry to an adult audience, and a Ministry official expressed the view the film violated public morals. The nation's Radio and Television Higher Board stopped a show called *He's a Lady Now* from being aired. The reality-based program would have shown men competing with one another to look and act like women.[716]

Turkey has a well-known transgendered population that includes homosexuals, transsexuals, and transvestites. Members identifying themselves with one or another group typically describe themselves by particular labels and distinguish themselves from members of other groups. Transsexuals, for example, may refer to themselves as *lubinya*. But members of the general population rarely make such distinctions and commonly view all crossdressers alike, using the label *travesti*.

Transsexuals are afforded legal recognition in Turkey under Article 29 of the Civil Code as amended by Law 3444 in 1988. However, their new status carries certain consequences, especially with respect to marriage. Article 29 states:

> All the necessary changes shall be made in the civil status of the transsexual in case of any sexual conversion which occurs after birth provided it is proved by a medical report. In all cases, for the correction of these records, action is brought against the spouse if the transsexual person is married. The same court shall indicate in its judgement to whom custody of the children shall be given. The marriage is automatically dissolved on the civil status record.[717]

As the above suggests, SRS is legal. Anyone seeking such surgery must obtain a medical certificate stating the change is 'necessary.' Curiously, however, no legal grounds were originally specified for what constitutes medical necessity. As a result, physician discretion became the determinative factor. Moreover, unlike societies like our own where established protocols mandate psychological evaluation prior to medical procedures, in Turkey no pre-operative evaluation of mental health was required.[718] However, in 2002 Turkish law was further amended (Article 40 of the new Turkish Civil Code) to regulate pre-surgical conditions as well as other procedures connected with a sex-change. Under the revised law, a candidate must be at least 18 years old, unmarried, demonstrate a reproductive deficiency such that infertility is chronic, and persuade that the surgery is needed on mental health grounds. These pre-conditions must be verified by an official medical report from a teaching hospital.[719]

Transsexuals became highly visible in urban Turkey in the late 1990s. Many gained notice through their participation in entertainment or the sex trade. With respect to the latter, Women for Women's Human Rights (WWHR) notes that transsexual women are only covered by the Turkish Penal Code if they are sex workers; under the Code they are accountable to all the rules and regulations covering sex work. Nevertheless WWHR observes that in actual practice these transsexuals are frequently maltreated by law enforcement: "They are often arrested and taken to the local police station, where they are beaten up, insulted, their hair is cut, and they are subjected to various other forms of ill treatment."[720]

Finally, with respect to Turkey's transsexual population, *Middle East Report* correspondent Deniz Kandiyoti notes that media attention has been widespread and includes mediums as diverse as cartoons, magazine articles, televised interviews, and book materials. Kandiyoti also observes that this attention has drawn complaints from the homosexual community, which is far greater in numbers.[721] As often seen elsewhere, the social response to minority groups often serves to drive those groups apart when they might be better served standing together.

Q. 54

Where is it found in Africa?

The Short Answer. Africa is a continent rich in cultural diversity. Befitting such diversity there are many transgender manifestations, and crossdressing accompanies a number of different contexts. Indeed, in sheer diversity of transgender realities the continent may be unrivalled. Yet, also perhaps more than for any other continent, the interpretation of what constitutes a transgender reality is a lively issue. Many African peoples construe sexuality and gender in ways different enough from our own perspective to cast serious doubt on the applicability of our Western terms. In fact, the struggle to match Western words and ideas to African cultural expressions is seen in the use of such labels as 'female husband,' 'boy wife,' and 'male daughter.' It is fair to argue that some of what we cover in this answer only fits a Western conception of a transgender reality. Nevertheless, whether by our own standard or by the local norms of the indigenous people, gender crossings occur, and prominent among them are instances of what we call crossdressing. Throughout the continent, in numerous tribes, transgendered people and cross-gender behavior have been known historically and remain a modern reality—sometimes in the face of official government pronouncements to the contrary. In some cases cross-gender behaviors have been part of religious rituals; sometimes transgendered people have occupied important roles. Yet, despite a long history of transgender realities in Africa, many modern transgendered people there experience well-warranted fear because of hostility in their families, tribes, or nations. Much of this modern hostile response has been placed on the influence of European culture, both because of a colonial past and because of contemporary pressure, or the influence of foreign religions. Nevertheless, as in the past, so now transgendered people are active members of their communities, seeking to effect positive changes. In some nations, such as South Africa, encouraging signs of progress have emerged amidst a lingering, disquieting legacy of harassment and violence.

The Longer Answer. As is the case with other continents the reality of transgender and the display of crossdressing in the countries of Africa present a subject too immense to be adequately covered in a work like this one. On the other hand, the matter cannot be ignored if we are to attain a basic sense of the role transgendered realities and crossdressing play in the world. So, as we have with other parts of the world, we will survey here some of the history and present issues with reference to crossdressing and transgender.

Unfortunately, the task of commenting on cultural matters of the past, especially pre-colonial history, is somewhat hindered by a number of significant obstacles. What we know about the traditional societies of Africa is often frustratingly little. Much of our knowledge is also overlaid with the selective records and interpretations of colonial observers and Western scholars since then.[722] In short, anything we venture to say about traditional societies in Africa has to be qualified by recognition of a host of complicating problems such as those noted above.

Still, we must venture an effort. Our first step is to acknowledge that African traditions relating to our Euro-American conceptions of gender and sexuality are inevitably distorted if we insist solely on relying on our own categories to understand them. While our ways of looking at things may make sense to us, and offer some utility, we must resist thinking of them as the only—or necessarily the best—ways of comprehending sexuality, gender, or transgender realities. In this material we want, as much as we can, to draw upon the work of native scholars as well as culturally sensitive nonnative scholars (principally ethnologists and anthropologists). This determination seems all the more desirable in light of the reality that our imposition of our culture's values and views on Africa have done more than cloud our conceptions of their past. There is evidence, as we shall see, that they have harmed past peoples and are harming modern African peoples.

How widespread are transgender realities in Africa?

Let us begin with an obvious question: how widespread are transgender realities across this continent? Roberta Perkins, writing for the Gender Centre Inc. in Australia, remarks that Africa provides more kinds of crossdressing than any other continent. The behavior, she notes, includes both males and females, and is employed in various contexts, sometimes briefly and at other times for extended periods.[723] Transgendered realities of one kind or another abound.

African languages have a number of terms for the transgendered, some descriptive and others more value-laden. Among the former, for example, is *wor sitabane*, a phrase in the Sesotho language of South Africa that identifies some individuals as "having both penis and vagina." Among the more value-laden words is *wobo*, used among the Maale people of Ethiopia, and meaning "crooked." Because the Maale have other words for transgendered people (e.g., *ashtime*), the use of *wobo* is pejorative. The meaning of words is context dependent. The same word can mean different things; for example, the Swahili term *shoga* (pl. *mashoga*) can be used as a term among women to refer to a 'girl friend,' or to name an older girl or woman in a mentoring role to another female, or to an impotent man, or to a homosexual man.[724] Obviously, we cannot explore fully such matters here. But we will indicate terms when illustrating different matters and we will investigate a number of transgender realities, especially from tribal societies listed in the following Table.

Table 54.1 Examples of Transgender Realities in Africa (By Tribe/Location)

Akan (Ghana)	Fon (Benin)	Lovedu (S. Africa)	Nzema (Ghana)
Amhara (Ethiopia)	Gabra (Kenya)	Luba (Congo)	Otoro (Sudan)
Ankole (Uganda)	Gisu (Uganda)	Lugbara (Uganda)	Ovimbundu (Angola)
Antandroy (Madagascar)	Hausa (Niger, Nigeria)	Lulua (Congo)	Pokot (Kenya)
Ashanti (W. Africa)	Hova (Madagascar)	Maale (Ethiopia)	Pondo (S. Africa)
Azande (Central Africa)	Ibibio (Nigeria)	Maasai (Kenya)	Sakalavas (Madagascar)
Bala (Congo)	Ibo/Igbo (W. Africa)	Mbuti (Congo)	Shona (Zimbabwe)
Bambara (Mali)	Ife (W. Africa)	Mende (Sierra Leone)	Siwan (Egypt)
Bangala (Congo)	Ihanzu (Tanzania)	Meru (Kenya)	Sotho (S. Africa)
Basongye (Zaire)	Jukun (Nigeria)	Mesakin (Sudan)	Swahili (Kenya)
Benin (W. Africa)	Kikuyu (Kenya)	Mindossi (Congo)	Tanala (Madagascar)
Bobo (Mali, Burkina Faso)	Konso (Ethiopia)	Moro (Sudan)	Thonga (Rhodesia)
Chokwe (Congo)	Kongo (Congo)	Mossi (Burkina Faso)	Tutsi (Rwanda)
Dagara (Burkina Faso)	Korongo (Sudan)	Nandi (Kenya)	Venda (S. Africa)
Dahomey (Benin)	Kwayama (Angola)	Ndonga (Angola)	Vili (Congo)
Dinke (Sudan)	Lango (Uganda)	Nuer (Sudan)	Yoruba (Nigeria)
Dogon (Mali)	Lovale (Zimbabwe)	Nuba (Sudan)	Zulu (S. Africa)

In the material that follows we will be drawing examples from these peoples.

As we proceed, we should keep in mind a point raised above, that transgender realities in Africa need not and frequently do not conform to Euro-American or Islamic conceptions and categories. At the same time, some modest application of classification schemes may help Western minds to sort out these realities. For example, the categories suggested by David Greenberg for kinship-structured societies like those common to Africa immediately assist us in understanding some transgender realities on that continent while reminding us that many of these realities are different from what we see in our own culture. Greenberg, focusing on same-sex relations as he constructs a taxonomy of sexual identity, offers three general categories for kinship-structured societies:

- ❏ *transgenerational*—where the relationship is defined by age, with the younger partner taking a passive role associated with femininity;
- ❏ *transgenderal*—where the relationship finds both gender roles enacted though the parties both belong to the same sex; and,
- ❏ *egalitarian*—where the relationship is not defined by age or gender role differences but reciprocity.[725]

While these categories hardly exhaust the lived realities in Africa, they provide some utility in understanding some of the variation found among tribal societies, as we will shortly see.

What role does gender play among traditional African societies?

Before we can understand how transgendered realities are viewed among African peoples we must grasp how gender is seen.[726] Because that task would require a hefty volume to do properly, all we can do here is note a few ideas organized around one key theme: indigenous variety at variance from European or Middle Eastern Islamic norms. African peoples display a range of conceptions and values concerning gender. Though influenced by colonization and conversion, the degree of influence and the creative maintenance of cultural traditions make for great diversity in which modern tribal societies operate within and across national borders and show signs of both continuity and discontinuity with tradition.

The impact of colonization, and the cultural pressures exerted by major religions, is undeniable and commonly remarked upon both by African scholars and others.[727] For example, sociocultural anthropologist Adeline Masquelier documents the struggle of modern Mawri youth in Niger, a struggle in no small measure reflecting the impact of colonial cultures and two major religions (Christianity and Islam) on a traditional society. Modern values and pressures daily interact with traditional ones. In a culture where bridewealth (a conveyance to the prospective bride's family to form a bridal contract) is key to forming marriage alliances, this interaction between tradition and modernity causes difficulties for many youth. Full maturity and adult social status is marked by assumption of primary obligations like marriage. But marriage requires transference of bridewealth to the woman's family. In modern society, Masquelier observes, many young men face twin obstacles: dwindling economic opportunities and inflated prices. These youth, unable to pay bridewealth, are confined to social immaturity longer than would likely have been the case in previous generations. As a result, there is a 'crisis of masculinity': young men are remaining longer in the domain defined by femininity—within the house. Men, for example, who perform any cooking task beyond the acceptably masculine task of grilling meat, are seen as effeminate and subject to ridicule. In short, Mawri males unable to marry cannot create a socially accepted masculinity and are thus culturally feminized.[728]

This example reflects the kind of dilemma modern Africans—caught among competing influences—may experience. Indigenous values, beliefs, and practices may not be fully compatible with foreign cultures, yet face pressures from those powerful other cultures to conform. And still variance persists. A few indications of this variance from European norms will serve to remind us of how the role and performance of gender need not proceed along lines familiar to Europeans and Americans.

In our culture, most people see gender closely tied to sexual anatomy. However, scholar and shaman Malidoma Somé says that "at least among the Dagara people, gender has very little to do with anatomy. It is purely energetic. In that context, one who is physically male can vibrate female energy, and vice versa. That is where the real gender is." Somé also says that gender is not used as a line to divide people. As for anatomical differences, these are used to guide the nature of the contribution made by each person in the service of the entire tribe.[729] This situation by no means pertains everywhere on the continent, but it should suffice to remind us that gender need not be seen exactly as our culture views it.

The fluidity of gender in some contexts can be glimpsed in other situations. For example, Brian MacDermot encountered an individual among the Nuer people of Ethiopia who not only appeared in feminine dress, and acted as a female, but was actually regarded as having become a woman. No physical change of sex had transpired, yet this person was free to occupy a feminine identity and role, even to the extent that marriage to a man was permissible. MacDermot was informed that the prophet of Deng had consulted the spirits and then had declared the change in this individual's status, which the people accepted.[730] Here transpired an outcome more certain and favorable than many individuals who actually undergo sexual reassignment surgery and legal identity change experience in our own culture (which so commonly arrogantly perceives itself as more enlightened).

In Euro-American culture, the family is structured along gender lines with reliable pairings of sex (male, female) to gender (masculine, feminine) to family role (husband/father, wife/mother). This structuring of the family is no more natural or inevitable than, for example, the structure found in the families of the Yoruba in Nigeria. Yoruba families are constructed not primarily along gender lines, but by relative age (Greenberg's 'transgenerational' category).[731] Similarly, social roles which in the Euro-American cultural tradition are strictly gendered, such as 'husband' and 'wife,' need not be so in African societies, as illustrated by the 'male wives' of the Azande of Sudan or the 'female husbands' of the Ibo of Nigeria.[732]

Another instance of gender behavior unlikely in Western societies is the practice of the people of Guinea-Bissau, an archipelago of 50 islands off the Western rim of the continent. In this society, the women choose the man they desire to marry. After she prepares a new home—one she builds herself—the new family can be officially recognized. As for men refusing marriage, refusal is highly unlikely—to do so would dishonor the man's family. However, in another sign of Western influence, signs of change are appearing. Though men proposing to women remains culturally opposed, the young people are reconsidering tradition.[733]

In terms of gender divisions, some groups, like the Pokot of Kenya, adhere to a relatively rigid binary system of masculinity and femininity—a scheme familiar to Europeans and Americans. Others, such as the Amhara of Ethiopia, the Igbo of Nigeria, or the Otoro of the Sudan, allow room for intermediate, mixed, or 'third gender' expressions. African societies vary, too, in when they see individuals becoming gendered. For instance, while the Igbo of Nigeria appear to assign gender around age 5, the Mbuti of Congo seem to find no need to do so before puberty.[734] The Dogon of Mali, in West Africa, offer yet another way of regarding gender and gender distinctions. They conceive the perfect human being as androgynous. In the male, the foreskin of the penis represents his femininity. Once removed, so also is his femininity and the fully male person is thus driven to seek a female as his mate, thus producing human community.[735]

Amidst this complex and varied gender context, African tribal cultures have a long history of transgendered realities and accompanying transgender behaviors like crossdressing. Some, like the Fanti people of Ghana, include cross-gender roles for both males and females.[736] The response to transgendered realities varies among different groups. Some have a history of little tolerance. Others have historically been quite tolerant. Some permit more flexibility of gender expression only at one end of the sex spectrum, male or female. Others allow some gender flexibility for all sexes. In a number of instances there are examples of Greenberg's 'transgenderal' category in phenomena often dubbed 'male wives' and 'female husbands' —examples of same-sex relationships with dual gender roles. This last notion leads us to consider instances of gender variance.

Are there instances of gender variance among females?

Female Husbands and Male Daughters

A number of tribal peoples traditionally have permitted some gender variance among those born female. One form is in same-sex marriages where one woman occupies the gendered role of 'husband' and the other the role of 'wife.' Female husbands (aka *gynegamie*[737]) are found across much of the continent, including nations in East Africa, West Africa and Southern Africa. Tribal societies include the Gikuyu and Nandi[738] of Kenya, the Ibo (or Igbo) and Dahomey peoples of Nigeria, the Dinke and Nuer[739] peoples of Sudan, and the Lovedu, Venda and Zulu peoples of South Africa. A few dozen African societies have been documented for this practice.[740]

Ifi Amadiune documents the phenomenon of so-called 'male daughters and female husbands,' a traditional practice among the Ibo of Nigeria. As in some other societies where patrilineage determines inheritance rights, in the traditional society that predominated before European colonization, where an Ibo man has no son to inherit, he may designate a daughter to occupy the role of a son for these rights—a 'male daughter' (*nhayikwa*).[741] She is placed into this position by ritual and gains access to masculine privileges. These include, in addition to continuing the line of descent, authority and possession of property associated with the position.[742]

Furthermore, some women attain enough wealth and power to take for themselves wives of their own. These women in the masculine matrimonial role become 'female husbands' (*nwanyi kwu ami*, 'a woman with balls'[743]). Their children are treated with the rights of patrilineal descent. These, and other traditional expressions of gender at variance with Western culture, commonly bowed before the immense pressure exerted by European colonization.[744]

Anthropologist Beth Greene, comparing the practice among the Igbo of Nigeria, Fon of Benin, and Lovedu of South Africa, highlights what she terms "positional succession." This means that a successor inherits a predecessor's position in the social system, including the predecessor's status and legal rights. Female same-sex marriage, then, accomplishes putting a woman in a more favorable position—one normally occupied by men. Such marriage might occur for one or the other of two important reasons. It could happen as part of a woman's establishment of her own power, complete with line of succession (so-called 'autonomous female husbands'), or in order to fill a vacant gender position for kinship reasons in a context of polygynous marriage with patrilineal descent (so-called 'surrogate female husbands'). Put more simply, woman-marriage either creates kinship or augments it.[745]

With regard to the first situation, a woman who secures adequate financial resources to do so can, in a traditional setting, lawfully contract marriage with another woman. She follows the same procedures as a male would, giving to the wife's family a payment (the 'bridewealth'), which establishes the giver in the role of 'husband.' Such marriage also puts the female-husband in position for passing on wealth in the role of 'father.' In these acts, Greene notes, woman-marriage pushes to the limits the social construction of gender. Females gain access to masculine roles ('husband' and 'father') through this kinship vehicle, and in attaining such roles experience some of the power associated with being male. The female 'husband' establishes for herself a masculine gender position and her own patrilineal descent.[746]

In the second situation, woman-marriage puts the female husband in a proxy position. She fills a gap in the kinship structure. We already have referenced such a process in the earlier example of how among the Igbo of Nigeria a girl might become a 'male daughter'; she is assigned a masculine gender position that ordinarily would belong to a male. Although not inevitable, such a person might grow up to become a female husband. A female husband who provides bridewealth supplied by a male (e.g., a kinsman) functions in a surrogate role for that male. The wife obtained, and any children, come under the male's authority. Among the Lovedu of South Africa, for instance, this might occur because a married woman was childless; by serving as a female husband she could still fulfill a role associated with feminine gender, securing children for her husband and a place for herself in the kinship structure.[747]

Similarly, transgender scholar Roberta Perkins notes variations among different societies in the practices of female-husbands. She observes that among the Nuer of Sudan an older, barren woman might use bridewealth acquired from a previous heterosexual marriage to contract with kin for a wife. Among the Dahomey of Benin there seems to be greater latitude; a woman need not be barren and may use bridewealth attained by other sources. Among the Venda of South Africa, writes Perkins, only a woman with high social status can become a female husband—an unusual situation. But among the Lovedu of the same country, she says, more than a third of marriages are same-sex female unions. These typically operate in a kinship structure where the female husband acquires a wife, and arranges for her to become pregnant, in order to secure an heir.[748]

Anthropologist John McCall provides examples of *gynaegamy* in a number of tribal societies, including the Dahomey, Dinke, Nuer, Nupe, and Ohafia Igbo.[749] Of particular interest is his portrait of an autonomous female husband, Nne Uko Uma Awa, of the village of Akanu in Ohafia, Nigeria. From an early age she seems to have identified with masculine identity and roles. In her youth she dressed in masculine fashion and sought out masculine activities. She gained honor as a *dike nwami* ('brave woman) when she succeeded as a warrior in a ritual hunt ordinarily performed by boys. Nne Uko enjoyed land privileges not typical for females and attained membership in masculine groups, such as the Leopard (*Ekpe*) society. She also became a female husband, taking two wives in order to acquire heirs (through Nne Uko's brother). As head of her own line her properties become the inheritance of those who claim descent from her.

She also serves her family (*ududu*) shrine as priestess, knowing that after her death she will be further honored as ancestor to her own line.[750]

The pre-20th century Gikuyu of Kenya were studied by Louis Leakey, who also observes the existence of woman-woman marriages, and describes these unions along lines similar to those observed above: the marriage happens when an older childless woman is widowed. She marries another woman, who becomes pregnant by a designated male, in order to secure lineage and inheritance rights.[751] However, Leakey's depiction, as well as the others already considered, are challenged by Wairimu Ngaruiya Njambi and William O'Brien, who reinvestigated the situation among the Gikuyu.

Njambi and O'Brien, noting that other descriptions emphasize the masculine nature of the 'female husband' role, contest the aptness of such characterization for all these marriages. They believe their interviews with women of the Gikuyu people of central Kenya refute any blanket application of a masculine role to one of the parties. In Gikuyu society the woman initiating the marriage alliance (the 'husband' role in Euro-American culture) is called *muhikania* (pl. *ahikania*)—the same term used when it is a male initiating marriage; the receptive partner is called *muhiki*. Njambi and O'Brien find that the women occupying the so-called 'female-husband' role do not identify this role as masculine. In fact, rather than apply the label *muthuri* ('husband'), the women involved in these marriages use the terms *mutumia wakwa* ('co-wife') or *muiru wakwa* ('marriage partner').[752]

Further, the basis of these unions does not appear to be sexual, or always for economic reasons (e.g., gaining land), or for lineage purposes. Instead, reciprocal affection plays a prominent role in some. Just as some of these marriages challenge the narrow models produced for African woman-woman marriages by other scholars, Gikuyu woman-woman marriages also challenge the Western notion of the nuclear family—with its ideas of heterosexuality, monogamy, permanence, and the presence of a father-figure—on all counts. They suggest that it is the difficulty outsiders have in seeing these marriages on their own terms within their own culture that produces misleading, Western characterizations. Because the masculine connotation for 'husband' is indispensable in Euro-American minds, perhaps a different term is needed.[753]

Of course, female gender variance also is found in the many ways lesbianism expresses itself in Africa. One notable instance is the conscious transvestism practiced by some lesbians in Uganda. Attorney and scholar Sylvia Tamale notes that among the homosexual subculture known as *Kuchuism*, female *Kuchus* typically self-consciously dress in masculine attire (e.g., trousers, shirt, and baseball cap). They proclaim this a simple assertion to dress as they please, while many observers interpret the behavior as an effort to be like a male.[754]

Are there instances of gender variance among males?

Boy Wives

Just as there are 'female husbands,' so there are 'male wives'—or more accurately, 'boy wives' (*ndonga-techi-la*)—among the Azande of the Central African Republic and Sudan. In this same-sex arrangement, the younger male in the same-sex relationship is the 'wife' while the older male is referred to as the 'husband.' As in a male-female marriage, the 'husband' contracts with the family of the 'wife.' Some men have both male wives and female ones. Traditionally, the boy-wife, unlike any female wife, might accompany the warrior husband when the latter was campaigning. The boy-wife would be dressed and adorned like a female, and attend his husband's possessions. The boy-wife, once into manhood as a warrior, was released to take on a boy-wife of his own, if he desired.[755]

Other tribal societies also have known 'boy-wives,' such as the Nuba of Sudan, the Thonga of Mozambique and South Africa, the Pongo people of South Africa (who call them tinkonkana), and the Siwan of Egypt. The reasoning and values behind such unions are marked both by common features and various dissimilarities. For instance, anthropologist Louis Tauxier describes in the early 20th century the practice among the Mossi of Burkina Faso of attractive boys being selected to gender perform femininity in dress and other ways, including sexual activity.[756] Or again, Italo Signorini notes that Nzema men marry attractive youth—who still present as masculine—principally for nonsexual reasons, though the male-brides are still expected to sleep with them.[757]

Another, unique variant is found in the 'wives' of the South African mines in the late 19th century. Tsonga migrant workers in the mines were bereft of women; instead, they formed unions in which younger, attractive males became *tinkonkana* ('mine wives'). Both parties—'husband' (*nima*) and 'boy-wife' (*nkhonsthana*)—benefited, the former by obtaining companionship, a domestic servant, and sexual services, and the latter by gaining protection, security, possessions, and a sexual partner. The husband occupied a masculine role, the wife a feminine role, though both were male. In the feminine role the *tinkonkana* would perform domestic duties associated with womenand occupy the passive role in sexual intercourse. The *tinkonkana* also adopted a more feminine appearance, shaving off his beard and, on occasion, crossdressing—sometimes with artificial breasts.[758]

Changed Men

Somewhat different is the *Mudoko Dako* ('changed man') known among the Lango people of Uganda. Such individuals have been reported by non-native observers since at least the early 20th century. Anthropologist John Driberg, writing in the early 1920s, remarks, "Being impotent, they have all the instincts and nature of women, and as such are recognized by men and women alike. They accordingly become women (*dano mulokere, mudoko dako*, a man who has been transformed, who has become a woman)."[759] In all respects the *Mudoko*

Dako lives as a woman, even adopting a feminine name. They wear their hair long, with feminine ringlets, and their dress includes feminine ornamentation and clothing. The occupation of the gender role associated with females sometimes may even include marrying a man. The identification with the female sex role is so complete the *Mudoko Dako* may even simulate menstruation. Driberg notes that while the Lango told him such individuals were rare among their people, they also claimed they were more common among neighboring tribes.[760] However, among the Iteso people of Uganda and Kenya a similar sort of person—who is feminine in manner, dress, ornamentation, and hairstyle, adopting a feminine name and doing work associated with females—reportedly does not live with other males as a wife.[761]

The Ashtime

Other instances of gender-crossing males who occupy feminine roles are well-known. For example, consider the *Ashtime* among the Maale people of Ethiopia. Anthropologist Donald Donham refers to them as 'male transvestites' whose proper social domain is among the women.[762] In another brief discussion of the *Ashtime*, Donham places them as part of a gender conception that avoids strict duality and instead conceives masculinity along a continuous grade. The most masculine is the ritual king; at some remove are the *Ashtime*. These anatomical males dress as women, take roles typically reserved for females, and may even form sexual relations with men (e.g., the ritual king), taking on the sexually receptive role assigned to women. Donham notes that the Maale claim there are fewer *Ashtime* today, and despite their once having occupied a recognized part in the kinship structure, by the mid-1970s they were likely to be viewed as abnormal.[763]

Other Crossdressing Males

Crossdressing males are common enough among African societies, and we shall cite further examples. The reason, extent, and permanence of the behavior may vary—and the possible imposition of European gender conceptions must always be considered—yet there is no reason to doubt that many such instances genuinely occur (just as elsewhere in the world). Anthropologists have been remarking on this matter for a long time. For example, Siegfried Nadel in the mid-20th century documented instances among the Moro, Nyima, Otoro, and Tira peoples.[764] Other scholars, before and since, have described such behavior among a wide and diverse number of tribal societies. Descriptions of 'crossdressing' or 'transvestism' have been applied to such a diversity of social contexts that at times it seems the only commonality among them is apparent gender-variant practice in dress. Often the term 'transvestism' has been applied to males who, in Euro-American eyes anyway, are homosexual, but heterosexual instances also seem to exist.

Interestingly, in the 1950s, Simon Messing describes crossdressing men among the Amhara of Ethiopia in terms not unlike those used by Havelock Ellis about European crossdressers: "Women tolerate a transvestite 'like a brother'; men are not jealous of him even when he spends all his time with the womenfolk. Often the transvestite is an unusually sensitive person, quick to anger, but intense in his personal likings, sensitive to cultural diffusions from the outside world . . . ." The Amhara call them *Wandar-Warad* ('male-female' persons).[765]

Anthropologist Christopher Hallpike points out that the Konso people of Ethiopia have four separate words for 'effeminate' males. Hallpike focuses on the term *sagoda*, a word wide enough in its reach to include males who never marry (certainly gender-variant behavior for males in a culture where masculine maturity is marked by marriage), and those who dress like women. Hallpike remarks that *Sagoda* of the latter sort are apparently uncommon. The one such person he observed was effeminate in manner and had taken a woman's role (curing skins) as his occupation. Sexually, the *Sagoda*—like females—play a passive role and engage in sex with other males.[766]

Among the Wolof people of Senegal are individuals termed *Gor-digen* ('men-women'). Geoffrey Gorer, early in the 20th century, remarks of them that they are feminine in their manner, dress, make-up and hairstyle. He also observes these people are not socially mistreated, though Islamic officials do not regard them favorably, denying them a religious burial. The *Gor-digen*, believes Gorer, practice same-sex sexual relations.[767] Some, in fact, interpret the term *Gor-digen* as 'homosexual,' though the emphasis on that aspect of behavior may misdirect attention away from a far more complex reality.

In an interesting gendered structure among the pastoral people known as the Gabra of Kenya older males reach an exalted status as *D'abella* (ritual experts), whose gendered identity is feminine rather than masculine. What makes this transformation particularly remarkable to Westerners is not only that these males' gender identity changes, but that they are then revered in a society that denigrates females and femininity. In this society, in Western terms, the apex of a man's life happens when he becomes a woman.[768]

What are other examples of gender-variant realities in Africa?

Variance in gender roles such as described above account for only some of the gender-variant patterns found in Africa. As noted earlier, the various native languages are rich with terms for differently gendered people, with the value connotation often easily inferred (e.g., the Swahili word *msagaji* (lit. 'grinder') is used for lesbians; the Ila of Zambia term transgendered males *mwaami* ('prophet')).[769] More importantly, as noted before, these terms and their applications typically demonstrate how contextually dependent a designation's interpretation is. The same word might be applied to two very different individuals whose performances of gendered roles or functions vary considerably (e.g. as seen above with reference to the terms *shoga* and *sagoda*). In fact, sometimes terms of relevance to gendered reality are not principally applied to individuals but to other things, such as an office.

Mugawe

An example of this situation comes readily to mind. Among the Meru people of Kenya there is a traditional leadership position whose holder is termed *Mugawe* (or *mugwe*, or *muga*; pl. *agwe*). This male role seems to have largely, perhaps entirely disappeared. As anthropologist Rodney Needham observed several decades ago, the *mugawe* serve a spiritual role, or perhaps more accurately, several related roles, including priestly, prophetic, and healing functions. As so often found in such matters, the service of joining the tribe to spiritual realities involves transgender behavior such as crossdressing. The extent to which the cross-gender behavior occurs varies, with some *agwe* actually marrying another man.[770]

'Dan Daudu

Transgender reality in a complex context of variously gendered roles is associated with holders of a different title: *'dan Daudu* ('son of Daudu,' an honorific; pl. *'yan Daudu*). These individuals are found among the Hausa people of Niger, Nigeria, and Sudan. The *'yan Daudu* are associated with a spirit possession cult known as the *bori* cult (cf. the answer to Q. 83). Some of them are *bori* performers and healers, but many are not. For these others, their activities occur around the performance of *bori* possession and their roles include both tasks typically assigned to females (e.g., preparing and selling food), as well as ones facilitative of the prostitution practiced by female members (*kuruwai*) of the cult (e.g., procuring customers). The *'yan Daudu* also use their freedom to live in the women's quarters to facilitate their own sexual contacts with men; when this happens with another *'dan Daudu* they call it 'lesbianism' (*kifi*). To further complicate matters in foreign eyes, some *'yan Daudu* also marry women and become fathers, even while retaining their *'yan Daudu* roles.[771]

Third Genders?

In some instances, the reality may be a 'third gender' phenomenon, though establishing this as the case is rarely a straightforward matter. For example, linguistic terms may distinguish gender-variant people from gender-conforming ones, but do such terms signify a distinct third gender or merely a deviation from what the culture sees as fixed norms? The Swahili use the term *mke-si-mume* ('woman, not man,' or 'wife, not husband') for someone a Euro-American would call homosexual. Is the *mumemke* ('husband-woman'), then, a third gender?[772]

Among the Basongye (Mbala) people of Central Africa there exists a distinctive gender role called *Kitesha* (pl. *Bitesha*), an unfortunately derogatory term. This role appears to be representative of a 'third gender' in which the individual performs gender that is neither typically masculine nor typically feminine but distinctive. More is known about the male *Kitesha* than the female, so the remarks that follow relate to the male *Kitesha*. Such a person dresses in a manner that incorporates feminine dress without being fully like that of a woman (e.g., they might wear a woman's skirt, but not otherwise be garbed in a feminine manner). They also engage in behavior unconventional for males, such as baring their chest or exposing their genitals. Others may view them as wanting to avoid work; when they do undertake tasks these are those associated with women, such as gathering firewood (and even this is seen by some as being selected simply because it is the easiest work). In terms of sexual relationships, the male *Kitesha* might establish a relationship with a female *Kitesha*. Or, the *Kitesha* might have sexual relations with either males or females who are not themselves *Bitesha*.[773]

Transgender and Sexuality

As seen in various instances cited above, transgendered people are no less sexual beings than others. Their intermediate position between the gender poles often positions them to occupy distinctive sexual roles. In terms of anatomical sex, some of these sexual couplings are same-sex and some are heterosexual. As is true in a number of other cultures, some transgendered people depend for their economic livelihood on the sex trade. This reality was noted by observers during the colonial period, such as the French scholar Armand Corre who observed males in feminine dress, performing feminine manners, who engage in prostitution in what is today Senegal.[774] Such crossdressing male prostitutes persist in Senegal today, and elsewhere in Africa. For instance, the *Mashoga* (sing. *Shoga*) are Kenyan prostitutes who present as feminine and take the subordinate sex role with their clients. Anthropologist Gill Shepherd, with reference to the area of Mombasa on the coast of Kenya, notes that the Swahili term *Shoga* (which we have considered earlier) is applied to the younger male who receives money from an older male (*Basha*), who may himself have once been a *Shoga*. These *Mashoga* exhibit gender-variant behavior that does not fit perfectly or consistently with what is expected of either a typical male or female.[775]

Situational Gender Crossings

Finally, we must note that crossing gender lines can occur in very transitory and specific situations, too. For example, Mtoro bin Mwinyi Bakari, in the 1890s, describes a Swahili *ngoma* (singing and dancing to musical instruments) in which men cross gender lines in the context of the dance. In the *mbenda*—a *ngoma* for men—the participants dance in female dress. This occurs in a social context where gender segregation is not as strict as it will become over the following century.[776] Other such transient gender-crossings occur in religious rituals and transition rites such as coming-of-age practices.

How do transgender realities display in transition rites?

Mainstream American society in the United States is woefully lacking in rites of passage, such as for when individuals leave childhood. But not so African peoples. Like many other cultures around the world, theirs are rich in transition rites that feature what Mircea Eliade calls the "temporary androgynization and asexuality of puberty rite initiates."[777] In some tribal societies this is reflected in behaviors like crossdressing. While these often involve males passing into adulthood (as in Liberia), they can also involve females, as in the female puberty rite among the Sotho people of South Africa.

The Sotho female passage into adulthood is marked by the girls putting on masculine clothing. Something similar happens among the Nandi of Kenya. However, this so-called 'ritual transvestism' can be understood in more than one way. While some scholars have seen in gender inversion a symbolic representation of the dangerous passage from childhood to adulthood, others favor more mundane explanations. The anthropological and linguistic scholars Jane and Chet Creider, for example, interpret what happens among the Nandi as a female's way of achieving equality with males. The masculine clothing girls receive is a gift from male significant others: "The apparel is given by the boyfriend to the girls as part of themselves, as something precious to them, to show the girls that they care for them, and to encourage the girls to bring honour to them (the warriors) by their brave behaviour during initiation."[778] We need not here take a stand one way or another as how best to understand this process for the points important to us remain in any instance: there is behavior that crosses gender lines and it involves a puberty rite of passage from childhood to adulthood.

Transition rites for males can also involve cross-gender behaviors, although again we face the issue of Western observers applying their own filter of gender consciousness on the behavior of African people. A prime example of the issue is seen in the interpretation of certain male puberty transition rites. The Maasai of Kenya, for instance, have a rite of passage that finds boys (*ol-ayioni*) changing their appearance through dress as part of their journey to adult warrior (*ol-murrani*) status. Anthropologist Alfred Hollis, in the early 20th century, characterizes the adornment, dress and overall appearance as like that of women.[779] More recent depictions shy away from such a judgment.

This transition for Maasai youth is a comprehensive one, entailing even where the boy lives. The Maasai live together in two kinds of enclosures (*kraals*), one including huts of families with their younger children are encircled by a fence (*enkang*), the other where circumcised males live (*manyata*). A boy's passage at puberty is but one rite of transition observed among the Maasai. Boys are circumcised at puberty (ages 11-14), after which they move out of their father's house to join the other circumcised males of the *manyata*. Their transitional status is marked by wearing a female's earrings as well as a black dress, fastened over one shoulder and cinched at the waist by cowrie shells; they will be thus clothed for several months. Only after circumcision are they permitted to engage in sexual relations with females.[780]

Comprehending that notions of sex and gender vary culturally helps explain why certain rituals transpire. For example, in our culture male circumcision is accepted and widely practiced while female circumcision is viewed as abhorrent. Many in our culture believe female circumcision is a barbaric practice that constitutes sexual abuse and is a violation of a female's basic human rights. In Africa, both male and female circumcision are practiced in many tribal societies and for reasons other than what most of us might expect or have awareness concerning. Consider the Dogon people of Mali, for instance. As religious scholar Geoffrey Parrinder explains:

> The Dogon are said to believe that man, like the primordial beings, has two souls of opposite sexes. One lives in his body and the other lives in the sky or water. When a boy is circumcised he is freed from the element of femininity, which he had had in childhood. Similarly when a girl is circumcised or excised she is freed from the male element and her clitoris no longer prevents intercourse. At circumcision prayers are offered for the stabilization of the soul, of the boy or girl, and spiritual force is thought to be released.[781]

For the Dogon, the transition effected by circumcision involves both sex and gender. The rite allows passage—'release' if you prefer—from childhood so that in adult the society's normative patterns of relationship may be pursued.

Are there sacred gender crossings?

Life is filled with important transitions and these are typically placed within a broader religious framework. Sacred gender crossings abound in the traditions of African peoples. Inasmuch as these are described in more detail elsewhere (see the answer to Q. 83), all we shall do here is highlight a few basic points:

- ❑ gender crossing is sometimes made by divine figures;
- ❑ gender crossings are sometimes used by human figures to signify a change in status; and,
- ❑ gender crossings for religious purposes may be either relatively permanent or occasional.

Gender as a characteristic of deity—whether as an inherent possession or a performance—may be incidental or intrinsic to any specific divine figure. Some deities are ambiguous in gender, others are androgynous, and still others are gender altering (see the answer to Q. 76). Examples of each of these gendered ways can be found among African deities. For example, the divine figure Cghene of the Isoko culture in Nigeria is a sexless and gender ambiguous deity. In Ghana, the figure of Nyame is gender androgynous in the sense of being depicted as either male or female. On the other hand, Inle of the Yoruba people of West Africa—noteworthy for prominence among certain groups in the Caribbean islands—is androgynous in a different way by being a hermaphroditic deity. The Egyptian deity Atum proclaims, 'I am that great He-She.' Another classical Egyptian deity, Ra, though normally depicted as masculine, is a gender-altering deity.

Gender crossing among human beings can signal a change in status with religious significance or for religious purposes. Already we mentioned the D'abella of the nomadic Gabra people of East Africa. Male masculinity, when a man attains this priestly position, is exchanged for an honored femininity. We also saw, in the story of Nne Uko Uma Awa, how a female husband serves as priestess of her family shrine. Ifi Amadiume offers, too, the example of Eze Agba, a male priest of the goddess Idemili, whom Amadiume describes as "a 'female man' in the sense that he had to tie his wrapper like women and not wear it loincloth fashion, like men."[782] Whether shamans or priests, gender crossings can be sacred markers for both the individual and the community.

The cross-gender condition for religious reasons may be highly transient or permanent. It may also involve a larger or smaller number of participants, together with observers. Ritual transvestism is confined to a specific ritual occasion, whereas some religious officials permanently assume an altered status upon entering into the sacred office. In spirit possession cults, several people may simultaneously enact one or another form of gender-crossing as they yield themselves to spirit personas of a different gender. The astonishing vitality and range of such phenomena should remind us of the power many people find in crossing gender lines for one reason or another.

How are crossdressing and transgendered realities viewed in modern Africa?

A Persistent Climate of Intolerance

When behaviors like crossdressing are in the news from Africa today they are often in a context emphasizing something violent. For example, the civil unrest in Liberia features crossdressing warriors. They are drawing on traditions where crossdressing is part of coming-of-age rites of passage. We may struggle to comprehend that for these lads they are participating in ancient ideas that proclaim the dangerous transition adolescents make as they become adults. This ritual transvestism, which in native eyes carries power, to European and American eyes may look darkly comical—a bizarre spectacle of heavily armed young men in dresses. However, seen in cultural context, the matter is deadly serious. As Stephen Ellis remarks, "For a young man to dress as a woman at moments when violence is in the air is tantamount to carrying a sign saying 'Look out, I am dangerous'."[783]

Modern Africa is a troubled continent in many respects. Instability among governments, famines, exploitation of various populations, and the ravages of AIDS are only a few of the significant difficulties African peoples face. Transgendered people's lives are additionally complicated in many societies by marginalization, intolerance, and violence. Human Rights Watch and the International Gay and Lesbian Human Rights Commission have specifically identified a number of nations concerning sustained harassment and violence against the transgendered. Such nations include Botswana, Namibia, South Africa, Zambia, and Zimbabwe.[784]

In many places incentives toward harassment, discrimination and violence flow down from the highest levels of government. In the late 20th century and early 21st century examples of hate speech aimed at sexual minorities, particularly homosexuals, could be found among both secular and religious authorities. For example, in Zimbabwe, former President Canaan Banana (1980-1987), a Methodist minister, was convicted in 1998 of sodomy. Robert Mugabe, who took the presidency from Banana and added it to his position as Prime Minister, has proven an outspoken enemy of sexual minorities, declaring them to be worse than dogs or pigs and denying their entitlement to basic human rights.[785] Other officials have followed this lead. In 1998, President Chiluba of Zambia called homosexuality unbiblical, abnormal, and the deepest level of depravity.[786] In 1999, President Museveni of Uganda publicly authorized state police to arrest homosexuals; at least five were tortured. (This happened despite his claim to the Commonwealth Heads of Government Meeting in Australia that his country has no homosexuals!)[787] In 2001, President Nujoma of Namibia in an address to college students said the country does not permit homosexuality and that known gay or lesbian people would be arrested and deported.[788]

Intolerance toward transgendered people at the highest levels of government can persist only because so many others in the societies involved either concur in it or accept it passively. For example, Norbert Brockman remarks that in modern Kenya "gender conflicted persons" are "invisible" because of social oppression.[789] This situation requires more than the ranting of government officials. That widespread hostility toward the transgendered exists in some societies is indisputable. The Pokot, for example, were reported by anthropologist Robert Edgerton in the mid-1960s to show little tolerance for the *sererr* (intersexed individuals). Infanticide of the intersexed is common, and those who are permitted to live lead marginalized lives.[790] Yet, given what can be reasonably pieced together about precolonial African life, this modern incivility may be reflective more of the impress of values imported from other cultures than from an indigenous history of intolerance.

Response of the Transgendered Community in Africa

Early in the 21st century more than two dozen African nations have laws against male homosexuality and nearly as many have laws against lesbianism. Even in nations where the environment is less hostile, such as among the half dozen countries where homosexuality is not illegal, it remains not unmixed. For instance, South Africa often has been held forth as exemplary in its reform efforts to protect sexual minorities. In a nation where research documents a significant portion of the population have sexual identity issues of varying intensity, subjects like homosexuality have been a substantial political issue.[791] As recently as 1969 the South African government passed the Prohibition of Disguises Act 16, which made male crossdressing illegal.[792] Yet less than thirty years later, in 1996, South Africa became the first nation in the world to include homosexual rights as a constitutional guarantee.[793] In 1998, the land's highest court ruled unconstitutional existing laws criminalizing homosexual behavior.[794] In 2000, 'The Promotion of Equality and Prevention of Unfair Discrimination Bill' passed, adding more protection to sexual minorities.[795]

Yet despite the legal gains made by transgendered people, many still face harassment and violence. Transgendered members of the community have not universally embraced additional legal reforms because these reforms continue the stigma of seeing realities like transsexualism as a mental disorder requiring treatment. For example, a bill entitled 'Alteration of Sex Description and Sexual Status,' passed in 2003, amended the 'Birth and Death Registration Act' so that a person must complete sex reassignment surgery before being able to obtain identity papers indicating their status.[796] There are also divisions within the transgendered community. For example, in 2004, the Gay and Lesbian Alliance banned crossdressers from membership on the grounds that such behavior harmed the image of the lesbian and gay community.[797]

In this complex continental climate transgendered people have not been silenced. In fact, in February, 2004, representatives from 22 organizations in 16 African nations met in Johannesburg, South Africa, where they drafted a statement to the African member states of the United Nations and its Commission on Human Rights. In it they make a forthright declaration:

> We say to you: We, African lesbians, gays, bisexuals, and transgender people, do exist—despite your attempts to deny our existence. We are part of your countries and constituencies. We are watching your deliberations from our home communities, which are also our communities. We demand that our voices be heard.[798]

The document discusses in frank terms the human rights abuses transgendered people experience in Africa. Yet it also affirms their resolve and recognizes the support of many non-transgendered people in their home countries. They conclude by reminding their audience that support of a UN resolution recognizing the need to protect sexual minorities is an act true to the real African tradition, "which, in culture after culture, before colonialism cast its stultifying shadow, recognized the interrelationship and interdependency of us all."[799]

As a continent filled with nations classified as 'emerging,' Africa's future is uncertain. That uncertainty extends to what life will be like for transgendered people. Unfortunately, at present, for every nation like South Africa making strides to protect all its citizens, there are several others dividing its people and singling out sexual minorities for persecution. The global community remains watchful but largely silent.

Q. 55

Where is it found in Latin America?

The Short Answer. The lands of Central and South America, including the islands associated with Latin America, are like most of the world in knowing crossdressing. Unlike many regions of the world, though, crossdressers have received more attention in Latin America. In part this is because the phenomena of male crossdressing in these lands raises particular challenge to the dominant cultural notions of *machismo*. Although traditional societies in the lands of this region knew people we today would call transgendered, these folk have received comparatively less attention than the contemporary transgendered whose visible appearance in the sex trade has occasioned much comment.

The Longer Answer. Latin America is generally characterized by well-defined and rigid roles along a strict dichotomy between two sexes and two genders. But that has not always been the case. Contemporary Latin American culture reflects the pressures exerted by European colonization. In ancient Mesoamerica, argues archaeologist/anthropologist Rosemary Joyce, the early Europeans own records indicate "a highly fluid Mesoamerican ideology of gender," one produced "from an original androgeny or encompassment of sexual possibilities, by creative action in mythological time and recreated by social means in individual time...." This gender fluidity is expressed in multiple ways: through the depictions of deities (e.g., Ometecuhtli) and original beings (e.g., Oxomocho and Cipactonal), through attributions of certain things as differently sexed at different times (e.g., maize as male or female at different points in its growth cycle), by crossdressed Mayan actors, and by high social status figures (e.g., the *chiucoatl*, 'woman-twin'—a male in mixed gender dress).[800]

Joyce says that among the Maya gender differentiated dress—applicable only to adults—is distinguished both by the material from which it was made, and by the symbolic axis used for markings. Maya female clothing employs woven textiles, while male apparel expanded beyond this to include natural products such as animal skins and bark cloth. Female clothing was marked symbolically as a horizontal surface akin to the cultivated earth, while male costume relied on the vertical axis of the World Tree of Maya cosmology.[801]

European conquest brought accommodations and substantive changes. All of these have implications for crossdressing, but the concept of *machismo* makes it especially difficult for male crossdressers to gain tolerance. Many have found that the only viable way to make a living is to ply the sex trade, a profession fraught with danger. Despite the fact that transvestite prostitutes are often protected by law, violence against them remains all too common. Throughout Latin America, these crossdressing pliers of the sex trade may be the most visible and probably most remarked upon segment of the crossdressing community. Their lives—difficult at best—have been chronicled in books by Jacobo Schifter based on interviews with male prostitutes and transvestites in the sex trade in Costa Rica.[802]

However, it would be misleading to reduce the complexity of the transgender phenomena in Latin America to only crossdressing male prostitutes. As in other lands, a variety of motives exist for crossdressing. Some are heterosexuals, some homosexuals. Some crossdress for sexual self-stimulation, others to attract sexual partners, and some show no connection to sexual interests in their crossdressing. While those who appear crossdressed in public, especially entertainers and prostitutes, garner the most attention, it seems plausible to speculate that most crossdressers remain carefully hidden from public view. As in many other places in the world, there are signs of change as efforts at education and the softening of rigid cultural expectations about gender occur.

Among the prominent leaders for change in Latin America have been Lohanna Berkins, Laura Bonaparte, Nadia Echazu (d. 2004), and Marcela Prado (d. 2004). Through the efforts of these and many others, a number of support groups and activist organizations have come into existence since the early 1990s. These organizations act in a number of countries. They embrace lesbian, gay, bisexual and transgender populations.

The following table offers examples of countries where crossdressing in one form or another has been studied or gained media attention:

Table 55.1 Examples of Countries Where Transgender Realities Are Documented

Argentina	Cuba	Mexico
Brazil	Dominican Republic	Nicaragua
Chile	El Salvador	Puerto Rico
Colombia	Guatemala	
Costa Rica	Honduras	

Various of these societies will be explored further below.

What are transgender realities in the Caribbean Islands?

The Caribbean Sea knows a number of disparate societies on its various islands. From Cuba to Puerto Rico and beyond transgendered people dwell in these lands.

Cuba

Cuba, largest of the Caribbean island nations, located only a short distance off the coast of the United States, possesses most of its notoriety in the modern world because of the Communist regime under Fidel Castro. As in a great many other societies, homosexual males receive disproportionately more attention than other transgender people. As far as homosexuals are concerned, evidence of some ambivalence is found in the irregular and arbitrary enforcement of existing law, which prohibits "publicly manifest" homosexuality (Article 303a of the 1988 Penal Code). This provision has been variously interpreted—and applied to crossdressing.[803]

As the above suggests, transvestites often are erroneously assumed to be homosexuals. The newspaper *Tribuna de la Habana*, in February, 2001, published an inflammatory anti-homosexual diatribe in which transvestites were singled out for special scorn. One study, involving 19 Cuban transvestites and transsexuals, found them socially marginalized with less education and greater employment instability than other Cubans. In such a climate, some turn to the sex trade to survive. But some hints of change can be glimpsed. A documentary featuring 7 transvestites discussing their life experiences was aired and positively received.[804] Unfortunately, it also reinforced stereotypes like the transvestite-as-homosexual.

Crossdressing entertainment exists, as in the transvestite stage shows found in the Havanna neighborhood of La Guinera. Spanish language and literature scholar Emilio Bejel, author of *Gay Cuban Nation*, writes that, "Cuban transvestites—like most transvestites in Western countries—are somehow related, directly or indirectly, to the tourist industry.[805] While that judgment is overly broad, there is ample evidence that many transgender people—and especially those who crossdress regularly—find public entertainment and the sex trade two of the few options open to them. But even those who work in entertainment face obstacles most entertainers don't. Sociologist Sujatha Fernandes remarks, "Transvestites have generally been an invisible and marginalized group in Cuban society. Although they acquired a somewhat higher profile in the 1990s, transvestite performers are still excluded from mainstream institutions and venues."[806]

Transsexuals may fare somewhat better, at least in terms of the law. While Cuban transsexuals seem to be permitted to seek sex reassignment surgery (SRS), it either is not available or it is not covered by the public health care system. They are, however, legally permitted to change their identity documents with respect to both name and sex. The legal situation for the country's transsexuals may be improving, too. Mariela Castro Espin, daughter of Raul Castro and director of the National Center of Sexual Education, supports making SRS available to all Cubans who seek it, at public expense.[807]

Dominican Republic

The Dominican Republic occupies the eastern two-thirds of the island of Hispaniola, part of the West Indies; its neighbor is Haiti. It boasts the oldest European settlement, Santo Domingo (founded 1496), in the Western hemisphere. After nearly three centuries of Spanish rule, it passed to the dominion of France, but it was a short-lived French possession. The history of the Republic has been marked by political turmoil, which has persisted into recent years. Nearly three-quarters of the population is of mixed ethnicity, but almost all the people (95%) claim Roman Catholicism as their religion.

Sexologists Paul Abramson and Steven Pinkerton regard the Dominican Republic as one of only two nations (Papua New Guinea being the other) where a three-gender system is socially embraced. In addition to 'masculine' (men) and 'feminine' (women) there is a generic 'other'—which fits particularly the intersexed.[808] In this regard, reporter Zachary Nataf points to the *machi-embra* ('male-female'), popularly known among the locals as *Guevedoche* ('balls at twelve')—intersex individuals assigned femininity at birth and raised as girls who at puberty become boys. Their condition has a biological basis—a hormonal deficiency that causes these genetic males to be mistaken as biological females at birth. At puberty, however, they begin developing male secondary sex characteristics. Not all *Guevedoche* transition to the masculine gender, however; some prefer to remain in the gender in which they were raised.[809]

The Dominican Republic has a dubious reputation as one of the more favored tourist destinations for the sex trade. The incidence of HIV infection has risen at an alarming rate, not merely in connection with same-sex sexual transactions, but among heterosexuals, too.[810] As found in other parts of Latin America, some crossdressing males earn a living through prostitution. In one incident that made the news and heightened local anxieties, a German national murdered a young male transvestite.[811] The boy, only 12 at his death in 1994, called himself 'Alice' and catered to tourists. His murderer bought freedom through bribery.[812]

Puerto Rico

With respect to crossdressers, Puerto Rico is typical of the situation across these island nations: though they are known they are little studied. As a result, comparatively little data exists about how widespread it is, about its various features, or concerning its relation to different transgender realities.[813] That transgender realities exist in the land—despite a general disavowal—is certain. Puerto Rican scholars Sheilla Rodriguez-Madera and José Toro-Alfonso, in material prepared for a 2002 international conference on AIDS, comment that both institutional and political practices effectively silence the island's transgender community through a denial of its existence. Their work documents the health price paid among members of this population. In a study of 50 transgender Puerto Ricans they found more than half (56%) engaged in risky sexual behaviors and 14% tested HIV positive.[814]

On the other hand, as seen in an increasing number of nations, legal advances have been made. For example, the Associated Press reported in the summer of 2000 on the case of Alexandra (formerly Andres) Andino Torres, who underwent sex reassignment surgery in 1976, and who in 1995 petitioned a local court for a change of both name and sex on her birth certificate. The matter wound its way through the judicial system to Puerto Rico's Supreme Court where a 4-3 decision in the petitioner's favor was granted.[815]

What are transgender realities in Central America?

Crossdressing occurs throughout Central America, but not without trouble. In fact, much of what is known about crossdressing in these lands comes from information in the context of the discrimination and violence crossdressers face. The best-known crossdressers are entertainers and sex workers. As a result, the ordinary lives led by those whose crossdressing remains secret is almost entirely unrevealed. We are left with a picture both decidedly imbalanced yet emphatic in depicting the difficulties transgendered people face wherever a rigid dichotomy in gender expectations exists.

Costa Rica

The best-known study of the transgendered in Costa Rica is Jacobo Schifter's study of male crossdressing prostitutes.[816] Schifter utilizes interview data collected in 1989 and 1997 by the Latin American Health Education and Prevention Institute, of which Schifter is a regional director. He uses the term 'transvestite' to encompass many different transgender types, including heterosexual and homosexual males, and transsexuals. Schifter notes that heterosexual crossdressers are less accessible to researchers because they generally keep their crossdressing secret. So his focus is on homosexual crossdressers engaged in the sex trade especially found in the cities. This group is especially at risk for sexually transmitted diseases such as HIV.

Schifter finds that transvestite prostitutes have undergone significant shifts within their population that, in turn, influence the heterosexual community. Using the city of San Jose as an example, Schifter describes a move of crossdressing sex workers from a poor district to a more affluent one. Those first making this move tended to be very feminine in appearance, some able to successfully pass as women. This makes them more acceptable to heterosexual clients. Though there may be some initial negativity, in time many clients allegedly begin to prefer the transvestite prostitutes to the available female prostitutes. In fact, Schifter claims, even some women begin to patronize the crossdressing sex workers. Another significant feature Schifter observes is how sexual orientation and gender identities among these transvestites appear 'plastic'—flexible and, apparently, circumstantial. Unlike such prostitutes in many other Latin countries, Costa Ricans seem not bound to especially rigid role expectations such as always being the passive partner in sex.

As his title *From Toads to Queens* suggests, Schifter notes the transformation intended by these men. However, despite the success some attain in presenting as women, there lives remain more 'toad' than 'princess' because of deeply rooted social discrimination, with its attendant restrictions, instances or violence, and self-despair. Unfortunately, limited by his reliance on interviews selectively utilized, there is little way to test Schifter's conclusions or to know how reliable his observations are. Nor does his work offer any real entry into the lives of the majority of Costa Rican crossdressers. We are left, instead, to rely on his considerable experience while remaining bereft of cross-validating research.

Guatemala

As in other Latin American countries, Guatemala has not proved a safe place for transgendered people to make themselves known publicly. In the late 1990s, a United Nations mission found 'planned and coordinated actions' of 'social cleansing' and 'extrajudicial execution' of crossdressers. Transvestites in public face a special conundrum: if they act in a feminine submissive role they face abuse; if they don't, those who work as prostitutes lose their customers, who desire maintenance of the illusion that they are heterosexual.[817] In the opening years of the 21st century the situation apparently has not grown safer. It has been reported that in the summer and fall of 2003 a number of transvestites were murdered with no serious investigation by law enforcement.[818]

Mexico

Mexico, the largest country of Central America, shares with other Latin American countries a long history of transgendered people that has remained largely shrouded in silence and secrecy.[819] The nation has not kept statistics on transgendered people, but Eusebio Rubio, writing in *The International Encyclopedia of Sexuality*, estimates that their number is not small. He points to a strongly dichotomous view of sex and gender as a principal factor in complicating life for the transgendered, especially transsexuals. Most medical professionals remain ignorant of the condition. Their response tends toward rejection, though Rubio does indicate some signs of change with regard to the treatment of transsexuals. He also notes an anecdotal report of one region of Mexico (Oaxaca near the Tehuantepec Isthmus) where it is claimed a more flexible gender scheme prevails with recognition of a 'third gender' or effeminate men.[820]

These individuals are known locally as *Muxe* ('like a woman'; pronounced Moo-shey). Biological males, they are comprehended as a third gender, "combining the assets of both the female and male, and sometimes equipped with special intellectual and artistic gifts." They are regarded as born *Muxe*, not made, and though some families have difficulty accepting them as such, they have a distinct place within Oaxacan society. They tend generally to occupy jobs traditionally associated with women and to perform traditional feminine tasks such as cooking, housecleaning, childcare, and elder care. As adults they occupy a sexual role like that assigned females—as passive, receptive partners. Men who pair with them are known as *Mayate* and are not seen as homosexual. No one knows how many there are, but they seem common enough that most everyone knows one and may count at least one among the extended family.[821]

With reference to Mexico as a whole, Rubio identifies four distinct forms of crossdressing in the nation: the heterosexual crossdresser seeking fetishistic arousal; the female impersonator, whether heterosexual or homosexual; the homosexual crossdresser who may use occasional drag to express gay pride or who may crossdress as an aspect of prostitution; and the person who experiences gender-conflict and utilizes crossdressing as a means of some relief.[822] These types generally correspond to those described in the discussion section of the *Diagnostic and Statistical Manual of Mental Disorders, 4th edition* (DSM-IV; see the answers to Q. 96, 99).

What are transgender realities in South America?

Crossdressing is well-documented in South America, both historically and in the present. As in Central America, cross-gender behavior, including crossdressing, is associated with a variety of negative matters, including violence. Juan Pablo Ordonez & Richard Elliott, reporting on transgender related violence in Colombia in the mid-1990s, observe that, "Deep-seated machismo spawns a hatred of women and 'homosexuals' (generally equated with transvestism and effeminacy in the popular mind), resulting in widespread domestic violence and stigmatization of sexual minorities."[823] Similar observations might be made about other Latin American nations.

Argentina
Crossdressing people have been known in Argentina for centuries. In the region of Patagonia, for example, the 18th century observer Thomas Falkner describes male 'wizards' generally selected for this position while still children who, in his words, "are obliged (as it were) to leave their sex, and to dress themselves in female apparel, and are not permitted to marry. . . ."[824] Their crossdressing began in childhood and continued as they learned and practiced their craft.

Argentina's modern day crossdressing population is among the best known in the world. The term 'transvestite' is used there to cover a number of disparate populations embraced in the U.S. under the broad use of the term 'transgender.' These include both homosexual and heterosexual crossdressers, but especially transsexuals.

Those crossdressers who are most visible are public entertainers. Sofia Kamenetzky notes that the attainment of some celebrity permits these crossdressers to be generally well-tolerated. But the situation is more problematic for other crossdressers. Crossdressing homosexuals, heterosexual crossdressers, and transsexuals all have a more difficult time finding tolerance. Kamenetzky does find, however, that some heterosexuals experience acceptance from spouses and even children so that crossdressing can occur at home. Yet the social expectations are such that crossdressing men typically conform to masculine stereotypes in work and social settings.[825]

Those seeking full-time expression of cross-gender identity/role are often subject to many hardships. There are reports of crossdressers facing widespread discrimination, being arrested and imprisoned without formal charges, and experiencing violence. Sex reassignment surgery is illegal. Many who live a cross-gender life full time find that prostitution is the only viable employment option for them. As a result, life expectancy is less among this group than in the general populace.

There are groups and organizations working to better the situation for at least some crossdressers. For example, in Buenos Aires the *Asociación de Lucha por la Identidad Travesti y Transexual* (Association Fighting for Transvestite Identity), also known by the acronym ALITT, is an activist organization aiming to improve matters through legislative means. Alongside others, Lohana Berkins, a male-to-female transsexual, founded ALITT in the mid-1990s. The Association lobbies for reforms especially in the areas of basic living: housing, employment, health and education.[826] Such efforts have made progress. In 1997, for instance, they were successful in Buenos Aires in securing the repeal of ordinances that allowed police to detain people up to one month without filing charges.

Brazil

This largest South American nation has a sizable transgender population. Roman Catholicism from Europe dominates indigenous religions, which refuse to disappear. Instead, they color the culture, just as other aspects of indigenous culture intermix with European influence from a colonial history under Portugal. As in other societies strongly influenced by Western culture, Brazilian notions of gender start from the duality of men (*homens*) and women (*mulheres*). But not all Brazilians adopt a gender identity as one of these alternatives.

Brazil's *Travestis* ('transvestites') view themselves in a separate gender identity—one between the gender poles. As in so many other places and times, this means crossdressers can occupy a space closed to other biological males. For example, social anthropologist Andrea Cornwall points to the *Travestis* of the city of Salvador, who in many temples of the Afro-Brazilian religion *Candombié* are accepted as 'daughters of the saint' (*filias de santo*), privileged to be possessed by the *orixás* (spirit intermediaries) to whom they are devoted. It has been estimated as much as 90% of the areas *Travestis* are devotees.[827]

Cornwall also reminds us that not all crossdressers are *Travestis*. What distinguishes the *Travestis* is the adoption on a full-time basis of feminine dress, behavior, and name. They may make transient or permanent body alterations, but unlike transsexuals, do not perceive themselves as females. There are transsexuals (*transsexuais*), and there are also *transformistas*—gender impersonators whose crossdressing is part of a specific context, typically an evening performance. Of course, nuances of difference may be lost on the wider public; crossdressers often are lumped together under the pejorative label *bicha* ('pest'). The great exception to this is the sanctioned crossdressing of Carnaval, when folk who ordinarily do not do so engage in gender crossing behavior.[828]

As in much of Latin America, crossdressers in Brazil tend to be grouped together, marginalized, and often ill-treated.[829] Crossdressing is not illegal, but social sanctions are strong enough to discourage much public expression, and where it does occur other means exist to punish its display. Some commentators have considered that crossdressing is considered *um fenômeno marginal* ('a marginal phenomenon'), an expression that puts crossdressers alongside criminals. Indeed, much of the crossdressing seen in public is practiced by transvestite prostitutes. Some of these are men who hold regular jobs in their gender-assigned clothing during the day but crossdress at night while engaged in solicitation.[830]

According to a 2005 Associated Press release, in the city of Nova Iguacu, near Rio de Janeiro, the city council addressed a problem with bathroom access concerning the city's transvestites. The crossdressing population there is estimated by a city councilman at some 28,000 in a total population of roughly 800,000 (3.5%). Regardless of the accuracy of this estimate, the number is sufficient to have motivated passage of a city ordinance mandating public facilities such as shopping malls, movie theaters, and night clubs to provide a third bathroom designated for transvestites.[831]

Chile

Among the indigenous Mapuche people of Southern Chile, various groups of individuals are known who would be termed transgender in contemporary Western terms. Two such groups have long enjoyed positive status. One is comprised of intersexed people, physical hermaphrodites called *alkadomo* ('male-female'), who traditionally are seen as co-gendered and positively regarded. The other group is anatomical males who historically, remarks anthropologist Ana Mariella Bacigalupo, "were culturally defined as possessing co-gendered status."[832] This meant such males could become either masculine or feminine, or both.[833] This ability opened up important avenues to function as mediators in this world and between this world and the realm of spirits. Like women, they could open themselves to possession by spirits.[834] Persons who performed this and other shamanistic functions are called *Machi*.

Most *Machi* are female; male shamans (*Machi weye*[835]) are transgendered people. Bacigalupo has studied the *Machi weye* extensively, both in terms of their historical presentation and perception, and in the modern world. Bacigalupo comments that the Spanish newcomers forged a complex relationship with the *Machi weye*, one characterized both by fear and concern over their appearance and spiritual practices, but also respect for their healing abilities and role in peace councils. The appearance of one *Machi weye* was described as 'like Lucifer':

he wore his hair long and straight, and wore an allegedly feminine garment (a puno[836]) in place of pants. Their atypical gender presentation was commonly construed as signifying a *puto*, or sodomite who engaged in devil worship.[837]

Misunderstood by the Spaniards who colonized the area, they remain misunderstood by other Chileans today. Not dissimilar to indigenous people in other countries, the Mapuche are a minority population relatively separated from other Chileans. The *Machi*, honored among the Mapuche, do not enjoy the same esteem from others. The *Machi weye* are even further separated from the majority population and if their dual status as Mapuche and *Machi* were not enough, their transgender characteristics further complicate their reception within the larger society. Bacigalupo cites a case in which "a *machi* who identifies as a woman but has a male body was jailed without trial under a false accusation of homicide and was described as a 'strange sexual deviant,' and a 'dangerous uncivilized indian' because she challenged Chilean gender and social norms."[838]

Bacigalupo presents a study of a modern *Mache weye* named Marta. Born male, Marta became feminine through a complex of developments, experiences, and behaviors that encompass past and present, traditional spirituality and modern life. These acts include such obvious gender markers as a change in dress, adopting feminine clothing and feminine manner. Marta's shamanic status represents a spiritual transformation accompanied and marked by a change in gender status and performance, including crossdressing.[839]

Another group of people who might be termed transgender are also known among the Mapuche. These are individuals called *maricones* or homosexuals. Bacigalupo comments that contemporary Mapuche often claim such persons were unknown prior to European colonization.[840] Their status is not as positive as that of *Machi weye* among the Mapuche. In this regard, the cultural view about homosexuality—strongly shaped by Roman Catholicism—has been influential.

Colombia

Bernardo Useche identifies two substantial groups among those he terms 'gender conflicted.' Interestingly, Useche differentiates these two groups by social class rather than behavior *per se*. Among the lower class there are both homosexual and heterosexual crossdressers, as well as MtF transsexuals. These individuals are socially isolated and found in areas associated with prostitution. Some work as entertainers, others as strippers, many as prostitutes. They tend to become sexually active at an early age and because of the relative ease of obtaining female hormones many self-medicate to effect physical changes. Among the upper class a different situation prevails. Though transvestites and transsexuals are also found in this social class, their affluence protects them from the limited options of the poor. Many use the internet to communicate with one another. Transsexuals with the financial means can seek sexual reassignment surgery in the larger cities like Bogotá, Cali, and Medellín. Neither group is likely to seek therapy; both face cultural resistance.[841]

Q. 56

Where is it found in Europe?

The Short Answer. Crossdressing has long exercised fascination in the European mind. Both male and female crossdressers have drawn attention. As we have seen in answering previous questions, most of the focus in the past was on female crossdressers. However, in recent decades this has changed so that today virtually exclusive attention is on male crossdressers. As was the case in pre-modern Europe, today's Europe witnesses crossdressing across its many nations. Since previous questions have engaged historical concerns in Europe, the emphasis in this answer is on the contemporary scene. The continent has been divided into regions and specific countries within each of these regions are given individual attention. Although on the whole Europe has been more accepting of crossdressing than the United States, the level of tolerance varies from place to place. Nevertheless, when it comes to legal reforms to ensure that transgender people are accorded civil respect and protection, Europe has typically exceeded the U.S.

The Longer Answer. Although various previous answers addressed historical matters in Europe, we will begin with a very brief historical summation, beginning with religion. Although these societies can fairly be called secular, Christianity has had an immense impact historically and remains a cultural force. In the examples offered below, the dominant religious form of Christianity (e.g., Orthodox, Roman Catholic, or Protestant) is often noted. Religious influences can have a significant impact on social responses to transgender realities.

The federal system embodied in the birth of the European Union in the later 20th century has proven beneficial to transgender people. Mazur remarks, "Much of the reason for the positive treatment of gay, lesbian, bisexual and transgender citizens in Europe is due to the pressure put on European Union states by their own definition and quest for human rights."[842] Nevertheless, because of the autonomy retained by member states, actual conditions vary and sometimes are worse than what the laws in place proclaim.

Crossdressing has a long and rich history in Europe.[843] There were crossdressing saints from early Christian times through the Middle Ages.[844] Crossdressing was well known as a phenomenon after the Medieval period, too, especially among women.[845] The early Modern period down to our own showed fascination with crossdressers, especially female ones, as evident in song, stage, literature, and historical records. From the 19th century forward, crossdressing has continued to be evident in Europe, though increasingly attention turned away from crossdressing women to crossdressing men.[846] This change in focus accompanied a variety of important developments covered earlier, such as the medicalization of sex, the success of the Women's Movement, and major conceptual shifts in the conversation on gender. In some respects, the coalescing of these various factors in our own time is calling into question exactly what kind of dress behavior truly qualifies as 'crossdressing.' Today, European fashion is producing skirts for men and a debate is developing over whether men who wear MUGs ('male unbifurcated garments') should be labeled as 'crossdressers.'

We lack the perspective of time to know how best to evaluate these changes and new perspectives. But our immediacy to the situation does permit description, which is the chief aim of these materials on societies around the world. It is important, however, to remember that what is recorded here is only a partial account of transgender realities existing in Europe (and elsewhere). Though the intent has been to report both important and interesting matters, every record proves a selective one. Thus, in studying transgender realities in Europe and elsewhere it is important to treat this account as a starting point and not as an ending place. We may begin with the following Table to provide an overview.

Table 56.1 Examples of Nations Where Transgender Realities Are Documented

Central & Eastern Europe	Northern & Western Europe	Southern Europe
Albania	Belgium	Crete
Austria	Denmark	Cyprus
Croatia	Finland	Greece
Czech Republic & Slovakia	France	Italy
Estonia	Germany	Malta
Hungary	Luxembourg	Portugal
Latvia	The Netherlands	Sicily
Lithuania	Norway	Spain
Macedonia	Sweden	
Poland	Switzerland	
Russia	United Kingdom	
Serbia		
Slovenia		
Ukraine		

Reports of the extent of crossdressing behavior and of the prevalence of transgender conditions vary among the countries. (To aid convenience of discussing crossdressing in Europe the area has been divided into overlapping regions, with countries grouped according to the table above.) As a preliminary note, we should be mindful that language like 'incidence' and 'prevalence' belong to the scientific enterprise connected with classifying human behavior. The European counterpart to the American *Diagnostic and Statistical Manual for Mental Disorders* (DSM) model is the *International Classification of Diseases* (ICD) model. Currently, the two classification systems (DSM-IV and ICD-10) are closely coordinated with respect to mental disorders. Thus the language used in research reports often employs terminology familiar to users of the DSM. This includes designations of 'Fetishistic Transvestism' (instead of DSM's 'Transvestic Fetishism') and 'Gender Identity Disorders' (including 'Transsexualism,' 'Dual-Role Transvestism,' and 'Gender Identity Disorder of Childhood') as mental disorders. However, not all European nations regard GID as a disorder, despite its presence in the psychiatric nomenclature.

What are transgender realities in Central and Eastern Europe?

For most of the 20th century, Central and Eastern Europe were in the shadow and under the pressure of the Soviet Union. Transgender realities were one aspect of life hidden from view. Since the collapse of communist domination a greater openness has emerged, but the weight of the past continues to be felt throughout the region. Like the rest of Europe, attention given to transgender people in this region is almost exclusively on males, especially male homosexuals. However, one notable exception to this is found among the Albanian people.

Albania
Female crossdressing behavior is found in the so-called 'sworn Albanian virgins.' These *virgjinesha* ('sworn virgins') are genetic females who by their manner of dress as males signal a male gender identity, assume a male gender role, are accorded status as males, but remain celibate. This unusual situation is found principally in northern Albania among families who adhere to the Kanun, a code governing gender and marital relations. As a part of this code, gender is clearly marked by dress. But unlike many societies, where biological sex governs perception of gender regardless of dress, under Kanun one's gender is as one presents it. A female may become male by swearing a vow, so long as certain conditions are met. One such is that the girl's family has no sons to inherit, thus threatening the loss of the family's wealth (because all wealth is transmitted from generation to generation through the males). Since a sworn virgin is treated as male—right down to being referred to as 'he'—this provides a male

heir.[847] In this social setting there is no shame in crossdressing; the sworn virgin is an honored part of society.

Austria

Like many other countries in this region, Austria is predominantly Roman Catholic and very conservative in social values. Strictly adhering to the Western gender binary, gender variant individuals have generally been unwelcome. That is not to suggest they are not a part of society. The younger generation appears more socially tolerant to transgender people, but the society itself remains discriminatory. Transsexuals have no formal legal standing. However, postoperative transsexuals do have the right to marriage; the first such marriage took place in 1997.[848]

Czech Republic and Slovakia

Czech sexologist Jaroslav Zverina, writing in *The International Encyclopedia of Human Sexuality*—a good starting point in investigating gender and sexuality issues around the world—offers a discussion of 'Gender Variant' people in the Czech Republic and Slovakia. He reports an apparently low incidence for both transvestic fetishism and transsexualism. He notes that in the case of heterosexual crossdressers presenting for therapy the reason for seeking counseling typically appears connected to a spouse or partner's hostility and the resulting difficulties in their sexual relationship.[849] It may be that the low incidence Zverina refers to is simply an artifact of reporting in a society very closed to discussion of such matters.

Transsexuals in the Czech Republic can seek reassignment surgery. A study published in 2000, of some 30 male and 52 female transsexuals, set the prevalence estimate for transsexualism at 1 in 10,000 people in 1990.[850]

In recent years the transgender community has made efforts to become more visible. For instance, in 1998 in Prague, the 'first official' Czech TG Group TransForum was initiated. The official website, with content last updated in 2000, claims 50 members drawn from male and female transsexuals, and transvestites. The site declares that transgender life in the nation "is at the very beginning," and that until very recently both transsexualism and transvestism had been "taboo" subjects.[851]

Latvia

A small nation bordering the Baltic Sea on the West, and sharing borders with the countries of Estonia, Lithuania, Belarus, and Russia. Religiously a mix of Russian Orthodox, Roman Catholic, and Protestant (Lutheran), Latvian society is strongly homophobic and few homosexuals live openly as such. There are no legal protections against discrimination in employment. The degree of homophobia is indicated in an example offered by the Asia-Europe Foundation: in 2001 a national Latvian paper ran a contest entitle 'Latvia without homosexuals' and urged readers to join it in combating homosexuality. Transsexuals do have a legal right to sex reassignment and afterwards can have their personal identity papers changed.[852]

Lithuania

Lithuania is a small country along the Baltic Sea. It borders Latvia, Byelorussia, Poland, and Russia. Culture scholar Arturas Tereskinas writes that, "Before 1989, the words 'gay, lesbian, bisexual and transgender' were rarely heard in Lithuania." This changed after the country declared independence from the Soviet Union in 1990. Same-sex sexual behavior was decriminalized in 1993. Lithuanian gay activists, says Tereskinas, brought increased media attention from 1995 onwards, and especially since 1998. The Lithianian Gay League (LGL), the first organization of its kind, was publicly registered in 1995. However, Tereskinas notes public opinion still ran highly against homosexuals as the 20th century closed, with more than three-quarters (78.2%) of respondents to a poll proclaiming intolerance of it.[853]

Lithuanian social researchers Jolanta Reingardiene and Arnas Zdanevicius, in a paper published in 2007, observe it remains difficult to research transgender people in the country and that population remains under-studied because of the difficulty in getting people to talk about the subject. In research they conducted using in-depth interviews of 38 GLBT people, only one participant identified as transgender. Most remained firmly 'in the closet,' at least with respect to work associates.[854]

Lithuania does not recognize transsexual identity as legitimate and sex reassignment surgery is not permitted. In Fall, 2006, a 28-year-old individual identified as 'Mr. L' brought suit in the European Court of Human Rights against the government of Lithuania for impeding transition from one sex to another. The female-to-male transsexual started treatment in 1998 and already had undergone hormone treatment and completed breast removal when his doctors refused further treatment. The Lithuanian government was slow to respond and by the end of 2006 no date had been set for a hearing.[855]

Poland

The 20th century was a troubled one for Poland as it found itself under fire from its neighbors Germany and Russia, being conquered at the beginning of the Second World War, and after it being a satellite in the Soviet Union for several decades. Though the nation has a transgender population, its extent and many of its characteristics are less known than in many other European countries. Polish psychiatrist Anna Sierzpowska-Ketner, in 1997, suggested that transvestism is "a marginal phenomenon" in Poland, and estimated the number of Polish transsexuals and transgenderists at about 1,000 persons, with male-to-female transsexuals about seven times as common as female-to-male.[856]

Transsexuals possess a legal right to sex reassignment, but postoperative transsexuals have only a limited right to changes in identity papers.[857] Unfortunately, strong homophobia and transphobia discourage much public visibility. Some transvestites and some transsexuals are active in 'escort' services; others make public figures through entertainment venues, such as nightclubs. Most remain invisible.

Russia

Russia is a transcontinental country that stretches from Europe in the West to Asia in the East. Most Americans are more familiar with Russia's association with Europe, which is why it is included here. The country's 20th century was dominated by the Communist Party. Under the first post-Communist leader, Boris Yeltsin, male homosexual behavior was decriminalized in 1993 (lesbian behavior had not been illegal).[858] According to Russian sexologist Igor Kon, research on transgender people, particularly transsexuals, dates back at least to 1960, when Aron Belkin conducted psychoendocrinology studies. He also notes as a landmark event the creation in 1992 of an Association of Transsexuals in Moscow to promote and advance human rights for that population.[859]

Among the peoples embraced in Russia's reach are a number of indigenous tribes. The Chukchi (or Chuckchee) people, the largest native population in the Asian Far North, are indigenous to the Chukchi Peninsula and shores of the Arctic Sea. At the turning of the 19th to 20th century, Russian anthropologist Waldemar Bogoras lived for nearly two decades among these people. He describes, in addition to masculine men and feminine women, seven other genders.[860] The range and fluidity of genders among the Chuki meant a number of kinds of individuals that fit our Westerner label of transgender. One such bear the name *Yirka-la Ul* ('soft man'). Born biologically male these individuals live like women and are highly respected by tribal shamans for their spiritual and healing powers.

Bogoras records his strong opinion of such people; the title of his section describing them is 'Sexual Perversion and Transformed Shamans.' Finnish anthropologist Edward Westermarck, in his early 20th century 2 volume work *The Origin and Development of the Moral Ideas*, which collects together a large number of moral judgments, includes the following made by Bogoras:

> It frequently happens that, under the supernatural influence of one of their shamans, or priests, a Chukchi lad at sixteen years of age will suddenly relinquish his sex and imagine himself to be a woman. He adopts a woman's attire, lets his hair grow, and devotes himself altogether to female occupation. Furthermore, this disclaimer of his sex takes a husband into the *yurt* (hut) and does all the work which is usually incumbent on the wife, in most unnatural and voluntary subjection. . . . These abnormal changes of sex imply the most abject immorality in the community, and appear to be strongly encouraged by the shamans, who interpret such cases as an injunction of their individual deity.[861]

Interestingly, Bogoras' moral judgment is not echoed by Krasheninnikoff in the late 18th century when he speaks of other native transgendered peoples, such as the *Ke'yev* (male concubines) or the *Koe'kcuc* (males who become women). "There is no indication," he writes, "that the North American aborigines attached any opprobrium to men who had intercourse with those members of their own sex who had assumed the. dress and habits of women."[862]

Setting aside the moral judgment, this observation documents both the importance of shamans among the Chukchi and the existence of gender crossing males. Anthropologist Conrad Kottak amends this picture by adding that female shamans also can cross gender lines, assuming masculine roles, including taking a wife.[863] Walter Williams writes that by the turn of the 20th century these 'soft men,' known also among other Eastern Siberian tribal peoples (e.g., Asiatic Eskimo, Koryak, Kamchadal), had declined significantly because of actions by the Russian government.[864]

What are transgender realities in Northern and Western Europe?

Defining crossdressing inevitably entails social judgments about what clothes belong to which gender. For example, in the United States a male found in any kind of unbifurcated outer garment like a skirt is likely to be judged a crossdresser. In this region of Europe, however, the Scottish kilt—an unbifurcated garment—is viewed as manly garb. On the continent young men may wear skirts designed exclusively for males.[865] Although the culture upholds a dichotomy of gender, the lines are not as inflexible for gender presentation as tends to be the case in the United States. Homosexual and heterosexual crossdressers are found throughout Northern and Western Europe. There also tends to be greater acceptance of gender diversity and transgendered people than in some other parts of the continent. Still, any generalization carries exceptions and this region is no different. The level of tolerance varies from one nation to another and, within nations, from city to rural areas, and from one place to another.

Denmark
An open and tolerant society, transgender people fare better in Denmark than in many other countries. Sex reassignment is legal and postoperative transsexuals are allowed to register changes in personal identity documents.[866]

Finland
Heavily Protestant (Evangelical Lutheran) Finnish society is generally open and tolerant of transgender people.[867] Some problem areas persist, but steps have been taken to address these. For example, in 2002, the nation legally recognized the rights of transvestites in an effort to combat discrimination.[868] As in most nations, transsexuals are more noticeable than other crossdressers. This is not merely because of the greater persistence among these individuals to present as a gender different than that assigned at birth. It has also to do with their greater likelihood to seek assistance (i.e., body modification), and the legal issues

accompanying sex reassignment.[869] Sex reassignment is legal and postoperative transsexuals are permitted to change personal identity papers and to marry.[870]

A number of agencies, organizations, and groups have arisen in Europe to support transgendered people, whether through education, social services, legal aid, or facilitating contact with other transgendered people. In Finland, *Seksuaalinen tasavertaisuus* ('Sexual Equality,' or SETA), founded in Helsinki in 1974, extends efforts for social justice and legal equality across all transgender populations. In addition to working for broad social change in Finland, SETA provides social services, education, and opportunities for transgender people to come together at cultural and social events.[871]

France

Heavily Roman Catholic, French society is largely tolerant toward sexual minorities. Homosexuals enjoy legal protections against employment discrimination and have a visible presence in society. Transsexuals are legally able to seek sex reassignment. Those that do so are permitted to register some changes in their personal identity documents.[872]

A French nonprofit organization headquartered in Paris, the Centre d'Aide, de Recherche et d'Information sur la Transsexualité et l'Identité de Genre (CARITIG; 'The Center for Assistance, Research and Information Concerning Transsexuality and Gender Identity'), has been visible both in that nation and internationally. Founded by its current President, Armand Hotimsky, in 1995, the organization operates at multiple levels of action. Besides providing local support meetings, CARITIG is active lobbying on behalf of transgender people at national, European, and international levels. In that last respect, in 2006, CARITIG took the lead in organizing the first International Transgender Rights Conference, held in Geneva. The organization has three main goals on its national political agenda: to see the law amended to permit change of registration of sex identity without sex reassignment surgery; to win for transsexuals the right to choose their own health care providers and still be funded by Health Care; and, attaining recognition of gender diversity as a natural part of social life—a recognition demonstrated, for example, by removing Gender Identity Disorder from the DSM and ICD diagnostic and classification systems. CARITIG maintains a website providing, among other things, information on transgender issues for transgender people, health professionals, and the general public.[873]

Germany

Few nations have had as turbulent a history as Germany over the course of the last century. Ravaged by two great wars, divided for decades, a reunited Germany is a vigorous leader in the European Union. German scholarship historically has contributed significantly to the study, and especially theorizing about transgender realities. Pioneering sexologists like Richard von Krafft-Ebing and Magnus Hirschfeld (1868-1935) helped establish the vocabulary common today, including words like 'transvestite' (see the answer to Q. 95).

Both transvestite and transsexual populations received important early investigation and support. Today there remains a vital transgender population in Germany.

Transvestites generally occasion less attention than transsexuals, but not in Germany. Hirschfeld coined the term and provided the first significant scientific study of them, early in the 20th century. They have been known to exist in German society for a long time and are perhaps the best known of Europe. For example, in the first quarter of the 20th century a series of so-called 'transvestite postcards' were issued, each bearing the image of a male crossdresser.[874] In POW camps of the First World War captive German officers employed female impersonation both on-stage and off.[875] Crossdressing males have been a staple of urban life in places like Hamburg and, especially, Berlin. Among the latter's crossdressers is a group of transvestites of Turkish immigrants, most notably examined in Kutlug Ataman's film *Lola + Bilidikid* (1999).[876] Arguably Europe's most famous transvestite, Charlotte von Mahsldorf (1926-2002), was a Berlin resident who survived both the Nazis and the Soviet occupation of East Berlin, and told her story in her autobiography, *I Am My Own Woman*.[877] Today, crossdressing in public seems to be met more by amusement than anxiety and some crossdressers have attained prominence through stage shows.[878]

Germany's transsexuals have a longer legal history than that found in most nations. In 1978, the Federal Constitutional Court (*Bundesverfassungsgericht*) ruled that transsexuals, age 18 or older, could have a change of identity recognized on their birth certificates if their condition was 'irreversible' and following sex reassignment surgery. Today, transsexuals possess two specific options under the amended 1980 German Transsexuals' Act (*Transsexuellengesetz* (TSG); formally and fully the Act is named *Gesetz über die Änderung der Vornamen und die Feststellung der Geschlechtszugehörigkeit in besonderen Fällen – Transsexuellengesetz*, 'Act on the Change of Christian Names and the Determination of Gender Identity in Special Cases). Most court petitions concern the 'small solution' (a change of first name) rather than the 'major solution' (change of sex status). The frequency of transsexual applications over a decade span was between 2.1-2.4 in 100,000 people, with a sex ratio of 2.3:1 (male predominant).[879] Those who pursue sex reassignment may postoperatively change all personal identity papers to reflect their new status. They also may marry.[880]

Perhaps the most prominent German website for the transgender community and interested others is provided by the nonprofit organization Deutsche Gesellschaft für Transidentität und Intersexualität e.V. (DGTI; 'German Society for Transgender and Inter-sexuality'), headquartered in Cologne. As the name indicates, its reach includes intersexed people as well as those more ordinarily covered under the transgender umbrella. While it tries to keep individuals always in view, DGTI also lobbies at the national level, seeking to educate and promote reforms beneficial to transgender people. The materials on the website range from information on legal developments to medical issues, to religious and ethical concerns.[881]

Luxembourg

Mostly famous in the United States for its size (being about half the size of Delaware), Luxembourg is predominantly Roman Catholic and generally tolerant toward transgender people. Transsexuals may obtain sex reassignment. Postoperatively they may change their personal identity documents.[882]

The Netherlands

Sexologists Jelto Drenth and Koos Slob, writing in the mid-1990s, report on the land's transsexuals. They point to legal reform occurring in 1985 (Article 29 of the Civil Code) as instrumental in removing many barriers to changing sex. Under the law no age limit is established for seeking sex reassignment, but candidates must be unmarried. With a medical professional's attestation that the post-operative transsexual is both infertile and irreversibly changed to the desired sex, a change can be obtained to the birth certificate. At that time, if the person was married a divorce had to occur before the birth certificate could be amended,[883] but since 2001 the country has permitted same-sex marriages.

Actual medical treatment of transsexuals, as sanctioned by a major hospital, dates even further back. Drenth and Koos relate that such treatment has been happening since 1976 at the Dutch Gender Foundation at the Academic Hospital of the Free University of Amsterdam. By the mid-1990s, some 1500 transsexuals had been assessed, with about 150 sex reassignment surgeries. They report an estimate of 1-in-12,900 males for male-to-female transsexualism and a much lower incidence of 1-in-30,400 for female-to-male transsexualism.[884]

Norway

Researchers Elsa Almas and Esben Esther Pirelli Benestad remark that transsexuals over age 18 have professional support available through a centralized team in Oslo. Treatment strategy typically follows the Standards of Care established by the Harry Benjamin International Gender Dysphoria Association. Unfortunately, many adult transsexuals find the level of support, both pre- and postoperative, less than desired; the care of transgendered adolescents and children lags behind that of adults.[885]

As of 2003, the country has two principal organizations for transgender people. The older, FPE-NE (inspired by the success of the American counterpart, today's Tri-Ess), dates to 1968 and originally targeted male heterosexual crossdressers, though today is broader in inclusion. The other, LFTS, originated in January, 2000. It targets the nation's transsexuals.[886] LFTS (*Landsforeningen for Transkjønnete*; National Organization for Transsexuals) was founded by Tone Maria Hansen, together with 6 other transsexuals. By the time Hansen addressed a conference in the U.S. in 2003, some 120 individuals were involved and 'significant' progress had been made in lobbying efforts with the government to improve conditions for transsexuals.[887]

Sweden

One of Sweden's most famous rulers, Queen Christina (1626-1689; see the answer to Q. 48), is attached to the transgender reality of crossdressing. Transgender people are a part of contemporary Swedish life. Swedish researchers Jan Trost and Mai-Briht Bergstrom-Walan, writing in the mid-1990s, declare that while transvestites have no special legal status, they are not regarded socially as either 'deviant' or 'sick.' Crossdresser support groups have chapters in the country (offshoots of Tri-Ess; see the answer to Q. 34).[888] Early in the 21st century, researchers at the Karolinska Institute surveyed 2,450 Swedish citizens (ages 18-60), both male and female. The study found 2.8% of Swedish men experience arousal from wearing feminine apparel (transvestic fetishism), and .4% of women crossdress for sexual arousal. However, no significant differences were found in lifestyles between crossdressers and the general public, save the obvious one of crossdressing itself.[889] Niklas Långström, who led this effort, remarks, "Our study shows that the majority who get turned on by dressing in women's clothes are well-adjusted and feel good."[890]

Sweden, in 1972, enacted specific legislations with respect to transsexuals. They enjoy a legal right to sex change procedures, provided they are age 18 or older and unmarried. Prior to surgery they must have followed a prescribed course of treatment. Postoperatively, they are able to legally change their identity status. Trost and Bergstrom-Walan estimate that while about half of the country's transsexuals pursue such surgery, only about a dozen operations are performed inside the nation each year.[891] Alongside this might be put an interesting comparative study of Sweden and Australia—both Western culture societies—published in 1981. The nations were examined with regard to prevalence, incidence, and sex ratio of transsexualism. Significant differences were found that the researchers attribute to social differences influencing how many transsexuals will present for treatment.[892]

United Kingdom (England, Northern Ireland, Scotland, Wales) & Ireland

Americans may be more aware of transgender realities in the United Kingdom than elsewhere in Europe because of the close ties between the U.S. and these island nations. Stephen Whittle and Gwyneth Sampson highlight the growing visibility of transgender people in the 1990s. They attribute the change to numerous factors, among which is greater support for transgender individuals afforded by organizations like the Beaumont Society, active since the late 1960s in supporting male heterosexual crossdressers and their families. In the last few decades other organizations also have arisen. They point, too, to the development of so-called 'gay villages'—areas within cities where the transgender population is higher and clubs and other meeting places have proliferated. Despite such changes, though, the number of transgender people remains unknown.[893]

As in the United States, most crossdressers remain invisible. Whittle and Sampson note that transvestites generally do not seek help from a mental health professional unless their crossdressing creates relational or social difficulties for them. They also follow current psychiatric thinking that some of these crossdressers, who display fetishistic transvestism earlier in life, go on to develop transsexualism (cf. the answer to Q. 38).[894]

Whittle and Sampson remark that transsexuals are better known than transvestites because of media coverage. Sex changes have been reported since 1944, when noted surgeon Sir Harold Gillies performed one on Michael Dillon, a female-to-male transsexual (see the answer to Q. 19). How common transsexualism is remains, like transvestism, unknown. However, Whittle and Sampson cite a 1995 study that estimated between 10,000-15,000 known transsexuals. One source for estimating this has been Gender Identity Clinics, of which perhaps the best-known remains Charing Cross Gender Identity Clinic, established by psychiatrist John Randell in the early 1970s. Historically, English law on transsexualism has been embedded in the decision of the famous case *Corbett vs. Corbett*.[895] In 1999, the UK enacted the Sex Discrimination (Gender Reassignment) Regulations, forbidding discrimination against transsexuals, but not providing them full legal recognition. The European Court of Human Rights, in the case *Goodwin vs. United Kingdom*, then found the UK in violation of Article 8 of the EU Convention on Human Rights, thus stimulating further legal reform.[896] Continued participation in the European Union has resulted in significant changes (see the answer to Q. 36).

Scotland, too, has a transgender population. A number of organizations, including the Beaumont Society, exist.[897] As is often true, more attention has been given to transsexuals, though much about this population remains unknown. In a study reported in 1999, the prevalence of 'gender dysphoria' in Scotland was estimated at 8.18 per 100,000 people, with a 4:1 ratio of males to females.[898] In order to improve access to services for such persons the Scottish Needs Assessment Programme (SNAP) convened a multi-disciplinary group to prepare a report on transsexualism in the country. The report, issued in 2001, concluded that about 300 people (4:1 ratio of males to females) were known to public sector health services in the land. These folk were being treated by various health care professionals, including psychiatrists, psychologists, speech and language therapists, and family planning and reproductive health care professionals. Research with care providers revealed certain themes, the principal of which are that ignorance of gender identity problems is widespread and professionals hold widely polarized views, ranging from strong moral disapproval to considerable empathy. The group offers several recommendations, including a call for ongoing research.[899]

Heavily Roman Catholic, Ireland is, for the most part, tolerant toward homosexuals. Other transgender populations appear not to enjoy quite as much tolerance. Physician and therapist Thomas Phelim Kelly calls transvestites and transsexuals so marginalized as to be "almost invisible." On the other hand, Kelly also notes that crossdressing is not against the law, people are generally aware such behavior exists, and that it actually seems to be "quite common."[900] In sum, as in many other places, crossdressing exists without sanction, support, or approval, but also without explicit civil condemnation or widespread social censure.

Transsexuals in Ireland hold a legal right to obtain sex reassignment. Some identity papers may be legally changed postoperatively, but not the birth certificate. The right of postoperative transsexuals to marry has in recent years been debated, but as of 2005 remained illegal.[901]

However, as elsewhere in the UK, the transgender population has become more visible. An Irish transgender organization named Sí (Gaelic for 'she'—and pronounced that way) began operating in 1999. Sí uses the internet to convey information through its website, and email to provide support. It is affiliated with the Gemini Club, a Dublin-based group where transgender people can meet on a regular basis.[902]

An important resource is Press for Change, a political lobbying and educational organization. The Home Page for the organization's website claims that, "Nowhere else in the world will you find such a comprehensive collection of information about the trans rights campaign, and details about the legal, medical, political and social issues surrounding the people it represents." Among the documents available on its website is the research prepared by the civil rights/human rights organization Liberty, entitled *Integrating Transsexual and Transgendered People*. This material contains information on government positions toward transgendered people in the members of the European Union.[903]

What are transgender realities in Southern Europe?

Transgender people have a long history in Southern Europe. As seen earlier in this volume, they are attested in classical Greek and Roman literature, evidence of their existence over more than two millennia.

Cyprus

The island nation of Cyprus is predominantly Greek Orthodox religiously. Transgender people predominantly live hidden lives. While the younger generation appears more accepting of sexual minorities, social tolerance is low. There are no specific civil protections against discrimination in employment. Sex reassignment remains illegal.[904]

Greece

The Mediterranean countries of southern Europe also know culturally accepted instances of dressing practice that in the US would likely be viewed as crossdressing. For example, Greek males dress in unbifurcated garments for various reasons, including dancing and military parading. The Presidential Guard—an instance of an elite military unit—wears either a pleated khaki skirt or a more formal short skirt (on Sundays) when performing their duties as honor guard at the Tomb of the Unknown Soldier in Athens.

Of course, dress behavior recognized as crossdressing has long been a part of Greek society. In ancient Greek theater crossdressing males played female parts. Social tolerance varies; though the general population seems generally tolerant, there have been reports of some transgender people experiencing arbitrary identity checks, body searches in public, and harassment by law enforcement.[905] Today, some male crossdressers still work as entertainers. Others find themselves in the sex trade. Dimosthenis Agrafiotis and Panagiota Mandi, referencing a source in Greece's Ministry of Health and Social Welfare, report that some of the nation's transsexuals obtain SRS abroad and then work as female prostitutes.[906]

Transsexuals in Greece hold the legal right to have their name and identity papers changed, and their birth certificate amended.[907] However, legal identity is still established by genetic sex. The number of transsexuals in the country appears not to be the subject of any reliable estimates.

Transgender people are supported by a variety of organizations, including the Greek Transvestites and Transsexuals Solidarity Association (GTTSA), headquartered in Athens. GTTSA works to promote transgender rights and also maintains a website to further its outreach.[908] The Transsexual Portal (*Το πρωτο Ελληνικο*) website provides a range of materials (e.g., news, referrals of books, information on transsexual celebrities), products, and a chat room.[909]

Italy

Home to the Vatican, Italian society is predominantly Roman Catholic religiously, but also secular. This has meant divisions and public debate over transgender realities—a situation mirrored throughout Western societies. Generally there is tolerance toward transgender people, though some voices remain strongly opposed based on their religious views.

In 1982, Italy enacted legislation (Act No. 164/82) specific to transsexuals. Under the law a person may attain, upon authorization of a legal tribunal, a change of legal sex and name on civil status records and papers. Such authorization must follow expert opinion on the applicant's psychological and physical condition. Any existing marriage is ended (though at the time of this writing the nation was debating legalizing same-sex marriage).[910]

Portugal

Heavily Roman Catholic, Portugal has a reputation as a society tolerant of transgender people. While transsexual people enjoy no specific legal right to seek sex reassignment, the possibility is not entirely closed to them. The Asia-Europe Foundation reports that petitions for sex reassignment are heard on a case-by-case basis. Upon approval of the Portuguese Medical Office sex reassignment surgery may be had, followed by postoperative changes to identity papers upon permission of the court.[911]

Spain

Spanish anthropologist Jose Antonio Nieto, with colleagues, observes that no term in Spanish is a clear equivalent to the English word 'transgenderism.' In that land, no distinction is made between what Americans call 'transvestites' (occasional crossdressers) and 'transgenderists' (individuals living full-time in a gender other than the one assigned at birth). Nieto writes, "For us, a transvestite is a person who reverses roles, dresses himself in clothing that does not correspond to his sex, regardless of whether this is permanent, chronic, episodic, or entertainment-related."[912] Regardless, this heavily Roman Catholic country is generally tolerant toward its transgender people.[913]

For the country's transsexuals, change of sex has been authorized since 1979, though the criminal code did not decriminalize sex reassignment surgery (SRS) until 1983. By the late 1990s, SRS was occurring in Madrid, Barcelona, and Zaragoza. Postoperative transsexuals are able to legally change their identity in the Civil Register.[914]

As all too common throughout the world, transgender people are disproportionately represented in the nation's sex trade. One study of 418 male sex workers found that 18% identified as either transvestites or transsexuals. Other research, conducted in Madrid, found among 132 transgendered street sex workers that nearly half (44%) were immigrants, mostly from Ecuador.[915]

Q. 57

Where is it found in the Pacific Ocean nations?

The Short Answer. The island nations of the Pacific Ocean are home to a great diversity of peoples and cultures. Crossdressing is documented in many societies and reflects the richness of diversity found in the region. From the continent of Australia to small islands unfamiliar to many Westerners crossdressing happens. As has proven the case in other parts of the world, the pressures exerted by Western culture have left their mark on the island nations of the region. The indigenous acceptance of gender variance ran headlong into the cultural intolerance of Western explorers and colonizers. As a result, as has happened elsewhere, indigenous peoples have been forced to either adopt Western conceptions and values or find creative ways to accommodate Western power while retaining some form of pre-existing realities.

The Longer Answer. Inevitably any attempt at grouping lands within geographic divisions meets with overlap between regions. Many of the lands that are found within the reach of the world's largest ocean also occupy the area known as the East. These include lands like Japan. But that nation is perhaps better known as belonging to the East and so is included in the answer to Q. 52. The nations that are covered in the answer to this question include those listed in the table below.

Table 57.1 Examples of Pacific Ocean Nations Where Transgender Realities Are Documented

Australia	Malaysia	Philippines
Cook Islands	New Zealand	Samoa
French Polynesia (Tahiti, etc.)	Okinawa	Singapore
Indonesia (Bali, Java, etc.)	Papua New Guinea	Tonga

What are transgender realities in Australia?

Crossdressing occurs in Australia. Reporting in the mid-1990s, Rosemary Coates estimates that 10% of men engage in some degree of crossdressing. Despite that number, no national support organization then existed; Coates found only local groups in four of Australia's states. Based on anecdotal and self-report measures, Coates concludes that the majority of crossdressers are heterosexuals. As in the United States, these men are often married, with children, and occupy professional positions in the workforce.[916] Interestingly, despite the origin of many of Australia's people in migrations from Europe, the question of cross-cultural differences in how transsexualism is approached have been studied by comparing Australia to Sweden.[917]

Australia's transsexual community may be among the more studied in the world. The nation itself has been progressive in recognizing transsexual's rights. For example, in 1982 the state of South Australia enacted a Sexual Reassignment Act affording transsexuals the right to legal recognition in their new identity.[918] By 2005, three Australian states afforded such legal rights.[919] Nevertheless, many find it difficult to fit within society and exist along the margins, such as working in the sex trade. King's Cross area in Sydney is one area well-known for its transsexual sex workers.[920]

What are transgender realities in the Cook Islands?

The Cook Islands are a nation formed from the alliance of 15 islands distributed across more than 850,000 square miles of ocean. Situated in the South Pacific, roughly midway between New Zealand and Australia to the west and South America to the east, the islands are geographically isolated by sheer distance. The entire population of Polynesian people is less than 20,000 although each island displays cultural diversity. The name for this group of islands derives from the famous sea explorer Captain Cook, who came upon them in 1770. They were made a British protectorate in 1888, with administration of the island handled by New Zealand after 1900. In 1965 the islands became self-governing.

Laelae

Transgendered people are known among the native people; men who act like women are called *laelae*, a word Kalissa Alexeyeff points out has no one exact translation as it embraces a range of meanings, including gendered acts and sexuality.[921] For example, *laelae* can refer to males who are either heterosexual or homosexual, who crossdress or don't. They typically have sexual relations with individuals who are not *laelae*. Their most defining qualities, says Alexeyeff, are feminine mannerisms and the adoption of work roles associated with women (e.g., cooking, sewing, or weaving). Alexeyeff says pointedly, "They become women through their work and how they display themselves."[922] Their mixing of maleness with femininity is met by other islanders with ambivalence.[923]

Tutuvaine/Tututane
   Crossdressing occupies another role in Cook Island life. It is an important element in entertainment, where it has strong comedic value. Alexeyeff observes that gender-imitating performances to elicit laughter occur both informally among both genders and also through venues such as drag shows and other entertainments. Drag performers are called *tutuvaine* or *tututane*, both words meaning bearing a likeness to appearance and manner of a member of the opposite sex. The principal mechanism for such imitations is dance.[924] Alexeyeff believes that "inversion of gendered movement and display is extraordinarily funny to Cook Islanders precisely because motility and performance are central to their experience of being male or female."[925]

What are transgender realities in French Polynesia?

French Polynesia is comprised of a number of islands located in the Pacific Ocean between New Zealand and Hawaii. The various, distinct island cultures, include Fiji, Hawaii, Samoa (both American Samoa and, some 60 miles to its west, Independent Samoa), Tahiti (part of French Polynesia), and Tonga, among others. Among the Polynesia people can be found a distinctive group of transgendered males, who occupy a place in society analogous to a 'third sex' or 'third gender.' Anthropologist Jeannette Marie Mageo interprets this phenomenon as reflecting an historical instability in male gender identity, one paralleled by a similar instability in female gender identity, where it gave rise to experiences of spirit possession rather than crossdressing. Because Polynesians conceive gender in terms of social role rather than as a stable, inner trait, the expression of atypical gender in Polynesian culture is reflected in the adoption of feminine dress and work roles.[926]

Fa'afafine
   These transgendered islanders have been well known in the modern West at least since reports of them from British sailors in the 18th century. In French Polynesia they bear the name *Mahu* or *Rae Rae*; in Samoa they are called *Fa'afafine*; in Tonga they are known as *Fakaleiti* (or, sometimes, *Tangata Fakafefine*, 'a man acting like a woman').[927] In the material that follows, primary reference is to the *Fa'afafine* unless otherwise noted.
   The *Fa'afafine* ('in the manner of a woman,' or 'like a lady') are genetic males raised as females. Traditionally, this family choice was neither arbitrary nor governed by sexual considerations. As sociologist Johanna Schmidt observes, Samoan culture, centered in villages, largely views gender in terms of what one contributes through labor; if a person fills feminine roles, then that person can be identified as a girl or woman. *Fa'afafine* do women's work (e.g., washing, cleaning, cooking).[928] The selection by a family of a boy to be *Fa'afafine* may transpire because the family decides it has enough sons but not enough daughters.[929] A male child thus chosen to fill a traditional feminine role is dressed as a

girl and accorded that gender role. Such an individual might, as an adult, eschew marriage and remain at home to care for aging parents.[930]

Today, under the influence of Western culture some males self-select this status. As Schmidt notes, Western emphasis on individuality has shifted the Samoan conception of gender and led to a greater reliance on appearance and bodily expression rather than labor role. When *Fa'afafine* leave their families and villages they simultaneously leave the primary markers used to identify their gender; new ones, emphasizing gender-specific Western forms of appearance and behavior, may now be adopted. This has resulted in two distinct kind of *Fa'afafine*—the traditional and socially approved 'womanly' *Fa'afafine* of the villages and the tolerated but often criticized modernized 'wild' *Fa'afafine* of the cities (and other lands).[931]

Some *Fa'afafine* continue to occupy the role because their parents placed them in it, often because their cross-gender behavior as a child led to parental recognition of them as transgendered. Though their numbers are not large, most villages know of a few and they hold an accepted place in the community.[932]

However, despite the long tradition of acceptance of the *Fa'afafine*, not all transgender children in Samoa receive warm support or approval from their parents, perhaps because of the encroachment of modern Western ideas about transgenderism. Still, research reported by psychologists Nancy Bartlett and P. L. Vasey in 2004 of 20 adult *Fa'afafine* finds that all warmly remember their childhood participation in female-typical behaviors, regardless of parental approval or resistance. Their study notes that—by Western psychiatric standards—the degree of gender dysphoria (see the answer to Q. 93) reported by the *Fa'afafine* does not differ significantly whether their parents opposed their transgender behavior or not, but where any difference was detected it correlated with parental opposition.[933]

Mahu

Tahiti merits some special mention. It is the largest island of French Polynesia, yet still with a population of less than 200,000 people. Its indigenous people are Polynesian. European adventurers discovered the island in the latter half of the 18th century; during that period it was the site of the infamous mutiny on the Bounty. By the end of the 19th century it had become a French colony. At the beginning of the 21st century it remained a part of modern French Polynesia.

The best-known transgender reality in Tahiti is the people called *Mahu* (the Polynesian term suggests 'abundance'; the *mahu* are known in other Polynesian lands such as the Marquesas and Hawaiian islands). The *Mahu* are variously characterized; locals are more apt to see them as a 'third gender' while foreign visitors apply Western labels like 'transvestites' or 'homosexuals.' There are *Mahu* who are anatomically male, intersex, and female.[934] However, male *Mahu* are the most often remarked upon. The native people regard the *Mahu* as special because they possess qualities of one sex but another gender. Identification of an individual as *Mahu* begins in childhood, based on gender behaviors. However, some families choose to raise a first-born son as a girl.

The *Mahu* who are anatomical males enact a feminine gender role, including crossdressing. They have been an important aspect of Tahiti culture for centuries. William Bligh, of H.M.S. Bounty fame, first described them in the later half of the 18th century; at least one he concluded was a eunuch.[935] The *Mahu* perform tasks typically associated with femininity, such as cooking and childcare. They are also known for their dancing, including ritual dance.

The sexuality of *Mahu* has been—and remains—prone to Western misunderstandings and censure.[936] Tahitian culture judges sexual activity not by anatomical sex but by gender. 'Homosexuality,' then, becomes a matter of same-*gender* sexuality rather than same-*sex* activity. A male *Mahu* having sex with another male is not viewed as homosexual. When the French military did atomic testing in the area, some *Mahu* entered into the sex trade to compensate for the lack of available women. This circumstance has further eroded the perception of them, especially by foreigners.

What are transgender realities in Indonesia?

Indonesia comprises an archipelago of some 13,700 islands stretching from Malaysia to New Guinea with one of the largest populations of the region. The more famous islands include Java (where Jakarta, the nation's capital is located), Bali, Borneo, and Sumatra. The people are a mix of various ethnic groups with a variety of languages and customs. A number of religions are represented, with Islam the predominant one. Not surprisingly, crossdressing in Indonesia reflects some of this rich diversity.

Crossdressers have not been a hidden group in Indonesian culture and even have on occasion figured in significant roles. Hayam Wuruk, a 14th century ruler, was reputed to don female garb and use a female name. In contemporary Indonesia there continue to be famous transgender performers, like Didik Nini Thowok, a master of the dance traditions of Java. The historic role of males in female parts in Indonesia dance and drama has had such wide acceptance that Sukarno, the first president of the modern independent nation, showed no hesitation in his autobiography of recounting in detail his own days as a young man embodying female roles as an entertainer.[937] Especially under Adi Sadikin, Sukarto's mayor from 1966-1977, the transgendered prospered under government protection. Generally, tolerance has held sway in Indonesian society, though it would not be unfair to observe that when and where Muslim conservatism has been strongest the transgendered have been most marginalized.

Bali Dance & Drama

Various dance and drama troupes have historically employed males in female roles, or occasionally females in male roles. In Bali, the *Arja*, developed in the late 19th century as a folk-opera, used all males, even for female roles. However, the Balinese *Ramayana*, a sacred Hindu dance, uses women in the roles of the two brothers, Rama and Laksama.[938]

Java's Waria

Though no official estimates exist for their numbers, transgendered people in Java—especially male crossdressers—are not uncommon. Transsexuals and transvestites are often called *Banci* ('hermaphrodite'; cf. *Béncong*, 'effeminate males' or 'she-males'), a term with negative coloring; female-to-male transsexuals are called *tomboi*. Another common designation, far less pejorative than *Banci*, is *Waria*, a contracted abbreviation of *Wanita* ('female') and *Pria* ('male')— 'feminine males' (or, 'lady boys')—that was coined in the 1970s. This term has also been misapplied to homosexuals, from whom there has been a clear distinction. Historically, the transgendered have not fared as well socioeconomically as the homosexual community, and tensions have existed between the groups, which persist to the present. The *Waria* have often been visible in society as entertainers, including street performers, and prostitutes.[939]

In fact, perhaps the crossdressers most likely to be noticed by a visitor are those who do so for entertainment. Even today, *Waria* entertainment in venues like the weekly show at Taman Remaja in Surabaya (East Java) are well-known and popular. In Ponorogo, East Java, feminine males known as *Gemblak* are well-known for their role in the traditional performance of the folk-dance known as the *Reyog*.[940]

Distinguishing transvestite from transsexual—both Western conceptions— among the *Waria* may be a futile effort. Certainly there are some of both Western categories, but in Indonesia there seems little need or desire for further differentiation than that the individual is *Waria*. Their developmental paths are not unlike the transgendered in other cultures, with early preference for atypical gender activities. Anecdotal accounts exist of males becoming *Waria* at various ages, from early childhood, adolescence, or occasionally adulthood. Some research indicates most identify as *Waria* by their early teens. Despite general social tolerance, many families respond negatively to the discovery that a son has identified as transgender.[941]

Transgendered individuals have often found themselves trapped in a life of prostitution. Organizations like *Perkumpulan Waria Kotamadya Surabaya* ('Association of Waria in Surabaya') offer assistance toward other alternatives.[942] But research in 2002 in Jakarta found the transgendered sex workers there at serious risk for sexually transmitted infections. HIV prevalence was more than 1-in-5 (22%) among them, and nearly 1-in-5 (19%) for syphilis. Most (59%) practiced unprotected sex and engaged in risky activities like anal intercourse.[943]

Still, it would be a mistake to conceptualize the general lot of the transgendered as either prostitutes or entertainers. Many are hairdressers and beauticians, or occupy other jobs, especially those traditionally associated with women. In modern Indonesia the *Waria* occupy an important and universally recognized cultural position.

Java's Theater Performers

Also on Java, social scientist Clifford Geertz, famed for his ethnographic studies of the island, tells of a group of female impersonators who do a form of drama called *Ludrig* (or *Ludruk*), which is popular farce.[944] This form of entertainment using crossdressed men dates back to at least the early 19th century. It has not been confined to one dance form. One of Java's most famous modern male dancers, Didik Nini Thowok, a figure with international renown who has performed throughout Asia and in Europe, often plays female characters, though the use of males in female roles has shown a decline in recent decades.[945]

Sulawesi's Bissu

Sulawesi, one of Indonesia's major islands, is home to the Bugis people, a predominantly Islamic (Sunni) group, with deep spiritual roots in indigenous traditions, who dwell mostly in the villages and cities of the isle's southwestern end. Anthropologist Sharyn Graham has identified a rich range of genders acknowledged among the Bugis, including 'male men' (*Oroane*), 'female women' (*Makunrae*), and transgendered people such as males living like females (*Calabai'*), females living like males (*Calalai'*), and symbolically intersexed individuals (*Bissu*), who transcend sex and gender.[946]

The *Bissu* are viewed as possessing the attributes of both males and females; they are perceived as both sexes and both genders. The Bugis believe such people may be marked from birth. Sometimes ambiguous genitalia at birth indicates the child will one day become *Bissu*. However, they are often unremarkably male (or female) anatomically; those who become *Bissu* are presumed to be a different sex/gender on the inside. By adolescence a child who demonstrates an affinity for the spiritual world may be apprenticed to an adult *Bissu* and began a long process of training and testing.[947]

Bissu present as a conscious mix of male and female. For instance, they may carry a knife like a man would, but wear flowers in their hair as a woman might. Their transcendence of the gender divide is paralleled by their transcendence of the ordinary mortal realm. Regarded as both partly human and partly spirit, they occupy an important role in indigenous spiritual traditions as a priestly people who mediate between this world and the heavens. Through elaborate rituals the *Bissu* contact the realm of spirits (*dewati*), allow a divine spirit to inhabit them for a time, and provide a blessing. These blessings cover a wide range of important events in the lives of the Bugis, including domestic matters (e.g., consecrating marriages), agricultural ones (e.g., blessing both plantings and harvests), and other religious events.[948]

Sulawesi's Calabai' & Calalai'

The *Calabai'* ('false women') are Bugis males who live as females, but without a transsexual's conviction of being female or a desire to become anatomically female. They occupy a distinct place within Bugis society. An important social role is played by the *Calabai'*, who are often asked to participate in a family's wedding as so-called 'wedding-mothers' (*indo' boting*) by superintending the preparation and many aspects of the day itself, such as the wedding party reception.[949]

The *Calalai'* ('false men') are Bugis masculine females; their numbers are fewer than the *Calabai'*. They are not transsexuals, for they clearly understand they are not males, nor do they desire to become male anatomically. Yet they refuse to conform to female gender role expectations. Instead, they develop a distinctive gender identity as *Calalai'*—women who live like men. Anthropologist Graham suggests that the rather limited way of being a woman in Bugis society contributes to the formation of *Calalai'* identity, though various ones come to it by different paths. While some may be motivated by same-sex sexual desires, many form their gender identity as *Calalai'* before their feelings of sexual desire develop. However they develop into *Calalai'*, their embodiment of the male gender role tends to be highly idealized. They adopt masculine dress (though in a distinctive way), choose occupations associated with men, and may avoid activities identified with women, such as cooking. In Bugis society their status as *Calalai'* permits them a range of obligation, privilege, and action somewhere between that of women and men.[950]

What are transgender realities in Malaysia?

Malaysia is a southeastern Asian country comprised of the northern third of the island of Borneo and the peninsula below Thailand that extends into the South China Sea. This area was colonized by Great Britain in the 18th-19th centuries, and seized by Japan during the Second World War. Independence was first gained in 1957, but modern Malaysia was formed in 1963, with its present configuration occurring even later than that. More than half of the population is drawn from the Malay people, with another third being of Chinese descent. Other groups include people who settled from India and an indigenous population that today accounts for only about 5% of the nation's populace.

Officially, gender crossing behavior has been discouraged. Any male behavior imitative of females, whether crossdressing, wearing feminine ornamentation, or body modification (e.g., hormone injections), has been forbidden. Male crossdressing has been an offense punishable by prison—up to six months. However, in early 2004 the government began considering decriminalizing the act.

Transgendered people are found in Malaysia as they are in other societies in the region. Malaysian people have terms for different transgender realities: effeminate men are called either *pondan* or *bapok*; transsexual men refer to themselves as *Mak Nyah* (*mak* being the word for 'mother'); and transgendered females are variously called *abang* ('brother' or 'man'), or *Pak Nyah* (*pak* being the term for 'father').⁹⁵¹

Mak Nyah

Mak Nyah ('men who are like women') persons are probably the best-known Malaysian transgendered population. Their number has been estimated at some ten thousand people, of which about three quarters (70-80%) are Malay. In 1987, *Mak Nyahs* attempted to officially establish a society, adopting the term *Mak Nyah* to refer to themselves. The Registrar of Societies denied their request. Inasmuch as Malaysia has adopted Euro-American ways of regarding transgender realities, *Mak Nyahs* are considered by many Malaysians to be deviant, and so they exist as a largely marginalized group.⁹⁵²

The Western category that seems to come closest to the *Mak Nyah* is 'transsexual.' Such individuals not only dress and act like women, they desire to be anatomically female. The identity for most of them is shaped in the context of Islam. Malaysian construction of what Islam (cf. the answer to Q. 78) permits in gender produces four possibilities: male, female, intersexed ('hermaphrodites' or *khunsa*), and the transgendered (*mukhannis* or *mukhannas*). The *Mak Nyah*, as transgendered people, are forbidden by Islamic law to seek sex reassignment surgery (SRS), a reality underscored by a religious fatwa in 1983 (that exempted the *khunsa*). In this context, the *Mak Nyah* is a marginalized person who must forego hope of SRS if he is to avoid committing a religious offense. Even so, a Muslim *Mak Nyah* is, essentially, a non-entity.⁹⁵³

What are transgender realities in New Zealand?

New Zealand has a vigorous population of transgendered people. Some legal protections and rights have been won in recent years. In a 1994 landmark case, New Zealand Attorney General vs. the Family Court at Otahuhu, the decision rendered made it possible for post-operative transsexuals to legally marry as members of their reassigned sex. In that decision it was observed that, "If society allows such persons to undergo therapy and surgery in order to fulfill that [the desire to alter their genital sex] desire, then it ought also to allow such persons to function as fully as possible in their reassigned sex, and this must include the capacity to marry."⁹⁵⁴

As in so many societies, some transgendered people find themselves plying the sex trade. A significant issue in New Zealand in this regard is the disproportionate representation of Maori people among the transgendered prostitutes. Although constituting only 9% of the country's population, in the early 1980s they represented about 90% of the transsexual prostitutes in Wellington, the capital city.⁹⁵⁵

What are transgender realities in Okinawa?

Westerners are perhaps most familiar with Okinawa as the scene of one of the fiercest Pacific battles of the Second World War. Formerly the Kingdom of the Ryukyus, Okinawa has its own rich history and distinctive culture, despite longstanding ties with Japan. Although it has not received as much attention as its more famous neighbors in the Pacific, observation has revealed that crossdressing occurs in this land as well.

Anthropologist Susan Sared, research director of the Religion, Health and Healing Initiative at Harvard's Center for the Study of World Religions, authored a work on the divine priestesses of Okinawa. In her study, Sared observed crossdressing males in the village of Henza. Curious, she investigated and discovered that, "a man wearing women's clothes, publicly and flamboyantly, is of no particular interest to villagers."[956] Her exploration of the culture led her to conclude:

> In Okinawa . . . gender—like other social categories—is loosely constructed, the connection between sex and gender is tenuous, and cross-dressing elicits almost no interest from onlookers: A man dressed in women's clothing presents no paradox, challenges no worldview, is given no label or diagnosis, and invokes no emotional reaction.[957]

What are transgender realities in Papua New Guinea?

Papua New Guinea constitutes the eastern half of the large island of New Guinea, bordering the Coral Sea, which separates it from Australia. The nation gained its independence from the Australian-managed United Nations' trusteeship in 1975. The nearly 6 million people are a mix of Melanesian, Micronesian, Negrito, Papuan, and Polynesian ethnicities. Religiously, the inhabitants are principally Christian (with Roman Catholics constituting the largest group), though indigenous beliefs remain a spiritual force for many.

Sexologists Paul Abramson and Steven Pinkerton regard Papua New Guinea as one of only two nations (the Dominican Republic being the other) where a three-gender system is socially embraced. Alongside 'masculinity' (men) and 'femininity' (women) is 'other'—a gender class especially reserved for intersexed individuals.[958] In this regard, Gilbert Herdt points to the *kwolu-aatmwol* of the Sambia in the eastern highlands. These are intersexed individuals ('male pseudohermaphrodites'), some raised as girls and others as boys. Herdt acknowledges that, "In certain regards one could argue that the adolescent *kwolu-aatmwol* constitutes a third-sex category for Sambia." However, he argues the matter is far from straightforward and the socialization of such individuals is "ambiguous."[959]

What are transgender realities in the Philippines?

The Philippines are an archipelago of more than 7,000 islands east of Vietnam, north of Indonesia, and south of Taiwan. The people are a diverse mix; Malaysian people with a liberal sprinkling of other groups (American, Arab, Chinese, Spanish, etc.). Religious diversity is indicated in the presence of Buddhism, Christianity (Catholicism is the dominant religious expression), and Islam, as well as other spiritual traditions. Both the ethnic and religious diversity reflect not only the island's proximity to other lands but also the impact of the nation's long colonial period. The Philippines were subjected to Spain's rule in the 16th century, then ceded in 1898 to the United States, and occupied by the Japanese during the Second World War. Modern independence was achieved in 1946.

Transgendered people have been a part of Philippine society both past and present. Prior to the arrival of the Spanish, evidence suggests that male crossdressers were viewed as an unremarkable aspect of the cultural landscape.[960] That situation changed with the power brought to bear by the Western world through first the Spanish and subsequently the Americans.

The Spanish conquerors of the 16th century observed a group of male crossdressers. These males the Spanish described as effeminate in manner, which appeared as feminine in dress and hairstyle. They played a religious role in the indigenous culture, as indicated by the various designations given them: *Asog* ('priest'), or *Baylan* ('priestess'), or *Bayog* ('shaman'). They were mediums to the spirit world and healers, assisting female priestesses. For some of them, at least, the crossdressing appears to have been confined to ritual practice. The weight of Spanish Catholicism and Western culture's imposition of a rigid gender scheme spelled doom to the *Asog*.[961]

Yet traces of these religious figures, and their influence, persist. The animism of this indigenous religious practice can still be found in scattered places among the islands. These *Baylan* (or *Babaylan*) might be either female, or males in female guise. Their religious function remains as it was, to communicate with and appease the spirits on behalf of the community. Interestingly, in recent times the role appears to be more often filled by males than by females.[962]

Transgender people are part of modern Philippine life. Social anthropologist Mark Johnson offers as an example the mainly Muslim Tausug communities found in the Southern Philippines. His work explores the complex ways gender and sexuality, especially ideas about sexual orientation, interweave among these people. The locals term a certain kind of male *bantut* ('impotent, effeminate, transvestite'). Another kind is called *bennie* or *billyboys* (transvestite-homosexual prostitutes). In a society where the masculine role in sexual interactions is active (*activo*), males taking a passive (*passivo*) role are feminine—in American terms, 'gay.' They are characterized as "having a woman's heart stuck in a man's body." In the ways they conceptually construct and speak about gender and sexuality, these people draw upon various sources to inform them, including Islam and, as

Johnson puts it, an 'imagined' America.[963] This society, then, affords yet another example of how dominant Western societies and their culture impact other places in the world.

Q. 58

Where is it found in North America?

The Short Answer. Crossdressing occurs across both Canada and the United States, down into Mexico and throughout Central America. In answering this question we will focus on its appearance in Canada and the United States. With respect to Canada, attention is given along lines similar to the other countries sampled in previous answers. In brief, Canadian society, like most others, exhibits a mixed response to transgender realities. The ambivalence of the society is seen, for example, in Canadian law with respect to transgender people. This not only varies from province to province, but has changed over time in a manner that suggests the still undecided social response to such things as sex reassignment surgery. Also like too many other lands, Canada has been troubled by violence toward transgender people and the society has—quite literally—paid a price for social intolerance. Yet many transgender people find Canada a more welcoming place than some other Western societies. There are a good number of support organizations and some transgender persons have attained social prominence through vehicles like entertainment. One interesting peculiarity of Canada's history with transgender realities are the so-called 'mock weddings' found in Canada's western prairie region. In these ceremonies most of the participants, male or female, crossdress. The relative brevity of this answer for the U.S. is accounted for by a number of things. First, since much of the material of this book derives from research done with North American people the bulk of the contents of this volume concerns transgender realities like crossdressing in the United States. Second, the answer to Q. 47 recounts the history of crossdressing in the United States. Third, the answer to Q. 59 provides an account of indigenous populations and so is only briefly treated here. Accordingly, the answer to this question aims to collect here certain materials that do not better fit elsewhere. In this respect, research on the health of this country's transgender people is looked at. This research reveals grounds for serious concern. Living in a culture that refuses to acknowledge the legitimacy of their gender identity creates great stress. Often marginalized and impoverished, these folk suffer. Finally, the transgender indigenous people of Hawaii are examined. Hawaii's *Mahu* people play an important role in the traditional culture, though the influence of Western culture has had a largely negative impact on them.

The Longer Answer. While North America geographically embraces the countries often differentiated as 'North' and 'Central' America, in answering this question, we will consider only Canada and the United States.[964] It may be easy to imagine that these friendly neighbors are so much the same that what has been said about transgender realities in the States can be applied to Canada. But though there are similarities, differences exist as well—and some of these may be significant.[965]

What are transgender realities in Canada?

Canada, like its southern neighbor, bears the imprint of a European legacy as English and French settlers brought Western culture to this continent. The views of this cultural perspective on sex, sexuality, and gender predominate. Canadian crossdressers, much like their counterparts in the United States, thus dwell in a culture with a relatively rigid gender dichotomy. Canadian attorney Barbara Findlay observes that, "the assumption that there exist two and only two genders in humankind is deeply entrenched in the Canadian legal system, as it is in Canadian society."[966]

Yet the history of recent decades has witnessed challenges to that dichotomy and increased flexibility in what is deemed acceptable gender behavior by males and females. Accordingly, social mores have loosened to the extent that more crossdressers feel comfortable expressing themselves. In turn, increased visibility has been accompanied by increased awareness, through education and media exposure. At the same time, the general public perception is more tolerant but not yet welcoming. As some scholars have put it, Canadian reaction to crossdressing and other cross-gender expression is "often a mixture of discomfort and fascination."[967]

Today, Canada has a robust transgender population, including those among the indigenous population.[968] However, the quality of life and legal protection available to transgender people varies in different places in this sprawling country. Egale Canada, a national organization advancing equality and justice for transgender people, records that discrimination in employment and housing, as well as in other respects, remains a problem.[969] More seriously, a 2001 study conducted through the Institute for Social Research at the University of Saskatoon estimates homophobia alone may account for between $1.9 to $8 billion dollars lost each year to the Canadian economy, and between 2,300-5,500 premature deaths annually.[970] If transphobia were added to this picture the already staggering numbers would be even greater. In this climate it is best we begin with a brief review of the legal situation in Canada.

Canadian Law

Canada is a nation organized into provinces. In addition to national law, provincial law must be considered. With respect to protection of transgender people, as in the U.S., law at the national level has not been as favorable as at the provincial level, where two provinces (Northwest Territories and Ontario) provide important protection. At the national level, Member of Parliament Bill Siksay introduced Bill C-392, An Act to Amend the Canadian Human Rights Act (gender identity), in May, 1995. The amendment aimed to add 'gender identity' and 'gender expression' as specific grounds for protection under the Act. But by the end of the year the bill died when Parliament was dissolved without having acted upon it.[971] Siksay has remained determined to keep the concern alive. He reintroduced the amendment (now Bill C-326) in the 39th Parliament, convened in 2006, on June 19th of that year. In April, 2007, he introduced a motion (M-309), which reads:

> That, in the opinion of the House, the government should: (a) endorse the Yogyakarta Principles on the Application of International Human Rights Law in Relation to Sexual Orientation and Gender Identity; (b) seek to fully implement these principles in Canada; and (c) work towards their acceptance and implementation worldwide through the United Nations, all other human rights and international law forums, and Canada's relations with other countries.[972]

No final disposition had been made at the time of this writing.

Among Canadian provinces, the Northwest Territories prohibits discrimination based on gender identity. They became the first region in Canada to do so when the Human Rights Act was passed in October, 2002. Article 2: 'Equal Rights and Effective Remedies' explicitly includes 'gender identity' as a ground for discrimination (see §724). The scope of the law covers both transsexuals and those transgender people who live full time in a gender identity different than that assigned them at birth.[973]

Ontario also provides protection from discrimination based on gender identity. Although gender identity is not specified in the code as a legal ground, the Ontario Human Rights Commission believes the Code's structure supports a progressive reading so that 'sex' is interpreted to include 'gender identity.' The Commission notes, "There are, arguably, few groups in our society today who are as disadvantaged and disenfranchised as transgenderists and transsexuals. Fear and hatred of transgenderists and transsexuals combined with hostility toward their very existence are fundamental human rights issues."[974] In March, 2007, Bill 186, An Act to Amend the Human Rights Code (respecting gender identity) was introduced to the Legislate Assembly of Ontario.[975] No final disposition had been made at the time of this writing.

In addition to the actions of the above provinces, British Columbia's Human Rights Commission also has urged prohibition of discrimination based on gender identity. In its 1998 publication, *Human Rights for the Next Millennium*, the Commission accompanied its call with the observation that the BC Law Foundation, through its Transgendered Law Reform Project, had demonstrated the inadequacy of bringing human rights complaints under existing law. They noted that adding 'gender identity' to the existing code as a ground of protection would ensure adequate protection for transgender people. Nearly a decade later, their call to action remains unanswered.[976]

Surely legal scholar Kathleen Ann Lahey is correct when she writes, "The Canadian approach to transsexualism and transgender issues may well change as time passes and understanding of the limitations of narrow categories in human rights legislation grows."[977]

Canadian Transgender People & Resources

Sex reassignment surgery (SRS) is legal in Canada. However, changes that take place with regard to public funding of operations reflects the controversy over SRS both within the professional community and the larger society. For example, in Ontario the Health Insurance Act provided coverage for SRS and related medical needs until changes in 1998. A similar situation pertains in British Columbia, but other provinces (e.g., Alberta, Saskatchewan) continue to provide health coverage for SRS.[978] In a similar fashion, the process for accomplishing changes in identity documents differs from province to province. Care for transsexual clients seeking body modification vary somewhat, but in general the Harry Benjamin International Gender Dysphoria Association (HBIGDA) guidelines are followed.[979]

As is true elsewhere in the world, Canada's most famous and visible transgender individuals tend to be those in entertainment. Arguably the most famous of Canadian crossdressers is Craig (or Graig) Russell (pseudonym of Russell Craig Eadie; 1948-1990), a noted female impersonator who rose to fame in both Canada and the U.S. in the 1970s-1980s. Two films, *Outrageous* (1977) and *Too Outrageous* (1987) featured him. He died October 31, 1990 of AIDs-related complications.[980] Two contemporary musicians, Dana Baitz, a self-identified 'transwoman.' Baitz, and Rae Spoon, a female-to-male transsexual, are among publicly known transgender people.[981]

Among Canadian organizations supporting transgender people, we already briefly mentioned Egale Canada. Founded in 1986, and headquartered in Ottawa, Egale was born in the wake of the government's consideration of a parliamentary committee's recommendations with respect to prohibiting discrimination based on sexual orientation.[982] Egale's 'About Us' webpage says that it has members in every province and has been vigorous in its efforts to advance the pursuit of equality for transgender people (in the widest sense) and their families.[983] Its extensive website contains resources and updated materials relevant to different segments of the transgender population. These include legislative initiatives, reports of hate crimes and acts of discrimination, educational issues, and so forth.

There are a number of other organizations supportive of transgender people in Canada. These include local chapters of Tri-Ess and PFLAG (see the answer to Q. 34). While Tri-Ess is an organization with international scope, many of Canada's support organizations are more localized. In British Columbia, for example, there is The Cornbury Society, an organization for crossdressers in Vancouver, founded in 1989 and functioning as a social and support group.[984] Gender Mosaic, located in Ottawa, Ontario, and another social and support organization, claims it is 'the oldest and most established transgender support group' in the country.[985] It was founded in the mid-1980s. There are many similar organizations across Canada and many of them maintain a presence on the internet.

Mock Weddings

Despite—or perhaps because of—the society's rigid gender order, there is a substantial history of transgendered realities in Canada. While gay drag in modern Canada is perhaps the best known public display of crossdressing, a long tradition of public heterosexual crossdressing remains in practice in the mock weddings of Canada's western prairie (and down into certain portions of the United States). The mock wedding is a form of costume folk drama connected with a social occasion, notably a milestone wedding anniversary. Except perhaps for the officiating clergy, all the participants crossdress; women occupy the masculine roles (e.g., bridegroom, best man, father of the bride), men the feminine parts (e.g., bride, maids of honor, flower girl, mothers of the couple). The mock wedding parodies the real ceremony, with specific ingredients added with reference to the couple being honored.

Michael Taft's study of these mock weddings reveals gender role reversal as a major reason for the event. Typically organized by women, the mock wedding offers them a chance to put the men around them into gendered roles they know all too well, but from which men remain generally distant. Indeed, Taft finds the men inhabit these roles in as ostentatiously masculine a manner as possible. Their portrayal of women is exaggerated and reflects masculine stereotypes of the way women are. In their posturing and behavior they remind witnesses that they are masculine despite their dressed appearance.[986]

What are transgender realities in the United States?

In the United States, crossdressing has a history as long as the nation's own. This we have already documented (see the answer to Q. 47). In this answer our focus is on contemporary America and we will address one or two matters not covered elsewhere in this work. In particular, that means examining indigenous people other than the Indian peoples covered in answering Q. 59. Often neglected by residents of the 48 contiguous states, many of the citizens of Alaska and Hawaii represent important and distinctive cultures. Also, the United States includes within its reach 'protectorates' such as Guam, Puerto Rico, and the

Virgin Islands, each with an indigenous population and native culture. In its rich diversity in peoples and cultures, the United States embraces a wide range of experiences and expressions that fall within our scope.

One indication of the changes occurring in both Canada and the U.S. is found in the business world. As in a number of other countries, these neighbors have witnessed a liberalization in certain clothing trends. Articles not long ago associated almost exclusively with one gender are now becoming unisex. Perhaps the most notable instance is hosiery. Shapings.com, a Canadian online business selling lingerie, disclosed in 2002 its estimate that 85% of its hosiery sales were to men. A market survey commissioned by the U.S. company G. Lieberman & Sons found strong support among men for regarding hosiery as unisex. As a result, a line of hosiery called 'Comfilon' was created for men.[987]

But such matters have been adequately covered elsewhere in this volume, and especially in volume 1 of this work. With respect to transgender experience in this society, the material that follows in question sets 6-7 offer much more. So in this material on the U.S. only a few remarks are in order. We will begin with a sobering fact: like elsewhere in the world, a disproportionate percentage of the American transgender population faces the hard consequences of social marginalization and family rejection. That means for many surviving by engaging in the sex trade or otherwise struggling with limited economic options and becoming mired in poverty.

Transgender Health

Only within the last decade has much effort been made to assess the health of transgender people in this country. A landmark study was conducted in 1997 in the City and County of San Francisco. Administered by the San Francisco Department of Health, the research involves both qualitative focus groups and compiling statistical data from surveys. The 'Transgender Community Health Project' (TCHP) had as its originating purpose the assessment of HIV risk among the area's transgender population. The results find that both transgender males and females are disadvantaged in many respects from members of the wider community, and that male transgender persons are especially at risk. Of those participating in the study, more than half the male individuals have no health insurance (52%; 41% for F), have unstable housing (53%; 21% for F), and have been jailed at one time or another (65%; 29% F). Most males (80%) and many females (31%) have histories of working in the sex trade, and identical percentages for each group (59%) have experienced forced sex. Surprisingly, only 2% of the females test HIV positive, but 35% of male participants do.[988]

In 2004, the National Coalition for LGBT Health issued an overview based on a meta-analysis of available research on U.S. transgender populations. The report utilizes 13 separate topic areas using Healthy People 2010 categories. The first of these concerns violence against transgender people. Murder reports in the U.S. reach across 89 cities in 20 states. The report notes GenderPAC's 1997 anti-violence report that finds 27% of its sample have been victims of violence.

The report concludes there is "sufficient evidence to document the existence of an epidemic of violence directed against transgender people in the U.S., especially transwomen of color."[989]

Other findings issued in the overview document high HIV prevalence in transgender women (studies indicate ranges from 14%-68% among populations in specific areas, with sex workers at greatest risk). Significant substance abuse problems are complicated by health provider insensitivity and hostility, among other things. Depression remains a major problem, with suicidal ideation rates as high as 64% in some locations and suicide attempts ranging from 16-37% in various studies. Thoughts of suicide are commonly linked to gender identity issues. Getting help, whether for psychological issues or other health concerns, is complicated by a pervasive lack of health insurance, underinsurance, exclusion of insurance benefits for health services important to transgender persons (e.g., hormone therapy and sex reassignment surgery(SRS)), and too few professionals trained in issues pertinent to transgender realities. Also, requiring a diagnosis of 'Gender Identity Disorder'—officially classified as a mental disorder—attaches an unnecessary stigma for those seeking services. For those who do seek services related to body alteration, treatments such as transgender hormonal therapy remain unapproved by the Federal Drug Administration, which complicates treatment. Additionally, SRS remains listed as an 'experimental' procedure, and is seen by many as 'elective' or 'cosmetic' surgery—all reasons used to exclude insurance coverage. In light of such obstacles, many transgender people turn to cheaper, more easily obtained procedures such as silicone injections, often under unsanitary conditions. Finally, health providers themselves often exhibit insensitivity or hostility, lessening the likelihood of transgender people seeking care or receiving quality help when they do seek it.[990]

Some interpret the high incidence of HIV, substance abuse, depression, suicide ideation, and suicide attempts as 'proof' that the problem resides inside transgender people, who are 'mentally disordered.' However, this less-than-charitable conclusion ignores the real and significant impact of social ostracism, marginalization, discrimination, discrimination-induced poverty, and the tremendous challenge of having a healthy gender identity in a culture whose gender system either denies its reality, or its legitimacy. It is less a wonder that so many transgender people suffer than it is that so many survive and do as well as they do given the obstacles they must overcome.

Hawaii's Mahu

Transgender realities are found among many of the indigenous peoples found within the United States. These include the so-called *berdaches* or 'two-spirit' people of American Indian tribes (see the answer to Q. 59), the shamans of the artic region included within Alaska (cf. the answer to Q. 76), and the Polynesian people of Hawaii. The first two of these groups have been much better studied than the last. Pauline Park and John Manzon-Santos, in testimony submitted to the President's Advisory Commission on Asian Americans and

Pacific Islanders, remark that to date there has been no community assessment of the transgender population among these people.[991]

With respect to the Polynesians, it has been estimated that about 70% of Hawaii's transgendered population are indigenous people. While this might be because of Polynesian acceptance of gender diversity, the reality of American culture means these people may face more obstacles and fare most poorly among native Hawaiians.[992] Indeed, though a popular perception exists that Hawaii is more tolerant of sexual minorities than other states, researcher Andrew Matzner says the reality is far different, with prejudice and discrimination a significant obstacle for transgendered people.[993]

Matzner observes that some among Hawaii's transgendered population embrace a traditional term, *Mahu*, to identify themselves. *Mahu* originally referred to people we today term intersexed; later its meaning was broadened to include all transgendered people.[994] Though this term today is often used disparagingly to refer to homosexuals, Matzner notes that in pre-contact Hawaiian culture mahu did not bear negative connotations. He remarks, "As males or females who behaved and/or appeared in ways associated with the opposite gender, it appears that mahu held privileged positions in their communities."[995] In former times they were revered as preservers of culture, and especially as teachers of the hula dance and chant. Like transgendered folk in other cultures, the *Mahu* fulfilled an important religious function. They served in the role of goddesses in the sacred hula dances performed in temples where women were not allowed.[996]

Q. 59

Where is it found in Native American groups?

The Short Answer. Among the most famous transgender expressions found around the world are those among the indigenous peoples of the Americas. Especially noted over the last two centuries are the so-called *berdaches*—a European term of pejorative content that nevertheless has stuck as a label for transgender Indian people. A modern alternative to this label is to term such folk 'two-souled' or 'two-spirit' people. While such individuals are known from North, Central, and South America, most attention until fairly recently focused on North America. In this area alone more than 150 tribes have been identified as recording transgender realities such as intersex, homosexuality, and cross-dressing. Transgender Native Americans might be either genetically male or female, though the former are more common. They are probably best understood as occupying within indigenous culture a distinct social group that might also be characterized as a 'third gender.' They typically play important and distinctive social roles. Among these the most famous is probably that of the shaman (cf. the answer to Q. 76).

The Longer Answer. Let us begin with two important observations: first, American Indians retain a long cultural heritage distinct from the conquering White culture that swept across the continent. Second, that distinctive culture is itself surprisingly diverse. Native American life is not monolithic. The Indian nations, despite the similarities often drawn among them by outsiders, constitute distinct and distinctive separate societies. Both of these critical facts converge in what we have to say about Indian conceptions of gender. As scholar Will Roscoe remarks, "The social universe of native North America was nowhere more at odds with that of Europe and Anglo-America than in its diverse gender roles."[997]

Many tribes have known members who adopt the dress, manners, and roles of a gender different than one typically associated with their anatomical sex. Over 150 different tribes have acknowledged gender roles beyond what we think of as masculine or feminine. Anthropologist Sabine Lang writes that more than 80% of all Native American tribes report crossdressing within their society.[998] Some of these tribes include:

Table 59.1 Indian Tribes (By Region) with Alternative Gender Roles[999]

East/ Southeast	North/ Northwest/ Plateau	Plains	Southwest	West
Algonkians	Aleut	Arapaho	Acoma	Achumawi
Caddo	Bella Bella	Arikara	Apache	Atsugewi
Cherokee	Bella Coola	Assiniboine	Chickasaw	Cahto
Creek	Carrier	Blackfoot	Choctaw	Chilula
Delaware	Chipewyan	Cheyenne	Coahuiltec	Chumash
Fox	Coeur d'Alene	Commanche	Cocopa	Costanaon
Illinois	Cree (subarctic)	Cree	Havasupai	Gabrielino
Iroquis	Eskimo (Inuit, etc.)	Crow	Hopi	Gosiute
Menominee	Eyak	Gros Ventres	Isleta	Hupa
Miami	Flathead	Hidatsa	Karankawa	Ipai
Micmac	Haida	Kansa	Laguna	Kawaiisu
Ojibwa	Haisla	Kiowa	Maricopa	Kitanemuk
Ottawa	Hare	Mandan	Mohave	Koso
Potawatomi	Ingalik	Ojibwa	Natchez	Lassik
Sauk	Kalispell	Omaha	Navajo	Luiseño
Tuscarora	Kaska	Osage	Papago	Maidu
Winnebago	Klamath	Oto	Pima	Mattole
	Kootenai	Pawnee	San Felipe	Miwok
	Kwakiutl	Ponca	San Juan	Modoc
	Lillooet	Quapaw	Santa Ana	Monache
	Naskapi	Sioux (Lakota, etc.)	Santo Domingo	Nisenan
	Nez Perce		Tesuque	Nomlaki
	Nisqually		Timucua	Paiute
	Nootka		Walapai	Patwin
	Ojibwa		Yamasee	Pomo

	Okanagan		Yavapai	Salinan	
	Quilute		Yuma	Shasta	
	Salish (Quinalt, etc.)		Zuni	Shoshone	
	Sanpoil			Sinkyone	
	Siuslaw			Tipai	
	Spokane			Tolowa	
	Takelma			Tubatulabal	
	Thompson			Ute	
	Tlingit			Wappo	
	Tsimshian			Washo	
	Tututni			Wintu	
	Wishram			Wiyot	
				Yana	
				Yokuts	
				Yuki-Huchnom	
				Yurok	

Most know of males who adopt the manner, dress, and role typically assigned women, but some tribes also know of females who occupy a masculine role; in many instances the manner and role presented are intermediate between masculine or feminine, or mix these genders, or otherwise show the individual is not a typical man or woman. The names applied to such people vary widely: *winkte*, *lhamana*, 'two-spirit,' and many others. Of these, the term 'two-spirit' has perhaps proved the most popular.[1000] But the label by which these transgendered people are most familiarly known is not a Native American term at all.

What does *berdaches* mean?

Outsiders have long called these transgendered people *berdaches*, a term derogatory in nature as it is derived from an Arabic term meaning 'sex slave boy.' The label first appears as early as the late 16th century America, apparently introduced by missionaries. The Spanish, encountering these Native American people, attempted to suppress the apparent crossdressing, and enlisted the power of the Christian missions to help reform the natives.[1001] The term *berdaches* soon became especially associated with Indian males in female dress and role, despite the fact that some women occupied a male gender role.

The latter are sometimes called 'Amazons,' after the legendary group of women who engaged in the masculine arts of hunting and warfare. The label is misleading. As Lang points out, many 'women-men' were motivated by the same desires that other females in different cultures feel, such as the wish to pursue work associated with men. Others may have been what our culture calls 'transsexual'—fully identifying as men; in addition to crossdressing they filled the masculine gender role in other respects, including their relationships, sometimes even marrying another female.[1002] Anthropologist Ana Mariella Bacigalupo lists as among the most prominent female *berdaches* 'Slave Woman' of the Chipewyan, 'Pine Leaf'' of the Crow, 'Running Eagle' of the Blackfoot, Qánqon of the Kutenai, Kuiliy of the Kalispel, and Kwisai of the Mohave.[1003]

Despite the derivation of the term, *berdaches* has become entrenched in usage. Moreover, as anthropologist Will Roscoe points out, no readily available term exists to replace it.[1004] We should also note that today it is defined in a scholarly manner using general and inoffensive terms. For example, anthropologists Henry Angelino and Charles Shedd, in the mid-20th century, offer as a definition that a *berdache* is "an individual of a definite physiological sex (male or female), who assumes the role and status of the opposite sex, and who is viewed by the community as being of one sex physiologically but as having assumed the role and status of the opposite sex."[1005] Similarly, anthropologists Charles Callendar and Lee Kochems 'roughly' define a *berdache* as "a person, usually male, who was anatomically normal but assumed the dress, occupations, and behavior of the other sex to effect a change in gender status."[1006] That new status is intermediate between masculinity and femininity—a 'third gender.' There is no opprobrium in such modern usage. So, with reluctance, it will be retained here as the broadest term encompassing various manifestations of the phenomenon among the Native Americans. However, as in the case with other words that have been cited with reference to transgender people, the negative connotations of the term are not here endorsed.[1007] Unless otherwise noted, the following material has male *berdaches* in view.

Who are the *berdaches*?

The traditional Native American comprehension of people that Europeans called *berdaches* is varied and different from that of the foreigners who displaced them from their native lands. Under the pressure of the culture embraced by their conquerors, some Indians have lost in part or in whole the sensibilities they once held about such people. For example, some whose tribal societies no longer retain multiple gender categories because they have adopted the Western dualistic gender scheme now conflate gender and sexuality, thus changing their perception of the *berdaches*.[1008] At this point in time, it is simply impossible to make any grand statement that could accurately reflect a broad consensus among Native Americans about the *berdaches*.

However, Roscoe believes it possible to identify a 'core set' of traits. He offers four:

- ❑ *specialized work roles* (cross-gender and unique work activities);
- ❑ *gender difference* (distinctive, 'third gender' characteristics);
- ❑ *spiritual sanction* (accepted as divine in causation); and,
- ❑ *same-sex relations* (typically, sexual relations with non-*berdache* people).[1009]

On this last point, it should be pointed out that though the sexed bodies of the partners may be the same, the gender identities and roles are not. Therefore, use of a term like 'homosexual,' in the way our culture understands it, would be misleading.

In contemporary Western culture's terms, the *berdaches* are transgender people in the broad sense. As such, they exhibit a range of distinctive characteristics. While some are intersexed individuals, most are not. Some are chosen by others, some choose themselves, and some claim to be born to the gendered identity and role. Various tribal societies differ in whether they call all their transgender people by the same name or by different ones. For example, the Acoma can refer to 'women-men' as *Mujerado* ('womaned'), *Qo-Qoy-Mo* ('effeminate person'), or *Kokwina* (translation uncertain).[1010] The Omaha people also distinguish among them, particularly the intersexed from other transgendered individuals, using different terms with varying regard. On the other hand, the Navajo use a single term, without distinction.[1011] As well, the translation into English of a particular word can be fraught with difficulties. For instance, the Cree term for people whom those outside the tribe might call *berdaches* is *Ayekkwew*, which can be understood either as 'both man and woman,' or 'neither man or woman'—a conceptual distance of some significance.[1012] However, Callendar and Ketchum contend that whatever the label, native terminology defines them within "a distinct gender status."[1013]

In this respect, Lang argues that we should distinguish the *berdaches* from others who might have crossed gender or sexual lines in some fashion. She differentiates them from the following:

- ❑ those who pursue same-sex sexual relations but do not change gender roles (i.e., people Western culture labels 'homosexuals');
- ❑ those who crossdress, perhaps for ritual purposes, but do not change gender roles (i.e., people Western culture labels 'transvestites');
- ❑ those who stretch the limits of their assigned gender, but do not change gender roles (i.e., people Western culture labels 'feminine men' and 'masculine women');
- ❑ those, like 'warrior women,' who cross gender boundaries, but without exchanging their gender status for an ambivalent one; and,

❑ those who are being socially shamed through forced crossdressing or assumption of another gender's role (i.e., what Western culture calls 'petticoat punishment').[1014]

While not everyone agrees that the *berdaches* should be regarded as a 'third gender,' it seems reasonably clear that is how they were viewed within at least some tribal societies.

Historian Richard Trexler finds that in some Indian societies the *berdaches* are consciously selected in early childhood or even before birth. He cites the historical instance of the Laches people of Colombia who permitted a family, after five boys, to "convert" one of them into a daughter (a situation echoed in the modern Artic Indian practice of permitting a girl child to be changed into a son). Other tribes have followed a similar practice of pre-selecting an unborn child to be *berdache*, although not always for the same reasons. Trexler, in surveying the literature of Latin American records at the time of the Spanish Conquest finds no instances of an individual self-selecting this place in society. Moreover, this general situation pertains to later times. In his estimation, even the notion of a 'test' to determine a child's 'true gender' is contrived; adult authorities construe the gender they want. An exception to this general practice is placing grown male warriors into the ranks of the *berdaches* after exhibiting cowardice.[1015]

Other evidence suggests that in some locations or instances the individual self-identified as transgendered, sometimes even in the face of opposition. We have the account of German naturalist Alexander Philipp Maximilian, *Prinz Zu Wiednuewied*, who between 1832-1834 visited the Great Plains and recorded his observations in two volumes.[1016] In a well-known passage, Maximilian writes of the *berdaches*:

> These generally assert that a dream or some high impulse has commanded them to adopt this state as their 'medicine' or salvation, and nothing then can turn them away from their purpose. Many a father has sought even by force to divert his child from this object, has reasoned with him at first, offered him fine weapons and masculine articles of dress in order to inspire him with a taste for manly occupations; and when this proved useless, has handled him sternly, punished and beaten him, yet all in vain.[1017]

Maximilian's account may or may not accurately reflect Indian sensibilities. His own European values intrude at various points, though overall he seems to have held a high opinion of American Indians. Perhaps he mistook a process of testing the youth's true nature; as Lang describes, likening it to the test Odysseus put to Achilles when the latter was disguised as a maiden: bring a spear and shield into the youth's presence, sound the battle alarm, and see what response transpires.[1018]

What roles are played by the *berdaches* in Indian society?

Berdaches in Socially Adaptive Roles

Unlike our own modern Western culture, which largely marginalizes transgendered people and censures crossdressing outside of entertainment venues, Indian societies traditionally often granted the transgendered a socially adaptive place. Roscoe, in his history of these people, writes that, "in this land, the original America, men who wore women's clothes and did women's work became artists, innovators, ambassadors, and religious leaders, and women sometimes became warriors, hunters, and chiefs."[1019] Sociologist H. Taylor Buckner notes that American tribes like the Dakotas, Mohave, Plains Indians, and Zuni provide a role for crossdressers that, in effect, puts the personal adaptation of an individual to societal use.[1020] Because they inhabit a space between masculine males and feminine females such individuals are often looked to as mediators between men and women. However, the idea of mediating often extends beyond being a go-between in only one respect. Often perceived as mixing masculine and feminine characteristics they may also be thought uniquely able to so 'see' better than either gender and so be called upon as 'seers' whose visions bridge this mundane reality with the spiritual realm. Accordingly, in some tribal societies they become shamans.[1021]

Trexler observes that the social role of the *berdaches* has been understood in different ways in different periods. The Spanish Conquistadores, for example, regarded them along the lines implied by the label—as males playing the woman's passive sexual role by allowing themselves to be penetrated by other males. Yet this unfairly denigrates their social role; Trexler shows that in Latin America at the time of the Spanish Conquests, even while submitting to a sexual act, the *berdaches* could fulfill a religious role within religious services. He concludes that, in general, the *berdaches* functioned as "representational emblems of subordination"—embodying the feminine role ruled by the masculine role—and that this was a "significant social role."[1022]

Trexler enumerates among the social roles and activities that might be played by the *berdaches* the following:

- ❑ domestic labor alongside genetic females;
- ❑ wives;
- ❑ sex surrogates for males to preserve marriageable females;
- ❑ substitutes for genetic females in ritual activities; and,
- ❑ possibly, to safeguard transfer of property between generations in instances where blood kin were not of a proper sex to inherit.[1023]

This list makes plain the value *berdaches* offered their societies, but it may not be plain why so many men found them especially valuable. Why might a *berdache* be preferred as a worker or as a wife? Anthropologist Walter Williams offers an answer: being biologically male, they never had the possibility of pregnancy and their greater size and strength meant they often excelled at the women's work assigned them. Such desirable features made them treasured members of a man's household because they added to its success.[1024]

Berdaches and Sacred Roles

To the above list we should add more broadly the many sacred roles often played by the *berdaches*. Indeed, this aspect has sometimes been made central to the understanding of them. Anthropologist Italo Signorini remarks that, "supernatural powers are attributed to *berdaches*, and they have specific ritual responsibilities (funerals, conferring of secret names, warfare, and others)."[1025] As noted by many scholars, shamanistic roles are often associated with them, and even where not specifically engaged in such a role the *berdaches* are often noted for their healing and spiritual prowess.

Lang, for example, offers that reports affirm the occupation of 'women-men' as shamans in 21 different Native American cultures. She elaborates:

> Women were the main practitioners in one-third of these cases, and the occupation was obviously chosen by the women-men as an aspect of their feminine gender role. Where men were the primary healers or medicine men, the women-men moved partly within the domain of the masculine gender role, both with respect to their status as medicine "men" and also with regard to acquisition of the necessary supernatural powers. Women's clothes and components of the feminine gender role appeared there as the expression of the personal "medicine" of a woman-man. In such cases, women-men were not healers in the framework of the feminine gender role, but—despite their ambivalent gender status—they were males with a special kind of supernatural power.[1026]

Varying Social Responses to the Berdaches

Regardless of the social niches the *berdaches* might occupy, the degree of social approval varies from society to society. Lang documents numerous studies covering a sizable number of tribal cultures. Tribal responses, as assessed by outside researchers, range from disapproval, even hostility (e.g., Choctaw, Eyak, Tolowa), through indifference (e.g., Achomawi, Southern Paiute, Ute, Wintu) to positive regard and support (e.g., Arapaho, Cheyenne, Cree, Eskimos, Hopi, Navajo). In some tribes, the response is varied; the *berdaches* may be seen by some with indifference and by others with disapproval (e.g., Atsugewi), or the tribe may provide evidence of the whole range of responses (e.g., Crow, Dakota, Flathead, Lakota, Omaha).[1027]

What is the relation between the *berdaches* and cross-dressing?

Not unexpectedly, the use of dress by *berdaches* helps signal their unique status. Anthropologist Arnold Pilling, who prefers the term 'two-spirit,' writes that the Zuni crossdressers of the past clearly belong under that designation.[1028] They merely exemplify the occurrence of a behavior that has been said to occur everywhere in some form or another.[1029] Callendar and Kochems note that in some instances their gender presentation means adoption of clothes associated with a gender different from their sexed body, such as a biological male taking on feminine dress. But in other cases the dress mixes masculine and feminine elements. Sometimes the dress proves distinctive enough it is not recognized as either masculine or feminine.[1030] Thus, Roscoe is correct in commenting, "The most visible marker of berdache status was some form of cross-dressing, although this occurred much less consistently than is usually assumed."[1031] He is also right in observing how sloppily terms are used—or misused—in many studies of Native American culture. Terms like 'transvestite,' 'transsexual,' and even 'homosexual' are sometimes freely and erroneously interchanged.[1032]

Today, under the immense pressure exerted by hegemonic Western culture, *berdache* expressions are much more limited than in the past. Callendar and Kochems claim that *berdache* status still exists in a few societies, more or less covertly, though they also observe that cross-cultural examination of the *berdaches* is sorely deficient.[1033] In all likelihood, the existence of *berdaches* persists to a greater degree than generally recognized. Indeed, in the more accepting climate of modern America the expression may be more visible now than even a couple decades ago when Callendar and Kechums made their observation.

What are some examples among Indian peoples?

American Indians do not comprise a monolithic culture. While there are similarities among various societies such that various attempts have been made to delineate Indian culture in a broad sense, we would do well to focus on discrete societal phenomena while acknowledging that these contribute to a wider sense. So the following examples are best seen as instances within individual tribal societies that in some sense reflect a more-or-less general Indian cultural value, belief, or practice. The examples selected, ranging from the far north to the American Southwest, include some of the most famous and remarked upon researches into the matter, but collectively represent only the tip of a sizable iceberg of study.

Konyagas' Achnutschik

In Alaska, among the Konyagas, an early 19th century Russian explorer observes males of Kodiak Island called *Achnutschik* (or *Achnuchik*), who live a fully transgendered role: they dwell among the women, do work assigned to women, and even have husbands. These individuals are identified early in life. Sometimes this is by virtue of their feminine manner, but it might also happen that parents who hoped for a daughter might likewise purposefully dedicate the child to being *Achnutschik*. This transgendered reality is positively appraised, with men having an *Achnutschik* as wife regarded as fortunate, and the tribe profiting from their spiritual work.[1034]

About these individuals Westermarck makes a brief comment in connection with alleged homosexual practices among the peoples in the vicinity of Behring's Straits. He writes:

> In Kadiak it was the custom for parents who had a girl-like son to dress and rear him as a girl, teaching him only domestic duties, keeping him at woman's work, and letting him associate only with women and girls. Arriving at the age of ten or fifteen years, he was married to some wealthy man and was then called *achnuchik* or *shoopan*.[1035]

This same description, based on a number of authorities, is offered by Sir Richard Burton in an appendix on pederasty at the end of his ten volume translation of *The Arabian Nights* (1885).[1036]

Kootenai Kupalke-tek & Other Plateau Tribes

The Kootenai, a people of the Plateau (Eastern Washington, Northern Idaho, Western Montana, Lower British Columbia), know transgendered people both male and female. One such, born female, we already have encountered. The story of Qánqon is told in the answer to Q. 48.

Male crossdressers among the Kootenai are called *Kupalke-tek* ('woman imitator'). Traditionally, such males never marry. They adopt feminine dress and gender role. According to some, the status follows instruction by the person's spiritual guide to take up the dress and manners of a woman. Ethnohistorian Claude Schaeffer offers as an example a male named Stámmiya ('Acts Like a Woman'), who lived in the latter part of the 19th century. According to Schaeffer's informant, who had known Stámmiya, others expressed a reserved tolerance and refrained from teasing. Catholic priests, who called Stámmiya by the Christian name 'Justine,' tried unsuccessfully to persuade Justine to abandon womanish ways.[1037]

Schaeffer, referencing other scholars, reports instances among a variety of Plateau tribes. The Southern Okanagon, located in north-central Washington State, knew males who dressed as women and pursued feminine occupations. At the same time, there were women who refrained from marriage and took up masculine pursuits such as hunting. Among the Couer d' Alene (northern Idaho), Pend Orielle (northern Idaho), Spokane (eastern Washington), and Flathead (western Montana), transgender males traditionally did not marry and frequently served as shamans and healers. They wore their hair like women, dressed like women, and followed feminine pursuits exclusively. Such persons were believed to have been guided into this way of life by their guardian spirits.[1038]

Mohave Alyha & Hwame

The Mohave (Mojave) people of the American southwest are traditionally associated with the Colorado River, alongside whose banks they dwelled. In their creation mythology, they envision an original state in which human beings were not sexually differentiated. When sex and gender entered the world, they did not do so in a dichotomous fashion. *Berdaches* were regarded as being as legitimately intended as men and women. Indeed, in the first third of the 20th century, anthropologist George Devereux distinguished four genders among the Mohave. They include the *Alyha* and *Hwame*—transgendered people.

The *Alyha* are identified early, before puberty. The family that sees in a child the characteristics of an *Alyha* might then plan a formal initiation ceremony, which serves both to test the youth's true nature and to introduce the child to the community in this new status. This includes a change of name as a feminine one is chosen, and of dress as the new *Alyha* dons a skirt. As adults, the *Alyha* occupy a sexual role like that of women. Consistent with the bias of the times, when a psychoanalytic interpretation of male crossdressing held sway, Devereux sees crossdressing as merely the outer sign of a homosexual orientation. He observes *Alyha* are often flirted with by men, and might even be engaged in formal courtship, though more for fun than seriously. But some men do marry *Alyha*, who are known to make hardworking spouses.[1039]

Devereux also describes female gender crossers called *Hwame*. As is the case with *Alyha*, some *Hwame* become tribal shamans.[1040] Roscoe, following Devereux, notes that *Hwame* exhibit more variability in behavior than their male counterparts. Some, in fact, do not become *Hwame* until after having birthed children.[1041] Perhaps this accounts for why *Hwame* can be described as "like lewd women who also throw away their house-keeping implements, and run wild."[1042]

Whether *Alyha* or *Hwame*, such persons might give hints as to their nature as early as while still in the womb, through dreams their mothers have. As children they differentiate themselves through activities that display preference for the gender role associated with the opposite sex. A tribal informant told Devereux, "When there is a desire in a child's heart to become a transvestite that child will act different. It will let people become aware of that desire. They may insist on giving the child the toys and garments of its true sex, but the child will throw them away and do this every time there is a big gathering."[1043]

Puberty provides the principal challenge. The *Alyha* or *Hwame* continue their preference for gender variant behavior, meet parental efforts to stop such behavior, and only through sheer persistence finally gain acceptance for who they are. The *Alyha* then undergoes an initiation ceremony into the gendered status; no parallel initiation takes place for the *Hwame*. As adults, confirmed in their gender status, they then live in conformity to the expectations associated with it. For *Alyha* that means living a life like that of a woman; the *Hwame* live like men.[1044] The *Alyah* might even go so far as to mimic menstruation and pregnancy.[1045]

Navajo Nádleeh

The Navajo are the largest tribe of North American Indians. They reside principally in Utah, Arizona and New Mexico of the Southwest United States. The Navajo Nation, like other indigenous populations, experienced pressure from encroaching foreign powers, including the Spanish and, later, settlers from the expanding United States. The Euro-American cultural dominance has impacted many aspects of Navajo life, including their conceptions of gender and sexuality.

Carolyn Epple notes that many Navajo see gender as situational in character.[1046] The relative fluidity of gender means traits associated with it are not static and independent but embedded in particular contexts that give rise to the meaning and assignment of 'man' and 'woman.' But Navajo weaver and anthropologist Wesley Thomas contends that when discussing the Navajo conception of gender recognition must be made of distinct periods. Prior to the 1890s, he says, traditional Navajo culture recognized multiple genders. Then, from the 1890s-1930s dramatic changes came about because of Western cultural pressure, especially that exerted by Christianity. Variant genders did not disappear, but in the face of this pressure went underground. Thomas writes that, "The traditional social gender system, although based initially on biological sex, divides people into categories based on several criteria: sex-linked occupation, behaviors, and roles. . . ."[1047]

In traditional Navajo culture a people called *Nádleeh* (or *Nádleehí*, or *Nádleehe*; sing. *Nadle*; 'other,' or 'transformed'), an alternate gender, are recognized alongside 'masculine men' and 'feminine women.' Crossdressing was traditionally associated with *Nádleeh*, at least prior to the 1930s-1940s, when White ridicule acted to curtail it.[1048] In the first third of the 20th century, anthropologist Willard Hill differentiated 'real' *Nádleeh* from 'pretend to be' *Nádleeh* on the basis of whether the person was intersexed or simply crossdressing.[1049] Thomas contests this characterization, arguing that the traditional Navajo view regarded as *Nádleeh* any male who demonstrated feminine gender characteristics. By the time Hill came around, says Thomas, the *Nadle* was already a figure receding into the past. Today the term is retained, but used sparingly and carefully.[1050]

While an emphasis on male *Nádleeh* reflects Euro-American fascination with male crossdressers, a *Nadle* might be biologically male, female, or intersexed. In fact, the *Nádleeh*, remarks anthropologist Lauren Wells Hasten, may be the closest physical manifestation of the Navajo conviction that the cyclical universal ideal is both male and female.[1051] The dual nature ('two-spirit') of the *Nádleeh* is represented in the unexpected disjunction of sex and gender; a male *Nadle* is like a woman in gender, and a female *Nadle* like a man. Accordingly, regardless of birth sex, the *Nadle* dresses like a member of the gender ordinarily associated with the opposite sex.

While an ambiguous genital presentation provides incentive to regard a child as one of the *Nádleeh*, that is not the only causal pathway. Parents might perceive in a child a marked preference for the activities typically associated with the gender paired with the opposite sex. They might then permit the child to grow into that gendered role.[1052] As adults in traditional Navajo society, *Nádleeh* often enjoyed success and Hill observes that families with an unmarried *Nadle* were considered especially fortunate.[1053] As for marriage and sexual relationships, scholars on the matter differ in their judgments. The Western conceptions of heterosexuality and homosexuality prove problematic in this regard.

Teton Dakota Winkte

The Teton Dakota, westernmost of the tribes collectively known as 'Sioux,' are part of the Indian tribal culture most Americans think of first when they recall historic Indian life—nomadic hunters dwelling in tipis (teepees). Likewise, when many people think of transgender Indians they think first of the *Winkte* (short for *Winyanktehca*, 'to be a woman'), often today translated as 'two souls person.'[1054]

Writing in the mid-1960s, anthropologist Royal Hassrick attributes the traditional adoption of this status as a socially acceptable option for those males unable to meet the strict demands of the Sioux warrior society. To become a *Winkte*, then, is an escape from the demands of masculinity in the society. Such males adopt the manner and dress of women. They might take up feminine activities like tanning hides, working beads, or quillwork. Hassrick remarks that some achieve great skill in such things. Others in the tribe hold mixed regard for a *Winkte*. To males such a figure might arouse mild disdain and avoidance, especially in terms of sexual contact. Yet this reaction is tempered by a certain regard for the spiritual status of the *Winkte*, who is believed called to this status. Indeed, Hassrick observes that some become tribal shamans, a role of power and respect.[1055]

Williams, through interviews with Native Americans, records a more contemporaneous perspective on the *Winkte*. They are, especially among the traditionalists, seen as special people with spiritual power. As one young informant puts it, "You never talked disrespectfully about a winkte because it is sacred. Every true winkte has sacred powers, some more, some less. They doctored illnesses and were wakan [sacred]."[1056]

But passing times have brought changes. Today's *Winkte* may dress more androgynously than femininely. For ceremonial purposes they might fully dress as a woman (an act construed as gaining more spiritual power), but otherwise might dress with mixed gender elements, or present in masculine clothing. One 32-year-old self-identified *Winkte* says, "I dress as a man, but I feel feminine and enjoy doing women's things. I would be terribly scared to be considered as a man."[1057] Similarly, today a *Winkte* may pursue a mix of activities associated with masculinity and femininity.

A contemporary *Winkte*, who holds a graduate degree in psychology, Marjorie Anne Napewastewiñ Schützer, tells in a speech to mental health professionals how she came to this status: "I was called through a vision, by 'Anog

Ite', (Double Face Woman) from out of the womb, to be that which I am. She offered me a choice. Lakota deities never order. My gender transformation was called for by the Spirits. She blessed me with skills of a supernatural kind."[1058]

Winkte are identified early in life. A 49-year-old self-identified *Winkte* explains that, "About age twelve, parents will take him to a ceremony to communicate with past winktes who had power, to verify if it is just a phase or a permanent thing for his lifetime."[1059] A spiritual vision guides the calling and once such a calling is confirmed the people accept the person henceforth as *Winkte* and as *wakan*.[1060]

Zuni La'mana

The Zuni, a Pueblo people of the Southwest, found in Colorado and New Mexico, have been the subject of various reports with respect to *berdaches* among them. They use the term *La'mana* ('man-woman') as a broad designation, further distinguishing among them as *ko'thlama* ('male-woman; a male *La'mana*) and *katsotse* ('girl-male' or 'girl-boy'; a female *La'mana*). Anthropologist Elsie Parsons, in a 1916 report, finds only a few among the Zuni and records that, "I got the impression that in general a family would be somewhat ashamed of having a *la'mana* among its members. In regard to the custom itself there seemed to be no reticence in general and no sense of shame."[1061]

Parsons recounts various connections made among the Zuni between the *La'mana* and Zuni mythology. These help provide background for *La'mana* participation in events such as the *ko'thlama* part in the *kia'nakwe* ceremonial dramatic dance.[1062] The path by which one becomes a *La'mana* is varied. Parsons notes that while there is never any external compulsion on a child to become one, in some households short on women a boy might be more readily permitted to become a *La'mana*. Initiation into the role occurs about age 12, when feminine dress is assumed. As adults, some male *La'mana* become wives to Zuni men. Because *La'mana* are neither men nor women per se, a logical question becomes how to deal with burial after death. The Zuni solution is to bury biological male *La'mana* on the men's side of the graveyard, but to dress them in a mix of feminine and masculine apparel.[1063]

Arguably the most renowned *berdache* among American Indians was the Zuni We'wha (pronounced 'WAY-wah'), dubbed by the American press the Zuni 'princess.' This individual, a biological male, was a gendered *La'mana*. At six feet tall, with a muscular build, We'wha cut an imposing figure. Acknowledged among the Zuni as a religious expert, and an accomplished potter and weaver, We'wha became acquainted with the anthropologist Matilda Coxe Stevenson as early as 1879. In 1886, Stevenson brought We'wha to Washington, D.C. Throughout that Spring, We'wha demonstrated Zuni weaving, cooperated with anthropologists at the Smithsonian, and met a variety of politicians, including President Grover Cleveland.[1064]

Q. 60

If it is so common, what role does it play in culture?

The Short Answer. Crossdressing, and the transgendered realities it represents, seems to occur virtually everywhere people make gendered distinctions. By virtue of its relation to gender, we can say that crossdressing offers both an experience and an expression of gender alongside but somewhat outside the basic duality of masculine and feminine. In so doing it offers new ways to be or do gender, and affords an important perspective on masculinity and femininity. Crossdressing also transcends transgender in the sense that not everyone who crossdresses experiences themselves as a transgendered person. Even those who fully identify themselves as masculine or feminine may on occasion utilize crossdressing for one or another reason. Thus crossdressing also fills a cultural role as a vehicle of escape from one's expected and usual gender performance.

The Longer Answer. While a rather large book might be written trying to answer questions about how gender, transgender, and crossdressing fit within culture, we can hardly use the excuse of the immensity of the question to avoid it altogether (and in fact we shall return to the matter at the conclusion of this volume). The ubiquity and persistence of transgender realities like crossdressing suggests that they play some role in culture. Whether that role is as a marginalized phenomenon or an honored one, virtually all cultures have made a place for transgender. Our task here is to see what place transgender might have in culture.

How do gender, transgender, and crossdressing fit into culture?

Across cultures, those who display gender variant characteristics are recognized as such, though the social responses vary widely. Since there is a ceaseless interaction between individuals and society, inevitably each influences the other, shaping self-identities as well as challenging or reinforcing cultural ideas. Any attempt to formulate a specific depiction of the way in which transgender people are the same around the world is doomed to failure. Only one broad generalization can be made: it appears that in every culture there exists some people who do not fit within the dominant genders known everywhere as masculinity and femininity. However different the particular shape of these variant gender expressions, all are recognized within their societies as not fitting the dominant categories—and some response is called for, whether official denial of their existence or celebration of them as an acknowledged 'other' gender.

While some crossdressing variance in different cultures should be expected, sometimes there is remarkable similarity. For instance, while Australia and the United States share roots in Europe, they have each developed distinctive cultures. Yet research into male transvestites in these two societies shows pronounced similarities in the development of their crossdressing behavior and its course.[1065] It would seem that because cultures rely on gendered distinctions in dress to indicate the gender a person belongs to, dress behavior serves as a near universal constant to show gender variance. But while some similarities may be observed, more often they are forced on realities in the interest of making them fit some particular conceptual scheme. Transgender realities, whatever they share in common, remain spectacularly diverse.

Let us turn, then, to a modest agenda: stating something about how gender, transgender, and crossdressing interact, albeit in broad strokes. First, crossdressing provides an easy, convenient, and recognizable way for transgender people to express their distinctive place within a culture's gender scheme. At the same time, as we saw in the first volume of this work, crossdressing enriches the gender experience of transgendered people just as dress does for other gendered people. In every culture, gender matters, dress matters—and something we in the West call transgender exists.

Yet the ways in which these fit into the culture differ. This necessarily results from the fact that cultures have different ways of understanding gender and different values they place upon it. In Western culture it seems a fair contention to claim that gender is central to self-identity, and that the rich possibilities of dress afforded by economic power make dress an especially rich source for individual experience and expression. Some cultures do not tie gender to sex as firmly as ours has, and some do not lend it the personal or social power it holds in ours. In such cultures dress, too, is likely to hold different value and meaning. Even so, crossdressing may be possible as a way to signal a gender crossing—whatever that means in a particular society.

What place do crossdressers occupy in society?

Given the manifold possibilities for how gender, transgender, and dress can interact, the place crossdressers may occupy in a society are multiple. In truth, even within a specific society, whether one with a small population of single ethnicity, or large with many ethnicities, the valuation of a crossdresser can vary.

In part this simply reflects the different ability individual persons have to see the humanity of others regardless of gender or dress. The best among us love and accept others *as they are*, however that might be. Others among us find tolerance difficult, especially where the gender or dress challenges comfortable securities relied upon for one's own self-definition. When enough such individuals exert sufficient social power there will be constraints set upon those who are different.

Yet, somehow, the pattern seems to be *adaptation*. It is not just transgender people who adapt. Cultures are flexible enough to wrap around realities that persist whether they formally sanction them or not. Sociologist H. Taylor Buckner speculates, "Where there are many transvestites in a society, a pattern of societal adaptation may arise wherein transvestites are given a specific job within the culture because there are too many of them to be ignored."[1066] In short, a place is either carved out by the transgendered, or permitted them. If this is so, we might reasonably ask for any given society what the specific job—or tasks—might be assigned to those who regularly cross gender lines, or exist in a separately gendered space.

We have seen in considering both history and geography that some tasks are more often allowed, or forced upon, or seized by the transgendered. Most notably these include various entertainment roles (especially in theater), the sex trade, helping and healing occupations, and religious roles. Yet we would err to suggest there is anything such as a formal 'transgendered occupation' in societies. Instead, transgendered people are mostly granted what leeway they find in staying to tasks and occupations associated with the dominant gender they present like. So transgendered males who crossdress, appearing and presenting femininely, typically seek and obtain work roles consistent with feminine females in their culture.

Gender bifurcation into two clearly dominant genders has always constrained transgender people. As a minority population in every society (with the possible exception of the Amazons!), transgender people lack social power. They are subject to bias, prejudice, and discrimination in patterns familiar to other minorities, whether based, for example, on race or religion. The place in culture they occupy is not one of choice so much as a niche reserved for them by the dominant genders in their power. Sometimes, as we have seen, that is benign or beneficent. But it never has to be and so transgender people are always at risk.

How does crossdressing serve noncrossdressers?

That risk might be alleviated somewhat if noncrossdressers could see any way in which they themselves might be advantaged by crossdressing's existence. The very idea probably seems surprising—crossdressing as a social *benefit*?! So accustomed are many of us in our culture to regard gender variance as bad that the very thought of crossdressing elicits distaste. Many of us tolerate crossdressers—so long as they stay at a distance—but accepting, even celebrating the notion they offer some good to all of us may seem completely absurd. Yet there may be some matters worth considering, and these shall serve in closing this answer. There are at least three dimensions worth exploring:

- how non-transgendered people utilize transgendered experience vicariously;
- how non-transgendered people experiment with transgender experience through occasional situational crossdressing; and,
- how non-transgendered people join with transgendered people in sanctioning crossdressing in certain social contexts.

Vicarious Cross-gender Experience Through Crossdressers

Crossdressers through public crossdressing express in actual practice a secret longing the rest of us experience from time to time. That secret desire is to somehow experience what it might be like to cross a gender line and walk awhile in the shoes of another gender. Men and woman are endlessly fascinated with the presumed differences that separate them. There is a commonly perceived 'gap' between the dominant genders that seems nearly impossible to bridge. Yet crossdressers bridge it.

The fact they do so through dress, and express a gender identity at odds with the one others may expect of them, raises objections. But perhaps, too, it prompts the tiniest of 'What would it be like?' imaginings. These probably are rapidly suppressed because they evoke anxiety. All of us have been subjected to sustained pressures toward gender conformity throughout our lives. We have learned to respond to gender variant feelings in ourselves with programmed rejection. So the prompt offered by obvious crossdressers pushes buttons.

And yet . . . such little instances of exposure crack open those imaginings, however briefly. Perhaps only for an instant they provide opportunity for vicarious experience. Certainly that seems to be in play when we seek out entertainments where we know crossdressing takes place. A significant difference between that and what happens on the street is that we go expecting to see the crossdressing, rather than being caught be surprise, and we diffuse anxiety by reminding ourselves that what we are seeing is merely play—purely for entertainment.

Transgender Experimentation Through Situational Crossdressing

More noncrossdressers than would like to admit it actually do crossdress! They reject the identity of crossdresser, typically hold the behavior in low regard, yet in very narrowly circumscribed situations engage in it. Some do it on occasion as an erotic act of play with a sexual partner. Others do it in order to draw comfort from a lover's clothing in their absence. Some do it for laughs at costume parties, and others try it once just to see what it's like.

There is no compelling reason why such behavior cannot be self-regarded as transgender experimentation. In fact, if it were, imagine how different might the social response become to actual transgendered people. If we could see that even the briefest engagement in crossdressing offers us the possibility of empathy—an imaginative placing of our own self in the experience of some other self—how much more tolerant we might become!

Perspective matters. We may be socially instructed to employ stereotypes to see transgender people, but we can by will and reason challenge those stereotypes. Every act of crossdressing, no matter the motivation or brevity, is an act ripe with potential. Rather than distance it and differentiate it from transgender, as though it had nothing in common, we could choose to find in it a microcosm of a larger universe of experience some of us dwell within all of the time.

Communal Experience in Sanctioned Social Crossdressing

Finally, there are occasions when crossdressers and noncrossdressers form a temporary community in which crossdressing matters and is sanctioned. Throughout history every society that heavily invests itself in keeping the genders separated and in strongly enforcing gender conformity has faced the need to manage the pressures that thereby arise. One important way to do so is through festivals, such as Carnival or Halloween. These times temporarily suspend normal gender conventions in dress and behavior. In permitting gender crossings they act as safety valves, reducing pressure.

The fact is, in our society (and in many others) we experience pressure to gender conform and that pressure produces mounting stress. All of us must find ways to deal with that stress. One such way is crossdressing. Crossdressers utilize it regularly; noncrossdressers may never use it, or may try it only in rare circumstances. But the holidays where crossdressing is sanctioned offer a perfect avenue for those who otherwise might never consider such behavior.

Some crossdressers who otherwise keep their crossdressing secret delight in these periodic opportunities to go out crossdressed in public, free of the fear of censure, or worse, that could befall them at other times. For a time, both crossdressers and noncrossdressers can be relaxed about gender presentation.

We are only left to wonder what the world would look like if we could be thus relaxed all of the time.

Notes

Q. 41 Notes

[1] Plato, *Symposium*, in *The Essential Plato*, translated by B. Jowett, with M. J. Knight (N. Y.: Quality Paperback Book Club, 1999), p. 719.

[2] Ibid. Cf. pp. 719-722. Aristophanes' speech elaborates the rather fantastic nature of these primordial beings, explains how sex and sexual attraction as we know it came to be, and also ventures that what we call sexual orientation is explained by the changes that have taken place since the original human beings. Thus, homosexuality stems from those who have a nature from the original Androgynous ('male-female') humans.

[3] Judith Ochshorn, "Sumer: Gender, Gender Roles, Gender Role Reversals," in S. P. Ramet (Ed.), *Gender reversals and Gender Cultures*, pp. 52-65 (London: Routledge, 1996).

[4] Sabrina Petra Ramet (Ed.), *Gender reversals and Gender Cultures* (London: Routledge, 1996), p. 3.

[5] Ibid, p. 1.

[6] Sextus Empiricus, *Outlines of Pyrrhomism*, ch. XIV. See Jason L. Saunders (Ed.), *Greek and Roman Philosophy After Aristotle* (N. Y.: The Free Press, 1966), p. 179.

[7] Juvenal, *Satires*, II, lines 93-97. Cf. Martial, *Epigrams*, III.lxxxii. On Juvenal and gender, see Barbara K. Gold, "'The House I Live In Is Not My Own': Women's Bodies in Juvenal's Satires," *Arethusa, 31* (no. 3), 369-386 (1998).

[8] Martial, *Epigrams*, III.LXIII.

[9] See "A Hymn to Inana for Iddin-Dagan (Idin-Dagan A)," lines 60-68 (ETCSL Translation: t.2.5.3.1) in Black, Cunningham, Fluckiger-Hawker, Robson, & Zólyomi. Accessed online at http://etcsl.orinst.ox.ac.uk/cgi-bin/etcsl.cgi?text=t.2.5.3.1#. For more on Inana, see the answers to Q. 53 & 76.

[10] Pierre Dufour, *Histoire de la prostitution chez tous les peuples du monde depuis l'antiquité la plus reculée jusqu'à nos jours* (6 vols., Paris, 1851-3; 8 vols., Brussels, 1861).

[11] The observation of Ctesias (from his *Persian History*, III) was preserved by Athenaeus (early 3rd century C.E.); see *The Deipnosophists*, XII, in Charles Burton Gulick (Trans.), *The Deipnosophists of Athenaeus of Naucratis*, vol. V: Books XI-XII (Cambridge: Harvard Univ. Press, 1983 reprint of 1933 ed. [Loeb Classical Library]), p. 529. Cf. Vern L. Bullough & Bonnie Bullough, *Cross Dressing, Sex, and Gender* (Phila.: Univ. of Pennsylvania Press, 1993), p. 23.

[12] Seneca, *Ad Lucilium Epistulae Morales* (*Letters to Lucilius*), vol. II, translated by William Heinemann (Cambridge: Harvard Univ. Press, 1920), Epistle LXVI (p. 35). The Latin context is: "Ut muliercula aut aliquis in mulierculam ex viro versus digitulos meos ducat?"

[13] Maragaret C. Miller, "Reexamining Transvestism in Archaic and Classical Athens: The Zewadski Stamnos," *American Journal of Archaeology, 103* (no. 2), 223-253 (1999). Miller reviews different lines of interpretation for the figures on the objects in question. These include the ideas that the figures are women wearing beards, crossdressed males engaged in religious practices, men crossdressed for some other reason, or men not crossdressed at all though their dress is culturally effeminate.

[14] Eva Cantarella, *Bisexuality in the Ancient World*, translated by C. O. Cuilleanain (New Haven, CT: Yale Univ. Press, 1992), pp.177-179.

[15] A. M. Harmon (Trans.), "The Dance," *Lucian*, vol. 5 (pp. 210-289). Loeb Classical Library (Cambridge: Harvard Univ. Press, 1936), p. 241.

[16] Miller, p. 233, with reference to Martin P. Nilsson, "A Krater in the Cleveland Museum of Art with Men in Women's Attire," *ActaArch, 13*, 226 (1942).

[17] Ibid, p. 244. Miller offers examples of both Macedonians (e.g., Alexander's general Polyperchon) and Greeks (e.g., Polystratus of Athens).

[18] Ibid; quote from Philostratus' *Imagines* 1.2.298 (italics added).

[19] Herodotus, *Histories*, 4.146.1-4. See Herodotus, *The Histories* (Rev. Ed.), translated by Aubrey de Selincourt (N. Y.: Penguin Books, 1972), p. 319.

[20] Licht, p. 500.

[21] Petronius, *The Satyricon*, translated by P. G. Walsh (N. Y.: Oxford Univ. Press, 1999), §81 (p. 69f.).

[22] Vern L. Bullough & Bonnie Bullough, *Cross Dressing, Sex, and Gender* (Phila.: Univ. of Pennsylvania Press, 1993), p. 26.

[23] The customs at Kos (or Cos) and at Argos are mentioned in Plutarch's *Lycurgus*, 15 and *Moralia*, 394 (Kos), and *Quaestiones Graecae*, 304e (Argos).

[24] Plutarch, *Lycurgus* 15, in *The Lives of the Noble Graecians and Romans*, translated by John Dryden (N. Y.: Modern Library, 1932 reprint of 1864 ed.), p. 60.

[25] Monica Cyrino as someone seeing Heracles' act as reaffirming traditional gender categories; see Monica Cyrino, "Heroes in D(u)ress: Transvestism and Power in the Myths of Herakles and Achilles," *Arethusa, 31* (no. 2), 207-241 (1998), p. 211. In reference to this comment, I would prefer the term 'role' to 'identity.'

[26] Pausanias, *Description of Greece*, IV.4.3.

[27] Herodotus, *Histories*, 5.18.1-20.4. See Aubrey de Selincourt's translation, pp. 346-347.

[28] Frontinus, *Stratagems*, 4.7.33. See Charles E. Bennett (Translator), *Frontinus. The Stratagems. The Aqueducts of Rome* [Loeb Classical Library] (Cambridge: Harvard Univ. Press, 1925), p. 324. The full text is available online at the LacusCurtius website. Accessed online at http://penelope.uchicago.edu/Thayer/E/Roman/Texts/Frontinus/Strategemata/4*.html#note123.

[29] Diodorus Siculus, *Library*, 12.16.1-2.

[30] See the discussion in John Boswell, *Same-Sex Unions in Premodern Europe* (N. Y.: Villard Books, 1994), pp. 147-155, especially p. 148. Boswell's translation of the 9th century *Passio antiquior SS. Sergei et Bacchi Graece nunc prima edita* accessed online at http://www.cs.cmu.edu/afs/cs/user/ scotts/ftp/wpaf2mc/serge.html. Cf. the answer to Q. 68.

[31] David D. Leitao, "The Perils of Leukippos: Initiatory Transvestism and Male Gender Ideology in the Ekdusia at Phaistos," *Classical Antiquity, 14*, 130-163 (1995). The Ekdusia was rooted in the story of Leukippos, recounted in the answer to Q. 43.

[32] Miller, p. 243.

[33] Robert Christopher Towneley Parker, "Oschoporia," in S. Hornblower & A. Spawforth (Eds.), *The Oxford Classical Dictionary*, 3rd ed. (N. Y.: Oxford Univ. Press, 1996), p. 1081.

[34] Miller, p. 242, with reference to Plutarch's *Quaestiones Graecae (Greek Questions)*, 58.

[35] Hans Licht, *Sexual Life in Ancient Greece* (London: Abbey Library, 1971 printing of 1932 ed.), p. 125.

³⁶ Ibid, p. 242, with reference especially to the Dionysiac cult.
³⁷ Licht, p. 500.
³⁸ Cf. Edward C. Whitmont, *Return of the Goddess* (N.Y.: Crossroad, 1984).
³⁹ Fritz Graf, "Transvestism, Ritual," in S. Hornblower & A. Spawforth (Eds.), *The Oxford Classical Dictionary*, 3rd ed. (N. Y.: Oxford Univ. Press, 1996), p. 1547.
⁴⁰ Richard L. Gordon, "Eunuchs," in S. Hornblower & A. Spawforth (Eds.), *The Oxford Classical Dictionary*, 3rd ed. (N. Y.: Oxford Univ. Press, 1996), p. 569. Cf. answer to Q. 44.

Eunuch priests of the Syrian Goddess (*Dea Syria*, aka *Atargatis*) are made fun of by Apuleius in *Metamorphosis*, as he recounts what happened when, still in the form of an ass, he was brought by a new owner to a bevy of eunuchs:

> As soon as he reached the threshold, he cried out, 'Girlies, troop up and spy the darling slavelet I've bought you.'
>
> The girls, however, turned out to be a band of eunuchs, who at once began squealing for delight in their splintering harsh womanish voices, thinking that it was really a man brought home trussed to do them good service. . . .
>
> [N]ext day the priesthood went out in a body, gowned in all the colours under the sun and hideously bedizened. Their faces were ruddied with cosmetics and their eyes ringed darkly; they wore little turbans; their linen was saffron-hued; and they were surpliced with silk. Some had donned white tunics covered with purple stripes pointing out every way spear-wise; and the whole mob displayed girdles and yellow shoes.

Excerpted from Apuleius, *Metamorphosis*, VIII, in Jack Lindsay (Trans.), *The Golden Ass by Apuleius* (Bloomington: Indiana Univ. Press, 1962), p. 181.

⁴¹ Jeannine Davis-Kimball, *Warrior Women. An Archaeologist's Search for History's Hidden Heroines* (N. Y.: Warren Books, 2002), p. 180.
⁴² Ibid.
⁴³ Ancient traditions about Attis are not uniform. However, it is clear that [1] the eunuch priests castrated themselves and crossdressed, and [2] the explanation offered for this was emulation of Attis. Among the most famous accounts from classical times about Attis is the Roman poet Catullus' poem #63 ('Attis'); for an online version of the poem, see Thomas J. Sienkewicz, *Catullus*. *"Attis" (#63)*, which has a translation of the poem, including the line uttered by Attis, "Witness me, a girl, a slave of Cybele, dressed like a girlish follower of Bacchus." Accessed online at http://department.monm.edu/classics/Courses/ISSI402/CourseHandouts/Attis.htm.
⁴⁴ Herodotus, *The Histories* (Rev. Ed.), translated by Aubrey de Selincourt (N. Y.: Penguin Books, 1972), pp. 84, 292.
⁴⁵ Davis-Kimball, p. 178. In a footnote on that page she calls attention to two efforts to translate the name 'Enaree': the first, by linguist Martin Schwartz sees the meaning as 'effeminate'; the other, by Martin Huld, views it as meaning 'unmanly.' With reference to the Hippocratic tradition, the treatise *Airs, Waters, Places* (§§20-22) offers a more extended consideration of the Scythian people and the Enaree (or 'Anarieis'). The author, while acknowledging that the Scythians themselves attribute the condition of the Enarees to "a divine visitation," nevertheless opines that their impotence has a natural

cause: a style of horseriding that afflicts them with varicose veins, which poorly treated leads to impotence. Concluding they have sinned against the deity they account responsible for such matters, they "then accept their unmanliness and dress as women, act as women and join with women in their toil" (§22). See J. Chadwick & W. N. Mann (translators), "Airs, Waters, Places," in G. E. R.Lloyd (Ed.), *Hippocratic Writings*, pp. 148-169 (N. Y.: Penguin Books, 1983), p. 166.

[46] Juvenal, *The Satires*, translated by Niall Rudd (N. Y.: Oxford Univ. Press, 1992), Satire 6 (p. 49f.).

Q. 42 Notes

[47] Ovid, *Metamorphoses*, IV.274f.

[48] Ibid, XII.146-209; cf. 429-535. Caenis is a beautiful woman, who catches the eye of the god Neptune. He rapes her, then offers her fulfillment of a wish. Caenis' understandable desire is to never again face such a wrong, so she asks to be made a man. Now Caeneus, he goes on to become a fighting man of renown. The story can be read online in the translation by A. S. Kline (2000), accessed at http://etext.Virginia.edu/latin/ovid/trans/Metamorph12.htm#_Toc486225989.

[49] Ibid, IX.714-719. Iphis' mother lies to her father that the child is a boy, because the father intends to expose the child if it is female. Iphis is raised as a boy, and grows up to fall in love with her arranged betrothed, the maiden Ianthe. The goddess Isis comes to the rescue, transforming Iphis into a male. The story can be read online in the translation by A. S. Kline (2000), accessed at http://etext.virginia.edu/latin/ovid/trans/Metamorph9.htm#_Toc483366552.

[50] Statius, *Achilleid*, 1.161-583. See Peter Heslin, *The Transvestite Achilles: Gender and Genre in Statius' "Achilleid"* (N. Y.: Cambridge Univ. Press, 2005).

[51] Ovid, *Metamorphoses*, XVIII.163-169, in Rolfe Humphries (Trans.), *Ovid's Metamorphoses* (Bloomington: Indiana Univ. Press, 1963), p. 310f. Cf. Ovid, *Ars Amatoria*, 1.681-704.

[52] See Apollodorus, *Library* 2.5.9. Translation by Sir James George Frazier, *Apollodrus. The Library*, 2 vols. (Cambridge: Harvard Univ. Press, 1921), vol. 1, p. 204. Cf. the comment in Strabo, *Geographica (Geography)* 11.5.1: "the right breasts of all are seared when they are infants, so that they can easily use their right arm for every needed purpose, and especially that of throwing the javelin; that they also use bow and sagaris and light shield. . . ." Translation by H. C. Hamilton & W. Falconer, *Strabo. The Geography of Strabo* (Cambridge: Harvard Univ. Press, 1924), vol. 5, p. 236.

[53] Jeannine Davis-Kimball, *Warrior Women. An Archaeologist's Search for History's Hidden Heroines* (N. Y.: Warren Books, 2002), p. 115.

[54] In the classical literature, see Homer, *The Iliad* 3.189, 6.186, and elsewhere for their involvement in the Trojan war; see Apollodorus, *Epitome* 5.1,2, Ovid, *Heroides* 21.118 and Diodorus Siculus, *Bibliotheke (Library)* 2.46 for more on Queen Penthesilea, whom Achilles kills, then falls in love with; see Apollodorus, *Bibliotheke (Library)* 4.16 for the account of Heracles' 9th labor, which is the taking of the Amazon Queen Hippolyte's girdle; see Plutarch, *Theseus* 26-27 for that hero's interactions with the Amazons, especially their leader Antiope; see Diodorus Siculus, *Bibliotheke* 17.77, and Plutarch, *Alexander* 46 for the legends of his involvement. These represent only a few of the many places where the Amazons are talked about.

⁵⁵ *Mahabharata*, Bk. 5, §CXCI, translated by Kisari Mohan Ganguli, *The Mahabharata of Krishna-Dwaipayana Vyasa*, (Calcutta: Bharata Press, 1883-1896), Bk. 5, p. 364. Accessed online at the Internet Sacred Text Archive website, at http://www.sacred-texts.com/hin/m05/m05191.htm.

⁵⁶ *Mahabharata*, Bk. 6, Bhishma Parva (especially §§CXIXff.). See the translation by Kisari Mohan Ganguli, accessed online at the Internet Sacred Text Archive website, at http://www.sacred-texts.com/hin/m06/m06119.htm. The complete text of the *Mahabharata* is available online and was accessed at http://www.sacred-texts.com/hin/maha/index.htm.

⁵⁷ Antoninus Liberalis, *Metamorphoseon Synagoge*, 13.

⁵⁸ See Kisari Mohan Ganguli (Translator), *Mahabharata*, Book IV: *Virata Parva* §§15-22. This translation of the *Mahabharata* completed 1883-1896. Text accessed online at http://www.sacred-texts.com/hin/m04/index.htm.

⁵⁹ Nicole Loraux, "Herakles: The Super-Male and the Feminine," in D.M. Halperin, J. J. Winkler, & F. I. Zeitlin (Eds.), *Before Sexuality: The Construction of Erotic Experience in the Ancient Greek World*, pp. 21-52 (Princeton: Princeton Univ. Press, 1990), p. 39. Loraux (p. 24) sees as an inherent contradiction in Herakles "the virile and the feminine."

⁶⁰ See Monica Cyrino, "Heroes in D(u)ress: Transvestism and Power in the Myths of Herakles and Achilles," *Arethusa*, 31 (no. 2), 207-241 (1998), p. 217.

⁶¹ Apollodorus, *Library*, 2.6.2-3. Cf. Sophocles, *Trachiniae*, lines 250, 355.

⁶² Ovid, *Heroides*, IX.153ff. in Harold Isbell (Trans.), *Ovid. Heroides* (N. Y.: Penguin Books, 1990), p. 79. Robert Bell has expressed the opinion that Omphale "bought Heracles as a sexual object, not as a servant. In a way she seemed to be evening the score with her husband by abasing Heracles, making him spin wool and dress in her clothes while she strode around in his lion's skin." Robert E. Bell, *Women of Classical Mythology* (N. Y.: Oxford Univ. Press, 1991), p. 382.

Also see Ovid, *Fasti*, 2.303-358, esp. 320-325. If anything, the depiction here is more lurid. The delicateness of the fine purple woman's tunic is emphasized, along with the softness of the belt Omphale had been wearing before it tried, in vain, to encircle Heracles. Likewise, her bracelets and slippers are too small for him. All this is set in an explicitly erotic context. In the darkness, groping for the softness of women's clothing, the lusty god Faunus instead finds Heracles, who dethrones him with a blow.

⁶³ Propertius, *Elegies*, 4.9.47-50. See Guy Lee (Translator), *Propertius. The Elegies* (N. Y.: Oxford Univ. Press, 1996), p. 125.

⁶⁴ Tara S. Welch, "Masculinity and Monuments in Propertius 4.9," *American Journal of Philology, 125*, 61-90 (2004), p. 61f. Welch refers to Micaela Janan as viewing Heracles' crossdressing as confounding traditional gender categories; see Micaela Janan, "Refashioning Hercules: Propertius 4.9," *Helios, 25*, 65-77 (1998). Welch points to Monica Cyrino as someone seeing Heracles' act as reaffirming traditional gender categories. Also see Matthew Fox, "Transvestite Hercules at Rome," in R. Cleminson & M. Allison (Eds.), *In/visibility: Gender and Representation in a European Context*, pp. 1-21 (Bradford: Univ. of Bradford Press, 1998). Also see Sara Lindheim, "Hercules Cross-Dressed, Hercules Undressed: Unmasking the Construction of the Propertian *Amator* in Elegy 4.9," *American Journal of Philology, 119*, 43-66 (1998).

⁶⁵ Cyrino, p. 215.

⁶⁶ The quoted material is taken from *The Saga of Hervör and Heithrek*, in Nora Kershaw, *Stories and Ballads of the Far Past*, (Cambridge: Cambridge Univ. Press, 1921), pp. 93 (ch. 4). Accessed online at http://www.home.ix.netcom.com/%7Ekyamazak/myth/norse/kershaw/Kershaw1s-hervor-and-heithrek.htm.

⁶⁷ Ibid, p. 101 (ch. VI).

⁶⁸ Ibid.

⁶⁹ Ibid, p. 113 (ch.X).

⁷⁰ Exposure of infants, especially daughters, remains a practice even today. Especially among the most impoverished child exposure was and is a means of practicing birth control *post facto* as a means to safeguard the family against starvation.

⁷¹ Antoninus Liberalis, *Metamorphoseon Synagoge*, 17 (offering a paraphrase of Nicander's earlier account in his *Metamorphoses*, 45).

⁷² Hans Licht, *Sexual Life in Ancient Greece* (London: Abbey Library, 1971 printing of 1932 ed.), p. 127f.

⁷³ Pausanias, *Description of Greece*, 8.20.2-4.

⁷⁴ Gaius Julius Hyginus, *Hygini Fabulae*, 190. Accessed online at the Theoi Project website, at http://www.theoi.com/Text/HyginusFabulae4.html. The translation at this site from Mary Grant, *The Myths of Hyginus* (Lawrence: Univ. of Kansas Press, 1960). This particular tale has themes common to many other stories, including some recounted in the material on crossdressing Christian saints (see the answer to Q. 68).

⁷⁵ Andrew L. Brown, "Odysseus," in S. Hornblower & A. Spawforth (Eds.), *The Oxford Classical Dictionary*, 3ʳᵈ ed. (N. Y.: Oxford Univ. Press, 1996), p. 1060f.

⁷⁶ Homer, *The Odyssey*, 5.333-353. The translation by Samuel Butler accessed online at http://classics.mit.edu/Homer/odyssey.5.v.html.

⁷⁷ Dianna Rhyan Kardulias, "Odysseus in Ino's Veil: Feminine Headdress and the Hero in *Odyssey 5*," *Transactions of the American Philological Association*, *131*, 23-51 (2001), p. 26.

⁷⁸ Ibid, p. 26 n. 10. On Athena, see the answer to Q. 76.

⁷⁹ Euripides, *Bacchae* (*Bacchanals*). Variations of the legend are found in other sources, such as Ovid's *Metamorphosis*, III.712ff., and the story is alluded to in various sources as well, such as Propertius' *Elegies*, 3.17.24.

⁸⁰ Pausanias, *Description of Greece*, 1.19.1. Typically, a man's tunic was shorter and his hair not done up; it is not entirely clear from the text whether the workmen really thought Theseus was a woman or whether they were mocking someone they saw as an effeminate male. (For an accessible account of this and other incidents concerning Theseus referred to in this answer, see Robert Graves, *The Greek Myths*, vol. 1 (London: The Folio Society, 1996), pp. 309ff.)

⁸¹ Plutarch, *Life of Theseus*, 23.2. See Plutarch, *The Lives of the Noble Grecians and Romans*, translated by J. Dreyden, revised by H. Clough (N. Y.: Modern Library, 1932 reprint of 1864 revision of 1686 Dreyden translation), p. 14f.

⁸² Plutarch, *Life of Theseus*, 23.2-3. See Karim W. Arafat, "Theseus," in S. Hornblower & A. Spawforth (Eds.), *The Oxford Classical Dictionary*, 3ʳᵈ ed. (N. Y.: Oxford Univ. Press, 1996), pp. 1508-1509.

⁸³Plutarch, *Life of Theseus*, 20.1. The translation is A. H. Clough's revision of Dreyden, p. 13. The word translated 'youth' is the Greek νεανισκος, 'a young man.'

⁸⁴ Hesiod, *Melampodia*, 2, 3. Especially see Ovid, *Metamorphosis*, III.316ff.

⁸⁵ Apollodorus, *Library*, 3.6.7; cf. 3.7.3-4.
⁸⁶ Sophocles, *Oedipus the King*, lines 300-460.
⁸⁷ Homer, *The Odyssey*, 11.90.

Q. 43 Notes

⁸⁸ Caroline Seawright, *Hatsheput, Female Pharoah of Egypt.* Accessed online at http://www.touregypt.net/historicalessays/hatshepsut.htm. For more on Hatsheput, see Catherine M. Andronik, *Hatsheput, His Majesty, Herself* (N. Y.: Atheneum, 2001), or see a somewhat different perspective by archaeologist Joyce A. Tyldesley, *Hatchepsut: The Female Pharoah* (N. Y.: Penguin, 1998; orig. work published 1996). Cf. Vern L. Bullough, *Sexual Variance in Society and History* (N. Y.: John Wiley & Sons, 1976), p. 66.

Queen Nefertiti, 18ᵗʰ Dynasty mate of Pharaoh Akhenaten and mother of Tutankhamun, is claimed by archaeologist Joann Fletcher also to have put on the false beard and regalia of the pharaoh and ruled after Akhenaten's death under the name of 'Smenkhare.' See Joann Fletcher, *The Search for Nefertiti* (N. Y.: William Morrow, 2004).

⁸⁹ Juvenal, *Sixteen Satires*, translated by Peter Green (N. Y.: Penguin Books, 1974), Satire VI (p. 139). Cf. Suetonius, "Life of Caesar," §6, in Robert Graves (Trans.), *Suetonius. The Twelve Caesars* (N. Y.: Penguin Books, 1989 reprint of 1979 rev. ed.), p. 15.

⁹⁰ For a full treatment, see A. A. Barrett, *Caligula, The Corruption of Power* (London: B.T. Batsford Ltd., 1989). On Venus (Aphrodite) and Diana (Artemis) as androgynous deities, see the answer to Q. 76.

⁹¹ Suetonius, "Life of Gaius," §52, in Robert Graves (Trans.), *Suetonius. The Twelve Caesars* (N. Y.: Penguin Books, 1989 reprint of 1979 rev. ed.), p. 179f.

⁹² Cassius Dio, *Roman History*, LIX.26.6-8, in Earnest Cary (Trans.), *Dio's Roman History*, VII (Cambridge: Harvard Univ. Press, 2000 reprint of 1924 ed. [Loeb Classical Library]), p. 347. The *thyrsus* was a wand wreathed in ivy and vine leaves, with a pine cone at its top; it was borne by devotees of the god Dionysius.

⁹³ Cassius Dio, *Roman History*, LXIII.9.1-4, in Earnest Cary (Trans.), *Dio's Roman History*, VIII (Cambridge: Harvard Univ. Press, 1995 reprint of 1925 ed. [Loeb Classical Library]), p. 151f.

⁹⁴ Suetonius, "Life of Nero," §28, in Robert Graves (Trans.), *Suetonius. The Twelve Caesars* (N. Y.: Penguin Books, 1989 reprint of 1979 rev. ed.), p. 228. Cf. Cassius Dio, *Roman History*, LXII.28.3, in Earnest Cary (Trans.), *Dio's Roman History*, VIII (Cambridge: Harvard Univ. Press, 1995 reprint of 1925 ed. [Loeb Classical Library]), p. 137; cf. LXIII.13.1-2 (p. 159).

⁹⁵ Tacitus, *Annals* XV.37 in Michael Grant (Trans.), *Tacitus. The Annals of Imperial Rome*, rev. ed. (N. Y.: Penguin Books, 1989), p. 362.

⁹⁶ Dio, *Roman History*, LXII.13.2 (Cary, p. 159).

⁹⁷ Suetonius, "Life of Nero," §51 (Graves, p. 244). On silk: "Silk dresses (*holoserica*) and half-silk dresses (*subserica*) began to be worn by ladies about the end of the Republic; under the Empire they were even adopted by men, notwithstanding the prohibitory law of Titus." E. Guhl & W. Koner, *The Romans. Their Life and Customs* (London: Senate, 1994), p. 485.

⁹⁸ Dio, *Roman History*, LXIII.13.3 (Cary, p. 159f.).

⁹⁹ Suetonius, "Life of Nero," §49 (Graves, p. 243).

¹⁰⁰ Scriptores Historiae Augustae, *Commodus Antoninus IX.6*, in David Magie (trans.), Scriptores Historiae Augustae, *vol. 1* (Cambridge: Harvard Univ. Press, 1991 reprint of 1921 ed. *[Loeb Classical Library]*), *p. 289*.

¹⁰¹ Ibid, Commodus Antoninus XI.9 (p. 293).

¹⁰² Edward Gibbon, *The Decline and Fall of the Roman Empire*, vol. 1 (London: The Folio Society, 1983; original work published 1776), p. 148.

¹⁰³ Cassius Dio, *Roman History*, LXXX.6.2, in Earnest Cary (Trans.), *Dio's Roman History*, IX (Cambridge: Harvard Univ. Press, 1982 reprint of 1927 ed. [Loeb Classical Library]), p. 451.

¹⁰⁴ Ibid, LXXX.13.2-4 (p. 463), and LXXX.14.4. Cf. Herodian, *History of the Roman Empire* V.ii.9; cf. V.v.3-5.

¹⁰⁵ Ibid, LXXX.16.5 (p. 469).

¹⁰⁶ Ibid, LXXX.16.7 (p. 471); cf. Herodian.

Q. 44 Notes

¹⁰⁷ Lesley Ferris (Ed.), *Crossing the Stage: Controversies on Cross-Dressing* (N.Y.: Routledge, 1993).

¹⁰⁸ For a comprehensive introduction to Indian theater, see Iravati, *Performing Artistes in Ancient India* (New Delhi: D. K. Printworld, 2003).

¹⁰⁹ For more, see Martha Bush Aston, "Yakshagana, a South Indian Folk Theatre," *The Drama Review: TDR, 13* (no. 3), 148-155 (1969). For a longer, more recent treatment, see Martha Bush Ashton & Bruce Christie, *Yakshagana: A Dance Drama of India* (New Delhi: Abhinav Publications, 1977).

¹¹⁰ John Campbell Oman, *The Great Indian Epics. The Stories of the Ramayana and the Mahabharata* (London: George Bell & Sons, 1994 reprint of 1894 ed.), p. 72.

¹¹¹ Ibid, p. 73.

¹¹² For a comprehensive introduction to Chinese theater, see Colin Mackerras, *Chinese Theater from Its Origins to the Present Day* (Honolulu: Univ. of Hawaii Press, 1983). Cf. Faye Chunfang Fei (Ed. & Trans.), *Chinese Theories of Theater and Performance from Confucius to the Present* (Ann Arbor, MI: Univ. of Michigan Press, 1999). Also cf. S. L. Li, *Gender, Cross-Dressing and Chinese Theatre* (Univ. of Massachusetts: PhD dissertation, 1995).

¹¹³ See Zuyan Zhou, *Androgyny in Late Ming and Early Qing Literature* (Honolulu: Univ. of Hawaii Press, 2003), p. 279 n. 6. Also see Wilt Idema & Beata Grant, *The Red Brush: Writing Women of Imperial China* (Cambridge: Harvard Univ. Press, 2004), pp. 677-684.

¹¹⁴ See S. Volpe, "Gender, Power and Spectacle in Late-Imperial Chinese Theater," in S. Ramet (Ed.), *Gender Reversals and Gender Cultures*, ch. 9 (London: Routledge, 1996).

¹¹⁵ Chou Hui-ling, "Striking Their Own Poses: The History of Cross-Dressing on the Chinese Stage," *TDR: The Drama Review*, 41 (no. 2), 130-153 (1997). Hui-ling places simultaneous appearances of men-dressed-as-women alongside women-dressed-as-men on stage in the Yuan Dynasty (1271-1368).

¹¹⁶ Yufu Huang, "The Changes in Chinese Women's Social Status As Seen Through Peking Opera (1790-1937)," *Ford Foundation Report* (2003, Spring). Accessed online at http://www.fordfound.org/ publications/ff_Report/view_ff_report_detail.cfm?report_index=399.

¹¹⁷ Yvonne Shang, "For Art's Sake," *Shanghai Star* (2002, June 6). Accessed online at http://app1.chinadaily.com.cn/star/2002/0606/fo6-1.html.

118 *People: Mao Weitao and Her Yueju Opera Dream* (2005). Accessed online at the China Economic Net website, at http://en.ce.cn/Life/entertainment/people/EP Groups/EPGArtist/ 200501/21/t20050121_2954844.shtml.

119 For a comprehensive introduction to Japanese theater, see Benito Ortolani, *The Japanese Theatre: From Shamanistic Ritual to Contemporary Pluralism* (Princeton: Princeton Univ. Press, 1995). For *Shirabyōshi* see Chapter V. An especially interesting volume to consider is Minoru Fujita & Michael Shapiro (Eds.), *Transvestism and the Onnagata Traditions in Shakespeare and Kabuki* (Kent, UK: Global Oriental Publishers, 2005).

120 Royall Tyler (Ed. & Trans.), *Nō Dramas* (N. Y.: Penguin Books, 1992), p. 88 n. 10.

121 Ibid, p. 7.

122 Lewis Crompton, *Homosexuality & Civilization* (Cambridge: Belknap Press of Harvard Univ. Press, 2003), p. 424.

123 Yoshiro Hatano & Tsuguo Shimazaki, "Japan," in R. T. Francoeur (Ed.), *The International Encyclopedia of Sexuality*, Vols. I-III (N. Y.: Continuum, 1997). Accessed online at http://www2.rz.hu-berlin.de/sexology/GESUND/ARCHIV/IES/JAPAN.HTM#7. %20GENDER%20CONFLICTED%20PERSONS. See §7. Gender Conflicted Persons.

124 Crompton, p. 424.

125 For more on Takarazuka theater, see Jennifer Robertson, *Takarazuka: Sexual Politics and Popular Culture in Modern Japan* (Berkeley: Univ. of California Press, 1998). An anthropologist, Robertson explores how this theater company affords access to larger questions about how modern Japanese understand and express sex and gender.

126 Mark Schilling, "The Rose of Versailles," in M. Schilling, *The Encyclopedia of Japanese Pop Culture*, pp. 206-209 (Trumball, CT: Weatherhill, Inc., 1997).

127 Peter A. Jackson, "Performative Genders, Perverse Desires: A Bio-History of Thailand's Same-Sex and Transgender Cultures," *Intersections: Gender, History and Culture in the Asian Context*, Issue 9 (2003), §74. Accessed online at http://wwwsshe.murdoch.edu.au/intersections/issue9/jackson.html.

128 Kalissa Alexeyeff, "Dragging Drag: The Performance of Gender and Sexuality in the Cook Islands," *The Australian Journal of Anthropology*, 11 (no. 3), 297-307 (2000).

129 Although it is conventional to say that males played all the parts, there is room to doubt that absolute claim. Some scholars think women had some involvement in Greek theater and clearly they were involved at least in the lower brow entertainments of the Roman world. On the debate with reference to Greek theater, see Z. Philip Ambrose, "Did Women Sing in the Thesmophoriazusae?" *Didakalia*, 1 (no. 6: Supplement) (1995). Accessed online at http://didaskalia.open.ac.uk/issues/supplement1/Ambrose.html.

130 Alan H. Sommerstein (Trans.), *Aristophanes. The Acharnians, The Clouds, Lysistrata* (N. Y.: Penguin Books, 1973), p. 23. On crossdressing in ancient Greek theater, see S. Case, "Classic Drag: The Greek Creation of Female Parts," *Theatre Journal*, 37, 317-327 (1985). Cf. Lesley Ferris, "Cross-Dressing: The Greeks and the Wily Phallus," in L. Ferris (ed.), *Acting Women: Images of Women in Theatre*, pp. 20-30 (N. Y.: New York Univ. Press, 1989).

131 Juvenal, *Sixteen Satires*, translated by Peter Green (N. Y.: Penguin Books, 1974), Satire III (p. 90).

¹³² Ambrose, "Did Women Sing in the Thesmophoriazusae?" Cf. John J. Winkler, "The Ephebes' Song: Tragoida and Polis," *Representations, 11*, 26-62 (1985).

¹³³ Sue-Ellen Case, "Classic Drag: The Greek Creation of Female Parts," *Theatre Journal, 37*, 317-327 (1985), p. 318.

¹³⁴ Froma I. Zeitlin, *Playing the Other. Essays on Gender and Society in Classical Greek Literature* (Chicago: Univ. of Chicago Press, 1996).

¹³⁵ Froma I. Zeitlin, "Travesties of Gender and Genre in Aristophanes' *Thesmophoriazouae*," in Helene Foley (Ed.), *Reflections of Women in Antiquity*, pp. 169-217. (Phila.: Gordon and Breach Science Publishers, 1981).

¹³⁶ Nancy Sorkin Rabinowitz, "The Male Actor of Greek Tragedy: Evidence of Misogyny or Gender-Bending?" *Didakalia, 1* (no. 6: Supplement 1) (1995). Accessed online at http://didaskalia.open.ac.uk/issues/supplement1/Rabinowitz.html.

¹³⁷ The three day festival was in honor of Demeter and excluded men; its secrets have remained largely unreveaded. The mythic story at the heart of the festival concerns Demeter's reclaiming of her abducted daughter Persephone from Hades.

¹³⁸ Aristophanes, *The Women at the Thesmophoria*, translated by Eugene O'Neill, Jr. in *The Complete Greek Drama*, vol. 2 (N. Y.: Random House, 1938); see lines 85-94. The full text of the play is available at the Internet Classic Archive. Accessed online at http://classics.mit.edu/Aristophanes/thesmoph.html. The Greek text and the same English translation are available through the Perseus Project, accessed online at http://www.perseus.tufts.edu.

¹³⁹ Ibid, lines 191-192.

¹⁴⁰ Ibid, lines 145ff. Agathon (lines 154ff.) also declares that, "What we don't possess by nature, we must acquire by imitation."

¹⁴¹ Although the character of Euripides does not appear onstage in woman's guise, one of his ploys is, from offstage, to mimic the nymph Echo.

¹⁴² Lauren K. Taafe, *Aristophanes and Women* (N. Y.: Routledge, 1993).

¹⁴³ Angeliki Tzanetou, "Something to Do with Demeter: Ritual and Performance in Aristophanes' *Women at the Thesmophoria*," *American Journal of Philology, 123* (no. 3), 329-367 (2002), p. 330.

¹⁴⁴ Ibid, p. 331.

¹⁴⁵ Pamela R. Bleisch, "Plautine Travesties of Gender and Genre: Transvestism and Tragicomedy in *Amphitruo*," *Didaskalia, 6* (no. 1) (1997). Accessed online at http://didaskalia.open.ac.uk/issues/vol4no1/bleisch.html.

¹⁴⁶ Ibid. For a translation of the play, see E. F. Watling (Trans.), *Plautus. The Rope, Amphitryo, The Ghost, A Three-Dollar Day* (N. Y.: Penguin Books, 1981 reprint of 1964 ed.), pp. 223-284.

¹⁴⁷ Terrence, *The Eunuch*, lines 356-358, in Betty Radice (Trans.), *Terrence. The Comedies* (N.Y.: Penguin Books, 1982 reprint of 1976 ed.), p. 180.

¹⁴⁸ Ibid, lines 378ff. (p. 181).

¹⁴⁹ Something was distinctive about the eunuch's garb. Unfortunately, much more is *not* known about the dress of eunuchs than is known. Part of the problem lies with how eunuchs were regarded. Sometimes they seem to be viewed as effeminate males, other times as female, and still others as a third gender. Regardless, there is little doubt that some eunuchs dressed in feminine clothes. See Arthur Darby Knock, "Eunuchs in

Ancient Religion," *Archiv für Religionswissenschaft, 23*, 25-33 (1925-1926). Accessed online at http://www.inoohr.org/eunuchsinancientreligions.htm.

150 Robert L. A. Clark & Claire Sponsler, "Queer Play: The Cultural Work of Crossdressing in Medieval Drama," *New Literary History, 28* (no. 2), 319-344 (1997). On crossdressing in the Medieval Mystery plays, see Meg Twycross, "'Transvestism' in the Mystery Plays," *Medieval English Theatre, 5*, 123-180 (1983).

151 Ibid, pp. 324-325. In the *Miracle de la fille d'un roy*, Ysabel's prowess as a knight wins the emperor's attention and approval, rewarding Ysabel with his daughter to wed. Of course, on the wedding night the truth comes out, though the emperor's daughter pledges to keep the secret. Unfortunately, a monk has discovered the secret and conveys it to a doubting emperor, who orders the couple to take a ceremonial bath in his presence. With divine interevention, when Ysabel disrobes a male body is seen. But this puts the monk in peril, so Ysabel reveals the truth to save his life. The play resolves matters by having the emperor wed Ysabel and his daughter is married to Ysabel's father.

152 Ibid, p. 327.

153 Ibid, pp. 337-339.

154 Steven K. Wright, "Joseph as Mother, Jutta as Pope: Gender and Transgression in Medieval German Drama," *Theatre Journal 51* (no. 2), 149-166 (1999), p. 150.

155 Helgi T. Daggson, William Conrad Karpen, & Eric Wodening, "Chapter XVII. Fro Ing (Freyr, Engus, Fraujaz Ingwaz)," *Our Troth* (2002). Accessed online at http://www.thetroth.org/resources/ ourtroth/freyr.html. Also see Alan Brody, *The English Mummers and Their Plays: Traces of Ancient Mystery* (Phila.: Univ. of Pennsylvania Press, 1970).

156 Consider, for example, the following: Lesley Ferris (Ed.), *Crossing the Stage: Controversies on Cross-Dressing* (N.Y.: Routledge, 1993). Jean E. Howard, *The Stage and Social Struggle in Early Modern England* (N. Y.: Routledge, 1994). Laura Levine, *Men in Women's Clothing: Anti-Theatricality and Effeminization 1579-1642* (Cambridge: Cambridge Univ. Press, 1994). Stephen Orgel, *Impersonations: The Performance of Gender in Shakespeare's England* (Cambridge: Cambridge Univ. Press, 1996).

157 Shasta Turner, "Disordered Subjects: Female Cross-Dressing and Sumptuary Regulation in Early Modern England," (1998). Accessed online at http://www. majorweather.com/projects/000040.html. A version of this paper was originally presented as part of the 1998 Huntington Library Graduate Seminars in Early Modern British History.

158 Laura Levine, *Men in Women's Clothing: Anti-theatricality and Effeminization, 1579-1642* (N.Y.: Cambridge Univ. Press, 1994).

159 Adapted to modernize the language and punctuation. Cf. the copy of the play at *Ben Jonson Page*, accessed online at http://www.hollowaypages.com/jonson1692 bartholmew.htm . The opening volley by Busy comes from Deuteronomy 22:5 (see the answer to Q. 61).

160 The play has been made available online as an Etext (PDF) by *Project Gutenberg*. Accessed online at *Manybooks.net* at http://manybooks.net/titles/jonsonbeetext03eotsw10.html.

161 Michael Shapiro, *Gender in Play on the Shakespearean Stage: Boy Heroines and Female Pages* (Ann Arbor: Univ. of Michigan Press, 1994). Cf. H. H. Chang, *Transvestite*

Sub/Versions: Power, Performance, and Seduction in Shakespeare's Comedies (Univ. of Michigan: PhD dissertation, 1990).

[162] See Casey Charles, "Gender Trouble in *Twelfth Night*," *Theatre Journal, 49* (no. 2), 121-141 (1997). The issues involved with Shakespeare are too involved to be treated here. A good starting point may be had with Catherine M. S. Alexander & Stanley Wells (Eds.), *Shakespeare and Sexuality* (N. Y.: Cambridge Univ. Press, 2001). On matters related to crossdressing, see the brief review of literature provided in chapter 1: Ann Thompson, "Shakespeare and Sexuality," pp. 1-13.

[163] Peter Berek, "Cross-Dressing, Gender, and Absolutism in the Beaumont and Fletcher Plays," *Studies in English Literature 1500-1900, 44* (no. 2), 359-377 (2004), p. 360. For the plays of Beaumont and Fletcher, see Francis Beaumont & John Fletcher, *Comedies and Tragedies* (London, 1647).

[164] See G. G. Bolich, *Conversing on Gender. A Primer for Entering Dialog* (Raleigh, NC: Psyche's Press, 2007), chapter 5 (pp. 83-103), for a discussion of the relation of gender to politics and power.

[165] Derval Conroy, "The Cultural Politics of Disguise: Female Cross-Dressing in Tragi-Comedy (1630-1642)," *Seventeenth-Century French Studies, 24*, 135-149 (2002).

[166] Mary Frith (Moll Cutpurse) is considered in the answer to Q. 48.

[167] Mary Beth Rose, "Women in Men's Clothing: Apparel and Social Stability in *The Roaring Girl*," *English Literary Renaissance, 14* (no. 3), 367-391 (1984). For a decidedly different interpretation see Susan Krantz, "The Sexual Identities of Moll Cutpurse in Dekker and Middleton's *The Roaring Girl* and in London," *Renaissance and Reformation/Renaissance et Reforme, 19* (no. 1), (1995).

[168] Jean I. Marsden, "Modesty Unshackled: Dorothy Jordan and the Dangers of Cross-Dressing," *Studies in Eighteenth-Century Culture, 22* (no. 1), 21-35 (1999).

[169] David A. Boxwell, "The Follies of War: Cross-Dressing and Popular Theatre on the British Front Lines, 1914-1918," *Modernism/Modernity, 9* (no 1), 1-20 (2002), p. 2. Boxwell cites Fuller's observation that many soldiers preferred watching their comrades-in-arms in drag to viewing touring female performers. See J. G. Fuller, *Troop Morale and Popular Culture in the British and Dominion Armies, 1914-1918* (N. Y.: Oxford Univ. Press, 1990), p. 106.

[170] Ibid, p. 13f.

[171] Alon Rachamimov, "The Disruptive Comforts of Drag: (Trans)Gender Performances Among Prisoners of War in Russia, 1914-1920," *The American Historical Review, 111* (no. 2), 362-382 (2006).

[172] See, for example, Laurel Halladay, "A Lovely War: Male to Female Cross-Dressing and Canadian Military Entertainment in World War II," *Journal of Homosexuality, 46* (nos. 3-4), 19-34 (2004).

[173] See Adele Seeff, "Recovering the History of the African Theatre," *Quarterly Bulletin of the National Library of South Africa, 58* (no. 3), 159-167 (2004), p.163.

[174] Juliana Azoubel, "The Cote d'Ivoire Mask Tradition from the Viewpoint of Dance Ethnology: Dancing the Gap Between Spirit and Human Worlds," *Journal of Undergraduate Research, 1* (no. 6) (2000). Accessed online at http://www.clas.ufl.edu/CLAS/jur/0003/papers/paper_azoubel.html.

[175] Kathleen DeGrave, *Swindler, Spy, Rebel. The Confidence Woman in Nineteenth Century America* (Columbia, MO: Univ. of Missouri Press, 1995), p. 120.

176 Pamela Brown Leavitt, "First of the Red Hot Mamas: 'Coon Shouting' and the Jewish Ziegfeld Girl," *American Jewish History, 87* (no. 4), 253-290 (1999), p. 255.

177 Cushman had an extensive female following, but drew decidedly mixed reviews from most men. See Etsuko Taketani, "Spectacular Child Bodies: The Sexual Politics of Cross-Dressing and Calisthenics in the Writings of Eliza Leslie and Catharine Beecher," *The Lion and the Unicorn, 23* (no. 3), 355-372 (1999), p. 355. Also see Faye E. Dudden, *Women in the American Theatre: Actresses and Audiences, 1790-1870* (New Haven: Yale Univ. Press, 1994).

178 Elizabeth Reitz Mullenix, *Wearing the Breeches: Gender on the Antebellum Stage* (N. Y.: St. Martin's Press, 2000).

179 Cf. the discussion of Schacht's "four emergent renditions of doing female drag" in the answer to Q. 17. See Steven P. Schacht, "Four Renditions of Doing Female Drag: Feminine Appearing Conceptual Variations of a Masculine Theme," *Gendered Sexualities, 6*, 157-180 (2002).

180 Helen Bode, "Is Drag Subversive of Binary Gender Norms?" *Dialogue, 1* (no. 3), 19-26 (2003), p. 21.

181 For an overview, see Rebecca Bell-Metereau, *Hollywood Androgyny* (N. Y.: Columbia Univ. Press, 1985).

182 See Lillian Schlissel (Ed.), *Three Plays by Mae West: Sex, The Drag, and Pleasure Man* (N. Y.: Routledge, 1997). Cf. Marybeth Hamilton, "'I'm the Queen of the Bitches.' Female Impersonation and Mae West's *Pleasure Man*," in Lesley Ferris (Ed.), *Crossing the Stage: Controversies on Cross-Dressing*, pp. 107-119. (N. Y.: Routledge, 1993).

183 Benmussa adapted a story by George Moore. For an interesting discussion of the play, see Amy Couchoud, "A Production Plan for Directing Simone Benmussa's *The Singular Life of Albert Nobbs* from a Materialist Feminist Perspective" (1998). Accessed online at http://www.smcm.edu/users/jrklein/couchoud.htm.

184 Schilling, p. 208f.

185 See Caryl Churchill, *Cloud Nine* (N. Y.: Metheun, 1984 rev. ed.).

186 See "*Man to Man*, Manfred Karge," in Michael Earley & Philippa Keil (Eds.), *The Contemporary Monologue: Women*, ch. 27 (N. Y.: Routledge, 1995).

187 For background, including a brief history, see *Hedwig and the Angry Inch*, accessed online at http://www.imagi-nation.com/moonstruck/albm51.html. Cf. *Hedwig in a Box* international fan site, accessed at http://www.hedwiginabox.com/. The play was made into a film released in 2001.

188 Background on the play accessed at the Imagi-nation.com website at http://www.imagi-nation.com/moonstruck/albm57.html.

189 See the *Hairspray* website accessed online at http://www.hairsprayonbroadway.com/.

190 See the *All Shook Up* official website accessed online at http://www.allshookup.com/.

191 See the *Official Tyler Perry Website* accessed online at http://www.tylerperry.com/.

192 For background and review, see S. I. Salamensky, "*I Am My Own Wife* (Review)," *Theatre Journal, 55* (no. 4), 700-702 (2003).

[193] See R. L. Bell-Metereau, *Cross-Dressing and Sex Role Reversals in American Film* (Indiana Univ.: PhD dissertation, 1981). Also see Dan A. R. Kelly, "Role Reversal," *Metro Beat*, 21-22 (2004, June 16-22), p. 21f.

[194] Interestingly, Brando's last role, voice work for the animated comedy *Big Bug Man* (scheduled release 2006), was for a female character and he reportedly did his work wearing a wig, dress, and white gloves. See *Brando's Last Role: An Old Lady* at *CBS News.com* (2004, July 16). Accessed online at http://www.cbsnews.com/stories/ 2004/07/02/ entertainment/main627273.shtml.

[195] Susan Donne, "Drag Addiction; Why Black Actors Keep Taking Cross-Dressing Roles, and Why It (Is/Is Not) Racist," *Hartford Courant* (2006, Feb. 24), D1.

[196] For a review, see Gary Morris, "Hong Kong's Who's the Man? Series," *Bright Lights Film Journal*, Issue 19 (1997, July). Accessed online at http://www.brightlights film.com/19/19_hkgender.html.

[197] For a description, see Garay Menicucci, "Homosexuality in Egyptian Film," *Middle East Report* (1998, Spring). Accessed online at http://www.merip.org/mer/ mer206/egyfilm.htm.

[198] For a review, see Gary Morris, "Poor Queen. Giorgios Katakouzinos's Angel," *Bright Lights Film Journal*, Issue 31 (2001, January). Accessed online at http://www. brightlightsfilm.com/31/angel.html.

[199] For a review, see Gary Morris, "Bugis Street," *Bright Lights Film Journal*, Issue 21 (1998, May). Accessed online at http://www.brightlightsfilm.com/21/21_bugis. html.

[200] Chris Nashawaty, "The Full Monty," *Entertainment Weekly*, #812, pp. 41-47 (2005, March 25), p. 44.

[201] Greg Kean appeared as 'Eric Hobart,' the crossdressing man, in an episode entitled "The Lying Game" (aka "A Difficult Cross to Bear").

[202] *A Girl Like Me* premiered on the Lifetime network on June 19th, 2006.

[203] See, for example, *Fantasy Island* (1983), where a husband and wife switch bodies (episode 131, 'The Big Switch'); cf. the family drama *Highway to Heaven* (1986), where Mark (played by actor Victor French) becomes a female movie star (episode 39, 'Change of Life'). Comedies are also well represented. See *The Munsters* (1965), where Grampa and Eddie are both transformed (episode 33, 'Lily Munster, Girl Model'); cf. *My Favorite Martian* (1965), where Martin changes bodies with the landlady, Mrs. Brown (episode 80, 'I'd Rather Fight Than Switch'). In science fiction and fantasy shows, gender crossing is always a possibility, as several instances of *Quantum Leap* (1989-1993) alone demonstrate. Cf. also *Star Trek* (1969), where Captain Kirk is forcibly switched with Janice Lester (episode 79, 'Turnabout Intruder').

Q. 45 Notes

[204] An indication of the breadth and vitality of the discussion can be seen in Martha A. Brozyna (Ed.), *Gender and Sexuality in the Middle Ages* (Jefferson, NC: McFarland, 2005).

[205] Robert L. A. Clark & Claire Sponsler, "Queer Play: The Cultural Work of Crossdressing in Medieval Drama," *New Literary History*, 28 (no. 2), 319-344 (1997), p. 320.

[206] Kathleen A. Bishop, "The Influence of Plautus and Elegiac Comedy on Chaucer's Fabliaux," *The Chaucer Review*, 35 (no. 3), 294-317 (2001), p. 309.

207 Ibid. Bishop herself is citing from Joan Cadden, *Meanings of Sex Difference in the Middle Ages* (N. Y.: Cambridge Univ. Press, 1993), p. 160.

208 Cited in James D. Cain, "Unnatural History: Gender and Genealogy in Gerald of Wales's *Topographia Hibernica*," *Essays in Medieval Studies*, 19 (no. 1), 29-43 (2002), pp. 31-32.

209 Cain, p. 32.

210 James M. Blythe, "Women in the Military: Scholastic Arguments and Medieval Images of Female Warriors," *History of Political Thought*, XXII (no. 2), 242-269 (2001). Accessed online at http://www.imprint.co.uk/hpt/179.PDF.

211 Ibid.

212 Cary J. Nederman & Jacqui True, "The Third Sex: The Idea of the Hermaphrodite in Twelfth-Century Europe," *Journal of the History of Sexuality*, 6 (no. 4), 497-517 (1996).

213 Peter Cantor, *De Vitio Sodomitico*, translated in John Boswell, *Christianity, Social Tolerance, and Homosexuality* (Chicago: Univ. of Chicago Press, 1980), p. 376.

214 Cited in Nederman & True, p. 512.

215 Joan Cadden, *Meanings of Sex Difference in the Middle Ages: Medicine, Science, and Culture* (N. Y.: Cambridge University Press, 1993). See chapter 4, 'Feminine and Masculine Types,' especially pp. 212-213.

216 For a comprehensive treatment, see Herbert Norris, *Medieval Costume and Fashion* (N. Y.: Dover Books, 1999 reprint of 1927 ed.). Also see, Mary G. Houston, *Medieval Costume in England and France. The 13th, 14th and 15th Centuries* (N. Y.: Dover, 1996). Cf. Francoise Piponnier & Perrine Mane, *Dress in the Middle Ages*, translated by C. Beamish (New Haven, CT: Yale Univ. Press, 2000). Especially see the immense website created by Dr. Tara Maginnis of the Theater Department of the University of Alaska Fairbanks, at *The Costumer's Manifesto*, accessed online at http://www.costumes.org/history/100pages/medievalinks.htm#General%20Medieval%20Costume. These and other resources inform the historical summary presented here.

217 Many Christians believed that the end of the first millennium (1000 C.E.) must mark the closing of history between the periods of Christ's first appearance on the earth and his second. This popular belief elicited some anxiety as people did their best to be ready for their Lord's return. We may recall similar anxieties felt by some people as the second millinium closed. The fact that Jesus did not reappear brought a reappraisal by many and is commonly thought to have facilitated a more secular turn in society in a variety of respects.

218 Ivan Illich, *Gender* (N. Y.: Pantheon Books, 1982), p. 95.

219 Lois Banner, "The Fashionable Sex, 1100-1600," *History Today*, 42 (no. 4), 37-44.

220 Blythe, p. 246.

221 Niketas Choniates, *O City of Byzantium, Annals of Niketas Choniates*, translated by H. J. Magoulias (Detroit, MI: Wayne State Univ. Press, 1994), p. 35 [2.1.60], cited in Blythe, p. 247.

222 Blythe, p. 248; Hervör/Hervath is briefly mentioned on p. 246.

223 See Sarah Roche-Made (Ed. & Translator), *Silence: A Thirteenth-Century French Romance* (East Lansing, MI: Michigan State Univ. Press, 1999). Also see Peter Allen, "The Ambiguity of Silence: Gender, Silence, and *Le Roman de Silence*," in J. Wassermann & L. Roney (Eds.), *Sign, Sentence, Discourse: Language in Medieval Thought and Discourse*, pp.

198-212 (Syracuse, NY: Syracuse Univ. Press, 1989). Other medieval romances featuring crossdressing include *Aucassin et Nicollete* and *Roi Flore et la belle Jeanne*—in both instances it is the woman who crossdresses. Male crossdressing occurs in the story *La Saineresse*, which evokes the ancient fear about male crossdressing that it is motivated by the desire to gain forbidden sexual access to women. In this case the crossdresser uses the masquerade to gain access to his mistress in her husband's domicile.

[224] Helmut Puff, "Female Sodomy: The Trial of Katherina Hetzeldorfer (1477)," *Journal of Medieval and Early Modern Studies*, 30 (no. 1), 41-61 (2000), pp. 43, 60.

[225] Ibid, p. 61. The trial manuscript describes the instrument as follows: "a red piece of leather, at the front filled with cotton, and a wooden stick stuck into it, and made a hole through the wooden stick, put a string through, and tied it round. . . ."

[226] Ibid, p. 50.

[227] For a collection of materials on this subject see Valerie R. Hotchkiss & Bonnie Wheeler (Eds.), *Clothes Make the Man: Female Cross-Dressing in Medieval Europe.* (London: Taylor & Francis, 1996).

[228] James Sprenger & Heinrich Kramer, *Malleus Maleficarum*, translated by Montague Summers (London: Pushkin Press, 1928), Part I, question 6. Accessed online at *The Malleus Maleficarum* website at http://www.malleusmaleficarum.org/. Quotation at http://www.malleusmaleficarum.org/part_I/ mm01_06a.html.

[229] Richard A. Carroll, "Assessment and Treatment of Gender Dysphoria," in S. R. Leiblum & R. C. Rosen (Eds.), *Principles and Practice of Sex Therapy*, 3rd ed., pp. 368-397 (N. Y.: Guilford, 2000), p. 370.

[230] Vern Bullough, "Transvestites in the Middle Ages," *American Journal of Sociology*, 79 (no. 6), 1381-1394 (1974). Bullough wrote often about sexuality and the Middle Ages.

[231] See, for example, Tova Rosen, "Circumcised Cinderella: The Fantasies of a Fourteenth-Century Jewish Author," *Prooftexts*, 20 (nos. 1-2), 87-110 (2000). This case is considered in the answer to Q. 77.

[232] Daniel Roche, *The Culture of Clothing: Dress and Fashion in the Ancien Regime* (N. Y.: Cambridge Univ. Press, 1994 [original work published in France, 1989]), p. 39.

[233] Betül Ipsirli Argit, "Clothing Habits, Regulations and Non-Muslims in the Ottoman Empire," *Akademik Arastirmalar Dergisi* (Sayi 24), 79-96 (2005), p. 79. Significant change in this system occurred in 1829 when Mahmud II replaced the traditions with a consciously European style—another marker of European cultural influence.

[234] Alan Hunt, *Governance of the Consuming Passions: A History of Sumptuary Law* (N. Y.: Macmillan, 1996).

[235] Ibid, p. 214.

[236] Ibid. Cf. Hunt's chapter 3, 'Tilting Against the Windmills of Fashion' for his consideration of the importance of clothing in general and with regard to gender.

[237] Julia Emberley, "The Libidinal Politics of Fur," *University of Toronto Quarterly*, 65 (no. 2) (1996). Accessed online at http://www.utpjournals.com/jour.ihtml?lp= product/utq/652/652_emberley.html.

[238] Hunt; see especially his chapter 1, 'Why Study Sumptuary Law?'

Q. 46 Notes

[239] Sharon E. Preves, "Sexing the Intersexed: An Analysis of Sociocultural Responses to Intersexuality," *Signs: Journal of Women in Culture and Society*, 27 (no. 2), 523-

556 (2001). Preves notes, for instance, that in 17th century France an intersexed individual was permitted to marry a member of which male/female sex was 'opposite' the male/female end of the continuum they had chosen to identify with. Thus, a hermaphrodite who elected to live as a woman could legally marry a man. But once such a choice was made, it was deemed irreversible. By the 18th-19th centuries, far less tolerance existed in Western Europe.

[240] See Marco Belfanti & Fabio Giusberti, "Global Dress: Clothing as a Means of Integration (17th – 20th Centuries)," p. 6f. Paper presented at the XIII Economic History Congress, Buenos Aires, July 22-26, 2002. Accessed online at http://www.eh.net/XIIICongress/cd/papers/64BelfantiGiusberti170.pdf.

[241] Thomas Laqueur, *Making Sex: Body and Gender from the Greeks to Freud* (Cambridge, MA: Harvard Univ. Press, 1990).

[242] Kate Chedgzoy, "Impudent Women: Carnival and Gender in Early Modern Culture," *The Glasgow Review, no. 1* (1993). Accessed online at http://www.arts.gla.ac.uk/SESLL/STELLA/COMET/ glasgrev/issue1/chefgz.htm.

[243] David Cressy, "Gender Trouble and Cross-Dressing in Early Modern England," *Journal of British Studies, 35*, 438-465 (1996), p. 451.

[244] Philip Stubbes, *The Anatomie of the Abuses*, ed. F. J. Furnivall (New Shakespeare Society, 1877-1879; original work published 1583, 1585, 1595), vol. 1, p. 73. I have modernized the language somewhat by changing spellings. This text is immediately followed by a quoting of Deuteronomy 22:5 (see the answers to Q. 61-65).

[245] Ibid, p. 73f. Cf. the answers to Q. 61-65; Stubb's application of this text is addressed in answering Q. 64.

[246] Cressy (pp. 442-444) offers a taste of these men's messages. Rainolds, for example, warned that "A woman's garment being put on a man doth vehemently touch and move him with the remembrance and imagination of a woman" (Cressy, p. 443, citing John Rainolds, *The Overthrow of Stage-Playes* (Middleburgh, 1599), p. 97).

[247] Ibid, p. 439.

[248] Ibid, pp. 446-450.

[249] Ibid, p. 453.

[250] Terry Castle, "The Culture of Travesty: Sexuality and Masquerade in Eighteenth-Century England," in G. S. Rousseau & R. Porter (Eds.), *Sexual Underworlds of the Enlightenment*, pp. 156-180 (Chapel Hill: Univ. of North Carolina Press, 1988), p. 163.

[251] Ibid, p. 163f.

[252] Sarah Carpenter, "Performing Diplomacies: The 1560s Court Entertainments of Mary Queen of Scots," *Scottish Historical Review, 82* (no. 2), 194-225 (2003).

[253] Jean E. Howard, "Cross-Dressing, the Theater, and Gender Struggle in Early Modern England," in Lesley Ferris (Ed.), *Crossing the Stage: Controversies on Cross-Dressing*, pp. 20-46 (N.Y.: Routledge, 1993), p. 21.

[254] Cressy, p. 460.

[255] K. V. Crawford, *The Transvestite Heroine in Seventeenth Century Popular Literature* (Harvard Univ.: PhD dissertation, 1984).

[256] Shasta Turner, "Disordered Subjects: Female Cross-Dressing and Sumptuary Regulation in Early Modern England," (1998). Accessed online at http://www.majorweather.com/projects/000040.html. A version of this paper was originally presented as

part of the 1998 Huntington Library Graduate Seminars in Early Modern British History.

[257] It may seem curious a female prostitute would advertise herself by dressing in masculine clothing. I am mindful, however, of the observation by Mary Ann Doane that while male crossdressing occasions laughter, female crossdressing elicits desire. See Mary Ann Doane, *Femmes Fatales: Feminism, Film Theory and Psychoanalysis* (N. Y.: Routledge, 1991).

[258] A few examples of recorded instances of female crossdressing in early modern England can be found in Jean E. Howard, "Cross-Dressing, the Theater, and Gender Struggle in Early Modern England," *Shakespeare Quarterly, 39*, 418-440 (1088), pp. 420-421. Cf. Cressy, pp. 460-461, who regards the incidents he recounts as "minor" transgressions that received appropriately "mild" punishments.

[259] Rudolf M. Dekker & Lotte C. van de Pol, *The Tradition of Female Transvestism in Early Modern Europe* (N. Y.: Macmillan Press, 1997; original work published 1989).

[260] Ibid, p. 3.

[261] Ibid, pp. 1-2. As we shall see, the judgment that it was lost in the 19th century is incorrect.

[262] Ibid, p. 9f.

[263] Ibid, p. 27.

[264] *A General History of the Robberies and Murders of the Most Notorious Pyrates* (N. Y.: Garland, 1972). Ostensibly written by a Captain Charles Johnson, this is thought to be a pseudonym for Daniel Defoe. On women pirates, see Marcus Rediker, "When Women Pirates Sailed the Seas," *Wilson Quarterly, 17* (no. 4), 102-119 (1993). Cf. Matthew Teorey, "Pirates and State-Sponsored Terrorism in Eighteenth-Century England," *Perspectives on Evil and Human Wickedness, 1* (no. 2), 53-63 (2003); on Anne Bonny and Mary Read, see p. 57.

[265] Gretchen van Slyke, "The Sexual and Textual Politics of Dress: Rosa Bonheur and Her Cross-Dressing Permits," *Nineteenth-Century French Studies, 26* (nos. 3-4), 321-335 (1998). Cf. Gretchen van Slyke, "Who Wears the Pants Here? The Policing of Women's Dress in Nineteenth-Century England, Germany and France." *Nineteenth-Century Contexts, 17,* (no. 1), 17-33 (1993).

[266] Theophile Gautier, *Mademoiselle de Maupin* (N. Y.: Heritage Press, 1944; original work published 1835).

[267] Honoré de Balzac, *Séraphita*, translated by K. P. Wormeley (original work published 1835). Accessed online at http://emotional-literacy-education.com/classic-books-online-c/sraph10.htm. The same translation is also available as part of Project Gutenberg's collection, accessed online at http://www.gutenberg.org/catalog/world/readfile?fk_files=38692.

[268] More than ten dozen have been identified in English alone. The lyrics quoted in this answer are from public domain sources. The commentary on the ballads is my own.

[269] Dianne Dugaw, *Warrior Women and Popular Balladry, 1650-1850* (Chicago: Univ. of Chicago Press, 1996). Also see Dianne Dugaw, "Balladry's Female Warriors: Women, Warfare and Disguise in the 18th Century," *18th Century Life, 9* (no. 2), 1-20 (1985). Cf. Dianne Dugaw, "'Female Sailors Bold': Transvestite Heroines and the Markers of Gender and Class," in M. Creighton & L. Norling (Eds.), *Iron Men, Wooden Women: Gender*

and Anglo-American Seafaring, pp. 34-54 (Baltimore, MD: John Hopkins Univ. Press, 1996).

270 Pauline Greenhill, "'Neither a Man Nor a Maid': Sexualities and Gendered Meanings in Cross-Dressing Ballads," *Journal of American Folklore, 108*, 156-177 (1995). Cf. Pauline Greenhill, "'The Handsome Cabin Boy': Cross-Dressing Ballads, Sexualities, and Gendered Meanings," in P. Greenhill & D. Tye (Eds.), *Undisciplined Women—Tradition and Culture in Canada*, pp. 113-130 (Montreal: McGill-Queen's Univ. Press, 1997).

271 Cf. Dugaw, pp. 82-84, under the title, 'Female Cabin Boy.'

272 A far less sympathetic tone is found in the comic country western ballad composed by the late 20th century musician Alice Cooper, whose "Saga of Jesse Jane" puts the protagonist in a Texas jail, dressed in his sister's wedding gown.

273 Cressy, p. 459.

274 Ibid, p. 463.

275 For more information, see David Williams, *The Rebecca Riots: A Study in Agrarian Discontent* (Cardiff, UK: Univ. of Wales Press, 1986 reprint of 1955 ed.). Also see *Rebecca Riots*. Accessed online at the Wales at Heart website at http://www.walesatheart.com/wah%20about%20wales/rebeccariots.htm. Also see the Powys Digital History Project webpage on the Rebecca Riots, accessed online at http://history.powys.org.uk/history/rhaeadr/rebecca.html.

276 A brief review of Ireland's Molly Maguires and the connection with those in Pennsylvania can be found in Kevin Kenny, *Making Sense of the Molly Maguires* (N. Y.: Oxford Univ. Press, 1998).

277 Natalie Zemon Davis, *Society and Culture in Early Modern France* (Stanford, CA: Stanford Univ. Press, 1975), pp. 147-148.

To the list of men disguised as women in politically charged acts we might add any number of incidents, but perhaps the most well-known is that of two butchers named Cumming who thus disguised themselves when they led the riots of 1736 in Edinburgh, Scotland associated with the Porteus uprising. This incident is recounted by Sir Walter Scott in his novel *Heart of Mid-Lothian*, volume 1.

278 Ibid, p. 149.

279 The text of the amendment and an accompanying brief history were found at the Knitting Circle Law Centre website maintained on the South Bank University web server and accessed online at http://myweb.lsbu.ac.uk/~stafflag/labouchere.html. The law remained in effect 82 years.

280 Cf. David A. Boxwell, "The Follies of War: Cross-Dressing and Popular Theatre on the British Front Lines, 1914-1918," *Modernism/Modernity, 9* (no 1), 1-20 (2002), p. 10.

281 Ibid, p. 9.

282 Jean E. Howard, "Crossdressing, the Theatre, and Gender Struggle in Early Modern England," *Shakespeare Quarterly, 39*, 418-440 (1988), p. 420.

283 Dekker & van de Pol, p. 97.

284 Howard, p. 22.

285 See Kari Boyd McBride, *The Woman Controversy. The Debate About the Nature of Womankind in Early Modern England* (n.d.). Accessed online at http://www.u.ari-

zona.edu/~kari/querelle.htm. McBride is a member of the Women's Studies Department at the University of Arizona.

[286] *Hic Mulier; or, The Man-Woman: Being a Medicine to cure the Coltish Disease of the Staggers in the Masculine-Feminines of our Times, Expressed in a brief Declamation: Non omnes possumus omnes.[we cannot all be everybody]* (1620). The pamphlet is linked from the *The Woman Controversy* cited above, and was accessed online at http://www.u.arizona.edu/~kari/querhm.htm.

[287] David Cressy, "Gender Trouble and Cross-Dressing in Early Modern England," *Journal of British Studies*, 35 (no. 4), 438-465 (1996). Cressy remarks, "these were mostly minor offenses, more jests and pranks than challenges to the gendered social order, and their punishment was appropriately mild" (p. 461).

Q. 47 Notes

[288] For an overview of intersex in early America, see Elizabeth Reis, "Impossible Hermaphrodites: Intersex in America, 1620-1960," *The Journal of American History*, 92 (no. 2) (2005). Electronic article accessed online at http://www.historycooperative.org/cgi-bin/justtop.cgi?act=justtop&url=http://www.historycooperative.org/journals/jah/92.2/reis.html.

[289] I am reluctant to go so far as Etsuko Taketani does in her claim that in the popular imagination of the 19th century sex was akin to dress and could likewise be donned or doffed. See Etsuko Taketani, "Spectacular Child Bodies: The Sexual Politics of Cross-Dressing and Calisthenics in the Writings of Eliza Leslie and Catharine Beecher," *The Lion and the Unicorn*, 23 (no. 3), 355-372 (1999), p. 356f. It seems more reasonable to me to read the evidence as suggesting gender was conceived as body-based but because the sexual body (specifically, its reproductive power), developed and changed across the lifespan gender could be seen as also relatively fluid. After all, if sex (read as reproductive ability) waxes and wanes, why not masculinity and femininity, too? Fascination with crossdressing, and being troubled by it, may thereby be seen as reflecting some anxiety over the implications of such an act for the stability of gender, rather than sex.

[290] Dianna DiPaolo Loren, "Social Skins: Orthodoxies and Practices of Dressing in the Early Colonial Lower Mississippi Valley," *Journal of Social Archaeology*, 1 (no. 2), 172-189 (2001).

[291] Kate Haulman, "Fashion and the Culture Wars of Revolutionary Philadelphia," *The William & Mary Quarterly*, 62 (no. 4) (2005), para. 2. Electronic article accessed online at http://www. historycooperative.org/cgi-bin/justtop.cgi?act=justtop&url=http://www.historycooperative.org/ journals/wm/62.4/haulman.htm.

[292] Nora Waugh, *The Cut of Men's Clothes 1600-1900* (London: Theatre Arts Books, 1964), p. 14.

[293] Nora Waugh, *The Cut of Women's Clothes 1600-1900* (London: Theatre Arts Books, 1968), pp. 23ff.

[294] John E. Crowley, "The Sensibility of Comfort," *The American Historical Review*, 104 (no. 3), 749-782 (1999). The electronic version accessed online at http://historycooperative.press.uiuc.edu/journals/ahr/104.3/ah000749.html. See §§10-12.

[295] Ibid, p. 10.

[296] Ibid, p. 14.

297 For explanation and illustration, see Linda Baumgarten & John Watson, with Florinne Carr, *Costume Close-Up. Clothing Construction and Pattern 1750-1790* (N. Y.: Quite Specific Media Group, 2000), p. 11. On the century's fashion in general, with discussion of the meaning attached to fashion styles by the people of the period, see Linda Baumgarten, *What Clothes Reveal. The Language of Clothing in Colonial and Federal America* (New Haven, CT: Yale Univ. Press, 2002).

298 Valerie Steele, "Fashion," *Microsoft Encarta Online Encyclopedia* (2005). Accessed online at http://encarta.msn.com/text_761585452__3/Fashion.html.

299 Ruth P. Rubinstein, *Dress Codes: Meanings and Messages in American Culture* (Boulder, CO: Westview Press, 1995), ch. 2 (pp. 16-30).

300 Sara Melissa Pullum-Piñon. *Conspicuous Display and Social Mobility: a Comparison of 1850s Boston and Charleston Elites* [Ph.D. dissertation] (Austin: The University of Texas, 2002), p. 147. Accessed online at http://www.lib.utexas.edu/etd/d/2002/pullumpinon 022/pullumpinon022.pdf.

301 Taketani, p. 355.

302 Vern Bullough, *Cross Dressing, Sex, and Gender* (Phila.: Univ. of Pennsylvania Press, 1993), p. 175.

303 Pullum-Piñon, p. 147.

304 Farid Chenoue, *A History of Men's Fashion,* translated by D. Dusinberre (Paris: Flammarion, 1993), p. 9.

305 Herbert Norris & Oswald Curtis, *Nineteenth-Century Costume and Fashion* (London: Dover Books, 1998; original work published 1933), p. 4f.

306 Pullum-Piñon, p. 151f.

307 Jill Fields, "Erotic Modesty: (Ad)dressing Female Sexuality and Propriety in Open and Closed Drawers, USA, 1800-1930," *Gender & History, 14* (no. 3), 492-515 (2002), p. 497.

308 Cf. Helene E. Roberts, "The Exquisite Slave: The Role of Clothes in the Making of the Victorian Woman," *Signs: Journal of Women in Culture and Society, 2* (no. 3), 554-569 (2977), p. 555.

309 Valerie Steele, *The Corset: A Cultural History* (New Haven, CT: Yale Univ. Press, 2001), p. 1.

310 Jill Fields, "'Fighting the Corsetless Evil': Shaping Corsets and Culture, 1900-1930," *Journal of Social History, 33* (no. 2), 355-384 (1999), p. 355.

311 Leigh Summers, *Bound to Please: A History of the Victorian Corset* (Oxford: Berg, 2001). See especially chapter 4, 'Corsetry and the Reality of Female Complaints.'

312 Jane Farrell-Beck & Colleen Gau, *Uplift: The Bra in America* (Phila.: Univ. of Pennsylvania Press, 2002), p. 4.

313 Though a patent application for a breast supporter was made in 1863 by Luman Chapman, it was Olivia Flynt's patent that made it to the market in the late 1870s. See Farrell-Beck & Gau, p. 1-7.

314 Fields places these becoming part of women's fashion in the early 19th century at a time when there was heightened gender differentiation accompanying changes in the importance of class distinctions and the "newly privatized woman's sphere." By the 1840s they were worn by most women of the middle class. See Fields, "Erotic Modesty," p. 495f.

315 Ibid, p. 493.

[316] Ibid. Fields remarks these drawers were feminized in three ways: choice of fabric, accompanying ornamentation (e.g., lace leg ruffles), and open-crotch construction.

[317] *The Tailor's Review* (1890, June), p. 108. Cited in Brent Shannon, "ReFashioning Men: Fashion, Masculinity, and the Cultivation of the Male Consumer in Britain, 1860-1914," *Victorian Studies*, 46 (no. 4), 597-630 (2004), p. 619. Shannon documents the trend in masculine fashion as shown in advertising of the time. He points out (p. 620), too, that for 19th century women the principal erogenous zone was the male leg—raising doubt as to exactly how dismayed the ladies were by this development in masculine fashion.

[318] Steele, *The Corset*, p. 2. Especially see Shannon (pp. 621-625), who provides evidence of the advertising effort in Britain to masculinize the garment, which may have been worn by thousands of men in the 1880s-1890s.

[319] Fields, "'Fighting the Corsetless Evil,'" p. 356.

[320] Fields, "Erotic Modesty," p. 495f.

[321] Ibid, p. 494.

[322] Claudia B. Kidwell & Margaret C. Christman, *Suiting Everyone: The Democratization of Clothing in America* (Washington, D. C.: Smithsonian Institution Press, 1974), p. 155.

[323] Jenna Weismann Joselit, *A Perfect Fit: Clothes, Character, and the Promise of America* (N. Y.: Henry Holt and Co., 2001). See the remarks in the answer to Q. 4.

[324] C. Willett Cunnington & Phillis Cunnington, *The History of Underclothes* (London: Michael Joseph, 1951), p. 220.

[325] Mary Lou Rosencranz, "Social and Psychological Approaches to Clothing Research," *Journal of Home Economics*, 57 (no. 1), 26-29 (1965), p. 29.

[326] Ibid, p. 220f.

[327] Helen Goodrich Buttrick, *Principles of Clothing Selection* (N. Y.: Macmillan, 1923), p. 4.

[328] Carolyn Kitch notes how such posters both reflect the increased gender flexibility and reinforce sex stereotypes such as the feminine role as inspiration for men. See Carolyn Kitch, *The Girl on the Magazine Cover: The Origins of Visual Stereotypes in American Mass Media* (Chapel Hill,NC: Univ. of North Carolina Press, 2001), p. 113f. These posters can be viewed on the internet; accessed online at http://www.history.navy.mil/photos/arttopic/pstr-rec/nrp-w1a.htm. The female model in the "Gee! I wish I were a man" poster is posed to emphasize her feminine sexuality and in the "I want you" poster the separation of those words from the remainder of the text clearly function as a double entendre.

[329] Diana Crane, *Fashion and Its Social Agendas. Class, Gender and Identity in Clothing* (Chicago: Univ. of Chicago Press, 2000), p. 106.

[330] Fields remarks that corsetry profited from the move away from the 'boyshform' silhouette of the 1920s to the 'womanly' figure of the 1930s. See Fields, "'Fighting the Corsetless Evil,'" p. 378.

[331] Shoulder pads in women's outfits became a common stylistic feature after this.

[332] Jane Cobb, "Girls Will Be Boys," *The New York Times Magazine* (1940, Nov. 3), p. 10.

[333] William I. Thomas, "The Psychology of Woman's Dress," *American Magazine*, 67, 66-72 (1908), p. 68. Accessed online at http://spartan.ac.brocku.ca/~lward/Thomas/Thomas_1908_b.html. Thomas, p. 71, quotes the remark of Sir Henry Maine that

the greatest calamity that might befall our modern society would not be war, pestilence or famine, but a revolution in fashion where women would dress as men—in one material of one color. (This observation was perhaps more pertinent in the early 20th century than today.)

Jill Fields briefly discusses the introduction of colored underwear for women in the 1860s, observing that such frilly, colorful garments are obviously meant to be seen, thus further attracting erotic attention at the same time the garments are protecting modesty. See Fields, "Erotic Modesty," p. 500.

334 Cunnington & Cunnington, p. 154.

335 For a brief history, see inventor Mary Bellis' online article *The History of Pantyhose?* at http://inventors.about.com/library/inventors/ blpantyhose.htm.

336 Mary Bellis, *The History of the Brassiere*, accessed at http://inventors.about.com/library/weekly /aa042597.htm.

337 Farrell-Beck & Gau, pp. 52-56, 81, 110.

338 The idea of fetishistic crossdressing has at least two major problems with regard to clothes. First, putting on the clothes is not necessary for the articles to have fetishistic power, so why they would be worn can at best be only partly answered by fetishism. Second, most crossdressers prefer to be fully crossdressed to partially crossdressed; partial crossdressing is typically a practical solution to environmental realities. Full crossdressing is hardly needed for sexual arousal and relief if the power of the fetish rests in the symbolic value of the clothing, for which undergarments would suffice. Clearly the notion of crossdressing for fetishistic purposes is dubious as a grand explanation for the behavior. For more on this matter see the answer to Q. 88.

339 It was at least as far back as the Fall of 1984 that fashion shows in London and Paris had men wearing skirts. An American designer, Stephen Sprouse, had earlier placed a male model in a black denim miniskirt over black denim jeans in an April, 1983 show. See John Duka, "Skirts for Men? Yes and No," *New York Times* (1984, October 27th). Also see the discussion in the answer to Q. 9.

340 As reported in answering Q. 9, a survey conducted by Mark Clements Research in 2000 in Los Angeles, New York, and Chicago of women ages 21-39 reveals that slightly more than 1-in-5 (20.8%) say they would be willing to date a man dressed in a skirt. Similar levels are found for the percentage of those surveyed who state they view men wearing skirts as "very" or "somewhat" acceptable (24%). Perhaps surprisingly, the survey finds a similar degree of support for accepting even a brother or father who engages in such dress (20.3%). A like percentage even express a willingness to share their own skirts with a man (22.3%). See Judith Thurman, "Would You Be Caught Dead with This Guy?" *Mademoiselle* (2000). Accessed online at http://users.pandora.be/tripticdesign/skirt10.html.

341 Elisabeth McClellan, *History of American Costume, 1607-1870* (N. Y.: Tudor, 1969; original work published 1904), p. 583.

342 Fields, "Female Modesty," p. 496.

343 Marjorie Garber, *Vested Interests: Cross-Dressing and Cultural Anxiety* (N. Y.: Routledge, 1992).

344 Kathleen DeGrave, *Swindler, Spy, Rebel. The Confidence Woman in Nineteenth Century America* (Columbia, MO: Univ. of Missouri Press, 1995), p. 120.

³⁴⁵ Dianne Dugaw, "Balladry's Female Warriors: Women, Warfare and Disguise in the 18th Century," *18th Century Life, 9* (no. 2), 1-20 (1985), p. 15.

³⁴⁶ Ute Kauer, "Masks and Masquerades in the 18th Century Novel: Sarah Fielding and Samuel Richardson," *Erfurt Electronic Studies in English*, article 1 (2003), § 1 'Narrative Cross-Dressing.' Accessed online at http://webdoc.sub.gwdg.de/edoc/ia/eese/artic 23/kauer/1_2003.html.

³⁴⁷ For more on Jemima Wilkinson's life see David Hudson, *Memoir of Jemima Wilkinson, A Preacheress of the Eighteenth Century, etc.* (Bath, N. Y.: R. L. Underhill & Co., 1844).

³⁴⁸ Catherine A. Brekus, *Strangers & Pilgrims. Female Preacing in America, 1740-1843* (Chapel Hill, NC: Univ. of North Carolina Press, 1998), p. 90.

³⁴⁹ Lucy Freeman & Alma Bond, *America's First Woman Warrior, The Courage of Deborah Sampson* (N. Y.: Paragon House, 1992). Also see Lonnelle Aikman, "Patriots in Petticoats," *National Geographic, 148* (no. 4) (1975). Her life has also been celebrated in a play titled "The Revolution of Deborah Sampson."

³⁵⁰ See the online memorial at the Canton Massachusetts Historical Society website, accessed at http://www.canton.org/samson/index.html.

³⁵¹ A variety of accounts exist for different events in the lives of both Anne Bonny and Mary Read. At this point no historical certainty exists for many details, though the general outline of their lives most likely conforms to the account offered here. The most famous account is found in a book generally believed to have been written by Daniel Defoe under the pseudonym of Captain Charles Johnson, *A General History of the Robberies and Murders of the Most Notorious Pyrates* (N. Y.: Garland, 1972; original work published 1724). Material from the book on these two female pirates accessed online at http://arthur-ransome.org/ar/literary/pyrates.htm. Also see Rictor Norton, "Lesbian Pirates: Anne Bonny and Mary Read," *Lesbian History* (2000 update of 1997 webpage version). Accessed online at http://www.infopt.demon.co.uk/pirates.htm.

³⁵² Patricia Bonomi, *The Lord Cornbury Scandal: The Politics of Reputation in British America* (Chapel Hill, NC: The Univ. of North Carolina Press, 1998), chapter 7 (pp. 147-165). Bonomi notes (p. 16) that fascination with male crossdressing was high at the time the rumor resurfaced in 1796. The keen interest centered around the renowned figure of Chevalier d'Eon de Beaumont, whose story is told in the answers to Q. 49, 70.

³⁵³ Ibid, pp. 54, 158-161. Four of the letters date between 1707-1709. They allege that Lord Cornbury was "addicted" to his pleasure, so dressing frequently and in public, even on holy days.

³⁵⁴ Ibid, chapter 1 (pp. 13-26); see p.14 for the portrait.

³⁵⁵ Ibid, p. 16; Bonomi refers to the crossdressing males known in London in the early 18th century.

³⁵⁶ Ibid, p. 15.

³⁵⁷ Though Bonomi presents a decent case against Lord Cornbury having crossdressed, at least three lines of evidence can be appealed to in support of the claim that he did. First, as a privileged man of power he was in a position to do so and succeed despite any complaints about it. Second, his alleged appeal to his reason for so doing makes sense in respect to such practice but not as much sense as a rationale applied by enemies. Third, the letters claim that he was well-known for his public presentation in women's dress—an unlikely claim if not true since it could easily be refuted.

358 Bonomi, chapter 5 (pp. 99-127).

359 Ibid, p. 141.

360 The case of British colonial governor Sir Edmund Andros is recounted in the answer to Q. 13.

361 Though their popularity diminished in the 19th century, crossdressing ballads continued to be sung, and even created. For example, an 1865 ballad by George Cooper and Henry Tucker entitled "Jeff in Petticoats" recounted with gleeful scorn the capture of Confederate President Jefferson Davis, declaring in its third verse and chorus:

> Now when he saw the game was up, he started for the woods,
> His band-box hung upon his arm quite full of fancy goods:
> Said Jeff, "They'll never take me now, I'm sure I'll not be seen,"
> "They'd never think to look for me beneath my Crinoline."
> (chorus)
> Oh! Jeffy D! you "flow'r of chivalry,"
> Oh royal Jeffy D! . . . your
> empire's but a tin-clad skirt, oh charming Jeffy D!

The complete lyrics accessed online at http://www.pdmusic.org/tucker/ht65a.txt. The account of Davis' capture is considered later in the answer.

362 Kauer, §1 'Narrative Cross-Dressing.' Cf. the discussion in the answer to Q. 5, especially with reference to the work of Judith Butler.

363 Herman Mann, *The Female Review: The Life of Deborah Sampson* (Boston: J. K. Wiggin & W. P. Lunt, 1866; original work published 1797). Accessed online at http://pds.harvard.edu:8080/pdx/servlet/ pds?id=2581268&n=8&s=4&res=3.

364 Charles Brockden Brown, *Ormond, or The Secret Witness* (1799), p. 93. Accessed online at http://www.blackmask.com/books61c/ormond.pdf. Also see Paul Lewis, "Attaining Masculinity: Charles Brockden Brown and Woman Warriors of the 1790s," *Early American Literature*, 40 (no. 1), 37-55 (2005).

365 Ibid, p. 95. Cf. the remarks in Merril D. Smith (Ed.), *Sex and Sexuality in Early America* (N. Y.: New York Univ. Press, 1998).

366 Daniel A. Cohen (Ed.), *"The Female Marine" and Related Works. Narratives of Cross-Dressing and Urban Vice in America's Early Republic* (Amherst, MA: Univ. of Massachusetts Press, 1997).

367 Sophia Griffith, *She Would Be a Heroine*, 3 vols. (London: Baldwin, Cradock, & Joy, 1816).

368 Catharine Maria Sedgwick, *Hope Leslie, or, Early Times in the Massachusetts* (1827). See especially Vol. 2, ch. III, pp. 45-53; ch. 9, p. 196f., 204ff.; ch. XII, pp. 249-250. Accessed online at the University of Virginia's website at http://etext.lib.virginia.edu/etcbin/browse-eaf?id=eaf339v2.xml&data =/texts/eaf&tag=public. The book has also been reprinted by Penguin Classics (N. Y.:, 1998).

369 Sedgwick, *Hope Leslie*, vol. 2, pp. 227ff. Hope Leslie masterminds the escape of her Indian friend Magawisca, who is persuaded to exchange clothes with Master Cradock to escape prison where she awaits execution. Interestingly, Cradock's reluctance is over aiding an infidel, not over crossdressing! When the deed is done, he remarks, "Thou woman in man's attire, it is given to thee to utter truth, even as of old, lying oracles were wont to speak words of prophecy" (p. 230).

[370] William Wells Brown, *Clotel; or, The President's Daughter* (N. Y.: Penguin Classics, 2004; original work published 1853). The president referred to in the title is Thomas Jefferson.

[371] See John Cooley (Ed.), *How Nancy Jackson Married Kate Wilson and Other Tales of Rebellious Girls and Daring Young Women* (Lincoln, NE: Univ. of Nebraska Press, 2001). Some of the stories covered in this volume include male or female crossdressing.

[372] Laura Skandera-Trombley lists nine of Twain's works in which crossdressing plays a part: "A Medieval Romance" (1868), "1,002nd Arabian Night" (1883), *Adventures of Huckleberry Finn* (1885), *Pudd'nhead Wilson* (1894), *Personal Recollections of Joan of Arc* (1896), *Following the Equator*, vol. 2 (1897), "Wapping Alice" (1898, 1907), "How Nancy Jackson Married Kate Wilson" (c. 1902), and "A Horse's Tale" (1907). See Laura Skandera-Trombley, "Mark Twain's Cross-Dressing Oeuvre," *College Literaure*, 24 (no. 2), 82-96 (1997).

[373] This kind of situation is found, for instance, in stories of crossdressing saints; see the answer to Q. 68. For Twain this plot twist left him, in his own words, in a pickle: "I have got my hero (or heroine) into such a particularly close place that I do not see how I am ever going to get him (or her) out of it again, and therefore I will wash my hands of the whole business." See Mark Twain, *The Complete Short Stories of Mark Twain*, rev. ed., edited by C. Neider (N. Y.: Bantam Classics, 1984), p. 56.

[374] Mark Twain, *Huckleberry Finn* (N. Y.: Courier Dover Publications, 1999; original work published 1885), pp. 26ff.

[375] Mark Twain, *The Tragedy of Pudd'nhead Wilson and the Comedy of Those Extraordinary Twins* (Hartford, CT: American Publishing Co., 1894). The text of the 1900 printing of this edition accessed online at http://etext.lib.virginia.edu/railton/wilson/facsimile/facsimilehp.html.

[376] Mark Twain, "Hellfire Hotchkiss," in F. R. Rogers (Ed.), *Mark Twain's Satires and Burlesques*, pp. 175-203 (Berkeley: Univ. of California Press, 1968), p. 187.

[377] Ibid, p. 199.

[378] Mrs. J. Wood, *Pantaletta: A Romance of Sheheland* (N. Y.: American News Co., 1882). Accessed online at http://srv2.lycoming.edu/~lewes/wood.htm/.

[379] Ibid, chapter VIII.

[380] Ibid, chapter IX.

[381] Ibid, chapter V.

[382] Ibid, chapter IX.

[383] Darby Lewes, "Gender Bending: Two Role-Reversal Utopias By Nineteenth-Century Women," in M. W. Elbert (Ed.), *Separate Spheres No More: Gender Convergence in American Literature 1830-1930*, pp. 158-178 (Tuscaloosa: Univ. of Alabama Press, 2000), p. 161.

[384] Ibid, p. 162.

[385] These summaries are based on the material in Taketani, pp. 356-362. For the works themselves, see Eliza Leslie, "Lucy Nelson; or, The Boy-Girl," *Juvenile Miscellany*, 3rd series, 1.2, pp. 149-159 (1831), and Eliza Leslie, "Billy Bedlow; or, The Girl-Boy," *Juvenile Miscellany*, 3rd series, 1.3, pp. 274-280 (1832)..

[386] Among the most famous—and controversial—accounts is that by Loreta Janeta Velazquez, a native of Cuba who fought for the Confederacy as 'Harry T. Buford.' Velazquez' account has been assessed as historically authentic by some, mostly fiction by

others. See Loreta Janeta Velazquez, *The Woman in Battle. The Civil War Narrative of Loreta Janeta Velazquez, Cuban Woman and Confederate Soldier* (Madison, WI: Univ. of Wisconsin Press, 2003). For her story see the answer to Q. 48. One account of a woman serving in the war while in disguise is offered in the biographical sketches at the end of this answer. For more such accounts, see Bonnie Tsui, *She Went to the Field: Women Soldiers of the Civil War* (Guilford, CT: Globe Pequot, Press 2003).

[387] Menie Muriel Dowie, *Women Adventurers: The Lives of Madame Velasquez, Hannah Snell, Mary Anne Talbot, and Mrs Christian Davies* (London: Unwin, 1893).

[388] Lillie Devereux Blake, *Fettered for Life, or, Lord and Master* (N. Y.: The Feminist Press at the City University of N.Y., 1996; original work published N. Y.: Sheldon, 1874). The original edition accessed online at Wright American Fiction, 1851-1875 website at http://www.letrs.indiana.edu/cgi/t/ text/text-idx?c=wright2;idno=wright2-0307. Cf. the remarks in Levander, p. 125f.

[389] "What a Michigan Woman Has Done," *The New York Times* (1869, Jan. 12), p. 2.

[390] Ibid, p. 29.

[391] Ibid, p. 35f.

[392] William Craft & Ellen Craft, *Running a Thousand Miles for Freedom; or, The Escape of William and Ellen Croft from Slavery* (London: William Tweedie, 1860). Accessed online at http://etext.lib.virginia.edu/toc/modeng/public/CraThou.html.

[393] In the Civil War alone about 400 women have been documented to have served in the ranks of either the Union or the Confederacy. See "Why Did Women Fight in the Civil War?" *The Smithsonian Associates Civil War E-mail Newsletter, 1* (no. 8). Accessed online at http://civilwarstudies.org/articles/Vol_1/women.htm. Also see Bonnie Tsui, *She Went to the Field: Women Soldiers of the Civil War* (Guilford, CT: Globe Pequot Press, 2003).

[394] "A Female Civil War Veteran," *The New York Times* (1898, Dec. 27), p. 1.

[395] Lauren Cook Burgess, *An Uncommon Soldier: The Civil War Letters of Sarah Rosetta Wakeman, alias Pvt. Lyons Wakeman, 153rd Regiment, New York State Volunteers* (Pasadena, MD: Minerva Center, 1994).

[396] For more on Mary Walker, see Charles McCool Snyder, *Dr. Mary Walker: The Little Lady in Pants* (N. Y.: Arno Press, 1974). For a shorter piece, see Rudi Williams, "Only Woman Medal of Honor Winner Ahead of Her Time," *American Forces Information Service News Articles* (2003) on the U. S. Dept. of Defense website. Accessed online at http://www.defenselink.mil/news/Apr1999/ n04301999_9904304.html.

[397] "Murray Hall Fooled Many Shrewd Men," *The New York Times* (1901, Jan. 19), p. 3.

[398] "The Woman Who Wore Men's Clothes," *The New York Times* (1882, Feb. 21), p. 3.

[399] "A Woman Married to a Woman," *The New York Times* (1856, Apr. 26), p. 2.

[400] "Woman Thief in Man's Clothes," *The New York Times* (1884, Nov. 14), p. 2.

[401] "Imposter," *The New York Times* (1874, Aug. 6), p. 2.

[402] DeGrave, p. 120.

[403] See *History of the American West, 1860-1920: Photographs from the Collection of the Denver Public Library*, at the American Memory website. Accessed online at http://memory.loc.gov/cgi-bin/query/D?hawp:2:./temp/~ammem_eduY::. See *History of the American West, 1860-1920*.

[404] Mock weddings persist in some places in the United States and in Canada. These are discussed in more detail in the answer to Q. 58.

[405] Such photos show White men in full American Indian apparel for a woman, including dress, bead necklace, and headband with a wig.

[406] Evelyn A. Schlatter, "Drag's a Life: Women, Gender, and Cross-Dressing in the Nineteenth Century West," in S. Armitage & E. Jameson (Eds.), *Writing the Range: Race, Class, and Culture in the Woman's West*, pp. 334-348 (Norman, OK: Univ. of Oklahoma Press, 1997).

[407] Elsa Jane Guerin, *Mountain Charley; or, The Adventures of Mrs. E. J. Guerin, Who Was Thirteen Years in Male Attire; An Autobiography Comprising a Period of Thirteen Years Life in the States, California, and Pike's Peak* (Norman, OK: Univ. of Oklahoma Press, 1985; original work published 1861). Guerin should not be confused with Charles Henry McKiernan (1825/30-1892), a Californian 'Mountain Charley.'

[408] Mary Canaga Rowland, *As Long as Life; The Memoirs of a Frontier Woman* (Seattle, WA: Storm Peak Press, 1994), pp. 106-108. Also see Patricia Dunn & Jeanne Gentry, *Lebanon Pioneer Cemetery*, rev. (Lebanon: City of Lebanon, 1995), pp. 86-87.

[409] Herbert Asbury, *The Barbary Coast. An Informal History of the San Francisco Underworld* (N.Y.: Knopf, 1933), p. 250.

[410] Such are the claims on the *Wild Women West* webpage, accessed online at http://users.wi.net/~maracon/lesson2.html. Unfortunately, I was unable to independently verify this information.

[411] "A Californian Romance," *The New York Times* (1874, Aug. 6), p. 2.

[412] Tania Modleski, "A Woman's Gotta Do . . . What a Man's Gotta Do? Cross-Dressing in the Western," *Signs: Journal of Women in Culture and Society*, 22 (no. 3), 519-544 (1997), p. 522.

[413] Ibid, p. 528. Cf. Henry Nash Smith, *Virgin Land: The American West as Symbol and Myth* (Cambridge, MA: Harvard Univ. Press, 1950), p. 118.

[414] Consider, for example, the case of one 'Miss Field,' who tried to persuade men to give up their long trousers in favor of knee-breeches, and was told in an editorial to "teach by practice as well as precept" if she hoped to gain male converts to her cause. See "Knee-Breeches," *The New York Times* (1882, Mar. 3), p. 4.

[415] Caroline Field Levander, *Voices of the Nation. Women and Public Speech in Nineteenth-Century American Literature and Culture* (N. Y.: Cambridge Univ. Press, 1998), p. 117.

[416] Susan Gubar, "Blessings in Disguise: Cross-Dressing as Re-dressing for Female Modernists," *Massachusetts Review*, 22 (no. 3), 477-508 (1981).

[417] J. C. Flugel, *The Psychology of Clothes* (London: Hogarth Press, 1930), p. 207.

[418] Although the date usually given for the start of what is termed the 'new costume' campaign is 1850 or 1851, Nancy Isenberg dates it to a 1849 article in the *Lily* about the dress of Fanny Kemble. See Nancy Isenberg, *Sex and Citizenship in Antebellum America. Gender and American Culture* (Chapel Hill, NC: Univ. of North Carolina Press, 1998), p. 48.

[419] For more on Amelia Jenks Bloomer see Amelia J. Bloomer & Dexter C. Bloomer, *The Life and Writing of Amelia Bloomer* (Boston: Arena Publishing, 1895).

[420] Isenberg, p. 53.

[421] Ibid, p. 96. Isenberg also refers to political cartoons of the day depicting feminists in bloomers as promiscuous, crossdressing hags, and men in disguise.

[422] Elizabeth Reitz Mullenix, "Private Women/Public Acts: Petticoat Government and the Performance of Resistance," *The Drama Review, 46* (no. 1), 104-117 (2002), p. 112.

[423] Fields, "Erotic Modesty," p. 497.

[424] A column in 1895 differentiated three garments women were wearing for bicycling: divided skirts, bloomers, and tight trousers. In this context, bloomers were regarded as more modest than tight trousers. See "A Plea for the Bloomers," *The New York Times* (1895, Aug. 4), p. 15.

[425] "Woman," *The New York Times* (1897, Oct. 3), p. 14.

[426] Robert Chandler, "Eliza Ann Hurd DeWolf: An Earky Case for Cross-Dressing," *Californians, 11* (no. 2), 28-30 (1993).

[427] "A Secret Revealed," *The New York Times* (1885, Aug. 15), p. 4. The notion that late 19th century men wanted in women the opposite of themselves is explored by Mullenix, p. 105, who deems the sentiment "ubiquitous" in the patriarchy that shaped opinion through pulpit and press.

[428] "New Fashions for Men," *The New York Times* (1871, July 26), p. 4. Mount Pleasant, Ohio, was a noted Quaker settlement, although the article does not mention if the men were Quakers.

[429] "Capture of Davis," *Harper's Weekly, IX* (no. 439), p. 1 (1865, May 27). Accessed online at http://www.sonofthesouth.net/ leefoundation/civil-war/1865/jefferson-davis-capture.htm.

[430] "Mr. Jefferson Davis in Costume," *The New York Times* (1880, March 6), p. 4. The article quotes the eyewitness testimony of a member of the Fourth Michigan Cavalry, which effected the capture, declaring that Davis was apprehended wearing a black dress and woman's shawl. Another witness called the garb a black gown, belted at the waist, with a shawl. Yet another eyewitness characterized the outfit as a waterproof skirt and shawl. Even Davis' own adjutant, Colonel Harrison, concurred, recounting that Mrs. Davis had placed a dressing-gown on him to aid escape.

[431] "Blinded by a Disguised Villain," *The New York Times* (1878, June 21), p. 5.

[432] "A Murderer's Escape," *The New York Times* (1873, Nov. 20), p. 8.

[433] "The Man Who Disguised Himself as a Woman," *The New York Times* (1879, Dec. 16), p. 8.

[434] Richard von Krafft-Ebing, *Psychopathia Sexualis. A Medico-Forensic Study*, 12th ed. (N. Y.: Pioneer Publications, 1939/1947; original work published 1886). Krafft-Ebing's work is discussed in the answer to Q. 95.

[435] "Caught a Bogus Policeman," *The New York Times* (1900, Nov. 21), p. 7.

[436] Julie Wheelwright, "Cross-Dressing," in W. Mankiller, G. Mink, M. Navarro, B. Smith, & G. Steinem (Eds.), *The Reader's Companion to U. S. Women's History*, p. 138f. (Boston: Houghton Mifflin, 1998).

[437] The history of the treatment of transgendered realities in the dominant psychiatric diagnostic model is discussed in the answers to Q. 96, 99.

[438] The material in this section is predominantly summary in nature because these matters are explored in depth in many other answers.

[439] Sherrie A. Inness, "Girls Will Be Boys and Boys Will Be Girls: Cross-Dressing in Popular Turn-of-the-Century College Fiction," *Journal of American Culture, 18* (no. 2), 15- 23 (1995), pp. 15-16.

[440] Ibid, pp. 16-21.

[441] Ibid.

[442] Radclyffe Hall, *The Well of Loneliness* (N. Y.: Anchor Books, 1990; original work published 1928).

[443] Djuna Barnes, *Nightwood* (Normal, IL: Dalkey Archive Press, 1995; original work published 1936). For a discussion of this work, see Clare L. Taylor, *Women, Writing, and Fetishism 1890-1950: Female Cross-Gendering* (N. Y.: Oxford Univ. Press, 2003), pp. 149-190.

[444] Laura J. Veltman, "'The Bible Lies One Way, But the Nightgown the Other': Dr. Matthew O'Connor, Confession, and Gender in Djuna Barnes's *Nightwood*," *MFS Modern Fiction Studies, 49* (no. 2), 204-227 (2003), pp. 204, 213.

[445] Hubert Selby Jr., *Last Exit to Brooklyn* (N. Y.: Grove Press, 1964).

[446] Leslie Feinberg, *Stone Butch Blues* (Ann Arbor, MI: Firebrand Books, 1993).

[447] These have a wide range, including historical fiction like an early entry in this wave of novels, Isabel Miller's *Patience and Sarah* (N. Y.: Fawcett-Crest, 1969), set in 1816 and featuring the lesbian love between the narrator, Patience White, and Sarah Dowling, raised by her father to perform the role of a son. Sarah, when we meet her is dressed "in boots, breeches, jerkin, fur mittens, fur hat with a scarf tied over it to cover her ears" (p. 8f.). The two go off together, Sarah masquerading as a man, though over time Sarah becomes more fully the woman Patience desires. While much of this fiction is erotic in nature—itself a reflection of the wider society's sexualization of all things transgender—most of it self-consciously aims at capturing a true-to-experience sense of what life is like for transgendered people. Alongside such literature are nonfiction works like Aphrodite Jones, *All She Wanted* (N. Y.: Pocket Books, 1996), the story of Teena Brandon/Brandon Teena, murdered after her masquerade as a man was discovered.

[448] In Atlanta a 39 year-old man dressed as a woman was arrested, apparently on suspicion of being a prostitute, by an officer after he tried to hide from him. See John Ghirardini, "Amateur Cross-Dresser Looks Too Professional," *The Atlanta Journal-Constitution* (2005, June 15). Accessed online at http://www.ajc.com/hp/content/metro/gwinnett/0605/15laworder.html.

[449] Pauline Weston Thomas observes in a review of fashion trends how designers have borrowed from boys' and traditional masculine fashion elements such as pinstriped fabrics, tweeds, and traditional fair isle patterning on knits. See Pauline Weston Thomas, "Fashion Trends 2004-2005. Autumn 2004 & Winter 2005. Part 2—General Trends," posted on Fashion.-Era.com, accessed online at http://www.fashionera.com/Trends/fashion_trends_05_gentex_autumn_2004_winter_2005.htm. Similar observations can be garnered from reviews of other fashion styles from the early years of the 21st century.

[450] A review of such trends and speculation as to their meaning is found in the answer to Q.9.

[451] Susan K. Freeman, "Book Reviews: In Style: Femininity and Fashion Since the Victorian Era," *Journal of Women's History, 16* (no. 4), 191-206 (2004).

Q. 48 Notes

[452] Rudolf M. Dekker & Lotte C. Van de Pol, *The Tradition of Female Transvestism in Early Modern Europe* (N. Y.: Macmillan Press, 1989).

⁴⁵³ For more on the life of Elena de Cespedes, see Richard L. Kagan (Ed.) & Abigail Dyer (Trans.), *Inquisitorial Inquiries: Brief Lives of Secret Jews and Other Heretics* (Baltimore, MD: John Hopkins Univ. Press, 2004), pp. 36-59.

⁴⁵⁴ William N. Eskridge, Jr., *The Case for Same-Sex Marriage: From Sexual Liberty to Civilized Commitment* (N. Y.: Free Press, 1996). See chapter 2.

⁴⁵⁵ Israel Burshatin's interest is described in the Haverford College *Media Resource Directory* section on History. Accessed online at http://www.haverford.edu/ publicrelations/expertsdir/ history/israelburshatin.html.

⁴⁵⁶ Mary Frith's story is also recounted in older works such as the *Newgate Calendar* (or *Malefactor's Bloody Register*), first published in 5 volumes in 1760. This collection—*The Complete Newgate Calendar*—is preserved in electronic text form in the 'Law in Popular Culture Collection' of the Tarleton Law Library of the University of Texas at Austin. Accessed online at http://tarlton.law.utexas.edu/lpop/etext/newgate/ frith.htm. Also see, "Moll Cutpurse and Jonathan Wild," in Charles Whibley, *A Book of Scoundrels* (Seattle: The World Wide School, 1999). Accessed online at http://www. worldwideschool.org/library/books/lit/historical/ABookofScoundrels/chap4.html.

⁴⁵⁷ *The Complete Newgate Calendar*, Vol. 1, p. 174. Accessed online at http://tarlton.law. utexas.edu/lpop/etext/newgate/frith.htm.

⁴⁵⁸ The play was written by Thomas Middleton (1580-1627) and Thomas Dekker (1570-1632). Accessed online at http://www.tech.org/~cleary/roar.html. For more on the play, see the answer to Q. 44.

⁴⁵⁹ See Ellen Galford, *Moll Cutpurse: Her True History* (Ann Arbor, MI: Firebrand Books, 1985).

⁴⁶⁰ See Catalina de Erauso, *Lieutenant Nun. Memoir of a Basque Transvestite in the New World*, trans. Michele Stepto & Gabriel Stepto (Boston: Beacon Press, 1996).

⁴⁶¹ See the entry "Nzinga, Queen of Angola," in C. Lewis, D. Barrett-Graves, J. Eldridge Carney, W. M. Spellman, G. Kennedy, & S. Witham, *Extraordinary Women of the Medieval and Renaissance World* (Oxford: Greenword Press, 2000). Also see Joseph Calder Miller, "Njinga of Matamba in a New Perspective," *Journal of African History*, 16 (no. 2), 201-216 (1975). Cf. David Sweetman, *Women Leaders in African History* (Oxford: Heinemann, 1984). On the internet, see John K. Thornton, *African Political Ethics and the Slave Trade: Central African Dimensions*, a seminar paper posted as part of 'The Atlantic World: An Electronic Exploration' website. Accessed online at http://muweb.millersville.edu/~winthrop/Thornton.html.

⁴⁶² "The Greatest Africans of All Time," *New African* (2004, Aug.-Sept.). Accessed online at the NewAfrican website at http://www.africasia.com/newafrican/na.php?ID=385.

⁴⁶³ See Georgina Masson, *Queen Christina* (London: Camelot Press, LTD, 1968); esp. see p. 370. Also see Veronica Buckley, *Christina, Queen of Sweden* (N.Y.: HarperCollins, 2004). Cf. Sven Stolpe, *Christina of Sweden* (N. Y.: Macmillan, 1966). Greta Garbo starred in the 1933 film, *Queen Christina*.

⁴⁶⁴ See Charles John Samuel Thompson, *The Mysteries of Sex: Women Who Posed as Men and Men Who Impersonated Women* (N. Y.: Causeway Books, 1974), pp. 54-69. Cf. Julie Wheelright, *Amazons and Military Maids: Women Who Dressed as Men in the Pursuit of Life, Liberty and Happiness* (London: Pandora, 1990). Also see "Christian Davies," in Henry Boylan (Ed.), *Dictionary of Irish Biography* (Dublin: Gill & Macmillan, 1998).

⁴⁶⁵ See Oscar Paul Gilbert, *Women in Men's Guise*, translated by J. L. May (London: John Lane, 1932). Also see Cameron Rogers, *Gallant Ladies* (N. Y.: Harcourt Brace, 1928). Also see the *Mademoiselle Maupin Home Page*, accessed online at http://home.comcast.net/~brons/Maupin/ MaupinIndex.html.

⁴⁶⁶ See Mary Anne Talbot, "The Intrepid Female, or Surprising Life and Adventures of Mary-Anne Talbot, Otherwise John Taylor," in R. S. Kirby (Ed.), *Wonderful Museum* (London, 1804). Also see Robert S. Kirby, *Life and Surprising Adventures of Mary Anne Talbot* (London, 1809). Cf. Thompson, pp. 84-94. Also see the ballad "The True History of Mary Anne Talbot," by Howard L.Kaplan (1990, 1991). Accessed online at http://www.thrinberry-frog.com/VirtualSongbook/TrueHistoryOfMaryAnneTalbot.pdf.

⁴⁶⁷ Claude E. Schaeffer, "The Kutenai Female Berdache: Courier, Guide, Prophetess, and Warrior," *Ethnohistory, 12* (no. 3), 193-236 (1965), pp. 193-196.

⁴⁶⁸ Ibid, p. 197.

⁴⁶⁹ Ibid, pp. 197-198.

⁴⁷⁰ Ibid, pp. 198-200.

⁴⁷¹ Ibid, pp. 200-207.

⁴⁷² Ibid, pp. 208-216. As with other events of her life, this one has alternate tellings. Some say Qánqon met her end by a Blackfoot ambush. In this telling, she was repeatedly wounded, each time the wounds miraculously self-healing until finally her chest was opened and the lower part of her heart cut out. Allegedly, after her death she continued to trouble the Blackfoot party, prompting the leader to declare they had killed a powerful woman.

⁴⁷³ See F. Winwar, *The Life Of The Heart: George Sand and Her Times* (N. Y.: Harper & Brothers Publishers, 1945); see esp. p. 100. Also see Andre Maurois, *Lélia: The Life of George Sand* (N. Y.: Harper & Brothers, 1953). Also see Belinda Jack, *George Sand: A Woman's Life Writ Large* (N. Y.: Knopf, 2000).

⁴⁷⁴ See Nadezhda Durova, *The Cavalry Maiden: Journals of a Russian Officer in the Napoleonic Wars*, translated by M. F. Zirin (Bloomington, IN: Indiana Univ. Press, 1989). Cf. Mary Fleming Zirin, "Durova, Nadezhda Andreevna," in R. Pennington (Ed.), *Amazons to Fighter Pilots: A Biographical Dictionary of Military Women*, pp. 128-131 (Westport, CT: Greenwood Press, 2003).

⁴⁷⁵ See Loreta J. Velazquez, *The Woman in Battle: A Narrative of the Exploits, Adventures, and Travels of Madam Loreta Janeta Velazquez, Otherwise Known as Lieutenant Harry T. Buford, Confederate States Army*, edited by C. J. Worthington (Richmond, VA: Gilman & Co., 1876). This text available through the Documenting the American South website and accessed online at http://docsouth.unc.edu/ velazquez/velazquez.html. Also see Loreta Janeta Velazquez, *The Woman in Battle. The Civil War Narrative of Loreta Janeta Velazquez, Cuban Woman and Confederate Soldier* (Madison, WI: Univ. of Wisconsin Press, 2003).

⁴⁷⁶ Velazquez, *The Woman in Battle*, p. 42. Cf. her remark later (p. 130), "I have no hesitation in saying that I wish I had been created a man instead of a woman."

⁴⁷⁷ Ibid, p. 6.

⁴⁷⁸ Ibid, p. 58f.

⁴⁷⁹ Ibid, p. 75.

⁴⁸⁰ Ibid, p. 128.

481 See Diane Wood Middlebrook, *Suits Me. The Double Life of Billy Tipton* (N.Y.: Mariner Books, 1999). Cf. the *Billy Tipton* webpage (with the photo of Tipton in 1934 in both male and female appearance); it was accessed at http://www.music.duke.edu.jazz_archive/artists/tipton.billy/01/.

Q. 49 Notes

482 See Ulrich von Lichtenstein, *The Service of Ladies. An Autobiography*. Tr. J. W. Thomas (Suffolk, UK: Boydell Press, 2004). Also see Brian R. Price, "Ulrich von Lichtenstein and the *Venus Fahrt* (Venus Journey)," *Chronique: Journal of Chivalry*, 7, 45-47. Von Lichtenstein's journey was the inspiration later for the well-known work, *Don Quixote de la Mancha*, and the film *A Knight's Tale*.

483 Katherine B. Crawford, "Love, Sodomy, and Scandal: Controlling the Sexual Reputation of Henry III," *Journal of the History of Sexuality*, 12 (no. 4), 513-542 (2003), p. 517.

484 Ibid, p. 517f.

485 Eugene de Savitsch, *Homosexuality, Transvestism and Change of Sex* (London: William Heinemann Medical Books, 1958), p. 16. Cf. James B. Collins, *From Tribes to Nation: The Making of France 500-1780* (Toronto: Wadsworth-Thomson Learning, 2002), p. 252f. About the riding dressed as an Amazon, Katherine Crawford (p. 524f.) notes only the king's contemporary L'Éstoile recorded such an incident. She speculates that some forms of crossdressing might have been common at the court entertainments Henry attended.

486 Pierre de L'Éstoile, *Le Cabinet du Roy de France* (Paris, 1581), 1:173, cited in Crawford, p. 527.

487 Crawford, p. 527.

488 Havelock Ellis, *Studies in the Psychology of Sex*, 2 vols. (N. Y.: Random House, 1941-1942; original work was published 1905-1928). See Vol. II, Part Two: 'Eonism and Other Supplementary Studies.' The work of Ellis is reviewed in the answer to Q. 95.

489 The Beaumont Society was founded in 1966 and today claims to be the UK's "largest and longest established transgendered support group." The Society maintains a website and was accessed online at http://www.beaumontsociety.org.uk/.

490 This volume was written by d'Eon's friend La Fortelle.

491 For more on Chevalier d'Eon's life, see Charles d'Eon de Beaumont, *The Maiden of Tonnerre: The Vicissitudes of the Chevalier and the Chevalière d'Eon*, Eds. and trans. Roland A. Champagne, Nina Ekstein, & Gary Kates. (Baltimore: The Johns Hopkins University Press, 2001). This work provides an introduction for context, together with translations of various works by d'Eon, including his never published autobiography *La Pucelle de Tonnerre*. For an interesting theatrical treatment, see the comedic play by Mark Brownell, *Monsieur d'Eon* (Theatre Communications Group, 2001). Among numerous online sites are a biography accessed at http://www.kirjasto. sci.fi/deon.htm and the French language site http://archives.chez.tiscali.fr/eon1.html.

492 Gary Kates, *Monsieur d'Eon Is a Woman: A Tale of Political Intrigue and Sexual Masquerade* (N. Y.: Basic Books, 1995). The Johns Hopkins University Press published a paperback edition of this book in 2001. Lest d'Eon be viewed as hopelessly disturbed in his reasoning, cf. the note in the much more contemporary account by Shere Hite: "A large part of teenage boys' 'mean and nasty' crazes are attempts by them to deal with their culturally imposed guilt; i.e., if one is 'bad' already, one might as well glorify being

an outlaw, being really tough and cruel, etc. Thus, the glorification of being mean and nasty as being 'really male' (for example, as frequently seen on MTV and in children's monster or war toy commercials) comes because men (by definition) can never be 'good.'" Shere Hite, *Women in Love. A Cultural Revolution in Progress* (N. Y.: Alfred A. Knopf, 1987), p. 689n.

[493] Gary Kates, "Introduction," in Charles d'Eon de Beaumont, *The Maiden of Tonnerre: The Vicissitudes of the Chevalier and the Chevalière d'Eon*, Eds. and trans. Roland A. Champagne, Nina Ekstein, & Gary Kates. (Baltimore: The Johns Hopkins University Press, 2001), p. ix. Concerning Joan of Arc, see her story in the answer to Q. 68.

[494] Riki Anne Wilchens, *Queer Theory, Gender Theory: An Instant Primer* (N. Y.: Alyson Books, 2004), p. 22.

[495] This material is drawn principally from the following sources: Dave King & Richard Ekins, *Pioneers of Transgendering: The Life and Work of Virginia Prince* (2000), accessed online at http://www.gender.org.uk/conf/2000/king20.htm. This material was prepared for the GENDYS Conference, 2000. Also see by the same authors, *Virginia Prince: Pioneer of Transgendering* (N. Y.: Haworth, 2006). Also see Jane Ellen Fairfax, *A Brief History of Tri-Ess* (2006), accessed online at the Tri-Ess website, at http://www.tri-ess.org/history.html. Also see Laura Granger & Joan Huff, *Tiffany Club of New England* (2004). Accessed online at http://www.tcne.org/club_history.htm.

[496] C. V. Prince, "Homosexuality, Transvestism and Transsexuality: Reflections on Their Etiology and Differentiation," *American Journal of Psychotherapy*, 11, 80-85 (1957). Reproduced in *Virginia Prince: Pioneer of Transgendering*, pp. 17-20.

[497] Fairfax, *A Brief History of Tri-Ess*.

[498] King & Ekins.

[499] Granger & Huff.

[500] Dennis Dailey calls Prince "an entrepreneur of transvestism"; see Dailey, *The Sexually Unusual: Guide to Understanding and Helping* (N. Y.: Haworth Press, 1988), p. 19.

[501] Virginia Charles Prince, *The Transvestite and His Wife* (Hollywood, CA: Chevalier Publications, 1967).

[502] This from Virginia Prince as recounted to Leslie Feinberg. See Feinberg, *Transgender Warriors: Making History from Joan of Arc to Dennis Rodman* (Boston: Beacon Press, 1996), p. x.

[503] Virginia Prince, "Seventy Years in the Trenches of the Gender Wars," in B. Bullough, V. Bullough, & J. Elias (Eds.), *Gender Blending*, pp. 469-476 (Amherst, NY: Prometheus Books, 1997). Quote is from p. 469.

[504] For a treatment of Twain's presentations of gender crossing and crossdressing, see the answer to Q. 47.

[505] Laura Skandera-Trombley, "Mark Twain's Cross-Dressing Oeuvre," *College Literaure*, 24 (no. 2), 82-96 (1997).

[506] Dennis Rodman (with Tim Keown), *Bad As I Wanna Be* (N. Y.: Delacorte Press, 1996), p. 178.

[507] Ibid.

[508] Ibid.

[509] Ibid, p. 179.

Q. 50 Notes

⁵¹⁰ See G. G. Bolich, *Conversing on Gender. A Primer for Entering Dialog* (Raleigh, NC: Psyche's Press, 2007). In fifteen chapters this volume moves from a thorough consideration of the meaning of basic terms ('sex,' 'gender,' 'transgender,' etc.), through a history of discussion of gender, into an array of spheres such as gender politics, the development of gender, gender identity, gender roles, and so forth.

⁵¹¹ Michel Foucault locates the transition in Western culture from the 17th century through the Victorian Age (19th century) down into the medicalization of sex in the late 19th-early 20th century. He views the Victorian period as one in which sexuality became more discussed in a particular way, one designed to control it. Science medicalized it and turned certain behaviors into scientifically classified illnesses. See *La Volonté de savoir Vol. 1 of Histoire de la sexualité* (1976). Trans. Robert Hurley as *The History of Sexuality Volume 1: An Introduction* (NY: Pantheon, 1978; also, Vintage Books, 1990). On medicine's pathological approach to sex, see pp. 54-56; on the medicalization of sex, see pp. 117-119. The modern Western emphasis on *whom* we have sex with rather than on *what* we do during sex (i.e., take the active or passive role) stands in contrast with previous centuries of sexual values in the West. The pre-modern Western stress on sexual acts and roles rather than on sexual objects also may have pertained to the East. Sam Winter of the University of Hong Kong, writing about sex and gender in classical China, has contended that "a Chinese male's sexuality was defined less in terms of whom he had sex with (man or woman) than what he did during sex (acting as inserter or insertee)." See Sam Winter, *'Country Report': Hong Kong: Social and Cultural Issues* (2002). Accessed online at http://web.hku.hk/~sjwinter/Transgender ASIA/country_report_hk_social.htm.

⁵¹² See, for example, John R. Clarke, *Looking at Lovemaking: Constructions of Sexuality in Roman Art, 100 B.C.-A.D. 250* (Berkeley: Univ. of California Press, 1998). Clarke, an art historian, shows how through their artistic depictions the ancients viewed sexual behavior in many ways, with variety of both 'objects' and 'aims' (to use Freud's terms) apparent. They were *not* focused on sexual activity for procreation—though they did not ignore that aspect—and they did not conceive of sexual behavior as 'sin.'

⁵¹³ Angus McLaren, *Twentieth-Century Sexuality. A History* (Oxford: Blackwell, 1999), p. 90.

⁵¹⁴ Ibid.

⁵¹⁵ Robert A. Nye, "Honor, Impotence, and Male Sexuality in Nineteenth-Century French Medicine," *French Historical Studies, 16* (no. 1), 48-71 (1989), p. 48.

⁵¹⁶ Numerous instances of this desire could be made, but the point is sufficiently illustrated by the persistent desire to explain homosexuality or transsexualism as hormones gone awry, or otherwise due to an 'unnatural' biology.

⁵¹⁷ The dubious heritage of this approach is the American Psychiatric Association's *Diagnostic and Statistical Manual of Mental Disorders*, now in its 4th edition. For an examination of this work, see Herb Kutchins & Stuart A. Kirk, *Making Us Crazy: DSM: The Psychiatric Bible and the Creation of Mental Disorders* (N.Y.: Free Press, 1997); with reference to issues of sex and gender, cf. chs. 3 and 5. Also see Stuart A. Kirk & Herb Kutchins, *The Selling of DSM. The Rhetoric of Science in Psychiatry* (N. Y.: Aldine de Gruyter, 1992). Cf. Paula J. Caplan, *They Say You're Crazy. How the World's Most Powerful Psychiatrists Decide Who's Normal* (N.Y.: Perseus Books, 1995). Also see Rachel Cooper, "What is Wrong with the DSM?" *History of Psychiatry, 15* (no. 1), 15-25 (2004). Finally, cf. Karen Eriksen

& Victoria E. Kress, *Beyond the DSM Story. Ethical Quandaries, Challenges, and Best Practices* (Thousand Oaks, CA: Sage, 2005).

[518] Bolich, *Conversing on Gender*. See especially pp. 30-38.

[519] Manuel X. Zamarripa, Bruce E. Wampold, & Erik Gregory, "Male Gender Role Conflict, Depression, and Anxiety: Clarification and Generalizability to Women," *Journal of Counseling Psychology, 50* (no. 3), 333-338 (2003), p. 333. Cf. J. M. O'Neil, "Patterns of Gender Role Conflict and Strain: Sexism and Fear of Femininity in Men's Lives," *Personnel and Guidance Journal, 60*, 203-210 (1981).

[520] Ruth E. Hartley, "Sex-Role Pressures and the Socialization of the Male Child," in J. H. Pleck & J. Sawyer (Eds.), *Men and Masculinity*, pp. 7-13 (Englewood Cliffs, NJ: Prentice-Hall, 1974), p. 7.

[521] Kenneth J. Zucker, Susan J. Bradley, & Mohammed Sanikhani, "Sex Differences in Referral Rates of Children with Gender Identity Disorder: Some Hypotheses," *Journal of Abnormal Child Psychology, 25* (no. 3), 217-227 (1997). The actual ratio was 6.6:1, boys to girls.

[522] In fact, these pressures are at the heart of one possible explanation for male crossdressing. In the literature, cf. J. M. O'Neil, "Patterns of Gender Role Conflict and Strain: Sexism and Fear of Femininity in Men's Lives," *Personnel and Guidance Journal, 60*, 203-210 (1981).

[523] Hartley, p. 7.

[524] For more on the role of homophobia as an important constituent in constructing a boy's masculinity, see Bolich, *Conversing on Gender*, p. 210f.

[525] Carol Lynn Martin, "Attitudes and Expectations About Children with Nontraditional and Traditional Gender Roles," *Sex Roles, 22* (nos. 3/4), 151-165 (1990).

[526] Francesco Alberoni, "A Freudian Skirt," *Mono Uomo, 79*, 44-45 (1994, March).

[527] American Psychiatric Association, *Diagnostic and Statistical Manual of Mental Disorders, 4th Edition, Text Revision* (Washington, D. C.: American Psychiatric Association, 2000), p. 574.

Q. 51 Notes

[528] Robert L. Munroe & Ruth H. Munroe, "Male Transvestism and Subsistence Economy," *Journal of Social Psychology, 103* (no. 2), 307-308 (1977). Interestingly, all of these societies are characterized by male predominance in subsistence activities in their economies. The authors suggest that the male transvestite role is more likely to become a social institution in societies where one of two conditions is present: either the distinction between gender roles is little, or there are high subsistence requirements placed on males.

[529] Robert L. Munroe, John W. M. Whiting, & David J. Hally, "Institutionalized Male Transvestism and Sex Distinctions," *American Anthropologist, 71* (no. 1), 87-91 (1969). The authors note that the traditional assumption had been that institutionalized male transvestism would be more likely in societies both where male-female sex roles are strongly differentiated and where some motive to escape the male role—such as avoidance of involvement in warfare—would be strongly present. Neither assumption held up to scrutiny. Interestingly, perhaps a rise in the incidence of transvestism has occurred in modern American society as sex role differentiation has modified and lessened.

530 Margaret Mead, *Sex and Temperament in Three Primitive Societies* (N. Y.: Morrow Quill Paperbacks, 1963; original work published 1935), p. 294. Mead mentions the practice among American Indians and people in Siberia in contradistinction to its manifestation in modern Europe and America.

531 Vern L. Bullough & Bonnie Bullough, *Crossdressing, Sex, Gender.* (Phila.: Univ. of Pennsylvania Press, 1993), p. 5.

532 Vicky Lee (Ed.), *Way Out of the Closet. The Tranny Guide*, 11th ed. (2003).

Q. 52 Notes

533 Magnus Hirschfeld, *Curious Sex Customs in the Far East* (N. Y.: Capricorn Books 1965 reprint of 1935 edition).

534 Ibid, p. xvi*f.*

535 See, for instance, V. N. Basilov, "Vestiges of Transvestism in Central-Asian Shamanism," in V. Diószegi & M. Hoppál (Eds.), *Shamanism in Siberia*, pp. 281-289 (Budapest: Akadémiai Kiadó, 1978).

536 In the Spring of 2005, Pakistani security agents, dressed in women's *burqas*, were able to capture a prominent Al Qaeda figure, Abu Faraj Al-Libbi. See Michael Isikoff & Mark Hosenball, "Got Him. Now What?" *Newsweek*, pp. 24-27 (2005, May 16).

537 Erick Laurent, "Sexuality and Human Rights: An Asian Perspective," *Journal of Homosexuality, 48* (nos. 3-4), 163-225 (2005), p. 169.

538 Shivananda Khan, Aditya Bondyopadhyay, & Carol Jenkins, *Eyes Wide Shut. Violence, Stigma and Social Exclusion, MSM, HIV, and Social Justice in South Asia* (Naz Foundation International, 2004). Accessed online at http://www.nfi.net/NFI%20Publications/Essays/2004/Eyes%20Wide%20Shut.doc. Also see "VI. Abuses Against Men Who Have Sex with Men," in *Bangladesh. Ravaging the Vulnerable: Abuses Against Persons at High Risk of HIV Infection in Bangladesh , 15* (no. 6 (C)) (N. Y.: Human Rights Watch, 2003), pp. 39-43. Accessed online at http://www.hrw.org/reports/2003/bangladesh0803/bangladesh0803full.pdf. A distinct group of transgendered males in Bangladesh self-identify as being *Kothis*, described in the section on India.

539 See Vern L. Bullough, *Sexual Variance in Society and History* (N. Y.: John Wiley & Sons, 1976), p. 299. Also see Fang Fu Ruan, "Taoism and Sex," in V. L. Bullough & B. Bullough (Eds.), *Human Sexuality: An Encyclopedia*, pp. 575-577 (N. Y.: Garland, 1994). Cf. A. Ishihara & H. S. Levy, *The Tao of Sex* (Yokohama: Shibundo, 1968).

540 See Fang Fu Ruan, "Confucianism and Sex," in V. L. Bullough & B. Bullough (Eds.), *Human Sexuality: An Encyclopedia*, pp. 139-140 (N. Y.: Garland, 1994). Cf. the section on social artifice in Confucianism in the answer to Q. 76.

541 Chou Hui-ling, "Striking Their Own Poses: The History of Cross-Dressing on the Chinese Stage," *TDR: The Drama Review, 41* (no. 2), 130-153 (1997).

542 *Lien-siang-pan* (*Love for the Perfumed Companion*) was written in 1638 by novelist Li Yu.

543 See S. Volpe, "Gender, Power and Spectacle in Late-Imperial Chinese Theater," in S. Ramet (Ed.), *Gender Reversals and Gender Cultures*, ch. 9 (London: Routledge, 1996). For more on crossdressing's role in Chinese theater, see the answer to Q. 44.

544 Zuyan Zhou, *Androgyny in Late Ming and Early Qing Literature* (Honolulu: Univ. of Hawaii Press, 2003), p. 279 n. 6

[545] Cao Xueqin, *The Story of the Stone*, 5 vols. Translated by David Hawkes (vols. 1-3) and J. Minford (vols. 4-5) (N. Y.: Penguin Books, 1973-1986). The original work appeared c. 1760.

[546] Shen Fu, *Six Records of a Floating Life*, translated by L. Pratt & C. Su-hui (N.Y.: Penguin Books, 1983), pp. 44f.

[547] Ibid.

[548] W. S. Chou, *Tongzhi: Politics of Same-Sex Eroticism in Chinese Societies* (N.Y.: Haworth Press, 2000).

[549] Sam Winter, 'Country Report': Hong Kong: Social and Cultural Issues (2002). Accessed online at http://web.hku.hk/~sjwinter/TransgenderASIA/country_report_hk_social.htm.

[550] Fang Fu Ruan & M. P. Lau, "China," in R. T. Francoeur (Ed.), *The International Encyclopedia of Sexuality*, Vols. I-III (N. Y.: Continuum, 1997). Accessed online at http://www2.rz.huberlin.de/sexology/GESUND/ARCHIV/IES/CHINA.HTM#7.%20GENDER%20CONFLICTED%20PERSONS. See §7. Gender Conflicted Persons.

[551] H. G. Hwu, E. K. Yeh, & L. Y. Chang, "Prevalence of Psychiatric Disorders in Taiwan Defined by the Chinese Diagnostic Interview Schedule," *Acta Psychiatrica Scandinavia, 79* (no. 2), 136-147.

[552] John Sik-Nin Ko, "Research and Discussion Paper: A Descriptive Study of Sexual Dysfunction and Gender Identity Clinic in the University of Hong Kong Psychiatric Unit, 1991-2001." Extracts from a dissertation submitted as part of the Part III Fellowship Examination for the Hong Kong College of Psychiatrists. Accessed online at http://web.hku.hk/~sjwinter/TransgenderASIA/paper_qmh_evaluation.htm.

[553] Fang Fu Ruan & Vern L. Bullough, "The First Case of Transsexual Surgery in Mainland China," *The Journal of Sex Research, 25* (no. 4), 546-547 (1988).

[554] Fang Fu Ruan, Vern L. Bullough, & Yung-Mei Tsai, "Male Transsexualism in Mainland China," *Archives of Sexual Behavior, 18* (no. 6), 517-522 (1989).

[555] Ko, 'Results' section. All the FtM had crossdressed, and all but two of the MtF.

[556] Emil Man-lun Ng & Joyce L. C. Ma, "Hong Kong," in R. T. Francoeur (Ed.), *The International Encyclopedia of Sexuality*, Vol. IV, pp. 216-245 (N. Y.: Continuum, 2001). Accessed online at http://www.sexquest.com/IES4/ies4hongkong.pdf. See §7. Gender Conflicted Persons, pp. 229-231. Also see Joyce L. C. Ma, "A Systems Approach to the Social Difficulties of Transsexuals in Hong Kong," *Journal of Family Therapy, 19* (no. 1), 71-88 (1997).

[557] Fang Fu Ruan, *Sex in China: Studies in Sexology in Chinese Culture* (N. Y.: Plenum Press, 1991).

[558] Ng & Ma, p. 230f.

[559] Ko, 'Results' section.

[560] For a detailed anthropological study, see Emma Tarlo, *Clothing Matters: Dress and Identity in India* (Chicago: Univ. of Chicago Press, 1996).

[561] Early British colonialists remarked on women dressed as men who served in various capacities, including as bodyguards. See Walter D. Penrose, Jr., "India," in C. J. Summers, *glbtq: An Encyclopedia of Gay, Lesbian, Bisexual, Transgender, and Queer Culture* (Chicago: glbtq, Inc., 2004), accessed online at http://www.glbtq.com/socialsciences/india,2.html.

⁵⁶² Cf. Devdutt Pattanaik, *The Man Who Was a Woman and Other Queer Tales from Hindu Lore* (Binghamton, NY: Haworth Press, 2002), p. 10.

⁵⁶³ Ibid.

⁵⁶⁴ Walter Penrose, "Hidden in History: Female Homoeroticism and Women of a 'Third Nature' in the South Asian Past," *Journal of the History of Sexuality*, 10 (no. 1), 3-39 (2001), pp. 6, 8, 17.

⁵⁶⁵ Akshay Khanna, *A Language for Love* (2006, Apr. 2). Accessed online at Boloji.com at http://www.boloji.com/wfs5/wfs577.htm.

⁵⁶⁶ Laurent, p. 172. *Zenanas* is a term more commonly heard in Pakistan.

⁵⁶⁷ Naz Foundation International, *Development Manual. Developing Community-Based Organizations Addressing HIV/AIDS, Sexual Health, Welfare and Human Rights Issues for Males-Who-Have-Sex-with-Males, Their Partners, and Families* (London: Naz Foundation International, 2005), p. 7. Accessed online at http://www.nfi.net/NFI%20Publications/Manuals/Book%201%20manual.pdf.

⁵⁶⁸ Ibid, p. 12. Also see Naz Foundation International, *Annual Report, 2003-2004. Planning for the Future* (London: Naz Foundation International, 2004), p. 25f. Accessed online at http://www.nfi.net/NFI%20Publications/Annual%20Reports/aAR2003-4.pdf.

⁵⁶⁹ Shivananda Khan, "Men Who Have Sex with Men and Disempowerment in South Asia," *Sexual Health Exchange 2005-2* (2005). Accessed online at the Royal Tropical Institute (KIT) website at http://www.kit.nl/frameset.asp?/ils/exchange_content/html/2005-2_men_who_have_sex_with_m.asp&frnr=1&.

⁵⁷⁰ More elaboration on this connection is found in the answer to Q. 79.

⁵⁷¹ Bullough, p. 30.

⁵⁷² Pattanaik, p. 11.

⁵⁷³ Penrose, p. 10.

⁵⁷⁴ For a complete account, see Serena Nanda, *Neither man Nor Woman: The Hijras of India* (N. Y.: Wadsworth, 1998).

⁵⁷⁵ Penrose, p. 4 n. 3.

⁵⁷⁶ National AIDS Control Organization (NACO), *Some Important Chapters of a Training Curriculum on VCT* (NACO, 2004), III/3-4 (p. 110f.), accessed online at http://www.nacoonline.org/ publication/trainingcuricullum.pdf. NSCO operates under India's Ministry of Health & Family Welfare.

⁵⁷⁷ Gayatri Reddy, "Crossing 'Lines' of Subjectivity: the Negotiation of Sexual Identity in Hyderabad, India," in S. Srivastava (ed.), *Sexual Sites, Seminal Attitudes: Sexualities, Masculinities, and Culture in South Asia*, pp. 147-164 (Thousand Oaks, CA: Sage Publications, 2004), p. 155.

⁵⁷⁸ Ibid. The *Kothi* are discussed separately in this answer.

⁵⁷⁹ Laurent, p. 172.

⁵⁸⁰ Bahuchara Mata is a 'mother goddess' like Cybele. See Pattanaik, chapter 4 for her story. Cf. Will Roscoe, "Priests of the Goddess: Gender Transgression in Ancient Religion," *History of Religions*, 35 (no. 3), 295-330 (1996).

⁵⁸¹ Many *Hijra* in Pakistan, an Islamic nation, are associated with the Sufi tradition of that religion. See the answer to Q. 78.

⁵⁸² On their contemporary struggles, see "Eunuchs Want Two Percent of Society," *India Briefly* (2006, May 26), accessed online at the Despardes.com website at

http://www.despardes.com/India/ newsbriefs/2006/20060530-india-news.html. The same place includes an account by Siddarth Narrain, "Being a Eunuch."

[583] Siddharth Narrain, "In a Twilight World," *Frontline, 20* (no. 21) (2003, Oct. 11-24). Accessed online at http://www.hinduonnet.com/fline/fl2021/stories/20031024002509800.htm. *Frontline* is a national publication in India.

[584] Jayaji Krishna Nath, & Vishwarath R. Nayar, "India," in R. T. Francoeur (Ed.), *The International Encyclopedia of Sexuality*, Vols. I-III (N. Y.: Continuum, 1997). Accessed online at http://www2.rz.hu-berlin.de/sexology/GESUND/ARCHIV/IES/INDIA.HTM#7.%20GENDER%20CONFLICTED%20PERSONS. See §7. Gender Conflicted Persons.

[585] See Serena Nanda, "Hijras: An Alternative Sex and Gender Role in India," in Gilbert Herdt (Ed.), *Third Sex, Third Gender: Beyond Sexual Dimorphism in Culture and History*, pp. 373-418 (N. Y.: Zone Books, 1993). For an account of modern *Hijra*, albeit with reference to Pakistan, see Nauman Naqvi & Hasan Mujtaba, "Two Baluchi *Buggas*, a Sindhi *Zenana*, and the Status of *Hijras* in Contemporary Pakistan," in S. O. Murray & W. Roscoe (Eds.), *Islamic Homosexualities: Culture, History, & Literature*, pp. 262-266 (N. Y.: New York Univ. Press, 1997).

[586] Bernard Rudofsky, *The Kimono Mind: An Informal Guide to Japan and the Japanese* (N. Y.: Doubleday, 1965).

[587] Richard Martin, "Our *Kimono* Mind: Reflections on 'Japanese Design Since 1950'," *Journal of Design History, 8* (no. 3), 215-223 (1995), p. 215.

[588] Akie N. Arima, "Gender Stereotypes in Japanese Television Advertisements," *Sex Roles, 49* (nos. 1-2), 81-90 (2003). A number of research studies have found that advertising in Asian countries has become more Western in its depiction of women and their dress. See, for example, Katherine Toland Frith, Hong Cheng, & Ping Shaw, "Race and Beauty: A Comparison of Asian and Western Models in Women's Magazine Advertisements," *Sex Roles, 50* (nos. 1-2), 53-61 (2004).

[589] Mark McLelland, "Living More 'Like Oneself': Transgender Identities and Sexualities in Japan," *Journal of Bisexuality, 3* (nos. 3-4), 203-230 (2003).

[590] Gary Leupp, *Male Colors: The Construction of Homosexuality in Tokugawa Japan* (Berkeley: Univ. of California Press, 1995). The book's time period is early modern Japan.

[591] Mark McLelland, "The Newhalf Net: Japan's 'Intermediate Sex' On-Line," *International Journal of Sexuality and Gender Studies, 7* (nos. 2-3), 163-175 (2002).

[592] Ibid.

[593] Keiji Hirano, "Transsexuals, Sex-Change Advocates Fight on Against Social, Registry Snub," *The Japan Times Online* (2003, February 6). Accessed online at http://www.japantimes.com/cgi-bin/getarticle.pl5?nn20030206b7.htm.

[594] Hiroshi Matsubara, "Sex Change No Cure for Torment," *The Japan Times Online* (2001, June 20). Accessed online at http://www.japantimes.com/cgi-bin/getarticle.pl5?nn20010620c1.htm.

[595] Hirano. Cf. "Transsexuals Set to File Civil Lawsuits," *The Japan Times Online* (2001, May 6). Accessed online at http://www.japantimes.com/cgi-bin/getarticle.pl5?nn20010506a6.htm.

596 Gary McLelland, "Why are Japanese Girls' Comics Full of Boys Bonking?" *Intensities. The Journal of Cult Media, 1* (2001, Spring/Summer). Accessed online at http://www.cult-media.com/issue1/CMRmcle.htm.

597 Mark Schilling, "The Rose of Versailles," in M. Schilling, *The Encyclopedia of Japanese Pop Culture*, pp. 206-209 (Trumball, CT: Weatherhill, Inc., 1997).

598 Yoshiro Hatano & Tsuguo Shimazaki, "Japan," in R. T. Francoeur (Ed.), *The International Encyclopedia of Sexuality*, Vols. I-III (N. Y.: Continuum, 1997). Accessed online at http://www2.rz.hu-berlin.de/sexology/GESUND/ARCHIV/IES/JAPAN.HTM#7 .%20GENDER%20CONFLICTED%20PERSONS. See §7. Gender Conflicted Persons.

599 Yang Sung-jin, "Trouble-Ridden Marriages for Sons," *Korea Times* (1999, Sept. 28). Accessed online at the *Korea Times* website archives at http://search.hankooki.com/times/times_view.php?term=cross-dresser++&path=hankooki1/ 14_6/199909/t465195.htm&media=kt.

600 Pauline Park & John Manzon-Santos, *Issues of Transgendered Asian Americans and Pacific Islanders*. Accessed online at the Asian and Pacific Islander Wellness Center website at http://www.apiwellness.org/v20/tg/tgtestimony.html.

601 Laurel Kendall, *Shamans, Housewives, and Other Restless Spirits. Women in Korean Ritual Life* (Honolulu: Univ. of Hawaii Press, 1985), p. 27.

602 For more on Korean shamanism, see S. A. Mousalimas (Ed.), *Christianity & Shamanism: Proceedings of the First Seoul International Consultation (25-30 June 2000, Seoul, Korea)*, accessed online at http://www.OxfordU.net/seoul (2001). See especially Cha Ok Soong, "Korean Shamanism," chapter 2 of the *Proceedings*.

603 Kim Rahn, "Ignorance Obstacle to Lesbian Human Rights," *Korea Times* (2005, Aug. 5). Accessed online at the *Korea Times* website archives at http://search.hankooki.com/times/times_view.php? term=transsexuals++&path=hankooki3/ times/lpage/nation/200508/kt2005080521593811970.htm&media=kt.

604 To its credit, the *Korea Times* has done excellent work in presenting factual information and correcting inaccurate media presentations. Among its accounts on transsexualism is the story of Kimbee, a MtF postoperative transsexual interviewed in 2002. Her story has many elements recognizable for transsexual experience elsewhere in the world, including her struggle to accept her assigned gender as a young person, her despair and attempts to harm herself, and her profound relief when once she began altering her body, first through hormones and then surgery. Kimbee says she has been far better accepted by her students, than by other adults—a generational gap in tolerance also mirrored elsewhere. See Cho Hyo-young, "Transsexuals Are Beautiful People Too," *Korea Times* (2002, Jan. 31). Accessed online at the *Korea Times* website archives at http://search.hankooki.com/times/times_view.php?term=transsexuals++&path= hankooki1/kt_special/200201/t2002013118193449110.htm&media=kt.

605 Park Soo-in, "Harisu Redefines Gender Identity," *Korea Times* (2001, June 28). Accessed online at the *Korea Times* website archives at http://search. hankooki.com/times/times_view.php?term=transgender++&path=hankooki1/kt_cul ture/200106/t2001062817032846110.htm&media=kt. Harisu's autobiography, *Adam-Turned-Eve*, was published when she was just 26 years old.

606 Yoo Dung-ho, "Transsexual Entertainer Permitted to Legally Change Sex," *Korea Times* (2002, Dec. 13). Accessed online at the *Korea Times* website archives at

http://search.hankooki.com/times/times_ view.php?term=transsexuals++&path=hankooki3/times/lpage/nation/200212/kt2002121317261412020.htm&media=kt.

607 *Korean Transsexual Singer Ties the Knot* (2007, May 20). Found at theage.com.au website, accessed online at http://www.theage.com.au/news/World/Korean-transsexual-singer-ties-the-knot/2007/05/20/1179601234751.html.

608 "Forum Addresses Row Over Gender Change," *Korea Times* (2002, July 10), published on the Transgender Crossroads website, accessed online at http://www.tgcrossroads.org/news/archive.asp? aid=306. Cf. Soh Ji-young, "Gender Changes Should Be Legally Recognized: Judge," *Korea Times* (2002, Apr. 4). Accessed online at the *Korea Times* website archives at http://search.hankooki.com/times/times_view. php?term=transsexuals++&path=hankooki1/kt_nation/200204/t20020402183919411 10.htm&media=kt.

609 Park Moo-jong, "'Adam-Turned-Eve'" [Times Colloquy], *Korea Times* (2001, Aug. 7). Accessed online at the *Korea Times* website archives at http://search.hankooki.com/times/times_view.php?term=transgender++&path=hankooki1/kt_op/200108/t2001080715262248110.htm&media=kt.

610 Chung Ah-young, "Transsexuals Call for Equal Treatment," *Korea Times* (2005, Oct. 23). Accessed online at the *Korea Times* website archives at http://search.hankooki.com/times/times_view.php? term=transsexuals++&path=hankooki3/times/lpage/nation/200510/kt200510231709 3710510.htm&media=kt.

611 Law Library of Congress, *Global Legal Monitor*, Issue 3 (2006, Aug.), p. 36.

612 Choi Tae-hwan, "Sexual Identity Disorder," [Thoughts of the Times], *Korea Times* (Aug. 23, 2001). Accessed online at the *Korea Times* website archives at http://search.hankooki.com/times/times_ view.php?term=transgender++&path=hankooki1/kt_op/200108/t2001082310512848110.htm&media=kt.

613 Michael G. Peletz, "Transgenderism and Gender Pluralism in Southeast Asia Since Early Modern Times," *Current Anthropology*, 47 (no. 2), 309-340 (2006), p. 318 n. 15.

614 This matter is explored further in the answer to Q. 82.

615 Eli Coleman, Philip Colgan, & Louis Gooren, "Male Cross-Gender Behaviour in Myanmar (Burma): A Description of the *Acault*," *Archives of Sexual Behavior*, 21 (no. 3), 313-321 (1992).

616 Ibid, p. 316.

617 Ibid, p. 317f.

618 Stephen O. Murray, *Homosexualities* (Chicago: Univ. of Chicago Press, 2000), p. 335. Cf. Coleman, Colgan, & Gooren, p. 317.

619 Coleman, Colgan & Gooren, pp. 315-316. Cf. Vern L. Bullough & Bonnie Bullough, *Cross Dressing, Sex, and Gender* (Phila.: Univ. of Pennsylvania Press, 1993), p. 15.

620 Peletz, p. 320. His observation is that the controversial *junta* may see in these matters an opportunity to secure popular support and enhance their claim to be a legitimate government.

621 The term is one applied by *Metis*. See Ramyata Limbu, *Rights-Nepal: Men Who Have Sex with Men Speak Up* (2003, Feb. 7). Accessed online at the Inter Press Service News Agency at http://www.ipsnews.net/interna.asp?idnews=15728.

622 See *Nepal: Police on 'Sexual Cleansing' Drive* (2005). Found at Human Rights Watch website, accessed online at http://hrw.org/english/docs/2006/01/12/nepal12422.htm. Also see *Nepal: 'Sexual Cleansing' Drive Continues* (N. Y.: Human Rights Watch, 2006). Accessed online at http://hrw.org/english/docs/2006/03/17/nepal13020.htm.

623 W. Qidwai, "Perceptions About Female Sexuality Among Young Pakistani Men Presenting to Family Physicians at a Teaching Hospital in Karachi," *Journal of the Pakistan Medical Association, 50* (no. 2), 74-77 (2000).

624 For more on this matter, see Yasmeen Sabeeh Qazi, "Adolescent Reproductive Health in Pakistan," in S. Bott, S. Jejeebhoy, I. Shah, & C. Puri (Eds.), *Towards Adulthood: Exploring the Sexual and Reproductive Health of Adolescents in South Asia*, pp. 78-80 (Geneva: World Health Organization, 2003).

625 Declan Walsh, "Pakistani Society Looks Other Way as Gay Men Party—Homosexuality 'Thriving' Despite Strict Criminal Code. Marriage and Cultural Factors Offer Camouflage," *The Guardian* (2006, Mar. 14), accessed online at the Pakistan News Report website at http://www.globalgayz.com/pak-news05-06.html.

626 The 42-year-old Afghani had paid a sizable sum to the parents of a 16-year-old Pakistani youth to become his 'male bride' and a large public wedding followed. See "First Gay Marriage in Pakistan," BBC News (2005, Oct. 5), accessed online at the Pakistan News Report website at http://www.globalgayz.com/pak-news05-06.html. Also available at http://news.bbc.co.uk/2/hi/south_asia/4313210.stm.

627 Tufail Muhammad & Naeem Zafar, *Situational Analysis Report on Prostitution of Boys in Pakistan (Lahore and Peshawar)* (Bangkok: ECPAT International in collaboration with Pakistan Pediatrics Association, 2006), p. 34. Accessed online at http://www.ecpat.net/eng/publications/Boy_Prostitution/PDF/Pakistan.pdf. ECPAT is a network of organizations; the acronym stands for 'End Child Prostitution, Child Pornography, and Trafficking of Children fro Sexual Purposes.'

628 Associated Press, "Pakistani Police Arrest Couple for Lying About Sex of Husband, Who Underwent Sex Change," *International Herald-Tribune* (2007, May 20). Accessed online at http://www.iht.com/articles/ap/2007/05/20/asia/AS-GEN-Pakistan-Sex-Change.php.

629 Asan Zaidi, *In Pakistan, the Biggest Star Is in Drag* (2007, Jan. 31). Accessed on the World Blog at the MSNBC website, at http://worldblog.msnbc.msn.com/archive/2007/01/31/45890.aspx. Also see *Begum Nawazish Ali. Ali Saleem's Alter Ego*, at Despardes.com, accessed online at http://www.despardes.com/newsmakers/default.htm. Also see Isambard Wilkinson, "How Pakistan's 'Dame Edna' Has Upset Musharraf," *The Daily Telegraph* (London) (2006, Apr. 22), p. 16.

630 Shahzad Sharjeel & Jim Rosenberg, *HIV/AIDS in Pakistan* (World Bank, 2005). Accessed online at http://siteresources.worldbank.org/INTPAKISTAN/ Country%20Home/20535956/HIV-AIDS-brief-June2005-PK.pdf. The presence of *Hijra* has been reported in every major Pakistani city. On the *Hijra* also see the remarks on the section on India, and see the answer to Q. 79.

631 Most of this information is derived from the following sources: Tahir Khilji, *Reaching Marginalized Populations: A Project on HIV/AIDS Prevention Amongst Men Who Have Sex with Men in the City of Lahore, Pakistan*. Presented at the "Reaching Men to Improve Reproductive Health for All" International Conference, Dulles, Virginia, September 15-18, 2003. Accessed online at http://www.jhuccp.org/igwg/presentations/

Wednesday/Plen4/ReachingMarginalized.pdf. Also, Muhammad & Zafar, pp. 48, 61-63.

[632] Khilji; Muhammad & Zafar, p. 34.

[633] Rosalind C. Morris, "Three Sexes and Four Sexualities: Redressing the Discourses on Sexuality and Gender in Contemporary Thailand", *Positions, 2* (no. 1), 15-43 (1994).

[634] Cf. Peter A. Jackson, "Performative Genders, Perverse Desires: A Bio-History of Thailand's Same-Sex and Transgender Cultures," *Intersections: Gender, History and Culture in the Asian Context, 9* (2003, August), §§10, 53-54. Accessed online at http://wwwsshe. murdoch.edu.au/intersections/issue9/ jackson.html. Also cf. Peter A.Jackson, "The Persistence of Gender: From Ancient Indian *Pandakas* to Modern *Thai Gay-Quings*," *Australian Humanities Review, Issue 1* (1996, April-June; original work published in *Meanjin*, 1996). Accessed online at http://www.lib.latrobe.edu.au/AHR/ archive/Issue-April-1996/Jackson.html. Also cf. Kittiwut Jod Taywaditep, Eli Coleman, & Pacharin Dumronggittigule, "Thailand," in R. T. Francoeur (Ed.), *The International Encyclopedia of Sexuality*, Vols. I-III (N. Y.: Continuum, 1997). Accessed online at http://www2.rz.hu-berlin.de/sexology/GESUND/ARCHIV/IES/THAILAND.HTM #7.%20GENDER %20CONFLICTED%20PERSONS. See §7. Gender Conflicted Persons.

[635] Ibid, §53.

[636] Ibid, especially §§1-25, 63-76. Jackson's history covers much more than what I have presented, dealing also with how the nation's authorities responded to criticisms of the Thai people's 'nakedness' and 'sexual excesses' in sanctioning polygamy.

[637] Ibid, §§32-37. Just as the women were commonly viewed as too masculine, the men were commonly regarded as too feminine by Westerners.

[638] Ibid, §39.

[639] Ibid, §49; cf. §62.

[640] Ibid, §69.

[641] Ibid, §60. Jackson references Lucien M. Hanks & Jane Richardson Hanks, "Thailand: Equality Between the Sexes," in B. E. Ward (Ed.), *Women in the New Asia: The Changing Social Roles of Men and Women in South and Southeast Asia*, pp. 423-459 (Paris: UNESCO, 1963), p. 447, with regard to dress distinctions instituted for children and gendered role differentiation in activities and professions.

[642] Ibid, §77.

[643] Ibid, §88. Jackson argues that today's *Kathoey* prominence in popular media is "thoroughly modern and utterly recent."

[644] Rosalind C. Morris, "Educating Desire: Thailand, Transnationalism, and Transgression," *Social Text, 15* (nos. 3/4), 53-79 (1997), p. 62.

[645] Taywaditep, Coleman, & Dumronggittigule, §7.

[646] Ibid.

[647] Andrew Matzner, *Thailand: Paradise Not (On Human Rights and Homophobia)*. Accessed online at http://home.att.net/~leela2/paradisenot.htm. This article originally appeared in the *Harvard Gay and Lesbian Review* (1998, Winter).

[648] Walter Irvine, *The Thai-Yuan 'Madman' and the Modernizing, Developing Thai Nation as Bounded Entities Under Threat: A Study in the Replication of a Single Image*. Ph.D. dissertation (London: University of London, 1982), p. 476.

649 Morris, "Three Sexes and Four Sexualities."
650 "Thai Army Draft Bans Gays, Transsexuals," *Transgender Crossroads*, from Gay.com UK (2003, March 25). Accessed online at http://www.tgcrossroads.org/news/archive.asp?aid=671.
651 Taywaditep, Coleman, & Dumronggittigule, §7.
652 Irvine.
653 Rosalind C. Morris, "The Empress's New Clothes: Dressing and Redressing Modernity in Northern Thai Spirit Mediumship," in L. Milgram & P. Van Esterik (Eds.), *The Transformative Power of Cloth in Southeast Asia*, pp. 53-74 (Toronto: The Museum for Textiles and the Canadian Council for Southeast Asian Studies, 1994). Cf. Rosalind C. Morris, *In the Place of Origins: Modernity and Its Mediums in Northern Thailand* (Durham: Duke Univ. Press, 2000), pp. 126-132.
654 Jacob Pastoetter, "Vietnam," in R. T. Francoeur (Ed.), *The International Encyclopedia of Sexuality*, Vols. I-IV (N. Y.: Continuum, 1997-2001). Accessed online at http://www2.hu-berlin.de/sexology/IES/vietnam.html. See §7. Gender Conflicted Persons.
655 Elliott M. Heiman & Cao Van Le, "Transsexualism in Vietnam," *Archives of Sexual Behavior, 4* (no. 1), 89-95 (1974).
656 Nga Pham, "Vietnam Man's Fight to Become a Woman," *BBC News* (2003, Sept. 24). Accessed online at http://news.bbc.co.uk/2/hi/asia-pacific/3132312.stm.
657 Amnesty International report #18726 (2003, Nov. 22; in German), referenced in the United Kingdom's Immigration and Nationality Directorate Home Office's *Vietnam Country Report* (2005, April), p. 45, §6.107. Accessed online at http://www.unhcr.org/home/RSDCOI/429f1a2b4.pdf.
658 "National Assembly Considers Making Sex Changes Legal," *Viet Nam News* (2005, May 13). Found at the VNS website, accessed online at http://vietnamnews.vnanet.vn/showarticle.php?num=01POL130505.
659 "Vietnam to Recognize Transsexual Plight," *Pink News* (2006, July 18). Accessed online at http://www.pinknews.co.uk/news/articles/2005-1996.html.
660 *Vietnamese Censors OK First Transsexual Singer's Musical Debut* (2006, Oct. 20). Found at the rawstory.com website, accessed online at http://rawstory.com/news/2006/Vietnamese_censors_OK_first_transse_10202006.html.
661 Vu Ngoc Bao, Lynellen D. Long & Yvonne Taylor, *"Suffered Lives": Assessment of Social and Behavioral Practices for HIV/AIDS Prevention in Can Tho*. Report prepared for Family Health International and the National AIDS Committee, Population Council, Vietnam Office (1998). Accessed online at http://www.undp.orgvn/projects/vie98006/Sex/CSW%CanTho.doc. This ethnographic study limited its scope to Can Tho Province and only a handful of men. In an unfortunately narrow definition of 'transgender' for the study, the authors confine the term to "a male who identifies as a female, prefers to dress as a woman, and has sex with other men."
662 M. L. Rekert, "Sex in the City: Sexual Behavior, Societal Change, and STDs in Saigon," *Sexually Transmitted Infections, 78* (Supplement I), i47-i54 (2002), p. i49.

Q. 53 Notes

663 "Enki and Ninmah," lines 75-78 (ETCSL Translation: t.1.1.2), in J. A. Black, G. Cunningham, E. Fluckiger-Hawker, E. Robson, & G. Zólyomi, *The Electronic Text Corpus*

of Sumerian Literature (1998-2005). Available from the Electronic Text Corpus of Sumerian Literature website, maintained by the Oriental Institute of the University of Oxford (2005 update). Accessed online at http://etcsl.orinst. ox.ac.uk/cgi-bin/etcsl.cgi?text= t.1.1.2#.

[664] "Enki and the World Order," lines 422-444 (ETCSL Translation t.1.1.3) in Black, Cunningham, Fluckiger-Hawker, Robson, & Zólyomi. Accessed online at http://etcsl.orinst.ox.ac.uk/cgi-bin/etcsl. cgi?text=t.1.1.3#.

[665] "A Hymn to Inana for Išme-Dagan (Išme-Dagan K)," lines 19-31 (ETCSL Translation: c.2.5.4.11) in Black, Cunningham, Fluckiger-Hawker, Robson, & Zólyomi. Accessed online at http://etcsl.orinst.ox.ac.uk/cgi-bin/etcsl.cgi?text=t.2.5.4.11#. Išme-Dagan was given by Enlil and Ninlil as Inanna's husband.

[666] "A *Sir-namsub* to Inana," lines 16-22 (ETCSL Translation t.4.07.9) in Black, Cunningham, Fluckiger-Hawker, Robson, & Zólyomi. Accessed online at http://etcsl.orinst.ox.ac.uk/cgi-bin/ etcsl.cgi?text=t.4.07.9#.

[667] "A Hymn to Inana for Iddin-Dagan (Idin-Dagan A)," lines 60-68 (ETCSL Translation: t.2.5.3.1) in Black, Cunningham, Fluckiger-Hawker, Robson, & Zólyomi. Accessed online at http://etcsl.orinst. ox.ac.uk/cgi-bin/etcsl.cgi?text=t.2.5.3.1#.

[668] "A *Tigi* to Inana (Inana E)," lines 46-49 (cf. 50-53) (ETCSL Translation: t.4.07.5) in Black, Cunningham, Fluckiger-Hawker, Robson, & Zólyomi. Accessed online at http://etcsl.orinst.ox.ac.uk/cgi-bin/etcsl.cgi?text=t.4.07.5#.

[669] W. G. Lambert, *Babylonian Wisdom Literature* (Oxford: Oxford Unity Press, 1960), pp. 225, 230.

[670] Michelle I. Marcus, "Dressed to Kill: Women and Pins in Early Iran," *The Oxford Art Journal,* 17 (no. 2), 3-15 (1994), p. 12. In support of this third hypothesis, Marcus points to an Egyptian tomb painting (dated c. 2134-2040 B.C.E.) depicting the deceased first in the color associated with men (dark red skin), and in old age in the color associated with women (yellow skin). Cf. the transition from masculine to feminine identity possible for an older male among the Gabra people of Kenya (see the answer to Q. 54).

[671] *Pyramid Text 1248-1249* has Atum procreating through masturbation. The hand that grasped his phallus is come to be seen as feminine and even depicted later as a goddess.

[672] Consider the lines from the *Contendings of Horus and Seth* (Chester Beatty Papyrus 1): "Now afterward, (at) evening time, bed was prepared for them, and they both lay down. But during the night, Seth caused his phallus to become stiff and inserted it between Horus's thighs. Then Horus placed his hands between his thighs and received Seth's semen." See "The Contendings of Horus and Seth," in W. K. Simpson (Ed.), *The Literature of Ancient Egypt: An Anthology of Stories, Instructions, and Poetry* (New Haven, CT: Yale Univ. Press, 1972).

[673] J. W. Wright Jr., "Masculine Allusion and the Structure of Satire in Early 'Abasid Poetry," in J. W. Wright Jr.& E. K. Rowson (Eds.), *Homoeroticism in Classical Arab Literature,* pp. 1-23 (N. Y.: Columbia Univ. Press, 1997), p. 6.

[674] For more on Hatsheput and Neferura, see the answer to Q. 43.

[675] *Women and Gender in Ancient Egypt from Prehistory to Late Antiquity,* an exhibition curated by Terry G. Wilfong at the Kelsey Museum of Archaeology (1997, Mar. 14-June 15). See the remarks in the section entitled "Other Genders," accessed online at http://www.umich.edu/~kelseydb/Exhibits/ WomenandGender/other.html. Exam-

ples of 'other genders' mentioned include eunuchs, hermaphrodites (intersexed), transvestites (both male and female), androgynous people, and asexual people.

676 See the legend of Aqhat (I iv 40-44), in C. R. Driver, *Canaanite Myths and Legends* (Edinburgh: T. & T. Clark, 1956), pp. 65-67.

677 Flavius Josephus, *Wars of the Jews*, Bk. V, ch. IX, §10, in William Whiston (trans.), *The Complete Works of Josephus* (Grand Rapids, MI: Kregel, 1981), p. 542f.

678 Everett K. Rowson, "The Effeminates of Early Medina," *The Journal of the American Oriental Society, 111* (no. 4), 671-693 (1991). For a more complete treatment in this text, see the answer to Q. 78.

679 Everett K. Rowson, "Gender Irregularity as Entertainment: Institutionalized Transvestism at the Caliphal Court in Medieval Baghdad," in S. Farmer and C. B. Pasternack (Eds.), *Gender and Difference in the Middle Ages*, pp. 45-72 (Minneapolis: Univ. of Minnesota Press, 2003); see especially pp. 51-52.

680 For a brief introduction relevant to understanding the moral thinking in the background of Islamic thought, see Everett K. Rowson, "The Categorization of Gender and Sexual Irregularity in Medieval Arabic Vice Lists," in J. Epstein & K. Straub (Eds.), *Body Guards: The Cultural Politics of Gender Ambiguity*, pp. 50-79 (N. Y.: Routlegde, 1991). Rowson observes that the conception of proper and improper sexual relations—the sexual ethos—of Middle Eastern lands owes more to the ancient worlds of Greece and Rome than to modern Western views. In this context male dominance is assumed and masculine sexuality is active and penetrative whereas feminine sexuality is passive and receptive. Males who willingly accept the feminine role in sexual acts with other men are viewed as homosexual; men who penetrate adolescent boys are not. Cf. Steven M. Oberhelman, "Hierarchies of Gender, Ideology, and Power in Ancient and Medieval Greek and Arabic Dream Literature," in J. W. Wright Jr. & E. K. Rowson (Eds.), *Homoeroticism in Classical Arab Literature*, pp. 55-93 (N. Y.: Columbia Univ. Press, 1997); see esp. pp. 67-68. Also see As'ad AbuKhalil, "Gender Boundaries and Sexual Categories in the Arab World," *Feminist Issues, 15* (nos. 1-2), 91-104 (1997), and Bruce W. Dunne, "Homosexuality in the Middle East: An Agenda for Historical Research," *Arab Studies Quarterly, 12* (nos. 3-4), 55-82 (1990). There are numerous books and articles exploring homosexuality in both early and modern Islamic societies.

681 Garay Menicucci, "Homosexuality in Egyptian Film," *Middle East Report* (1998, Spring). Accessed online at http://www.merip.org/mer/mer206/egyfilm.htm.

682 Paula E. Drew, "Iran," in R. T. Francoeur (Ed.), *The International Encyclopedia of Sexuality*, Vols. I-III (N. Y.: Continuum, 1997) [hereafter *IES*]. Accessed online at http://www2.rz.hu-berlin.de/sexology/GESUND/ARCHIV/IES/IRAN.HTM#7. %20GENDER%20CONFLICTED%20PERSONS. See §7. Gender Conflicted Persons. Drew speculated on the possibility that such theater might provide a 'niche for gender-conflicted males.'

683 See the *Café Trans Arabia* website. Accessed online at http://www.thesisterhood.net/transsexualallianceofthekingdomofjordan/id3.html.

684 "Turkey: No Security Without Rights," *Amnesty International Reports* (London: Amnesty International, 1996). AI Index: EUR/44/84/96, pp. 38-39.

685 In a 2000 decision, a Saudi court ordered nine male defendants convicted of 'deviant sexual behavior' for crossdressing to receive up to 2,600 lashes each, to be administered at 15 day intervals over a two year span. See *Alleged Transvestites Sentenced to*

Brutal Flogging (2000, April 20), accessed online at http://www.iglhrc.org/site/iglhrc/section.php?id=5&detail=412. Amnesty International, in 2000, noted that six Saudi men were executed on charges of 'deviant sexual behavior' (including transvestism and homosexuality). AI Index: MDE 23/058/2000.

[686] See Rex Wockner, "Saudi Gays Beheaded," *International News* #325 (2000, July 17). Accessed online at http://www.qrd.org/qrd/world/wockner/news.briefs/325-07.17.00.

[687] "Kuwait Sex-Change Upheld," *BBC News World Edition* online (2004, Apr. 25). Accessed online at http://news.bbc.co.uk/2/hi/middle_east/3657727.stm.

[688] Megan K. Stack, "Iran Warms Up to Sex Changes, But Still Shuns Homosexuality," *LA Times* (2005, Jan. 30), accessed online at http://www.freenew mexican.com/news/9882.html.

[689] Julanne McCarthy, "Bahrain," in R. T. Francoeur (Ed.), *The International Encyclopedia of Sexuality*, Vols. I-III (N. Y.: Continuum, 1997). Accessed online at http://www2.rz.hu-berlin.de/sexology/GESUND/ARCHIV/IES/BAHRAIN.HTM#7.%20GENDER%20CONFLICTED%20PERSONS. See §7. Gender Conflicted Persons.

[690] Jakob Skovgaard-Petersen, "Sex Change in Cairo: Gender and Islamic Law," *The Journal of the International Institute*, 2 (no. 3) (1996, Spring), accessed online at http://www.umich.edu/~iinet/journal/ vol2no3/sex_in_cairo.html.

[691] Afsaneh Najmabadi, *Women with Moustaches and Men without Beards: Gender and Sexual Identities in Iranian Modernity* (Berkeley: Univ. of California Press, 2005), p. 3.

[692] See the blog posting by Yoshie entitled "Changing Sex, Changing Islam" (2004, Aug. 31), at the *Critical Montages* website, accessed online at http://montages.blogspot.com/2004/08/changing-sex-changing-islam.html. The posting incorporates material from various sources. For a briefer piece, see Stack, "Iran Warms Up to Sex Changes, But Still Shuns Homosexuality."

[693] "A Fatwa for Freedom," *The Guardian* (2005, July 27), maintained on the Guardian Unlimited website, accessed online at http://www.guardian.co.uk./g2/ story/0,,1536658,00.html.

[694] Ibid. Also see, Frances Harrison, "Iran's Sex-Change Operations," *BBC News* (2005, Jan. 5), accessed online at http://news.bbc.co.uk/2/hi/programmes/ newsnight/4115535.stm.

[695] Nazila Fathi, "As Repression Lifts, More Iranians Change Their Sex," *New York Times* (2004, Aug. 2). With NYTimes.com membership the article can be accessed online at http://www.nytimes.com/2004/08/02/international/middleast/02iran. html?hp=&adxnnl=1&adxnnlx=1091489991-2sBf34Gerj 3nlXAaASXZcQ.

[696] Drew, "Iran," *IES*, §7. Gender Conflicted Persons.

[697] See Dana International's autobiography accessed online at http://www.dana-international.net/.

[698] B. Modan, R. Goldschmidt, E. Rubinstein, A. Vansover, M. Zinn, R. Golan, A. Chetrit, & T. Gottlieb-Stematzky, "Prevalence of HIV Antibodies in Transsexual and Female Prostitutes," *American Journal of Public Health*, 82 (no. 4), 590-592 (1992), cited in T. Nemeto, D. Luke, L. Mamo, A. Ching, & J. Patria, "HIV Risk Behaviors Among Male-to-Female *Transgenders* in Comparison with Homosexual or Bisexual Males and Heterosexual Females," *AIDS Care*, 11 (no. 3), 297-313 (1999).

699 Larry Derfner, "Openly Gay Knesset Member Ripples the Establishment," *The Jewish News Weekly of Northern California* (2002, Oct. 11), accessed online at http://www.jewishsf.com/content/2-0-/module/displaystory/story_id/19055/edition_id/385/format/html/displaystory.html.

700 Nina Gilbert, "First Gay MK Sworn In," *Jerusalem Post* (2002, Nov. 5), p. 4. Also see Derfner, "Openly Gay Knesset Member Ripples the Establishment," who observes that another publicly known homosexual member of the Knesset, Marcia Freedman, did not disclose she was a lesbian until *after* her stint in the Knesset in the early 1980s.

701 "First 'Out of the Closet' Gay Man Elected to Tel-Aviv City Council," *GayMiddleEast.com News* (2003, Oct. 30), at GME GayMiddleEast.com website, accessed online at http://www.gaymiddleeast.com/country/Israel.

702 See the Agudah website accessed online at http://www.geocities.com/WestHollywood/Stonewall/2345/.

703 Viva Sarah Press, "TA Gay Pride Parade a Colorful Celebration," *Jerusalem Post* (2004, June 27), p. 4.

704 For more on the Transgender Day of Remembrance, see the official website that is part of the Gender.org website accessed online at http://www.gender.org/remember/day/. In 2004, nations represented in observing this day (November 20th) included Canada, France, Israel, Italy, and the United States.

705 The *Banot* website was formerly accessed online at http://banotmag.co.il/. Its operation by 2004 was difficult to verify.

706 Ronny A. Shtarkshall & Minah Zemach, "Israel," in R. T. Francoeur (Ed.), *The International Encyclopedia of Sexuality*, Vols. I-IV (N. Y.: Continuum, 1997-2001), accessed online at http://www2.hu-berlin.de/sexology/IES/israel.html#7.

707 Esther Hecht, "Gender Bender," *Jerusalem Post* (1998, May 8), p. 8.

708 Unni Wikan, "Man Becomes Woman: Transsexualism in Oman as a Key to Gender Roles," *Man*, 12 (no. 2), 304-319 (1977); originally published in *Tidsskriftfor Samfunnsforskning*, 17 (1976).

709 Ibid. See Unni Wikan, "The Omani *Xanith*—a Third Gender Role?" *Man*, 13 (no. 3), 473-476 (1978). Also see Unni Wikan, *Behind the Veil in Arabia: Women in Oman* (Chicago: Univ. of Chicago Press, 1982). See chapter 9, 'The *Xanith*: a Third Gender Role?' (pp. 168-186).

710 "Saudi Arabia: Men 'Behaving Like Women' Face Flogging," *Human Rights Watch* (2005, Apr. 7), at the hrw.org website accessed online at http://hrw.org/english/docs/2005/04/07/saudia10434.htm.

711 *Sydney Star Observer*, no. 421 (1998, Sept. 3), p. 6.

712 "Sex Change for Five Saudi Sisters," *Sydney Morning Herald* (2004, June 16), found online at smh.com.au and accessed online at http://www.smh.com.au/articles/2004/06/16/1087244946830.html.

713 Sebastian Usher, "Gender Correction for Saudi Girls," *BBC News* (2004, June 17), accessed online at http://news.bbc.co.uk/2/hi/middle_east/3814041.stm.

714 "Saudi Court Rules in Favor if Transsexual . . ." [News], *Al Bawaba* (2004, Dec. 16), accessed online at http://www.albawaba.com/en/news/178356.

715 Türker Özkan & Timo Lajunen, "Masculinity, Femininity, and the Bem Sex Role Inventory in Turkey," *Sex Roles. A Journal of Research*, 52 (nos. 1-2), 103-110 (2005).

[716] The Associated Press, "Turkey Blocks Cross-Dressing TV Reality Show" (2006, May 4). Also see Nicholas Birch, "Cross-Dressing Show Falls Victim to Disquiet; Conservative Attitudes About Family Also Reveal Skepticism Over EU," *The Washington Times* (2006, May 24), p. A15.

[717] Committee of Experts on Family Law, *Information Concerning the Legal Situation of Transsexuals in Turkey* (1988). Accessed online at http://www.pfc.org.uk/files/Turkey_1988.pdf. Cf. "Turkish Civil Law Number 743, Article 29," *Resmi Gazete* (1988, May 12).

[718] Sahika Yüksil, Isin Baral Kulaksizoglu, Nuray Türksoy, & Dogan Sahin, "Group Psychotherapy with Female-to-Male Transsexuals in Turkey," *Archives of Sexual Behavior*, 29 (no. 3), 279-290 (2000).

[719] Women for Women's Human Rights, *Turkish Civil and Penal Code Reforms from a Gender Perspective: The Success of Two Nationwide Campaigns* (Istanbul: WWHR-New Ways, 2005). Accessed online at http://www.wwhr.org/images/CivilandPenalCodeReforms.pdf. See p. 65f. Also see Yesim M. Atamer, "The Legal Status of Transsexuals in Turkey," *International Journal of Transgenderism*, 8 (no. 1) 65-71 (2005).

[720] Ibid, p. 66.

[721] Deniz Kandiyoti, "Transsexuals and the Urban Landscape in Istanbul," *Middle East Report 206* (1998, Spring), accessed online at http://www.merip.org/mer/mer206/turksx.htm.

Q. 54 Notes

[722] This is a point often made, including by Stephen Murray, whose work pointed me in many fruitful directions for the answer to this question. See Stephen O. Murray, *Homosexuality in "Traditional" Sub-Saharan Africa and Contemporary South Africa* (2000), accessed online at http://segai.fr.dri_ etpdf20/06/2003. Cf. Appendix II, "Organizations of Homosexuality and Other Social Structures in Sub-Saharan Africa," in Stephen O. Murray & Will Roscoe (Eds.), *Boy-Wives and Female Husbands: Studies in African Homosexualities*, pp. 283-298 (N. Y.: Palgrave, 1998).

[723] Roberta Perkins, "Cross-Dressing Magic, Intersexuals & Female Husbands," *Polare 9* (1995). Accessed online at http://www.gendercentre.org.au/9article7.htm, part of the Gender Centre Inc. website.

[724] On *shoga* see Yale University's Kamusi Project dictionary, accessed online at http://www.yale.edu/swahili/. The discussion board on the term *mzenge* (*msenge*), another word employed for a gay man, also provides insight into the varied, often controversial, use of words; accessed online at http://research.yale.edu/swahili/learn/?q=en/node/8718.

[725] David F. Greenberg, *The Construction of Homosexuality* (Chicago: Univ. of Chicago Press, 1988); see chapter 2 (pp.25-88), 'Homosexual Relations in Kinship-Structured Societies.' Each of the three categories is covered, as follows: Transgenerational (26-40); Transgenderal (40-65); and Egalitarian (66-73).

[726] A useful introduction to the subject, at manageable length, is offered by Oyeronke Oyewumi, "Conceptualizing Gender: The Eurocentric Foundations of Feminist Concepts and the Challenge of African Epistemologies," *Jenda: A Journal of Culture and African Women Studies*, 2 (no. 1) (2002). Accessed online at http://www.jendajournal.com/vol2.1/oyewumi.html. Cf. Oyeronke Oyewumi, *The Invention of Women: Making an African Sense of Western Gender Discourses* (Minneapolis: Univ. of Minnesota Press, 1997).

Also see Oyeronke Oyewumi, "Discourse on Gender: Historical Contingency and the Ethics of Intellectual Work," *West Africa Review, 3* (no. 2) (2002). Accessed online at http://www.westafricareview.com/vol3.2/owomoyela.html. Another helpful examination may be found in C. Otutubikey Izugbara, "Patriarchal Ideology and Discourses of Sexuality in Nigeria," *Understanding Human Sexuality Seminar Series 2* (Africa Regional Sexuality Resource Centre, 2004). Accessed online at http://www.arsrc.org/en/resources/documents/izugbara.pdf.

727 The work of African scholar Oyeronke Oyewumi is only one example among many works chronicling the effects of colonialism. Also see A. Adu Boahen, *African Perspectives on Colonialism* (Baltimore: John Hopkins Univ. Press, 1987).

728 Arlene Masquelier, "The Scorpion's Sting: Youth, Marriage and the Struggle for Social Maturity in Niger," *Journal of the Royal Anthropological Institute, 11* (no. 1), 59-83 (2005).

729 Burt H. Hoff, "Gays: Guardians at the Gates. An Interview with Malidoma Somé," *MEN Magazine* (1993, Sept.), accessed online at http://www.menweb.org/somegay.htm.

730 Brian H. MacDermot, *Cult of the Sacred Spear: The Story of the Nuer Tribe in Ethiopia* (London: Hale, 1972), p. 119.

731 Oyewumi, "Conceptualizing Gender."

732 Cf., too, the discussion on the tribal chief and his—or her—'wife' in Kwesi Yankah, *Speaking for the Chief: Okyeame and the Politics of Akan Royal Oratory* (Indianapolis: Indiana Univ. Press, 1995).

733 Rukmini Callimachi, "Women, Not Men, Choose Spouses On African Archipelago," *USA Today* (2007, Feb. 3). Accessed online at http://www.usatoday.com/news/world/2007-02-02-ladies-choice_x.htm.

734 See Edwin S. Segal, *Gender Transformation in Cross Cultural Perspective*. Paper prepared for presentation at Women's Worlds 99, the seventh International Interdisciplinary Congress on Women, Program Section II: New Constructions of Gender, session 2, Friday, June 25, Tromsø, Norway, June 20-26, 1999. Accessed online at http://www.skk.uit.no/WW99/papers/Segal_Edwin_S.pdf.

On the Mbuti, cf. Colin Turnbull, "Sex and Gender. The Role of Subjectivity in Field Research," in T. Larry & M. E. Conaway (Eds.), *Self, Sex, and Gender in Cross-Cultural Fieldwork*, pp. 17-27 (Urbana, IL: Univ. of Illinois Press, 1987).

735 Mircea Eliade & Ioan P. Couliano, *The Eliade Guide to World Religions* (S. F.: HarperSanFrancisco, 1991), p. 16.

736 James Boyd Christensen, *Double Descent Among the Fanti* (New Haven: Human Relations Area Files [HRAF], 1954).

737 The term *gynaegamy* was coined by Victor Chikezie Uchendu in the late 1960s with reference to the Igbo. See V. C. Uchendu, *Ezi Na Ulo—The Extended Family in Igbo Civilization* (1995). Ahiajoku Lecture Series. Accessed online at the IgboNet website at http://ahiajoku.igbonet.com/1995/.

738 The Gikuyu are discussed later in this section; on the Nandi see Regina Smith Obolier, "Is the Female Husband a Man? Woman/Woman Marriage Among the Nandi of Kenya," *Ethnology, 19* (no. 1), 69-88 (1980). Also see Myrtle S. Langley, *The Nandi of Kenya: Life Crisis Rituals in a Period of Change* (London: C. Hurst and Co., 1979).

[739] On the practice among the Nuer, see Edward E. Evans-Pritchard, *Kinship and Marriage Among the Nuer* (Oxford: Clarendon Press, 1951).

[740] Roberta Perkins notes more than two dozen, Denise O'Brien puts the number at more than thirty, and Beth Greene at more than forty; suffice it to say the practice has been well-established and widespread. Cf. Joseph M. Carrier & Stephen O. Murray, "Woman-Woman Marriage in Africa," in S. O. Murray & W. Roscoe (Eds.), *Boy-Wives and Female Husbands: Studies in African Homosexualities*, pp. 255-266 (N. Y.: Palgrave, 1998).

[741] The term 'male daughter' is Amadiume's way of referring to a female assuming a gender position traditionally assigned to a male. Thus one ordinarily expected to be a daughter has become like a male son. In our gender vocabulary we might be more likely to use the label 'female son,' because the biological sex is female, but the gendered role is masculine.

[742] Ifi Amadiume, *Male Daughters, Female Husbands: Gender and Sex in an African Society* (London: Zed Books, 1987).

[743] Biko Agozino, "Between Divas and Dimpers: A Review of Ifi Amadiume's *Daughters of the Goddess, Daughters of Imperialism: African Women, Culture, Power & Democracy*, London, Zed, 2000," *Jenda: A Journal of Culture and African Women Studies*, 1 (no. 1) (2001). Accessed online at http://www.jendajournal.com/vol1.1/agozino.html.

[744] Amadiume.

[745] Beth Greene, "The Institution of Woman-Marriage in Africa: A Cross-Cultural Analysis," *Ethnology*, 37 (no.4), 395-412 (1998). Greene notes that not all female husbands fit into the classification scheme of 'autonomous' or 'surrogate,' a scheme proposed by Denise O'Brien, "Female Husbands in Southern Bantu Societies," in A. Schlegel (Ed.), *Sexual Stratification: A Cross-Cultural View*, pp. 109-126 (N. Y.: Columbia Univ. Press, 1977).

[746] Ibid, especially pp. 399-403.

[747] Ibid, especially pp. 401-406.

[748] Perkins.

[749] John C. McCall, *Dancing Histories—Heuristic Ethnography with the Ohafia Igbo* (Ann Arbor, MI: Univ. of Michigan Press, 2000).

[750] John C. McCall, "Portrait of a Brave Woman," *American Anthropologist*, 98 (no. 1), 127-136 (1996).

[751] Louis S. B. Leakey, *The Southern Kikuyu Before 1903* (N. Y.: Academic Press, 1938; reprinted 1977).

[752] Wairimu Ngaruiya Njambi & William E. O'Brien, "Revisiting 'Woman-Woman' Marriage: Notes on Gikuyu Women," *NWSA Journal*, 12 (no. 1), 1-23 (2000). Accessed online at http://iupjournals.org/nwsa/nws12-1.html#f3.

[753] Ibid; see section subtitled 'Beyond Common Explanations.'

[754] Sylvia Tamale, "Out of the Closet: Unveiling Sexuality Discourses in Uganda [Standpoint]," *Feminist Africa* (2003). A publication of the Gender Institute of Africa, accessed online at http://www.feministafrica.org/fa%202/02-3003/sp-tamale.html.

[755] Edward E. Evans-Pritchard, "Sexual Inversion Among the Azande," *American Anthropologist*, 72, 1428-1434 (1970). Also see, E. E. Evans-Pritchard, *The Azande: History and Political Institutions* (Oxford: Clarendon Press, 1971), p. 83. Cf. Adolphe L. Cureau,

Savage Man in Central Africa: A study of Primitive Races in the French Congo, trans. E. Andrews (London: T. Fisher Unwin, 1915).

756 Louis Tauxier, *Le noir du Soudan. Pays mossi et gourounsi* (Paris: Larose, 1912).

757 Italo Signorini, "Agonwole Agyale: The Marriage Between Two Persons of the Same Sex Among the Nzema of South Western Ghana," *Société des Africanistes, XLII* (no. 2), 221-234; cf. Italo Signorini, "Agonwole Agyale: il matrimonio tra individui dello stesso sesso degli Nzemi del Ghana sub-occidentale," *Rassegna Italiana de Sociologia, 12* (no. 3), 529-545 (1971).

758 See Murray & Roscoe, pp. 178-182. Also see M. Wa Sibuye, "Tinkoncana etimayinini: The Wives of the Mines," in M. Krouse (Ed.), *Invisible Ghetto: Lesbian and Gay Writing from South Africa*, pp. 52-64 (London: Gay Men's Press, 1993). Cf. Amanda Lock Swarr, "Moffies, Artists, and Queens: Race and the Production of South African Gay Male Drag," in S. P. Schacht & L. Underwood (Eds.), *The Drag Queen Anthology. The Absolutely Fabulous But Flawlessly Customary World of Female Impersonators*, pp.73-89 (Binghamton, NY: Haworth Press, 2004), p. 78.

759 John H. Driberg, *The Lango. A Nilotic Tribe of Uganda* (London: Thorner Coryndon, 1923), p. 210.

760 Ibid. Cf. C. Ford & F. Beach, *Patterns of Sexual Behavior* (N. Y.: Ace Books, 1951).

761 J. C. D. Laurance, *The Iteso: 50 Years of Change in a Nilo-Hamitic Tribe of Uganda* (Oxford: Oxford Univ. Press, 1957).

762 Donald L. Donham, *Work and Power in Maale, Ethiopia* (N. Y.: Columbia Univ.Press, 1994), p. 24.

763 Donald L. Donham, *History, Power, Ideology: Central Issues in Marxism and Anthropology* (N. Y.: Cambridge Univ. Press, 1990), pp. 92, 112-113. The *Ashtime* provide an instance in which the continuum between the sex poles of male (*atinke*) and female (*lali*) may lead to an interpretation of the *Ashtime* (sexual anatomy of *atinke* but gender role of *lali*) as a 'third gender' or as a low grade of 'maleness.' The determination reflects the categorizer's assumptions about the pairing of sex and gender.

764 Siegfried F. Nadel, *The Nuba: An Anthropological Study of the Hill Tribes in Kordofan* (London: Oxford Univ. Press, 1947). Also see S. F. Nadel, "Two Nuba Religions: A Comparison," *American Anthropologist, 57* (no. 4), 661-679 (1955).

765 Messing is quoted in Murray & Roscoe, p. 22.

766 Christopher R. Hallpike, *The Konso of Ethiopia. A Study of the Values of a Cushite People* (Oxford: Clarendon Press, 1972), pp. 150-151.

767 Geoffrey Gorer, *Africa Dances: A Book About West Africa Negroes* (London: Eland Publishing, 2003 reprint of 1935 ed.).

768 See John Coleman Wood, *When Men Are Women. Manhood Among Gabra Nomads of East Africa* (Madison, WI: Univ. of Wisconsin Press, 1999).

769 Murray & Roscoe, p. 176.

770 Rodney Needham, "The Left Hand of the Mugwe: An Analytical Note on the Structure of Meru Symbolism," in R. Needham, *Right and Left Essays on Dual Classifications*, pp. 109-127 (Chicago: Univ. of Chicago Press, 1973).

771 See Rudolph P. Gaudio, "White Men Do It Too: Racialized (Homo)sexualities in Postcolonial Hausaland," *Journal of Linguistic Anthropology, 11* (no. 1), 36-51 (2001). Also see Rudolph P. Gaudio, *Men Who Talk Like Women: Language, Gender, and Sexuality in a Muslim Hausa Society* (Stanford, CA: Stanford Univ. PhD dissertation, 1996). Also

see Renee Pittin, "Houses of Women: A Focus on Alternative Life-Styles in Katsina City," in C. Oppong (Ed.), *Female and Male in West Africa*, 291-302 (Allen & Unwin, 1983). Cf. Susan O'Brien, "Pilgrimage, Power, and Identity: The Role of the *Hajj* in the Lives of Nigerian Hausa *Bori* Adepts," *Africa Today, 46* (nos. 3-4), 11-40 (1999). Also cf. Fremont E. Besmer, *Horses, Musicians and Gods: The Hausa Cult of Possession Trance* (South Hadley, MA: Bergin and Garvey, 1983).

[772] Cf. the *Internet Living Swahili Dictionary*, at the Kamusi Project website, accessed online at http://research.yale.edu/cgi-bin/swahili/main.cgi?right_frame_src=http%3A//www.yale.edu/ swahili/home.html.

[773] Alan P. Merriam, *An African World: The Basongye Village of Lupupa Ngye* (Bloomington: Indiana Univ. Press, 1974). See Murray & Roscoe, pp. 144-146. Cf. Louis A. Berman, *The Puzzle. Exploring the Evolutionary Puzzle of Male Homosexuality* (Wilmette, IL: Godot Press, 2003), p. 186.

[774] Armand Corre, cited in Murray.

[775] Gill Shepherd, "Rank, Gender, and Homosexuality: Mombassa as a Key to Understanding Sexual Options," in P. Caplan (Ed.), *The Cultural Construction of Sexuality* pp. 240-270 (London: Tavistock, 1987), p. 250.

[776] Kelly M. Askew, "Female Circles and Male Lines: Gender Dynamics Along the Swahili Coast," *Africa Today, 46* (no. 3/4), 67-102 (1999).

[777] Mircea Eliade, *Rites and Symbols of Initiation: The Mysteries of Birth and Rebirth*, translated by W. R. Trask (N. Y.: Harper & Row, 1975; original work published 1958), p. 44.

[778] Jane T. Creider & Chet A. Creider, "Gender Inversion in Nandi Ritual," *Anthropos, 92* (no. 1), 51-58 (1997), p. 56.

[779] Alfred Claud Hollis, *The Maasai: Their Language and Folklore* (Oxford: Clarendon Press, 1905). Hollis draws a similar conclusion about the circumcision rituals involving Nandi boys. Cf. A. C. Hollis, *The Nandi: Their Language and Folklore* (Oxford: Clarendon Press, 1909).

[780] See S. Bagge, "The Circumcision Ceremony Among the Naivasha Maasai," *Journal of the Anthropological Institute*, 167-169 (1904). Joy Adamson, *The Peoples of Kenya* (N. Y.: Harcourt, Brace & World, 1967), p. 224. Cf. Joseph Lemasolai-Lekuton & Herman Viola, *Facing the Lion: Growing Up Maasai on the African Savannah* (Washington, D. C.: National Geographic Society, 2003), which though aimed at young adults offers a friendly entry into the subject.

[781] Stephen Ellis, *Young Soldiers and the Significance of Initiation: Some Notes from Liberia* (2003). Accessed online at http://asc.leidenuniv.nl/pdf/conference24042003 -ellis.pdf. Cf. Mary Moran, "Warriors or Soldiers? Masculinity and Ritual Transvestism in the Liberian Civil War," in C. R. Sutton (Ed), *Feminism, Nationalism and Militarism*, pp. 73-88 (Association for Feminist Anthropology/American Anthropological Association, Arlington VA, 1995). Also cf. Donal B. Cruise O'Brien, "Review Article: Satan Steps Out from the Shadows. Religion and Politics in Africa," *Africa, 70* (no. 3), 520-525 (2000), p. 522.

[782] Amadiume, *Male Daughters, Female Husbands*, p. 53.

[783] Geoffrey Parrinder, *Sex in the World's Religions* (N. Y.: Oxford Univ. Press, 1980), p. 130f. Cf. Aud Talle, "Transforming Women into 'Pure' Agnates: Aspects of Female Infibulation in Somalia," in V. Broch-Due, I. Rudie, & T. Bleie (Eds.), *Carved Flesh/Cast Selves. Gendered Symbols and Social Practices*, pp. 83-106 (Oxford: Berg, 1993). Talle explains

how infibulation (removal of clitoris and labia minora, followed by stitching) constructs body sexuality by further emphasizing the differences between male and female.

[784] See *State-Sponsored Homophobia in Southern Africa* (2003). Accessed at the Human Rights Watch website, page online at http://hrw.org/press/2003/05/safrica051403.htm.

[785] See *Mugabe: Gays Are Not Better than Pigs & Dogs*, on Voice of Africa website (2004-2005). Accessed online at http://www.voiceofafricaradio.com/ newsdetails.php?id=11.

[786] Chiluba's remarks are quoted in "Chiluba Blasts Gays," *Times of Zambia* (1998, Oct. 19), cited in "II. The Spread of Homophobic Rhetoric in Southern Africa," *More Than a Name. State-Sponsored Homophobia and Its Consequences in Southern Africa* (Human Rights Watch and the International Gay and Lesbian Human Rights Commission, 2003). Accessed online at http://www.hrw.org/reports/2003/ safrica/ safriglhrc0303-02.htm#P599_118723.

[787] From Amnesty International's "Uganda," *Report 2003*. Accessed online at http://web.amnesty. org/report2003/Uga-summary-eng.

[788] See "II. The Spread of Homophobic Rhetoric in Southern Africa."

[789] Norbert Brockman, "Kenya," in R. T. Francoeur (Ed.), *The International Encyclopedia of Sexuality*, Vols. I-III (N. Y.: Continuum, 1997). Accessed online at http://www2.rz.hu-berlin.de/sexology/GESUND/ARCHIV/IES/KENYA.HTM#7.%20 GENDER%20CONFLICTED%20PERSONS. See §7. Gender Conflicted Persons.

[790] Robert B. Edgerton, "Pokot Intersexuality: An East African Example of the Resolution of Sexual Incongruity," *American Anthropologist, 66*, 1288-1299 (1964).

[791] For example, research reported in 1994 finds in a survey of more than 2,000 South African Black university undergraduates that about 1-in-6 indicate a 'moderate' to 'high' need for help with issues of sexual identity. L. J. Nicholas, "A Profile of 2,209 UWC First Year Students: Career Interests, Guidance Experiences, Knowledge and Attitudes towards AIDS and Sexuality and Religiosity" (An unpublished report: Centre for Student Counseling, University of the Western Cape, 1994). Cited in Lionel John-Nicholas, Priscilla Sandra Daniels, & Mervyn Bernard Hurwitz, "South Africa," in R. T. Francoeur (Ed.), *The International Encyclopedia of Sexuality*, Vols. I-III (N. Y.: Continuum, 1997). Accessed online at http://www2.rz.hu-berlin.de/sexology/GESUND/ ARCHIV/IES/SAFRICA.HTM#7.%20GENDER%20CONFLICTED%20PERSONS. See §7. Gender Conflicted Persons.

[792] Swarr, p. 79.

[793] This followed the inclusion of a similar provision in the 1993 Interim Constitution. The protective clause (9.3) reads as follows: "The state may not unfairly discriminate directly or indirectly against anyone on one or more grounds, including race, gender, sex, pregnancy, marital status, ethnic or social origin, colour, sexual orientation, age, disability, religion, conscience, belief, culture, language, and birth." See the World Legal Survey webpage for South Africa at the International Lesbian and Gay Association website. Accessed online at http://www.ilga.info/Information/Legal_survey/africa/southafrica.htm.

[794] Ibid; see subsection entitled, 'October 1998: South Africa's Constitutional Court Confirms that Laws Criminalizing Sex Between Men Are Unconstitutional.'

[795] Ibid; see section entitled, 'Anti-Discrimination and Anti-Vilification Legislation.'

[796] See Charles Phalane, "Transgender Group Calls for More Time to Consider 'Inhumane' Bill on Sex Status," *CapeTimes* online edition (2003, Sept. 10). Accessed online at http://www.capetimes.co.za/ index.php?fSectionId=271&fArticleId=224963.

[797] "News and Opinion: Brief: International: South Africa," *MCV Victoria and Tasmania* (2004, July 2), p. 6.

[798] Gays and Lesbians of Zimbabwe (GALZ), *Statement from African Lesbian, Gay, Bisexual, and Transgender Organizations* (2004, Feb. 13). Accessed online at the Kubatana.net website at http://www.kubatana.net/html/archive/sexual/040213galz.asp?orgcode=gay001&range_start=1.

[799] Ibid.

Q. 55 Notes

[800] Rosemary A. Joyce, "Negotiating Sex and Gender in Classic Maya Society," in C. F. Klein (Ed.), *Gender in Pre-Hispanic America*, pp. 109-141 (Washington, D. C.: Dumbarton Oaks, 2001). Quote is from p. 109. Cf. her "Beauty, Sexuality, Ornamentation and Gender in Ancient Mesoamerica," in S. Nelson & M. Rosen-Ayalon (Eds.), *In Pursuit of Gender*, pp. 81-92 (Walnut Creek, CA: AltaMira Press, 2002).

[801] Ibid, p. 117.

[802] Jacobo Schifter, *From Toads to Queens: Transvestism in a Latin American Setting* (Binghamton, NY: Haworth Press, 1999). Cf. Jacobo Schifter, *Lila's House: Male Prostitution in Latin America* (N.Y.: Harrington Park Press, 1998). This latter volume focuses on *cacheros*, heterosexual males who occasionally engage in sex with other men, sometimes for pleasure, more often for money.

[803] Information found at The International Lesbian and Gay Association website, accessed online at http://www.ilga.info/Information/Legal_survey/americas/cuba.htm.

[804] *Gay and Lesbian Rights in Cuba* (2006). Found at the www.cuba-solidarity.org.uk website. Accessed online at www.cuba-solidarity.org/faqdocs/Cuba-sexual-diversity.pdf.

[805] Emilio Bejel, *Gay Cuban Nation* (Chicago: univ. of Chicago Press, 2001), p. 20.

[806] Sujatha Fernandes, *Cuba Represent! Cuban Arts, State Power, and the Making of New Revolutionary Cultures* (Durham, NC: Duke Univ. Press, 2006), p. 148.

[807] Leslie Feinberg, "Sex-Changes in Cuba Will Be No-Cost, Like All Health Care," *Workers World* (2007, Feb. 22). Found at the www.workers.org website, accessed online at http://www.workers.org/2007/world/sex-change-0301/.

[808] Paul R. Abramson & Steven D. Pinkerton, *With Pleasure: Thoughts on the Nature of Human Sexuality*, rev. ed. (N. Y.: Oxford Univ. Press, 2002), p. 127.

[809] Zachary Nataf, "Whatever I Feel, That's the Way I Am," *New Internationalist*, pp. 22-25 (1998, Apr. 1). On the debate within medicine over whether hormones contribute decisively to the adoption of gender identity, see both Juliane Imperato-McGinley, R. E. Peterson, T. Gautier, & E. Sturla, "Androgens and the Evolution of Male Gender Identity Among Male Pseudo-Hermaphrodites," *New England Journal of Medicine, 300* (no. 22), 1233-1237 (1979), and Jean D. Wilson, "The Role of Androgens in Male Gender Role Behavior," *Endocrine Review, 20* (no. 5), 726-737 (1999).

[810] Jon Cohen, "A Sour Taste on the Sugar Plantations," *Science, 313*, 473-475 (2006, July 28).

[811] Denise Brennan, *What's Love Got to Do with It? Transnational Desires and Sex Tourism in the Dominican Republic* (Durham, NC: Duke Univ. Press, 2004), p. 83.

[812] Julia O'Connell Davidson & Jacqueline Sanchez Taylor, *Child Prostitution and Sex Tourism. Dominican Republic* (1995), p. 12. This is a research paper written as part of a series of papers in preparation for the World Congress Against the Commercial Exploitation of Children (August, 1996). Accessed online at http://www.ecpat.net/eng/ecpat_inter/Publication/Other/English/Pdf_page/ecpat_sex_tourism_dom_rebublic.pdf.

[813] Luis Montesinos & Juan Preciado, "Puerto Rico," in R. T. Francoeur (Ed.), *The International Encyclopedia of Sexuality*, Vols. I-III (N. Y.: Continuum, 1997). Accessed online at http://www2.rz.hu-berlin.de/sexology/GESUND/ARCHIV/IES/PUERTORI.HTM#7.%20GENDER%20CONFLICTED%20PERSONS. See §7. Gender Conflicted Persons.

[814] S. L. Rodriguez-Madera & J. Toro-Alfonso, *Gender as an Obstacle in HIV/AIDS Prevention: The Transgender Community in Puerto Rico* (2002). Abstract no. ThPeE7845 prepared for the International Conference on AIDS (July 7-12, 2002). Accessed online at http://gateway.nlm.nih.gov/MeetingAbstracts/102251329.html.

[815] For the case, see the *LexJuris Puerto Rico* website; the case accessed online at http://www.lexjuris.com/LEXJURIS/tspr2000/lex2000109.htm.

[816] Schifter, *From Toads to Queens*.

[817] Andrew Reding, "In Guatemala, Bashing is Just the Beginning," *Gay Guatemala* (1999), at the *Global Gayz* website, accessed online at http://www.globalgayz.com/g-guatemala.html.

[818] Manuel Fernandez, "Guatemala," in Claude J. Summers (Ed.), *glbtq: An Encyclopedia of Gay, Lesbian, Bisexual, Transgender, and Queer Culture* (2004). Accessed online at *glbtq* website at http://www.glbtq.com/social-sciences/ guatemala.html.

[819] See Ben. Sifuentes-Jauregui, *Transvestism, Masculinity, and Latin American Literature: Genders Share Flesh* (N. Y.: Palgrave Macmillan, 2002). This book focuses on the arrest of 41 men, some of them crossdressed, at a private party in Mexico City on November 20, 1901. It exposes the way the transgendered experience has been handled in the culture. For a focus on a more contemporary situation, see Annick Prieur, *Mema's House, Mexico City: On Transvestites, Queens, and Machos* (Chicago: University of Chicago Press, 1998).

[820] Eusebio Rubio, "Mexico," in R. T. Francoeur (Ed.), *The International Encyclopedia of Sexuality*, Vols. I-III (N. Y.: Continuum, 1997). Accessed online at http://www2.rz.hu-berlin.de/sexology/GESUND/ARCHIV/IES/MEXICO.HTM#7.%20GENDER%20CONFLICTED%20PERSONS. See §7. Gender Conflicted Persons.

[821] Julie Pecheur, "The Third Gender," *Oaxaca Times* (2004). Accessed at the Oaxaca Times.com website, online at http://www.oaxacatimes.com/html/third.html#. Also see Lynn Stephen, "Sexualities and Genders in Zapotec Oaxaca," *Latin American Perspectives*, 29 (no. 9), 41-59 (2002).

[822] Rubio.

[823] Juan Pablo Ordonez & Richard Elliott, *'Cleaning Up the Streets.' Human Rights Violations in Colombia and Honduras—1996*, (International Lesbian and Gay Association, 1999). Accessed online at http://www.ilga.info/Information/Legal_survey/americas/supporting%20files/cleaning_up_the_streets_.htm.

[824] Cited in Edward Carpenter, *Intermediate Types Among Primitive Folk. A Study in Social Evolution* (London: George Allen & Co., Inc., 1914), p. 37. Accessed online at http://www.sacred-texts.com/lgbt/itp/itp05.htm.

[825] Sofia Kamenetzky, "Argentina," in R. T. Francoeur (Ed.), *The International Encyclopedia of Sexuality*, Vols. I-III (N. Y.: Continuum, 1997). Accessed online at http://www2.rz.hu-berlin.de/sexology/GESUND/ARCHIV/IES/ARGENT.HTM#7.%20GENDER%20CONFLICTED%20PERSONS. See §7. Gender Conflicted Persons.

[826] For more information, contact the Association at: Asociación de Lucha por la Identidad Travesti y Transexual, Defensa 920—Dpto D, Ciudad Autonoma de Buenos Aires Argentina. Telephone: 54 11 43815854. Also see the information at the Astraea website, accessed online at http://www.astraea.org/PHP/Grants/AssociationFightingForTransvestiteIdentity.php4. For more on Lohana Berkins see the profile on the occasion of her receiving the 2003 International Gay and Lesbian Human Rights Commission's Felipa Award, accessed online at http://gaytoday.com/world/050103 wo.asp.

[827] Andrea Cornwall, "Gendered Identities and Gender Ambiguity Among Travestis in Salvador, Brazil," in A. Cornwall & N. Lindisfarne (Eds.), *Dislocating Masculinity: Comparative Ethnographies*, pp. 111-132 (N. Y.: Routledge, 1993), p. 111.

[828] Ibid, p. 113.

[829] Luiz Mott, *Epidemic of Hate: Violations of the Human Rights of Gay Men, Lesbians and Transvestites in Brazil* (S. F.: International Gay and Lesbian Human Rights Commission, 1996).

[830] Sérgio Luiz Gonçalves de Freitas, Elí Fernandes de Oliveira, & Lourenço Stélio Rega, "Brazil," in R. T. Francoeur (Ed.), *The International Encyclopedia of Sexuality*, Vols. I-III (N. Y.: Continuum, 1997). Accessed online at http://www2.rz.hu-berlin.de/sexology/GESUND/ARCHIV/IES/BRAZIL.HTM#7.%20GENDER%20CONFLICTED%20PERSONS. See §7. Gender Conflicted Persons.

[831] Michael S. Rose, "The News You May Have Missed: A Third Place to Do Number 1 & Number 2," *New Oxford Review* (2006, March). Accessed online at http://www.newoxfordreview.org/article.jsp?did=0306-news.

[832] Ana Mariella Bacigalupo, "The Struggle for Mapuche Shamans' Masculinity: Colonial Politics of Gender, Sexuality, and Power in Southern Chile," *Ethnohistory, 51* (no. 3), 489-533 (2004), p. 505.

[833] Ibid, pp. 505, 524. In the latter place Bacigalupo adds, "The Reche had co-gendered identities in which *machi weye* oscillated between masculine and feminine poles. They combined women's and men's behavior, dress, and style in varying degrees, and this co-gendered condition could be associated with passive or active sexual acts or with celibacy, the meanings of which varied according to context." [Italics added.]

[834] Ibid, p. 505. Bacigalupo argues that *Machi weye* primarily became feminine to receive spirits. This ability was instrumental in healing practice, important religiously, and conferred social status and power to the individual.

[835] Bacigalupo (ibid, p. 517) notes that today some such males are labeled *domo-wentru* ('woman-man').

[836]Ibid, p. 504. Bacigalupo observes that this loincloth among the Reche-Mapuche was a garment worn by men in battle or to play a war-like game, but to Spaniard eyes it resembled a woman's skirt. Though the *Machi weye* might incorporate feminine items

(e.g., rings and necklaces), their gender presentation was more feminine to Spanish eyes than to their own people.

[837] Ibid, pp. 489f., 503. Bacigalupo notes that the Spanish view of sex, sexuality, and gender prompted them to view all crossdressing males as homosexuals who, like women, took a passive, receptive role in sexual activity.

[838] Ana Mariella Bacigalupo, "Rethinking Identity and Feminism: Contributions of Mapuche Women and *Machi* from Southern Chile," *Hypatia, 18* (no. 2), 33-57 (2003), p. 37.

[839] Ana Mariella Bacigalupo, "The Mapuche Man Who Became a Woman Shaman: Selfhood, Gender Transgression, and Competing Cultural Norms," *American Ethnologist, 31* (no. 3), 440-457 (2004). Cf. Ana Mariella Bacigalupo, "The Mapuche Man Who Became a Woman Shaman: Conflict and Conformity in the Life and Spiritual Practice of Machi Marta," in S. Marcos (Ed.), *Gender, Orality, and Indigenous Religions* (Cuernavaca, Mexico: ALER Publications, 2002).

[840] Bacigalupo, "The Struggle for Mapuche Shamans' Masculinity," p. 506.

[841] Bernardo Useche, "Gender Conflicted Persons," in Jose Manuel Gonzales, Ruben Ardila, Pedro Guerrero, Gloria Penagos, & Bernardo Useche, "Colombia," in R. T. Francoeur (Ed.), *The International Encyclopedia of Sexuality*, Vols. I-III (N. Y.: Continuum, 1997). Accessed online at http://www2.hu-berlin.de/sexology/IES/colombia.html#7. Cf. Jose Manuel Gonzales, Ruben Ardila, Pedro Guerrero, Gloria Penagos, & Bernardo Useche, "Colombia," in R. T. Francoeur (Ed.), *The International Encyclopedia of Sexuality*, Vol. IV, pp. 48-85 (N. Y.: Continuum, 2001).

Q. 56 Notes

[842] Paul Mazur, "The Developed World," in W. Shawn (Ed.), *Handbook of Gay, Lesbian, Bisexual and Transgender Administration and Policy*, pp. 1-16 (N. Y.: Marcel Dekker, 2004), p. 10.

[843] See Question Set 6 (Q. 41-50) for more information on the history of crossdressing in Europe and elsewhere.

[844] See the answer to Q. 68 (and cf. answers to Q. 69-70).

[845] For example, researchers have documented female crossdressers across Europe, from Denmark in the north to Italy in the south; see Rudolph M. Dekker & Lotte C. van de Pol, *The Tradition of Female Transvestism in Early Modern Europe*. (N. Y.: Palgrave Macmillan, 1997; original work published 1989). For more, see the answer to Q. 46.

[846] See the answer to Q. 95 for a history of how modern mental health scientists—many of them European—have tried to understand crossdressing.

[847] Antonia Young, Women Who Become Men: Albanian Sworn Virgins. (N. Y.: Berg Publishers, 2000). Cf. Rene Grimaux, "Woman Becomes Man in the Balkans," in Gilbert Herdt (Ed.), Third Sex, Third Gender: Beyond Sexual Dimorphism in Culture and History, pp. 241-282 (N. Y.: Zone Books, 1993).

[848] Asia-Europe Foundation (ASEF), *Coming Out in Dialogue: Policies and Perceptions of Sexual Minority Groups in Asia & Europe* (2005), p.16, 3.2.1 Austria. 5th 'Talks on the Hill' Conference held in Singapore, Mar. 6-8, 2005. Final report published as ASEF website, accessed online at http://asef.org/go/subsite/ccd/documents/COUNTRY STUDIESFinal.pdf.

[849] Jaroslav Zverina, "The Czech Republic and Slovakia," in R. T. Francoeur (Ed.), *The International Encyclopedia of Sexuality*, Vols. I-III (N. Y.: Continuum, 1997). Accessed

online at http://www2.rz.hu-berlin.de/sexology/GESUND/ARCHIV/IES/CZECH.HTM#7.%20GENDER%20CONFLICTED%20PERSONS. See §7. Gender Conflicted Persons.

[850] L. Jarolim, "Surgical Conversion of Genitalia in Transsexual Patients," *BJU International,* 85 (no. 7), 851-856 (2000).

[851] Czech TransForum website accessed online at http://www.fortunecity.com/village/newcompton/153/.

[852] ASEF, p. 29, §3.2.14 Latvia.

[853] Arturas Tereskinas, "Toward a New Politics of Citizenship: Representations of Ethnic and Sexual Minorities in Lithuanian Mass Media," in M. Sükösd & P. Bajomi-Lázár (Eds.), *Reinventing Media: Media Policy Reform in East-Central Europe,* pp. 203-238 (Budapest, Hungary: Central European University Press, 2003), p. 207.

[854] Jolanta Reingardiene & Arnas Zdanevicius, "Disrupting the (Hetero)Normative: Coming Out in the Workplace in Lithuania" (2007). Working paper 2007-1, published on the Lithuanian Social Science Forum website, accessed online at http://www.socforumas.lt/files/articles/2007-1(reingardiene&zdanevicius).pdf.

[855] *Transsexual Takes Lithuania to European Court* (2006, Oct. 19). Article prepared by 365Gay.com staff, accessed online at http://www.365gay.com/Newscon06/10/101906 lithuania.htm. Also see *Lithuania Sued Over Transsexual* (2006, Oct. 17), at BBC News website, accessed online at http://news.bbc.co.uk/2/hi/europe/6060114.stm.

[856] Anna Sierzpowska-Ketner, "Poland," in R. T. Francoeur (Ed.), *The International Encyclopedia of Sexuality,* Vols. I-III (N. Y.: Continuum, 1997). Accessed online at http://www2.rz.hu-berlin.de/sexology/GESUND/ARCHIV/IES/POLAND.HTM#7.%20GENDER%20CONFLICTED%20PERSONS. See §7. Gender Conflicted Persons.

[857] ASEF, p. 34, §3.2.19 Poland.

[858] Igor S. Kon, "Russia," in D. J. West & R. Green (Eds.), *Sociolegal Control of Homosexuality: A Multi-Nation Comparison,* pp. 221-242 (N. Y.: Plenum Press, 1997).

[859] Igor S. Kon, "Russia," in R. T. Francoeur (Ed.), *The International Encyclopedia of Sexuality,* Vols. I-III (N. Y.: Continuum, 1997). Accessed online at http://www2.rz.hu-berlin.de/sexology/GESUND/ARCHIV/IES/RUSSIA.HTM#7.%20GENDER%20CONFLICTED%20PERSONS. See §7. Gender Conflicted Persons.

[860] Waldemar Bogoras, *The Chuckchee* (N. Y.: Memoirs of the American Museum of Natural History, 1907). On Bogoras' work, see Williams, *The Spirit and the Flesh,* pp. 252-254.

[861] Edward Westermarck, *The Origin and Development of the Moral Ideas, vol. 2* (N. Y.: Macmillan, 1908), p. 458.

[862] Quoted in Edward Carpenter, *Intermediate Types Among Primitive Folk. A Study in Social Evolution* (London: George Allen & Co., Inc., 1914), p. 17. Accessed online at http://www.sacred-texts.com/lgbt/itp/itp04.htm.

[863] Conrad Kottak, *Cultural Anthropology: The Exploration of Human Diversity* (10th ed.) (Boston: McGraw-Hill, 2004), p. 358.

[864] Williams, *The Spirit and the Flesh,* p. 254.

[865] For examples of European businesses selling unbifurcated garments to men, visit any of a number of websites. While this volume was being prepared I sampled various places online, such as a German fashion site accessed at

https://ssl.Ekundenserver.de/menintime.de/start_en.php3?VID=pwYIqgr5sRhjtLvF& P ID=no. Also see the German fashion site Persus de accessed at http://www.persus.de/index2.htm. Cf. the British site for Midas Clothing in Manchester, England, accessed at http://www.persus.de/ index2.htm. See the answer to Q. 9.

866 ASEF, p. 20, §3.2.5 Denmark.

867 ASEF, p. 22, §3.2.7 Finland.

868 *Fundamental Rights in the EU in 2002* (2002). European Parliament text, accessed online at http://www.europarl.europa.eu/pv2/pv2?PRG=CALDOC&TPV=PROV&FILE=20030904&TXTLST=2&POS=1&LASTCHAP=6&SDOCTA=6&Type_Doc=FIRST&LANGUE=EN.

869 Osmo Kontula, & Elina Haavio-Mannila, "Finland," in R. T. Francoeur (Ed.), *The International Encyclopedia of Sexuality*, Vols. I-III (N. Y.: Continuum, 1997). Accessed online at http://www2.rz.hu-berlin.de/sexology/GESUND/ARCHIV/IES/FINLAND.HTM#7.%20GENDER%20CONFLICTED%20PERSONS. See §7. Gender Conflicted Persons.

870 ASEF, p. 22, §3.2.7 Finland.

871 See SETA's English website accessed online at http://www.seta.fi/en/. Cf. Kontula & Haavio-Mannila.

872 ASEF, p. 23, §3.2.8 France.

873 Centre d'Aide, de Recherche et d'Information sur la Transsexualité et l'Identité de Genre, acceesed online at http://www.caritig.org/index.php.

874 For more on this collection, see the *Guide to the German Transvestite Postcards, 1903-1920*, accessed online at http://rmc.library.cornell.edu/EAD/htmldocs/RMM07636.html.

875 Alon Rachamimov, "The Disruptive Comforts of Drag: (Trans)Gender Performances Among Prisoners of War in Russia, 1914-1920," *The American Historical Review, 111* (no. 2), 362-382 (2006).

876 For a review of *Lola + Bilidikid*, see Georg Seesslen, *Between Cultures—Third-Generation Immigrant Cinema* (2003, June), found at the Goethe-Institut website, accessed online at http://www.goethe.de/ges/pok/prj/mig/fli/fum/en47146.htm.

877 Charlotte von Mahlsdorf, *I Am My Own Woman. The Outlaw Life of Charlotte von Mahlsdorf, Berlin's Most Distinguished Transvestite* (San Francisco: Cleis Press, 1995). For more information, see the I Am My Own Wife website, focused on the play made about von Mahlsdorf, but with materials about her as well, accessed online at http://www.iammyownwife.com/explore.asp.

878 Rudiger Lautmann, Ph.D., and Kurt Starke, "Germany," in R. T. Francoeur (Ed.), *The International Encyclopedia of Sexuality*, Vols. I-III (N. Y.: Continuum, 1997). Accessed online at http://www2.rz.hu-berlin.de/sexology/GESUND/ARCHIV/IES/GERMANY.HTM#7.%20GENDER%20CONFLICTED%20PERSONS. See §7. Gender Conflicted Persons.

879 See Cordula Weitze & Susanne Osburg, "Transsexualism in Germany: Emperical Data on Epidemiology and Application of the German Transsexuals' Act During Its First Ten Years," *Archives of Sexual Behavior, 25* (no. 4), 409-425 (1996). Also see, for a specific case, "As to the Admissibility of Application No. 31176/96 by Theodor (Dora) ROETZHEIM Against Germany" (1996), accessed online at http://www.pfc.org.uk/files/legal/r-v-ger.txt.

[880] ASEF, p. 24, §3.2.9 Germany.

[881] Deutsche Gesellschaft für Transidentität und Intersexualität e.V. website accessed online at http://www.dgti.org/.

[882] ASEF, p. 31, §3.2.16 Luxembourg.

[883] Jelto J. Drenth & A. Koos Slob, "Netherlands and the Autonomous Dutch Antilles," in R. T. Francoeur (Ed.), *The International Encyclopedia of Sexuality*, Vols. I-III (N. Y.: Continuum, 1997). Accessed online at http://www2.rz.hu-berlin.de/sexology/GESUND/ARCHIV/IES/NETHER.HTM#7.%20GENDER%20CONFLICTED%20PERSONS. See §7. Gender Conflicted Persons.

[884] Ibid.

[885] Elsa Almas & Esben Esther Pirelli Benestad, "Norway," in R. T. Francoeur (Ed.), *The International Encyclopedia of Sexuality*, Vol. IV, pp. 460-462 (N. Y.: Continuum, 2001). Accessed online at http://www.SexQuest.com/IES4. See §7. Gender Conflicted Persons.

[886] Elsa Almas & Esben Esther Pirelli Benestad, "Norway," updated material (2003), p. 781, accessed online at http://www.indiana.edu/~kinsey/ccies/no.php#top.

[887] Tone Maria Hansen, *Treatment in Norway for Transsexuals* (2003), found at the LFTS website, accessed online at http://www.lfts.no/?module=Articles;action=ArticleFolder.publicOpenFolder;ID=182.

[888] Jan E. Trost & Mai-Briht Bergstrom-Walan, "Sweden," in R. T. Francoeur (Ed.), *The International Encyclopedia of Sexuality*, Vols. I-III (N. Y.: Continuum, 1997). Accessed online at http://www2.rz.hu-berlin.de/sexology/GESUND/ARCHIV/IES/SWEDEN.HTM#7.%20GENDER%20CONFLICTED%20PERSONS. See §7. Gender Conflicted Persons.

[889] Niklas Långström & Kenneth Zucker, "Transvestic Fetishism in the General Population," *Journal of Sex & Marital Therapy, 31* (no. 2), 87-95 (2005).

[890] "Single Skint Transvestites," *The Local. Sweden's News in English* (2004, July 2). Accessed online at http://www.thelocal.se/245/20040702/.

[891] Ibid.

[892] Michael W. Ross, J. Walinder, B. Lundstrom, & Inga Thuwe, "Cross-Cultural Approaches to Transsexualism: A Comparison Between Sweden and Australia," *Acta Psychiatrica Scandinavica, 63* (no. 1), 75-82 (1981).

[893] Stephen Whittle & Gwyneth A. Sampson, "7. Gender Conflicted Persons," in Kevan R. Wylie, et al., "The United Kingdom of Great Britain and Northern Ireland," in R. T. Francoeur (Ed.), *The International Encyclopedia of Sexuality*, Vols. I-III (N. Y.: Continuum, 1997). Accessed online at http://www2.rz.hu-berlin.de/sexology/GESUND/ARCHIV/IES/UK.HTM#THE%20UNITED%20KINGDOM%20OF%20GREAT%20BRITAIN%20AND%20NORTHERN%20IRELAND. See §7. Gender Conflicted Persons.

[894] Ibid.

[895] Ibid.

[896] Christopher McCrudden, "United Kingdom," in European Commission: Employment and Social Affairs, *Bulletin. Legal Issues in Equality*, pp. 36-37 (Tilburg, The Netherlands: European Commission, 2002). See §2.2 'Rights of Transsexuals,' p. 37. Accessed online at http://ec.europa.eu/employment_social/equ_opp/newsletter/bulletin02_3_en.pdf.

⁸⁹⁷ For a short list, see Scottish LGBT organizations listed at the LGBT Centre for Health and Wellbeing website, accessed online at http://www.lgbthealth.org.uk/links.php#scotorgs.

⁸⁹⁸ Philip Wilson, Clare Sharp, & Susan Carr, "The Prevalence of Gender Dysphoria in Scotland: A Primary Care Study," *British Journal of General Practice*, 49, 991-992 (1999).

⁸⁹⁹ Scottish Needs Assessment Programme, *Transsexualism and Gender Dysphoria in Scotland* (Glasgow: Scottish Needs Assessment Programme, 2001). Accessed online at www.phis.org.uk/doc.pl?file=publications/Transsexuals%20Report.doc. Also see Susan V. Carr, "Scotland's Transsexuals—Towards a National Gender Dysphoria Service?" Abstract prepared for The Third International Congress on Sex and Gender. An Interdisciplinary Conference, Exeter College, Oxford University, September 18-20, 1998, published in *The International Journal of Transgenderism*, 2 (no. 3) (1998). Accessed online at http://www.symposion.com/ijt/whittle_congress.htm.

⁹⁰⁰ Thomas Phelim Kelly, "Ireland," in R. T. Francoeur (Ed.), *The International Encyclopedia of Sexuality*, Vols. I-III (N. Y.: Continuum, 1997). Accessed online at http://www2.rz.hu-berlin.de/ sexology/GESUND/ARCHIV/IES/IRELAND.HTM# 7.%20GENDER%20CONFLICTED%20PERSONS. See §7. Gender Conflicted Persons.

⁹⁰¹ ASEF, p. 26, §3.2.11 Ireland.

⁹⁰² Sí website accessed online at http://www.transgender.org/si/.

⁹⁰³ Press for Change website accessed online at http://www.pfc.org.uk/.

⁹⁰⁴ ASEF, p. 19, §3.2.4 Cyprus.

⁹⁰⁵ *Excerpts Pertaining to LGBT – and HIV/AIDS-related Incidents* (2006). Taken from U.S. Department of State Country Reports on Human Rights Practices, found at the glaa.org website and accessed online at http://www.glaa.org/archive/2007/Country Reports2006.shtml.

⁹⁰⁶ Dimosthenis Agrafiotis & Panagiota Mandi, "Greece," in R. T. Francoeur (Ed.), *The International Encyclopedia of Sexuality*, Vols. I-III (N. Y.: Continuum, 1997). Accessed online at http://www2.rz.hu-berlin.de/sexology/GESUND/ARCHIV/IES/GREECE.HTM#7.%20GENDER%20CONFLICTED%20PERSONS. See §7. Gender Conflicted Persons.

⁹⁰⁷ ASEF, p. 35, §3.2.20 Portugal.

⁹⁰⁸ The GTTSA website accessed online at http://clubs.pathfinder.gr/transsexoyal.

⁹⁰⁹ The Transgender Portal website accessed online at http://www.transs.gr/.

⁹¹⁰ Stefano Fabini, *The Rights of Transsexual and Transgender Persons: The Italian Legal Framework and New National and European Challenges* (2002). Paper presented at the Workers Out! 2nd World Conference of Lesbian and Gay Unionists, Sydney, Autralia, Oct. 31-Nov. 2, 2002. Accessed online at http://www.cgil.it/org.diritti/transex/transtrans.htm. Fabini is part of the Center for Research and Legal Comparative Studies on Sexual Orientation and Gender Identity. Cf. ASEF, p. 28, §3.2.13 Italy.

⁹¹¹ ASEF, p. 25, §3.2.10 Greece.

⁹¹² Jose Antonio Nieto, with Jose Antonio Carrobles, Manuel Delgado Ruiz, Felix Lopez Sanchez, Virginia Maquieira D'Angelo, Josep-Vicent Marques, Bernardo Moreno Jimenez, Raquel Osborne Verdugo, Carmela Sanz Rueda, & Carmelo Vazquez Val-

verde, "Spain," in R. T. Francoeur (Ed.), *The International Encyclopedia of Sexuality*, Vols. I-III (N. Y.: Continuum, 1997). Accessed online at http://www2.rz.hu-berlin.de/ sexology/GESUND/ARCHIV/IES/SPAIN.HTM#7.%20GENDER%20CONFLICTED%20PERSONS. See §7. Gender Conflicted Persons.

[913] ASEF, p. 38, §3.2.23 Spain.

[914] Nieto.

[915] M. J. Belza for the EPI-HIV Study Group, "Risk of HIV Infection Among Male Sex Workers in Spain," *Sexually Transmitted Infections, 81*, 85-88 (2005).

Q. 57 Notes

[916] Rosemary Coates, "Australia," in R. T. Francoeur (Ed.), *The International Encyclopedia of Sexuality*, Vols. I-III (N. Y.: Continuum, 1997). Accessed online at http://www2.rz.huberlin.de/sexology/GESUND/ARCHIV/IES/AUSTRAL.HTM#7.%20GENDER%20CONFLICTED%20PERSONS. See §7. Gender Conflicted Persons.

[917] Cf. Michael W. Ross, J. Walinder, B. Lundstrom, & Inga Thuwe, "Cross-Cultural Approaches to Transsexualism: A Comparison Between Sweden and Australia," *Acta Psychiatrica Scandinavica, 63* (no. 1), 75-82 (1981).

[918] Thomas Martin Franck, *The Empowered Self: Law and Society in the Age of Individualism* (Oxford: Oxford Univ. Press, 1999), p. 172.

[919] Robert Reed, "Transsexuals and European Human Rights Law," in H. Graupner & P. Tahmindjis (Eds.), *Sexuality and Human Rights: A Global Overview*, pp. 49-90 (Binghampton, NY: Harrington Park Press, 2005), p. 62. Simultaneously published as *Journal of Homosexuality, 48* (nos. 3-4), 2005.

[920] Viviane K. Namaste, *Invisible Lives: The Erasure of Transsexual and Transgendered People* (Chicago: Univ. Of Chicago Press, 2000), p. 100.

[921] Kalissa Alexeyeff, "Dragging Drag: The Performance of Gender and Sexuality in the Cook Islands," *The Australian Journal of Anthropology, 11* (no. 3), 297-307 (2000), p. 298.

[922] Ibid, p. 303.

[923] Ibid, p. 304. Alexeyeff notes that it is especially among young males that *laelae* are discussed derisively.

[924] Ibid, pp. 298-299.

[925] Ibid, p. 302. Alexeyeff finds the islanders principally enunciate sex and gender through dress, comportment, and work roles (p. 300).

[926] Jeannette Marie Mageo, "Male Transvestism and Cultural Change in Samoa," *American Ethnologist, 19* (no. 3), 443-459 (1992). Cf. Jeannette Marie Mageo, "Samoa, on the Wilde Side: Male Transvestism, Oscar Wilde, and Liminality in Making Gender," *Ethos, 24* (no. 4), 588-627 (1996).

[927] Paul Miles, "Transgender in the Pacific: Fa'afafine, Fakaleiti and Mahu," *ACP-EU Courier Transgender in the Pacific*, No. 183, pp. 45-48 (2000, Oct.). Accessed online at http://europa.eu.int/comm/development/body/publications/courier/courier183/en/en_045_ni.pdf.

[928] Johanna Schmidt, "Redefining Fa'afafine: Western Discourses and the Construction of Transgenderism in Samoa," *Intersections: Gender, History and Culture in the Asian Context, 6* (2001, August), §12. Accessed online at http://wwwsshe. mur-

doch.edu.au/intersections/issue6/schmidt.html. Cf. Johanna Schmidt, "Paradise Lost? Social Change and Fa'afafine in Samoa," *Current Sociology, 51* (nos. 3-4), 417-432 (2003).

[929] This context may help explain the observation of late birth order for *Fa'afafine*; see Kris Poasa, Ray Blanchard, & Kenneth Zucker, "Birth Order in Transgendered Males from Polynesia: A Quantitative Study of Samoan Fa'afafine," *Journal of Sex and Marital Therapy, 30* (no. 1), 13-23 (2004).

[930] Antonia Young, *Women Who Become Men: Albanian Sworn Virgins*. (N. Y.: Berg Publishers, 2000), p. 114.

[931] Schmidt, "Redefining Fa'afafine," §§13-17. Cf. the notion of Mageo that the increase in numbers of *Fa'afafine* in the 20th century helps meet a cultural need for expression of feminine sexuality—a need partly frustrated by Western missionaries when they curbed indigenous women from traditional sexuality displays. The *Fa'afafine*, for example, now occupy the place in evening entertainments once held by females.

[932] See the *Charting the Pacific* website page on 'people,' accessed online at http://www.abc.net.au/ra/pacific/people/hazy.htm. Also cf. Laura Fraser, "The Islands Where Boys Grow Up to Be Girls," *Marie Claire* (2002, Dec.). Accessed online at http://www.laurafraser.com/fafafine.html.

[933] N. H. Bartlett & P. L. Vasey, *Does Your Mother Know? Parental Reactions to Childhood Cross-Gender Behaviors in Samoan Fa'afafine*. Poster presented at the Annual Meeting of the International Academy of Sex Research (IASR), June 16-19, 2004. Abstract accessed online at http://www.iasr.org/meeting/2004/abstracts2004.pdf (p. 10). Apparently, in Samoa (as elsewhere), transgender behavior is unlikely to be stopped by parental rejection of it, but such opposition may prompt more gender dysphoria.

[934] On the *mahu* see Raleigh Watts, "The Polynesian Mahu," in S. O. Murray (Ed.), *Oceanic Homosexualities*, pp. 171-184 (N. Y.: Garland, 1992). On female *mahu* see the work of anthropologist Deborah A. Elliston, "Negotiating Transnational Sexual Economies: Female Mahu and Same-Sex Sexuality in Tahiti and Her Islands," in E. Blackwood & S. Wieringa (Eds.), *Female Desires: Same-Sex Relations and Transgender Practices Across Cultures*, pp. 230-250 (N. Y.: Columbia Univ. Press, 1999).

[935] Michael Sturma, "Dressing, Undressing, and Early European Contact in Australia and Tahiti," *Pacific Studies, 21* (no. 3), 87-104 (1998), p. 92.

[936] Elliston. Cf. Leila J. Rupp, "Toward a Global History of Same-Sex Sexuality," *Journal of the History of Sexuality, 10* (no. 2), 287-302 (2001). Also cf. R. I. Levy, "The Community Function of Tahitian Male Transvestism," *Anthropology Quarterly, 44* (no 1), 12-21 (1971).

[937] Jane Perlez, "For These Transvestites, Still More Role Changes," *NY Times* (2003, July 24). Accessed online at ButchDikeBoy.com website at http://p074.ezboard.com/fbutchdykeboy5326frm7.showMessage?topicID=634.topic.

[938] On these Balinese dance forms see *Dance Forms* on the Bali Xtranet website; the page on art forms was accessed online at http://balix.com/travel/guide/chapters/balinese_art/perform_forms.html.

[939] See the account by Dede Oetomo, National Coordinator of *Gaya Nusantara*, Indonesia's gay network, entitled "Gay Identities," *Inside Indonesia, 46* (1996, March). Accessed online at http://www.insideindonesia.org/edit46/dede.htm.

[940] Josko Petkovic, "Waiting for Karila: Bending Time, Theory and Gender in Java and Bali (with Reflections for a Documentary Treatment)," *Intersections: Gender, History*

and Culture in the Asian Context, 2 (1999, May). Accessed online at http://wwwsshe.murdoch.edu.au/intersections/ issue2/Josko.html.

[941] Tom Boelstorff, "Playing Back the Nation: Waria, Indonesian Transvestites," *Cultural Anthropology, 19* (no. 2), 159-195 (2004); see esp. pp. 165-166.

[942] Wimpie Pangkahila, & J. Alex Pangkahila, "Indonesia," in R. T. Francoeur (Ed.), *The International Encyclopedia of Sexuality*, Vols. I-III (N. Y.: Continuum, 1997). Accessed online at http://www2.rz.hu-berlin.de/sexology/GESUND/ARCHIV/IES/INDONES.HTM#7.%20GENDER%20CONFLICTED%20PERSONS See §7. Gender Conflicted Persons.

[943] E. Pisani, P. Girault, M. Gultom, N. Sukartini, J. Kumalawati, S. Jazan, & E. Donegan, "HIV, Syphilis Infection, and Sexual Practices Among Transgenders, Male Sex Workers, and Other Men Who Have Sex with Men in Jakarta, Indonesia," *Sexually Transmitted Infections, 80*, 536-540 (2004).

[944] Clifford Geertz, *The Religion of Java* (Glencoe, IL: The Free Press, 1960), p. 219f.

[945] For more on the artist, see the Didik Nini Thowok Dance School website, accessed online at http://www.didikninithowok.info/.

[946] Sharyn Graham, "Sex, Gender, and Priests in South Sulawesi, Indonesia," *ILAS Newsletter*, #29 (2002, Nov.). Accessed online at http://iias.leidenuniv.nl/iiasn/29/IIASNL29_27.pdf. Cf. Matthew Kennedy, "Clothing, Gender, and Ritual Transvestism: The *Bissu* of Salawesi," *The Journal of Men's Studies, 2* (no. 1), 1-13 (1993).

[947] Ibid. Also see Leonard Andaya, "The *Bissu*: A Study of a Third Gender in Indonesia," in B. Andaya (Ed.), *Other Pasts: Women, Gender and History in Southeast Asia*, pp. 27-46 (Honolulu: University of Hawaii Press, 2000).

[948] Ibid. For an account of such a ceremonial blessing, also see, Sharyn Graham, "Sulawesi's Fifth Gender," *Inside Indonesia*, no. 64 (2001, Apr.-June). Accessed online at http://www.insideindonesia.org/ edit66/ Bissu2.htm. Cf. R. Anderson Sutton, *Calling Back the Spirit. Music, Dance, and Cultural Politics in Lowland South Sulawesi* (N. Y.: Oxford Univ. Press, 2002), pp. 74-78.

[949] Sharyn Graham, "While Diving, Drink Water: Bisexual and Transgender Intersections in South Sulawesi, Indonesia," *Journal of Bisexuality, 3* (nos. 3/4), 231-248 (2004). Cf. Sharyn Graham, "Hunters, Wedding Mothers, and Gender Transcendent Priests: Conceptualizing Gender Among the Bugis of South Sulawesi, Indonesia." Abstract for a speech delivered at the *AsiaPacifiQueer 1* Conference, University of Technology, Sydney, Australia (2001, Feb. 16). Accessed online at http://apq.anu.edu.au/abstracts.html#sharyn.

[950] Graham, "Sex, Gender and Priests in South Sulawesi, Indonesia." Also see, Sharyn Graham, "Negotiating Gender: *Calalai'* in Bugis Society," *Intersections: Gender, History and Culture in the Asian Context, 6* (2001, August).

[951] Yik Koon Teh, "*Mak Nyahs* (Male Transsexuals) in Malaysia: The Influence of Culture and Religion on Their Identity," *International Journal of Transgenderism, 5* (no. 3) (2001), accessed online at http://www.symposion.com/ijt/ijtvo05no03_04.htm.

[952] Ibid. Also see Yik Koon Teh, *The Mak Nyahs: Malaysian Male to Female Transsexuals* (Singapore: Eastern Universities Press, 2002).

[953] Ibid.

[954] *Attorney-General v. Otahuhu Family Court*, (1994) 1 NZLR 603, 607. A summary of the case accessed online at the Press for Change website at http://www.pfc.org.

uk/legal/ellisj.htm. Franck (p. 172f.) notes the Wellington High Court's reasoning that, "allowing those few who qualify [by operative procedure] to marry will not impact greatly on society, but it will provide relief and recognition for the few individuals affected."

[955] D. F. MacFarlane, "Transsexual Prostitution in New Zealand: Predominance of Persons of Maori Extraction," *Archives of Sexual Behavior, 13* (no. 4), 301-309 (1984).

[956] Susan Sered, *Women of the Sacred Groves. Divine Priestesses of Okinawa* (N. Y.: Oxford Univ. Press, 1999), p. 238.

[957] Ibid, p. 239.

[958] Paul R. Abramson & Steven D. Pinkerton, *With Pleasure: Thoughts on the Nature of Human Sexuality*, rev. ed. (N. Y.: Oxford Univ. Press, 2002), p. 127.

[959] Gilbert Herdt, "Mistaken Sex: Culture, Biology, and the Third Sex in New Guinea," in G. Herdt, *Sambia Sexual Culture: Essays from the Field*, pp. 243-264 (Chicago: Univ. of Chicago Press, 1993); quote is from p. 257.

[960] Mark Johnson, *Beauty and Power: Transgendering and Cultural Transformation in the Southern Philippines* (N. Y.: Berg, 1997).

[961] Carolyn Brewer, "*Baylan, Asog*, Transvestism and Sodomy: Gender, Sexuality and the Sacred in Early Colonial Philippines," *Intersections: Gender, History and Culture in the Asian Context, 2* (1999, May). For a description of their appearance, drawn from Spanish sources of the period, see §§13-15.

[962] Carolyn Brewer, *Holy Confrontation: Religion, Gender and Sexuality in the Philippines, 1521-1685* (Manila: Institute of Women's Studies, 2001). Brewer's focus is on the conflict between the Catholic officials who came with colonization and the *Baylan* women of the islands, who were re-characterized by the Spanish as *bruja* (female witch). She also discusses the *bayog*, or men who dressed as women in undertaking religious rituals. On the modern phenomenon, see especially pp. 153-181.

[963] Mark Johnson, "Global Desirings and Translocal Loves: Transgendering and Same-Sex Sexualities in the Southern Philippines," *American Ethnologist, 25* (no. 4), 695-711 (1998). Quote is from p. 696f.

Q. 58 Notes

[964] For the lands of Central America, see the answer to Q. 55.

[965] While such differences are not pursued in this work, there are materials that do so. See, for example, Viviane K. Nemaste, *Invisible Lives: The Erasure of Transsexual and Transgendered People* (Chicago: Univ. of Chicago Press, 2000), p. 66f.

[966] Barbara Findlay, *An Introduction to Transgendered Women: An Equality Analysis* (Vancouver, B. C., 2000), p. 6. This 39 page booklet was prepared for TransAction from the Justice and Equality Summit, June, 1999. Accessed online at http://www.barbarafindlay.com/articles/42.pdf.

[967] Michael Barrett, Alan King, Joseph Lévy, Eleanor Maticka-Tyndale, & Alexander McKay. "Canada," in R. T. Francoeur (Ed.), *The International Encyclopedia of Sexuality*, Vols. I-III (N. Y.: Continuum, 1997). Accessed online at http://www2.rz.hu-berlin.de/sexology/GESUND/ARCHIV/IES/CANADA.HTM#7.%20GENDER%20CONFLICTED%20PERSONS. See §7. Gender Conflicted Persons.

[968] See, for example, Claude E. Schaeffer, "The Kutenai Female Berdache: Courier, Guide, Prophetess, and Warrior," *Ethnohistory, 12* (no. 3), 193-236 (1965).

[969] Francis Plourde, *The Demise of House Government Bill C-392 on Transsexuals Rights* (2006, Nov. 1). Found at the AlterHeros website, accessed online at http://www.alterheros.com/english/Edito/?recordID=95.

[970] Christopher Banks, "The Co$t of Homophobia: Literature Review on the Economic Impact of Homophobia on Canada and The Cost of Homophobia: Literature Review on the Human Impact of Homophobia on Canada," *CUISR News, 1* (no. 8), p. 8 (2004). On the problem of violence, also see Douglas Janoff, *Pink Blood. Homophobic Violence in Canada* (Toronto: Univ. of Toronto Press, 2005).

[971] Gilles Marchildon, "Off to the Polls. Harper Puts the LGBT Community on Notice: A Conservative Government Will Reverse Our Gains," *INFO Egale, 2* (no. 6), p. 1 (2005, Fall).

[972] *Motions. M-309* (2007, Apr. 18). Found at Bill Siksay MP Burnaby-Douglas website, accessed online at http://action.web.ca/home/billsiksay/attach/Motion-309-Yogyakarta-Apr18.doc

[973] David Garmaise, "NWT Prohibits Discrimination Based on Gender Identity," *Canadian HIV AIDS Policy Law Review, 7* (nos. 2-3), 37 (2002). Also see the province's Human Rights Commission website, accessed online at http://www.nwthumanrights.ca/english/general.html. Also see specifications of Article 2 at the Canadian Human Rights Program website, accessed online at http://www.pch.gc.ca/progs/pdp-hrp/docs/fifth_iccpr/nt_e.cfm.

[974] *Policy on Discrimination and Harassment Because of Gender Identity* (2005; last modified June 5, 2007), found at Ontario Human Rights Commission website, accessed online at http://ohrc.on.ca/english/publications/gender-identity-policy.shtml.

[975] *No. 144. Votes and Proceedings. Legislative Assembly of Ontario* (2007). Accessed online at http://72.14.205.104/search?q=cache:rk30UgeZu1sJ:www.ontla.on.ca/house-proceedings/votes-and-proceedings/files_pdf/March_21_2007.pdf.

[976] British Columbia Human Rights Commission, *Human Rights for the Next Millenium* (Victoria, BC: British Columbia Human Rights Commission , 1998), §6. Accessed online at http://www.bchrcoalition.org/files/Human%20Rights%20for%20the%20Next%20Millennium%20Report%20(1998).rtf.

[977] Kathleen Ann Lahey, *Are We 'Persons' Yet? Law and Sexuality in Canada* (Yoronto: Univ. of Toronto Press, 1999), p. 26.

[978] *Sex Reassignment Surgery Backgrounder* (2004). Found at the Egale Canada website, accessed online at http://www.egale.ca/index.asp?lang=E&item=1086.

[979] The subject of these guidelines and of treatment for transgender people is covered in volume 4 of this work. One source of guidelines for Canadian transsexuals is provided by the Trans Care Project in Vancouver. See Cameron Bowman & Joshua Goldberg, *Care of the Patient Undergoing Sex Reassignment Surgery (SRS)* (Vancouver: Transgender Health Program, 2006). Accessed online at www.vch.ca/transhealth/resources/library/tcpdocs/guidelines-surgery.pdf.

[980] Donald W. McLeod, *Lesbian and Gay Liberation in Canada: A Select Annotated Chronology, 1964-1975* (Toronto: ECW Press/Homestead Books, 1996), p. 48f.

[981] For Baitz, see her website accessed online at http://www.danabaitz.com/groove.php?s=2&t=a. For Spoon, see his website accessed online at http://www.raespoon.com/bio.html.

⁹⁸² *History of 'Egale'* (2007). Found at the Egale Canada website, accessed online at http://www.egale.ca/index.asp?lang=E&menu=2&item=791.

⁹⁸³ *About Egale Canada* (2007). Found at the Egale Canada website, accessed online at http://www.egale.ca/index.asp?lang=E&menu=2&item=1152.

⁹⁸⁴ *About Us* (n.d.). Found at The Cornbury Society website, accessed online at http://www2.cornbury.org/?q=node/2.

⁹⁸⁵ See the Gender Mosaic website, accessed online at http://www.gendermosaic.ca/.

⁹⁸⁶ Michael Taft, "Folk Drama on the Great Plains: The Mock Wedding in Canada and the United States," *North Dakota History, 56* (no. 4), 17-23 (1989). Also see Brenda Verandi, "I *do*? Northern New York's Mock Weddings," *Voices: The Journal of New York Folklore, 26,* 37ff. (2000, Fall-Winter).

⁹⁸⁷ Matthew Temple, "Men in Tights," *FT.com Financial Times* (2002, June 7). Accessed online at http://news.ft.com/home/us.

⁹⁸⁸ *The Transgender Community Health Project: Descriptive Results* (1999, Feb. 18). Material found at HIV InSite website, accessed online at http://hivinsite.ucsf.edu/InSite.jsp?doc=2098.461e.

⁹⁸⁹ National Coalition for LGBT Health, *An Overview of U.S. Trans Health Priorities* (2004). Found at the National Center for Transgender Equality website, accessed online at http://nctequality.org/HealthPriorities.pdf.

⁹⁹⁰ Ibid.

⁹⁹¹ Pauline Park & John Manzon-Santos, *Issues of Transgendered Asian Americans and Pacific Islanders* (2000). Testimony submitted to the President's Advisory Committee on Asian Americans and Pacific Islanders. Found at the Asian & Pacific Islander Wellness Center website, accessed online at http://www.apiwellness.org/v.20/tg/tgtestmony.html.

⁹⁹² Carol Odo & Ashliana Hawelu, "Eo na Mahu o Hawai'i: The Extraordinary Health Needs of Hawai'i's Mahu," *Pacific Health Dialog, 8* (no. 2), 327-334 (2001). This situation is all the more sad when we recall the honored role played by the *mahu* in Hawaiian culture. Even today they are important in the performance and teaching of the sacred *hula* dance. On the *mahu* of Hawaii see Andrew Matzner, *'O Au No Keia: Voices from Hawaii's Mahu and Transgender Communities* (Philadelphia: Xlibris, 2001). On the *mahu* of Tahiti see the answer to Q. 57.

⁹⁹³ Andrew Matzner, "'Transgender, Queens, *Mahu*, Whatever': An Oral History from Hawaii," *Intersections, 6* (2001), §9. Accessed online at http://wwwsshe.murdoch.edu.au/intersections/issue6/ matzner.html.

⁹⁹⁴ Andrew Matzner, *O Au No Keia: Voices from Hawaii's Mahu and Transgender Communities* (Phila.: Xlibris, 2001), Preface.

⁹⁹⁵ Matzner, "'Transgender, Queens, *Mahu*, Whatever'", §2.

⁹⁹⁶ Ibid, §7.

Q. 59 Notes

⁹⁹⁷ Will Roscoe, *Changing Ones: Third and Fourth Genders in Native North America* (N.Y.: St. Martin's Press, 1998), p. 4.

⁹⁹⁸ Sabine Lang, *Men as Women, Women as Men: Changing Gender in Native American Cultures* (Austin, TX: Univ. of Texas Press, 1998), p. 256.

⁹⁹⁹ Table adapted from Roscoe's *Changing Ones*, pp. 223-247. Roscoe lists 157 tribes or tribal groups with alternative gender roles and/or sexuality. In each case he also cites sources and the nature of the alternative role.

¹⁰⁰⁰ Writing in a volume that adopts this term, one author offers the following: "'Two-spirit' refers to persons who are a blend of the feminine and the masculine, the woman and the man." Arnold R. Pilling, "Cross-Dressing and Shaminism Among Selected Western North American Tribes," in S-E. Jacobs, W. Thomas, & S. Lang (Eds.), *Two-Spirit People: Native American Gender Identity, Sexuality, and Spirituality*, pp. 69-99 (Champaign, IL: Univ. of Illinois Press, 1997), p. 69. In the same volume, Lang (p. 100) makes clear that the term is meant to replace *berdaches*. However, gender historian Elizabeth Reis argues that using a designation like 'two-spirit people' would distort the past because in contemporary usage it typically refers to homosexuals. See her "Teaching Transgender History, Identity, and Politics," *Radical History Review, 88*, 166-177 (2004), p. 170.

¹⁰⁰¹ John D'Emilio & Estelle B. Freedman, *Intimate Matters. A History of Sexuality in America* (N. Y.: Harper & Row, 1988), p. 91.

¹⁰⁰² Lang, p. 273.

¹⁰⁰³ Ana Mariella Bacigalupo, "The Struggle for Mapuche Shamans' Masculinity: Colonial Politics of Gender, Sexuality, and Power in Southern Chile," *Ethnohistory, 51* (no. 3), 489-533 (2004), p. 525, n. 35.

¹⁰⁰⁴ Will Roscoe, *Changing Ones: Third and Fourth Genders in Native North America* (N.Y.: Palgrave Macmillan, 2000), p. 19; cf. his discussion pp. 17-19.

¹⁰⁰⁵ Henry Angelino & Charles L. Shedd, "A Note on Berdache," *American Anthropologist, 57*, 121-126 (1955).

¹⁰⁰⁶ Charles Callendar & Lee M. Kochems, "The North American Berdache," *Current Anthropology, 24* (no.4), 443-456 (1983), p. 443. With comments, the article extends to p. 470.

¹⁰⁰⁷ Indeed, to underscore this point, the word is left uncapitalized—it is not a self-designation adopted by Indian transgendered people and does not identify a distinct social group in the way the capitalized terms in this question set do. The term is a broad label covering individuals with certain traits across many different tribal societies.

¹⁰⁰⁸ Cf. Sue-Ellen Jacobs, Wesley Thomas, & Sabine Lang, "Introduction," in S-E. Jacobs, W. Thomas, & S. Lang (Eds.), *Two-Spirit People: Native American Gender Identity, Sexuality, and Spirituality*, pp. 1-20 (Champaign, IL: Univ. of Illinois Press, 1997), p. 12.

¹⁰⁰⁹ Roscoe, p. 8.

¹⁰¹⁰ Lang, p. 248; see Table 6 (pp. 248-251) for terms in different tribal cultures.

¹⁰¹¹ Callendar & Kochems, p. 444.

¹⁰¹² Walter L. Williams, *The Spirit and the Flesh: Sexual Diversity in American Indian Culture* (Boston: Beacon Press, 1986), p. 83.

¹⁰¹³ Ibid, p. 443.

¹⁰¹⁴ Lang, p. 10; see p. 61 for examples.

¹⁰¹⁵ Richard C. Trexler, "Making the American Berdache: Choice or Constraint?" *Journal of Social History, 35* (no. 3), 613-636 (2002).

¹⁰¹⁶ Prince Alexander Philipp Maximilian, *Reise in das innere Nord-America in den Jahren 1832 bis 1834*, 2 vols. (*Travels in the Interior of North America, 1832-1834*), excerpts of which are offered in an English translation by D. Thomas & K. Ronnefeldt (Eds.), *Peo-*

ple of the First Man: Life Among the Plains Indians in Their Final Days of Glory (N. Y.: Dutton, 1976).

[1017] Maximilian, *Reise in das innere Nord-America*, II, p. 133; cited in Carpenter, *Intermediate Types Among Primitive Folk*, p. 43.

[1018] Lang, p. 3.

[1019] Roscoe, *Changing Ones*, p. 4.

[1020] H. Taylor Buckner, "The Transvestic Career Path," *Psychiatry, 33* (no. 3), 381-389 (1970), p. 387. Accessed online at http://www.tbuckner.com/TRANSVES.HTM. For more on Buckner's ideas, see the answer to Q. 22.

[1021] Williams. See especially Part I: The Character of the *Berdache* (pp. 17-130).

[1022] Trexler, pp. 615-615. Also see Richard C. Trexler, *Sex and Conquest: Gendered Violence, Political Order, and the European Conquest of the Americas* (Ithaca, NY: Cornell Univ. Press, 1995), pp. 106-114.

[1023] Ibid. Throughout his article Trexler identifies social roles and functions.

[1024] Williams, p. 114.

[1025] Italo Signorini, "Comment" on Callendar & Ketchum, "North American Berdache," p. 463.

[1026] Lang, p. 167.

[1027] Ibid, Table 10, pp. 314-318.

[1028] Pilling, p. 69.

[1029] Jacobs, Thomas & Lang, p. 9.

[1030] Callendar & Kochems, p. 447.

[1031] Roscoe, p. 8.

[1032] Ibid, p. 122.

[1033] Ibid, p. 443.

[1034] Edward Carpenter, *Intermediate Types Among Primitive Folk. A Study in Social Evolution* (London: George Allen & Co., Inc., 1914), p. 37. Accessed online at http://www.sacredtexts.com/ lgbt/itp/itp05.htm.

[1035] Westermarck, vol. 2, p. 457.

[1036] Sir Richard Francis Burton, "Terminal Essay: Section D: Pederasty," in *The Arabian Nights*. See the material following footnote 53. Accessed at the People with a History website, online at http://www.fordham.edu/halsall/pwh/burton-te.html.

[1037] Claude E. Schaeffer, "The Kutenai Female Berdache: Courier, Guide, Prophetess, and Warrior," *Ethnohistory, 12* (no. 3), 193-236 (1965), p. 218.

[1038] Ibid, p. 219.

[1039] George Devereux, "Homosexuality Among the Mohave Indians," *Human Biology, 9,* 498-597 (1937).

[1040] Ibid, p. 516.

[1041] Roscoe, p. 141.

[1042] Robert C. Owen, J. F. Deetz & A. D. Fisher, *The North American Indians: A Sourcebook* (N. Y.: Macmillan, 1967), p. 413.

[1043] Devereux, p. 503.

[1044] Ibid, pp. 501-506.

[1045] Ibid, pp. 511-512.

[1046] Carolyn Epple, "Coming to Terms with Navajo *Nádleehí*: A Critique of *Berdache*,'Gay,' 'Alternative Gender,' and 'Two Spirit'," *American Ethnologist, 25* (no. 2), 267-

290 (1998). Cf. the much earlier work, W. W. Hill, "The Status of Hermaphrodite and Transvestite in Navaho Culture," *American Anthropologist, 37*, 273-279 (1935).

[1047] Wesley Thomas, "Navajo Cultural Constructions of Gender and Sexuality," in S-E. Jacobs, W. Thomas, & S. Lang (Eds.), *Two-Spirit People: Native American Gender Identity, Sexuality, and Spirituality*, pp. 156-173 (Champaign, IL: Univ. of Illinois Press, 1997), p.p. 156-157; quote is from p. 157. Also see his Table 7.1 (p. 157).

[1048] Roscoe, p. 42.

[1049] Willard W. Hill, "The Status of the Hermaphrodite and Transvestite in Navaho Culture," *American Anthropologist, 37*, 283-289 (1935).

[1050] Ibid, p. 159.

[1051] Lauren Wells Hasten, *In Search of the 'Berdache': Multiple Genders and Other Myths* (1998). Accessed online at http://www.laurenhasten.com/berdache.htm#navaho.

[1052] Sabine Lang, "Various Kinds of Two-Spirit People: Gender Variance and Homosexuality in Native American Communities," in S-E. Jacobs, W. Thomas, & S. Lang (Eds.), *Two-Spirit People: Native American Gender Identity, Sexuality, and Spirituality*, pp. 100-118 (Champaign, IL: Univ. of Illinois Press, 1997), p. 105.

[1053] Hill, p. 284.

[1054] See Marjorie Anne Napewastewiñ Schützer, *Winyanktehca: Two-souls Person* (1994). Paper presented to the European Network of Professionals in Transsexualism, August, 1994. Found at the gender.org website and accessed online at http://www.gender.org.uk/conf/trilogy/winkte.htm.

[1055] Royal B. Hassrick, *The Sioux: Life and Customs of a Warrior Society* (Norman: Univ. of Oklahoma Press, 1964), pp. 121-123.

[1056] Walter L. Williams, "Persistence and Change in the Berdache Tradition Among Contemporary Lakota Indians," in L. D. Garnets & D. C. Kimmel (Eds), *Psychological Perspectives on Lesbian and Gay Male Experiences*, pp. 339-347(N. Y.: Columbia Univ. Press, 1993), p. 343.

[1057] Ibid, p. 344.

[1058] Schützer.

[1059] Williams, "Persistence and Change," p. 345.

[1060] For more on *Winkte*, see John (Fire) Lame Deer & Richard Erdoes, *Lame Deer, Seeker of Visions: The Life of a Sioux Medicine Man* (N. Y.: Simon & Schuster, 1972).

[1061] Elsie Parsons, "The Zuni La'mana," *American Anthropologist, 18* (no. 4), 521-528 (1916), p. 523.

[1062] Ibid, pp. 524-525.

[1063] Parsons, pp. 526-528.

[1064] *The Zuni Man-Woman* (2005). Article posted on SantaFe.com. Accessed online at http://www.santafe.com/history/zuni_man-woman.html. For much more detail, see Will Roscoe, *The Zuni Man-Woman* (Albuquerque: Univ. of New Mexico Press, 1991).

Q. 60 Notes

Please note: related matters on how crossdressing fits into society are discussed in the answer to Q. 40, where the principle question is, 'Why does society tolerate crossdressing?'

[1065] Neil Buhrich & Trina Beaumont, "Comparison of Transvestism in Australia and America," *Archives of Sexual Behavior, 10* (no. 3), 269-279 (1981).

[1066] H. Taylor Buckner, "The Transvestic Career Path," *Psychiatry, 33* (no. 3), 381-389 (1970), p. 387. Accessed online at http://www.tbuckner.com/TRANSVES.HTM. For more on Buckner's ideas, see the answer to Q. 22.

Crossdressing in Context.
Dress, Gender, Transgender, and Crossdressing.

Table of Contents for 5 Volume Set

Volume 1: Dress & Gender
Preface. Can we be honest?
Introduction. What do you need to know to get started?
Question Set 1: What is all the fuss about clothes and gender?
- Q. 1 Why do clothes matter?
- Q. 2 How do we experience clothes?
- Q. 3 How do clothes affiliate us with others?
- Q. 4 Does what we wear communicate our morals?
- Q. 5 Why do sex and gender matter?
- Q. 6 What do clothes say about gender?
- Q. 7 How is crossdressing related to gender and dress?
- Q. 8 What happens when what clothes express doesn't make sense to us?
- Q. 9 Do clothes express something unchangeable?
- Q. 10 What does crossdressing express?

Volume 2: Today's Transgender Realities
Question Set 2: Who crossdresses—and why?
- Q. 11 How many people crossdress?
- Q. 12 Why would anyone crossdress?
- Q. 13 Do men crossdress?
- Q. 14 Do women crossdress?
- Q. 15 Do children crossdress?
- Q. 16 What do people find entertaining about crossdressing?

Q. 17   Why do some homosexuals crossdress?
Q. 18   What is 'transvestism'?
Q. 19   What is 'transsexualism'?
Q. 20   What does 'transgender' mean?

Question Set 3: What causes crossdressing?

Q. 21   Is crossdressing 'natural'?
Q. 22   Is crossdressing learned behavior?
Q. 23   Is crossdressing developmental (i.e., "just a 24phase")?
Q. 24   Is crossdressing caused by sexual abuse?
Q. 25   Is crossdressing a choice?

Question Set 4: What is it like to be a transgendered crossdresser?

Q. 26   How do crossdressers describe themselves?
Q. 27   What is the profile of a 'typical' crossdresser?
Q. 28   When does crossdressing usually start?
Q. 29   What is childhood and adolescence like?
Q. 30   What is adulthood like for a crossdresser?
Q. 31   Does crossdressing lead to a sex change operation?
Q. 32   Is crossdressing harmful?
Q. 33   What is involved in crossdressing?
Q. 34   Where do crossdressers find support?
Q. 35   Are all crossdressers homosexual?

Question Set 5: How are transgender realities regarded by others?

Q. 36   What is the legal status of crossdressers?
Q. 37   How are crossdressers treated in public?
Q. 38   How do partners handle the crossdressing of their significant others?
Q. 39   How does crossdressing affect families?
Q. 40   Why does society tolerate crossdressing?

Volume 3: Transgender History & Geography

Question Set 6: What is the history of crossdressing?

- Q. 41 What did the ancient world think?
- Q. 42 Who are some famous crossdressers of mythology?
- Q. 43 Who are some famous ancient crossdressers?
- Q. 44 What is the history of crossdressing and the theater?
- Q. 45 What was the history of gender, transgender and crossdressing in the Middle Ages?
- Q. 46 What is the history since the Middle Ages?
- Q. 47 What is the history in the United States?
- Q. 48 Who are some famous crossdressing women?
- Q. 49 Who are some famous crossdressing men?
- Q. 50 What will the present likely be noted for?

Question Set 7: Where in the world is crossdressing found?

- Q. 51 Is crossdressing only found in the Western world?
- Q. 52 Where is it found in the East?
- Q. 53 Where is it found in the Middle East?
- Q. 54 Where is it found in Africa?
- Q. 55 Where is it found in Latin America?
- Q. 56 Where is it found in Europe?
- Q. 57 Where is it found in the Pacific Ocean nations?
- Q. 58 Where is it found in North America?
- Q. 59 Where is it found in Native American groups?
- Q. 60 If it is so common, what role does it play in culture?

Volume 4: Transgender & Religion

Question Set 8: What does the Bible say about crossdressing?

- Q. 61 Where does the Bible address crossdressing?
- Q. 62 What are the key issues for understanding what the Bible says?
- Q. 63 What do Jewish commentators say?

Q. 64   What do Christian commentators say?

Q. 65   What constitutes a 'reasonable' position to take?

Question Set 9: What does Christianity say about crossdressing?

Q. 66   What does the New Testament say?

Q. 67   What did the Church Fathers say?

Q. 68   Are there crossdressing saints?

Q. 69   Are there notable crossdressing Christian women?

Q. 70   Are there notable crossdressing Christian men?

Q. 71   Are there Christian festivals where crossdressing is accepted?

Q. 72   Has the Church said anything "officially" about crossdressing?

Q. 73   What do Christians today who oppose transgender realities say?

Q. 74   What do transgender Christians and their supporters today say?

Q. 75   Are there resources for transgender Christians?

Question Set 10: What do other religions say about crossdressing?

Q. 76   How did crossdressing figure in ancient and pre-modern religions?

Q. 77   What stance does Judaism take on crossdressing?

Q. 78   What role has crossdressing played in Islam?

Q. 79   How does Hinduism regard crossdressing?

Q. 80   Is Buddhism tolerant of crossdressing?

Q. 81   Is crossdressing found in Japanese religions?

Q. 82   Can transgender elements be found in other Eastern religions?

Q. 83   What roles do crossdressing and transgender play in African religions?

Q. 84   Are transgender realities found in Native American religiosity?

Q. 85   What role does crossdressing play in religion?

Volume 5: Transgender & Mental Health

Question Set 11: How does crossdressing relate to sexual behavior?

- Q. 86   What role do clothes play in sexual behavior?
- Q. 87   What is the relationship between crossdressing and sexuality?
- Q. 88   What is a crossdressing 'fetish'?
- Q. 89   Is there a relationship between crossdressing and certain sexual practices?
- Q. 90   Can crossdressing be a part of 'normal' sex?

Question Set 12: Are transgender or crossdressing behaviors sick?

- Q. 91   What is the historical context needed to understand the modern mental health view of crossdressing and transgender issues?
- Q. 92   When do transgender conditions come to the attention of mental health professionals?
- Q. 93   What is 'gender dysphoria'?
- Q. 94   Is crossdressing associated with any forms of mental illness?
- Q. 95   How has crossdressing been understand by past mental health experts?
- Q. 96   How have transgendered conditions been understood in the DSM model?
- Q. 97   How do mental health experts today treat crossdressing and other transgendered behaviors?
- Q. 98   What constitutes a 'supportive model' of treatment for transgendered people?
- Q. 99   What is the future of transgendered conditions in psychological evaluations?
- Q. 100 Do transgendered people need to be changed?

Conclusion. Where Do We Go From Here?

Author Index

A

Abramson, Paul, 264, 296
Abu Nuwas, 231
Agrafiotis, Dimosthenis, 284
Alberoni, Francesco, 189
Alexeyeff, Kalissa, 288f.
Almas, Elsa, 280
Amadiume, Ifi, 247, 257
Angelino, Henry, 310
Argit, Betül Ipsirli, 83
Aristippus, 20
Aristophanes, 18, 54-56
Asclepiades, 24

B

Bacigalupo, Ana Mariella, 269-270, 310
Banner, Lois, 77
Barnes, Djuna, 145
Bartlett, Nancy, 290
Benjamin, Harry, 172
Bentler, Peter, 173
Berek, Peter, 61
Bergstrom-Walan, Mai-Briht, 281
Bishop, Kathleen, 74
Blake, Lillie Devereux, 130
Bleisch, Pamela, 56f.
Blythe, James, 75, 78, 79
Bogoras, Waldemar, 276-277
Bonomi, Patricia, 120f.
Boswell, David, 98
Boxwell, David, 62
Brekus, Catherine, 117
Buckner, H. Taylor, 313
Bullough, Bonnie & Bullough, Vern, 82, 105, 196
Burton, Sir Richard, 316
Buttrick, Helen Goodrich, 110

C

Cadden, Joan, 74
Cain, James, 75
Callendar, Charles, 310-311, 315
Carroll, Richard, 81
Castle, Terry, 88
Chappelle, Dave, 67
Chase, Sue-Ellen, 54
Chedgzoy, Kate, 86
Chenoue, Farid, 106
Clark, Robert, 58, 74
Cohen, Daniel, 124
Cornwall, Andrea, 268
Corre, Armand, 254
Crane, Diane, 110
Crawford, Catherine, 169
Creider, Jane & Creider, Chet, 255
Cressy, David, 87-89
Croft, William, 130-132
Crompton, Louis, 51f.
Crowley, John, 104
Ctesias, 22
Cunnington, C. Willet, & Cunnington, Phillis, 109-110
Cyrino, Monica, 25, 36

D

Davis, Natalie Zemon, 97
Davis-Kimball, Jeaninne, 27-28, 31
DeGrave, Kathleen, 116
Dekker, Rudolph, 89-90, 99
De L'Éstoile, Pierre, 168
Devereux, George, 317
Dio Cassius (Cassius Dio), 43-46
Diodorus Siculus, 36
Donham, Donald, 251
Dowie, Menie Muriel, 130
Drenth, Jelto, 280
Drew, Paula, 235
Driberg, John, 250f.
Dugaw, Dianne, 91, 117

E

Edgerton, Robert, 258
Eliade, Mircea, 255
Elliott, Richard, 267
Ellis, Havelock, 172, 251
Ellis, Stephen, 257

Enheduanna, 229
Epple, Carolyn, 318
Erikson, Erik, 367-368
Eskridge, William Jr., 150

F

Falkner, Thomas, 267
Fathi, Nazila, 235
Feinberg, Leslie, 146-147
Ferris, Leslie, 48
Fields, Jill, 107, 113

Findlay, Barbara, 300
Foucault, Michel, 221, 361 n. 511
Freeman, Susan, 147f.
Freud, Sigmund, 189
Frontinus, 25f.

G

Garber, Marjorie, 116
Geertz, Clifford, 293
Gibbon, Edward, 45
Gorer, Geoffrey, 252
Graham, Sharyn, 293

Greenberg, David, 244
Greene, Beth, 247f.
Greenhill, Pauline, 93
Gubar, Susan, 138

H

Hall, Radclyffe, 145
Hallpike, Christopher, 252
Hartley, Ruth, 184-185
Hassrick, Royal, 319
Hasten, Lauren Wills, 318
Hatano, Yoshiro, 51f., 214
Haulman, Kate, 103
Heiman, Elliott, 224
Heldris de Cornuälle, 79
Herdt, Gilbert, 296

Herodotus, 23, 28
Hill, Willard, 318-319
Hirschfeld, Magnus, 172, 201f., 278f.
Hollis, Alfred, 255
Homer, 38
Howard, Jean, 98
Huang, Yufu, 50
Hui-ling, Cho, 204
Hunt, Alan, 83

I

Illich, Ivan, 77
Ikeda, Ryoko, 213f.

Inness, Sherrie, 144

J

Jackson, Peter A., 53, 221-223
Jacopo de Flori, 75
Johnson, Mark, 297f.
Jonson, Ben, 59-60

Jordan, Dorothy, 62
Josephus, 231
Joyce, Rosemary, 261
Juvenal, 20, 28, 42

K

Kamenetzky, Sofia, 267f.
Kandiyoti, Deniz, 240
Kardulias, Dianna Rhyan, 38f.
Kates, Gary, 171
Kauer, Ute, 122
Kelly, Phelim, 282f.

Ko, John Sik-Nin, 206, 207
Kochems, Lee, 310-311, 315
Kon, Igor, 276
Kottak, Conrad, 277
Krafft-Ebing, Richard von, 141, 278

L

Lacroix, Paul, 21
Lahey, Kathleen Ann, 302
Lang, Sabine, 308, 310-312, 314
Långström, Niklas, 281
Laurent, Erick, 202
Levander, Caroline Field, 139
Leakey, Louis, 249

Ma, Joyce L. C., 206f.
MacDermot, Brian, 245
Mandi, Panagiota, 284
Mann, Herman, 122
Manzon-Santos, John, 215, 305
Marcus, Michelle, 229f.
Martial, 20
Martin, Richard, 211
Masquelier, Adilene, 244f.
Maximilian, Alexander Philipp, 312
Matzner, Andrew, 223, 306
McCall, John, 248f.

Nadel, Seigfried, 251
Najmabadi, Afsaneth, 234
Narrain, Siddharth, 209
Nataf, Zachary, 264
Needham, Rodney, 253

O'Brien, William, 249
Ochshorn, Judith, 19
Oman, John Campbell, 49

Park, Pauline, 215, 305
Parrinder, Geoffrey, 256
Parsons, Elsie, 320
Pausanius, 25
Perkins, Roberta, 242, 248
Peter Cantor, 75
Petronius, 24
Philostratus, 23
Pilling, Arnold, 314

Leslie, Eliza, 129
Lewes, Darby, 129
Licht, Hans, 37
Loraux, Nicole, 35
Loren, Diana DiPaolo, 103
Lucian, 23

M

McClellan, Elisabeth, 112
McCarthy, Julanne, 233f.
McLaren, Angus, 181
McLelland, Mark, 213
Mead, Margaret, 196
Menicucci, Garay, 232
Messing, Simon, 251f.
Miller, Margaret, 23
Modleski, Tonia, 138
Morris, Rosalind, 222-224
Munroe, Robert & Monroe, Ruth, 196
Mwinyi Bakari, Mtoro bin, 254

N

Ng, Emil Man-lun, 206f.
Nieto, Jose Antonio, 285
Niketas Choniates, 79
Njambi, Wairimu, 249
Nye, Robert, 182

O

Ordonez, Juan Pablo, 267
Otto of Freising, Bishop, 78
Ovid, 35f.

P

Pinkerton, Steven, 264, 296
Plato, 18
Plautus, 56f.
Plutarch, 24, 39f.
Portius Azo, 75
Prince, Virginia, 143, 171-173
Propertius, 36
Puff, Helmut, 80
Pullum-Piñon, Sara Melissa, 105, 106

Q, R

Rabinowiyz, Nancy, 54
Ramet, Sabrina Petra, 19
Reingardiene, Jolanta, 275
Roche, Daniel, 83
Rodman, Dennis, 175
Rodriguez-Madera, Sheilla, 264
Roscoe, Will, 310-311, 313, 315, 317
Rose, Mary Beth, 61
Rosencranz, Mary Lou, 109
Ruan, Fang-Fu, 206, 207
Rubio, Eusebio, 266f.
Rubenstein, Ruth, 105
Rudofsky, Bernard, 211

S

Sampson, Gwyneth, 281-282
Sarad, Susan, 296
Schaeffer, Claude, 316
Schifter, Jacobo, 265f.
Schmidt, Johanna, 289-290
Schützer, Marjorie Anne Napewastewiñ, 319f.
Sedgewick, Katherine, 125
Selby, Hubert, 146
Seneca, 22
Sextus Empiricus, 20
Shapiro, Michael, 60
Shedd, Charles, 310
Shepherd, Gil, 254
Shimazaki, Tsuguo, 51f., 214
Shtarkshall, Ronny, 237
Signorini, Italo, 250, 314
Skandera-Trombley, Laura, 174
Slob, Koos, 280
Somé, Malidoma, 245
Sponsler, Claire, 58, 74
Steele, Valerie, 105, 107
Stubbes, Philip, 87
Suetonius, 43-44

T

Taafe, Lauren, 56
Taft, Michael, 303
Taketani, Etsuko, 105
Tamale, Sylvia, 249
Tauxier, Louis, 250
Taywaditep, Kittiwut Jod, 222
Tereskinas, Arturas, 275
Terrence, 57
Thomas, Wesley, 318
Thu Nan, Nguyen, 225
Toro-Alfonso, José, 264
Trexler, Richard, 312-313
Trost, Jan, 281
Turner, Shasta, 59, 89
Twain, Mark, 125-126
Tyler, Royall, 51
Tzanetou, Angeliki, 56

U, V

Useche, Bernardo, 270
Van de Pol, Lotte, 89-90, 99
Van Le, Cao, 224
Vasey, P. L., 290
Velazquez, Loretta Janeta, 162-165

W

Weitao, Mao, 50
Welch, Tara, 36
Westermarck, Edward, 276, 316
Wheelwright, Julie, 142
Whittle, Stephen, 281-282
Wikan, Unni, 237
Wilchens, Riki Anne, 171
Williams, Walter, 313, 319
Wilson, Glen, 351
Winkler, Jack, 54
Winter, Sam, 206
Wood, J., 127-129
Wright, Steven, 59

X, Y, Z

Zdanevicius, Amas, 275
Zeitlin, Froma, 54
Zemach, Minah, 237
Zverina, Jaroslav, 274

Country Index

A

Africa, 241-260
Albania, 273-274
Argentina, 267-268

Australia, 288
Austria, 274

B

Bahrain, 233-234
Bangladesh, 203, 208

Brazil, 268-269
Burma (*see* Myanmar)

C

Canaan, 230-231
Canada, 300-303
Chile, 269-270
China, 21, 49-51, 203-207
Colombia, 270

Cook Islands, 288-289
Costa Rica, 265-266
Cuba, 263-264
Cyprus, 283
Czech Republic and Slovokia, 274

D

Denmark, 89, 90, 277

Dominican Republic, 264

E

Egypt, 21, 230, 232, 234

England, 83, 89, 98, 107, 207

F

Finland, 277-278
France, 278

French Polynesia, 289-290

G

Germany, 278-279
Greece, 53-56, 283-284

Guatemala, 266

H, I

India, 21, 30, 32-33, 34-35, 48-49, 69, 207-210
Indonesia, 53, 291-294
Iran, 19, 234-235

Ireland, 97, 282f.
Israel, 22, 230-231, 235-238
Italy, 284

J

Japan, 51-52, 83, 210-214

K

Korea, 20f., 53, 214-217

Kuwait, 233

L

Latvia, 274f.
Lithuania, 275

Luxembourg, 280

M

Malaysia, 294-295
Mesopotamia, 228-230

Mexico, 266-267
Myanmar (Burma), 217-218

N

Nepal, 218
Netherlands, 89, 280

New Zealand, 295
Norway, 280-281

O

Okinawa, 296

Oman, 237

Pakistan, 219-220
Papua New Guinea, 296
Philippines, 297f.

Russia, 276-277

Saudi Arabia, 238
Scotland, 282

Thailand, 53, 220-223

United Kingdom, 281-283

Vietnam, 224-225

P
Poland, 275f.
Portugal, 284
Puerto Rico, 264-265

Q, R

S
Spain, 285
Sweden, 7, 281

T
Turkey, 31, 239-240

U
United States, 101-148, 303-306

V, W
Wales, 96

Subject Index

A

Acault, 217-218
Achilles, 24, 30-31, 32
Achnutschik (or *Achnuchik*), 315-316
'Age of Disguise,' 88
Albertus Magnus, 74
Alexander the Great, 25, 32

Ali Saleem, 219
Alyha, 316f.
Amazons, 31-32
Amba, 32-33
Ashtime, 251
Astygetes, 33-34

B

Baitz, Dana, 302
Ballads, 91-95, 121, 123
    "Devilish Mary," 123
    "Handsome Cabin Boy," 93
    "The Holy Nunnery," 96
    "Mary Ambree," 121
    "The Soldier Maid," 94
    "The Young Shepherd," 95
    "Young Sailor Bold," 95
Bartholomew Fair, 59-60
Baylan, 297
Beaumont Society, 169, 281, 282
Berdaches, 307-320
    characteristics, 311-312

Berdaches (cont.)
    crossdressing and, 314-315
    definition, 309-310
    roles, 314-315
Bhishma, 32-33
"Billy Bedlow," 129
Bima, 34-35
Bissu, 293
Bloomers, 106, 139-140
Bonnet, Jeanne, 137
Bonny, Anne, 90, 119-120
Boy wives, 250
Boys Don't Cry, 68
Butler, Judith, 178, 221

C

Calabai'/Calalai', 294
Caligula, 43-44
CARITIG, 278
Carnival, 82, 97, 136, 169, 174
Changed men, 250-251
Chevalier d'Eon, 169-170
Chukchi, 276
Clodius Pulcher, 42
Clotel, 125, 127
College fiction, 143-144
Commodus, 45
Corset, 107
Croft, Ellen, 130-132

Crossdressing
    ancient world and, 17-28
    ballads, 91-95
    cultural considerations, 198-199
    martial strategy, 25f.
    protest and rebellion, 96f.
    puberty rites, 26, 254-256, 317
    sacred, 26, 256-257, 314
Crossdressers
    female, 81, 89-90, 117-120,
        130-136
    male, 82, 95-98, 120f.
        140-142, 180
    marriage and, 24-25

D

Dana International, 236
Dan Daudu, 253
Davies, Christian, 155-156
Davis, Jefferson, 123, 141, 351 n. 361
De Cespedes, Elena, 150-151
De Erauso, Catalina, 152-153
Diagnostic and Statistical Manual of Mental Disorders (DSM), 181, 183f., 189, 267, 273

Dillon, Lawrence Michael, 282
Dress
   ancient world, 18-19
   Golden Rule of Dress, 188
   medieval world, 76-77
   post-Medieval world, 86-87
   theories of origin, 105
   U.S. history of, 102-114
Durova, Nadezhda Andreevna, 161

E

Egale Canada, 300, 302
Elagabulus, 45
Enarees, 28, 329f. n. 45

Eunuchos (*The Eunuch*), 57-58
Eunuchs, 27-28, 329 n. 40, 329. n. 43, 336f. n. 149,

F

Fa'afafine, 289-290
Female husbands, 247-249
Female Marine, 123-124, 127
Feminine males, 187
Festival of Ekdusia, 26
Flower Boys of Silla, 20f., 215

French Revolution, 106, 122
Frith, Mary, 61, 151-152
From Toads to Queens, 266
Fu Sheng Liu Ji (*Six Records of a Floating Life*), 204-206

G

Galli, 27f.
Gender identity, 23f., 80
   experience and expression, 80, 96
'General Ludd's Wives,' 97
GID (Gender Identity Disorder), 185, 273

Gilgamesh Epic, 228
Gillies, Sir Harold, 282
Guevedoche, 264
Guerin, Elsa Jane ('Mountain Charley'), 137

H

Haec-Vir (*This Man*), 61, 99
Hall, Murray (Mary Anderson), 134
Hall, Radclyffe, 144
"Handsome Cabin Boy," 93
Harisu (Ha Ri-su), 216
Hathsheput, 21, 41-42
"Hellfire Hotchkiss," 126
Heracles (Hercules), 24, 35-36
Hermaphrodites (*also see* Intersex), 75, 85
Hervör, 36-37, 79
Hetzeldorfer, Katherina, 80-81

Hic Mulier (*This Woman*), 61, 99
Hijra/Hijrin, 209-210
Homosexuality/homosexuals, 233, 236, 238
Hong Lou Meng (*The Story of the Stone*), 204
Hope Leslie, 125
Huckleberry Finn, 126
Hwame, 316f.
Hyde, Edward (Viscount Cornbury), 120-121

I

IFGE (International Foundation for Gender Education), 171
Inanna, 229-230

Intersex/intersexed (*also see* Hermaphrodites), 85

J

Joan of Arc, 79
Jogoppa/Jogamma, 208

Jonson, Ben, 59-60
Jordan, Dorothy, 62

K

Kathoey, 222-223
Kaúxuma Núpika/Qánqon Kámek Klaúla, 159-160
Khomeini, Ayatollah Ruhollah, 235
Kimono, 211-212

King Henry III, 168-169
King James I, 89
Kothis, 208
Kupalke-tek, 316

L

Labouchère Amendment, 98
Laelae, 288-289
La'mana, 320
Last Exit to Brooklyn, 145

Leonard, Ray/Rae, 137
Leucippus (Leukippos), 37-38
Lombards, 79

M

Maa Khii, 223-224
Machi weye, 269-270
Mademoiselle de Maupin, 90f., 156-158
Mahu, 290-291, 305-306
Mak Nyah, 295
Male daughters, 247-249
Malleus Maleficarum (The Witch Hammer), 81
Manga, 213-214
Mary Queen of Scots, 89
Masculine gender role, 184-186
Mayate, 267

Medicalization of sex, 97-98, 108, 142f., 180-184
Metis, 218
Mock Weddings, 303
Molkara, Maryam, 235
Moll Cutpurse (*see* Frith, Mary)
'Molly Maguires,' 97
Movies, crossdressing and, 65-69
Mudang, 215
Mugawe, 253
Mummer's theater, 59
Muslim crossdressing, 231

N

Nádleeh, 318-319
Nero, 44-45

Nightwood, 145
Nzinga a Mbande, 153

O

Odysseus (Ulysses), 38-39, 312
Oman, 237

Ormond, 122

P, Q

Paksu, 215
Pantaletta: A Romance of Sheheland, 127-129
Pentheus, 39
Petticoat punishment, 23, 26, 312
Plato, 18, 74-75

Prince, Virgina, 142, 171-173
Psychopathia Sexualis, 141
Pudd'nhead Wilson, 126, 127
Queen Christina of Sweden, 154-155, 281

R

Read, Mary, 90, 120
'Rebecca and Her Daughters,' 96-97
Religion, 75, 76, 208, 214, 229, 231, 236, 256-257, 271, 297, 318
Roaring Girl, 61-62, 152

Rodman, Dennis, 174-175
Romance of Silence (Le Roman de Silence), 79
Rose of Versailles, 52, 71, 213f.
Russell, Craig (Craig), 302

S

Samson, Deborah, 117-119, 122
Sand, George, 91, 161-162
Sardanapolis, 22
Séraphita, 91
Shakespeare, 60-62
She Would Be a Heroine, 124
Spoon, Rae, 302

Talbot, Mary Anne, 158-159
Television, crossdressing and, 69-71
Terrence, 57
Theater, crossdressing and, 47-65
    African, 62
    American, 63-64
    Chinese, 49-51
    European, 58-62
    Greek, 53-56
    Indian, 48-49
    Indonesian, 53
    Iranian, 232
    Japanese, 51-52
    Javanese, 293
    Korean, 53
    Roman, 56-58
    Thai, 53
Theseus, 39-40
Thesmophoriazusae (Women at the Thesmophoria), 54-56
Third gender, 207, 212f.

Velazquez, Loretta Janeta, 162-165
Von Lichtenstein, Ulrich, 167-168

Wakeman, Sarah Rosetta, 132-133
Walker, Mary Edwards, 133-134
Ward, Josephine, 138
Waria, 292-293
Well of Loneliness, 144
We'wha, 320

Xanith, 237

Stanton, Elizabeth Cady, 139
Stone Butch Blues, 145-146
Stubbes, Philip, 87
Sukarno, 291
Sumptuary regulations, 82-83
Sworn virgins, 273-274

T

Tien, Nguyen Trong, 224f.
Timoleon, Francois (Abbe de Choisy), 169
Tipton, Billy, 165-166
Tiresias, 40
Torai, Masae, 213
Transgenderist, 173
Transphobia, 275, 300
Transsexuals/Transsexualism
    health, 304-305
    prevalence, 279
    sex reassignment surgery, 142, 173, 207, 214, 216, 220, 232f., 237, 259, 263, 265, 281f., 284, 295, 299, 302, 305
Travesti, 268-269
Tri-Ess, 172, 303
True Description of a Child with Ruffles, 86
Tutuvaine/Tututane, 289
Twain, Mark, 125-127, 174
'Two-spirit,' 305, 307, 309, 314, 318

U, V

Von Mahlsdorf, Charlotte, 279

W

Wilkinson, Jemima, 117
William of Conches, 74-75
Winkte, 319-320
Witches, 81, 88, 224
Women's Movement, 106-107, 138-139, 186, 272

X, Y, Z

www.ingramcontent.com/pod-product-compliance
Lightning Source LLC
LaVergne TN
LVHW010959250326
834688LV00003B/24